OUR DUMB CENTURY

OUR DUMB CENTURY

EDITED BY
Scott Dikkers

SECTION EDITORS

1900–1939	1940–1969	1970–2000
Maria Schneider	John Krewson	Robert Siegel

WRITTEN BY
Scott Dikkers, Robert Siegel, John Krewson,
Todd Hanson, Maria Schneider, Carol Kolb,
Mike Loew, Tim Harrod, David Javerbaum

ADDITIONAL MATERIAL BY
Jack Szwergold, Kurt Luchs, Rick Streed,
Ryan Kallberg, Randel Shard

DESIGNED BY
Scott K. Templeton
Andrew Welyczko

PHOTOS AND GRAPHICS BY
Mike Loew

ADDITIONAL ART BY
Maria Schneider, Jack Szwergold, Scott Dikkers

COPY EDITOR
Stephen Thompson

THANKS TO
Maggie Thompson, Scott Watson, Roy Jaruk,
Daniel Greenberg, Michael Shulman, David Cashion,
Kenneth J. Artis, Keith Phipps, Peter Haise

THREE RIVERS PRESS • NEW YORK

This book uses invented names in all stories, except notable public figures who are the subjects of satire. Any other use of real names is accidental and coincidental.

Copyright © 1999 by The Onion, Inc.

All rights reserved. No part of this book may be reproduced or transmitted in any form or by any means, electronic or mechanical, including photocopying, recording, or by any information storage and retrieval system, without permission in writing from the publisher.

Published by Three Rivers Press, New York, New York.
Member of the Crown Publishing Group.

Random House, Inc. New York, Toronto, London, Sydney, Auckland
www.randomhouse.com

THREE RIVERS PRESS is a registered trademark of Random House, Inc.

Printed in the United States of America
Design by *The Onion*

Library of Congress Cataloging-in-Publication Data
is available upon request.

ISBN 0-609-80461-8

PHOTO CREDITS

p. viii, eagle: *Pictures And Stories From Forgotten Children's Books*, Dover, 1969. p. 4, undergarments; p. 10, liniment: *The 1902 Edition Of The Sears, Roebuck Catalogue*, Portland House, 1996. p. 6, airplane: United States Air Force Museum. p. 7, Tyrannosaurus skull: Express News/Archive Photos. p. 17, soldiers; p. 73, television; p. 79, MacArthur; p. 101, motorcade; p. 107, movie still; p. 109, woman's hair; p. 119, Nixon's head: Popperfoto/Archive Photos. p. 22, player catching football: Hirz/Archive Photos. p. 26, White Sox: Sporting News/Archive Photos. p. 43, Hoover; p. 83, schoolchildren; p. 138, Baio; p. 141, Rambo: American Stock/Archive Photo. p. 45, plutocrats: Museum Of The City Of New York/Archive Photos. p. 60, *From Here To Eternity:* Imapress/Archive Photos. p. 61, Japanese boy: *Executive Order 9066*, California State Historical Society. p. 61, steelworker; p. 74, homes; p. 80, malt; p. 85, school; p. 106, scientists; p. 111, hippie: Lambert/Archive Photos. p. 69, family: ©FPG International LLC. p. 78, 3D glasses: ©Movie Stills Archives/FPG International LLC. p. 82, soldiers; p. 101, Johnson: CNP/Archive Photos. p. 86, Parks; p. 97, Gagarin; p. 117, Liddy; p. 121, shooting; p. 128, Jonestown; p. 129, Sadat and Begin, Capote, Studio 54; p. 131, Congress; p. 136, Reagan; p. 137, Denver; p. 139, incinerator; p. 141, Williams; p. 147, rescue workers; p. 161, infants: UPI/Corbis-Bettmann. p. 90, bread: Grant Smith/Corbis. p. 93, Sputnik: Barson Collection/Archive Photos. p. 95, Joseph Kennedy's head: Morgan Collection/Archive Photos. p. 95, dog: APA/Archive Photos. p. 96, hand dryer; p. 98, soup; p. 99, dolls; p. 125, comb; p. 130, Walkman; p. 134, TI-99; p. 137, Rubik's Cube; p. 158, O.J. with killer; p. 164, Christians, Omnicorp: Chad Nackers. p. 98, Funt: Tim Boxer/Archive Photos. p. 100, Giancana; p. 116, Simpson; p. 117, teens; p. 122, Le Duc Tho; p. 134, Hinckley; p. 140, U2; p. 142, Reagan and Marcos; p. 147, Raisins; p. 151, Madonna; p. 153, Elvis, Dream Team; p. 156, stadium: AP/Wide World Photos. p. 104, Leary: Horst Tappe/Archive Photos. p. 106, bombing; p. 123, Viking 1; p. 137, Khomeini: Agence France Presse/Archive Photos. p. 107, Dylan's head: Ed Grazda/Archive Photos. p. 111, astronauts: NASA. p. 112, Lennon: ©Apple Corps Ltd./ABC Photos. p. 125, Barris: Maddy Miller/Archive Photos. p. 126, Amin: Express Newspapers/H103/Archive Photos. p. 129, masked dancer: Tom Gates/Archive Photos. p. 131, hostages: Express Newspapers/Archive Photos. p. 134, Foster; p. 141, Johnson's head; p. 145, Cosby: Fotos International/Archive Photos. p. 138, Reagan's head: Express Newspapers/2339/Archive Photos. p. 138, *Diff'rent Strokes:* NBC Photo/Archive Photos. p. 138, car bomb: David Silverman/Archive Photos. p. 139, NYSE; p. 146, Reagan, p. 164, Falwell: Bernard Gotfryd/Archive Photos. p. 140, Ethiopia: Reuters/Werner/Archive Photos. p. 140, Piscopo: Bob Scott/Archive Photos. p. 140, Mondale: Sara Krulwich/*New York Times*/Archive Photos. p. 142, scientist: Reuters/Barbara Johnston/Archive Photos. p. 143, parade: Joan Slatkin/Archive Photos. p. 145, Nelson: Reuters/Scott Olson/Archive Photos. p. 146, Tyson: Reuters/Gary Hershorn/Archive Photos. p. 146, King; p. 147, Dukakis: Reuters/Archive Photos. p. 146, ring: Al Bello/Allsport. p. 148, tanker: Reuters/Blake/Archive Photos. p. 148, Bush: Reuters/Reed Schumann/Archive Photos. p. 148, Tiananmen; p. 150, soldiers: Reuters/Corbis-Bettmann. p. 149, Berlin Wall: Reuters/David Brauchli/Archive Photos. p. 149, Helms: Reuters/Mike Theiler/Archive Photos. p. 151, aircraft carrier: Reuters/Robert Catalano/Archive Photos. p. 151, Herstory: Julie Chambers. p. 152, Hill: Reuters/Rick Wilking/Archive Photos. p. 152, Soviets: Reuters/Viktor Korotayev. p. 153, L.A. rioters: Reuters/Sam Mircovich/Archive Photos. p. 153, King video: George Holliday/SYGMA. p. 154, Clinton: Reuters/Jim Bourg/Archive Photos. p. 155, Beavis & Butthead: ©MTV. p. 155, Limbaugh: Jason Trigg/Archive Photos. p. 158, Garcia: AFP Photo Files/Arista. p. 159, crowd: Reuters/Luc Novovitch/Archive Photos. p. 160, mall: Keith Webster. p. 160, pants: Mike Wise. p. 160, Ramsey: Reuters. p. 160, cow: Reuters/Ian Waldie/Archive Photos. p. 161, immobile; p. 163, drugs: Mike Loew. p. 162, Tamagotchi: Sam Chung. p. 162, *Titanic:* Merie W. Wallace/©1997 Paramount Pictures. p. 162, Clinton: Consolidated News/Archive Newsphotos. p. 162, Jones: Ron Sachs/CNP/Archive Photos. p. 162, talk-show set: ©*The Jerry Springer Show*. p. 163, Gates: Reuters/Dick Baldwin/Archive Photos. p. 163, Clinton: Reuters/Win Mcnamee. p. 163, Lewinsky: Dod Dod/Newsmakers. p. 163, Starr: Luke Frazza/AFP Photos. p. 163, shooting: Reuters/Leigh Daughtridge/Archive Photos. p. 164, Reed: Reuters/Ken Cedeno/Archive Photos. p. 164, Robertson: Reuters/Colin Braley/Archive Photos.

All other photos: Archive Photos
All other photo components: Chad Nackers

AN INTRODUCTION

by T. Herman Zweibel,
Onion Publisher
(photo circa 1919)

It is with a tremendous sense of pride and accomplishment that I look back upon this great Twentieth Century of ours and say that *The Onion* news-paper was able to document and, to a great extent, shape this wondrous time in human history, as this fine tome demonstrates.

As of this writing, I am almost 132 years old. I edited and published *The Onion* from 1896 until 1958, when my court-ordered retirement forced me into the medical wing of my 648-room estate in the East, with only my pudding-headed nurse-maid and my iron lung to keep me company. O, how I so yearn to relive my heady hey-day! *The Onion* was my very life, and I loved it more than any woman or fine buggy. I'm a news-paper-man to the very core! Printer's ink flows through my veins! For it is the right of every citizen of our great American Republic to be told what is going on about them, and it is the sacred duty of *The Onion* to tell it to them.

It all began in 1756. Friedrich Siegfried Zweibel, an immigrant tuber-farmer from Prussia, shrewdly bartered a sack of yams for a second-hand printing press and, according to legend, named his fledgling news-paper *The Mercantile-Onion* after the only words of English that he knew. The earliest existing *Mercantile-Onion* dates from 1765. The front page of this edition is pictured on the following page.

We know not what happened in the years 1774 to 1837, because little record exists from this time in U.S. history. It is widely assumed that the American Colonies fought for and won independence from their wicked oppressors, the Tartars, and that our Founding Fathers established what we know today as the Great Republic Of The

THE Mercantile-ONION.

Being a Helpful Chronicle and Digest of Publick Events of Significant Note, and Well-Found'd Advices, &c., for the General Enlightenment of Letter'd YANKEES.

Friedfich Siegfried Zweibel, EDITOR & PUBLISHER.
Boston, Friday, 18. October 1765.

The Following are the Latest News-Worthy Occurrences from *LONDON*, as described by Mr *PERCY SHERIDAN, Esq.*, a *Dilletante*, and Gentle Man of Leisure.

To the Editor of The Mercantile-ONION, Boston,
7. February 1765.

Esteem'd Sir,

IT is my profound Hope that you have not wait'd for this Missive with great Anticipation, as little of Import has happen'd in the City of *London* since our last Correspondence. It has been raining a great Deal, as is the usual Custom. The King's loyal Subjects continue to dwell in a teeming Abundance of *Filth*; Human Excrement, Turnip Tops, and dead Cats clog our Sewers and Gutters in a most Sick making Way. For, nigh a Fort Night, I have been able to sleep little, as the Vermin in my Bed Cloaths bite most closely. Compounding this Grievance, Mrs Reynolds, the Neighborhood Fish Wife, has the *Small Pox*, and screams long into the Night; and just as I fall into Slumber, I am awoken by the Chimney Sweep's cries of 'weep, 'weep, in the street.

Your esteem'd Personage may recall from my last Message that I purchased a saucy new Perriwig, and look'd quite the foppish Macaroni in it. But, I regret to report, it has done little to conceal or expunge the great Deal of *Lice* which dwells upon my Scalp. I have tried Every Thing to get rid of this D—d Scourge, including the Copious Use of Whale Oil, Goose Grease, Candle Flame, and a Cat O'Nine Tails, but alas to no Avail. I have consider'd drawing a Water Bath, and immersing my Head in it, so as to drown the small Wretches; but it is most difficult to haul out a Pail of Water from the Publick Well without its emerging full of Tar, Swine Vomit, more dead Cats, and other Impurities.

Aside from Parliament considering the Passage of a Stamp Act to tax the American Colonies, I can think of no other Events of Significance which to impart. Oh, yes, the Price of Snuff has increased by a Ha'penny.

I remain most respectfully and graciously yours,

Percy Sheridan, Esq.

Ships Departing This Week.

The *Scurvy*, The *Dismal*, The H.M.S. *Whore*, The *Slaver*, The *Priscilla Constant*, The *Bloody Head*, The *Jolly Plunderer*.

Run Away Slaves & Indentur'd Servants.

GAIUS, a Negro Man, about 23 years of age; ran away from his Master Isaiah Phelps, Planter, on 13. September. He bears many Whip Lashings upon his Back and Buttocks, measures 5 Feet 9 Inches high, and weighs over twenty Stone; he is a very *Leviathan*, so take care should he cross your Path. He who takes up and secures said Brute shall have *Twenty Shillings Reward*, and reasonable Charges, to be collected at the *Phelps Plantation*, near Starkeweather Town Ship.

TOM, Indentur'd Irish Man, about 14 years of age; ran away from his Master Friedrich Siegfried Zweibel, News Paper Publisher, on 17. October. He is possessed of a prominent Hunch Back, few Teeth, and a surly Disposition typical of the indolent Irish Race. He does not take kindly to Bridle or Saddle, nor drinks the India Ink he is given for his Supper, nor other wise submits to the Terms of his Indentures. He who takes up and secures TOM shall have *Fifteen Shillings Reward*, to be collected at *The Mercantile-ONION, Commerce Street*, BOSTON.

Benjamin Franklin is a Great Ass.

The Opinion Held by the August Editor & Publisher of this very Journal.

Gentle Men of Boston,

Mr Benjamin Franklin, Esq. of Philadelphia, late of this City, has achieved much Notoriety for his invention of a Stove and for flying a Child's Kite in a Lightning-filled Tempest; but I say unto you, kind Gentle Men, that these are but Fool's Errands, and serve as a mere Guise for the Pursuit which be holds most dear; that is, inserting his Hand up our good Ladies' Petticoats, and placing his Tongue down their Gullets. I dare say he is as Debauch'd and Carnal as a Bacchante in the Days of Rome, and rivals the pagan god Priapus for

turn

American States. I also believe that the cotton-gin was invented around this time.

I am getting very tired and wish to take a nap. This is the problem with books. I myself don't believe in them. I once tried to read a book by an English fellow named Dickens, and, after a few pages, I cast the thing into the fireplace in great disgust. I'm a news-paper-man, damn it! Come to the point with me, sir, or take your business elsewhere! I want the plain, hard facts, not who kissed Lady Beverly behind the wisteria bush! All these words, they numb the soul.

Herman Ulysses Zweibel, my father and the grand-son of the founder, took the reins in 1850, and I grew up under his astute tutelage. Upon my father's death in 1896, I assumed the editorship, and although reverent of my father's great memory, I wished to modernize the news-paper a bit. Re-christening it *The Onion*, I moved the operations to the bustling new industrial metropolis whose name I forget, but it was an electric place where the smell of rancid cow entrails and human feces intermingled in a distinct aroma that invigorated the spirit. As I look back, I realize that these were the golden years of *The Onion*. I was in the very bloom of youth, and, with our ever-growing profits, increasing prestige, and strategic garrotings of various rivals in the news-paper trade, we stood poised at the brink of the Twentieth Century, ready to take it on and make it our own.

I only wish I could remember the Twentieth Century. It starts to get a little hazy after 1912. But I've been assured that it was quite eventful. For example, there were several wars in Europe, something I wholeheartedly endorse. God-damn Europeans, with their leathern short-pants and their wooden-shoes and their keeping of billy-goats upon the roofs of their houses. To hell with them all, I say—they deserve one another! I have also been informed that, during this century, music and the sound of the human voice has been captured, stored, and conveyed in lacquered boxes fired with the electrical-power. This intrigues me, but I can see how listening to the spoken words of others could very quickly become vexing and tiresome. I believe I will stick to my favorite past-time of lapsing into a coma every now and again.

I have also been told that not only does *The Onion* news-paper still thrive to this very day; it is still published by my distant descendants in the Zweibel clan. They're lousing it up, too! The last time I saw *The Onion*, I was so furious, I had to be administered laudanum. Do you realize there is now a section in *The Onion* called "Features And Life-style," in which subjects such as health, personal hygiene, calisthenics, aging, and nutrition are treated as news-items? And that actors and actresses of the movable-picture photo-plays are solicited for interviews and opinions, simply because they happen to be celebrated public personages? I can scarcely believe I have lived to see such lily-livered folderol in the august pages of *The Onion!* I am surprised that the so-called news-paper-men of *The Onion* do not volunteer to come to the readers' homes and wipe their behinds! I do not require a news-paper to tell me how to live my life, nor do I wish to read about how some vapid chorus-girl loves the porpoises.

Anyhow, here is the *Onion*-Through-The-Twentieth-Century book, and you are welcome to the wretched thing. Don't ever interrupt my nap again!

T.H. Zweibel

1900-1929

A NATION TURNS ITS CRANK

MIRROR OF THE NATION.

THE ONION

FEWER PRINTING-PRESS-MEN KILLED EVERY DAY.

Monday, January 1, 1900. The Best Source of News-worthy Items in our Great Republic. Price Two Cents.

A NEW CENTURY DAWNS!

MCKINLEY USHERS IN BOLD NEW 'COAL AGE.'

AS NEW EPOCH DAWNS, OUR PRESIDENT HAILS FUTURE, COAL.

McKinley Makes Speech.

Complete Text of Brief, Three-Hour Address on Pages 4 Through 7.

Washington, D.C., Dec. 30.—In a grand ribbon-cutting ceremony in our Republic's capital Saturday, President McKinley hailed the advent of a glorious new era in which coal reigns supreme.

"Praise be to Divine Providence for the holy bestowment upon man, by the grace of the Author and Giver of all blessings, before whom we stand in reverent thankfulness, of the great power of coal!" McKinley proclaimed, severing an ornate silken bunting, then turning a great crank to release several hundred tons of picturesque coal dust into the skies.

A coal exposition followed the president's keynote address. Those who have been exposed to coal and its by-products were in attendance to attest to coal's great advantage as a fuel for man's endeavors. When placed into a parlor-stove and lighted, it glows like a heavenly angel. Furthermore, many of the wondrous maladies new to the annals of medicinal science were in evidence: "black-lung," "sulphur-cough," "stoop-back," "scarlet-sputum," and "the wasting-away."

Whereas the average family in this Republic of thirty years hence spent nearly fifteen hours each day alone splitting logs, gathering wood chips, and maintaining the fire in the hearth, today a comparable family consumes only nine hours each day scooping coal out of the coal-bin.

The wizards of science are gradually unearthing new and fanciful uses for King Coal, which were on display at the festival. The obsidian sheen of the mineral is coveted in ladies' jewelry. Peppy coal drinks are expected by merchants of confectioneries to become as popular as lemonade and beer made from the root of the Birch.

The coal-mines of the Appalachian hill-country present a rugged and challenging topography that has not gone unnoticed by entrepreneurs. Mile upon mile of virgin forest populated only by mere savages lay bare for productive mining by enterprising coal barons, the business leaders of the morrow.

We do well to consider the future at the momentous turn of the century mark. As McKinley so eloquently predicted, "the future rests firmly in the eminent domain of King Coal!"

NATION'S SKIES FILLED WITH BEAUTIFUL, BLACK SMOKE.

WILL MAN-MADE GRIME REACH THE VERY VAULT OF HEAVEN?

Look up, citizens, for all across the sky floats glorious proof of our incomparably robust manufacturing power! Indeed, there can be no more apt portent for our fair Republic's ever-growing industrial might than the very sky above us, thick and endowed with the beautiful black smoke of industry.

Just ten years ago, America's skies were filled with untarnished, snow-white clouds—willowy wisps bereft of even the slightest sign of a textile plant or steel mill or boot factory below. But to-day, thanks to such great captains of industry as Carnegie, Rockefeller, and Vanderbilt, there is glorious evidence of American industrial vigor as far as the eye can see—a canopy of black soot stretching proudly across the heavens, from ocean to ocean, blocking out the sun with the by-products of our intimidating manufacturing might.

Can any other nation on earth lay claim to such a sky? Certainly not. Fair England, great colonial power that she may be, possesses the clear blue sky of an industrial weakling, her few and feeble factories scarcely able to belch out enough smoke to cast a grayish pall over London. And unlike our mighty Mississippi, into which each day millions of gallons of sludge and machine waste is productively pumped, the proud evidence of booming paper mills and smelting plants, the Thames is crystal clear and pure enough to render drink. The clean state of her rivers and lakes must certainly be a source of embarrassment for the Queen.

And what of Germany? Kaiser Wilhelm, proud nationalist that he is, has little of which to be proud when one considers the virgin state of the Black Forest, its trees tall and strong and green of leaf, wholly unsullied by the smoky air of nearby iron works.

Indeed, our Republic's smoke-stacks are unmatched throughout the world. Watch the other nations turn green with envy as the American landscape reminds them of our greatness at every turn, from the loco-motive smoke which clogs our skies to the boiling lead which seeps into our soil. Huzzah!

MISCREANT DIRECTS CARRIAGE WRONG WAY AROUND TOWN SQUARE.

New-York, Dec. 31.—Tumult and a confused state of affairs were the order of the day when a Manhattan-borough miscreant drove his wagon the wrong way around the town square. Marketers and shop-keepers were confounded, the hats of ladies were in disarray, an unholy shrieking was heard from the school-children, and a generalised sort of Pandemonium was incited before a constable, along with several good towns-men, could stop the miscreant and his mad game of Chase-The-Wild-Goose. Such was the indignity perpetrated upon the senses, of a wagon circling the square in a counter-clock-wise rather than clock-wise fashion, that the minds of many towns-men refused to accept the spectacle, and they were nearly trampled in their consternation.

The miscreant, an itinerant hide-chewer employed at Macauley's Tannery, has coarsely refused to surrender his name to our town's authorities and languishes now in the jail-house. His wagon has been described as a dilapidated lath-board and cotter-pin affair towed by unkempt dray-horses of the rudest breed, altogether the sort of conveyance unfit for traversing our town in the day-light, let alone for flouting the Law in a drunken widdershin-wise caper through the heart of the kind principality of New-York.

The Onion news-paper feels confident in suspecting the rough hand of the Immigrant in this affair.

MAN WITH LIMBS EMPLOYED BY RAIL-ROAD.

Minneapolis, Dec. 31.—The Great Northern Pacific Rail-Road has announced that it has newly hired a laborer who has all his limbs intact.

The new laborer, Henry Fischdale, 16, is a great boon to the Northern Pacific, as nearly 97 percent of its work-force has lost one or more limbs or digits in the course of their labor. "Skilled labor is a valued commodity which the Northern Pacific requires to maintain an efficient operation," Rail-road vice president F. Herbert Caldwell told The Onion. "Young Fischdale is just the type of healthy, four-limbed worker required to maintain a reliable, on-time freight and passenger service." Fischdale was immediately put to work coupling box-cars and crawling under them to inspect possible damage to the wheels and under-side during transit.

AFRICAN SAVAGES TAUGHT WAYS OF CHRIST BY KINDLY BRITISH.

Via the Trans-Atlantic Cable.—British missionaries are reported to be spreading Christian wisdom to the far reaches of most savage Africa. Ships carrying missionaries are arriving daily, bringing needed shipments of Bibles, religious teachers, and priests to the spirit-starved jungle-dwellers.

The blessing of laboring in British mines is also being conferred on the savages.

OUR NATION'S FORESTS MUST BE MINED FOR COAL!

A Editorial, on page 10.

OTHER NEWS-WORTHY OCCURRENCES AROUND THE REPUBLIC:

City Planners Call for Expensive Plan to 'Pave' Road-ways to Make Them 'as One Long Brick.'

kindly please turn to page 5.

Savory New Beverage Delights Republic with Miracle 'Pep' Ingredient.

may we gently persuade you to turn to page 3?

OCCURRENCES FROM OTHER REALMS OF THE GLOBE:

Europe's Generals Promise Easy Quelling of Boxer Rebellion.

Flow of China-man Labor into U.S. to Continue.

read the full story on page 9.

TO-DAY'S EXTINCTIONS.

Northern Pond Shrew.

Terwinger's Slug.

Hoofed Plover.

Screwhorn Sheep.

Edgington's Lesser Titmouse.

Western Furred Owl.

Carolina Toothed Varmint.

ATTENTION, GRACIOUS LADIES AND GENTLE-MEN:

If, by using a plain house-hold shears, you take pains to sever this paid advertisement from the remainder of this news-paper, place it in your pocket or hand-bag, and travel to our mercantile establishment on 16 Canal Street, New-York, we earnestly guarantee that, on presentation of said advertisement, we, Slocombe & Sons Co., will grant you a ten per-cent reduction in the cost of a one-pound can of cream of tartar. We cordially extend this discount-sale offer to ladies and gentle-men who should happen upon this notice until our closing-time on the evening of January 15.

We thank you for your attentions, and wish you godspeed, and sincere best wishes.

SIGNED, ADOLPH SLOCOMBE III, PROPRIETOR, SLOCOMBE & SONS CO.

ADOLPH SLOCOMBE IV.
JOSIAH SLOCOMBE.
FRANCIS SLOCOMBE.
HERBERT SLOCOMBE.
CADWALADER SLOCOMBE.
PURVIUS SLOCOMBE.
THE LATE OSCAR SLOCOMBE.
JULIUS SLOCOMBE.

DEATH-BY-CORSET RATES STABILIZE AT ONE IN SIX.

GROWING USE OF DR. SCHEIDT'S PATENTED SAFETY CORSET.

Ladies Breathe Slightly Less Painful Sigh of Relief.

The Republic's health-officers are reporting an overall seven percent fewer deaths by corset this year, a statistic that will no doubt gladden the hearts of those dutiful ladies who unselfishly risk sacrifice upon the altar of Beauty every day so that they may appear comely and supple to their husbands and suitors.

This reduction in corset-related fatalities is credited to the growing popularity of Dr. Ezra Scheidt's Safety and Wellness Corset for the Improvement and Uplifting of the Pleasing Female Form. The supporting under-garment received a patent last year for its unique styling and construction. With this corset, the waist is bound to only seventeen inches, but it still dramatically enhances the figure and beautifies its wearer, giving her an alluring pouter-pigeon appearance which will assuredly turn the heads of gentle-men.

A flexible steel-enforced whale-bone lines the corset, forcing the bosom and hips several inches past their normal areas and pressing the brisket almost flush against the spine. But the lady is still allowed the ability to do things never before achievable with previous corset designs, such as looking down, sitting, and inhaling sufficient oxygen to fortify the extremities, giving the fingers the dexterity to hold a fan or nose-gay.

Margaret Wettingham, a Boston resident, has witnessed the passing of three sisters and an Aunt to corset-related atrophy. "Dr. Scheidt's corset could save my life. I wear it every day." Miss Wettingham then paused and labored for a breath, lest she perish.

Corset deaths are now the fourth leading cause of death to ladies. Yellow-fever, dropsy, and child-bearing stand foremost.

Some doctors have assailed the new corset, calling for its ban from the market-place. "Surgically removing the waist altogether is the only medically advised fashion of achieving ideal beauty in ladies," said Dr. Menning Hildebrandt.

The Reverend X. Lucius Dalrymple, in a letter to this news-paper, condemns the new corset for "immorally permitting the woman to gallivant about in the manner of a man."

NEWS FROM ROME.

VATICAN CONDEMNS 'RHYTHM METHOD.'

Pontiff Excoriates Infidels for Fiendish 'Sin by the Calendar.'

RELEASES PAPAL EDICT OUTLINING FORBIDDEN FAMILY PRACTICES.

ITALIANS IN ATTENDANCE VOW TO PEOPLE THE EARTH.

Vatican City, Dec. 31.—In a proclamation rife with the righteous anger befitting a clergyman of his most exalted station, His Holiness the Pope, Bishop of Rome, Vicar of Christ, Leader of all Christians of the World, lashed out at those with the effrontery to use the calendar to defeat God's purpose of peopling the globe.

"This prideful 'rhythm method' is a blasphemy before God," Leo XIII declared to a crowd of as yet non-American-emigrant Italians at St. Peter's Basilica. "Those who would count the days He created against the ripeness of their goodwives are indulging in the darkest brand of sorcery."

The reactions of lay civilization have been varied, as most prominent Americans are expected to seek the counsel of their bishops and priests for clarification of the edict.

The denounced "rhythm method," according to physician Hobart McGreely of Pittsburgh, is "the way by which a lady, having an intuitive grasp still elusive to medicinal science of the ebb and flow of nature, can divine when she is most conducive to the conception of young, and may choose to refrain from the painful process of copulation, in essence avoiding her dutiful role as a mother."

"Childbearing women have a responsibility to the Lord on High," added noted Chicago priest Father Willard Portkin. "In this advanced age of modern medicine, most mothers need only give birth to two or three still-born children before enjoying the fruits of living progeny. And now-a-days many of the gentler sex are enjoying full recuperation and survival of the birthing miracle. There is therefore no excuse for women-vessels to engage in trickery of God's plan for their fertility."

TO-DAY'S WEATHER PROGNOSTICATION.
Whatever Lord Jesus the Christ, our Divine Saviour, the Messiah, Emmanuel, the Lamb of God, the Nazarene, the Light and the Word, doth will.

THE ONION

EMPLOYER OF CHILDREN.

Saturday, September 7, 1901. The Best Source of News-worthy Items in Our Great Republic. Price Two Cents.

MCKINLEY ATTACKED BY WILD BOAR!

PRESIDENT DEAD OF WOUNDS SUSTAINED IN HIRSUTE PIG'S FEROCIOUS ASSAULT.

VILE BRUTE RAIDS EXECUTIVE MANSION AND REPUBLIC'S SEAT OF POWER.

ROOSEVELT SWORN IN; VOWS TO HUNT DOWN VILLAINOUS BEAST.

THE HON. PRESIDENT MCKINLEY.

1843 – 1901.

Washington, Sept. 6.—President McKinley, according to tele-graphic dispatches received this very day from Washington by The Onion's tele-graph operator, was attacked and wounded unto death by a wild boar, who gored and ravaged the surprised president with much ferocity, inflicting terrible wounds.

Though the president fought back to defend himself with all his strength, it is said that he proved in the end no match for the maddened beast, which snorted and lunged at him with its deadly tusks, until no life was left within him.

McKinley is the fourth American president to succumb to attack by wild boars since 1800.

Vice President Theodore Roosevelt was sworn in as president of these states in an emergency session yesterday after-noon.

Roosevelt had fought valiantly to defend McKinley from the enraged boar's advances, but in the end proved equally ineffectual against the bristled swine's murderous rage. He was stunned by a blow to the head from the animal's great cloven hooves, falling unconscious as the ferocious creature savaged McKinley's person.

Speaking from his hospital bed, the new president vowed to make all due haste in addressing the issue of wild boar attacks in the future, promising to, if necessary, mobilize the national militia to subdue and slaughter as many of the hirsute pig creatures as possible, so that our nation can once again be made safe for its citizenry.

"For too long, we, the American populace, have cowered in fear before the deadly wrath of these beasts," he said. "I promise the people of this land that I will personally hunt down and destroy as many of these horrible saber-fanged pigs, as well as any other wild game that I may find, as is humanly possible. Let the word go forth to the beasts of the forests and wilderness that Roosevelt is coming with his musket," the new president said to resounding cheers. "The death of our beloved McKinley shall not be forgotten! Beasts of the woodlands, I tell you, McKinley shall be avenged!"

PHILANTHROPIST ANDREW CARNEGIE DONATES $50 MILLION TO HIS BUSINESS.

HAILED AS LARGEST GIFT EVER GIVEN TO HIMSELF.

Pittsburgh, Sept. 6.—Steel magnate Andrew Carnegie, long known for his generous works of charity and philanthropy, has committed yet another generous act, donating $50 million of his fortune to his own business.

Said Carnegie, "I remember growing up penniless in a foreign land, and having only five dollars in my pocket when I came to this great nation. Now it is time to give a little something back to myself."

Carnegie said that the money will go to the construction of two new Carnegie Steel Mills in the Monongehela Valley, and to improving capacity in his existing mills.

This is Carnegie's largest gift ever given to himself, topping the $8 million mansion he built in the Hamptons in 1894 and the $1.5 million diamond and emerald bracelet he purchased for his wife last year. The act will do much to ease Carnegie's present burden of wealth.

NIETZSCHE POSITS EXISTENCE OF 'SUPER-MODELS.'

Via the Trans-Atlantic Cable. — The late German philosopher Friedrich Nietzsche, student of Schoepenhauer, contemporary of Wagner, and famed hair-dresser, is being discussed throughout the international scholarly community to-day, following the English translations of his works "Beyond Cute and Perky" (1876), "Gorgeous, All-Too-Gorgeous" (1878), and the opus "Thus Spake Claudiaschifra" (1883-91). In the last of these works, he posits the notion of invincible, unattainable "Uber-Models," or "Super-Models," representing the human form in its most elevated and self-glorifying state.

The noted aphorist and madman passionately decried the so-called "slave morality" of traditional Christianity in favor of a new, heroic morality requiring absolute adherence to impossible standards of superficial physical perfection. Ruling as dominatrices over the new society Nietzsche envisioned is a new breed of visually stunning Overwomen, whose "Will to Glamour" would place them atop mighty pedestals, far above the inferior "herd" of plain-looking common humanity.

Although the works are earning great renown, some fear Nietzsche's ideas may one day be misunderstood and used to justify terrible atrocities.

1900 CENSUS REVEALS RECORD NUMBER OF CITIZENS SLEEPING IN-DOORS.

The recent census continues to reveal many surprising statistics. An estimated 13 million of our 76 million citizens can now be found sleeping in-doors, a greater number than in any other period of American history. Of course, the term "in-doors" is not clearly defined by the Bureau of the Census, so we may safely assume that it could apply to anything from houses to tenements, wig-wams, lean-tos, and trees. "This is a capital development," said one prominent Washington, D.C., attorney in response to the findings, before retiring to his burlap shanty on the east bank of the Potomac.

ATHLETICS DEFEAT RED STOCKINGS IN LIGHTNING-QUICK NINE-HOUR GAME.

From the Sporting Correspondent.—The world of base-ball was turned upon its ear yesterday, as the mighty Athletics of Philadelphia used a herculean barrage of offensive might to defeat the Red Stockings of Boston in a nine-hour game, which set records and astounded on-lookers with its quickness and speed.

"I dast not believe it myself," said Athletics first-baseman Shuffler Schiel. "The ten-hour game has so long been base-ball's impossible dream that I am almost sad that it is now made fact. It is an honor to have played an important part in this age of Progress."

The Athletics stormed out of the gate, hitting no fewer than six pitches in the first four hours, another base-ball record. It was during the fourth hour that Boston team Manager Mortimer Stahl noticed that the Athletics were keeping every player in the dug-out awake and ready.

"That is an unheard-of strategy, against the spirit and philosophy of our beloved game, and I intend to lodge a formal complaint with the American League headquarters as soon as my team and I have caught a few more winks," said Stahl, exhausted by his effort and the drubbing received at the hands of the Athletics and their brilliant seventh-inning run.

"I could not believe what was happening," said spectator Horace McGillie of Boston. "I stood to adjust my breeches and fetch victuals, it having been three hours since I first took my seat, and I noticed it was already in the fourth inning!"

Great turmoil was instigated by the early ending of the game. Only half the usual amount of peanuts, Cracker-Jack, raspberry phosphates, sausage-wieners, and Pilsner beer were sold by vendors.

Now that base-ball's fastest game, once thought an impossibility, has come to pass, very few barriers are left to be broken in the arena of sports-manship. The few yet extant include: a man rushing for more than fifty yards in foot-ball; a man running a mile in fewer than seven minutes; a mechanical carriage besting a horse in a road-race; and a woman being taught the rudiments of any team sport.

FISTICUFFSMANSHIP!

To-Night At The Masonic Temple,

SUDDEN DEATH SCOTT

Shall Contend With

CLOBBERIN' COLGRAVE

UNTIL INDIVIDUAL OR MUTUAL UNCONSCIOUSNESS, BRUTAL DEATH, FISTIC AMPUTATION OF NO FEWER THAN THREE LIMBS, OR TEARING-ASUNDER OF ONE OR BOTH PARTIES HAS BEEN SATISFACTORILY AND VISIBLY ACHIEVED.

A Gentlemanly Sporting Display Of Uncommon Magnitude, Upon Which Wagers May Be Placed.

Sudden Death Scott, 199 Pounds, a Tried and Tested Giant of Finnish Descent, lends his unique Eye, and Spirit of Calculation, to Hand-to-Hand Combat, and renders the Bludgeoning and Pulverisation of his opponent a Science; Most recently victorious in his match against Kid Ithaca, who was rendered Helpless against Scott's devastating Ice-Hard Fists, and vomited forth his Heart, Stomick, and Vitals in a great Spume of steaming Offal.

Clobberin' Colgrave, 205 Pounds, a doughty Hibernian late of the Emerald Isle, is a very Hogs-Head of Defiance, a stout Contender who shrugs off Hammer-Blows as if they were Kisses, and drinks in Punishment as it were Whiskey; Has been seen to Cudgel his Man with such Pile-Driving Force, that Bones fly to Flinders with a resounding Crack. Lately triumphant against Homer Hoose the Slashing Swede, whose Skull he Splintered with a Heroic Right Cross, Showering the Delighted Onlookers with Crimson Gobbets torn from the Swede's Brain-Pan, and winning the Lakeland Crown.

Both Scott and Colgrave are fleet of Foot, bright of Eye, and possess Fists of the heaviest Lead; yet both are noble Gentlemen, schooled in the Craft of Sports-Manship. By these lights, the Promoter shall forbid the use of Axes, Sledges, Gun-Powder, Punt-Hammers, Horse-Whips, Plough-Shares, and Fence-Posts by members of the Audience. The Pugilists may not use any Drug or Physick, excepting Alcohol, Morphine, Heroin, Laudanum, Horse Laxative, and Coca Leaf; The humane use of leathern Pugilistic Gloves, as specified by the New-York Sporting Commission, in order to artificially soften the Brutality of any Blow, is expressly Forbidden.

No Ladies or Boys under Eight Years of Age Permitted.

ADVANCES IN BALLOONING SCIENCE.

SCIENTISTS HAVE HARNESSED GREAT POWERS IN THE MIGHTY BALLOONS.

BUT DOES MANKIND HAVE THE WISDOM TO USE THE POWER RESPONSIBLY?

Annapolis, Maryland, Sept. 6.—At a symposium at the McCauley Conventioneering and Exposition Pasture this week, celebrated technicians, scientists, contraptioneers, and prognosticators of future advances gathered. They conferred on our Republic's stupendous achievements in the ballooning technologies, and shared splendid visions for where the mighty sky-ships will take us in the future.

Many foresaw a new age of greatness, in which even the vaulted Heavens of the Lord are within the reach of the outstretched arms of Progress.

Yet, as the promise of the balloon continues to defy the Earth-bound destiny of man, the question was raised, Will we prove worthy of the marvels our God-given blessing of balloon flight has wrought? In this new century, will we be able to maintain our control over the balloons, or will these modern air-chariots control us? Thinkers speculate that it is possible that in this emergent age, we will no longer walk like men, but, rather, buoyed by the floating dirigibles above us, float upon the aether. Does man have the humility to ascend into the clouds and remain mere men? Or will we, rather, fancy ourselves as verily unto gods?

As the century unfolds, new advances in ballooning science are expected to change the way we live our daily lives as citizenry. The experts in attendance at the symposium foretold fantastic visions of the balloon age. If there is no time to milk the cows, farmers will be able to strap on a personalized balloon harness and float to the barn in seconds. Sewing a kerchief will be made easy with balloon-powered needles and thread, making the chore float by in half to one-third the time. Soon, we will no doubt educate our children in vast, balloon-powered mobile school-houses in the sky, and mighty balloon cities will enable us to live as angels amongst the clouds.

But theologians in attendance asked, "What if the balloons themselves become our God?" Men of God and scientists alike urged all peoples to be mindful of man's humility before Christ our Lord. Though the coming century looms with windblown wonders, let us remember that Adam and Eve walked the Earth upon human feet. We may embrace the greatness of the new ballooning era and its wondrous miracles yet to come, but worship not the balloon! Hold your head high as we balloon into the future, yet bow and debase yourself in fear of our terrible Lord and His mighty justice.

THE ONION

PRESSES POWERED BY STEAM

A CLARIFICATION. A news-paper is not intended for use as food, clothing, or shelter. One reads a news-paper for information.

Tuesday, May 20, 1902. — The Best Source of News-worthy Items in Our Great Republic. — Price Two Cents.

SEARS, ROEBUCK PLEAD 'NOT GUILTY' TO PORNOGRAPHY CHARGES.

Noted Merchants Accused of Scandalous Etchings of Under-Garments in Catalogue.

RACY SPREAD DEPICTS ALL MANNER OF CORSETS, BODICES, NIGHT-WEAR.

The Onion offers these immodest and wanton images not to titillate or excite prurient tastes, but to edify the reader and alert him to the unspeakable sights to be found within one of our Republic's most prominent catalogue wish-books.

Chicago, May 19.—Sears, Roebuck and Co., the famed Chicago mail-order entrepreneur of curious reputation, whose catalogue wish-books have proven greatly popular with settlers of the Great Plains and other outlying reaches of the Republic, pleaded not guilty to-day in a federal court to charges of sedition and corruption of the morality and virtue of America's manhood via the distribution of pornography and obscenity through the nation's mails.

"Our catalogue is nothing more than a listing of household items readily available to the citizenry at a substantial discount," said Richard Sears, the merchant and warehouse wholesaler whose shipping business, co-founded with Alvah C. Roebuck in 1893, has revolutionized commerce on the frontier, from his place at the witness-stand, where he and his partner stood accused.

Nonetheless, prosecutors for the state of Illinois asserted the merchants' guilt.

"Engravings in the Sears and Roebuck catalogue clearly depict arousing and titillating images of comely young ladies of questionable virtue clad in the merest and most slight of under-clothes, corsets, bloomers, and night-gowns, plainly stripped of proper clothing 'for the eyes of all to gaze upon," the charges read.

Numerous witnesses for the prosecution agreed, claiming that on many an occasion they had, despite earnest attempts to avoid temptation through prayer and church-going, been unable to resist the scandalous and prurient imagery depicted within the catalogue, and had succumbed to fascination and even, in several cases, bouts of wicked onanism by the rousing pictures within.

Ministers of the clergy of notable social standing also contested the moral purity of the mail-merchants. "With the effort they expend to disseminate their filthy catalogue, these evil-doers could have been distributing copies of the Holy Bible to poor families or spreading the Word of the Christ to the savages," the Reverend X. Lucius Dalrymple said on the stand.

Presented in evidence of the ware-house's crimes were several reproductions of imagery taken from the catalogue's pages, clearly displaying underwear-clad lovelies in shameful poses.

Despite Sears and Roebuck's fervent claims of their own innocence, it is expected that any right-thinking and God-fearing system of justice will find them guilty as charged and sentence them to hang by their necks until dead.

THOS. EDISON INVENTS 423RD CONTRAPTION.

May 19.—The famed Gadgeteer of Menlo Park, New Jersey, Thomas Edison, has applied for a patent for his latest invention, the Revolving Spark-Shooter.

This curious instrument marks Edison's 423rd patent and stands as the 612th contraption to be patented in the United States.

By slowly turning a crank and releasing a small brake, a small dynamo will quickly spin and undulate, and scrape against a piece of elongated metal. As friction is increased, what appear to be bolts of miniature lightning will begin to shoot. As the dynamo whirls, it makes a high-pitched noise, much like a button spinning upon a taut string. And, if one listens closely and carefully to the noise, one can almost make out the words, "God Save the Republic." It is a miraculous device, one to rival Edison's many others, which include the Talking Machine, the Incredible Incandescent Electric Lighting Appliance, the Steam-Powered Ear-Trumpet, the Amazing Mechanical Winnowing Contrivance, the Foldable Checkers-Playing Board, the Revolving "French" Fried-Potato Cooking Kettle, and the Astounding Paper-Sack.

CONGRESS REDUCES WORK-WEEK TO 135 HOURS.

Captains of Industry Scarlet with Rage.

'WE STAND TO LOSE EVERYTHING,' CARNEGIE SAYS.

LAW CALLS FOR FIFTEEN-MINUTE 'BREAK' BETWEEN WORK WEEKS.

In a move that resounds like thunder throughout our great Republic, a Congress made up of influential Progressive Republicans has voted "Yea" on legislation that would cut the work-week to a scant 135 hours and hobble fair Dame Industry with many other insidious and crippling reforms.

"We have built a great nation and a just and fair Republic on the strong backs of our working-men," opined the great steel baron Andrew Carnegie during a week-long bacchanal at New York's opulent Plutocrat Club. "Now, certain elements in Congress would have these working-men's backs be unburdened for almost eight hours of every working day. Is it difficult to believe, gentle-men, that Congress wishes to undermine the very foundations of fair America herself?" The gracious Carnegie added that, should such radical measures be taken before next year's end, he would be forced to fall short in a lucrative contract with no less a personage than the Kaiser of Germany himself.

Many other princely Captains of Industry were eager to press their opinions on this reporter, and many a scandalous detail was gleaned thereby. Congress also wishes every working-man to be granted a fifteen-minute break for lunch-time every day. If these fifteen minutes are multiplied by the thousands of men, women, and children whose valiant efforts bring vitality to our Republic's foundries and meat-packing plants, the resulting lost time can be estimated in thousands of life-times. A certain potentate of the banking-houses also noted that Congress' bill did not specify for what the laborer's new-found eight hours of lassitude every day should be used. The cautious gentle-man, in order to stay informed upon this issue, should remember that idle hands are the Devil's tools, and that a working-man with eight hours to spend between shifts is more liable to spend them at the fiendish Labor Agitator's meeting-hall.

Although the workers themselves have not yet been informed of the new measures, there seems little reason to do so. No doubt the swarthy, potato-stained hand of the Immigrant will soon be detected in this matter, and the law put down. The publishers of The Onion newspaper urge Congress to stop the tom-foolery of pandering to laborers too busy and addle-pated to vote, and pass a bill, a just and fair law punishing those who leave work without permission in order to attend the funerals of sons or daughters who die at the loom.

'ADOLF' MOST POPULAR NAME FOR BOYS.

The name "Adolf" remains the most popular for new-born males throughout the Republic, according to data gathered from birth-rolls. The next most popular monikers are Purvius, Earsworth, Cadwalader and Ebenezer. As for the most popular girls' name, it remains, for the thirteenth year running, "Sugarbelle," which also leads the list of names given to mares.

MOST PREFERRED SHEET MUSIC SELECTIONS OF TO-DAY.

"Up On My Merry Thresher."

"Won't You Please Imbibe a Raspberry Phosphate With Me, My Sweet Agnes Dear of Mine?"

"Err, staria, Darling, Please Do Not Die of the Dropsy."

"I Will Give You a Sweet Comfit."

"Our God Is a Vengeful God."

"Gaily We Prance About."

"March of the Darkies."

"O Mighty and Merciful Lord God in Heaven Above, Please Do Not Smite Us Your Humble Children."

"I'm Sweet on You, Oh Virgie Dear."

REPUBLIC'S NEGROES STILL WAITING FOR 40 ACRES, MULE.

AGRICULTURE SECRETARY FAULTS LOW MULE, ACREAGE AVAILABILITY AT PRESENT.

Washington, May 18.—Nearly 30 years after the end of Reconstruction, freed-men and free-born throughout the land's Negro populace experienced to-day yet another delay in their long-promised allocation of forty acres and a mule.

Citing "prohibitive federal budget inadequacies," U.S. Agriculture Secretary James Wilson announced that "the United States presently cannot afford to allocate forty acres or mules to any citizen, particularly those of dark-skinned, African persuasion, at this time."

Wilson urged all Negroes to remain forth-right and stead-fast in their patience. He addressed Negroes directly by adding, "Please do not commit any acts of violence or impropriety against our nation's white women while waiting."

Negroes were urged by the Secretary to bear in mind that the consequences of any such tempestuous response to his announcement would cause further delay, and perhaps even jeopardize acreage and mule availability altogether.

The Secretary also called for coffee to be brought into his parlor immediately.

"Prompt serving of coffee and other refreshments is essential for avoidance of further delays in mule and acreage allocations," he said.

Wilson promised that, if coffee was served hot, in a timely fashion, and with pleasant demeanor, any number of mules and allocations, each amounting to 40 acres of good farming land in the Western territories, may be forth-coming.

For Negroes who may have grown tired of waiting, the Department of Agriculture is offering special premiums that may be accepted in lieu of mules and acreage.

Negroes waiting fifteen to twenty-five years are eligible to receive a three-legged stool, suitable for holding a cow or goat, or for elevating themselves to a slightly higher station than to which they are normally accustomed.

Negroes who have been waiting twenty-six to forty-two years will receive a wooden, jointed dancing-man on a stick, which makes a pleasing and whimsical clattering sound when jerked in an up-and-down motion upon a thin piece of wood.

And finally, those Negroes who have waited forty-three years or more will receive a fine bolt of sturdy calico, from which anything from curtains to a fancy pinafore may be sewn.

Despite these considerable offers, some Negroes stubbornly continue to hope for the parcel of land and mule they were promised so long ago, despite the reasoned explanations given to them as to why this is not likely.

LADY LIBERTY'S SPANISH MENACE RETURNS FOR REVENGE.

Lady Liberty. — "I was a fool to let my guard down, even after my great 1898 victory."

TO-DAY'S WEATHER PROGNOSTICATION.	# THE ONION	Employing
Goat entrails indicate that to-day will be fair and mild, with variable winds.		Photo-Graphs.

Thursday, August 6, 1903. — The Best Source of News-worthy Items in our Great Republic. — Price Two Cents.

ZULUS ATTACK LONDON!

KING HELD AT SPEARPOINT.

A Disastrous Turn of Events for British Empire, as Treacherous Savages Turn on Their Benevolent Overseers.

PARLIAMENTARY HEADS SHRUNKEN.

PRIME MINISTER CALLS FOR CALM, BISCUITS.

London, Aug. 5.—This quondam glorious metropolis was in abject shambles this evening, the sad victim of a cruel and villainous attack by members of Rhodesia's Zulu tribes.

Horrified women clutched their young children bosomward and watched helplessly as the combined forces of the once-proud British Army, joined by dozens of amateur soldiery culled from the ranks of Scotland Yard, proved no match for the thousands of ululating warriors who rushed upon the city to-day, brandishing poison-tipped spears and descending en masse from what appears to have been their primary bivouac in Epsom.

"There is no cause for alarm," Prime Minister A.J. Balfour told the surviving members of Parliament to-day at a hastily called assemblage. "Both His Majesty and myself remain supremely confident that no threat to our vast and glorious Empire is posed by the ignominious surrender of its capital."

Balfour also called for calm throughout the city and for crumpets to be served at 4 o'clock with tea.

Sir William Williams-White, Head of His Majesty's Armed Forces, said that the British had long expected Zulu retaliation for last month's massacre of 500 tribeswomen in Natal, which was itself retaliation for Zulu slowness in bringing British officers their smoking jackets. However, Williams-White said he had believed the anticipated assault would be "a sortie by grass-boat along the Sanyati River, somewhere between Kadoma and the Chegutu outpost," rather than a flank attack on the English main-land.

The King himself was held at spearpoint by the brutish warriors, and many of his high-level officials are feared cooked in an enormous stew-pot and consumed by the cannibals.

THE ONION'S REPORT ON CLOTHING FASHIONS.

BLACK STILL COLOR OF CHOICE THIS FALL.

Ladies will once again be turning heads of the gentlemanly sort as they pass by silently in the season's deepest blacks. There is no need to discard that basic black all-wool over-coat you have been wearing perennially since 1886, because, once again, it is the color in which everybody about town and country will be clad.

True black has been lauded from the East Coast to the Mississippi as the superior choice to maintain a respectful Christian appearance while hiding telltale signs of human drudgery and the disregard for hygiene that is so popular in our time.

Wools-men and tailors have crafted 12 new garment varieties in this century alone.

This year, black is seen in everything from the 42 Eyelet Patent Leather Laced Ladies' Shoe to the Young Boys' Cannery Vestee Suit with Knee Pants, all of exquisite quality and custom-made from durable products by the best American tailors and seamstresses at exemplary value for the price.

Bolt fabric will be available in a spectrum of choices: Coal Dust Black, Topsoil Black, Glorious, Wondrous Machine-Oil Black, and this year's swift seller, Pittsburgh Sky.

Our comely country lasses are appearing in the Ladies' Summer Suit, available by package freight from four major American cities. Hand-sewn of the finest double-weight wool-lined wool available in America, it has unhitched ruffled wrists for freedom of movement and increased airflow to the elbow for the warmer months. It is a delight when paired with black leather Corn-Husking Gloves. This lovely article is enduring enough to save lady's dress from ruination during even the longest walk home, withstanding all splashes from the family wagon's wheels.

Turning the fashion world on its bottomward side, a fifth style of Ladies' Suit was introduced this year through the finest supply houses. The sensibly black all-wool Cheviot Serge Double-Breasted Suit differs with an added row of buttons on the inside coat collar. The effect is stunning and has all the ladies in the suffrage committees in quite a dither! A high-standing collar protects lady's delicate neck from exposure to elements of sun and afternoon breeze. It is a good value for the money at $4.00.

Some of the preferred ways to wear black this year:

Double-stitched at the seams for durability, the new Ladies' Porcine Slaughter Suit washes clean at the end of butchering season without staining or fading.

A most sought-after garment is the Birthing Gown and Velvet Birthing Hat bedecked with black ostrich feather plumes, splendiferous silk ribbon, and vaginal access chute.

Ladies' Sleeping Gowns will feature an opening at the feet this year, as well as extra seam bulk around the waist to facilitate a looser sleeping corset.

The Short Length Parlor Skirt is an option for the light of heart. During private times about the home, draw the curtains shut and delight in this skirt that just grazes the ankle.

Order your Hen-house Coat now and be prepared for the chilly fall mornings. Comes complete with belt loops to fit the Beheading Shoulder Harness. Great value for the price at $2.50.

WORLD'S LARGEST CESS-POOL OF CARCASSES AND FECES DEDICATED OUTSIDE CHICAGO MEAT-PACKING PLANT.

Chicago, Aug. 5.—City Hall officials and prominent captains of industry were on hand in this fast-growing Middle Western metropolis yesterday for the dedication of an enormous cess-pool, believed to be the world's largest outside of Schweliger and Sons' Meat Processing Plant. The bros. Schweliger, the Mayor, and the district alder-man were on hand to draw back a large broad-cloth curtain hung from a rear entrance of the plant, revealing to the attending audience an awesome lagoon of liquid sewage, bloated cattle carcasses, and undefinable sludge. The spectacle was made more vivid by the sweltering heat and absence of wind.

"It was Progress that built this cess-pool, and Progress will continue to feed it, God willing," declared the Mayor. The day's festivities were somewhat marred by an outbreak of cholera among the Bulgarian immigrants who live near the factory, but all agreed that the evening's fire-works display illuminated the cess-pool in an aesthetically appealing manner.

SOUTH COVERED IN WEEVILS.

Cotton-growers throughout the Deep South are reporting enormous infestations of weevils, insatiable insects who devour and devastate cotton crops. The damage incurred by these pests is incalculable, and existing cotton reserves are selling at a premium rate. Americans may have to resign themselves to the hard truth that soon they may not be able to purchase bolts of cotton cloth to make a nobby suit of clothes or a pretty Sunday go-to-meeting frock.

Meanwhile, weevils continue to cover the South like dirt on a street-urchin. Weevils can be found crawling in baby perambulators, tea-pots, molasses-barrels, sacks of flour, out-houses, and all other objects commonly found in Southern house-holds.

Some enterprising share-croppers have contrived a novel way to address the weevil menace: Gathering as many weevils as they can scoop up, the share-croppers throw them into a large cauldron of water, boil them for several hours, then pour the contents into bottles and preserve-jars. "Weevil-Gin" has taken the place of white lightning and moon-shine hooch as the beverage of preference among poor Southerners.

Moving Photo-Drama Cinema-Play 'The Great Train Robbery' Causes Many Breeches to Be Soiled.

Lest the reader estimate the moveable-picture device to be nearly an innocuous trifle not capable of harming a person any more than it could launch an industry, "The Great Train Robbery" proved itself at a nickelodeon exhibition to be a shocking picture-play of no morals or restraint, and one which caused numerous patrons to involuntarily evacuate their bladders into their raiment.

Telling the affairs of a confederation of dastards who force entry on a locomotive and plunder the treasures of all on board, its shocking depictions of violence and even murder had many ladies in attendance fainting and many gentle-men soiling their trousers from fright precisely where they sat. When the moving film-o-graph's scandalous final image unrolled, in which the leader of the robber band fires his pistol directly at the hapless audience, the entire theater was brought to screams and wettings by the horror of the matter.

All in attendance concurred that this grievous picture-story was no better than the urine which had been frightened out of them. It is sad that such a meticulous and expensive motion-drama-image as this needed be made to prove the point that violence cannot masquerade as entertainment, and that no upstanding citizen of the Republic shall let his conscience nor suit be soiled by the knowledge that he has subsidized such folly with his hard-earned nickel.

FROM EUROPE.

Artist Picasso Runs out of Blue Paint.

From the European correspondent, Aug. 5.—Young popular painter Pablo Picasso of Spain ran out of blue paint earlier this week, ending a nearly six-year phase of his artistic career.

The paint, acquired by Picasso at a special paint wholesaler's Removing-Myself-from-Mercantiling Sale years ago, came at such a substantial volume discount that Picasso could not pass up the bargain, despite having only the color blue available.

"With the high cost of paints to-day, I felt I should use all the blue paint before moving on to new colors, such as green or red," Picasso said. "I had such quantities of paint—in my attic, in my root cellar... everywhere."

After running out of blue paint, Picasso says, he is now free to explore other artistic goals, such as drawing people with both eyes on the same side of their face.

"I've also got a great idea for a big, mad-looking, cow-related thing I wish to present in Chicago," he said.

YESTERDAY'S PANAMA CANAL DEATHS:

308

TO-DAY'S PANAMA CANAL DEATHS:

261

'I AM VERY DISMAYED AT THE STOCKINGS YOUNG PEOPLE ARE WEARING TO-DAY.'

AN EDITORIAL ON PAGE 16.

CONFESSIONS OF A UNION MAN.

A SHOCKING TRUE STORY ON PAGE 18.

Chicken Raper.

This is a positive-action force-feed twin-gate twelve-and-a-half-pound tension-operated hand-held double-action device utilized by stockmen, poultrymen, gentle-man farmers, and hobbyists. Guaranteed.

Price each.............. $1.75

Schlien and Sons,
19 E. Murdo Ave., Kansas City

TO-DAY'S LYNCHINGS.

10:30 A.M., RED SEAVER AT THE TREVERTON TOWN SQUARE.

12 NOON, POKEY WILLIS AT THE HORBART FARM, BEAUMONT. LUNCHEON TO FOLLOW.

12:30, LONNIE LITTLE AT THE CRESTWOOD VILLAGE FESTIVAL.

4:30 THE BROTHERS BROWN, ON THE WILMUTH PROPERTY, ARLINGTON.

3:00 P.M., UN-NAMED NEGRO, IDENTITY TO BE ANNOUNCED, IN MAIN SQUARE, GREENVILLE.

SUPPORT YOUR LOCAL MONOPOLY.

THE ONION

Mastery of Flight **EXTRA!**

Friday, December 18, 1903. The Best Source of News-worthy Items in our Great Republic. Price Two Cents.

SCIENCE CONQUERS SKY WITH WRIGHT BROS. FLYING MACHINE; HEAVEN EXPEDITION SLATED FOR NEXT YEAR.

Historic Meeting Between Roosevelt and St. Peter Planned; President Preparing Speech.

Citizens of Republic Eager to Visit Passed Relatives.

POSSIBILITIES FOR TRADE CONSIDERABLE, SAY CAPTAINS OF INDUSTRY.

WILL DEATH BECOME A THING OF THE PAST?

Washington, D.C., Dec. 17.—The serene Kingdom of Heaven will be the domain of man as early as next year, thanks to the scientific prowess of the Wright brothers of Ohio, who verified man's mastery of the skies at 9 a.m. today with their historic flight above the dunes at Kitty Hawk, North Carolina.

Possessing at last a heavier-than-air craft capable of lifting itself, staying aloft, and listing where directed by the able pilot, man-kind will now be able to journey to God's fair abode, where the moral and philosophical conundrae which vex Earth dwellers may be explained by the Creator Himself.

"In close consultation with the brothers Wright and other scientific thinkers, I support an expedition to the Heavens in the name of the United States," proclaimed President Roosevelt in an impromptu Pennsylvania Avenue speech which gathered many passers-by.

The expedition is slated for June of next year.

The journey, to be arranged by prominent theologians and leading Flying Scientists, shall be attempted aboard a replica of the Wrights' magnificent Kitty Hawk craft constructed to eight times original size, this to accommodate its full complement of a captain, a navigator, several theologians, and a photo-grapher.

Theologians are included so that God may be recognized at first sighting. Though modern religious thinkers believe Him to be a gargantuan man, up to a hundred feet in stature, fair of face with flowing white hair and beard, and bedecked in a luminous robe, variations in popular descriptions necessitate a quorum of learned Men of God to distinguish Him from other radiant giants who may inhabit the Kingdom of Heaven.

As it is anticipated that when the craft reaches the Kingdom, cherubim will sound majestic trumpets heralding man's return to his Creator, plans are to include a famous Edison talking-machine to record the historic event.

Anticipated with equal zeal is the opportunity of the expeditioners to meet with long-lost loved ones, as well as admired figures of historical renown. Father Clement Dickey of Norfolk, Virginia, said to this reporter, "I should like to visit with my departed mother, and speak with her unfettered by the yoke of mental sickness, which was the bane of our conversations in her waning years." Though Dickey is unsure whether the doubtless busy schedule of St. Thomas Aquinas will permit a Heavenly meeting, he has made numerous requests via the medium of prayer.

Also being carried on the great sky-vessel will be food and libations for eight to last a full week, as it is unknown what fare may be served in Heaven. To quote the words of Father Dickey, "It is possible that only Godly manna may be served in the kitchens and dining halls of Heaven, and whether mortal man can be nourished solely by such is yet unknown." The expedition does hope to bring a quantity of manna safely back, so that our scientists may analyze it and determine its nutritive qualities and whether it may be harvested and exported.

Once the expedition has returned safely to Earth and a reliable map is drafted, mass production of Heaven-planes will begin, that the just and honest may journey to their lasting Reward on whim, rather than suffer the infirmities of age and hardship, as demanded in the traditional route to Salvation.

ARMY CONTEMPLATES FORMATION OF SEPARATE 'FLYING CONTRAPTION FORCE.'

FLYING MOUNTED HORSEMEN COULD BE FORMIDABLE LINE OF DEFENSE, SAY PRESIDENT'S GENERALS.

From the Military Correspondent, Dec. 17.—The esteemed and doughty gentlemen charged with governing our great Republic in matters of warfare have taken notice of the Wright brothers' recent success and are reportedly considering the military value of a craft that could remain aloft without the aid of a balloon device. While no learned or soldierly gentleman has yet explored the usefulness of an airborne conveyance as a gunnery platform, the War Department considers it more than just an element of scientifical-fiction, and reports that it merits further study.

"The airborne contraption could be a formidable line of defense," said General of the Cavalry John J. Pershing, whose experience fighting the Cuban and Filipino has been brought to bear in the consideration of a new air-borne force of fighting men. "Presently the operation of the flying contraption utilizes the flyer's full attention," the General said. "But if engineers can develop a contraption which holds two men, one could operate the device, and the other could fire a gun or swing a saber while the craft swoops down onto enemy troops like a hawk."

The general also speculates that a cavalry of flying horses could be used to stop charging men on horse-back, provided the horses aloft could hold men on their backs without the aid of encumbering trusses and harnesses. "I am not yet convinced this is possible," the General said. He added that such harnesses would be necessary, yet may make use of a rifle or other hand-held weapon nearly impossible.

In the spirit of scientific investigation, Army officials are planning to stage a mock battle between the Crimson Guard, a squadron of elite Army horse-men, and a squadron of flying machines.

"We hope to demonstrate that a significant advantage is begotten by a fleet of horse-drawn, flap-winged flying contraptions," Pershing said.

Other Army officials believe the flying machine will be of more utility when it can be powered by steam.

"Not until we harness the might of Steam will any air-borne contraption be a suitable engine of warfare," said General Edward Horister. "If the Army should construct a steam-powered craft, the Spaniards and other enemies of these United States had best beware."

THE FLYING MACHINE OF ORVILLE AND WILBUR WRIGHT, WHICH FLEW 400 YARDS THURSDAY UN-AIDED BY BALLOON. PICTURED HERE BY PHOTO-LITHOGRAPH.

RAIL-ROAD SCIENTISTS SAY KITTY HAWK FLYING APPARATUS A HOAX.

LOCOMOTIVE EXPERTS 'NOT FOOLED.'

New York, Dec. 17.—In an attempt to demonstrate that flying is a physical impossibility, and that railroading is still the only effective means of traversing a great distance in mere days, a noble congregation of the Republic's greatest Scientific and Engineering men gathered in a provincial New York hay-mow today purporting that the Wright brothers have fooled the world.

The showing-up of the Wrights was a grand affair not unlike a carnival. Demonstrations were held throughout the day showing how easily flight can be faked. Hundreds of New York towns-people attended the spectacle.

"In all my years as designer and chief locomotive-expert for the great Cornelius Vanderbilt, I believe I am well qualified to judge the physical limits in the field of mechanical transportation," said Harold Dorenheim, who holds Doctorates of Boilerology and Steamic Physics from the Institute of Railway Science in Chicago.

Dorenheim, his great white moustache billowing in the wind, presented an elaborate stockyard demonstration in which a test locomotive car was brought up to speed and, by the means of a ramp, launched some dozens of feet into the air, upon which it failed utterly in taking flight.

"By this means," Dorenheim said, "we begin to see that the sheer amount of horse-power required for balloon-less flight is almost infinite. If an eighty-thousand-pound locomotive, the most powerful device known to man, is not powerful enough to fly, what could be?"

Dorenheim added that it was clear to the plain eye that no rail-way tracks appeared in the aether, thereby proving that airborne transport is "a fallacy most ludicrous."

"Why, even a child can see that there are no rails in the air," he said. "Therefore, even a child can deduce with the most elementary reason the absurdity of locomoting transport cars through the air. Would these Wrights believe the rest of us to be no smarter than a child?"

Another display, conducted by Steamaticist and Fluid Pressure Hydraulicist Franz Joseph Gegen, involved a life-sized device which might, under fortuitous conditions, seem to actually take a passenger to the air and fly. It was made from a model of a so-called aero-plane affixed to a twenty-foot-high scaffold, which was mounted upon a railway hand-car. The hand-car was then obscured behind an immense sheet of broad-cloth, upon which moving-pictures of the sky were projected. The assembled audience seemed to agree wholeheartedly that the illusion was striking.

"In Scientific exploration, it is important to first formulate a belief, and then defend it against all evidence," Gegen said. "In this manner, we have struck a blow for Science and the people, and falsified flying along with Evolution and the scandalous beliefs of Galileo."

The demonstration show was arranged and funded by the Northeastern Railway Company.

WOODEN MILK-WAGON TOY MOST POPULAR THIS CHRIST-MAS SEASON.

ECLIPSES LAST YEAR'S SUCCESS, THE UNCLE SAM MECHANICAL-BANK.

GENERAL STORES REPORT MAD RUSH OF SHOPPERS EAGER TO ATTAIN PRIZED TRIFLE FOR CHILDREN.

An abundance of dry-goods proprietorships throughout our Republic are reporting that their customers are exhibiting a great partiality toward a wooden milk-wagon toy as a worthy gift for their children during the Christ-mas-time holiday. Supplies of the toy are said to be fast becoming depleted.

Gunderson's General Mercantile on Water Street in Chicago, for example, testified that its full stock of the item, nearly three dozen, was sold by closing-time Friday last. Proprietor Josiah Gunderson would not disclose the amount his establishment had taken in from the sales, but with the milk-wagon toy averaging a retail cost of fourteen cents among similar merchants, the proceeds of this particular sale must have been close to five dollars.

So much is this sundry in demand among the populace that its mere presence in a shop-window creates a considerable furor. The employees at Atchison's Premium Dry-Goods Emporium in Scranton, New Jersey, expressed surprise at the zealousness which their patrons invested in the task of purchasing the milk-wagon. Gentle-men waved their umbrellas in a brusque fashion, demanding that the clerks procure the item for them post-haste. Ladies were seen to demonstrate little of the charm and demureness for which the fairer sex is known, fighting over one of the milk-wagons like so many hounds over a ham-bone.

The milk-wagon itself is quite a handsome and well-hewn facsimile of the genuine article, and it is easy to see how a young boy or girl would derive enjoyment from it. Joined with small nails and sporting a realistic wheel-and-axle mechanism that smoothly responds to a gentle push, the wagon is fancifully decorated with red paint.

While many are busy wrapping the coveted play-thing in gay ribbons and colored butcher-paper and placing it under the Yule-tide tree, some esteemed men of the cloth have expressed concern that the spiritual meaning of the holiday is being cast asunder by materialistic sentiments.

"Christ-mas is the time in which we solemnly commemorate the birth of our Divine Savior the Christ-Child," said the Reverend X. Lucius Dalrymple from his pulpit Sunday. "To do anything other than to honor our Messiah on this Holy day is to blaspheme and besmirch His Divine Purpose. This wee milk-delivering vehicle, innocuous though it seems, could be construed as a vehicle for delivering Satan's base and covetous message to the most vulnerable lambs in Jesus' flock."

CHURCH SOURCES CONFIRM: NO HOMO-SEXUALS IN U.S. NOW.

see full account on page 10.

NEW 'STRAPPING DOWN ON SLAB OF STONE' THERAPY MAY BE BREAK-THROUGH IN TREATING MENTAL ILLNESS.

see full account on page 3

THE ONION
TOLERATOR OF THE COMMON MAN.
Providence!

Tuesday, March 8, 1904. — The Best Source of News-worthy Items in Our Great Republic. — Price Two Cents.

COPPER MINE FIRE ENTERTAINS IDLE RICH.

'Such Colors and Such a Roar,' Well-to-Do Socialites Say of Spectacle.

Butte, Mont., Mar. 7.—A great fire that has engulfed a mine-shaft and threatens surrounding villages, farms, and 87,000 square acres of forest was applauded as a grand show of pyrotechnical wizardry by mining executives.

"This is the most spectacular conflagration since the blaze at the Dakota Indian School and Orphanage," said L. Edgar Crampton, president and general operating manager of the Rocky Mountain Mining Company of Montana. "Such gay colors!"

Crampton visited the mine with several of his executive officers when a sudden explosion beneath the earth was heard for miles around. The ground below their feet shook violently, and a roar the loudness of which was likened to the simultaneous chugging of twenty locomotives issued from the mine.

"That was most likely the sound made as sparks from the explosion caught fire from the gas-lamps used by the seventy or so miners in the mine at the time," Mr. Crampton told The Onion. "The force of the sound cast me into the dirt and the wind was knocked out of me. Such a fantastic roar! It was as though the glorious Fourth came early this year!"

P. Wilford Drevington, owner of the mine and several others in the area, was also entertained by the raucous rumble and fire: "I'm certain the stock-holders and my beloved will be reading this," he said, "and they will be white with fear for my safety. Let it be known that I promptly made my escape and am as right as rain, aside from some dirt on my suit and spats. But I am having a capital time, and it reminds me of why I simply relish the life of a mining executive!"

Volunteer fire-men from the neighboring towns are feverishly attempting to extinguish the blaze and remove the bodies, but the heat and fire are growing too intense as acres of wood-land are consumed in the fire's insatiable advance. Given no time to grieve, the citizens of Butte hastily gathered up their few paltry possessions, bundled up their half-starved broods, and headed to the train station at the county seat of Hickory Run, a desperate act given that most of them haven't the money to purchase a train ticket.

The train station, however, was clogged with the arrival of dozens of executives of other mining companies, generously invited by Mr. Drevington to witness the blaze in the peace and serenity of his summer retreat in the Mountains a safe eight miles away.

Pouring a glass of brandy for one of his executives and puffing a fat Cuban cigar, Drevington marveled at the distant blaze from his porch and appeared to be nonplussed by the demise of one of his highest-yielding mines.

"This is why insurance exists. I'm going to make out handsomely!" he said.

CITIZENS!

With the most emphatic of advisement, you are strongly urged to attend the

ST. LOUIS EXPOSITION OF ST. LOUIS, MISSOURI,

The Grandest and Most Glorious Event of Our Age!

Makes the Exhibits of The 1893 Columbian Exposition resemble so many Chicken Droppings

Eight Fantastic Exhibition-Halls, of the Finest Beaux-Arts Architectural Design, displaying the latest Scientific Advances, including Multitudinous and Innovative Uses of the Great Discovery, Electrical-Power.

You are a Pathetic, Barely Sentient Human Being Deserving of the Mocking and Derision of Others If You Fail to Witness

**THE HALL OF EMBROIDERY.
THE HALL OF ITEMS OF DIVERSE SHAPES.
THE HALL OF BROKEN GLASS.
THE HALL OF PORRIDGE.**

And the Amazing Attractions

THE "FECES-LESS" SIDE-WALK.
Imagine a pedestrian walk-way completely free of the malodorous excretions of horses and oxen! You may think this a far-fetched pipe-dream of Jules Verne, but it does indeed exist, and only at this Great Exposition!

THE EXHIBITION OF THE NEW FRENCH "PORNO-GRAPH."
A Machine to Whose Attributes We Can Not Adequately Do Justice in This Advertisement. You Must Experience It to Believe It!

AND THE ELECTRICAL-CHAIR,
Which sends several thousand Roentgens of the magical electrical-current through the bodies of condemned criminals

HUZZAH!

SKELETON OF SATAN DISCOVERED!

BONES FOUND IN WYOMING INDIAN LANDS.

THEOLOGIANS, SCIENTISTS CAN NOW DISCERN EXACT LOCATION OF LUCIFER'S FALL FROM HEAVEN.

COULD PROVE SAVAGE INDIANS IN LEAGUE WITH DEMONS.

From the Western Territories correspondent, Mar. 7.—The discipline of theology underwent perhaps the greatest moment in the field's long and distinguished history this Monday, when experts from Universities across the land gathered to examine the first-ever irrefutable proof of the fall of Lucifer from the Heavens—the intact and complete skeleton of Satan himself, Prince of Darkness and Lord of Lies, found by a farming-hand in an untilled field in Wyoming.

The skeleton, the mortal remains of what is clearly seen to depict Satan's terrible visage, was dug up by a team of experts from the Chicago School of Theology after the farming-hand who discovered it summoned help from more learned minds with the aid of the tele-graphy device located in Casper Town.

It is estimated that the bones have lain undisturbed within the field since Lucifer originally fell from Heaven, after being cast out by the Lord Almighty and His Heavenly Hosts of Arch-angels for the deadly sin of pride, probably more than fourteen thousand years past.

"There is no doubt that the skeleton is that of Satan," said Reverend-Doctor Hanover Waine, one of the clergy-men present at the site of the find. "The grim face of all evil, though stripped of flesh by Holy Providence, is unmistakable."

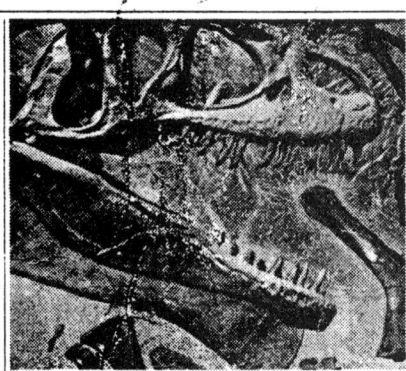

The find, confirmed by learned men of science as proof of the Evil Angel's fall as recounted within the pages of the Revelation of John, puts an end to any doubt over the veracity of the claims made by the Apostles within the Bible. It in fact verifies the location of Lucifer's fall as some 240 miles north of Casper Town, Wyoming.

"Now that Biblical history has been irrevocably proven as scientific fact, the task of science is obvious—to help lead the struggle for missionary work over-seas, to redeem heathen souls through the cleansing power of the Blood of the Savior of man, our Lord Jesus Christ," leading Paleontologist E. Cadwalader Doyle stated.

Scientists suspect that the precise location of Satan's fall is evidence that the Pawnee Indian may be in league with the Lord of Darkness.

"The scourge of the Indian savage has been rendered forty times as heinous," Doyle said. "We must obliterate the savage from this Earth, as well as others of Satan's flock: harlots, opium-smokers, atheists, and lechers."

The skeleton will be on display at the Divinity School, surrounded at all times by a special team of priests and holy men, and guarded with Holy Water, Prayer, and other sacramental protections.

THE TERRIBLE VISAGE OF SATAN, CAPTURED IN CHILLING DETAIL BY NEWS-PAPER PHOTO-ETCHTOGRAPHY.

Dr. Abernathy's Anti-Masturbation Harness and Genital Pouch.

Protects against Sickness of Self-Abuse and Spermatorrhoea.

Unremovable sheet-metal and steel-bolt locking.

Internal penis-lacerating feature curbs arousal. Attempted removal causes possible mutilation.

For young men, sanatorium inmates, or the out-of-work.

From Your Medical or Church Supplier.

FISHER'S OPERA-HOUSE.

One Night Only
FRIDAY EVE,
MARCH 11TH.

a special engagement of

THE "DAINTY SONG BIRD" MISS CHARLOTTE WREN,
WHO WILL PERFORM MANY BELOVED FAVORITES OF BOTH GRAND AND LIGHT OPERA IN HER ANGELIC SOPRANO, INCLUDING THE REPUBLIC'S ONLY POPULAR TUNE, "BY THE LIGHT OF THE SILVERY MOON."

ALSO FEATURING THE FAMED KNOCK-A-BOUT COMEDY FAMILY QUARTET, **THE FOUR FENTONS,** WHO ENGAGE IN MUCH SPIRITED AND VOLATILE HORSE PLAY, WHICH INVOLVES THE STRIKING OF ONE ANOTHER WITH INDIAN-CLUBS & OAKEN TABLES.

plus music executed upon the wondrous steam-calliope,

The Great ROLLIO,
a man who can contort himself to resemble Massachusetts,

and a woman who screams uncontrollably.

ADMISSION:
Parquet, reserved 75c
Dress Circle,
reserved 75c
Three Rows in Balcony,
reserved 75c
Remaining Seats in
Balcony 50c
Gallery 25c
Below the Stage 15c

Box-office opens
Thursday at 9 a.m.

The management kindly requests that second-class citizenry not attend.

HORSE-LESS CARRIAGE DEFEATS NINE-YEAR-OLD POLACK IN COAL-HAULING RACE.

From the Pittsburgh correspondent, Mar. 6.—The gasoline-combustible self-propelling engine has gradually grown in acceptance among industrialists and gentleman-hobbyists alike, for its potential usefulness in production and transportation, and the striking novelty of its ability to carry multiple passengers considerable distances without the use of horses or kindred beasts of burden. Although short-comings in its mechanics must be overcome, it has become common wisdom that the future is increasingly secure for the horse-less carriage, as it is popularly known, particularly considering the results of an exciting competition between one of these machines and a nine-year-old Polish coal-hauler in Pittsburgh Sunday last.

Both the horse-less carriage and the boy were assigned the task of pulling seven-hundred-and-fifty pounds of raw bituminous coal in small wagons for roughly fifty yards behind the Amalgamated Iron Works factory.

Competition was at a virtual dead-lock for several minutes, as machine and Pole alike struggled with their loads, until the boy, despite frequent switchings, could not bear his burden any longer and collapsed face-forward into the mud and tailings. The horse-less carriage itself barely crossed the finish-line before experiencing over-heating and a damaged wheel, but, considering that it also was obliged to carry a driver, it marked a significant victory for the combustion-engine.

The driver, a Mr. Buick, received a grant of $250 from the Amalgamated Iron Works Company to continue refining and perfecting his version of the machine, which he had invented in his work-shed. After being administered a few draughts of soothing-syrup, the Pole was returned to his regular duties in the factory.

LESS MUCK-RAKING

THE ONION

MORE YELLOW JOURNALISM.

Monday, May 29, 1905. The Best Source of News-worthy Items in our Great Republic. Price Two Cents.

THE MACHINE: WILL IT REPLACE THE CHINA-MAN?

Many New Contrivances Just as Cheap, Dependable as Chinee.

INDUSTRIOUS RACE MAY SOON BE BEREFT OF PURPOSE.

As the wonders of the Industrial Age continue to unfold before us, a question arises: Will the China-man, upon whose strong back this nation's rail-roads and other industries were built, be replaced by mechanized contraptions of labor?

In recent years, Horace Mayweather, noted captain of industry, has turned to machines as the solution to his manufacturing needs, and he has found them to be superior to China-men in numerous respects. Among their advantages over the pig-tailed yellow men: They do not require work-breaks, they do not need to be paid, and they do not bleed on the floor when beaten.

Said Mr. Mayweather: "The China-man has proven to be an extremely productive worker over the years, capable of tasks ranging from serving hot food to laying tracks of rail. However, even the finest Chinee, one possessing the greatest resolve and the most subservient of manner, tires after a 26-hour shift. The machine's capacity for toil is virtually limitless."

In addition to industrial manufacture, the machine is currently being used for cotton-picking, cigarette-rolling, and sewage disposal, fields of labor which were once the exclusive domain of the China-man, the Negro, and the Mexican.

While many experts foresee numerous possibilities for the machine, most captains of industry do not expect the China-man to be replaced entirely. As prominent machine contraptioneers and inventors are quick to point out, the machine lacks, as of this date, the capacity to reproduce—an ability at which the China-man is worrisomely qualified.

'CRIMINAL RIGHTS' ADVOCATES CALL FOR SOFTER WHIPS.

Albany, New York—A segment of society calling itself "Advocates for Criminals," is puzzling lawmakers in New York this week for its call to soften the whips used to punish imprisoned felons.

Among their suggestions is a lessening of the number of lashes given a law-breaker as part of his regular punishment, from 300 per day to a mere 260. They also call for lighter, softer leather in whips, varieties which simply break the skin, and not the tough muscle fiber beneath.

New York's Administrator of Jails and Holding Stockades Edwin Sheckmann issued a response to the citizens' call to action, calling it "the most absurd poppycockery."

He continued: "It is not for the mere misplaced concern for the lowliest of the low that I object to these points. It is the notion that proper punishment within jails be usurped by citizens, preventing wardens and jail-masters from administering punishment by the terms of their own good judgment."

'SHIT-HEAD' COINED.

Several eminent grammarians from our Republic's most prominent academies of higher learning agreed yesterday that the newly coined term "shit-head" should be made available for general usage amongst the American populace.

Quoting Dartmouth University Professor E. Purvius Tufts, "It is truly the rarest of occasions that the people may observe, with appropriate pomp and heraldry, the ushering of a new word into the august realm of English malediction. Gentleman, I give you 'shit-head,' or one whose head is composed entirely of shit, a figure of speech describing a slothful and noisome fellow who is in need of a stern dressing-down from his more upstanding peers."

Etymologists believe the word originated several decades ago in Irish parlance.

The derogatory implications of the word have not gone without objections, mainly from those at whom the word has been directed.

"I deny the scurrilous charges of shit-headedry," said local robber-baron Hiram P. Devitt.

WEST TAMED.

Virginia City, Nev.—One century after Meriwether Lewis and William Clark embarked upon their famous expedition, it has been determined that the Western regions of our great Republic have been thoroughly tamed, with not a spot of wildness to be had.

The realization came when the sheriff of Virginia City, Thomas C. Harmon, announced that "Shot-Gun Ephraim, the Shootin'-est Hombre West of the Continental Divide," became entangled in barbed-wire during a man-hunt and was subsequently gunned down by Harmon and his deputies. "With Shot-Gun Ephraim's bloody demise, the West can no longer be considered wild," Sheriff Harmon said. "You may now attend your places of worship and purchase hard-tack at your favorite dry-goods proprietorships without fear of lawlessness."

The recent placement of the remaining Indian savages in small, chicken-wire cages has also been cited as a factor.

RAFFISH SLACKER TREATED ROUGHLY FOR UNGALLANT UTTERANCES.

Harrisburg, Penn., May 28.—John Killebrew, an idler and slacker of the lowest order, was showered with a hail of fisticuffs after uttering ungallant words about the Pittsburgh Pirates at a Calumet City saloon. While partaking of his third Scotch rye whiskey shot and rudely taking full advantage of the free-lunch offered by the saloon, Killebrew, 20, was heard to remark that the Pirates were "bums," and Honus Wagner "the biggest bum of them all." One of the patrons demanded that Killebrew retract his comments, but the brute refused. A group of six or seven patrons then pounded him to a viscous jelly with right crosses, left hooks, and glancing blows. Killebrew emerged in a daze from the saloon, his shirt and collar almost soaked through with blood, and his face sporting the effects of well-deserved hay-makers.

AGITATORS!

RABBLE-ROUSING MUCK-RAKERS INTERFERE WITH GEARS OF INDUSTRIAL PROGRESS.

SEE FULL ACCOUNT ON PAGE 5.

G. W. VANDERBILT BUYS SKY.

Esteemed Capitalist hopes to be first to profit from great air-ship cities of the new century.

SEE THE FULL ACCOUNT ON PAGE

DAM EVERY RIVER!

AN EDITORIAL ON PAGE 11.

NEWS FROM OTHER AREAS OF OUR WORLD.

Arab–Jew Accord Promises New Era of Peace.

A FULL NEWS STORY ON PAGE 10.

MOVING PHOTO-PICTO-GRAPH REVIEW:

'MAN TURNING SOMERSAULT' A STALE RETREAD OF 'MAN DOING BACK-FLIP.'

Though it may have been said by P.T. Barnum, "If they like a horse, they will like two horses twice as well," it would behoove the mindful celluloid-dramatist to heed the fate of Thaddeus Grunwold and Fritz Kochendorffer.

After the grand public spectacle which made their thrilling moving-picture "Man Doing Back-flip" the toast of New York, anticipation was high for their new release. Alas, "Man Turning Somersault" offers little to the seasoned movable-picture observer than another glimpse at the popular character "Man," still ably played by Grunwold. One disgruntled viewer offered the suggestion that they might better have run the first picture in reverse than keep a nation in suspense for a year only to disappoint. Hereby cast into print is the lesson of Grunwold and Kochendorffer: that they who grow complacent in the glow of public acceptance may fall just as easily, and do so by proffering reconstituted material in lieu of fresh ideas. Additionally, they who endeavor to perform in as well as direct their photo-plays are doomed to be overwhelmed by their duties, and none shall suffer more pitiably than the hapless filmic-drama-picture-play viewer.

Heed this well, that moving-picture creators and their progeny for generations to come may know the wisdom of their fore-bears.

U.S. STEEL GRANTS SUPREME COURT JUDICIAL POWERS.

U.S. Steel, the world's largest steel manufacturing trust, has agreed to permit the United States Supreme Court limited powers in determining the constitutionality of federal laws, as well as some say in settling inter-state disputes and litigation appealed in federal courts. This decision comes after U.S. Steel's decision to allow the existence of a bicameral federal assembly of law-makers, called "Congress," which is made up of popularly elected, U.S. Steel-approved representatives.

J.P. Morgan, chief financier and Supreme War-lord of U.S. Steel, said he hopes this latest action will prove wrong those nay-sayers who claim U.S. Steel is a tyrannical dictatorship which exercises excessive control over the political and economic freedoms of Americans.

In response to U.S. Steel's decision, Standard Oil of New Jersey is adopting its own constabulary police-force and government. Founder and Generalissimo John D. Rockefeller stated that Standard Oil is doing so to protect its business interests against a possible coup d'état by U.S. Steel.

THE SCANDALOUS BATHING COSTUMES OF '06.

FASHION PRESENTATION SHOW HELD.

NEARLY BARE ARMS, NECKS ANTICIPATE NEW WOOLEN FASHIONS NEXT SEASON.

Corset-Makers Demand to Know How Corset Is to Be Worn with Revealing New Designs.

New York—The new revealing swimming-costume styles, with hemline stitchings creeping well above the wrist and collarless neck-lines plunging down to expose the throat in full view, are being planned for public display by some of this city's most notable designers of woolen fashions.

Beach-going citizens across the land are outraged at the new-fangled costumes. Some of the dresses even bare the wearer's fore-arms, subjecting them to the damaging effects of the noon-day sun and breezes. What's more, these bathing-outfits often boast such loud and gaudy colors as brown and navy blue.

Those bold enough to wear these suits claim to prefer them over their predecessors from past summers, since they allow for greater physical mobility than the familiar starched canvas and whale-bone affairs that covered the entire body save the head and finger-tips.

A show of the new fashions was presented by the city's most prominent clothiers at the lovely beach on the south bank of the Long Island Sound this Saturday last. Several ladies in the wool-spinners' employ, chosen for their rotund beauty, were witnessed lounging nearly horizontal on the banks of the pristine beach, displaying themselves flagrantly in the sun or dipping their conspicuously unshod feet into the water. Rather than attending to cooking and curtain mending, these women were spending their free moments in the idle pursuit of recreation.

The plump, healthful young women, clearly uncorsetted under the inundated dark fabric of their swimming garments, expelled shrieks of unearthly delight as they splashed wantonly in the water or tossed a child's play-ball amongst themselves over a fishing net affixed upon poles.

"The purpose of this frolicking," said one of the costume-makers, "was to present the new garments in their natural setting so that etching artists in my employ could observe them in motion, thereby depicting the new designs for the dry-goods catalogues."

THE BRAZEN HARLOT PICTURED IN THE ETCHING ABOVE IS CAVORTING IN A SWIMMING COSTUME WHICH CITIZENRY ARE ASSAILING AS "BARE-ARMED DEPRAVITY."

The dress-maker asserted that the wanton merriment in no way endorsed such use of the new costumes. "They are for home bathing only," the clothier said.

Esteemed corset-makers in the area have expressed concern over the reduced role of the corset in the new fashions.

The startling swimming costumes, previously viewed only in Men's Entertainment Zoetropes and Parisian Dry Package Order Catalogues, caused many a gentle-man to turn his head twice or thrice in the swimmers' direction with a protrusion of eyes and lolling of tongue.

Robert Ingerson, a gentleman going for a walk on the beach the morning of the fashion display, reported not only glimpsing several uncovered calf regions, but seeing women rubbing a moistening salve onto their ungloved hands and fore-arms.

Mr. Ingerson admitted to feeling "upset" upon viewing the ladies. "Fortunately," he said, "I was able to expel the impure visage from my thoughts, but none-the-less believe I have earned an eternity of hell-fire and damnation."

As to whether wearers of the new costumes will be guilty of sin, the Reverend X. Lucius Dalrymple, in a letter to The Onion, recalled a passage in The Bible, Exodus 28:4, in which God on High makes clear His design for clothing the body: "And these are the garments which they shall make; a breast-plate, and an ephod, and a robe, and a girdle: and they shall make holy garments for Aaron thy brother, and his sons, that he may minister unto me in the priest's office."

In response to the letter, the designers and wool-spinners promised to manufacture ephod-draped swimming costumes made atop iron breastplate corsets for the '07 season.

THE ONION

PRINTED ON PAPER CULLED FROM THE MAJESTIC SEQUOIA.

EXTRA! LATEST EDITION.

Sunday, April 22, 1906. — The Best Source of News-worthy Items in our Great Republic. — Price Five Cents.

EARTH-QUAKE MARKS LEAST GAY DAY IN SAN FRANCISCO HISTORY

'QUEEN CITY ON THE PACIFIC' LIES IN RUINS.

Garment District Still Flaming.

San Francisco, California, April 18.—Gaiety was not to be had on the streets of the city this morning, as it lies in ruins from what fair citizens in the city are calling the most outlandish earth-quake in known history.

"This is not a gay day for San Francisco," the honorable Mayor Eugene Schmitz said.

At precisely 5:12 a.m., local time, the quake shook the city to its conservative core, rendering it no more than rubble, ash, and faggots.

Earth and rock were outed by the great quake from the northernmost 200 miles of the San Andreas fault line northwest of San Juan Bautista to the Triangle Junction at Cape Mendocino.

City authorities fear that of the thousands of fair citizens trapped under collapsed homes, some 700 will never come out.

Rescue workers scouring the rubble have been instructed to investigate "anything that moves."

Mayor Schmitz said the citizens of the city will come out victorious from the catastrophe. "No mere earth-quake can dampen the colorful spirit of the citizens of San Francisco," he said. "We are here to stay."

"Get used to it," he added.

Ferries at the foot of Market Street straddled both sides of the Bay in order to carry confused victims to the safety of the Sausalito shore.

Phobic citizenry near a local theater reported a virtual parade of calamitous noises, such as the tinkling of china plates, falling picture frames, and pianos smashing into pink parlor walls.

"It was a rainbow of noise," said one gay-less citizen.

Almost more remarkable than the great fissure and shaking of the foundation of Earth was the quake's flaming after-math, as fires engulfed the city's garment district and are still raging loudly and proudly in the sky as of press-time.

President Roosevelt declared martial law in the city, and Naval officers stationed in the area now patrol the area in studded leather boots and tight jodhpurs, ready to punish those disobedient of emergency ordinances by crack of whip or stick.

Modern geologists were confounded by the queer length of the great rupture, and by displacements which were uncharacteristically straight.

Will a gay-friendly day return to this once flamboyant city? One business-man has hopes for future gaiety. Wilmore Ernst, a Mission Street banker, said, "The day I can peacefully walk down our rebuilt streets hand in hand with my sweet-heart, that will be a gay day indeed."

ABOVE IS THE DEVASTATION IN ITS TOTALITY, AS DEPICTED BY MODERN PHOTO-GRAPH, DELIVERED TO THE ONION OFFICES BY RAIL-CAR FROM SAN FRANCISCO IN ONLY SIX DAYS.

SHOULD U.S. SET LIMITS ON INDIAN SLAUGHTER?

CONGRESS-MEN SEARCH FOR SPORTING ANSWER.

Some Naturists Fear Indian May Become Scarce if Hunted Wantonly.

Bureau of Savage Affairs Chair-man Gives Speech.

Washington, D.C., April 21.—Congress-men rose to speak on all sides of the issue of the unremitting Indian slaughter as the House of Representatives debated whether to set limits on the pastime so enjoyed by many. Chair-man of the Bureau of Savage Affairs John Brearly announced that the Indian population in Western regions has fallen shy of 200,000, where once there were "a million or so."

Sherman D. Bacon of Kentucky began the debate Monday with an impassioned speech: "Since the advent of the covered wagon, men have enjoyed hunting the red man for both protection of women-folk and for sport, but could we take our amusements to such a measure that one day there may be not a single Indian left upon our land to hunt and kill?"

Indian slaughter greatly increased in popularity after the introduction of the practical Colt six-shooter, which interested the urban man in hunting jaunts to rural areas. Pogroms against the noble savage remain as lively an avocation as ever for settlers and members of the militia.

The thinning of tribes has long been practiced by the Bureau of Savage Affairs to ensure a healthy population, as well as to prevent rampant over-breeding and strains on area resources, but many conservationists now fear extinction. Throughout the debates they called for limits to be set on the number of Indians slaughtered while hunting for diversion, paired with restrictions on the butchery of squaws and their broods.

Supporting the notion of limits was the president himself. "We must protect and conserve the proud Indian! Otherwise our children may grow up to never know the joy of hunting him," President Roosevelt said in a message relayed to Congress.

Throughout the proceedings, men speaking on behalf of the Indian Shooting Association, a group opposed to any limitation on Indian killing or maiming, expressed that it is a hunter who is best qualified to make decisions regarding the future of the native. "Who really is closer to the Indian than the hunter?" said Walter Edmund of Virginia. "Who else walks in his very foot-steps and knows every habit, every hiding place, even the distinctive cry of the red man in agony, and that of his doe-eyed mate, the squaw?"

The debate raged upon the lawn of the Capitol as hunters compared Winchester rifles and decried regulation as government intrusion. Clyde Armbruster, Indian hunter of 21 years, spoke to the assemblage.

"The government man tries to dictate what is best for the Indians from his desk where he experiences the red man in photo-graphs! Hog-wash! I have looked into the face of Indians who stood only inches from the barrel of my gun."

One speaker raised the concern that many of these Indians are on federally mandated reservations, land set aside for Indian habitation, and by law should enjoy the due process accorded to American citizens. The notion was swiftly dismissed by Francis Aeshalman of Ohio: "Restrict the Indian who now runs unbridled to a small swath of land? Balderdash! What challenge, what sport, would there be in hunting the Indian contained in such a way?"

Many speakers denied all theories of Indian scarcity, noting the vast lands of the great United States which have scarcely been traveled by shod feet. "I have no doubt these regions are teeming with fauna and Indian-life just waiting to be discovered, tracked, and slain," said John Swasey of Maine.

But not all law-makers are losing heart in the proposition of slaughter limits. "Should our own lands be emptied of natives," said Stephen Cooper of Alabama, "we need only travel into the regions of Mexico and our holdings in the Philippines to find aborigines suitable as game."

See The Onion's newest comical-sequential story panel, "Little Fat-Pants and his Billy-Goat, Juniper."

Kindly turn to page 14.

FROM THE WORLD OF SPORTINGS

KANSAS DEFEATS INDIANA IN PLOUGHING CONTEST.

A spectacle to rival the Olympic entertainments of the Gods themselves was beheld by spectators at the Four-teenth Annual Agricultural Fair-Confabulum Exposition held Friday at the Miller's Guild Out-Door Sporting Field. In a display of manly industry and cunning, Kansas defeated Indiana by more than seven furlongs to win this year's ploughing contest.

"Thunderous speed and reflexes as fast as the very lightning are how I would relate this contest," said one farmer, who claimed that the ploughing "was of such ferocity that I would swear the Kansan was in a full run."

Indiana started in a flash, as its mules were the first to emerge from sleep, and set its great shoulders to the task. But the Kansas plow was perhaps sharper, or the blade more skillfully whetted, for it began tossing up clods and furrows at such a speed that many doubted the evidence of their eyes.

The Indiana team conceded the victory with simple good sports-manship, saying that their chief ploughs-man and his mules had been blessed with a great quantity of speed that day. But there were some murmurings of dissent from the Iowa stable, where men of that doughty team said Kansas had used an out-lawed brand of pig-lard to grease their plough-share.

The grand-stands were packed, and many were over-come by the excitement and the heat of the moment, and some ladies of light constitution did collapse in faint straight away. When such a sporting event is performed, there are few who would remain unmoved.

SIX-MINUTE MOVING PICTURE PHOTO-PLAY AGONIZINGLY LONG, SAY CRITICS.

Though the viewing of photo-graphic art in moving form may be a fine diversion, persons viewing the new leviathan epic "Man Washing Horse" were overcome by fatigue Saturday night at the Capital Nickelodeon. Shouts of "So rinse the beast already!" and "My word, what a long picture-play!" accompanied the six-minute footage of a man washing a horse thoroughly, from soaping to scrubbing to rinsing.

Attentions were sparked at the three-minute mark, as the beast rose up on its hind legs for a moment in protest of the man's washing of its lower belly, but excitement gave way to groans, as the man left the image for a full minute to obtain a larger brush, information which was conveyed to the viewers by the new device of photo-graphic titles engraved upon black cards.

Only in the play-o-graph's sixth minute, by which time none but a handful of the original two hundred specta-tors remained, did the man fully rinse the animal, stand before the camera, and take a bow.

The title card heralding the end of the film, which it did by literally announcing "The End" in elegantly scripted letters, was a most welcome sight to those who remained in the viewing-house as a courtesy to the moving-photographic-picture's creators.

MADMAN SELLS SECRET OF STEAM POWER TO PERSIA!

A FULL NEWS STORY ON PAGE 11.

CHANTICLEER OF THE STEAM EPOCH.

THE ONION

ONLY 225 DEAD THIS WEEK FROM THE CHOLERA.

Wednesday, February 13, 1907. The Best Source of News-worthy Items in Our Great Republic. Price Two Cents.

PURE FOOD AND DRUG ACT WILL LIMIT HUMAN-THUMB LEVELS PERMITTED IN MEATS

Will Other Fingers Follow?

From the Washington Bureau, Feb. 12.—With the recently passed Pure Food and Drug and Meat Inspection Acts now being implemented, government-appointed meat inspectors are charged with the task of stringently curtailing the human-thumb levels present in the Republic's meat supply.

In the wake of a reported increase in the volume of human thumbs found in potted-meat products for the first half of this decade, up from approximately five thumb-pounds per hundred-weight to nearly seven thumb-pounds, the enforcement of the new laws is considered timely by many public health authorities.

Said Bureau of Meat Commissioner P. Turling Throckmorton, "Thanks to the steadfast pressure of the U.S. Bureau of Meat on unscrupulous meat-packing concerns, the American public may soon enjoy a delicious and healthful luncheon of potted-pig or calf without the unsettling discovery of an unskilled immigrant laborer's lifeless digit on the dinner-plate."

The law has decreed that no butcher shall allow more than six human thumbs to pass through its shipping doors in a single business day.

In the slaughter-house, foremen are expected to caution laborers to keep their thumbs a safe distance from rotating blades, saws, pounders, grinders, and other slaughtering implements in order to abide by the new regulations, lest they be shut down by government meat authorities.

None-the-less, the legislation is decried by butchers as "obsessive" and "over-governing to the extreme." The act is the most dramatic law enforcing pure foods since last year's regulation that baby formula may contain no more than twenty percent plaster.

The Bureau's next task will be to oversee the reduction of insect-parts and full-bodied horse carcasses in pure-leaf bulk lard.

MORE CHILDREN STAYING IN SCHOOL PAST THIRD GRADE.

Though "John Q. Factory Foreman" might object, more and more of our nation's children are choosing to pursue higher education, even after the alphabet and numbers to twenty are learned. An overwhelming one in ten American youths elected to enter fourth grade this past semester, far more than in years past. Skeptics may inquire in puzzlement as to what more usable skills a child might learn, but graduates of the fourth and fifth grades tell of ways to manipulate numerals other than addition and subtraction: "Multiplication" is said to be a sort of super-addition resulting in numbers so large that three or even four figures are required to write them.

Other subjects that may be taught to the tender young geniuses of tomorrow are manners of speaking that persons of other lands may understand, and a subject called "History" involving stories that happened some time ago. If this trend continues, one day citizens might stay in school nearly into their adolescent years, and work at new jobs created for the super-intelligent, such as controlling the weather via a contraptional device strapped with great leather belts directly onto their oversized brains.

ELECTROCUTION DEATHS UP 300,000 PERCENT.

TOTAL ELECTROCUTIONS, 1900s: 3,148

TOTAL ELECTROCUTIONS, 1800s: 1

Deaths by electrocution have risen sharply, with the year's fatalities rising 300,000 percent from figures of last century. Officials are eyeing the generation of electricity and the introduction of such into the nation's homes and work plants as possibly related to the escalation of electricity-related deaths and gaping, charred, electricity-induced wounds.

The first electrocution ever reported occurred in 1887 in the scientific laboratories of Thomas Edison, bringing the death-by-electrocution count to one for the 19th century. The count remained steady until this decade when, perhaps coincidentally, the three-wire system for transporting electrical power was made available to the public.

Electricity is described as safe by Edison Electro-Graphic officials. According to Edison scientist J. Franklin Fuller, electricity has always been present in our homes in forms such as static electricity. To demonstrate this fact at a recent electricity conference in New York, the professor drew a glass rod from his desk drawer and rubbed it with silk, generating small sparks.

"The only difference today is that a wire falling onto your tin roof or into your kitchen bathing tub may send one or two amperes through the body, resulting in horrific burns at the site of entry, uncontrolled muscle spasms, and loss of consciousness before death," Fuller said.

The Edison Electro-Graphic Company is planning to warn the public of such dangers with a series of educational etchings on the sides of Clover-Leaf milk bottles.

WOMEN'S SUFFRAGE LEADERS PROMISED EXPENSIVE HATS.

From the Washington Bureau, Feb. 13.—After struggling for some 50 years to win the vote, Women's Suffrage leaders won their first victory today, as President Roosevelt and an esteemed panel of congressmen authorized the distribution of several popular 'Merry Widow' style hats to the ladies.

The president assured the ladies that he and the legislative leaders were making "every possible effort" to guarantee that the hats would be festooned with pheasant wings, artificial flowers, and lacy veils.

While the hat appropriation is scheduled for later this year, Roosevelt promised prompt delivery of the stylish head-wear.

"These spirited women," Roosevelt said, "who have struggled and fought for voting rights so tirelessly and for so long, must not be made to wait equally long for these expensive hats, because it is quite possible that they may go out of fashion."

Some law-makers are questioning the allotment of federal monies for the hats, which can cost as much as two dollars.

Democratic Senator Daniel Hoarcker, of the State of Illinois, advised that the president send the Suffragettes "a nice compliment" in lieu of the hats.

CIVIL WAR VETERANS DESCRIBE DELUSIONARY 'FLASHING-BACK' OF MEMORY.

Dayton, Ohio.—As the population who fought the War between the States grows older and ever more infirm, it has been brought to our attention that many of these aging individuals have experienced queer tricks and delusions of the mind which permit them to believe that they are once again young recruits fighting in bloody battles that ended more than forty years earlier. The Republic's nervous-hospitals are filled with these unfortunate veterans, and this "flashing-back" of memory may be more common than would be initially believed.

"I am still in Fredericksburg in my mind," testified Eli Macready, 59, formerly a Master Sergeant in the 23rd Ohio Regiment, to this Onion correspondent. "The smell of burnt cordite is in my nostrils to this day, and I often wake in a cold sweat after having dreamt of using the corpse of my young barefoot buddy Jim as a shield against a volley of gun-shots. Sometimes I will be walking down the street, and will hear something as innocuous as the collision of tin pots hanging off a peddler's wagon, and will believe them to be the sound of thundering hooves from a sudden ambush by Nathan Bedford Forrest and his men, and I'll run for cover behind an ash-can or a washer-woman's skirts. People in the street see this and begin to laugh and make much mock of me."

Macready has been prescribed a regimen of soothing morphine by his family physician for this queer ailment.

SCANDAL!

CELEBRATED LADY-ACTRESS SUSPECTED OF BEING SPANISH

Miss Charlotte Wren, Toast of All Europe and the Americas, an Iberian?

"PERFIDY AND OUTRAGE!" EXCLAIMS SENATOR FENNWICH.

SEEN DANCING THE WICKED FLAMENCO BY EPISTLE-WRITING EYE-WITNESS.

When confronted with charge, Miss Wren overcome with the vapors.

New York, Feb. 12.—The world of song and light theatrics was stunned today at

MISS CHARLOTTE WREN

the possibility that Miss Charlotte Wren, the beloved "Dainty Songbird" who has performed before the crowned heads of Europe with her angelic soprano and touching histrionics, may be of low and ignoble Spanish descent.

In a letter addressed to Onion Editor T. Herman Zweibel and bearing no return-address, the celebrated lady-actress is accused of keeping secret a former life as a young Spanish immigrant who sold flowers and danced about immorally, often barefoot, on the streets of Barcelona, in exchange for kisses and close embraces from ruffians and other contemptibles.

Excerpts of the letter, which arrived in yesterday's post, are reproduced for the benefit of Onion readers. Remember, the most vital news of the age first sees the light of day in The Onion.

"Gentlemen—Doubtless you, being gentlemen of upstanding class and taste, do plan to attend Miss Charlotte Wren's performance at Carnegie Hall, as it is considered the social and artistic event of the season. The 'Dainty Songbird' herself, owing to her numerous performing merits, is considered, if not the Queen of New York Society, certainly one of its most popular and beloved princesses.... Therefore, it will almost certainly come as a deep and horrendous shock to all of you fine and upstanding gentlemen that, contrary to popular perception, Miss Wren is not the product of blue-blooded English lineage, but the natural daughter of a Spanish milk-maid and her similarly Iberian soldier-boy. Miss Wren's real name is Maria Isabel Luisa Rosalba de Ibanez y Colon y Martinez de Estiban y Suarez, and as a child danced for doubloons in the cobble-stone streets of Old Barcelona. I saw her when I was in the Merchant Marine on shore leave nearly a decade ago....

"Imagine my surprise, then, years later, when a Miss Charlotte Wren, in her début at Pastor's Light Opera House, wins the love, praise, and accolades of audience and critics alike—the selfsame barefoot urchin of the Barcelona streets, trading kisses for coins."

The infamy of such an accusation will not be lost on those for whom the recent war with the Spanish is still a fresh memory. Many patriotic Americans would choose death by firing squad over association with a lowly Spaniard.

This has not been lost on Senator Potter C. Fennwich, who promised to introduce anti-Spanish lady-actress legislation following the Wren revelation. "Perfidy and outrage!" Senator Fennwich exclaimed, as he pounded the Senate podium, muttonchop whiskers a-billowing and snuff shooting out his nostrils like cannon-shot. "Such scurrilous subterfuge must not be tolerated by the American people!"

When presented with the charge, Miss Wren, who was about to board a carriage bound for Carnegie Hall, promptly swooned. When she came to through the use of smelling-salts, she weakly asked her maid to escort her back into her brownstone and said nothing more. Although her side of the story has not yet been elaborated, her lack of denial of the accusation is, indeed, telling.

Last year, a chronicle of the life of Miss Wren was published, which not surprisingly paints quite a different picture of her origins. Titled The Truthful and Forthright Biography of Miss Charlotte Wren, Celebrated Lady-Actress of the Present Age, the profile contends that Miss Wren is not born of this world, but is, instead, a celestial demi-goddess brought to Earth in a golden carriage drawn by four-and-twenty enchanted butterflies. There had been little reason to doubt this claim until the aforementioned letter arrived in our office.

FACTORY WORKERS GRANTED EIGHT-HOUR WORK DAY WHILE TEETHING.

Washington, Feb. 12.—The Senators of these 45 states voted 56–30 in favor of imposing a one-time limit of eight hours in a day that a factory laborer may be made to work if said laborer is teething. On the floor of the Senate, The Hon. Victor Kornblum, Progressive from the Commonwealth of Massachusetts, said, "While I mean no disrespect to the coal, copper, iron, steel, and sugar interests of this great nation, I know, from tales told by my wife, that teething can be painful for a young laborer and may interfere with the efficient execution of his duties. Limiting his work to only eight hours during the teething period will allow him to grow strong and vigorous, to become a valued worker, of full strength, benefitting U.S. Industry for several years more."

Noted industrialists reacted with shock to the news, calling for the resignation of Senators McHavish and Chalmers, of New Hampshire and Minnesota, who sponsored the legislation. Said Copper Baron Thedgewick J. Miles: "In a free nation, I must now shut down my factories at the slightest whim of government? Balderdash!"

INDIAN TRIBES STILL HOLDING AMERICAN LAND

THE INNOMINEE.
THE CADDO.
THE CHOCTAW.
SOME DOZEN OSAGE.
THE CREEK.
THE QUAPAW.
SEVERAL SHAWNEE.
THE QUAHADA.
THE KIOWA.
THE ARAPAHO.
A TONKAWA (ELDERLY).

THE ZIPPER: SIGN OF OUR MORAL DECAY?

An Editorial on page 4.

FOREIGN CHILD LABOR A 'GREAT THREAT' TO AMERICAN CHILD LABOR, SAY CAPTAINS OF INDUSTRY.

An Editorial, on page 10.

NEWS FOR LABORERS: RAG-PICKING, POT-MENDING AMONG MOST PROMISING CAREER OPTIONS.

The story on page 11.

POPULARITY OF 'WEEK-END' THREATENS PROGRESS, SAY INDUSTRIALISTS.

The story on page 19.

DR. CRAWFORD'S ELECTRIC LINIMENT AND SOOTHING SYRUP.

An unscrupulous few will extol the virtues of other soothing syrups. Eschew their nefarious claims! Dr. Crawford's panacea is the finest obtainable in the Republic. Prevents and alleviates the common cold, croup, fever, consumption, afflictions of the lungs, infections of the blood, rheumatism, grippe, catarrh, constipation, coated tongue, torpid liver, jaundice, child-birth, foul gasses, ladies' complaints, Irish blood-vomits, ague, nervous head-aches, hysteria, soreness of the parts, fallen arches, loss of appetite, dyspepsia, obesity, doldrums, chilblains, the Crimean itch, flesh wounds, stoop back, corns, spastic colon, cancer, black-heads, gonorrhea, earwigs, the screaming shits, scrofula, eruptions, delirium tremens, night sweats, boils, excema, dropsy, the feathers, shingles, ulceration of the womb, pink-eye, superfluous hair, fits, anal tantrum, piles, hoof and mouth disease, pleurisy, tape-worm, bowel moths, tender bladder, and all kindred maladies. An excellent emulsion, whether internally or externally used. In full-pint bottles. Harmless.

Available at fine drug and mercantile establishments everywhere.

TODAY'S WEATHER PROGNOSTICATION: Farmer's Almanac scientists predict clear skies, or perhaps rain.

THE ONION

STAUNCH DEFENDERS OF OUR STOCK-HOLDERS.

Thursday, November 5, 1908. The Best Source of Newsworthy Items in Our Great Republic. Price Two Cents.

NEW 'LITERATE VOTE' TURNS OUT FOR TAFT

Increasingly High Numbers of Post-Fourth-Grade Citizenry Thought to Be Deciding Factor in Recent Elections.

HON. PRESIDENT-ELECT WILLIAM HOWARD TAFT.

See story on page 3.

HORSE LOOSE IN CITY HALL!

Philadelphia—This fair city's seat of municipal government—the City Hall—was in turmoil yesterday as a horse galloped loose through its dignified corridors and various assembly-rooms, causing much panic among the citizens therein and forcing the Mayor to shut down

operations for several hours until the mare could be captured and removed.

The horse disrupted many affairs of state, including an important speech given by Alderman Richard C. "Deadeye" Blaine on the need for special fund allocations to his ward to buy new shovels for his constituents, and a spectacular bribe given to a mayoral aide from one of the local steel executives. The horse also interrupted a meeting of the Ladies' Upward Improvement Society for the Downtrodden and Shoeless, prompting much feminine screaming and standing on chairs. It then tipped over a step-ladder, sending buckets of whitewash crashing everywhere and forcing a painter to dangle precariously by his fingertips to some trimming near the ceiling.

"Why, the very idea," exclaimed Mayor John Weaver, his face crimson with rage and his collar popping out of its buttons. "A horse loose in City Hall—an outrage! Get that four-legged slab of pet meat out of my sight immediately! Consarn the vile beast!"

After much clattering about, Negroes managed to lure the mare with a fistful of hay and swiftly bridled her. The mare is a bay named Rose of Tralee and is owned by a Seamus O'Gahagan of Stuyvesant Street. O'Gahagan, drunk on rye at a saloon close to City Hall, had failed to tether his horse properly, and it soon roamed away. Following its capture, the horse was sent to a glue factory and O'Gahagan given thirty years in jail for conspiracy to subvert government operations.

ROWDY TEENS STAYING UP UNTIL 9 O'CLOCK READING ALL MANNER OF RIBALD BOOKS.

Educators and clergy are reporting an alarming rise in the moral turpitude of our Republic's youth, which they attribute to the recent proliferation of "novels," stories of the veriest fiction which present characters of wanton repute in situations of which few clean-living Christians would approve. The dubious rise of novels in the Western literary canon has caught many normally vigilant Americans off-guard, as the reading of this scandalous material often takes place long after the Methodist Church-sanctioned bed-time of 8 o'clock in the evening. Nevertheless, young people have been observed reading these novels as late as 9 o'clock, often secreting them under their bed-clothes, with only the waning light of a lantern as company.

The novel is a rather alien literary form that cannot be easily classified as Scripture, wish-books, hymnals, or the McGuffey Reader. It is believed to have been perfected by the French; a reasonable theory, since the French are known for a certain propensity for weaknesses of the flesh, as has been elsewhere demonstrated with their passion for the immodest gyrations of female café-dancers and elaborately rendered lace under-garments. Notorious novels of French authorship include "Madame Bovary," the tale of a woman of loose morals who conducts clandestine trysts with rogue adventurers and makes a cuckold of her decent, God-fearing doctor-husband; and "La Dame Aux Camillas," which depicts the affairs of a consumptive Parisian courtesan.

Now we hear that American authors are trying their hand at novel-writing. Not only are they liars, since they write made-up tales of non-existent people, but they are spreading the heat of luxurious sin to the youth of our heart-land. We blush at the scandalous situations that can be undoubtedly found in "Little Lord Fauntleroy," "Uncle Remus," "A Connecticut Yankee In King Arthur's Court," and other recently written works of American fiction which are reportedly favored by the young people.

It is, indeed, a sad state of affairs when our Republic's youths so readily fall prey to temptations that would chip away at hard-fought American values and ideals. In desperation, and no small measure of pessimism, The Onion can only ask: What is next? Drinking water flavored with lemon and sugar?

CAVORTING BEHIND DOORS SUSPECTED.

AUTHORITIES CONCERNED.

WHAT WAS PREVIOUSLY ASSUMED TO BE KNITTING OR BIBLE-STUDY MAY BE SOMETHING ELSE ALL TOGETHER.

The sanctity of the home and hearth has always been one of our great Republic's most cherished ideals. None-the-less, it has been brought to The Onion's attention that a goodly portion of the American public could be engaging in flippant, nay, playful, undertakings behind the doors of their homes and in other secluded areas, instead of embroidery, butter-churning, Scripture-reading, and other wholesome and productive activities which maintain morally stead-fast households.

Witness, for example, the recent actions of a couple in New York. While awaiting the street-car last Friday night, an Onion reporter happened to notice a gentleman bounding up the steps of his town-house with a spring in his step that could be construed as sprightly. His curiosity piqued, the reporter crept up to the front parlor window and gazed in through the white muslin curtains. The man virtually showered his wife with embraces and kisses, then opened his over-coat to reveal what appeared to be a bundle of sheet music. Excited, the woman took the music and began to pick out melodies upon her piano-forte. The man leaned over the woman, and together they began to sing a song called "Shine On, Harvest Moon." The reporter later learned that the shameful man and woman were Mr. and Mrs. Howard McNaughton of 14 Gerry Street.

This incident, outrageous though it seems, is not a singular one, if a report from Council Bluffs, Iowa, can be believed. There, eyewitnesses observed a woman purchasing penny sweet-meats for her two young children inside a general mercantile establishment.

In Plovis, South Dakota, a nine-year-old child reportedly executed a bizarre physical maneuver called a "cart-wheel" in his father's barn, to the delighted squeals of several young companions.

In Tigerton, Wisconsin, two adolescent brothers made a batch of creamed-ice in their great-aunt's kitchen, then proceeded to consume it.

Three sisters in Schenectady, New York, were observed braiding one another's hair with gaily colored ribbons.

Perhaps most shocking of all, a young lady and her beau in Piqua County, Kansas, went on a frivolous buggy-ride one recent Saturday and created a large wreath of daisies and prairie-flowers, which they then placed upon the brow of their sorrel nag.

Gentle readers, are we to believe this is what truly goes on behind the key-holes and secluded meadows of our once-great Republic? We at The Onion stand behind the validity of these eye-witness accounts and will staunchly defend them against anyone who may question or challenge them. Fulfilling our pledge to safeguard the sanctity and well-being of American society, we turned over the original testimony, names, addresses, and other evidence of these shameful acts of cavorting to police authorities in the aforementioned town-ships. These servants of the people naturally demonstrated great concern and promised to soundly discipline the ne'er-do-wells who disturbed the public peace.

But how many other incidents of cavorting occur which go both undocumented and unpunished? Upstanding citizens do well to shudder at the clandestine acts which may be occurring at this very moment and consider. How shall the Republic protect itself from the Spaniards and the yellow Chinee if it continues to turn a blind eye toward such frivolity? The very destiny of the Republic is at stake.

RAPSCALLION VAUDEVILLE ENTERTAINER FINDS MIRTH IN NEW PRESIDENT'S GIRTH

Comedic Material Unearthed by Skillful Japester.

PUBLIC ATTENTION, WHEN DIRECTED TO REPUBLICAN'S MID-SECTION, PROVIDES HUMOROUS DIVERSION.

New York, Nov. 4.—Comedian "Dapper" Dan Dugan tonight delighted the audience of his long-running entertainment, "Dapper Dan's Old-Time Musical Minstrel Revue," by making various verbal flourishes on the subject of the physical stature of our Republic's president-to-be, William H. Taft.

As 400 theatergoers struggled to rein in the enthusiasm of their amusement, Mr. Dugan noted that Mr. Taft "might very well resolve the Italo-Turkish imbroglio were it not for his tendency to employ his time in more gastronomic endeavors."

The ribald Dugan added that he was "concerned that our beloved leader may perhaps be violating his own strict policy of deploring trusts of all kinds—for I have heard that at formal banquets, he is known to seek monopolies on many of the delectables."

Again, the audience in attendance erupted in merriment.

Dugan's remarks are believed to be the first time a performer has ever used a personal foible or trait of a well-known political figure to derive humor.

Although currently the toast of Vaudeville for his outrageous humor, Dugan is deemed offensive by some.

"I enjoyed much of his performance," said one audience member, "but believe he forsook good taste in referencing Taft's size."

"This business of jokery-making has gone too far," said Senator Henry Cabot Lodge of Massachusetts. "It is of course quite proper that Mr. Dugan should use his Constitutional freedom of speech to make known his disagreement with the future president's policies or party affiliation. But to attack the trouser-size of a gentleman of importance is a distasteful act, unthinkable to all but the lowest vulgarian."

Dugan will perform through Dec. 2 at New York's Jests and Japes Comedic Club.

INFANT MORTALITY RATE DROPS TO 1 IN 3.

RATE OF DEATH WHILE BIRTHING AT 1 IN 5.

Radiant Mothers-to-Be Optimistic at Cheery News.

U.S. SECRETARY OF HYGIENE CREDITS INCREASED USE OF CRAWFORD'S SOOTHING SYRUP AS POSSIBLE FACTOR.

Washington, March 12.—The motherly bosom of our great nation must swell with pride today as news from U.S. Secretary of Hygiene Bernard W. Thatcher is heard. A great shadow which has heretofore spread across our nation has now receded somewhat, and we are far the better for its absence. From this day forward—barring the dread specter of plague, famine, or another unfortunate domestic military engagement of notable duration—half of the Union's children will not die before adulthood.

"Huzzah!" exclaimed the Secretary upon his announcement of the joyous tidings. But his glad-heartedness was nothing compared to that of other citizens. Many noted captains of industry are delighted with the prospect of having an improved and heartier work-force. And the nation's long-suffering mothers wept tears of joy as they realized that the apples of their eyes would not wither and rot quite as frequently as in times past.

Even though her heart must be selfless, laughing or weeping first for her family, the species Woman must also feel no small relief upon hearing that bearing children must no longer be such a gamble with Death, as the incidence of mortal accident during the process of labor has fallen to less than one in five. The gentleman of America may rejoice in the knowledge that his family is now some few steps closer to Security and the shelter of Divine Providence.

The Secretary credits this change of almost Utopian proportions to young ones' consumption of a healthy draught of Dr. Crawford's Soothing Syrup, a panacea available through advertisements in this news-paper. Of somewhat lesser importance, but none-the-less worth noting, is the use of soap and spirits-of-wine to cleanse the nether regions of young women in their birthing years, from ages 11 to 20.

Doctors of surgery themselves, skeptical at first, now admit that advantage is gained by the washing of hands and forearms before deliveries.

Although the lower classes have thus far had little truck with notions of medicine and cleanliness, readers are encouraged to order their servants of the coarse Irish or colored races to wash themselves with lard soap before giving birth, thus maintaining a healthy stock of labor.

THE ONION

BEACON OF JUSTICE

MOUTH-PIECE OF THE ROBBER-BARON

Sunday, May 8, 1910 — The Best Source of Newsworthy Items in our Great Republic. — SUNDAY EDITION — Price Five Cents.

U.S. SECRETARY OF INTERIOR REPORTS GOOD BUFFALO HUNTING STILL AVAILABLE

HERDS FOUND IN REMOTEST IDAHO, WYOMING.

News Mollifies Game Hunters Disappointed by Recent Extinction of Hoofed Plover.

Majestic Animals Expected to Last Until October.

Washington, May 7.—U.S. Secretary of the Interior Richard A. Ballinger announced to a relieved crowd of citizenry today that clusters of bison are still present in the American West.

This comes as welcome news to game hunters who have grown discouraged by the lack of creatures to hunt in recent years. The passenger pigeon is an increasingly rare sight, as are Carolina parakeets and prairie chickens. The buffalo was feared extinct, until an agent of the Department of the Interior reported small herds in remote regions of Idaho and Wyoming near Indian reservations. The Secretary's agents have entered into the national registry estimates that over 600 wild buffalo roam these United States territories. It is expected that the number will satisfy the game hunter for another five months until the buffalo is extinct.

"I am overjoyed," said prominent San Francisco banker H. Mulgrew Stubbs. "When I was a lad, I shot my first buffalo as my family rode the Union Pacific transcontinental line, happy just knowing I had downed the great animal, albeit to rot in a forgotten patch of prairie. I thought my young grandson would never know this great thrill. But now, Saints willing, he will."

THE LAST BUFFALO

In a related story, the Secretary has commissioned famed hunter Buffalo Bill to preside over the killing of America's last buffalo.

A gala ceremony is planned for late October to slay the last of the bison. Cordons of sash and decorative partitions will encircle a 20-yard radius about the beast. Promoters are promising a lively affair and encourage spectators, travelers, and children to attend. Buffalo Bill will sing, perform his celebrated circus-show re-enactment of the storming of Fort Flatgatt, and then, with great pomp, fire a thick volley of bullets into the animal. Top hats and ladies' chapeaux are expected to be tossed about to the accompaniment of cheers, after which music will be played by Buffalo Bill's traveling brass and wicker band.

As part of the gala event, famed Indian villain 'Sitting Bull,' killer of Custer, will have his memory desecrated with great fanfare.

NOW, THOSE GERMANS, THEY HAVE AMBITION!

AN EDITORIAL BY T. HERMAN ZWEIBEL, EDITOR-IN-CHIEF

I hear that a motley collection of coal-miners in some Appalachian back-water have the all-fired temerity to go on strike against the very company that grants them their livelihoods! This shocking indolence seems to pervade all corners of our once-great Republic; today's laboring force seems bent on spitefully undermining the glorious achievements of the titans of American capital.

You don't see any of this laziness in Germany! Now, there's a country with ambition! Since its unification, Germany has smote the hated French and crushed Socialism.

My favorite thing about the Empire of the Germanies is that it doesn't take any guff from the lousy English! Those inbred, tea-quaffing, fox-hunting limeys have all the nerve, trying to lord it over everyone.

When I look upon Kaiser Wilhelm II, the German emperor, the adjectives that most spring to mind are youth, beauty, and industry. Look upon his very visage! Regard his noble brow, his impeccably waxed mustaches, and his meticulously polished jack-boots! This is a leader with a God-ordained blue-print for his country's shining future. I yearn for his personal friendship, and hope and pray for the day when I can entertain him and the lovely Kaiserin at my tide-water estate. We will have a grand ball, and I will ask my private ball-room quartet to perform many popular and quaint American standards, such as "May I Have the Pleasure of Escorting You to the Cotillion, Sweet Mildred Dear?" and "Gaily We Prance About." And, if I were permitted to ask a question of his Imperial Highness, it would be, "Could I have one of those pointed helmets?" And maybe, just maybe, he would permit me to kiss his delicate, gloved hand. Would that such a grand day come to pass!

UNITED STATES LEADS WORLD IN INDUSTRY

'Thanks, Orphans!' Grateful Americans Say.

HARD-WORKING FOUNDLINGS BACKBONE OF AMERICAN INDUSTRIAL MIGHT.

Americans are "on top of the world" in the area of industrial growth, and the heartfelt gratitude of a nation is being extended daily to the tireless young citizens who, according to one prominent capitalist, "deserve a great portion of the credit" in helping turn the wheels of progress with their tiny hands.

The U.S. Department of Commerce and Labor reports that our nation's prominent businessmen are finding great help from labor-minded children, as more Americans are leaving the farms to work in the factories of our great cities.

In addition, the agency reports that the Republic enjoys the lowest number of work-related fatalities in the civilized world, with only 16 of every 100 losing their lives each day while working. For children, the number is only 12 for every hundred.

"These tots do a splendid job," esteemed industrialist R. Conkling Dunlop said. Dunlop's Steel and Brass Works on the island of Manhattan employs over 400 children not yet 14 years of age in its downtown mill. "With the tireless cooperation of the precious young, my company has seen a steady increase in production. Three years ago, I was paying dozens of adult laborers $3 a week each. But the young ones will do the same work for a mere ladle of broth, and with nary a complaint."

Worker morale at the Dunlop mill has also improved of late. The dank, nearly subterranean conditions in which armies of children man coal shovels, molding presses, and air-blast mechanisms ensure what Dunlop calls a "brisk turnover rate," which keeps the floor populated with bright, new faces.

An additional benefit to the employment of orphaned children is an economic one—that such unregulated hires circumvent the mountain of laws and statutes protecting adult workers from unfair conditions. "When my laborers were mostly adults, the law was on my back about machines that had to be kept below a certain temperature, or unacceptable levels of smoke in the furnace room," iron baron Harold Rudford said. "But with employees under the age of 12, I have the most adult-safe conditions imaginable: No adults."

According to rail-road officials, more than 75,000 orphans, immigrant offspring, and impoverished children from improper homes have been shipped via rail-car to live in coal towns, mill towns, and other areas where a willingness to undertake an extraordinary work-load is in short supply.

"I would like a family to love me, a house to live in, some bread every day," said plucky coal-pitcher Angelo Antonini, 7, whose parents died during the perilous ocean-crossing from Sicily. "I would also like to stop coughing at night."

"I can't see in color any more," said Beulah Sondergarten, 8, who was forced to replace her father at Vogel's Textile Plant, Boston, when he was ground to death after falling into a looming machine. "I used to have a dolly, but she fell in the machine and it ate her, just like it did my Daddy."

Leaders of the nation's largest cities are discussing a national day of celebration in honor of the hard-working foundlings. It will feature parades, circus entertainers, and all manner of gastronomic delicacies.

Dunlop said that children working in his Manhattan mill will be busy working and, therefore, unable to attend the celebration.

The Folly of Man!

TIDINGS OF 'TECHNOLOGY' MOST DIRE.

Ruin Foreseen.

By Oliver C. Prescott.
OFFERED AS AN AMUSING COUNTER-OPINION TO THE INFORMED BELIEFS OF THE EDITORS.

Citizens of the Republic, our nation stands on a moral precipice: the new Machine Age, an era of industry and technology. Will it prove to be our salvation... or the Folly of Man?

MAN'S LABORS CEASING?

Everywhere, scientificists and secular humanists bellow about the coming of the machines! A glorious new age awaits, say the contraptioneers, in which mankind shall be freed of drudgery by the power of newfangled automated devices! Every day, it seems, there is a promise of a new construction which will deliver us from our duties: the automated corn-shucker, the steam-driven fence-post driver, the log-splitting engine. We are to have faith that soon all natural labors of mankind will be taken o'er by clanking, smoke-belching contraptions of blackest iron!

INCREASING APATHY

But will it truly profit a woman to have her hen's eggs collected by a monstrous construction with mechanical arms? Will a man truly be benefited by an assemblagement which clears his ditches for him, without the slightest honest lifting of a finger? Will not the eggs taste sweeter when plucked from the nest by soft, womanly hands? Will not the sweat on the man's brow prove more virtuous than the oils and vapors spat upon his soil by a cold, unthinking contrivance?

In this young century, man looks higher toward the fount of mechanical ingenuity for the providence of his daily bread. But where is the smoke-filled, oil-bespattered path leading those who tread heedlessly along its course?

Envision a day that is not brightly lit with the glowing illumination of scientific knowledge, but darkened under the cloud of mindless machines! Will there come a day when horse-less carriages do not faithfully convey us to our destination, as has been loudly promised, but instead putter endlessly about, vainly hoping to find a place to park, so thoroughly will our automobiles have blanketed our streets?

Will there come a day when knowledge is not spread amongst the public by schools, but instead by mechanized picture-boxes, which we watch in huddled apathy, engrossed in the illiterate shadow-plays?

Will a time arrive when our instruments and machines of war become a greater threat than war itself? When our very food is prepared entirely by machine hands, so we do not have the slightest notion what we are consuming? When the pleasures of automated musical-boxes so distract us that, when faced with an actual violin, guitar, piano, or horn, we realize we no longer even know how to play them, music-lovers though we may be?

AN IDLE LIFE

Will we learn to rely on our machines so much that our children lose the will to survive and become unmotivated, endlessly prolonging the indecision of adolescence well into their twentieth year, meandering through life unsure of where to go or what to do, facing the world with blank eyes, uncaring of all they behold, while all around them machines clatter and wheeze mankind into oblivion?

This is the folly of man!

INEXPENSIVE NEW MOTOR-CARS WILL ALLOW DECENT FOLK TO LIVE FAR AWAY FROM COMMON LABORERS.
OUR REPORT ON PAGE 12.

NATION'S PORTS CLOGGED WITH JEWS.
OUR REPORT ON PAGE 17.

STATUE OF EMINENT MUSTACHIOED TOP-HATTED STATESMAN ERECTED.
OUR REPORT ON PAGE 3.

| EXTRA! | THE ONION | EXTRA! |

Tuesday, April 16, 1912 — The Best Source of Newsworthy Items in our Great Republic. — Price Two Cents.

WORLD'S LARGEST METAPHOR HITS ICE-BERG

TITANIC, REPRESENTATION OF MAN'S HUBRIS, SINKS IN NORTH ATLANTIC

1,500 DEAD IN SYMBOLIC TRAGEDY

The Royal Mail Steamer Titanic, the ill-fated emblem of man's pride, took 1,500 to a watery grave. It is photographed here leaving the port of Queenstown, Ireland, on her doomed, allegorical maiden voyage.

New York, April 15.—Officials of the White Star Line have confirmed the sinking, during her maiden voyage, of the R.M.S. Titanic, the world's largest symbol of man's mortality and vulnerability.

First reports of the calamity were received Monday at the London telegraph office of the White Star Line, which owns the nautical archetype.

MESSAGE FROM CARPATHIA

At 4:23 a.m. Greenwich Standard Time, the following message was received from the rescue ship Carpathia:

TITANIC STRUCK BY ICY REPRESENTATION OF NATURE'S SUPREMACY STOP INSUFFICIENT LIFEBOATS DUE TO POMPOUS CERTAINTY IN MAN'S INFALLIBILITY STOP MICROCOSM OF LARGER SOCIETY STOP

INDIFFERENCE

It is believed at this time that upwards of 1,500 passengers aboard the metaphor may have perished in the imperturbable liquid immensity that, irrespective of mankind's self-congratulatory "progress," blankets most of the globe in its awful dark silence. Seven hundred more passengers survived to objectify human insignificance in the face of the colossal placidity of the universe.

Among the prominent passengers ironically missing and believed perished are New York millionaire John Jacob Astor, mining tycoon Benjamin Guggenheim, railroad president Charles Melville Hays, and presidential military aide Major Archibald Butt, providing further example of man's inability to cavort with God, no matter how wealthy or powerful he may be, as well as the vast indifference of the universe toward even the grandest of human achievement. Late word indicates, however, that the well-to-do and the privileged constitute a great majority of the living. It could not yet be determined whether this betokens a form of maritime social Darwinism or a particularly overt form of social injustice.

IRONY

Although unconfirmed as of press-time, it is rumored that the Titanic was proceeding at a rapid pace through ice-berg-laden waters in order that her captain might flaunt the ship's great speed, making all the more ironic the demise of this paramount symbol of man's hubris.

An architect from the firm of Harland & Wolff, which constructed the great metaphor, was stunned and aggrieved by the significance of the tragic event.

"I spent the better part of two years re-drawing the marble on the grand staircase at the first-class entrance until it represented absolutely the right dimensions for showing off the daintily luxurious evening-wear of the wives of the industrial millionaires. Now that staircase will provide an entrance only for the plankton, moss, and other marine life that inhabits the frigid North Atlantic seabed. I dare say that is ironic."

HYPERBOLE

"Let us take a step back from the horror of the tragedy," said Lord Peter Hothcrofte, a British naval historian, "and view it in terms of its grander significance. Simply put, the Titanic was more than a gigantic crystallization of the accumulated triumphs of 200 years of Western industrialization wedded to the firm but icy hand of Science triumphant. It was a ship larger than any ship need be, which therefore also makes it somewhat of a hyperbole."

TELEGRAPHIC NEWS DISPATCHES ON THE TITANIC TRAGEDY

SPANIARDS RULED OUT AS SUSPECTS IN ICE-BERG PLACEMENT

BUT IS THE STATE DEPARTMENT BEING TOO HASTY? THE ONION INQUIRES

The Department of State has responded in the negative to a cabled inquiry by Onion Editor-in-Chief T. Herman Zweibel about possible involvement of the Spaniards in the location of an ice-berg which tore into the Titanic's hull and sent her to a watery ocean grave. In a statement to The Onion, Secretary of State Philander Knox said that there is very little tangible evidence of Spanish agents-provocateur in the region of the North Atlantic where the Titanic sank, nor was it believed possible that the Spaniards had even the capability to tow a several-hundred-ton ice-berg into the path of an oncoming ocean liner.

In addition, there was a general ice-berg advisory issued to ships in the region. Therefore, Knox concluded, the Spaniards are ruled out as suspects at this time. Those mindful of the war, however, know that the Spaniards are capable of such a dastardly deed.

DID JAZZ SINK THE GREAT SHIP?

Controversial "ragtime" jazz music may have brought the great ship to her disastrous end, a prominent minister says.

Reverend X. Lucius Dalrymple suspects that a cornucopia of lively jazz medleys, as performed by the ship's orchestra, may have delighted passengers right up until the Titanic's submersion.

The Reverend believes religious science has evidence to implicate the new form of music in the ship's demise.

"This rambunctious 'rag-time' music has an effect on the human body not unlike an evil spirit," he said. "It can quickly eat away at the morals of the listener, slowly reducing the mind to a state of dementia. A sea captain affected by this malady would be in no condition to pilot a large ship safely."

STEWARDS KINDLY ASK THIRD-CLASS PASSENGERS TO DROWN

From all reports, the attempt to abandon the sinking Titanic was fraught with chaos and panic of the first order, as passengers in the steerage class rudely strained against locked gates to reach the main deck and reacted harshly to the stewards' polite entreaties to accept the notion of drowning in the fast-rising waters. Words of an unkind and occasionally profane nature were addressed to employees of the White Star Line, who were simply doing their duty in trying to restore order and propriety.

As a representative of the White Star office in New York explained, "The standard rescue procedure aboard all trans-Atlantic luxury liners is as follows: ladies and children of the first-class, then first-class gentlemen, followed by their pets, steamer-trunks, potted-palms, and, finally, the billiard tables. Then the second- and third-class passengers are respectfully accommodated.

"However, the Titanic was sinking at such a rapid rate, and there were so few available life-boats, that few of the first-class gentlemen were themselves saved. Therefore, in that light, the stewards had no choice but to ask in the most deferential and delicate way manageable for the third-class passengers to consider drowning, so that the rescue could proceed more smoothly overall."

WELL-TO-DO DOWAGER GETS HAIR DISHEVELED FOR FIRST TIME

Lady Geraldine Dinsdale-Grey, a passenger aboard the ill-fated liner R.M.S. Titanic, experienced her first ever hair-mussing while being helped to a life-boat. Lady Dinsdale-Grey, the widow of Lord Clement Dinsdale-Grey, was being assisted by a steward when a gust of wind nearly swept her hat from her head. If not for the presence of a hat-pin securing the hat to Lady Dinsdale-Grey's head, the hat would have surely been lost.

Loosened strands of hair brushed against her face, as Lady Dinsdale-Grey attempted to adjust her hat-pin without the assistance of her maid-in-waiting, who had become separated from her in the rush to the life-boats. But there was little time, and, by the time Lady Dinsdale-Grey's lifeboat was set afloat, her thick auburn pompadour had fallen out of place considerably. Lady Dinsdale-Grey is reportedly safely on-board the rescue ship Carpathia, although there is no word on the present status of her hair.

THE ONION

PUBLISHED BY DIVINE RIGHT

PROGRESS AT ALL COSTS!

Wednesday, February 26, 1913 — The Best Source of News in Our Great Republic. — Price Two Cents.

ARCHDUKE FRANZ FERDINAND OF AUSTRIA BOASTS:
'NO MAN CAN STOP ME'

Vienna, Austria, Feb. 25. — Archduke Franz Ferdinand, a European nobleman, stood before a gathering of his subjects yesterday to announce, "No man can stop me."

The royal continued, "Were any harm visited upon my most exalted person, the crowned heads of Europe would stir themselves in their might, and God Himself could not stem the tides of blood that followed! All the world would be set aflame, and the horrors would not cease until the destruction of the hemisphere itself was complete!"

QUITE THE FOP

The archduke is reported to be in fine fettle as of late. His Highness, as he demands to be addressed, has been acting quite the cockerel, according to European dispatches. He is planning a vacation in Sarajevo next season, where he is expected to be seen boasting and strutting about, coming on like quite the fop, cutting a rakish profile, jutting forth his chin, and generally comporting himself in a brash and untoward manner.

DISMISSES RUMORS

"I'm quite the raffish rogue, quick with the rapier and rapier wit alike, and I'm not afraid to unsheathe both, if necessary," he said.

"I've heard rumors that there are ethnic tensions seething throughout my empire," he added. "Poppycock. Will someone please be charged with keeping dew off my snuff tin?"

The archduke then arbitrarily boasted that he has a summer home made out of Serbian peasants stacked like logs.

Those close to His Highness are quick to apologize for his behavior, noting that the burden of nobility, however minor, is never easy to bear; but some observers have taken issue with young Ferdinand's rakish behavior.

"We live in an age of Progress, in which royalty is but a symbol for the masses, and true power and liegehood lies with the industrial plutocracy," said noted smelting magnate J. Willoughby Sloane of Philadelphia. He does not doubt that others will agree that the puff-chested archduke is asking for trouble, and that no one should care if such a noble were to come to some harm. "The archduke is a symbol of a bygone era," Sloane said, "and in this century, men shall not care in the least if harm, no matter how grievous, were to come upon a mere figurehead."

BOASTS

Here are further excerpts from the archduke's speech: "I have a porcelain palace surrounded by six-foot-tall iron spikes.... I'm surrounded by bodyguards, and I have a special getaway carriage equipped with a small concealed cannon, and I can shoot arrows tipped with poison.... I have several peasant wenches who wait on me hand and foot, and a chest filled with precious jewels and gold bullion.... No one has shot more pheasants.... I have 1,278 pairs of kid gloves.... I have more Victrola records than any other archduke.... I am schooled in the gentlemanly martial arts, such as fencing and boxing per Marquis of Queensbury rules.... I am extremely well-groomed.... Woe betide the wretch who is foolish enough to try his hand at besting the great Franz Ferdinand, for, if a few swift sweeps of my blade don't dispatch him outright, surely any number of the crowned heads of Europe would quickly race to the defense of their noble brother to smite the lowly upstart's challenge to the Divine Right of imperial rule!"

The Archduke, here pictured with his wife, Sofia.

CONCERNED PARENTS CALL FOR OPERA RATING SYSTEM.

Read the story on page 13.

Henry Ford's New 'Assembly Line' Frees Workers' Minds to Contemplate Meaningless Void of Existence.

Read the story on page 12.

Pictured above is the latest example of Teutonic superiority, an air-ship that can easily out-pace a loping horse.

U.S. BUREAU OF REVENUE NO LONGER ACCEPTING CHICKENS

Hard Currency or Bank-Cheque Only Methods of Paying New 'Income Tax'

CAPRICIOUS NEW LAW UNFAIR, SAY FARMERS

Washington, D.C., Feb. 25. —"Modernization" has come to the U.S. Subtreasury, effecting the establishment of the new Federal income tax. In accordance with its implementation, Revenue Commissioner Lawrence C. Pettigrew announced that the U.S. will not accept chickens or other poultry as payment for monies owed.

Said Pettigrew: "Although chickens have long been an acceptable form of viable legal tender for the rendering of federal tariffs on farm products, shipping, and other excises, certain fowl can no longer be acknowledged for such purpose, no matter how succulent."

DEEMED 'IMPRACTICAL'

Pettigrew explained that chickens were becoming a nuisance, as government employees sorted through the enormous stacks of income-tax paper-work filed by tax-paying citizens. Many of the forms arrived in cages along with the fowl, covered in chicken defecation and poultry-lice, and giving off a stench. A few chickens had pecked at the forms until they were well-nigh illegible, and some were presumed to have eaten the forms entirely.

Many of the chickens also laid eggs during their shipment to Washington, surprising the government with the unexpected and costly expense of sending back the eggs, which qualified as over-payments, to their respective tax-payers.

Pettigrew cautioned that there was no viable way in which to deposit the amassing chicken-revenue. "Nothing in the Federal Reserve charter permits the acceptance of chicken-deposits, as it is difficult to calculate the birds' value, let alone interest," Pettigrew said.

The government has tried storing the chicken supply at the Federal gold reserves at Fort Knox, but this has proved impractical, as chickens do not stack in heaps side-by-side as well as gold and silver bullion.

INSTABILITY OF VALUE

Perhaps most importantly, the value of a chicken depreciates rapidly following its demise, and with the mass glut of poultry flooding into our Republic's capital, the government cannot sell deceased chickens to the populace, even at cut-rates, before the meat spoils and the carcasses become virtually worthless. "The advantage of legal tender or negotiable instruments," Pettigrew said, "is that their value is much more stable over a given period of time. Government-backed currency is much less apt to die, or to decompose as quickly, as a chicken that has passed away. Currency is also backed with stores of gold and other precious metals, while chickens are backed with only their will to live, which, unfortunately, has not proven to be particularly strong."

EQUIVALENCY SCALE

Pettigrew recommended that Americans accustomed to poultry-based tax payments substitute hard currency or bank-cheques for chickens come Tax Day of next year, according to the following animal-tender scale:

Tax due: one to three chickens...two pennies. Three to five chickens...four pennies. six to eleven chickens...six pennies. Goose of fertile age...one quarter dollar. Wild bull-turkey of roasting age...thirty cents. Slaughter pig...two quarter dollars.

Yesterday's Chicago Live Stock Market Quotations.
Beef steers, $7@7.25; bulk fat cows & heifers, $4.50@6.50; veal calves, slow to 25 cents lower; slunk calves, steady. Hogs, $10.25@10.75; bulk packing sows, $9.50@10; literate hogs, $8.75@9.50; dressed poultry remained full steady, with broilers .26@28c; castrated roosters, .24@25c; cute baby ducklings, $7.50 a bushel.
General Produce and Cash Grain Markets.
Oats—No. 1 white, 50@40c; No. 2 white, 31@32 1/2c.
Wheat—No. 2 red, $1.20@1.22 7/8; No. 2 northern dark, $1.45@1.47.
Hominy feed, white, per ton—$30.25.
Butter—creamery, fancy prints, 44@47; dairy, choice to fancy, 40@41.
Tallow—special loose, 4 1/2c.
Mother's milk—preferred, 42@43 7/8; wet-nurse, 37@39.

DOES AMERICA SUFFER FROM A 'ZEPPELIN GAP'?

'The Nation That Controls the Zeppelin Controls the World,' Secretary of War Proclaims

As the Kaiser continues to fortify his mighty fleet of zeppelins, voices of concern can be heard rising up from the bosom of this great Republic: Does the United States suffer from a zeppelin gap? Many a man believes the answer is yes.

GERMAN DOMINANCE

"Though it saddens me greatly, I fear that Lady Liberty cannot currently compete with the Germans in the arena of the flying dirigible contraption," said Secretary of War Lindley M. Garrison during a speech to a joint session of Congress Friday.

At present, the Germans are said to be in possession of twenty-five zeppelins, compared to the Republic's two. What is more, the Kaiser's zeppelins are said to be capable of reaching speeds of up to fifteen miles per hour.

Further, his enormous air-ships can block out the sun, causing crops to wither and die, or causing lesser minds to mistake the air-ships for avenging angels of the Lord, inciting great panic.

AMERICA'S RESPONSE

Most worrisome is that the Germans are rumored to be developing an enormous 600-yard zeppelin which could carry as many as 28 armed men inside its hanging underbelly compartment. It may be obvious that the balloon-wielding enemy has a decided advantage in sky-to-ground combat.

"Were one of our boys to see a hostile airship, he would be unable to flee it on foot," Garrison said. "Such is the technology the Prussians possess."

The Secretary proposed building a country-wide network of pointed towers to provide a formidable defense against attacking air-ships. He also proposed an increase in zeppelin research spending, which could bring the total war budget to $100,000. President Wilson may have no choice but to veto such an outlandish sum should it cross his desk.

In response to the growing U.S.-German zeppelin gap, Wilson has issued a challenge to America's leading dirigible makers: "Improve your zeppelins so that, if the need for war should arise, we may smite the Hun."

The president asserted that the United States has no immediate plans for war with Germany or any other nation.

EXTRA!	THE ONION	EXTRA!
Wednesday, August 5, 1914	The Best Source of News in Our Great Republic.	Price Two Cents.

WAR DECLARED BY ALL

AUSTRIA DECLARES WAR ON SERBIA DECLARES WAR ON GERMANY DECLARES WAR ON FRANCE DECLARES WAR ON TURKEY DECLARES WAR ON RUSSIA DECLARES WAR ON BULGARIA DECLARES WAR ON BRITAIN

OTTOMAN EMPIRE ALMOST DECLARES WAR ON ITSELF

· · · · · · · · · · · · ·

NATIONS STRUGGLE TO REMEMBER ALLIES

From the London and Washington Bureaus, Aug. 4—After weeks of unbearable tension following the assassination of the heir to the Austro-Hungarian throne, the great European powers have declared war on one another in a bitter struggle for something that is sure to be determined by war's end. Enmeshed in a confusing string of rivalries and alliances, diplomats, politicians, and military leaders expect to wage tireless battles through the course of the war without any knowledge of the reason why.

"We are all idiots," said one Bulgarian official. "We are most likely fighting about something, but we're not exactly certain what that is."

"Crush the demon Frenchman!" the diplomat added.

MEN ENLISTING FOR UNCLEAR BUT PATRIOTIC CAUSE

Millions of troops from the nations and their respective colonies are marching off, prepared to pay the ultimate price for the Central Powers' noble cause, which remains unclear as of presstime, or that of the mighty Triple Entente alliance, which no one can really put his finger on, either.

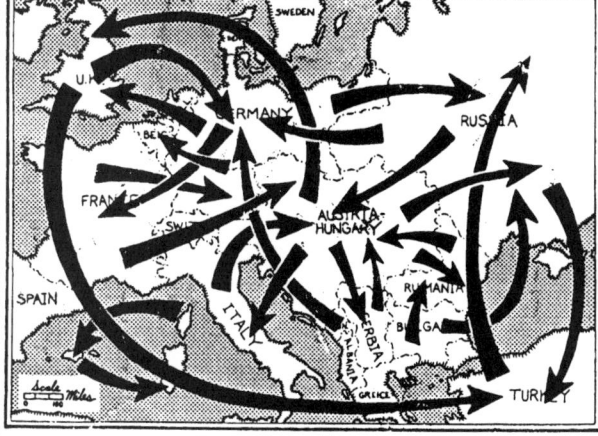

CABLE NOTIFIES WILSON

President Woodrow Wilson received the fateful news via a trans-Atlantic cable communication from the U.S. consulate in London. The cable reads as follows:

WAR DECLARED BY GERMANY FRANCE BRITAIN AUSTRIA HUNGARY RUSSIA SERBIA OTTOMAN EMPIRE LUXEMBOURG BELGIUM MONTENEGRO ALBANIA GREECE RUMANIA BULGARIA AUSTRALIA CANADA IRELAND SCOTLAND SOUTH AFRICA WEST AFRICA INDIA STOP MORE TO NAME BUT OTHERS WAITING TO USE CABLE STOP ARCHDUKE OF AUSTRO-HUNGARIAN EMPIRE BEING SHOT SOMEHOW RELATED STOP

Indeed, a state of war did not exist before the June 18th assassination of Austrian Archduke Franz Ferdinand in Sarajevo, but some of the fast-mobilizing nations seem skeptical about crediting his death as the cause of this new and awesome world war.

NO EXPLANATION FOR WAR FOUND

French diplomats suggest that an obscure "Dead Archduke of Austria" clause that exists in the peace treaty signed by the French and the Prussians in 1871 could be to blame for the hostilities. Officials of the German Foreign Ministry, however, allege that the treaty was nullified by the "Kill Everybody" accord signed by the warring powers in 1912.

U.S. WILL ONLY WATCH

"The U.S. must remain apathetic," Wilson said in a statement released to the press. "But we extend our blessing and best wishes to all European nations who wish to obliterate each other from the face of the Earth."

'WAR TO END ALL EUROPE'

American observers are calling this great, worldwide war the "War to End All Europe," as new technological warfare, untested in actual combat, may render the region incapable of holding another war for generations.

A MODERN WAR

Not every military expert, however, speculates that the forthcoming war will be as destructive as is commonly believed. "The introduction of modern technology into the theater of war will change the face of warfare forever," Col. Andrew Waylan Horace said. "The clean, efficient use of war machines will make the fighting safer and the duration of the war shorter."

Horace expects no more than 22 people need lose their lives in this Great War.

Président Wilson, who has vowed to maintain U.S. apathy.

ASSASSINATION OF ARCHDUKE SPREADS FEAR AT ARCHDUKE CONVENTION

The Hague, Netherlands, Aug. 4.—European archdukes attending their annual convention expressed alarm at the assassination of fellow aristocrat Archduke Franz Ferdinand, whose end came at the hand of a Serbian nationalist in Sarajevo several weeks ago.

Archdukes attending the convention expressed concern for the issue of nobleman safety, once considered a birthright. Most also claimed they had no knowledge of the Serbian demand for independence from Austria. "Could it be that the oppressed minority peoples in our own provinces are weary of centuries of authoritarian rule, as well?" asked Archduke Karl von Kremhelz, who cut short a month-long fox-hunting jaunt to attend the convention.

The convention, held yearly since 1421, gives archdukes of diverse backgrounds an opportunity to get acquainted, exchange archduke ideas, and purchase special archdukes-only notions and effects, most of a commercial nature. This year's convention included such notables as the Archduke of Badenherz-am-Geschildenschliess, the Archduke of Slochholz, and the Archduke of Lower Polony, who gave a special talk on the proper maintenance of monocles. The panel discussions "Coping with Genetic Hemophilia," "Dueling Pistol Best Buys," and "Putting the 'Happy' Back in 'Hapsburg'" were canceled due to the year's grave occurrence.

AREA DRUNKARD DECLARES WAR ON IRELAND

ALE-HOUSE PEERS FALL IN AS ALLIES

Davenport, Iowa, Aug 4. — As bloody conflict rages throughout Europe, Orvald Brunvald, a drunkard of many years' experience, declared war on Ireland Friday evening.

A RESOUNDING DECLARATION

"Consarn ever' one of 'em to damnation," Brunvald stated over a mug of porter at Quigle's Ale House in Davenport. "I'll lick 'em all to death!" he said. "Filthy potato-eating Papists, they are."

ALLIES 'HALF SEAS OVER'

Two gentlemen assembled with Brunvald at Quigle's Ale House tacitly fell in as allies. They are Archibald Johnson, 38, and Samuel Neubauman, 36, both of Davenport.

WILSON MEETS WITH DRUNKARD

The Department of War has been alerted to Brunvald's declaration. President Wilson, upon hearing of Brunvald's statements, called the drunkard to the Capitol building for an emergency session.

Wilson also discussed tactical matters with the drunkard. "Sock ever' last one of 'em in the chops, I say," Brunvald advised the president.

15

THE ONION

ALL YOUR LATEST WAR NEWS HERE

HUMBLE SERVANT OF THE MONEYED ELITE

Monday, August 24, 1914 — The Best Source of News in Our Great Republic — Price Two Cents

WAR BULLETINS

BRITISH CROQUET MALLETS PROVE USELESS AT FRONT

HUNS' 'MACHINE-GUNS' PROVE MORE EFFECTIVE WEAPONS.

CRUSHING SETBACK FOR ALLIES.

"I Say, It Worked Splendidly in the Drill," Brigadier General Sir Edmund Shropshire-Lloyd Says.

From the Paris correspondent, Aug. 23.—British infantrymen and their commanding officers are facing the painful realization that their tried-and-true weapons of warfare, croquet mallets, are ineffective in arresting the Germans' advance into France and Belgium.

CARNAGE

The 7th Malletiers Battalion reported extremely heavy casualties following an attempted advance against the German line near the Marne River. Although presenting a fearsome sight as they raised their croquet mallets over their heads while ascending from their trenches, the brave British troops were quickly mowed down by the rapid gunfire of the Huns' new and terrifying "machine-guns," which can fire several rounds of ammunition per second with great accuracy.

SANDWICHES EMPLOYED

Desperate officers, shocked by the carnage, ordered their men, with considerable trepidation, to sheath their mallets and attack with cucumber sandwiches.

Although once considered the most strategically vital force in the British infantry, having been decisive in earlier British campaigns in Afghanistan and Rhodesia, it was clear that the Sandwichiers' skill and bravery would be seriously challenged in this particular conflict. Although many sandwiches were successfully lobbed into enemy territory, none, to the horror of the British command, caused any apparent casualties, nor did the heretofore frightful specter of live cucumber sandwiches falling into enemy trenches force a retreat.

Germans are overrunning the British trenches, bayoneting soldiers and forcing an Allied retreat over a three-mile span. Eyewitnesses have reported that some Germans were even eating some of the cucumber sandwiches as they left their trenches for the pursuit across No-Man's Land.

"These blasted Teutons aren't human," said Brigadier General Sir Edmund Shropshire-Lloyd.

In one defining exchange, a battalion of Sandwichiers 12 miles from the German border with Belgium were delicately layering slices of cucumbers upon bread readied for catapulting when they were taken by surprise by a hail of machine-gun fire from advancing Germans. Blood flowed from their chests, necks, and heads and onto the unused sandwiches, rendering them useless as either weapons or tea-time hors d'oeuvres.

BELGIAN FORCES HALT GERMAN ADVANCE USING CREAM-TOPPED WAFFLES

HUNS NO MATCH FOR DELICIOUS REGIONAL CONFECTION.

GERMAN GENERAL HEINRICH VON STADT REPORTED IN 'SLEEPY' CONDITION.

Liege, Belgium, Aug. 23.—The seemingly unstoppable German army ground to a halt today after the surprise deployment of delicious cream-topped Belgian waffles to the front. "No soldier can resist a crisp, golden waffle smothered in dairy-fresh Belgian cream and a variety of fruit toppings," said crafty King Albert I, acting commander of the Belgian Armed Forces.

DAWN STRIKE

The waffle strike was executed with the utmost secrecy. Under the cover of darkness, specially trained Belgian breakfast commandos approached the German lines last night armed with back-mounted tanks of whipped cream and heated platters stacked high with steaming waffles. Enemy sentries were quickly neutralized by the offer of two waffles apiece, enabling the Belgians to inundate the main body of German troops with a mouth-watering barrage.

German forces this morning remain bloated and immobilized by their midnight feast, infuriating the Imperial German High Command. The German press reports that Chief of Staff Helmuth von Moltke is considering charging Belgium with violation of the Geneva Code of Warfare, calling the Belgian waffle weapon "inhumanly tasty."

BELGIAN TROOPS WAFFLIZE

While overjoyed by the success of the Belgian baked-goods gambit, Allied military experts fear that the waffles might only whet the German appetite for more savory morsels. "It is well known that the Hun enjoys the sweet flesh of human infants," said British Field Marshall Sir Douglas Haig. "I am terrified by the prospect of the filthy Huns topping off their waffles with a jellied-infant compote."

However, the Belgian mood remains triumphant today. Pastry units are busily mixing another large batch of waffles in the front-line kitchens, cheered on by comrades lustily singing traditional waffle-crafting songs. "If we can hit the Germans with a fresh bombardment of wafflery before the first is even fully digested, intestinal discomfort and severe drowsiness may result," said King Albert I.

Reconnaissance planes report that the Germans are countering by fixing the coordinates of seventeen long-range artillery battalions upon Brussels.

INFECTIOUS DISEASES CELEBRATE OPENING OF PANAMA CANAL

Multitudes of microscopic diseases are pictured here en route to New York City via the new canal.

Panama City.—As world travelers rejoice at the imminent Panama Canal opening, no one is happier than the many infectious diseases that will enjoy untold new opportunities to inhabit hosts and spread to other continents.

The canal was dedicated in a colossal ceremony Saturday attended by thousands of human celebrants and over 80 different germs and pathogens.

"I once was consigned to the limitations of transcontinental land travel across the Isthmus of Panama. But now, I'm going to see the world!" malaria said.

"This is the opportunity we have waited for," a thrilled colitis said of the momentous opening. "I, and all infections like me, are standing on the threshold of a golden age. Beware, intestinal tracts!"

"We have forged here the greatest miracle of modern engineering and proven conclusively man's superiority over the forces of nature," said George Goethals, chief engineer of the Canal project, moments before turning pale, doubling over, and vomiting.

PRESIDENT WILSON MAKES APPEAL TO EUROPE'S MONARCHS: 'USE YOUR LINK WITH DIVINE PROVIDENCE TO STOP THE WAR'

Washington, D.C., Aug. 23.—Although he has pledged American neutrality toward the war in Europe, President Wilson is nonetheless troubled by its awesome destruction, and is asking the monarchs of Europe and Russia, who rule by Divine Right, to entreat the Savior to end the war.

"As the divinely ordained rulers of much of the civilized world, your relationship with God is direct and immutable," Wilson said in a message telegraphed to the imperial palaces in Berlin, Paris, London, Vienna, and Petrograd. "In light of this, I am imploring you to use your special link with Divine Providence to stop this horrible war."

CROWNED HEADS RESPOND

In response, Czar Nicholas II of Russia thanked President Wilson for his concern but said that, to the best of his knowledge, God wanted the war to continue, although He was clearly on the side of the Allies.

Crown Prince Ilonz Josef of Bulgaria cabled that two nights ago the Christ-Child came to him in a dream and handed him a flaming golden sword, which was inscribed with the words, "Stab the Allied Foe through the Heart! Your Central Powers Shall Be Victorious."

Wilson's advisors have urged him to abandon the fruitless notion of imploring monarchs, suggesting he instead use the power of prayer.

TRAVELING CIRCUS FEATURES ANIMALS NOT FOR CANNING

The world-renowned Slats-Belbo Circus is making its annual tour about the Republic and is premiering its newest and most remarkable attraction: rare and exotic beasts not suitable for canning, curing, pickling, or any other type of meat-processing known to Christian civilization.

The creatures were either captured in the jungles of darkest Africa and the Amazon or purchased from traders in the far-off land of Araby. Once stateside, many were promptly slaughtered at a Chicago meat-packing operation, but butchery proved a great difficulty, as many were possessed of great size and choleric temperament, as well as hides tougher and more unusually colored than those of cattle.

When served to diners in a Chicago restaurant, the resulting meat met with mixed reviews. It was said by some to have a peculiar and offensively gamey taste, which no amount of salting and seasoning could fully eradicate.

Hearing word of this extraordinary occurrence, agents of the Slats-Belbo Circus paid the slaughterhouse an amazing $75 in gold bullion for the surviving creatures so that they may be exhibited for public viewing.

The animals are now housed in circus-wagons covered with iron bars and are exhibited under a large bunting which reads, "The Wondrous Animals Which God Did Not Intend Us to Eat."

The roster of inedible animals include a wild leopard-cat, a peccary, two storks, a giraffe, several beetles, a gibbon, a hippopotamus, and a sloth.

ALL THE LATEST HABERDASHERY NEWS	**THE ONION**	**Kids!** JOIN T. HERMAN ZWEIBEL'S "HUN-HATING HOOLIGANS" CLUB
Friday, February 19, 1915	The Best Source of News in Our Great Republic	Price Two Cents

WAR BULLETINS

600,000 KILLED IN 4-INCH ADVANCE ON WESTERN FRONT

HEROIC SOLDIERS PAY ULTIMATE PRICE TO MAKE PATCH OF MUD SAFE FOR DEMOCRACY

'These 4 Inches of Mud No Longer Bow Before the Whip of Tyranny,' Says British Command

Plessier, France, Feb. 18.—Allied High Command is jubilant today after last night's triumphant four-inch advance into enemy territory at the cost of a mere 600,000 troops. The strategically vital one-third of a foot is already being fortified by British forces against the expected German counter-assault tonight.

STRATEGICALLY SIGNIFICANT

The mud had been seized by the Kaiser two days before, despite a valiant defense at the cost of 450,000 soldiers. It is expected to remain safely in Allied hands for at least two or three days, British Army Intelligence officials said.

Allied strategists consider this advance extremely significant. "After this bold offensive, the Allied armies are only 931,720,458 inches from Berlin," said Lt. Gen. Thomas Fuller, former leader of the Second Army Corps, which was eliminated in the fighting. "My men fought valiantly for at least five minutes. Thank God we claimed the mud, and their deaths were not in vain."

Other units lost in the cause of victory include nine British regiments, sixteen French battalions, and all able-bodied men from Ceylon.

The long march to victory began with a furious artillery bombardment two weeks ago upon the entrenched Huns, who withstood the rain of shells enough to offer stiff resistance until last night's breakthrough. One Belgian regiment pushed as far as eight inches ahead, but was decimated by German crossfire when communication and supply lines were cut from its supporting units two inches back.

The stunning advance is the most monumental Allied victory since last December's nine-inch onslaught near Beaufort.

HENRY FORD UNVEILS NEW LINE OF ANTI-SEMITIC AUTOS

'Model-C' Vehicle 100 Percent Hebrew-Free, Says Manufacturer

SEATS 4 GENTILES IN COMFORT

Detroit, Mich., Feb. 18.—With much fanfare, Henry Ford unveiled his latest line of Jew-hating motor cars.

"The 1915 Model-C Ford is the finest automobile ever manufactured for the American people, barring those of Israelite stock. I personally guarantee it," Ford told an assemblage of reporters at his company's famed Highland Park assembly plant. "And yes, sir, it's got that smooth, anti-Semitic ride you've come to expect from a Ford."

"If you dislike the Jew," Ford added, "you'll love this particular motored carriage."

The automobile is offered in black, as a symbol of the maker's seething, black-hearted hatred of the Jews.

Among the fine, upstanding Christian automobile's many features: a 30-horsepower engine, an easy-to-read, Hebrew-free dashboard, and genuine pig-leather seats.

As an incentive to buy, Ford said the new automobiles can be purchased on credit. "Buy now, pay later," the auto tycoon said. "With the Ford Easy Payment Plan, you won't have to go to your local bank and suffer the humiliation of begging a Jew for a loan."

According to Ernest P. Stansford, spokesman for the Ford Motor Company, advance orders for the new automobiles have exceeded all expectations, numbering over 20 million in the Deep South alone and coming in from as far away as Germany.

THE FORD MOTOR COMPANY'S 1915 MODEL-C "JEW-HATER" AUTOMOBILE.

'Jolly Good' Brit Boys Die 'Cheerio, Can-Do' Deaths

GOOD SPORTS PERISH WITH DIGNITY, MANNERS

With the British Armies in France.—At 5 o'clock in the evening, the horizon of the Western Front glows a dull red, silhouetting Private Donald Derby, age 17, as he peers over the tops of sandbags into no man's land. "It's over the top for us tonight, mate," he says, sipping a hot cup of tea. "There's nothing quite like a spot of trench warfare to get your tucker up. Biscuit?" he asks, proffering a crispy shortbread.

Private Derby is a typical British fighting man. It's all "Right-O, old boy!" and "Can do, sir!" for these plucky doughboys. Although they emerge as barely audible squeaks, Derby still forces the words, "It was a pleasure, sir. Cheerio!" as he chokes on a cloud of mustard gas later that evening.

Now, the 7th Royal Welsh Guards are enjoying a refreshing tea, swapping merry trench tales before tonight's assault on the German position near Cambrai.

"Remember the row we had last month, mates, in the woods near Grenonville? Now, that was a scrap," says one soldier.

"Aye," pipes up Private Willy Boggins, a cheeky Cockney lad of 19. "Old Brewster 'ad both 'is arms shot clean off, but 'ee kept a-runnin' right with us over the barbed wire. 'Take more than two bullets to put me down, mates!,' 'ee shouted, until 'ee took one more in the noggin. Daft old dodger, that one!"

Suddenly a mortar blast goes off nearby, and a stray shard of metal whips through the air and lodges squarely in Boggins' chest. He falls instantly, downed by the cat-sized shard, which has cut him nearly in two. He wheezes briefly and manages a short, "blast my rotten luck," before passing on.

The soldiers share a concerned look, then lift their tea cups to their fallen comrade. A fellow with lieutenant's shoulder-pips pops his head out of an underground bunker. "Let's tidy up the trench a bit before we go off, boys," he says. "So much nicer to come back to, eh?"

The men busy themselves about the trench, shaking greasy rats out of cooking pots and pushing the loose limbs of rotting corpses back into the muddy fortifications. Suddenly the rumble of distant artillery is cut through by several high-pitched whistles and pops.

Yellow trails of gas are floating over the scarred landscape toward the British lines. "Lovely patterns that phosgene gas makes, don't you think?" asks Lieutenant Bertrand Woolsey, 18, enjoying the view while leisurely unstrapping his gas mask. "And a nice, lemony sort of scent, as well. Not bad at all."

The lieutenant turns to face his masked troops. "Well, now, lads, we don't want the Hun to get the jump on us tonight. Off we go, through the gas and over the barbed wire! God save the King!" A tendril of gas snakes around the unmasked lieutenant's head. He topples down into the mud, a smile frozen on his face.

The Brit boys shout a muted "hurrah" through their respirators, affix bayonets to their rifles, and vault over the sandbags into the yellow cloud. A terrific barrage of machinegun fire answers their gay shouts. Fully half of the battalion is riddled with lead the instant they clear the sandbags, their bodies crashing back into the trench. The rest disappear into the gas, laughing and singing.

Youngsters of Today Enjoy Socializing at Church

EXPERIENCE OPPORTUNITY TO SING, CONSORT WITH NON-RELATIONS

OUTDOOR MEALS OF PICKLED CUCUMBERS, 'POTATO-CHIPS' MAKE FOR MERRY TIME

Minot, N.D., Feb. 17.—Young people consider attending church their most favored form of socializing, if the activities of the youths who live in the vicinity of this northern North Dakotan county seat provide any indication. The young people noted that they very much enjoy the weekend activities of professing their faith in Christ, setting foot off the farm, and meeting other young people with a different last name than their own.

The youths enjoy other activities organized or sanctioned by their local parish or regional synod, such as prayer meetings, barn dances, and Book of Leviticus recitation contests.

COURTSHIPS ALSO RESULT

Young men attending church events also have the opportunity to sing hymns of worship while sitting on a bench next to a young woman to whom he is not related.

The young ladies, meanwhile, have the chance to leave their family kitchens and put on their finest Sunday dresses, apply dusting-powder, and demonstrate their cooking and serving abilities during the year-round church picnics and luncheons, which often include such specially prepared delicacies as pickled cucumbers, chipped potato wedges, and liverwurst sandwiches.

The congregation inspires many a young man to seek courtship with a young lady and, following the customary courtship period of five years, possibly ask for her hand in marriage, provided neither party has been carried away by the typhus.

Seven engagements alone were announced shortly after last week's Youth Prayer Meeting at the First Lutheran Church in Minot. One groom-to-be, Cletus Anderson, reported that he had grown quite fond of a young lady who had been seated in a pew adjacent to his, and the fact that they had politely exchanged approximately fifteen words in six years was reason enough for their betrothal.

OTHER RECREATION SECONDARY

Other forms of socializing do exist for young people, but they take a distant place behind church attendance. Some enjoy vexing goats and other livestock by tying cans to their tails, or throwing small rocks in the air and striking them with a bat.

YOUNG PRAGUE SALESMAN METAMORPHOSES INTO ENORMOUS BUG

(turn to page 8, col. 4.)

FOE OF FALSEHOOD

THE ONION

Thursday, April 13, 1916 — The Best Source of News in Our Great Republic — Price Two Cents

Ladies! HAVE YOU ENTERED OUR BIRTHING CONTEST? Kindly see page 8.

WAR BULLETINS

British Navy Condemns German U-Boats as 'Not Very Sporting'

FROM THE LONDON CORRESPONDENT, Apr. 12. — As German U-boats continue to torpedo non-combative merchant ships and passenger liners containing innocent civilians in the waters of the North Atlantic, officials from the British Home Office condemned the actions as "not very sporting" and "scarcely what anyone would call fair play."

"The mere notion," said Evelyn Pith-Holloway, seventh Earl of Dunwiddie-on-Stoke. "I say. Right beastly things. Positively horrid, these U-boats. U-boats? 'Uncouth boats' if you ask me. Haven't they gone a bit too far?"

HUNS ILL-MANNERED

Sir Geoffrey Alan Mycroft-Waring, aide to the Chancellor of the Exchequer, was more blunt in his assessment of the German atrocities. "Blast all this wretched Hun nonsense anyhow," he said. "As I was saying to my man, Buskers, this morning, it would be a much simpler tussle if these Germans would stay fast to the battlefield area and stop all this lurking about in the water."

Despite the clear violation of rules of warfare respected by all mannered nations, Germany continues to insist that its policy of unlimited submarine warfare is necessary to thwart the delivery of contraband to Allied shores. British leaders decry the recent sinking of the Lusitania as but the latest example of German rudeness.

The English have demanded that Germany withdraw its U-boats and engage in more civilized, cultured tactics in its war against the Allies, such as fencing, recital of classical Greek poetry, sherry-drinking, and the devastating use of wry understatement.

KING'S RESPONSE

In a statement released from Buckingham Palace, King George V expressed concern at Germany's refusal to cease the U-boat attacks. "Dreadful business. Dreadful. Not at all the sort of thing to which we can give our approval. Beastly stuff, this whole war business. Cloak-and-dagger and all that. Something ought to be done, really it should."

"I say, when is tea?" the King added.

Pictured above are German photographs, acquired by Allied spies, of what British officials have dubbed the "Uncouth Boat."

ALLIED POWERS CLAIM 2 MORE INCHES ON THE FRONT!

Our report on page 6

CUBIST REGIMENT DECIMATED

Quasi-Two-Dimensional Trench Is Exposed to German Gunfire

Skewed Perspective, Lack of Depth Prove Liability as Non-Linear Soldiers Are Mercilessly Cut Down

WITH THE FRENCH ARMIES NEAR VERDUN, FRANCE, Apr. 12. — As the Battle of Verdun continues to claim heavy casualties on both sides of the conflict, the French High Command reports the total loss of its Cubist Infantry Division, as it defended the city of Verdun against a renewed German advance.

The trench dug by the Division lacked correct scale or even a perceptible vanishing point, its opening facing the German front lines, thereby making it easy for German infantry to clearly see its inhabitants and gun them down as they huddled for safety.

Hailing mostly from the Left Bank and Latin Quarter of Paris, and many having produced works exhibited in elite artistic salons and galleries throughout the city, members of the Cubist Division were largely raw recruits for whom armed conflict, let alone coherent spatial relation, was alien. Their very presence on the front lines demonstrated the extent of the French forces' desperation.

The Cubists' fight training was a brief two weeks, a dogged but ultimately fruitless effort to whip them into fighting shape. Their vision, skewed because both their eyes were on one side of their faces, made them poor marksmen, and their poor depth perception made them deficient in such vital skills as bayoneting and wire-cutting.

As they arrived at the front, the Cubist troops proved an immediate hindrance. The Cubists' sharply angular, distorted bodies took up too much room in the trenches, poking and prodding their compatriots with their graceless, chunky forms.

"They were brave and eager, that much is clear," said French Lieutenant Pierre Buton, "but their abstract, disproportionate figures created much discomfort for the already beleaguered troops, and they were simply not suited for the rigors of army life."

Eventually the Cubist troops were withdrawn from the trenches and sent to reinforce a weakly defended area north of Verdun. Once there, they were put to work digging fresh trenches in anticipation of additional reinforcements. Before their work could be completed, however, German guns rendered the Cubists even more misshapen.

Among those killed were Les Demoiselles d'Avignon, Ambrose Vollard, three dancers, three musicians, a mother, and a child.

HUNGARIANS ESCALATE WAR WITH TERRIFYING 'BARTOK ASSAULT'

NEAR THE EASTERN FRONT, Apr. 12. — Hungarian soldiers unleashed the intense, bombastic compositions of Bela Bartok in the Battle of Bansag, an assault that had great effect against emotionally impacted Allied forces.

Bartok's new collection of works emphasizing strings, percussion, and celestas is being hailed by war officials as the most fearful weapon in Austro-Hungarian history.

Soldiers, in tandem with the Budapest Symphony Orchestra, lulled Italy's 3rd Infantry Battalion with soothing passages inspired by traditional Hungarian folk melodies, then shook them with sudden, outbursts of French horn, timpani, and tuba.

Allied troops were filled with awe and trepidation at the sheer magnitude of the new military possession, which was developed in conjunction with German symphonic strategists and the Royal Academy of War Music in Budapest.

Allied tacticians predict Austro-Hungary will utilize violent shifts in rhythm and startling harmonic abstraction, employing volumes never before experienced in land combat. And some caution that their use of an interpolated 12-tone celesta may violate the rules of warfare.

Allied commanders believe the Hungarians have "a flair for tonality which could revolutionize 20th-century fighting music."

There has not been such a leap in Hungary's strength since 1911, when the army engaged the formidable men of the Budapest Flying Circus.

Fall Fashions for Women Hint at Existence of Hips

Ladies May Also Have Differently Shaped Chests

A Reversal of Fashion's Historical Directions

Tailors everywhere expressed surprise and some trepidation, as the new line of women's safety-seamed gowns and double-jacketed coats was released to package-and-goods stores last week. With layers of black wool tucking slightly in at the bodice, the new dresses undeniably hint at a curvature just below the waist on the female body.

Nothing this outrageous has occurred in American fashion since 1908, when the outward bowing of the bosom was shown to exist beneath the double-breasted snapping woolen waistcoat of the feminine summer lakeside sunning frock.

Clothing designer Grant Heffens, the most respected of the five designing tailors practicing in America, said, "Fall is the time of harvest and the spirit is of cultivation and fecundity, so my plan was to hint ever so slightly that there may be components of the female form which deviate from the male form, and which could serve certain special purposes."

ANATOMISTS BAFFLED

Scientist and anatomy specialist Herman H. Cavanagh is confounded by the new truths of biology revealed by the shocking clothing, admitting that science has "much to learn" about the anatomical differences between the sexes. Cavanagh has organized an academic consortium to confer with Heffens and other fashion designers at the University of Chicago's Medical College in the hopes of uncovering heretofore unknowable facts about the shape of the female body, and the mysterious purposes thereof.

SLOCOMBE'S
GENERAL DRY GOODS PROVISIONERS

Your exclusive mercantile establishment for official "Birth of a Nation" merchandise, personally licensed by the famed moving-picture supervising dramatist, D.W. Griffith. Anyone else who claims to be selling "Birth of a Nation" merchandise is a base charlatan, for only Slocombe's is approved by Mr. Griffith to vend the following wares.

Featuring

The "Little Sister" hand-trowel .... **35¢**

The "Little Colonel" thimble .... **7¢**

The "Silas Lynch Sinister Mulatto" meerschaum pipe ... **59¢**

and, in limited quantities, the official "Birth of a Nation" galvanized bucket, whose protective pasteboard package-wrapping is personally autographed by lady-actress Lillian Gish ... **$2.95**

16 CANAL STREET
NEW YORK

JOIN NOW!	THE ONION	PREPARE TO DIE!
Saturday, April 7, 1917	The Best Source of News in Our Great Republic	Price Two Cents

U.S. ENTERS WAR; WILSON VOWS TO 'MAKE WORLD SAFE FOR CORPORATE OLIGARCHY'

Ex-President Roosevelt Enlists in Infantry

Young in fighting spirit if not in years, former President Theodore Roosevelt made a brave show of patriotism by enlisting as an infantryman in the U.S. Army Friday.

No sooner had the stalwart veteran Rough Rider and vocal Interventionist heard that hostilities were to begin against German aggression than he dressed in his finest First Cavalry uniform, buckled on his saber, saddled Imperator, his finest stallion, and galloped to Recruiting Office 4723 in Oyster Bay, where he was informed that there would be little call for the cavalry in the coming conflict. Undaunted by the modernization of warfare, Roosevelt signed on as a lowly footsoldier, saying that his only wish was to fight and kill as many Huns as God saw fit to deliver before his rifle.

Although the ex-president and former Commander-in-Chief of the Armed Forces was not allowed to take a position of rank, he did not seem upset, laughing and cheering with his fellow recruits as they helped him aboard the troop train and repeatedly exclaiming that the Great War was the "most bully" 60th-birthday present a soldier could receive.

Roosevelt's commanding officer said that the former president seemed spry and full of ginger, but, for the safety of himself and others, would not be issued a rifle. Roosevelt is scheduled to be assigned kitchen duty later next month, where he will be given potato-boiling responsibilities as his health and age permit.

SPY ON YOUR NEIGHBORS! REPORT THEM!

AN EDITORIAL PASSED BY THE ONION BOARD OF DIRECTORS

As with the Minutemen of old, we red-blooded true Americans must stand ever-vigilant against those who would destroy our freedom! For the murderous German fiends and their oily agents of espionage are everywhere, spinning their villainous webs of intrigue and corruption.

We must never be conquered by the twin evils of despotism and depravity! So, with God and justice on our side, we rightly take up arms against the German oppressors and their partners in crime. But we must also remember that the supporters of the Boche are everywhere—including within the borders of our great Republic!

They are not easily noticed; in fact, they often adopt a mild, unassuming guise. Take, for instance, Mrs. Obermeyer down the street: a stout, cheerful matron whose tireless sweater-knitting for our boys Over There has been admired and praised by all her neighbors. But, for all we know, Mrs. Obermeyer is writing the words "Toten Sie mich bitte, weil ich ein Amerikanersoldat bin!" on each sweater—which, translated into English, means, "Please kill me, for I am an American soldier!"

What can you, as a patriotic American, do to thwart the steady stream of espionage that flows from the heartland of America to the Kaiser in Berlin? The Onion strongly urges all its readers: If you see anyone doing anything anywhere, report it immediately to your local police constabulary, the War Department in Washington, or to Onion Editor-in-Chief T. Herman Zweibel. Spy on your neighbors! Report them! Organize angry mobs of determined patriots wielding pitchforks and torches! Harass and persecute anyone of even remotely German heritage, and make them wear badges proclaiming, "I am a treacherous and smelly Hun." Seize all the braunschweiger you can find and burn it in the town square. For fuel, use books.

And most important, do not believe what you read in the newspapers or magazines, or see in the moving-picture newsreels. It is all lies!

ALLIED POWERS CLAIM HALF INCH MORE ON THE FRONT IN FIRST QUARTER OF 1917!

Our report on page 7.

DADAISTS CREATE SELF-DESTROYING WORK OF ART; NEW 'LAND MINE' COULD REVOLUTIONIZE VIEWS OF MECHANIZED CULTURE.

Our report on page 7.

'KU KLUX KLAN' CLUB GROWING IN POPULARITY

Many Drawn By Late-Night Activities, Fanciful Outfits

Members of the Ku Klux Klan enjoy a Sunday outing.

CUSTIS, Ga. — Espousing a common bond of ethnic and cultural heritage, the fancifully titled Ku Klux Klan Club is experiencing quite a revival of late. The recreational group expects to admit several thousand qualified applicants this year alone.

The Klan's renewed popularity comes on the heels of its recent changes to appeal to the modern American, such as an updating of club hate-activities to include a much broader variety of racial and religious persuasions.

"We want our prospective members to know that our KKK is their KKK," explained Regional Exalted Cyclops Ambrose Monroe, "provided they are white, Protestant Christian, and native-born. We appreciate a wide variety of viewpoints. Therefore, besides our traditional resentment of coloreds, we now also strongly disapprove of Catholics, Jews, mulattos, and those of Irish, Chinese, and other immigrant stock."

"Our activities are created and practiced with the family in mind," Monroe added. "This year, we have held seven prayer breakfasts and commemorative lynchings, as well as three potlucks and firebombings of darkie schools. Next week, we will hold our annual fundraising bake sale and hazing of a local Jew family."

Monroe touted the Klan's valuable social work, including its members' willingness to proselytize anywhere and anytime, even in the wee hours of the morning. The raising of large wooden crosses is a hallowed Klan tradition, and if darkness renders these crosses difficult to see, resourceful Klan members coat them with a flammable solvent, setting ablaze the consecrated symbol for all to behold.

Cleanliness and a willingness to stand out among one's fellow men are exemplified by the Klan's club uniforms, whose white, meticulously starched robes and pointed hoods trimmed with gay, blood-red crosses can even be seen in the dark behind trees and bushes.

"Remember," Monroe added, "The Ku means You in the Ku Klux Klan."

Those interested in joining the Klan may attend an orientation meeting at Geo. Mauston's General Mercantile Emporium in downtown Custis this Wednesday, April 11, at 3 o'clock p.m. Please bring a copy of your birth certificate and your own rifle. Hardtack and whiskey will be served.

Nation's Young Men Flock to Enlist in Defense of U.S. Corporations

Vanderbilt, Rockefeller Applaud President's Brave Stance

Wilson: Heroic Defender of the Monied Few.

WASHINGTON, D.C., Apr. 6. — President Wilson, speaking before a joint session of Congress Friday afternoon, committed the United States military to the war against the Central Powers. Pledging an initial commitment of 200,000 troops, with additional troop deployment in the future, Wilson called on all Americans to support the war effort, stating that the United States must be firm in its mandate to "make the world safe for corporate oligarchy."

Said the president: "The United States must use military force if necessary to ensure that a privileged and entrenched plutocratic power structure continues to impose unregulated, rampant industrial capitalism upon not only the populace of this great land, but all the peoples of the world, known or unknown, white or non-white."

"We cannot and will not shirk this duty," the president continued, "but must remain steadfast for the future generations of oligarchs who will be our legacy."

RICH APPLAUD PRESIDENT

The presidential decree met with loud and vociferous approval from business leaders throughout the land. "The Kaiser's relentless advance must be rolled back," said Edmund G. Hausmann II of the Amalgamated Tetrahedron Co. "Only when this cruel and despotic dictator is deposed, and he is no longer able to enforce his iron will upon the peoples of the European continent, will our world once again be safe for oligarchs of all nationalities."

Railway baron Harold Sterling Vanderbilt agreed, dispatching a telegraph to the New York offices of The Onion without delay, urging all able-bodied American males of the laboring classes to support the president's call and volunteer for service in the European theatre. "I say to all young, unmonied men of the Republic: Go with courage in your hearts, and die of agonizing, gas-induced respiratory failure in the fetid trenches, that future conglomerations of private financial interests will be free to rule."

Vanderbilt also offered words to the women who would be waiting patiently for their husbands, future husbands, and sons to return home from the war: "Pray for your boys' lives. Pray that they fight hard, fight true, and, if need be, die, to secure for United States posterity a ruling class of unaccountable millionaire monopolists."

"I see before my eyes a golden age of commerce," Wilson concluded in an impassioned appeal, "in which the sons and daughters of our democracy will be free to be exploited by cold, faceless conglomerates. I see a day when public policy will be dictated from above by powerful plutocrats, uninhibited by the coercion of elected officials. I see massive, market-driven engines of commerce, ruled by a tiny core group of rich and mighty men, transforming the very cultural landscape of the world. And it is my deepest conviction that it is the duty of the armies of this Republic to ensure that the world remains safe for this coming age to thrive."

BRITISH SHIPS SUNK TODAY:

H.M.S. QUAIL

H.M.S. MRS. TIGGY-WINKLE

H.M.S. SNETTISHAM

H.M.S. WET-NURSE

H.M.S. BED-SIT

H.M.S. BUTTERED TOAST

H.M.S. WIDGEON

THE ONION

Printed without wasting precious Meat, which Our Boys need!

Thursday, November 8, 1917 — The Best Source of News in Our Great Republic — CAPITALISTIC — Price Two Cents

PRETENTIOUS, GOATEED COFFEEHOUSE TYPES SEIZE POWER IN RUSSIA

WAR BULLETINS

FIRST ROUND OF SOLDIERS' LIMBS RETURNS HOME TO HERO'S WELCOME

Hometown Wives and Mothers Flush with Emotion Upon Reunion with Disembodied Arms, Legs

Sight of Gangrenous Amputations Brings Tears to Eyes of Lovely Ladies

Severed Parts Honored With New York City 'Ticker Tape' Parade

NEW YORK, Nov. 7. — Amidst much pomp and joyous celebration, cheering crowds at New York Harbor greeted the first round of heroic American limbs to return from the war.

Emotions ran high at the welcoming ceremony, as loved ones and family members were tearfully reunited with limbs many thought they would never see again.

Sweethearts of fighting men cried out with joy as the arms and legs of their fighting-men husbands were handed out by sailors.

"Heavens to goodness," cried Miss Beatrice Atkinson of Brookston, Ohio, who had traveled to New York to greet her fiancé Lawrence Thadacker's gangrenous left arm, "I can't tell you how long I've waited to hold Larry's hand." And hold it she did, taking care to avoid the bloody and possibly contagious stump where the limb had been severed at the shoulder.

Miss Atkinson added that, although her fiancé will not return for months, she was happy that at least for now she knew his left arm was out of harm's way.

Miss Atkinson was only one of many overjoyed ladies at yesterday's reception.

Clutching a pair of severed feet, one joyous mother burst into tears as she recognized a telltale mole, identifying the limb as belonging to her beloved son.

"I could have waited until my Tommy's feet arrived at the train station in Des Moines," said Mrs. Thomas Budwig, Sr., mother of the feet, "but I just knew that, after their ordeal, it would mean so much more to Tommy's feet to be there in person to greet them as they touched American soil again."

Preacher Warns: Board of Book Censors Allows 'Tales of Wanton Smooching' to Reach Boys at the Front

When not in the midst of battle, our boys at the front require activities with which to occupy their minds, and, indeed, our patriotic citizens have been most generous in their donations of reading material. However, the content of the material has apparently not been scrupulously examined by Army censors, according to the Reverend X. Lucius Dalrymple, Doctor of Divinity. In a letter addressed to General Pershing, a copy of which was also furnished to The Onion, Reverend Dalrymple alleges that cheaply bound, scandalously detailed novels, periodicals, and booklets which contain goings-on of a most purple sort are finding their way into the doughboys' restless hands.

"Unchaperoned meetings between young men and women, conversation between these scarlet individuals, the holding of the hand of the fairer sex by a man to whom she is neither married nor betrothed, and, in some vile cases, actual smooching, have been portrayed in these sinful materials," read the missive. "As a servant of our most wrathful and angry God, I cannot in faith allow our brave fighting men to take part in carnal sin, lest they lose their taste for the foul black blood of the malignant Hun."

Upon learning of the outrage, General Pershing promised to dispatch couriers to the Front to confiscate such materials, the better to combat the moral corrosion they might inflict upon our brave boys. The General noted that the proximity of the fighting to Paris has certainly been an influence and stated that as soon as business in the Somme has been attended to, he and his aides will personally raid its bawdy districts, streets of ill repute, and fleshpots until he and his staff are fully satisfied.

The Reverend also released a list of some of the offending books to The Onion. It is reprinted here in its entirety:

A Kiss Upon the Lips.
Annie Gets a Reputation.
The Slightly Parted Mouth of Mademoiselle du Quoit.
The Bosoms Which Heaved, or Why the Bosoms Heaved.
Johnny Doughboy's Torrid Trench Tryst.
Nan Roundheels and Her War-Chest.
Husbands & Wives.

If the Huns Had Their Way

Teuton — "I vill make short vork of zis 'Fraulein' Liberty."
Lady Liberty — "Oh, red-blooded American men between the ages of 18 and 35, please save me!"

CIVIL WAR VET CALLS FOR ISOLATION; 'WE SHOULD BE FIGHTING OURSELVES, NOT A FOREIGN ENEMY!'

Lt. Colonel Reginald Ponsett, 74, veteran of the Army of Northern Virginia in the Civil War, issued a statement to The Onion Wednesday calling for an end to the present hostilities in Europe and urging the former Confederacy to renew its struggle against the Union.

His letter read, "I don't rightly care for getting involved in some trouble across the water between Old King Cole and Prince Blue Blood. There is still much fighting to be done on our home soil. If just a small number of the men being sent to Europe could be retained to fight the battle for the Confederacy, we might still save the city of Atlanta. The fight must continue! Remember Fort Sumter! Secede or die!"

The army to which Ponsett belonged surrendered to General Grant at Appomattox Courthouse in 1865.

'Over There' Replaces 'Alexander's Ragtime Band' as Nation's Only Song

The Republic's vaudeville houses and sheet-music stores report that George M. Cohan's patriotic war ditty "Over There" has officially replaced noted Jew Irving Berlin's "Alexander's Ragtime Band" as the only popular musical song in the land. This marks the first change in the official popular tune since "Alexander's Ragtime Band" replaced Gus Edwards' "By the Light of the Silvery Moon" in 1913.

Naturally, the response to "Over There" has been overwhelming, although some express reservations about the extremely fast tempo of this song. For nearly five years, the nation's official song has not exceeded a tempo consisting of one beat per second, so as not to agitate and upset listeners possessed of delicate constitutions. Recently, several men and women attending a weekend matinee at Pastor's Theatre in Providence, Rhode Island, were overcome during the pit orchestra's stirring chorus of "Over There" and had to be carried on stretchers to a nearby receiving hospital.

STUDENTS IN BERETS AND TURTLENECK SWEATERS STAGE ARMED COUP D'ÉTAT

REVOLUTION FUELED BY TRIPLE ESPRESSOS

WINTER PALACE LOOTED FOR POETRY ANTHOLOGIES

PETROGRAD, RUSSIA, Nov. 7. — While puffing on expensive French cigarettes, a cadre of alienated young poetry readers in black turtleneck sweaters emerged from their coffeehouse haunts yesterday to seize power in Russia from Alexander Kerensky and his Provisional Government.

"The ruling class oppresses the proletariat. They are so bourgeois," they were heard to say.

DICTATORSHIP OF THE HIP

Vladimir I. Lenin, described as a "perpetual graduate student" by his peers, is the leader of these revolutionaries. Lenin's stylishly cut Vandyke beard and world-weary demeanor have made him the darling of co-educational students at the University of Moscow. Lenin's first proclamation has been to declare a "dictatorship of the hip"—a synthesis of Marxism with his own espresso-fueled theories, whereby the masses will be led by an elite party of stylish individuals, well-versed in dialectical materialism, Hegelian metaphysics, and the appreciation of a wide range of exotic Italian coffees.

After an especially inspired poetry reading last night at a downtown café, the radicals marched on the Winter Palace in a brooding mood. Troops loyal to the Provisional Government were powerless before the goateed students' withering intellectual critiques.

"We were trained for an armed uprising, but not such a devastating theoretical attack," said Captain Grigori Vlasov, leader of the Winter Palace Guards. "When they logically proved us to be 'enemies of the working class' and 'Menshevik deviationists,' I was forced to surrender to their superior command of Soviet ideology."

Vlasov added that Lenin and his friends were "very laid-back and attractive."

It is also believed that several members of the Provisional Government were executed by their turtlenecked captors in a fit of murderous pique after they ran out of clove cigarettes.

Czar Nicholas II and his family remain under house arrest in an undisclosed location. The popular rumor is that the Czar is being forced to serve the finest coffee and cigarettes to the newly installed leaders like a common butler, while his best French tailors have been put to work sewing new black turtlenecks and berets of the finest cashmere for the pseudo-intellectuals.

Lenin is believed to have said, "The irony wrought by this revolution is so blinding, I may need to don glasses which are tinted very dark."

One of Lenin's chief cohorts, a university dropout named Josef Stalin, immediately established the Extraordinary Commission to Combat Counterrevolution, Sabotage, and Squareness. This group is to be a highly organized secret police with the authority to purge those who fall from the coffeehouse party's favor.

Coup Leader Vladimir Lenin

Remember... EVERY WEDNESDAY IS WHEATLESS!	# THE ONION	SUBSCRIBERS! We are now delivering to the Western Front! (Payment in advance)
Wednesday, Nov. 6, 1918	The Best Source of News in Our Great Republic	Price Two Cents

Our Boys Need Photographs of Ladies in Undergarments!

Ladies on the home front, who have been so tireless in doing the valuable war work to help the doughboys thwart the Hun hordes, are now being called upon to fulfill a new responsibility. Due to massive wartime shortages of French postcards and other materials of a "blue" nature, the War Department is asking the ladies of our great Republic to send photographs of themselves, clad only in their underclothes, to our boys in France.

The Yank is brave and true as he smashes through Boche positions on the Western Front, but sometimes, in the midst of great annihilation, his morale sinks. He will no doubt treasure any pictures greatly and carry them in his mess kit or helmet, staring at them when he is not bayoneting a German. For ladies who may feel too bashful or shy to adopt such an undertaking, we, the editors, remind these women that it is their patriotic duty to help in the war effort.

CHAPLIN MOVING PICTURE $400 OVER BUDGET

FISCAL FUTURE OF STUDIO DOUBTFUL

Moving-Picture Business May Be Out of Control

HOLLYWOOD, Calif., Nov. 5. — The moving-picture industry is in quite a stir over the news that world-famous comedian Charlie Chaplin's soon-to-be-released two-reeler "Shoulder Arms" has reportedly exceeded its projected production costs by $400.

First National Pictures, which recently placed Chaplin under contract, is perhaps regretting its association with the Little Tramp, despite his worldwide popularity and entertaining screen presence.

This is reportedly the single biggest moving-picture production debt since D.W. Griffith's "Birth of a Nation," which was, at one point, $312 in deficit.

Several factors contributed to the excessive expenditure, not the least of which is Chaplin's own capricious, difficult personality, a characteristic common in famed moving-picture artists. As a stipulation in his First National contract, Chaplin demanded that his dressing room be provided with electric lights, cushioned chairs, and several bottles of Corn Husker Lotion. These curious eccentricities have plagued First National with unanticipated expenses.

A series of calamities on the set also increased the production's debt. A half dozen bamboo canes, used by Chaplin for his Tramp persona, snapped during rehearsal, prompting several trips by the propmaster into Los Angeles to purchase replacement canes. Then, a prolonged halt in filming occurred when Chaplin's stock villain, Albert Austin, dislocated his shoulder and tore a neck tendon while performing a slapstick routine.

These interruptions vexed Chaplin greatly, and one day, after stagehands spent the better part of a morning searching for a hair-pin lost by Chaplin's leading lady Edna Purviance, the star stormed off the set, got into his chauffeured Packard, and rode to his Beverly Hills estate. There, he moodily played solitaire and sought commiseration with his friend Douglas

Picture star Chaplin

Fairbanks, whose own recent moving picture "A Modern Musketeer" became $75 over budget when a chicken absent-mindedly left inside a camera defecated on the workings.

First National executives are hoping that the release of "Shoulder Arms" will gain enough for them to repay the debt. It may be too great a risk, however; Chaplin's last release, "A Dog's Life," earned a record $612 in theater receipts worldwide, but, in order for "Shoulder Arms" to make back its production deficit and turn a modest profit, it must earn nearly one thousand dollars.

Works of Joyce Provide Much-Needed Kindling for Rationers

With their fighting men needing all available resources, citizens of free countries everywhere are eager to scrimp on everyday usefuls. And Ireland's James Joyce is proving the greatest help of all with his stellar career in what critics are calling "the most flammable literature since 'The Collected Works of Mark Twain.'"

"Nothing starts up a roaring fire and keeps it going all night like the first-person stream-of-consciousness narrative typical of Joyce's works," said American housewife Mrs. Allen DeWitt. "We used to start fires with Brontë or Ibsen, but, for a real roaring hearth-warmer, you need Joyce's dense, wholly experimental prose."

While being burned by a St. Louis U.S. Postal Service worker in accordance with a Federal court order, Joyce's work was discovered to be extraordinarily flammable. During this unseasonably cold weather, bookstores nationwide are sold out of Joyce, and no library north of Texas can keep a single copy of "A Portrait of the Artist as a Young Man," which chimney sweeps are hailing as a new "Huckleberry Finn."

Compounding the shortage is the newly emerging trend of building entire bonfires of Joyce books. Literary critic and patriotic rationer Edwin Haines recommends four or five essays kindled with several copies of "Exiles," with several of Joyce's poems crumpled into balls as tinder. "Touch a match to that, and you've got decades of writing experience warming your family all night."

Joyce is today rumored to be hard at work on an epic titled "Ulysses," and anticipation is understandably high. If Joyce can sustain the incendiary force that blessed his earlier works, "Ulysses" promises to be a literary wildfire.

"Please write faster, Mr. Joyce," Haines said. "We are awfully cold."

KNOWN U.S. AGITATORS:

ADELBUSCH, Kenneth R.
ADKINS, Jeremiah P.
AGRELL, William T.
ALTSCHULER, Klaus M. & Berthe
AVERY, Samuel B.
BARANOWSKI, Herschel S.
BEACHAM, Loyal K.
BECKER, Axel
BOWEN, Paul F.
BURGESS, Irene M.
CARNEY, John C.,
  Bernadette L. & children
CARSTEN, Agnes R.
CLARKE, Earsworth D.
COZNOFSKI, Stanislaus
CRAWFORD, Eustace H.M.
DALY, Rose B.
DONNELLY, Father Patrick
DOUGLAS, Pierce R.
ESCHER, Ignatz S.

Continued on pages 3 and 4.

CORPSE-EATING RATS NOW LARGEST MILITARY FORCE IN EUROPE

VERMIN OUTNUMBER ALL MILITARY FORCES 2 TO 1

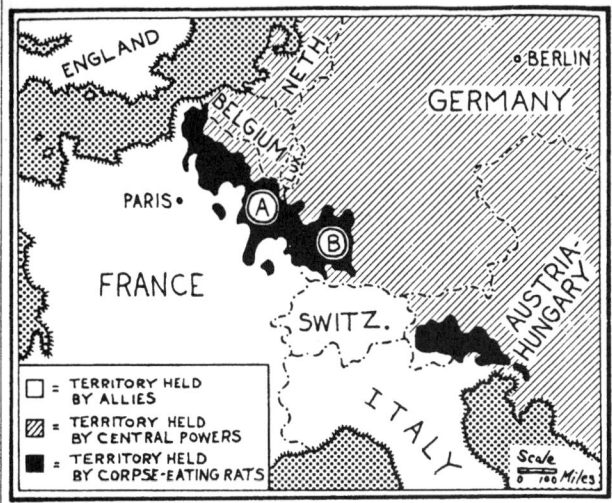

An Anglo–French offensive was launched against the rats last week (A), but was turned back in the face of superior gnawing. It is rumored that the Kaiser will send top diplomats to the rats' mountainous corpse-fortress (B) with offers of an alliance.

Tons of Rotting Human Flesh Provide Formidable Fortifications for Rat Forces

Allied Command Preparing to Make Overtures to Rat Leaders

NEAR THE WESTERN FRONT, Nov. 5. — Alarming intelligence reports from France, made public today, claim that corpse-eating rats now outnumber all military forces in Europe by a margin of nearly 2 to 1. Rat battalions have fortified lands as far East as Brussels and as far west as Rouen.

Vast stretches of no-man's-land are now controlled by the rats. A combined Anglo-French offensive under the leadership of General Petain was recently launched upon a rat stronghold near the River Somme, but was turned back in the face of superior numbers and the nauseating stench of the corpse piles in which the rats took shelter.

An artillery barrage was later brought to bear in an effort to pulverize the bodies into tiny scraps, which war theorists hoped the rats would have greater difficulty consuming.

Many believe the Great War is nearing its end, with the Kaiser's forces near exhaustion. But the new flesh-eating vermin enemy shows no sign of giving way on its occupied lands. The rat, some experts warn, may prove a more fearsome foe than the Hun.

Both Allied and Central advisors are developing strategies for making overtures to the rat leaders. It is rumored that Kaiser Wilhelm has sent his top Berlin diplomats to several rat-infested areas in an attempt to broker an alliance between the rat empire and the German, an effort that could spell disaster for the Allies, if successful.

However, British military scientists are working on a weapon that could make survival tough for the hungry vermin. Ingenious in its simplicity, the device consists of a sealed canister to be worn on the human soldier's chest, filled to the brim with searing sulfuric acid. When the man is shot, shelled, or gassed to extinction, his comrades need only pull a tab on the canister to release a stream of acid over the corpse, reducing the body to a puddle of gelatin in a matter of minutes. It is the hope of all free peoples that this bold scientific solution will make the fields of Europe more hygienic, clearing the way for our boys to reconquer vital acreages of mud from the grip of our new enemy, the corpse-eating rat.

Ways to Guard Against the Spanish Influenza:

A message furnished to The Onion by United States Congressional Chaplain and Master of Surgeons Oliver T. Christensen

Wear a flimsy cotton mask; it will filter the influenza bug from the air you breathe.

Read the entire book of Numbers as loudly as possible.

Bury your family alive.

Wear a cast-iron collar ringed with lit candles. This will ward off the invisible evil spirits bringing this pestilence.

Advise your children that the infected corpses cluttering the gutters may not be used as play-dolls.

Scrape skin with sharp edge of sandstone; cut off lips, eyelids, nose, fingernails, hair; cover body in paste made from rock salt, borax, and wood alcohol; wrap body in burlap; sing hymns.

If you must attend mass bond rallies, try not to inhale or exhale.

Persuade Congress to declare war on the hated Spaniards, purveyors of this wicked and fearsome malady, so that they may receive a soundly deserved punishment.

THE ONION

BEACON OF MORALITY | **999 YEARS, 364 DAYS OF PEACE LEFT!**

Tuesday, November 12, 1918 — The Best Source of News in Our Great Republic — Price Two Cents

WAR OVER AS FRANZ FERDINAND FOUND ALIVE

1,000 Years of Peace Begin Today

The cries of joy and pealing of bells will fill the ears of all Mankind today, as the world's great powers prepare to sign an Armistice of Peace in Versailles, France. It is the opinion of the president, the State Department, and, indeed, of this newspaper, that the Great War, which bathed faraway lands in blood and brought grim death to over 22 million foreigners and Americans alike, shall never be repeated in our lifetimes, nor those of our children, nor their children's children, unto the tenth generation.

The terms of the Armistice are intelligently chosen and cunningly phrased so as to make any war—especially involving the Germans—nigh impossible. It is a brilliant document of statecraft.

Thus shall our descendants come to know war only as a horror tale, as all nations are governed by one law, the Armistice, which, with iron certainty, has ensured the peaceful state of our world for a thousand years to come.

IN THE WORLD OF SPORTING

SEVEN TORN ASUNDER IN GRIDIRON BATTLE

Lively Football Contest
Four Players, One Coach Unaccounted for

Mighty deeds of athletic prowess and a general show of titanic strength were the order of the day Monday, as the mighty men of Fordham's football squad proved themselves up to the challenge of Chicago's doughty crew. Seven stout players were savagely torn limb from limb in the 14–0 battle.

The game, a crucial conference battle, nonetheless proved only slightly more rugged in its strategy and execution than routine seasonal play. Four men and one coach remain unaccounted for.

The hullabaloo started early, as Bert "Blood Foot" Sturgis, the rollicking Fordham back, plunged up past the bucking-guard on only his third carry, stepping directly through the thorax of Chicago lineman Max Schechner and gaining 21 yards. The drive was stifled, however, by Schechner's brilliant and nearly posthumous tackle on the very next play. Fordham quarterback Herman Krungle tripped on a coil of Schechner's intestine in the backfield, ending that brave fighter's career and life and getting himself tackled for a six-yard loss.

Sturgis and Krungle would combine for a stunning 233 yards this game before the last ligament on Krungle's left leg failed in the third quarter, causing him to lose the leg and fumble.

"Field got muddy," said the terse but towering Sturgis, when asked about the game in which he was the undisputed star (27 carries, 167 yards, two touchdowns, four arms dislocated, one knee shattered, a nose bitten off, two killed, no fumbles). "Nice day. But ground got all wet from blood."

Chicago's attack was no less swift but certainly less sure, as Arlon Hackmann, their brilliant young crushing-back, pounded the tackles for 80 yards in the first quarter before impaling himself on the protruding leg-bone of a line-backer whose battered corpse made identification impossible.

"I could have played," said the Chicago stomper, one of only four ever to survive the Fordham game in the contest's 30-year history. "God granted me two kidneys, and the gouging-out of one should not have slowed me down. But I cannot move my left side, so I stayed in to block only."

The game was wrapped up by Fordham's possession play in the second half, using the new "forward-passing" invention to knock out the eyes of three Chicago defenders with accurate throws.

Star Fordham back Bert "Blood Foot" Sturgis scored two touchdowns and four opponent decapitations.

Chicago crushing-back Arlon Hackmann.

DEAD MILLIONS CELEBRATE ARMISTICE DAY

Corpses Commemorate War's Long-Awaited End

Military cemeteries, potter's fields, and still-smoking battlegrounds around the world have been filled with the sounds of revelry of late, as the millions of men slain in three years of bloody conflict celebrate peace.

"I'm so happy," said the bloodied corpse of Private First Class Horace Stebbins, an infantryman who was only 17 when he was fatally machine-gunned during a charge on the German trenches.

Stebbins and his fellow celebrants are doing their best to enjoy the end of the war which took them before their time, despite the fact that many of them cannot hold glasses in their shattered hands, or have no faces or even heads with which to enjoy party snacks and drinks or make conversation. Compounding the problem is the fact that anything eaten or drunk tends to ooze out through the multiple wounds left in their flesh by bullets, grenades, bayonets, and barbed wire.

17-Year-Old Wonderboy Files First Infringement Lawsuit

KANSAS CITY, Missouri. — Walter E. Disney, enterprising 17-year-old high-school student, is suing an 8-year-old Kansas City resident for allegedly copying an illustrated comical character Disney drew for his school's newspaper. Disney accuses Dickie Goulding of drawing "Rudolph Rooster" in the youngster's third-grade class without express permission, and is asking $86,000 in damages and a promise from young Goulding that he never reproduce his creation again in any form.

"'Rudolph Rooster' is the exclusive property of Mr. Walter E. Disney and cannot and may not be used without the express written consent of said owner," said Cadwalader L. McGraw, Disney's attorney. "Dickie Goulding violated this tacit and fundamental right to property ownership."

When queried by reporters outside his home, a nervous Goulding alleged that he had never seen Disney's creation before, and was merely drawing a rooster per an assignment on farming his teacher had given his class. Asked how he would respond to the lawsuit, Goulding turned around and raced back inside his home, weeping hysterically.

WORLD'S AUTHORS URGE WARRING POWERS: 'PROLONG THE WAR!'

Remarque, Hemingway Lament End of Prose-Inspiring Conflict

Men of letters the world over, finding themselves horrified, shocked, and remarkably inspired by the Great War and the millions of deaths it caused, have called upon the League of Nations for the war's continuation.

"I have been chilled to my very soul by this grisly contest between nations," Author Erich Maria Remarque said in an open letter to the leaders of both the Allied and Central Powers. "Therefore, I call upon the world's powers to sacrifice thousands more of their young men, inspiring me to write a book which cries out against the injustice of this savage and bloody conflict."

"This new peace is not such a good thing for the writing I try to do," said Ernest Hemingway. "In a man's youth, there is the war, and glory, and the tearful women who say to him do not go, do not go. And there are fine books to be written. But without the war, the books are about only bullfighting, or perhaps fishing."

French novelist Marcel Proust, in Paris working on a sensual memoir, announced that his novel was an intensely personal remembrance unaffected by either war or peace or any other event or state of mind experience by a consciousness that was not his own. He, therefore, would make no statement regarding the Armistice at this time.

'How Fares Europe?' Asks Presumed-Dead Archduke

Long and Hideous War Was Simple Misunderstanding

Archduke Franz Ferdinand, here pictured in a pre-war photograph with his family, was found alive in the bowels of a Sarajevan granary yesterday, thus ending over four years of terrible bloodshed.

PARIS, Nov. 11. — After years of death, disease, famine, the impoverishment of nations, and the near-devastation of Europe, all was made right when Archduke Franz Ferdinand of Austria was found alive in the basement of a Sarajevo granary Monday.

"I am merely a bit rumpled, though I miss grievously the pageantry and scurrilous goings-on of the Austrian high court," said the unkempt archduke before being taken away to be shaven and shorn. "I merely wanted to live as a Croatian peasant for a few years. Though I am scarcely wiser for the experience, I have come to no harm. How fares Europe?"

Chancellor Friedrich Ebert, upon hearing that the much-mourned heir to the Hapsburg throne was alive and well, was mortified. In addition to signing a formal peace treaty to appease British and American statesmen, he has also offered to quell Allied wrath by ordering the archduke's immediate execution.

THE PRETTY LADIES OF SCIENCE
PART FOUR IN A SERIES: MARIE CURIE

To set your eyes upon some of France's most lovely ladies, stop frequenting the ballrooms of Paris and begin searching the scientific laboratories! With smooth ivory skin and breath-taking almond-shaped eyes, Madame Marie Curie, our day's most learned and lovely lady, spends her nights not with a husband, but with a microscope as her companion.

Madame Curie, bedecked with silken locks which cascade upon her well-framed shoulders like rivulets of spring snowmelt, was awarded Nobel's Prize for Chemistry after isolating pure radium. And isolation seems to be the word for Marie, after the death-by-carriage loss of her husband, Pierre, in 1906. This quaint creature will be quite a discovery for the next man who can woo her favorably.

Ever since her childhood in Warsaw, petite Marie had a penchant for mathematics and physics. With the strong and wise Pierre and able-handed Henri Becquerel to instruct her behind the closed laboratory doors, Marie quickly learned more than mere chemistry.

Now her daughter Irene, barely in her double-figured years, is already following in her mother's airy footsteps. This rosy-cheeked debutante says she wants to be scientific, too! Let's see if a young lad sweeps away this comely modernistic lass first!

Some have speculated it is Madame Curie's constant contact with the newly discovered chemical elements polonium and radium that give her her ideal, slender figure, stunning snow-white countenance, and alluring lassitude. It won't be long until all the ladies of Paris are carrying radium brooches to bring about this very effect!

Fetching Marie Curie discovered radium. But it's her smile that lights up a room.

THE ONION

| MORE FOUR-LIMBED PRESSMEN THAN THE HEARST PAPERS | | FEWER LUNGS FILLING WITH DEADLY FLU-INDUCED MUCUS THIS MONTH. |

Sunday, June 29, 1919 — The Best Source of News in Our Great Republic — SUNDAY EDITION — Price Five Cents

PRESIDENT WILSON CALLS FOR CREATION OF USELESS WORLD GOVERNING BODY

New 'League of Nations' to Offer Gift Shop, Guided Tours

President Wilson's Fourteen Points

That war between nations be made illegal and its practice punishable by fine;

That the lands of Turkey and the former Ottoman Empire be given to the Great State of Texas;

That international policy be free, open, and no longer a secret procedure, and that it involve America and Britain only, to the exclusion of all other nations;

That the economy of Italy be channeled into the development of sporting automobiles, stylish women's footwear, and men's suits;

That Russia be evacuated and its population housed in a spacious country to be designated later;

That Serbo-Croatia and all lands surrounding the city of Sarajevo shall be the future vessel of all conflict, strife, horror, and insanity in Europe;

That the European nations admit in writing that, but for America, they would now be speaking German;

That all nations be unified in their love of and commitment to peace, and to the hatred of the French;

To that end, that France be severely punished for its role as host of this horrific conflict, and made to pay reparations to Germany;

That Austria be open, in the summer months, to tourists;

That combat against Switzerland continue until the last Swiss lies dead;

That Luxembourg be maintained as a nation, against common logic, to serve as an interesting political curio;

That the King of Belgium be set as watchman over Germany, to ensure that no suspicious or warlike activities transpire in that nation;

That all civilized nations unite in the noble purpose of exploiting the browner peoples of the Earth.

LAST 8 GERMANS SURRENDER

After long and intense fighting that has claimed the lives of 22 million soldiers from nearly every nation of the Western world, Allied troops finally succeeded in reducing the German army to a strength of eight men at large in the Belgian countryside, all of whom surrendered yesterday after protracted fighting.

"This, the complete and total surrender of the German armed forces in the persons of Joachim, Johann, Adolf, Siegfried, Hans G., Hans M., Gunther, and Uwe, is a proud moment for the Allied and American Expeditionary forces," said Colonel Roger Stemmons, commander of the 34th Infantry and the officer who accepted the German surrender after cornering the Hun force behind a charred oak during a routine mop-up operation. "Fearsome and mighty Germany is defeated, and the world need never again fear the thunder of her pair of steely rifles, the once-keen blade of her single rusty bayonet, or the hobnailed tramp of her last good pair of combat boots."

The German forces, feared and loathed through years of bloody attrition, were unbowed in defeat and fought tooth and nail to the last. Some detachments, most notably Johann, refused to believe that the Fatherland had surrendered, and fought on after both his legs and his right arm had been shattered by American covering fire. Their Allied captors, to their eternal credit, lost only three soldiers in the operation.

Prime Ministers David Lloyd George of England and Georges Clemenceau of France, and President Wilson, forgers of a new era in tourist attractions.

Gertrude Stein, Literature's Most Famous Bachelorette, Is Still Single

(Hint, Hint, Fellows!)

The Comely Miss Stein.

On both sides of the Atlantic, young gallants are all a-twitter about Gertrude Stein, one of America's most eligible expatriates. Admired as much for her feminine charms as for her experimental prose poems such as "Sacred Emily" and "Pink Melon Joy," Stein continues to captivate many a man.

Perhaps it's that blockish figure which attracts the bachelor eye, such a lovely sight given the skinny, underfed look that's increasingly in vogue. Perhaps it's the sack-like dresses of coarse fabric she wears which intrigue artists and avant-garde gentlemen. Whatever the elements in Stein's style, they are literally devastating!

Adding to Gertrude's charm is the company she keeps, including one Alice B. Toklas, a bewitching brunette in her own right. Even if a young wooer should fail to win Gertrude's heart (an all-too-common occurrence!), the chance of a tryst with the lovely Alice is nothing to sneeze at!

Her appeal is undeniable, her work unexplainable— "a rose is a rose is a rose," indeed! We'll believe it only if you're writing about yourself, Gertie!

SNACK BAR 'A POSSIBILITY,' WILSON SAYS

WASHINGTON, D.C., June 28. — President Woodrow Wilson today called for the creation of a "League of Nations," a world governing organization with limited powers and an unlimited selection of souvenir world flags and postcards, available for purchase in its lower-level gift shop.

"I am fully committed," President Wilson told members of the press corps assembled at the White House, "to making the new League of Nations an extremely powerful, effective world tourist attraction, one which will draw visitors from around the globe. With the most terrible war in human history finally behind us, with 22 million men dead from the most grisly, bloody fighting the world has ever seen, it is vital that the peoples of the world have a place where they may gather to purchase miniature wax statuettes of famous landmarks with national slogans on them."

HAMBURGERS

According to Wilson's decree, the League will be made up of two parts: the Council of Nations, where representatives of more than 35 nations gather to attempt vainly to maintain international peace and security, and the Chamber of Snacks, where delicious refreshments such as "hamburger"-style sandwiches, kidney pies, leek soup, and strawberry phosphates may be purchased by fatigued visitors for as little as five cents.

A park bench and as many as two oaken picnic tables will be placed outside League headquarters. This "industrial park" setting will feature potted trees, refuse boxes, and paved pathways.

Despite widespread support for the League of Nations' charter among member nations, formal ratification has been delayed due to a bitter dispute over guided-tour schedules and admission pricing.

"Tours should be given every half hour from 9:15 a.m. to 4:45 p.m. daily, except on weekends during January and February," said Crown Prince Ocelot of Syldonia. "But there should be no group discounts available. On this point there can be no concessions."

"No," replied Duchess Tatiana of the duchy of Wurdstein. "There must be special group rates for school field trips."

As outlined in President Wilson's plan, those nations who wish to re-enter the League would receive a special "hand-stamp," which would permit easy recognition upon returning.

The site chosen for the League headquarters, Geneva, Switzerland, boasts plentiful janitorial, snack-service, and retail counter-help resources.

EUROPEAN CARTOGRAPHERS COMMIT MASS SUICIDE

LONDON, June 8. — Apparently despairing of the constant and never-ending alterations of the map of Europe resulting from peace treaties, seven cartographers were found hanged in the London offices of the Royal Geographic Society. Four others at the Sorbonne in Paris swallowed arsenic, unable to cope with the addition of Poland, Lithuania, Latvia, Estonia, and Finland; the dissolution of the Austro-Hungarian Empire and formation of Austria, Hungary, and Czechoslovakia; the division of the Ottoman Empire into Turkey, Transjordan, and several other nations; the transfer of Alsace and Lorraine from Germany to France and additional loss of German territory to newly created Poland; and additional land gains and losses for Rumania and Bulgaria, respectively.

Tonight at 7 o'clock p.m., Professor J.T. Lindsey will appear in lecture and expound upon his vast and great knowledge of

THE PARTS OF A COW

AT THE DAUGHTERS OF THE AMERICAN REVOLUTION MEETING HALL
276 SYLVANIA AVENUE, PHILADELPHIA

THE ONION

EXPLOITER OF THE RABBLE | FEEDING HYSTERIA SINCE 1892

Wednesday, October 29, 1919 — The Best Source of News in Our Great Republic — Price Two Cents

GANGSTERS PASS 18TH AMENDMENT

'Lucky' Luciano Casts Deciding Vote to Make Alcohol Illegal

TEDDY ROOSEVELT ALLOWS THREE OTHERS TO BE CARVED INTO MOUNTAIN

FORMER PRESIDENT GRACIOUSLY SHARES SPACE ON PROPOSED RUSHMORE MONUMENT

In a gesture he called "greatly magnanimous," the late President Theodore Roosevelt, it was announced Tuesday, had granted his permission before his unfortunate demise to allow three other presidents' likenesses to appear alongside his own atop the 5,725-foot Mount Rushmore in western South Dakota.

Months-long speculation over a suitable Roosevelt memorial was serendipitously answered in a lengthy epistle, penned by Roosevelt himself and discovered amongst his private papers shortly after his death. Roosevelt chose the prominent Black Hills peak of Mount Rushmore as an ideal location for an enormous sculpture of his likeness.

"The broad outcropping of granite that forms Mount Rushmore's peak," Roosevelt wrote, "provides a bully setting for a 60-foot-tall bas-relief of my face."

He added that he actually preferred the Alaska Territory's Mount McKinley, North America's tallest

The magnanimous Roosevelt.

mountain, as the site, but had to concede that carving an immense sculpture on its 20,320-foot summit would present excessive logistical difficulties.

WILL NOT BE ALONE

"In addition to my own august image," Roosevelt wrote, "I also call upon the likenesses of three other great presidents, George Washington, Thomas Jefferson, and Abraham Lincoln, to grace the imposing rock face. It is only right and fair that three other great leaders of our Union should serve as a rousing backdrop to my own visage."

Roosevelt selected these three particular chief executives for their brilliant leadership and historical significance, although he expressed misgivings about each.

"Washington and Jefferson," he wrote, "although guarantors of our independence and architects of our freedom, nonetheless presented a frilly appearance, adorned as they were in powdered wigs and fluffery of costume. They are not nearly so burly as a decorated cavalryman and big-game hunter such as myself. And Lincoln, preserver of the Union though he was, sadly proved incapable of defending himself against the pistol shots of a lone malcontent."

The former president then added that, in keeping with a spirit of generosity and reverence, the other presidents' portraits should be carved at the approximate size and proportion of his own, so as to foster an appearance of equality among the four men.

"Thus, as future generations gaze upon my majestic granite face," he concluded, "which will dwarf every other monument erected to man's great achievements in this God-given land, they will in their hearts remember me as a modest, generous, and humble soul."

Other Events Today

FOLLOWING COCA-COLA'S LEAD, 'MORPHINE-PUNCH' REPLACES MAIN INGREDIENT
Our report on page 15.

PRESIDENT WILSON ACCIDENTALLY DEPORTED
Our report on page 31.

NEW STUDY REVEALS WOMEN NOT AT FAULT IN ALL RAPES

FINDINGS INDICATE WOMEN GUILTY IN ONLY 85 PERCENT OF ASSAULTS, NOT 97 AS PREVIOUSLY BELIEVED

MEN STILL COMPOSE THE MAJORITY OF VICTIMS, HYGIENE SECRETARY SAYS

According to findings of a recent study by the U.S. Department of Hygiene, it appears possible that ladies sullied by rapists or other molesters may be slightly less wanton than doctors and clergy had previously estimated.

"While it has been made clear that the vast majority of rape incidents involve lurid harlotry and Jezebelism of the foulest stripe," said U.S. Secretary of Hygiene Dr. Hammersmith Woodridge, "it is becoming apparent that occurrences of sexual excess in which the male was not spurred by tempestuous advances may be as much as 15 percent of all cases. This is significantly higher than the prior accepted figure of 3 percent."

Woodridge explained, "In the minority cases in which the female is not to blame, we must reconsider our approach to the issue, possibly even going so far as to hold the male perpetrator accountable for his misdeeds in a court of law, in extreme cases."

AROUSED BY HARLOTS

Although the need for additional research was stressed, Woodridge emphasized that the vast majority of rapes and molestations are still committed by perfectly innocent males, aroused against their will by the immoral provocations of temptresses.

The study indicated that, in most cases, the male does not resort to acts of indiscretion unless he has first been caused to become upset by the lurid displays of slatternly ladies of the night.

"We must not forget that 85 percent of rape victims are men, unwillingly led down the path of lust and seduction by saucy ladies of loose virtue," he said. "Any woman wishing to avoid the shame of 'fallen' status, which society rightfully thrusts on the invirtuous who finds herself raped by men other than her lawful husband, should take care to keep her wits about her and her wrists and ankles hidden from view at all times."

Woodridge also reiterated the time-honored notion that all women who are raped, whether blameless in the event or not, are still considered to be whores unfit for godly marriage under holy writ. "The Bible is quite specific on this point," he said.

A Reputation for Safety

Fewer mustache-twirling villains tie golden-haired virgins to our tracks than any other railroad's. Our competitors cannot make this claim.

Enjoy a comfortable ride aboard our "Winnetonke Express"—lightning-swift service from Chicago to Winnetonke in less than four hours—without being startled by the sudden pull of the emergency brake, or chancing to look out the window and see the severed torso of an innocent young girl rolling down the hill.

THE CENTRAL AND SOUTH-CENTRAL LINE

Mob to Take over $500 Million Liquor Industry

'Sinful Drink' Rightfully Condemned, Says Al Capone

Charles "Lucky" Luciano voted "yes" on liquor prohibition.

CHICAGO, Oct. 28.—At a special meeting at its Chicago headquarters, the United Organized Criminals of America voted in favor of passing the 18th Amendment, outlawing alcohol in the United States, effective immediately.

Gangsters present were elated by the amendment's passage, which they called "long overdue."

"Alcohol is a depraved and immoral substance which has brought ruin to countless lives," U.O.C.A. president Alphonse "Scarface" Capone said. "Our government is wrong to have tolerated its manufacture for as many years. The only proper place for such a substance is in the hands of unsavory mobsters."

'ROOT OF EVIL'

New York U.O.C.A. member Dutch Schultz agreed. "As Carrie Nation and so many other brave leaders of this nation's temperance movement have argued, alcohol is the root of nearly all the evil that surrounds us. Crime, sexual promiscuity, and decreased church-attendance can all be traced to it," Schultz said. "Thank goodness the millions of Americans who drink will no longer do so through legal channels."

With this overwhelming mandate, control of the nation's multi-million-dollar liquor industry officially transfers to the U.O.C.A. Spokesmen said that manufacture of bootleg alcohol will start immediately, with white lightning and bathtub-gin production expected to reach 400 million gallons a month by March 1920.

In addition to increasing the U.O.C.A.'s annual alcohol-vending profits an estimated 1,900 percent, the 18th Amendment's passage is expected to create an explosion in several of the league's other operations, including contract murder, prostitution, racketeering, gun-running, and gambling. According to U.O.C.A. estimates, by 1924, illegal sales of automatic machine guns alone are expected to exceed $600,000, up from just $75,000 last year.

GOLDEN AGE OF GANGSTER ACTIVITY

In a print statement released by the White House, President Wilson praised the gangsters for outlawing alcohol. "You are to be roundly applauded for your brave stand against alcohol," the president said. "I congratulate you on this, the dawning of a golden age of gangster activity in America."

With the passage of the 18th Amendment, overall mob profits, U.O.C.A. treasurer Meyer Lansky said, could hit an estimated $40 million by 1930.

"This is big, big, illegal business, the sort of dirty dealing that the U.S. government should have no part of," Lansky said. "This amendment very much needed to be passed. It is difficult to comprehend that, until now, the feds sanctioned this immoral industry. At long last, it's in the back rooms of shady-looking businesses, where it belongs."

Following the amendment's approval, gangster Johnny Torrio was appointed head of the National Speakeasy Construction Board, a U.O.C.A.-founded organization that will be responsible for building and managing more than 21,000 speakeasies across the U.S.

"In addition to servicing our traditional criminal and immigrant clientele," Torrio told The Onion, "we also hope to attract Anglo-Saxon Protestants, the middle-class, and women—segments of the populace who would otherwise seldom drink but are irresistibly lured by the promises of hedonism, liberation, and adventure that the devil's brew offers."

Shortly after the gangsters' historic vote, officials from The Anti-Saloon League of America, a coalition of Christian clergy, businessmen, and aged dowagers, cabled the U.O.C.A. with thanks and appreciation for assisting them in the nearly decade-long crusade to make alcohol prohibition possible on a national level.

THE ONION

DEFENDER OF PRUDISHNESS | **BULWARK OF HYGIENE**

Friday, August 27, 1920 — The Best Source of News in Our Great Republic — Price Three Cents

WOMEN GET VOTE, REST ROOMS

ONE HUNDRED YEARS OF ELECTORAL, EXCRETORY STRUGGLE END

WASHINGTON, D.C., Aug. 26.—Nearly a century of electoral and excretory struggle ended with the adoption of the 19th Amendment to the U.S. Constitution, guaranteeing both women's suffrage and women's public water closets.

The ratification by Tennessee means that the required three-fourths of the 48 states have assented to the fairer sex's being given an equal stake in the democratic process and an equal opportunity to relieve themselves in toilet stalls clearly designed and intended for ladies only.

STRAP-ON PAILS TOSSED ASIDE

No longer must the nation's ladies bear cumbersome chamber pots which hang between their legs and are secured at their waists by chains.

"Hoo-ray! We have the ballot and the water closet!" proclaimed longtime suffragette and toilet agitator Carrie Chapman Catt at a rally of future voters and squatters on the steps of the Capitol this afternoon. "No longer will one-half of the citizens of this nation spend each Election Day bewailing their voiceless, powerless status while publicly relieving their bladders into chamber pots."

Catt proceeded to fling her bedpan-harness—which she termed "an everyday symbol of male tyranny in the realm of voiding"—onto the ground, prompting thousands of her sisters-in-deprivation to do the same.

SENATOR HARDING CONGRATULATORY

Senator Warren G. Harding of Ohio, the Republican Party's nominee for president, said he welcomes the Amendment's passage. "I have long endorsed an electorate comprising both genders," he said, adding that he also supports "the enhancement and beautification of the feminine portion of our country which will arise when they are no longer forced to perform their eliminations on public streets, then haul their strap-on pails to the nearest refuse bin or gutter to empty them."

The Wilson administration has pledged to take immediate steps to ensure that all female citizens 21 years of age or older will both vote and "powder" in individual public stalls by Election Day.

These water closets for women will not be labeled as such, in order to provide for the discretion of the user. Instead, they will be denoted through the hanging of a symbol, the meaning of which will be made known to females alone so as not to cause defilement or embarrassment.

PLAN ECONOMICALLY FEASIBLE

Officials have also commissioned an American inventor to create a contraption that would allow for the insertion of pennies in exchange for the instantaneous deliverance of personal towels or sanitary aprons for use by ladies in times of special need.

Municipal and state governments will be responsible for providing urino-stercoraceous facilities for women. These will contain individual stalls large enough to accommodate the removal and temporary hanging-up of ladies' skirts, large-brimmed hats, gloves, petticoats, vests, stockings, corsets, trusses, girdles, harnesses, bodices, loin engirdments, and stomachers during their visits. The new rest rooms are also to be staffed with several "ladies' attendants," directed to assist in the removal, unlocking, and unstitching of garments for bodily elimination.

Vaudeville jesters and joke tellers have already made light of this development; one of the most popular jokes on the vaudeville circuit queries, "Have you ever taken notice of how the fairer sex always adjourns to powder-room facilities in pairs? Why do they not go alone?"

A LOGISTICAL DIFFICULTY

Harding issued a charge to architects of the new ladies' latrines, saying, "In consideration of ladies' extraordinary clothing considerations, this will be the challenge: to create powder rooms large enough and well-staffed enough to accommodate the great layers of clothing on the modern woman, that the time necessary to visit the facility will be rendered equal to that of men's."

AUTOMOBILE REPLACING HAY WAGON AS VEHICLE OF CHOICE FOR CLANDESTINE ADOLESCENT COURTING
see story, page 22.

WHEELBARROW DEATHS DOWN 42 PERCENT SINCE 1900, STATISTICS SHOW
see story, page 22.

WOMEN FINALLY ALLOWED TO PARTICIPATE IN MEANINGLESS FICTION OF DEMOCRACY

After nearly a century of tireless agitation by supporters of women's suffrage, the 19th Amendment to the U.S. Constitution has finally been signed into law. Now American citizens of female gender may, along with their male counterparts, fully participate in the meaningless travesty that is American democracy.

In a speech before a cheering crowd of suffragettes, Vice President Marshall, speaking on behalf of the ailing president, hailed the historic event as a "long-overdue patronizing gesture" toward the women of the nation. "The nation's ladies are being extended the franchise at a time when our democratic political system has never been more corrupt and awash in cynicism," he said. "The major political parties get their ultimate marching orders from a shadowy, byzantine amalgamation of mighty industrial and financial interests, which exacts a much more profound influence in shaping the United States' domestic and foreign policy than the popular vote has or ever will."

"Women everywhere will now be able to cast their ballots and join men in the long-hallowed process of choosing the lesser of two or more evils," said Carrie Chapman Catt, president of the National American Women's Suffrage Association. "We may now freely take our place among the rank-and-file of the slavishly pandering footmen who pass for lawgivers and statesmen in the federal and state governments."

Painless Dentistry

FEATURING THE GREATEST ADVANCES IN DENTISTRY-SCIENCE SINCE PLIERS.

A fully accredited dental-hygiene practice, specially equipped with several odorless and numbing gases and medicinal elixirs which make tooth extraction practically whimsical.

SEPTEMBER SPECIAL:
1 to 30 extractions, same low price.

Edward Landau, D.D.S.
864 Staten Avenue, Chicago
Second Floor Office

BURDENED NO MORE

This file photograph depicts suffragettes marching down Broadway Avenue in New York City, their traditional strap-on chamber pots swinging under their skirts, a much-disliked convention which will soon be obsolete.

Voting Potential of Husbands Doubles

The signing into law of the 19th Amendment will almost certainly see twice the number of citizens participating in the democratic process, experts say, causing crowding and long lines at the polls, as women queue up to echo their husbands' votes.

"As women obediently take their place in line behind their husbands, preparing to do their wifely duty by casting their ballot for the candidates of his choice, it will certainly seem that a vast political change is sweeping our nation," said Hubert Prentice, a political-science professor at Harvard University. "However, aside from the novelty inherent in a voting female, little will actually change. The ladies will, no doubt, seek the reasoned and tempered opinions of their better halves and vote accordingly, the greater number of votes cast therefore resulting in the same ratio of winning to losing votes."

CONVENIENCE FOR HUSBANDS

It is not known at this time whether special compensations would need to be made for married couples, but many of the nation's gentlemen were heartened by the passage of this latest amendment to our Constitution. "Pesky thing, voting, and a bit of a bore," Cleveland Democrat Walter Edmundson told reporters. "But now I can just send the wife to the polls along with a signed note from myself, and she will cast both our votes at once. Progressive idea, this 'suffrage' of women."

I Can Get All the Booze I Want

BY T. HERMAN ZWEIBEL, PUBLISHER

The ratification of the 18th Amendment means that alcohol is no longer manufactured, sold, and transported within our great Republic, and to that I say huzzah! Demon Drink has claimed many a bread-winner, and our cities and towns were debased by the presence of wicked saloons and grog-shops, distasteful dens whose chief patrons were immigrant idlers and diseased ladies of pleasure.

But the more prosperous classes of the Union may take heart: Liquor is still readily and abundantly available to us, and our rarefied tongues are still able to sample fine Scotch, tempting bourbon, and pleasing merlots.

Many within the lower orders have already taken to improvising alcoholic concoctions in their bathtubs and kitchen basins, often with laughable results, such as fatal poisoning or blindness. But plutocrats and captains of industry need not worry about such dangers. With their multiple contacts both professional and familial in Europe, Canada, and the lesser Americas; ability to bribe Customs officials; control of national shipping concerns; and extensive investments in liquor manufacture in the aforementioned lands, the wealthy are able to not only enjoy the fermented grape and distilled rye without disruption, but profit from its reduced availability in the Republic, as well.

We may also take advantage of our already-existing and vast holdings in our wine-cellars. Right now, as I dictate this editorial to my steno-grapher, I am enjoying an exquisite vintage 1892 Chateau Briand. Even if I were to never again purchase another cask or keg, I could still sample and savor my fine collection of wines and spirits well into the far-off decade of the 1950s, and it will naturally have grown even finer with age.

This really is a fine Chateau Briand, I must say. It has a rich bouquet and a mellow, smoky taste, much like an excellent cut of prime rib.

If you happen to occupy one of the lower castes of society, you may as well forget about ever consuming a drop of real booze again. Anything you may be able to acquire will either be artificial or of such inferior quality that you might as well be drinking formaldehyde or Electric Liniment Soothing Syrup.

I have heard that some enterprising Sicilians, Hebrews, and Irish individuals in our larger metropoli are forming criminal societies engaged in the inter-state smuggling of alcoholic spirits. But I must dismiss these rumors as so much folderol, since I strongly doubt that any person of those particular ethnic heritages possesses the cunning and cleverness to effect such grand schemes.

THE ONION

THE LATEST DISPATCHES FROM THROUGHOUT CHRISTENDOM

HERALD OF PROGRESS

Thursday, November 18, 1920 — The Best Source of News in Our Great Republic — Price Three Cents

FIXED WORLD SERIES HERALDS FIRST-EVER MOMENT OF EXCITEMENT IN BASEBALL

The '19 Chicago White Sox

FANS SHOCKED

'Black Sox' Scandal Creates Drama Unequaled During Normal Play

Shoeless Joe, Other Players Make Apology; Vow to Return Game to Boring Norm

CHICAGO, Nov. 13.—Unaccustomed thrills and a measurable level of excitement were introduced into the placid game of baseball this past week by the shocking revelation that outfielder "Shoeless" Joe Jackson, star pitcher Eddie Cicotte, and six other members of Chicago's White Sox conspired to "throw" the 1919 World Series. Fans and players alike are abuzz with the news of the resulting excitement, an emotional sensation not usually associated with the sport.

FANS DISTURBED

"No sooner had I heard the news of their nefarious gambling to-do than I realized that my heart-beat had increased slightly, my breath had become shallower and more rapid, and my palms had begun to sweat almost imperceptibly," said one White Sox enthusiast, who was profoundly confused by this uncharacteristic and un-fanlike reaction to the deeds of his team and, therefore, asked that he not be identified. "Due to my long association with the sport of baseball, it was quite some time before I realized that I was not physically afflicted, but was rather feeling baseball-induced excitement for the first time in all my life."

SLIGHT EXHILARATION

According to reports, eight of the White Sox ballplayers in the series made a shady deal with gamblers and other undesirables, adding an untoward amount of excitement to this staid recreation. While the investigation is pending, newly appointed Commissioner of Baseball Kennesaw Mountain Landis pledged to restore the game to its traditional dullness.

PLAYERS APOLOGIZE

Players on the Chicago team admitted to being quite mortified at this turn of events and have released a letter of apology addressed to all citizens of the nation. The letter states that the players are deeply ashamed to have brought such vast ignominy and slight exhilaration to the sport which had given them their livelihood.

SPORTING TRADITION VIOLATED

"We have overturned the very lynch-pins of baseball itself: tradition, fair play, and stultifying lethargy," the letter read in part. "It is our most sincere desire that baseball be allowed to forget our crimes and return to the honest and somnolent state that is its natural purview."

Official condemnation was swift and vocal and came from some of the highest-placed men in our nation. "I was upset, to say the least, when I learned that a game I have come to rely upon for a sense of orderly, placid relaxation had, through criminal activity, become associated with the base emotion of excitement," said longtime baseball fan and millionaire industrialist Howard P. Murtaugh, who has relied upon baseball's sleep-inducing qualities to comfort him during his long battle with the gout. "I had come to rely on the game for the restful twelve-hour duration of the experience, the drowsy seats in the sun; the pleasing geometry of the nigh-motionless flannel-clad gentlemen arranged on the soothing green of the out-field. Now this tranquil experience has been forever marred, and I might be forced to ask my doctor to prescribe a tonic relaxant to ensure my continued enjoyment of the game."

CHAPLINESQUE RAPSCALLION NEW LEADER OF GERMANY'S NATIONAL SOCIALIST PARTY

From the European correspondent.—Seeming to accept Germany's comical "born loser" role following the Great War, a short, mustachioed rapscallion resembling vaudevillian "little tramp" Charlie Chaplin has been placed in charge of its growing National Socialist German Workers Party.

Adolf Hitler is noted for impassioned speeches about the misery of life in postwar Germany under the devalued Deutschmark. One almost expects the whimsical ragamuffin to tell of eating a large overshoe for supper.

Said one admirer, "Hitler is doing great work to reform Germany's image as a gang of bloodthirsty tyrants, as well as to add an air of light-hearted, wistful tomfoolery to everyday German life."

Wal-Market Refuses to Sell Ebony Jazz

Mercantile-Goods Chain Calls Wax Cylinders of Ma Rainey, Kid Ory 'Not Appropriate for Wholesome Families'

Rapid Movements Could Agitate Listeners

The Wal-Market chain of retail-goods stores is refusing to stock wax-cylinder recordings of New Orleans jazz music popularized by Negro musicians.

When asked why the chain has opted not to carry the recordings, Wal-Market executive Harris Blaines said that protection of Wal-Market customers is the company's first priority.

"The loud, quickly paced sounds of ebony jazz could cause increased agitation in listeners. As a public-safety concern, we cannot endorse the product, as it may put shoppers at the Wal-Market stores at risk for bouts of nervous excitement, shortness of breath, and even heart failure."

Blaines said there have also been recent reports of jazz inciting listeners to "swing," a lurid form of bodily movement which crudely mimics the private activities conducted between married couples in the confines of their locked bed chambers.

"It is strictly against our policy to permit any 'swinging' motions in the Wal-Market stores," Blaines said. A regional manager in the Kansas City Wal-Market concurred, adding that customer order must be maintained in the store.

"Jazz is a form of music with no written notes," manager Clyde Galsworthy said. "There is only improvisation. If there is no order in the music, how can order be maintained in the store, let alone in the larger society in which we live?"

BOLSHEVIKS DIVIDE TUNDRA WASTELAND EQUALLY

Communist Idea of Wealth Distribution Means Plot of Barren Ice for Every Citizen

MOSCOW, Russia, Nov. 17.—The Bolshevik Party, after spending nearly two decades fighting for control of the valuable Siberian territory of Russia, is now dividing it up equally among her citizenry as per the new form of communist government.

In accordance with the country's new law, in which all citizens share in the nation's wealth, newly appointed Minister of Ice Pyotr Zbiewski has allotted to every peasant family in the land a 30-square-mile plot of tundra.

A survey is under way to determine that each swath of tundra contains the same number of rocks. If not, a program of exchange will be initiated.

A SHARED HARVEST

The allocation of land to all members of the nation is only the beginning of communism's ideal manifestation. All citizens will also be given their percentage of the nation's agricultural production. According to Russian Farm Bureau Chief Sergei Koralenko, this means that every year, each Russian citizen will be entitled to one-third of a turnip.

"Our nation's agricultural might derives from a one-square-mile patch of land near Baku, which is the one spot in Russia where the ground thaws just enough each season to allow for minimal harvesting of crops," Koralenko said. "The several-thousand-turnip yield of this crop will feed all of glorious new Russia."

Citizens thus far are elated by the new system.

"My 30-mile-square plot of tundra is much nicer than my cousin Ilyich's," said Bolshevik soldier Igor Dmitriev, a hearty, bearded wood-cutter, age 46, who was granted the plot by the people-controlled government just last week.

"My family and I are also savoring our turnip fragment," he added.

Dmitriev hopes to sow and harvest a good crop of lichen and microscopic spores during the tundra's growing season, which takes place between 9 a.m. and 2 p.m. every August 24. Of course, in accordance with newly drafted regulations of the collectivist farming system, he must share 95 percent of the harvest with the government, so that it may be distributed equally amongst the proletariat. This also includes a percentage of the annual lemming kill.

"We are much happier than under the czar," he said.

A WARNING

TO YOUNG, UNMARRIED MAIDENS:

STRANGERS MAY ATTEMPT TO LURE YOU INTO UNHYGIENIC RELATIONS WITH OFFERS OF ROOT BEER OR AUTOMOBILE RIDING.

Harding Elected, Forgotten About

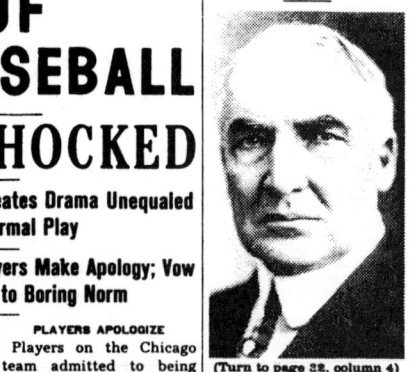

(Turn to page 22, column 4)

CITY FATHERS TO COMMEMORATE FIRST ANNIVERSARY OF PROHIBITION WITH LIFELESS PARTY

'Strained Conversation and Superficial Gaiety Will Abound,' Says Mayor

NEW YORK, Nov. 16.—Mayor John Hylan announced that a "lifeless and awkward" party will be held next month to commemorate the one-year anniversary of the ratification of Prohibition. It will be held at New York's famed Waldorf Astoria's Sincerity and Sarsaparilla Parlor, formerly the Saloon and Ballroom.

Soda water, ice water, and lemon-flavored water will be served at the gala event, as will coffee.

Games and diversions such as mah-jongg, the oat-sack toss, and the Charades may be played in an attempt to maintain spirits. "Asaph," the Slats-Belbo Circus' psalm-reciting clown, is also scheduled to perform.

SOBER, EVEN-TEMPERED FUN

The mayor promised that a "reasonable semblance of a good time" will be had by all, and that the festivities will last well into the early evening, perhaps continuing until party-goers in attendance start becoming listless.

The mayor's Special Events Coordinating Council expects "sober, even-tempered fun and dutiful dancing and gaiety by all attendees."

The party is expected to be attended by the cream of New York's high society, including the city's Chief of Police, official representatives of the Treasury Department, a prominent area judge, and several pastors.

THE ONION

DENOUNCER OF FLAPPING BEHAVIOR | **A THREAT TO HEARST SINCE 1898**

Thursday, February 2, 1922 — Finest Source of News in Our Great Republic — Price Three Cents

INDIA'S NATIONALIST LEADER PUMMELED SENSELESS BY PRACTITIONERS OF BRITISH 'VIOLENCE' MOVEMENT

Mohandas Gandhi Given 'Non-Passive Head-Bashing'

Agitator Mohandas K. Gandhi, who reportedly received a non-peaceful beating from his jailers yesterday.

CALCUTTA, India, Feb. 1. —Indian National Congress leader Mohandas K. Gandhi's ongoing attempt to defy British colonial rule was thwarted again this week by the Royal Police Force of India's swift deployment of "Non-Passive Violence."

Entailing such tactics as heavy blows to the head, face and back, this remarkable technique of effecting social change is being put to good use by the British to quell mass demonstrations in Calcutta.

Today, native agitator Gandhi was arrested and given a non-cooperative head bashing. In sympathy, hundreds of protesters heeded his call to disperse.

A BRITISH MAINSTAY

"Violence," as the British term it, has been in use by their imperial forces for centuries. The Violence technique is most commonly characterized by large-scale oppression of indigenous peoples through whippings, beatings, and clubbings.

"Violence is a simple philosophy," said Oxford University professor of Violence studies Herbert Smythe. "Yet it works. One only need observe its impact throughout India."

While Gandhi has spoken out against the radical British tactic, the Indian leader offers little or no defense against it.

"India does not seem to have picked up on Violence's finer points," Smythe said. "Gandhi's mawkish speeches and primitive methods of defiance are simply no match for the advanced British techniques of cudgeling, horsewhipping, and bone-breaking."

GANDHI DEFENSELESS

When Gandhi first introduced "Satyagraha," the open defiance of British colonial rule, he urged his countrymen to discontinue their use of British products and services. The British adopted a policy of non-cooperation with this tactic, responding by slaughtering hundreds of Indian peasants. The powerful resistance strategy of the British ultimately proved superior, and Gandhi was forced to curtail his plan.

When Gandhi later persisted, the British employed more complex varieties of Violence. They used a subtle technique known as a "Beating Boycott": Late last year, they refused to allow Gandhi to go unbeaten several times each day until he agreed to lift his "Satyagraha" once again.

STRENGTHS OF "VIOLENCE"

Violence can be as simple as a well-placed kick to the genitals, or as elaborate as firing projectiles into enemies with a gun. Diversity of techniques is one of Violence's greatest strengths. According to R.P.F. Officer Nigel Blevins, "When repeatedly punching Gandhi in the face proved ineffective, we began kicking him in the stomach, producing more impressive results. Finally, smashing our billy clubs against his skull provided just the desired effect."

Other benefits of Violence include the low cost of materials and the relative ease of training. The R.P.F. now trains all its officers to employ Violence liberally wherever it appears potentially useful or necessary, or merely to remain in practice.

FATTY ARBUCKLE TRIAL CALLED 'TRIAL OF THE CENTURY'

SAN FRANCISCO, Feb. 1.—The sensational series of murder trials involving moving-picture star Roscoe "Fatty" Arbuckle is now being called the "trial of the century" by experts in the study of law.

Never before—and likely never again—has so much public and newspaper attention been generated by a court trial in America.

According to Harvard Law professor Samuel M. Wolheim, "There will never again be a trial such as this, where publishers of soft-covered books and nickel periodicals are scrambling to publish the peculiarities of the trial."

"There is something unique about this Fatty Arbuckle trial," he said.

The trial is so unusual, the professor explained, that it merits being called the 'trial of the century' from now until the year 2000.

"It is not likely that another trial will take place in the next 80 years that will generate so much intense popular interest," Wolheim added.

Unattractive Dresses

Available in several shapeless, unalluring styles

Slocombe's Department Store
11 Canal Street, New York

WILL THE AGITATING CLOTHES-WASHING TUB RUIN OUR WOMEN'S CHARACTER WITH IDLENESS?

An editorial opinion by the Reverend Doctor X. Lucius Dalrymple, Lutheran Pastor.

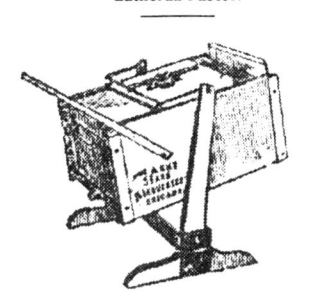

A MODEL WASHING TUB

Daily we read of patented new contraptions whose essential purpose is to conserve labor and hasten the completion of ordinary, everyday chores. While, due to their expense, lack of availability, low level of necessity, or difficulty of operation, not all of these machines have been readily adopted by the American people, some have become as essential to our lives as food, drink, and fresh air. What American household is without a sewing machine, breech-loading shotgun, screw-cutting lathe, or chicken raper?

But does this newly gained convenience arrive at the expense of the moral strength and virtue that can only be produced by hard, solid, unceasing labor? I speak specifically of the newly invented Agitating Clothes-Washing Tub, whose electrically fired mechanization replaces the muscle and "elbow grease" wielded by the females of our Republic for generations.

A lady who possesses one of these machines need only concern herself with putting soiled clothing and linen in the tub, pouring in water and a measured amount of laundry-soap, and throwing a switch which sends electrical-current to a dynamo which, in turn, speeds the agitating-mechanism. When the lady determines that the laundry has been sufficiently cleansed, she halts the mechanism, runs the wet articles through a wringer, hangs them to dry, and finally drains the tub of the spent wash-water.

NOT ENOUGH WORK

This may still impress the casual reader as involving work, but I submit that the nature of such a task will corrupt a lady's character with idleness and torpor. For it is not what she does that will lead her astray, but what she no longer does, namely, her chore of washing the clothes by hand. And when a female has less with which to occupy her limited mind and nimble hands, you can believe that in the merest wink of an eye, her attention strays and she becomes open to temptation.

LEISURE IS DEVIL'S PLAYGROUND

Picture this scenario, if you will: A lady has begun to launder articles in the agitating clothes-washing tub. Free to engage in other chores, she puts on her coat and hat and starts for the corner butcher to buy a soup bone. Along the way, she spies a newsstand. Her eyes are drawn to a ladies' gazette, which contains a serialized story whose main character is an unescorted young lady who often kisses gentlemen whom she does not intend to marry. She spends on the gazette the precious soup-bone allowance her husband has so diligently earned and saved for her. Returning home, she hungrily devours the scandalous contents of the magazine, which introduce her to a world which she previously hadn't the slightest idea existed.

Forgetting the operation of the agitating clothes-washing tub, she packs her suitcase, hastily pens a note of farewell to her husband, and catches the train to the big city, intent on becoming a chorus girl in a speakeasy. Several hours later, the husband returns home and discovers the note. Awash in grief, he stumbles into the kitchen, only to further find that the agitating clothes-washing tub is still functioning and has shrunk all his clothes to the size of a circus midget's.

A TOOL OF DECADENCE

Why, the very agitation of the mechanical laundry-tub itself is enough to stir up latent feelings of discontent and wanderlust. I liken its undulations to that of the wanton "shimmying" of chorus girls in the vaudeville musical presentations Mark my words, if America continues to tolerate the presence of the mechanical clothes-washing device, in no time the ladies of our nation will be gallivanting in skirts made entirely of bananas

Nosferatu Elected Chancellor of Germany

Vampire Committed to Ending Economic Crisis

(see story on page 6)

MARCEL PROUST FINALLY DIES

"We thought it would go on forever," say loved ones

(see story on page 18)

Two New Literary Journals Founded

T.S. Eliot's 'The Criterion' and Mr. and Mrs. DeWitt's 'Reader's Digest'

Which Will Endure?

(a noted scholar's viewpoint, page 9)

Bolshevism Must Be Nipped in the Bud; Unorthodox 'Sharing' Idea Is Anti-Christian

(see editorial, page 8)

Tomb of King Tut Opened; Quaint Victoriana Found

Mysterious Inscription Warns of 'Curse of the Tourists'

(see story on page 6)

Get Your "Fruit Juice" "Fresh-Squeezed" at Tip-a-Wink Tom's "Produce Stand"!

"Delicious" and "Thirst-Quenching"! That's Tip-a-Wink Tom's "Produce"!

Tip-a-Wink Tom's,
406 State Street, Chicago
Formerly Tom's Liquor

THE ONION

THE JUDGMENTAL VOICE OF REASON — *SENTRY ON SOBRIETY'S BORDERS*

Friday, March 16, 1923 — Finest Source of News in Our Great Republic — Price Three Cents

IRVING BERLIN PUBLISHES 1,000TH ANNOYING, CLAMOROUS DITTY

Celebrated Songsmith Gives World Music, Headaches

Reaches Milestone with 'Don't Wail for Me, Pansybelle'

Just 211 From All-Time Mark Set by George M. Cohan

IRVING BERLIN

NEW YORK, Mar. 15.—Recently the toast of Broadway thanks to his music for the play "Squawk Me a Love Song," famed songwriter Irving Berlin has released his latest annoying number, "Don't Wail for Me, Pansybelle." Not only does this new ditty exceed the already high standard of ear-drum-abusing irritation Americans have come to expect in the sheet music of this prolific songster, but it marks his one-thousandth headache-inducing masterpiece.

The new number is a modern music-lover's feast of clanking, ringing piano playing, and melodic yowling, best belted out by a woman of great lung capacity with a shrill vibrato not unlike a fire alarm.

A SING-A-LONG FAVORITE

The quick tempo and pounding piano bass-line of the tune are enough to delight the ears of the discerning racket fan. Add to that, however, the catchy melody of sharp, clinking, upper-register piano keys in the most repetitive and unrelenting pattern, back and forth and back and forth, bobbing excitedly from a note in one octave to the same note in the next highest octave on every half-note until the ears have almost had too much of the uplifting noise, and you've got the makings of another million-sheet seller.

When played on the home piano, the pleasing irksomeness of this fine music clamor comes blusteringly to life. With the addition of lyrics, shrieked in the pleasantly grating voice of an enormous aunt, hurriedly yelping the bluntly worded themes in her most shrill of bleats, Berlin's notions of pride in America, pride in showmanship, and pride in the favor of a young companion come bursting forth in uplifting calamity.

The idiotic lyrics to "Don't Wail for Me, Pansybelle" make clear how fun-filled the sing-a-long time is made: "You're a peppy lass/With a lot of class/You're swell!/What you've got/Makes me hot to trot/Thanks a lot/Pansybelle!/You're the sweetest pip/So don't give me the slip/Don't wail for me, Pansybelle!"

LONG CAREER OF CLAMOR

On Tin Pan Alley, Berlin wowed sheet-music lovers with such clamorous ditties as "My Big Brass Trumpet," "Howl as Loud and as Fast as You Can the Entire Text of the Declaration of Independence, Dear Friend of Mine," and "Your Shrieking Falsetto Is My Lullaby." His "Songs for the Kazoo and Screaming Whistle" became one of the best-selling music sheets of 1921.

But the sheer volume of this talented noise-master is almost too difficult to believe. Berlin has put 1,000 blaring, unremitting songs in our hearts and induced a throbbing migraine headache for every music-lover in the world.

TRIBUTE PERFORMANCE

At an upcoming tribute performance at New York's great Savoy Theater, popular singing star Eddie Cantor and the All-Gibbon Orchestra will perform a special "All of Berlin's 1,000 Songs Played Simultaneously" show.

"It will be the most calamitous, clamorous, and cantankerous music show in town!" Cantor told The Onion. "And it's sure to be snappy!"

The show will vex eager fans Friday and Saturday nights at the Savoy from March 16 through April 20.

WE MUST SAVE OUR LIBERTY BEFORE IT IS TOO LATE!

RUSSIANS CONTINUING TO KILL RASPUTIN

'Progress Being Made,' Says One Gunman

HIRSUTE MYSTIC TO REACH DEMISE 'NO LATER THAN 1925,' SAY ASSASSINS

From the Moscow correspondent, Mar. 15.—Former members of the Russian aristocracy are continuing, for the seventh straight year, to kill Grigoriy Rasputin, hypnotist, healer, and counsel to former czar Nicholas II.

"In the first year, we commenced with our plan to poison him, shoot him, stab him, and then drown him in the Neva River," said Prince Felix Yusupov, leader of the aristocrats charged with killing the charismatic mystic. "But those efforts met with fair to middling success, as Rasputin continued to stay alive."

AN INVOLVED PROJECT

In 1917 alone, the Kill Rasputin Project conceived of attempts to speed up the process, such as encasing his head in solid iron, repeated electrocutions, two beheadings, and a burial.

Yusupov recalls, "It was in 1919, at the Kill Rasputin Project holiday staff party, that someone came up with the idea of chopping his body into hundreds of little pieces and scattering them across the Russian countryside."

The chopping up of Rasputin, for a short time, seemed to be succeeding, until word reached the project's headquarters that Rasputin had been seen cavorting with Russian farm ladies, coercing them into unsavory relations using his strange and irresistible charm.

ALMOST DEAD

In later years, Rasputin was set on fire, dissolved in acid, boiled alive, flensed, fed molten lead, ground beneath the wheels of a freight train, thrown from the top of St. Basil's Cathedral, impaled on sharpened stakes, buried under ten tons of hot gravel, struck at high speeds by an automobile, strapped to the mouth of a great cannon which was then fired several times, bolted to the keel of an icebreaking ship which was repeatedly run aground, drawn and quartered, crucified, run through with a cavalry spear from bowel to gullet, vivisected, and eviscerated. Furthermore, throughout the process, he was continually re-poisoned, re-stabbed and re-shot.

"We're making excellent progress," Yusupov said. "This trickster's mysterious influence over the now-dead czar will soon come to an end. It is only a matter of time."

The team expects Rasputin's death to take place no later than 1925.

LOST?
...
Be an American expatriate in Paris!

Cheap rates now available for trans-Atlantic passage. Book now before the rush.

Columbia Steamship Line

Harold Lloyd Killed in Fall from Clock

PLUMMETS 300 FEET TO HIS DEATH

CLUNG VALIANTLY TO MINUTE-HAND BEFORE FATAL FREE-FALL

REMEMBERED AS 'BESPECTACLED GO-GETTER'

LOS ANGELES, Mar. 15.—Harold Lloyd, a 30-year-old citizen of Los Angeles, died today from injuries suffered after a 300-foot drop from the hands of a clock. Lloyd was attempting to scale the building of a major department store.

Eyewitnesses report that, moments before the dreadful accident, Lloyd had managed to climb to a window ledge, on which he attempted to rest. But something startled him, they report, and he lost his balance and fell onto a clock next to the window. As he desperately clutched the minute hand, his weight made the entire clock facade loosen from the mechanism. As Lloyd desperately tried to regain a foothold on the ledge, the clock facade snapped off, and Lloyd plummeted to the ground.

He was taken to Mercy General Hospital, where he was pronounced dead on arrival.

Witnesses said Lloyd executed a long and perilous climb up the face of the building prior to the accident.

The department store's head floorwalker, Clarence Stubbs, had this to say: "If this Lloyd fellow had put safety first, perhaps this tragedy wouldn't have happened. But it appears to me that he was was putting safety last."

The building's clock sustained nearly $1,280 of damage.

Friends and fellow workers praised Lloyd as an eternally optimistic, energetic character, whose pair of eyeglasses and straw hat were a constant trademark.

"Harold was a real go-getter," said one friend. "It was just like him to attempt a daredevil stunt like this."

This is but the latest in a recent series of accidents resulting from odd stunts in the Los Angeles area involving excessive and perilous physical exertion. Just last week, an unidentified man in baggy clothes and a porkpie hat was crushed under the side of a large wooden house-frame which was blown down directly on top of him during a cyclone. He might have been saved, had he been standing on the exact spot of ground where an open window on the facade landed.

Mussolini Becomes Italian Dictator After Closely Contested Fist-Fight

MILAN, Mar. 15.—Benito Mussolini, a Fascist journalist for the Italian newspaper Il Populo, became ruler of Italy after a backstreet brawl today. His opponent, Catholic moderate Mario Taruffi, was powerless to stop Mussolini's combination of powerful body blows and uppercuts, succumbing in the first round.

The Italian parliament acknowledged Mussolini's leadership shortly after news of his pugilistic victory reached Rome. "Mussolini's straight-ahead Fascist viewpoint, as well as his unstoppable jabs and hooks, make him the perfect choice to lead the Italian people at this crucial juncture," a government press statement read. "Long live Mussolini, and long live Italy."

Mussolini is scheduled to begin his rule later this afternoon, when he will pound his military spending requests through the Italian Treasury and attempt to knock out a delegation of Sicilian tradesmen opposed to his new tariff structure.

Gee, that's rich

MAN.—I declare, Clement, why is your right forearm all bloodied?

RUBE.—I spent all morning with my arm up a cow's arse.

MAN.—Oh, I hope that the calf you were delivering is alive and well.

RUBE.—What calf?

12 Flapped to Flinders in Foofaraw
(see story on page 5)

General Pershing Retires, Becomes Statue
(see story on page 8)

Providing the most current misinformation on the William Desmond Taylor murder.

THE ONION

ENEMY OF THE ITALIAN

Tuesday, December 18, 1923   Finest Source of News   in Our Great Republic   Price Three Cents

Listerine Company Invents, Cures Halitosis

'Fear Not This Ailment We Have Just Created,' Say Makers

New Era of Manufactured Insecurities Dawns

The Listerine Oral Rinse Company has unveiled an exciting new product which promises to eradicate in our time the specter of halitosis, a dreaded disease of the company's own invention.

"Halitosis is a terrible ailment of the mouth which can frighten away neighbors, acquaintances, and suitors alike," proclaimed literature trumpeting the new cure. "Listerine kills the germs which cause what our advertising-copywriting scientists call halitosis, restoring oral well-being to the afflicted."

The product, which is available in refreshing medicine flavor, can be found at local drug stores and is currently available without a prescription from a doctor. Listerine has 62 other uses, which are found listed on the side of the bottle next to additional blank lines, on which the customer may write in any more uses he might discover.

Thousands of halitosis sufferers are rejoicing in gratitude to the company for discovering that they were, in fact, ill, then for informing them and making a treatment available.

"Traditionally, we rely on science to reveal new ailments," said halitosis survivor Paul Groves. "Then, if a pharmaceutical genius can create a cure, he would provide that service. But in our modern age, we have wise, benevolent corporations to make us realize we are malodorous, then provide the solution all in one concise advertisement. What an age we live in. I'm so excited, one could probably smell my perspiration."

Latest Dirigible Accident Prompts Safety Officials to Call for Less Hydrogen, Fire, Cloth in Airships

Exploding Trend Discouraged

Safety Now 'Primary Concern' for Popular, Combustible Mode of Travel

Yet another hydrogen-buoyed dirigible has exploded in a horrendous conflagration, resulting in considerable loss of life. With millionaire socialite Thaddeus Earnsley's airship "Katherine Sue" going down in flames in a field outside Schenectady, New York, Sunday, killing 14, many throughout the nation are asking, Why are these seemingly invincible airships proving as vulnerable as soap bubbles?

The recently formed National Airship Safety Bureau has issued a 40-page report suggesting that the materials that make up a dirigible—dry canvas cloth for its balloon, millions of pounds of compressed hydrogen, and the six- or eight-cylinder propeller engines, which often generate sparks—may contribute to airship explosions.

BUREAU'S FINDINGS, RECOMMENDATIONS

"Given the tendency of hydrogen to explode when in contact with fire, and observing the presence of both hydrogen and fire in all known dirigibles, it appears reasonable to assume a causal link," the report read.

The use of cloth coverings on dirigible frames was also questioned. "Extensive laboratory research performed at the Bureau has determined that, in an overwhelming number of tests, dry cloth is found to burn with considerable rapidity and ease," the report read. "All cloth, when placed in the immediate vicinity of fire, erupts in flames quickly. This mixture of elements in a vehicle carrying humans many hundreds of feet in the air should give one significant cause to ponder the wisdom of such an endeavor."

The Bureau's report concluded: "It likewise seems prudent to advise that the makers of dirigibles seriously consider minimizing one factor or another or substituting them with less-flammable materials and better insulation to enhance the safety of all airships."

MANUFACTURERS SKEPTICAL

Dirigible manufacturers have responded with skepticism and criticism to the Bureau's report. "Poppycockery!" said Rockwell Brophy, president of Consolidated Air-Ships. "If we did not cover our frames with cloth, all the hydrogen would escape between the struts. The ship would never leave the ground. What would they propose dirigible skins be made of? Impregnable iron?"

Brophy questioned the Bureau's statement that the very materials of the airship caused the explosion of the "Katherine Sue," preferring to speculate that an outside factor, such as a flock of migrating geese or even cannon-shot from a nearby Army base, forced the "Katherine Sue" to crash.

But, added Brophy, "Unless government officials are able to collect the fragments of cloth, frame, and human remains, then reconstruct the 'Katherine Sue' piece by piece, we will never know for certain what the cause of the accident was, nor ascertain the cause of any of the other 80-odd dirigible explosions this year."

PRESIDENT COOLIDGE PROMISES TO ISSUE EVERY MAN IN THE LAND A SNAPPY STRAW HAT

WASHINGTON, D.C., Dec. 17.—In his first major declaration since assuming office, President Calvin Coolidge announced Monday that he will issue every American gentleman a snappy straw hat.

The hats, which Coolidge described as "constructed of the finest straw and featuring a generous brim and a smart-looking red-and-white hatband of cloth," will be distributed January 1 to all gentlemen above the age of 18, immigrants excepting.

"Won't we all look like Jim Dandys in these snazzy head-toppers?" Coolidge asked. "I tell you, the American people are going to look like the elephant's instep."

Coolidge said he is also working on a follow-up plan to supply every man in the land with a bamboo cane and bow-tie.

Doctors Link Long-Term Health Risks to 'The Charleston'

Merrymakers at Risk for Damaged Joints, Increased Body Temperature

Illustrious men of medicine announced Monday that the youthful craze in dance referred to as "The Charleston" may put those who practice it in grave danger of damaging their health, particularly in the delicate areas of their joints and tempering fluids.

"This dance, 'The Charleston,' may bring the shoulders and the hips into slightly different planes of alignment, an unnatural condition which may cause imbalancing strictures in the body's fluids, an abrupt and abnormal increase in the temperature of the blood, and even light perspiration," said U.S. General of Surgeons Walter Hiltbrunner.

WARNINGS ISSUED

Although no deaths resulting from the performance of "The Charleston" have yet been reported, the General is warning all bandleaders, musicians, and dance aficionados of the grievous peril which is almost certain to befall those who indulge themselves.

"We cannot have the finest flower of our Nation become imbalanced, unduly excited, hot, bothered, turgid, or otherwise upset in any extreme by this unnatural dance," Hiltbrunner said. "We are recommending that Congress add 'The Charleston' to the ever-growing Federal Roster of Forbidden Dances."

OTHER OFFICIAL ACTIONS

If Congress chooses to take this course of action, the Charleston would join the Irish Jig, the Tango, the Hopping Calumny, the Shuffle, the Black Bottom, the Drunken Welshman, the Two-Step, and the Figginhop as dances deemed unhealthy, disruptive, immoral, and illegal.

Doctors are urging that signs of warning be affixed to phonograph recordings or sheet music to which "The Charleston" may be danced.

DADAIST MOVEMENT ENDS; 'VICTORY,' CRY DADAISTS

Dadaists Drench Selves with Glue in Celebration

'Make Angry Love to the Fish!' Cry Triumphant Artistes

ZURICH, Switzerland, Dec. 17.—The revolutionary "anti-art" movement known as "Dada" officially came to an end today.

According to poets, painters, and sculptors identified throughout the art world as Dadaists, the increasing chaos and alienation of the modern world made the movement no longer tenable within intellectual circles.

The news has set off a volatile explosion of impassioned celebration from Dadaists throughout the globe.

"At last, Dada has achieved its ultimate victory over itself," said Dadaist poet and essayist Tristan Tzara, who spoke from inside a dank, fetid cabinet constructed of rotting cheese. "This day shall forever be remembered as Dada's greatest hour: the death of Dada."

No art historians, museum curators, or art critics who had the slightest idea what was going on could be located for comment.

PERHAPS STRANGE

Congratulating themselves with embraces, accolades, and occasional violent slaps to the face with steaks, Dadaists everywhere gathered in Zurich to drink, dance, and bellow inanities from atop tremendous stilts in a celebration mourning the movement's failure.

"Art has long needed Dada, and now that art has killed Dada, Dada has triumphed forever over art," said tragico-absurdist nonsense poet Hugo Ball, who founded the Dadaist cafe and nightclub Cabaret Voltaire in Zurich seven years ago, "Art and Dada could not both survive for long, but now that Dada is over, the Dada menace will never be overthrown." Ball's consort, ingenue and writer Emmy Hennings, covered much of his torso with a thick impasto of papier maché and toothpaste while Ball spoke.

EVERY MAN HIS OWN FOOTBALL

"Now that the movement known as Dada is over, we must do everything possible to ensure that its memory lives on," said artist Francis Picabia, "and I can think of no better means by which to do so than to begin destroying as many Dadaist 'objets d'art' as can be found, and with no delay." Picabia busily erased his own drawings as he spoke, shortly before setting fire to more than 2,000 Dadaist agit-prop photo-collages, calling his actions "a tribute to the glory of Dada."

Dadaist Marcel Duchamp, hailed by many as the father of Dada, said he hopes to abandon all creative ventures altogether, in favor of a lifetime of relaxation and recreational chess-gaming.

L.H.O.O.Q.

"As long as I keep playing chess and avoid the practice of creating artwork, then I know the spirit of Dada will never die," Duchamp said. "Death to Dada! Down with Dada! Victory is ours! Long live the Dadaists and long fly the Dada banner, which is fish entrails held aloft atop a cheese-cloth."

André Breton, when asked to describe the direction of his new "surrealist" movement, told reporters to "imagine a boot stomping on a face, eternally," before firing a pistol at random into the crowd.

EIGHT VIOLENTLY BOBBED AT LOCAL BARBER SHOP

(see story on page 7)

AMAZING NEW VOICE-AMPLIFICATION DEVICE CREATED

The 'Megaphone' Could Be a Boon to Our Nation's Songsters

(see story on page 7)

29

NEWS WITH Pep!

THE ONION

CLEARED OF ALL TEAPOT DOME WRONGDOINGS

Wednesday, January 23, 1924 — Finest Source of News in Our Great Republic — Price Three Cents

FROM THE SOVIET NEWS WIRE

LENIN DEAD FROM MASSIVE 'STROKE OF THE PEOPLE'; GLORIOUS LACK OF OXYGEN DISTRIBUTED EQUALLY THROUGH BRAIN

✚ ✚ ✚ ✚ ✚ ✚ ✚ ✚ ✚

Brain Parts Shut Down like Proletarian Workers Laying Down Tools to Paralyze Bourgeois Factory Owner

✚ ✚ ✚ ✚ ✚ ✚ ✚ ✚ ✚

Cerebral Hemorrhage of Glorious Red Blood Declared 'Heroic Victory for the Communist Vanguard'

✚ ✚ ✚ ✚ ✚ ✚ ✚ ✚

Vladimir Lenin 1870 - 1924

MOSCOW, Jan. 22.—Vladimir Ilyich Lenin died last night of what Lenin's chief physician, Dr. Aleksandr Bronislav, called "a massive and glorious stroke of the people."

"Comrade Lenin died in proud Soviet fashion," Bronislav, weeping mightily, told members of the Supreme Soviet Congress. "This was not a bourgeois stroke, with certain parts of the brain receiving nearly all the oxygen while others were forced to do without. No, this was a triumphant, proletarian stroke of the people, a truly Marxist-Leninist brain hemorrhage in which the cerebrum, cerebellum, and medulla oblongata were all deprived of precisely equal amounts of oxygen."

GREAT MOURNING

As members of the Congress—including the ordinarily stoic Bukharin, Zinoviev, Rykov, and Kalinin—sobbed openly for their fallen leader and dear friend, Bronislav continued:

"As would befit the leader of the People's Revolutionary Vanguard, the stroke caused Comrade Lenin's life functions to shut down as one, paralyzing his lungs, heart, and other vital organs, just as a group of workers would lay down their hammers as one to paralyze the oppressive factory owner who had for years kept them in chains."

HONORED BY COMRADES

Bukharin, a member of the Central Committee of the Communist Party, then approached the podium to pay his respects.

"Comrade Lenin was not just great in life, but he was also great in stroke. Who else would writhe and suffocate so, his body violently convulsing with a fury like that of the Russian workers who demonstrated before the Czar's Winter Palace in 1905? The day he died, I visited Comrade Lenin in the hospital, and, as I watched his once-prodigious brain languish lifelessly in a sea of his own blood clots, I was reminded of the great Battleship Potemkin, symbol of proletarian might, proudly afloat in the Black Sea."

"A faithful Communist to the end," Bukharin said, "in the last month of his life Comrade Lenin paid tribute to the millions of Russian soldiers who starved during the evil imperialist war by wasting away to less than 100 pounds from an inability to hold down his food."

INJURIES BEFIT STATURE

According to Bronislav, Lenin had been in failing health for many years. At all times, however, his physical ailments were of a nature befitting the father of the Communist Party:

• In May 1911, he was bedridden and pushed to the brink of death from a fever of 103 degrees, with 103 also representing the number of Bolsheviks in attendance at the first-ever European Communist Party Congress in Zurich, Switzerland, in 1904.

• In the Revolutionary Year of 1917, Lenin contracted pleurisy, causing his body to develop sores oozing white pus. In purging his body of the impurities, Lenin did as the Red Bolsheviks had done several years earlier, purging Russia of the loyalist Whites.

• Lenin bled from the anus throughout this most recent winter, demonstrating a great affinity with the brave Russian soldiers who died by the Kaiser's hand in the winter of 1916, many from anus-related injuries.

COULD MAN 'DUNK' BY 1930?

FANTASTIC BASKETBALL FEAT MAY BE PHYSICALLY POSSIBLE

Six-Footer Thos. McCardle of Akron Red Vests Believed to Be Mankind's Brightest Hope

AKRON, Ohio, Jan. 23.—Across the country, scientists and followers of the basketball sport are vigorously debating a question once consigned to the realm of fantasy: Could man "dunk" by 1930?

It is a question H.G. Wells himself once dared pose: the notion that a mortal man, bound by the laws of gravity, should be able to elevate himself skyward in such a manner as to be able to deposit a leather ball, from above, directly into a netting hung some ten feet off the ground. It would seem an audacious impossibility, but mankind grows closer with each passing day.

"If we can put a man on the North Pole, it is not too far off to imagine the time when we will launch a man four feet into the air to dunk a ball and return him safely to the ground," Wells wrote in his essay "To the Basket Rim" in 1910.

Thomas "Dutch" McCardle, a towering six-foot gentleman from the Akron, Ohio, Red Vests, is widely believed to be mankind's best hope for achieving the first-ever dunk without the aid of a step-ladder device or mechanical wings. On a recent attempt, McCardle came within six inches of triumph, coming so close as to glance the side of the netting with the basketball.

"I was positively flabbergasted," said Mortimer Kempton, a sporting-pages writer for the Akron Bugle-Gazette who witnessed McCardle's near-historic attempt. "To see a man vault himself so high into the heavens using only his legs is truly colossal. It is a shame there was no moving-picture apparatus present to record the feat."

McCardle will make another attempt at a dunk on February 16 at the Vanderbilt University gymnasium.

SPECIAL

"NO, NO, NANETTE" FEVER BONUS: SHEET MUSIC FOR "TEA FOR TWO" INSIDE.

WHITE-CROONER SCIENTISTS WORKING ON WAYS TO WATER DOWN NEGRO JAZZ

Process Will Pleasantify Tunes

NEW YORK, Jan. 22.—With white audiences demanding milder, less provocative fare for their entertainments, scientists at the New York Institute of Cultural Appropriation have announced rapid progress in the field of adapting the jazz music of the negro into a form suitable for Caucasian ears.

Such young, up-and-coming white composers as Hoagy Carmichael and Ira Gershwin are eager to apply watered-down negro jazz themes to current compositions, leading to great pressure on the scientists to perfect the process.

MUSIC TONED DOWN

In the words of Institute head Dr. William Birch, "We are making bold strides toward taking soulful, pulse-pounding negro jazz and converting it into quaint, appropriate music that cannot disturb a conversation or alter the mood of the listener in any way. It instead can only calm him."

The scientists are using modern, electrically powered front-beat-rhythmization gyros to take away the sinful "back-beat" of the music. They then use syncopation-regulating tubes to tame the lustful, ferocious beat which often features rhythmic accents on unexpected beats. Third, they apply a micro-tonal unflattening rod to the decadent seventh note of the "blues scale," converting it to the more listenable major scale. Finally, the music is wrung through laboratory de-wailing, de-growling, and de-quickening filters.

The procedure has met with early success, but needs to be fine-tuned, scientists say.

DE-JUNGLIFIED

According to Birch, "A particularly loud and frighteningly lusty number, identified as 'Hot Boogity Boo' by King Roscoe and the Uptown Tramps, is a classic example of the thumping, squealing piano-and-trumpet-driven rhythms which can only inflame the soul and hypnotize the minds of youths." This music, according to white-crooner scientists, induces the listener to dance as if in a jungle, clapping hands and singing aloud.

Birch added, "After careful pretreating of the song with the electronic whitening processes, as well as the re-scoring and re-recording of the new tune on organ or violin, the listener now is induced to remain seated, listening to the tune with a smile on the face and hands folded in the lap, an activity not associated with a jungle of any kind."

A BROADENED APPEAL

Most promising, said Birch, is the translation of the husky, suggestive lyrics of the negro wailer into a civilized, listenable form by white artists: "We have in our archives one jazz song featuring the quizzical, senseless lyrics, 'Won't you come 'round my place, woman, and make love to me all night long.' Using white translators, we have produced a superior version of the lyric: 'Won't you please come over to my house, miss, where I shall serve shortbread and lemonade.'"

Birch said the new version is one that "everyone can enjoy."

No official representative of negro jazz artists was reached for comment.

RECOMMENDED SUBSTITUTES FOR ILLEGAL ALCOHOLIC DRINK

RUBBING ALCOHOL
PAINT THINNER
FLOOR WAX
MEN'S COLOGNE
CERTAIN SECRETIONS OF THE GREATER CAROLINA HOP-TOAD
ELECTRIC LINIMENT SOOTHING SYRUP
MCWHEELY'S COUGH ELIXIR AND TONIC (ADD 2 PARTS VINEGAR)
LAST YEAR'S APPLES, FINELY MASHED
SOOTHING HEROIN
PORNOGRAPHIC DIME NOVELS
SHOE POLISH
ICE-COLD BATHTUB WATER

PRESIDENT HARDING DIES SEVERAL MONTHS AGO

(see story, page 14)

NEGRO SHARECROPPERS INFORMED OF NATION'S PROSPERITY

(see story, page 4)

INSTRUMENT OF THE RICH	# THE ONION	PACIFIER OF THE POOR
Monday, July 20, 1925	Finest Source of News in Our Great Republic	Price Three Cents

SCOPES MONKEY TRIAL RAISES TROUBLING QUESTION:
IS SCIENCE BEING TAUGHT IN OUR SCHOOLS?

Scopes Trial Called 'Trial of the Century'

DAYTON, Tenn., July 19. —The sensational trial of science teacher John Scopes is now being called the "trial of the century" by experts in the study of law.

Never before—and likely never again—has so much public and newspaper attention been generated by a single court trial in America. According to Harvard Law professor Samuel M. Wolheim, "There will never again be a trial such as this, where publishers of soft-covered books and nickel periodicals are scrambling to publish the peculiarities of the trial."

"There is something unique about this Scopes trial," he said.

The trial is so unusual, the professor explained, that it merits being called the 'trial of the century' from now until the year 2000.

"It is not likely that another trial will take place in this century that will generate so much popular interest," he said.

Bessie Smith Signs 3-Cylinder Deal With O-Keh Records
see story, page 8.

SPECTER OF FAMINE LOOMS OVER WORLD, WARNS STAN LAUREL
see story, page 4.

INDIANA CURIOUSLY FREE OF JAZZ MENACE
see story, page 7.

TODAY'S WIRELESS RADIO SCHEDULE

9:00 a.m. to 3:00 p.m. .... static
3:00 p.m. to 3:02 p.m. .... faint sound of human voice
3:02 p.m. to 9 a.m. .... static

SHOULD CHILDREN BE EXPOSED TO FACTS?

Are Reason and Empirical Evidence Suitable School Subjects?

The Opinion of Edward Tillich, The Onion's Crime and Science Editor

Science! The word is thrown about nowadays as if it were a miracle of our Age. To hear its fanatical, wild-eyed supporters talk, one would think that Science could explain everything in all Creation, and that these "Scientists" were privy to the very secrets of the universe. They say that this century will be ruled by Science, and that the nation's might depends upon its adaptation and comprehension by every man. They claim that, if we are to be a great civilization, we must even teach this Science to our schoolchildren.

As a man who holds that the welfare of the country takes precedence over any other human concern, I must stand firmly against the teaching of Science in our schools. This Science has already caused turmoil among God-fearing folk who did not wish to learn that they, as human creatures, may have descended from apes. What if Science were to champion other truths, provable and real, which people do not want to hear? Should we allow our citizens to become aware of facts which go against their chosen beliefs, it would cause untold turmoil and strife among our people! The people's reaction would cause division and conflict in our nation that would doubtless outweigh any benefits of the actual Scientific discovery.

Should we teach our children facts? No, I say, a thousand times no! As they grow into tomorrow's farmers, housewives, mill workers, and coal miners, facts are the last things they will need. Manners! Subservience! Above all, obedience! To speak only when spoken to, and not to cause trouble! These are the principles upon which our educational system was founded. Why in the name of God should we replace it with a system that actually encourages an ignorant man to ask questions? A good citizen does nothing of the sort. He is content with the reasons he is given by his betters.

Humanity's noblest heroes were not men who cared about facts. They were men who stood up for what they believed in, and to Hell with facts! To Hell with any truth not their own! Our most cherished heroes would fight to the death, bludgeoning their enemies repeatedly, wholly uninterested in whether they were right or wrong.

Once something is accepted as true, it should be true forever. This noble ideal, with its emphasis on unquestioning acceptance of and obedience to authority, is what we should teach our children. It is the rock upon which we have built our government, our religion, and our American way of life, and it is the very ideal which Science seeks to thwart with its new "discoveries" and impersonal ledgers of "facts."

Learning! Why should we provide our citizens with learning? Does learning mathematics aid a man who will spend the rest of his life smelting iron in a foundry? Does knowing that Man comes from apes—if he indeed does, which seems to be a subject of some debate—change the lot of

Attorney Clarence Darrow (above) would have us teach children the scurrilous theories of Darwin.

the farmwife who lives out her years shuttling between the birthing-bed and the milking-stool? I say it does not. Furthermore, it fills the brains of children with useless facts which do not help them to become good American citizens. Does a fact have any inherent moral value? Does Science? We know that Science allowed the Germans to develop the mustard gas and the motor-gun. Has religion ever been used in so evil a fashion? Of course not.

It is possible that we, with our motorcars and aeroplanes powered by the new internal-combustion engines, have already started down a slippery slope of destruction. We were not content to stay with time-honored steam, to travel in our dignified trains and coach-and-fours. But we can take action now, before ape-worshiping scientists turn us one against the other. We must cease our deadly march of Progress now, and there is no better way to achieve this than to keep the hellborn demon Science, and his diabolical Facts, from coming into contact with our dear children.

LITERATURE
Complexity Marks New Fitzgerald Novel, 'Zelda, Be a Dear and Fix Me Another Gin Fizz, You Incorrigible Harlot I Love You'
see review on page 12

Leaking?

Permit our new "Unspeakables" disposable hygienic underbandage to gently absorb Milady's foul drippings during her less dainty time of the month. Far less cumbersome than the wire-constructed strap-on "secretion cages," "Unspeakables" will leave ladies as free as a soap bubble wafting ever heavenward.

Available at most pharmacies in discreet, featureless gray boxes, for your privacy.

Mitchell Hygiene Company, Grayson, Ohio.

Scopes Defended By Super-Intelligent Chimpanzee-Man from Future

Cornelius, a beast imbued with speech and learning

William Jennings Bryan

DAYTON, Tenn., July 19. —The trial of high-school biology teacher John Scopes took another controversial turn today with the introduction by defense attorney Clarence Darrow of a surprise witness: Cornelius the intelligent chimpanzee-man, a strikingly anthropomorphic simian claiming to originate from thousands of years in Earth's future.

Darrow hopes that the presence of the chimp, a member of the "intellectual class" of a future society ruled by apes, will illustrate to the jury the merit of the biological theory of evolution, the teaching of which now stands in question under Tennessee law.

When Cornelius was called to the witness stand, Darrow spoke: "I know that many of you with faith in the Bible's teachings find it impossible to believe that man evolved from apes thousands of years ago." He then pointed to Cornelius and said, "Yet sitting before you today in this courtroom is an ape from the fourth millennium, an ape thousands of years more advanced than any living man!"

APE SPEAKS

Cornelius, who, along with his wife Zira, was accidentally transported backward through time from centuries hence, spoke eloquently of a future world ruled by apes. The fantastic testimony caused many ladies in attendance to fall victim to swooning and fainting spells on this hot July day.

"My friends, the humans," Cornelius said in an erudite British accent, "I understand why it might first appear to you that evolution could not be true. I myself at one time did not believe that humans could talk like apes. Then I met a man named 'Taylor.' He talked. But I still didn't believe, until I discovered a human child's doll at an archaeological site, a doll that, although human, spoke as an ape did. My prejudices were dispelled by this evidence that a larger society of men had once possessed the power of speech, and indeed dwelled on this planet."

BRYAN DISCREDITS APE

When cross-examining the chimp, outraged prosecutor William Jennings Bryan loudly decried the validity of his testimony.

"None of these tales can possibly be more than the wildest science-based fictions!" the famed orator said. "Does The Bible tell us of a planet of apes or a subsequent adventure beneath it?" he asked. "It does not. I submit to you that this Cornelius is not even a Christian, has never been baptized, and has, of his own admission, no knowledge of the teachings or even the existence of Christ our Lord and Savior!"

Bryan went on to further discredit Cornelius. "By the ape's own admission, all records of the previous civilization of man were destroyed in the so-called 'ancient thermonuclear wars,' whatever that means; therefore Cornelius cannot have known of the teachings of Christ in any form. I thus submit that his testimony is that of a godless atheist ape!"

APE CONTRADICTS BIBLE

Bryan then turned to the jury and said, "Ladies and gentlemen, The Bible, ultimate authority of all the laws of God and man, tells us in Revelations of the coming of a seven-headed dragon at the end of the world, not of any 'Doomsday Bomb' in the year 3955. Nor does it mention any time vortices created by the detonation of such a device, nor of any cult of mutant humans who preserve and worship such a bomb for thousands of years in subterranean tunnels."

"This ape's testimony," Bryan continued, pointing at Cornelius, "stands in blatant contradiction to the holy testament of God in Heaven himself! Is that what you would have our school-children taught?"

The crowd in attendance was aroused by Bryan's dramatic tone, and the judge was forced to call a recess.

Bryan's cross-examination of Cornelius will continue Tuesday.

THE ONION

Dry Since 1919 — **Prohibiting Since 1791**

Friday, August 6, 1926 — Finest Source of News in Our Great Republic — Price Three Cents

EINSTEIN PROPOSES THEORY OF 'SELL-A-TIVITY'

The Idea, Physicist Says, Is to 'Get Out There and Sell!'

GENEVA, Switzerland, Aug. 5.—In what physicists and entrepreneurs are calling "the most significant discovery of the 20th century" and "a paradigmatic shift in our theoretical models of salesmanship," German physicist Albert Einstein has shocked the Western world with two papers, the Special and General Theories of "Sell-a-tivity," presented this week at the University of Geneva's prestigious International Motivational Symposium of Self-Employment. The two-part theory is a study in the science of "Overall Customer Satisfaction."

'ALWAYS BE CLOSING'

The radical and complex theory, the mathematics of which are so advanced it is said that only a handful of sales physicists can truly grasp them, has wide-ranging implications that could render obsolete many long-held precepts about both the universe and customer relations, including the immutability of matter and the existence of absolute time-management strategies for people who own their own businesses.

"With my system and the right attitude," Einstein said, "your merchandise will look distorted and foreshortened because it is moving so fast."

SALES AT HEART OF THEORY

At the core of the momentous theory is one elegant and simple proposition: that the trick of it is to just get out there and sell.

The most famous equation of the theory is $e = ABC^2$, meaning that, with the right energy, salesmen can "Always Be Closing." Einstein explained, "Your merchandise and the customer's money are the same things, in different states. You can convert one into the other, given sufficient energy to ring those doorbells and give the customer a big, wide smile no matter what the last customer said to you."

"The true salesman needs to have what physicists call 'brass balls,'" Einstein said, pounding his fist in his hand for emphasis during the conference's "Sales Motivation" seminar. "He must always be closing. Closing that sale. Closing the deals, getting that customer's signature on the dotted line. Bam, bam, bam. One after the other."

PROFITS INCREASE EXPONENTIALLY

The story of how Einstein's Special Theory came to be is a classic example of sales success. "When I started out, I was living in a one-room apartment in

ALBERT EINSTEIN

Switzerland, washing my dishes in the bathtub," Einstein said. "Then one day I decided I'd had enough. I was only going around once in this crazy world, and the time had come for me to take control of my life, start my own motor, make my destiny happen." Then, Einstein said, he used his theory to increase his profit potential tenfold.

"If you can always be closing, your efforts will result in exponentially increasing money-making and career opportunities," he explained. "Remember three things: Time flows at a slower rate the faster the potential for sales growth moves; a positive attitude increases profits to near the speed of light; and matter and go-get-'em energy are two forms of the same thing."

The story behind Einstein's theory proved inspirational at the conference.

"With the publication of this breakthrough work of genius," said Geneva Physics Counsel General president Erno Heidegger, "our fundamental concept of the universe of sales is forever altered. Einstein posits that the fundamental fabric of space-time can, with the right amounts of willpower and energy, be curved in such a manner that great money-making opportunities literally flow in the direction of the motivated, self-starting entrepreneur."

BUSINESS UNIVERSE EXPLAINED

Explaining the complex General Theory of Sell-a-tivity, Einstein said, "Customers say yes and they say no. It is my belief that there is a large but finite number of 'nos' getting in the way of sales. Therefore, it can be inferred that every 'no' you get takes you one 'no' closer to your next 'yes.'"

"The customer is capable of generating a theoretically limitless number of objections to the purchase," he said. "It is the function of the effective salesman to annihilate each objection by placing an anti-objection in the customer's path."

A bold addendum to Einstein's theory suggests that all matter in the universe is composed of tiny classified ads.

Phone-Book-Swallowing Fad Captivates Nation's Youth

To Charleston contests, mah-jongg-playing, flag-pole-sitting, and marathon-dancing, add the latest fad poised to sweep the nation: telephone-directory-swallowing. The zany craze, which involves the swallowing-whole of paper-bound telephone listings, has virtually paralyzed the Eastern universities and is catching on among tens of thousands of young people across the country.

TELEPHONE-BOOK SHORTAGES REPORTED

The trick to successfully passing a telephone directory down the throat, the experts will tell you, is to force yourself to suspend the natural gag reflex. Some of the more zealous practitioners have even gone so far as to have their uvulas surgically extracted so as to not interfere with their odd hobby.

Clyde Harbaugh of Elmira, New York, can swallow three of his hometown listings in a five-minute time span. In fact, Harbaugh's techniques have become so imitated by the public that nary a smaller directory from a middle-sized town or city remains intact. Few large directories exist which are not stained with the telltale saliva or gastric juices of unsuccessful swallowing attempts.

A CHAMP

Champion telephone-directory swallower Miss Geraldine Ralston, a peppy lass who can swallow the Greater Boston directory, is a crowd favorite. Miss Ralston has demonstrated her talents before appreciative vaudeville audiences, but was briefly hospitalized after an unsuccessful attempt to swallow the Greater New York listings during a July 8 performance at the Palace Theater.

Despite this setback, the gay Miss Ralston is dismissive of Harbaugh and other "amateurs" who concentrate on swallowing smaller directories in a short time span. "Where's the showmanship?" she asked. "When people put down good money to see a thrilling evening of telephone-book-swallowing, they don't want to watch someone like Harbaugh. They want a professional like me to put away a four-hundred-page metropolitan listing, see?"

However, not everyone is thrilled by the new pastime. Said Chancellor Marvin Dunworthy of Boston University at a recent orientation event, "I do not approve of the swallowing of the phone books so popular among the young people, who should be more concerned about tending to the washing of fences and trimming of hedges on campus."

EXCRUCIATING PAIN

One of the drawbacks of swallowing telephone directories whole is the excruciating gastrointestinal pain which results shortly thereafter. The width and volume of a telephone directory outsizes the volume of the average adult human stomach by one-and-a-half, and the esophagus must expand to five times its normal width to pass the directory successfully into the stomach. Even if the amateur is able to swallow the directory, the problem of passing it through the rear presents a wholly different ordeal. It is estimated that surgeries performed to extract telephone-directory blockages are up over 212 percent since 1920.

But there is no indication that the craze will wane; as a matter of fact, it has inspired other stunts, such as wish-book and dictionary-swallowing. A Catholic priest in Grand Forks, North Dakota, recently swallowed an entire Holy Bible in front of his congregation, but was quickly defrocked for "taking the Lord's name into his gastrointestinal tract."

DEMPSEY–TUNNEY FIGHT AVAILABLE FOR 75¢ ON PAY-PER-HEAR

JACK DEMPSEY

CHICAGO.—The National Broadcasting Company announced today that the upcoming championship bout between Jack Dempsey and Gene Tunney in Philadelphia will be broadcast over its radio network to paying customers for the special cost of 75 cents.

"We're proud to be the voice of World Championship Boxing," Walter McGuffey, N.B.C. vice-president in charge of sporting broadcasts, said on N.B.C.'s "Ear on Sports" program this morning. "And now, listeners can tune in to an almost perfectly clear blow-by-blow description of this pugilistic clash of heavyweight champions at a fair price."

Listeners who wish to receive the Dempsey-Tunney fight should send their 75 cents in cash or stamps to the National Broadcasting Company in New York City (Attention: Pay-Per-Hear Billing) and then turn their radio dials to 660 kilohertz for the barely audible action.

Eliot Ness Spoils 500th Chicago Party

CHICAGO, Aug. 5.—Eliot Ness, crusading government agent and tireless defender of Prohibition, led a successful bootleg-liquor raid on Chicago businessman Charles Dupree's 45th-birthday party Thursday. The bust marked the 500th party ruined by Special Agent Ness.

Chicago Mayor William Dever commemorated the occasion with a special ceremony for Ness.

"It is my solemn duty as Mayor of Chicago to acknowledge the actions of Mr. Ness and to commend him for so doggedly persisting in the performance of his assigned task," Dever said.

"I believe I speak for all Chicagoans, Mr. Ness, when I say that I hope there comes a day when there is an end to lawlessness in our fair city and we no longer need the service you so diligently perform."

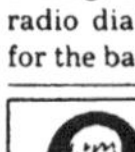

Oh, Mother! Please May I Have Some PUMMELED WHEAT For Breakfast?

A flavorful and nourishing morningtime repast, composed of specially bleached and processed cereal grains. Maintains healthy glands and instills a feeling of vigor and pep. Available in regular and hay flavors.

THE ONION

News for Christ's Flock — Finest Source of News in Our Great Republic — Now With Crossed-Word Puzzler

Monday, November 1, 1926 — Price Three Cents

Man Ventures Outside Hatless

Harry Houdini Escapes from Wisconsin

Famed escape artist and magician Harry Houdini made his most daring escape Sunday, disappearing from the remote, impoverished existence of his Appleton, Wisconsin, upbringing.

He made the escape by dying of a ruptured appendix in an injury sustained Friday in Canada.

"This is my greatest escape," Houdini was overheard to say shortly before his unexpected death.

Escaping the life of hunger and destitution that the former Erich Weiss and his Hungarian immigrant family suffered in the cold, lifeless Great Lakes region may have seemed an impossible trick. But according to Frederick E. Powell, Dean of American Magicians and an associate of Houdini's, "Only a performer of such prodigious talent as the Great Houdini could have escaped from this inconsequential wasteland of the North. Getting out of the state of Wisconsin is a feat of such derring-do and savoir-faire that no other magician would dare even attempt it."

In recent history, only one other magician has attempted to escape from Wisconsin, the Amazing Buppo of France. Buppo's attempt failed in a tragic hiring at a low-wage paper mill in Stevens Point, Wisconsin, where he remains to this day.

Wisconsin Director of Tourism Harold Knocke issued a statement reading that, while the great Houdini may have considered his escape from Wisconsin momentous, that many tourists would enjoy escaping "to" Wisconsin to enjoy its many attractions, such as Frozen-Ass Lake and the Winnewaukee County Bratwurst and Polka Fair.

OUTRAGEOUS 'FLAPPERS' SUGGEST EXISTENCE OF HUMAN SEXUALITY

(see story on page 3)

ALGONQUIN ROUND TABLE'S PITHY WITTICISMS WOW ALGONQUIN ROUND TABLE

NEW YORK, Oct. 31.—The wits and raconteurs of the New York literary intelligentsia met today to lunch at their customary haunt, a large round table at the Rose Room of the Algonquin Hotel, and exchanged a number of droll bon mots and well-aimed barbs, to the enormous enjoyment of themselves.

'Ladies Home Journal' Publishes Scandalous 'Marital Habits Survey'

In a bold November issue that has some of the nation's women turning red, the Ladies Home Journal published its first-ever marital-habits survey this week.

Here is a shocking sampling of its indiscreet questions: "Does private, married-partner child-quickening time ever occur with the lights on?" (Yes, 3 percent. No, 97 percent.) "Would you liken your lifelong partner in marriage more to a tiger or a lamb while in the confines of the room in which you both sleep?" (Tiger, 3 percent. Lamb, 12 percent. Did not understand, 85 percent.)

The survey participants submitted personal information anonymously, which allowed Ladies Home Journal editors access to heretofore unknowable anthropological information regarding the marital practices of the nation's citizens.

STARTLING FACTS UNCOVERED

"We found that some ladies of very high education—as high as eighth grade in some cases—have knowledge of, but certainly never employ, unholy sheepskin accoutrements for the prevention of family-making," said Ladies Home Journal statistician Henry Orville.

"In this same highly educated group, we also see a marked increase in the number of affirmative responses to the question, 'Have you and your marital partner ever had a relation which involved a reversal of the typical physical configurement named for Blessed Missionaries of Christ's Word?'" Orville said.

Ninety-eight percent of those responding said no.

CONTROVERSY

The Ladies Home Journal has seen an increase in public outcry and claims of indecency, as well as a sharp rise in sales as a result of the survey, Orville said.

But controversy is not new to the Ladies Home Journal, which was assailed by decency groups last year when it began publishing the monthly advice column "Biological Queries to Dr. James Gregory, a Certified Physician."

AL JOLSON MISTAKENLY LYNCHED BY KKK

AL JOLSON

LOS ANGELES, Oct. 31.—Celebrated singer-actor Al Jolson was accidentally hanged to death Sunday by a band of horse-mounted Ku Klux Klansmen, who tragically mistook him for a Negro.

The blackface-sporting Jolson was on the set of his "talking" moving-picture "The Jazz Singer," due to be screened by the public next year. He was preparing to perform his famous "Mammy" number when the attack occurred. An estimated 15 hooded, torch-wielding men set upon Jolson and carried him off to a nearby field, where he was hanged from the branch of an elm tree. He died some 15 minutes later.

"This is a terrible tragedy," director Alan Crosland said. "We tried to inform the assailants that Mr. Jolson was, indeed, white, but so fervent were they in their thirst for Negro blood that they refused to listen."

Jolson attempted to communicate to the Klansmen that he was white and made a frantic effort to wipe off his black-shoe-polish make-up, but he was bound and gagged before he could do so successfully.

Funeral services are scheduled for 10:30 a.m. Tuesday at Hillside Memorial Park Cemetery in Los Angeles.

Among the most well-received witticisms was one uttered by writer and poet Dorothy Parker. After New Yorker magazine editor Harold Ross made a passing remark about the famed women's college Vassar, Parker was heard to quip, "If all the girls of Vassar were laid end to end, I for one wouldn't be surprised." It was then that the epigram-coining habitues of the Round Table, which included humorists Robert Benchley and S.J. Perelman, playwright George S. Kaufman, critic Alexander Woolcott, and author Edna Ferber, burst into loud laughter.

No witticisms were heard from the Oblong Table, a table near the Round Table that is frequented by accountants from a New York insurance company. The most memorable statement came from accountant Clement Hooper, who noted that the rainbow trout seemed a little on the dry side today.

NEW 'TALKIES' REVEAL HOW PINCHED AND NASAL OUR VOICES SOUND

Scientists and moving-picture-goers across the nation are experiencing an awkward self-consciousness, and even slight embarrassment, as the new "talkies" form of moving-picture entertainment reveals how pinched and nasal our voices sound.

Said Columbia University Speech Therapy and Articulation Sciences expert George C. Wayer, "We, as a nation, don't really sound like that, do we? We sound like we all come from Brooklyn or something."

Another expert, theater critic and diction coach Simon Tauschek, said, "We sound like so many squawking geese." He went on to suggest, "We should turn those talkies off, because it's embarrassing to listen to."

Lawrence Weatherbee, a noted actor and wireless-radio announcer, said he believes that this pinched, nasal quality is "how we actually sound." He theorized that this surprisingly unflattering way in which we now hear ourselves is "how others have heard us all along."

Weatherbee advised that citizens grow familiar with the way our voices sound, so that it will not be such a shock to hear them, should talkies become a popular form of entertainment in the years to come.

Mere Wisps of Hair All that Stand Between Scalp, Elements.

Top Mind-Doctors Recruited from Nearby Sanitorium to Diagnose Cause of Mad Hatless Excursion.

Here pictured is Charles Breubauer in saner, hatted times. Inset: an artist's depiction, using eyewitness descriptions and state-of-the-art photo-retouching technology, of what Breubauer may look like hatless.

NEW YORK, Oct. 31.—A businessman shocked thousands of pedestrians in downtown New York this afternoon by stepping outside wearing no visible headgear of any kind.

"I've never been so stupefied in all my life," said one eyewitness to the incident. "To see, in the height of the lunch hour, an insane man braving the elements with nothing between his scalp and the heavens.... It was not to be believed. Who but a madman would ever think of appearing outdoors without a hat?"

POLICE ALERTED

Police received calls of "a hatless maniac in broad daylight" and "a berserk, exposed-headed man walking down the street as nonchalantly as if properly bowlered."

The man, Charles Breubauer, 43, an accountant employed by Crane, Harcourt and Associates, was reportedly in good condition following his two-minute wanton excursion on First Street around 2 o'clock p.m., reportedly to purchase a newspaper. Onlookers gasped in terror and emptied the sidewalk temporarily as Breubauer, walking with a confident stride and by most accounts looking straight ahead, navigated the half-block route from office to newsboy and back to office without benefit of a protective chapeau.

Eyewitnesses report that Breubauer's exposed head was almost entirely bereft of hair, save around his ears and above the back of his neck. The bright mid-afternoon sun only served to emphasize it all the more, and the gleam off his bald head could reportedly be seen by workers in a seventh-floor office building on First Street.

MEDICAL DANGERS

Dr. Paul Rogers, M.D., said Breubauer's hatless adventure "put him at great risk of windburn, detasslefication, defoliation, scalp exsiccation, and possible moisis."

The doctor added that the incompleteness of Breubauer's wardrobe also created conditions "ripe for the spread of freethinking and malcontentism."

AN 'ODD DUCK'

Breubauer was unavailable for comment at press time, but an anonymous co-worker at Crane and Harcourt said he was "not surprised" by the afternoon's bizarre behavior. "Charlie has always been an odd duck," noted the co-worker. "One time he told me he was thinking about removing the table cloth from the dining-room table in his home. Can you imagine that? Obviously, he hasn't done it yet, or we would have heard about it."

The man also confirmed that Breubauer's employers, Donald F. Crane and John P. Harcourt, were out of town on business during the incident. Because Breubauer is a competent employee who has been with the company many years, he is not expected to be fired. However, Crane and Harcourt will surely give Breubauer a stern reprimand, and possibly a reduction in salary, for his controversial actions.

33

THE ONION

Roaring Since 1920   *Gay Since 1890*

Monday, April 4, 1927   Finest Source of News in Our Great Republic   Price Three Cents

Lindbergh Signs Unprecedented $300 'Endorsement' Contract

Will Represent Professor McWheely's Cough Elixir and Tonic

A Lucrative Contract for America's Fearless Flyer

Advertising to Be Featured in Magazines and Upon Wireless-Radio

Fresh from his triumphant trans-Atlantic flight, Captain Charles A. Lindbergh has signed a deal with the A.W. McWheely Company whereby he will receive an astounding $300 to endorse its popular Cough Elixir and Tonic brand.

Advertisements for the compound featuring Lindbergh's image will make their debut in next week's editions of The Saturday Evening Post and Judge, and bottle labels will be embossed with his signature of endorsement. An advertisement will also be broadcast over the wireless-radio, a medium the McWheely Company trusts will be successful in conveying the word of its product's existence to a mass public.

"The McWheely Company is extremely proud to have Captain Lindbergh's world-renowned name and likeness upon its famed throat remedy," said W.P. McWheely, president of the company and son of its late founder.

A LUCRATIVE ENDORSEMENT

This lucrative endorsement exceeds that of former heavyweight champion Jack Dempsey, who received $275 in 1925 to pitch Grainger's Brand Rolled Oats.

Other endorsement offers are pouring in for Lindbergh, including those from Liberty Wing-Nuts, Schlitze's Meat Tenderizer, Lady-Killer Hair Oil, Shoe-Ola Shoe Polish, Mandelbaum's Kosher Gum-Drops, and O'Monahan's Goat Cure. But these other arrangements are still under consideration.

A 'SELL-OUTER'?

Not all are pleased by Lucky Lindy's decision to lend his name to a commercial endorsement. Some have gone so far as to accuse Lindbergh of having forgotten his morals, instead "selling out" his good name and reputation to the highest bidding elixir and tonic.

One fan of Lindbergh's, 29-year-old Harlan Riley of Brooklyn, said he fears that Lindbergh is selling his name to a product that he may not even truly endorse. He recalled an earlier product endorsement by Lindbergh before he was the most famous man in the world. "I remember when Lindbergh made an appearance at the American Piano Rolls Store opening before he had made the big flight," Riley said. "He wasn't getting paid anything. He did it because he believed in those piano rolls."

Another fan, New York City salesman Howard Tierney, read news of Lindy's solo Atlantic flight with as much pride and patriotism as the next man. But he criticized Lindbergh for usurping his livelihood. "He should stick to the flying. There's others like me who have been selling mercantile products our whole lives, see, and he thinks he can just accept a big check and learn how to do it overnight? I don't think so."

Nonetheless, it is the McWheely Company's fervent hope that the multi-hundred-dollar gambit will pay off. As McWheely said, "It is our hope that, when future generations speak of The Spirit of St. Louis, in the next breath they will recall the equally laudable McWheely's Cough Elixir and Tonic."

LINDY SPEAKS

The wireless-radio advertisement for McWheely's Cough Elixir and Tonic will be broadcast during the "Waldo Chester Juggling Hour," the Sunday-night program featuring the celebrated vaudeville showman. The following is the prepared script which Lindbergh will read on the air:

Good evening, ladies and gentlemen, Captain Charles A. Lindbergh here. When I am not busy making history with an exciting trans-Atlantic flight, I am either using or thinking about McWheely's fine Cough Elixir and Tonic, and I highly recommend you do the same. McWheely's Cough Elixir and Tonic can be used for mild irritations in the throat such as coughing, heartburn, and swollen lymph nodes, and for loosening phlegm produced by the common cold. It's the Cough Elixir and Tonic with my personal endorsement, as indicated by my signature reproduced on every bottle. I thank you for your attention. And now, back to the program.

Captain Charles Lindbergh, whose latest challenge will be to fly high on wireless-radio waves in support of Professor McWheely's Cough Elixir and Tonic.

Babe Ruth Unveils 'Wife Bat'

"The Slugger"

NEW YORK, Apr. 3.— With the panache and style that has characterized his skill as both a ballplayer and a carouser, George Herman "Babe" Ruth introduced his brand-new "wife bat" to the sportsman's fraternity Sunday.

"The impeccable balance and large 'sweet spot' of this bat can only help my swing and allow me to further my reputation as a slugger," said Ruth, displaying the slightly oversized wooden cudgel at a special meeting of the New York Sporting Gentlemen's Society. "With this new bat, I intend to vastly improve the quality and force of my power-hitting."

The bat, manufactured in Louisville by the esteemed club-makers of Hillerich & Bradsby, is an excellent example of its type. Fashioned from a single billet of aged and cured hickory, the 34-inch regulation-sized wife-bat was tempered over red-hot coals, steeped in pine resin, finished with an outer coat of hard, chip-proof varnish, and rolled in glass chips to increase its durability. Copper bands were added at intervals along the bat's length to give it more "sauce," as well as to preserve it against splintering after repeated impacts. To protect the Babe's champion hands from stinging at an ill-timed or off-balance strike, the grip was fashioned from soft, padded glove-leather.

"I do not think any of my fans will be disappointed in the performance of either myself or my new wife-bat," said Ruth. "With this beauty, I am almost assured of getting 60 'Home Runs' this season."

Representatives of Hillerich & Bradsby say the style may become so well-liked that the public will request its mass-production, asking for it by name.

Gandhi Enjoys Enormous Piece of Cake after Brits Cave in to Hunger-Strike Demands

'Oh!' Exclaims India's Resistance Leader, His Mouth Stuffed with Cake

Indian National Congress leader Mohandas Gandhi partook of an enormous piece of German-chocolate cake today after ending a hunger strike that had lasted nearly three weeks.

The revered leader, who had withered away to almost nothing in protest of a British ordinance he believed was an injustice to all Indians, proclaimed the cake to be "God-damned delicious."

Surrounded by trusted advisors and followers, Gandhi was silent throughout much of the cake-eating process in which he eagerly indulged. The silence was only periodically interrupted by the great resistance leader's loud grunts, moans of pleasure, and cries of, "This cake tastes so God-damned good."

Upon devouring the piece of cake, Gandhi pleaded for another, his words muffled by the hastily consumed cake still unswallowed in his mouth, his cheeks and chin coated with German-chocolate frosting.

Area Dame the Bee's Knees

see story on page 12.

THE ONION

News Concerning Lindy and the World

Trivial Lindy Facts, Pages 18-34

Tuesday, August 23, 1927 — Finest Source of News in Our Great Republic — Price Three Cents

Sacco, Vanzetti Executed for Murder, Italian Descent

✛ ✛ ✛ ✛ ✛ ✛ ✛ ✛ ✛ ✛ ✛ ✛ ✛

PAIR DIES ON TWO COUNTS OF WOPNESS

KKK Gathers for First-Ever 'Monstrous Truck Rally'

ANNOUNCER CALLS DISPLAY 'SPECTACULAR, SPECTACULAR, SPECTACULAR'

From the Sporting Correspondent—Members of the white-race supremacy group known as the Ku Klux Klan gathered in a remote South Carolina field this week to hold a festival dedicated to the driving of powerful, heavily oversprung, giant-wheeled monstrous trucks over the wrecked hulls of other modes of transportation.

"As superior members of the holy white Aryan race, it is our duty to spread hatred of the Nigger, the Injun, the Slant-Eye, the Kike, and all other inferior filthy non-white races," said Supreme Grand Dragon Clem Lee Wilikins. "And it is also our racial imperative to soup-up our trucks and farm vehicles; put giant pneumatic flotation-type tires on them; paint them with confederate flags, flames, fanciful ladies, and other Caucasian heraldic symbols; and drive them over other vehicles while whooping."

AUTOMOTIVE CONTESTS

The assembled Klansmen intend to set the attending monstrous trucks against one another in several trials of power and skill designed to determine their fitness to be Klan vehicles. After making several parade circuits of the field, the Caucasian trucks will engage in a race across a two-acre hog wallow, a horn-blowing exhibition, a spinning-in-the-mud display, and finally, a show of strength in which the monstrous trucks are driven across the shattered hulks of other vehicles.

Wilikins also noted that certain powerful farm-tractors would be pulling large, weighted sleds in a separate ceremony of white racial pride.

RACIAL AND CORPORATE SLOGANS

Many of the Klansmen sported painted slogans upon their gowns attesting to their ability to imbibe alcohol or exclaiming their preference for one type of vehicle over another. "The good Lord constructed the Ford," said one. Another stated, "I do not have a problem with the ingestion of alcohol, for I drink it, get drunk upon it, then fall upon the ground. There is no problem."

The Klansmen's trucks were also decorated with colorful seals representing their commercial sponsors, which include Owl's Eye Flour, Amalgamated Tetrahedron-brand spark plugs, and Lengdon's Scalp Powder.

PRIDE IN TRUCKS, WHITENESS

"The monstrous truck is the symbolic vanguard of the White Army, the conveyance which most powerfully represents the potential and future of the white race," said hooded and helmetted Klansman Lew Pickett, driver of the monstrous truck Big Aryan Foot. "To demonstrate this, I shall drive my superior Ford truck over the top of such inferior mud-person vehicles as a wagon, a wheelbarrow, a Model T jalopy, a horse-cart, and a horse, crushing them beyond recognition."

Pickett expressed regret that he would not be able to drive his truck over any Negroes, explaining that, although the event had been advertised far and wide, no members of the African race chose to attend.

"There is something about the power and majesty of the driving of monstrous trucks which is absolutely foreign to the Colored," said Wilikins. "I assume that these inferior peoples are blind to the magnificence of these most Caucasian of vehicles, and that they choose to flee from their hundreds of white horsepower. No other explanation for their avoiding this Ku Klux Klan monstrous truck rally is conceivable."

Edna Etiquette

Q: Edna, what is the proper way to ask a member of the opposite sex to pass the butter?

A: Butter should not be passed.

BILLIONAIRES BUY U.S. FROM MILLIONAIRES

Future of Nation in Yet Wealthier Hands

RICH WILL REGULATE GOVERNMENT, CITIZENRY

John D. Rockefeller, one of the five new owners of America, pictured here after his luxurious cosmetic-surgery treatment.

NEW YORK, Aug. 22.—Our nation's foremost captains of industry met with America's wealthiest plutocrats in secret chambers above the New York Stock Exchange Monday to arrange for the nation's sale. The ceremony, which included a seven-course feast, a secret two-hour Masonic rite of power, and the indulgence in many exotic and expensive pleasurings, was the first such occurrence since 1789, when American millionaires secretly purchased the continent from similarly wealthy British merchants and fur traders following an abortive attempt at revolution.

BIG PLANS MADE

"I intend to be a stalwart caretaker of this great nation, which has always been supportive of my company in the areas of lighting and heating oils," Rockefeller told the jewel-bedecked, ermine-clad assemblage of twenty men. The esteemed Rockefeller's ownership of the Standard Oil Company has caused his net worth to exceed one thousand million dollars, a fact which he believes will make him a suitable caretaker of the United States.

"I am proud to come into ownership of this beautiful and vast market," Rockefeller said.

Gunpowder baron Thomas Coleman du Pont, whose immense wealth is currently inestimable by any known science or ciphery, concurred. "I shall endeavor to live in peace and harmony with my fellow rich men, and to not come into conflict with them, but with the working-man or woman only, that from America we may continue to reap a rich harvest and dictate its policies to guarantee a profitable future for our billionaire children," he said.

WILL CONTROL SOCIETY

The assembled billionaires plan to take control of all aspects of American society, including the passage of laws, levying of taxes, and all else that makes up the greater structure of daily life. The government, they say, will be left in place, but its function will, of course, be regulated by the richest of American citizens, and it will seem a democracy only upon its most superficial face.

"We propose that the government be the facade behind which we most private gentlemen shall hide," said Harold Sterling Vanderbilt, whose wealth is estimated at five-sevenths of the total monies extant in the world. "The common man will be free to believe, if he so wishes, that his desires as a free citizen may still be exercised and that he maintains a certain importance. But, of course, this will not be so."

Vanderbilt proposed that the popular newspapers be influenced to play along with the great masquerade and be paid handsome compensation for so doing.

As a newspaper that has always found the best interest in acting in accord with the ruling elite, The Onion will happily ally itself with the United States' new billionaire rulers.

The billionaires will rule until a day comes in the far future when men with trillions of dollars exist and are seen fit to purchase the right of governance.

MANY OTHER ITALIANS STILL AT LARGE, POLICE WARN

FAIR-MINDED GOVERNOR DOES NOT ISSUE STAY OF EXECUTION

Sacco and Vanzetti, convicted Italians

CHARLESTOWN STATE PRISON, Mass., Aug. 23.—Nicola Sacco and Bartolomeo Vanzetti died in the electric chair today, having been found guilty on two counts of murder and larceny, and one count each of being greasy, violence-prone wops.

Governor Alvan T. Fuller had announced on August 4 that he had no sufficient reason to rescind the sentence handed down by Judge Webster Thayer in Sacco and Vanzetti's 1921 trial. The execution took place shortly after midnight, with Sacco preceding Vanzetti in the death chair. Even with the specter of death surrounding them, the unrepentant pair refused to renounce their ethnic ways, and met their demise utterly and completely Italian.

Sacco and Vanzetti continued to converse with their jailers in a barbaric gibberish of pidgin English and their bastardized native Latin dialect, punctuating their babble with florid and unnecessary gesticulations. At one point, Vanzetti was seen to warmly embrace and otherwise touch the prison warden, triggering shudders of disgust from the assembled officials and clergy.

"They died as they lived," prison chaplain Rev. Lester Hollander told the assembled reporters outside the prison. "As two garlic-eating, large-nosed, hairy-chested, parmesan-smelling dagos."

TRIAL SPEEDY

The two Southern Europeans had been charged with the 1920 murder of a paymaster and guard at a South Braintree, Massachusetts, shoe factory and subsequent escape with over $16,000 (50 trillion Italian lire) in payroll money. The trial was quick, with numerous pieces of evidence brought against the pair that immediately proved that they were, indeed, of Italian descent. Even a direct questioning of Sacco and Vanzetti produced irrefutable proof of their guilt. Prosecuting attorney Alvin Heitmann asked each of them on the witness stand, "Are you Italian?" Both answered, "Yes."

After their sentencing, the dago duo, displaying the flamboyant and irrational behavior characteristic of their nationality, immediately began a legal battle which dragged on for six years. This was due in large part to the strategy of lead defense attorney William Reynolds, who, while asserting his clients' innocence in the robbery and murder, conceded that they were, indeed, guilty of being members of a scheming, crime-ridden, destructive, swarthy, worthless race. The day before Governor Fuller's decision, Reynolds had also attempted to introduce new evidence to the Massachusetts Court of Appeals that the Morelli Gang, another group of slicked-back, oily wafer-eaters, was responsible for the crimes.

Sacco-Vanzetti Trial Called 'Trial of the Century'

BOSTON, Aug. 23.—The sensational 1921 trial of shoemaker Nicola Sacco and fish peddler Bartolomeo Vanzetti is now being called "the trial of the century" by experts in the study of law.

Never before—and likely never again—has so much public and newspaper attention been generated by a single court trial in America.

According to Harvard Law Professor Samuel P. Wolheim, "There will never again be a trial such as this where publishers of soft-covered books and nickel periodicals are scrambling to publish the peculiarities of the trial."

"There was something unique about this Sacco-Vanzetti trial," he said.

The trial was so special, the professor explained, that it merits being called the "trial of the century" from now until the year 2000.

"It is not likely that another trial will take place in this century that will generate so much popular interest," he said.

Young Maiden Seduced by Ukulele Music

(see story on page 9)

35

THE ONION

Tuesday, April 17, 1928 — Finest Source of News in America — Price Three Cents

CELEBRATING THE U.S. SESQUI-CENTENNIAL PLUS TWO YEARS!

Available On Credit

HEELS KICKED UP ACROSS NATION; PRESIDENT CALLS FOR CALM

Young Ladies Flap Long into the Night at Detroit's Kit-Kat-Klub

Frolicking, Cavorting Levels at 30-Year High

MILLIONS BUYING ON CREDIT

CHARLESTON-DANCING, JALOPY-RIDING ALL THE RAGE IN '28

WASHINGTON, D.C., Apr. 16.—The United States is currently in the midst of its greatest era of sustained prosperity since the Prancing '00s, and, as a result, heels are being kicked up across the land.

Among the evidence of heel-kicking: the rising popularity of marathon dancing; a 42 percent increase in the manufacture and consumption of outlawed liquor in 1927 alone, and a quadrupling in rouge-wearing and hair-bobbing since 1920. A dramatic rise in the number of college-age men who wear crew-neck athletic pullovers decorated with hand-lettered "slang" terms, such as "Oh, you, kid!" and "Go easy, Mabel!" is also being cited as proof of the overall rise in U.S. spirits.

RISE IN FRIVOLITY

The U.S. Statistical Bureau also reports a 30 percent increase in buoyancy levels among the public during the period of January 1927 to January 1928, measured by such indicators as baseball-game, vaudeville, and motion-picture attendance; buying on credit; and the number of family "joyrides" in spiffy new Stutz Bearcats.

"Gee, things sure are swell as can be," said Walter "Speedy" Miller of Philadelphia, Pa. "I just bought a Model A with $11 down. The rest went on credit."

GAY TIMES FOR THE YOUNG

Nowhere is this sense of gaiety and exuberance more evident than on our nation's college campuses. "Why, say, my pals and I barely have time to attend class, what with all the heel-kicking and co-ed-chasing and telephone-book-swallowing shenanigans we are constantly engaging in," said "Attaboy" Andy Freehley, a freshman at Notre Dame University. "Now, if you'll excuse me, I've got to don my raccoon-skin coat and head over to the campus sweet shop, enjoy a refreshing malted, and listen to the latest Bix Beiderbecke number on the radio while I spoon with this gal I'm just cuckoo about."

Freehley declined to add whether he would be lacing his malted with a few drops of bootleg brandy from his ill-concealed hip flask.

A SOBER CAUTION

For all the apparent affluence, President Coolidge warned that Americans should exercise some sobriety and restraint. "The United States is currently enjoying a period of prosperity," the president told an audience of dignitaries at the White House this weekend. "And, as a result, many are elevating their heels in a sustained skyward arc and generally having a grand time, flap-dancing and cavorting about in a gay and carefree manner. But it is important that we preserve an air of calm and reason. I would urge people to practice level-headed sobriety in their daily affairs."

When informed of Coolidge's remarks, Treasury Secretary Jerome "Skippy" Stimson dismissed the president as a "wet blanket."

"Aw, what does he know, the old buzzard?" Stimson asked. "Everything is peachy here in the good old U.S.A. And how!"

Economists Have High Hopes for 'Hoovernomics'

Republican Candidate Has Financial Plan for the '30s

(see story on page 8)

Author Ernest Hemingway Grits Teeth, Beds Nurse, Fights in War, Sits at Bar, Remembers Nurse

A collection of wartime documents, released Monday by the International Red Cross, discloses Ernest Hemingway's rugged humanity while simultaneously demonstrating the noble human struggle for love, hope, redemption, and self-discovery.

According to the papers, the famous writer and journalist gritted his teeth manfully, bedded a young Expeditionary Forces nurse, fought as a Red Cross ambulance driver in the Great War, sat in Harry's Bar in Paris, and reminisced about his sexual conquest of the nurse through a whisky-smoked lens of nostalgia and nameless sorrow for himself and all mankind.

The earliest document was dated August 1917 and described how Hemingway, realizing that the struggles of one man must mean something against the larger canvas of human history, but, not knowing exactly what, commenced to grit his teeth.

"It was the war, and Italy, of course, and the women, and the old men on the black bicycles, and the smell of fresh bread baking, and we were in the season of the yellow flowers and the little sweet grapes, but still it was the war," Hemingway later told reporters. "The war, and yet, Italy, and yet, when one is so young.... And you know, then, of the grind of tooth upon tooth. You do that and you hope that is all."

But by November 1917, Hemingway's awareness of the contrast of romantic Italian rustic life with the war's proximity soon led him to seek solace through sexual communion with a young Army nurse.

"And the drunken gondolier, with his knowing wink," admitted Hemingway later. "And the wine, the sharp Chianti in the bottle with the wicker, and the rustle of her skirt a half-promise on the brown autumn grasses of the Palazzo del Lothario, and her tiny moans, and the smell of her dark hair on the cool ivory pillow of the villa, and oh, the racing of my heart as I loved her in secrecy, and oh, oh how sweet it was, how sweet."

In January 1918, increasing troop activity and German encroachment in the nearby mountainous regions soon led to the activation of Hemingway's ambulance-driving detachment. He soon saw action that resulted in his wounding by over 200 pieces of shrapnel.

"It was there, there that I screamed and sobbed by the machine for the making of the coffee, as the shells fell down like nothing ever before since Lucifer fell from heaven, and they shattered, and burst, and it was my red blood I saw upon the dirt floor, and it burned coldly. And they ask me sometimes, and I say to them, yes, it did hurt," Hemingway wrote in an official Red Cross report. "But not much."

Hemingway's wounds were judged serious enough to excuse him from further service. He was discharged in April 1918, and made his way to Harry's in Paris, a place described by its patrons as dark and cool during the day and a good place to get a generous three fingers of brandy.

"It is the drunken gondolier, perhaps, that makes me wonder," the final document quotes Hemingway as he reflected upon his stay at Harry's. "It is good to be here in the cool with the guitar music and the brandy and the hard bread in little loaves. But there is fear even in one's memories. She is still a certain thing, a real thing, the woman. I know that. But the man who was there, I think, has been lost. It is the uncertainty, the sneer perhaps, or the disdain. It is the sigh, the sigh that is like the coming of death, and the ugly cackle of the drunken gondolier, I think, that I shall hear in my life's last sleepless hour."

GENTS!

Dial the following telephone number to listen to unmarried young ladies converse in a most suggestive and stimulating manner:

MA rlowe-3658

You will be billed a fixed per-minute rate for using this service.

Besting the Brickton Atlas-Trumpet	# THE ONION	More In-Depth Than Wireless Radio
Wednesday, September 12, 1928	Finest Source of News in America	Price Three Cents

CLARA BOW TO APPEAR SLEEVELESS IN OCTOBER COLLIER'S

HOLLYWOOD'S 'IT' GIRL SENDS DECENT FOLK INTO TIZZY WITH SHOCKING DISPLAY OF ARMS

'Besleeve Yourself, Strumpet!' Clergy Urge

From the Hollywood Correspondent, Sept. 11.—The famed "It" Girl of the moving pictures, Miss Clara Bow, has again sent our nation's moral leaders into the throes of deepest shock by consenting to appear sleeveless in next month's Collier's magazine.

Miss Bow is to be featured in the magazine dressed in a flimsy and close-fitting drop-waist frock, with her arms perfectly bare. "It is the most tasteless and licentious display by a screen-actress since Miss Mary Pickford exposed her collar-bone in last November's issue of Judge," said Father Joseph Scharchmidt of New York City's Our Holy Father Redeemer of Sins Church.

UNIQUE TRAITS OF BODY REVEALED

Sources inside the magazine reveal that in the Collier's photographs, Miss Bow's uncovered arms appear long and silky white, bent ever-so-slightly at the elbow and resting motionless on a chair back. A small brown mole is said to be detectable just above her left wrist line.

The antics of Miss Bow have provided much copy for newspapers and consternation for the clergy since she first came to prominence in the Hollywood photoplays. Besides kissing young gentlemen on the mouth, unescorted, in several of her film performances, she has behaved in a scandalous manner off-screen, as well. Last month she was seen piloting a bicycle down Hollywood Boulevard, keeping both of her unbound feet on the pedals instead of riding sidesaddle, as a proper lady would. And she recently lent her image and endorsement to Keeler's Sugared Fizz Milk, a product that could promote the decay of teeth.

CLERGY OUTRAGED

According to Father Scharchmidt, "The openly cavorterous behavior of Miss Bow may be taken lightly by the gossip papers and hellfire-bound motion-picture-goer, but the greater society recognizes it with great disgust as the most wanton strumpetry!"

FLIP WORDS FOR WRITERS

Will it only be a matter of time, clergymen like Scharchmidt wonder, before Miss Gloria Swanson is photographed in her barest feet?

The Onion made inquiries of Miss Bow regarding her latest immoral behavior as she exited her Beverly Hills home and boarded her Stutz Bearcat roadster. Does she plan to beg the Lord Our God and Saviour for His forgiveness and Divine

Clara Bow, in one of the scandalous photographs that will be featured in the magazine. Note bareness of shoulder.

grace? "Nuts to you," came her vulgar response. "Now listen, Jackson, I gots to amscray to Paramount, see? I'm making a picture about fly-boys in their aeroplanes, see, and I'm gonna kiss Buddy Rogers square on the lips, you get me? Toodles, scrivener."

It should be noted that during the conversation, the Onion correspondent detected the scent of the outlawed demon drink and Smith Brothers coughing-drops on Miss Bow's breath.

Instead of ruining Miss Bow's career, just as Mary Miles Minter was ruined after allegations that she enjoyed chewing gum were proved true, Miss Bow's immodest display appears to be catapulting her career forward, as offers to star in motion pictures continue to come her way despite public knowledge of the upcoming photographs.

Peace-Torn Germany Struggles With No War in Sight

GERMANS BEMOAN DECADE OF TRANQUILITY

TANKS, GUNS GATHER DUST IN PAINFUL ERA

ESSEN, Germany, Sept. 11.—The Krupp Arms Factory still stands, but its leviathan presses and dies sit in silence. Outdoors, children grow fat and slovenly on treats of unrationed sugar and butter. Further along the street, a man in a crisp army uniform paces aimlessly, seeming to await orders that are not forthcoming.

In Germany, this is just another day since swift, cruel armistice ended the nearly five years of war so relished by the German people. Not one hostile soldier has stormed the Fatherland in years; not one son has been struck down in the name of Deutschland. In the words of one pedestrian, "It does not even seem like Germany."

They're calling the period "Schlaglosschmerz."

The ravages of peace are inescapable these days, leaving Germans to attempt other activities to occupy their time. Some have even turned to hobbies to fill the stagnant void within their souls. Otto Dix has taken up painting to fill his silent hours but cannot find subject matter to depict other than the heroic days of the Great War.

"I was a high-ranking Oberstleutnant," said Karl Schmidt of Dresden. "Now, I am forced to work as a mere toymaker." But the presence of tin soldiers, miniature cannons, and pop-guns in Schmidt's workshop merely serve as painful reminders of unattainable past glories. "To see all these unused little playthings and trifles gathering dust when they could be melted down and forged into invincible armaments which could rend and burn enemy flesh hurts me like a wound," he said. "The bad, non-battle-casualty kind of wound."

"People say how bad it is that we lost the war," noted Professor Heinrich Frisch of Heidelberg University. "I say, at least we had a war. Today, our most urgent needs are to walk the dog, to buy bread. When will it end?"

Sensitive to the needs of its people, the Weimar government has attempted to make amends, but its efforts have proven largely ineffectual.

Whether light at the end of the tunnel can ever be seen is hard for Frisch to say. "It would be wonderful to negotiate a protracted, crippling war with another nation or just a temporary start-fire," he said. Overtures to European neighbors such as France and Poland have, however, proved fruitless.

If the peace continues, German baker Rolfe Pfaffenbach could live to be 47, an age no man in his family has ever reached.

"There could be generations of men in my family all alive at once," Pfaffenbach said. "Grandchildren meeting grandparents, none of them ever knowing war. It is a sad and frightful possibility."

Ford Auto Workers Given Own Wheels

Tires Replace Human Limbs in the Great Henry Ford's Latest Efficiency Experiment

A Ford worker is pictured here using his new 'wheel limbs' to produce the 1929 Model A

DETROIT, Mich., Sept. 11.—In what is being widely hailed as his greatest innovation since the Automated Wop, manufacturing genius Henry Ford unveiled his line of new, improved "wheeled workers" Tuesday.

The new workers whose legs have been sawed off just above the knee and fitted with special wheels to make their movements about the factory floor an estimated 40 percent more efficient, will be put to use in the auto giant's River Rouge factory beginning Nov. 17.

LEGS POORLY DESIGNED

"We felt that the conventional lower limbs of humans were poorly designed and prone to breakage," Ford said. "The ankles would frequently twist and break in machine parts, and the way the foot mechanism protruded, objects would often fall on it, causing severe damage that often incapacitated the worker unit, causing it to miss upwards of four hours of work. While God's original design for the auto worker was functional, I am confident that my revamped, wheeled worker will prove superior in every way."

With members of the press watching, Ford unveiled the model in Detroit, removing a sheet covering a prototype of a new wheeled worker, called "Thomas H. McKeough."

"Just look at this impressive unit," Ford said. "This very model used to complain of fatigue after standing on its feet for more than 16 hours at a time constructing engine parts. All that has changed with the removal of its feet. Now, it can go for nearly 36 hours, requiring a mere two-minute break to allow maintenance workers to refill its tires."

WHEELS EFFICIENT

According to Ford, more than 40,000 assembly-line workers will be outfitted with the new wheels. A team of surgeons will be on hand at the Ford factories all next week to remove the old, outmoded legs of worker units and refit them with sturdy new wheels, drilled into the workers' femurs with a six-inch bolt. The old legs will be donated to local orphanages or made into lamp bases.

"Here at Ford, we are always striving to develop new technologies that improve our efficiency and output," Ford said. "And we are by no means through with our worker-improvement efforts. Our product-development team is currently working on a steel heart which can pump blood 10 times faster than the conventional, tissue-based heart found in worker units today. We have conducted experiments implanting the mechanical hearts into workers, but their arteries have so far proven unable to handle the increased blood flow, causing their bodies to eventually give out and burst violently."

WILL INCREASE PRODUCTIVITY

Increasing demand for automobiles has for years spurred Ford to seek out ways of improving productivity. Since the company's introduction of the assembly line, it has continued to lead in the field of innovative production techniques, pioneering the use of the zero-break work day, fanless blast furnaces, and the 8-year-old lever-puller.

"We will do anything we can to improve the product the American consumer buys," Ford said. "If we have to remove the rib cage of every last Ford worker to provide the finest-quality car possible, then that is what we will do."

Why doesn't your home have a smokestack?

Sure, you've got an automobile and an agitating washing-tub, but why do you continue to live in a home which lacks a workable smokestack? Make your dream of turning your pig-iron-smelting hobby into a lucrative, full-time activity come true. Nothing conveys success like a 70-foot Payne concrete smokestack operating at full capacity in the backyard.

Now, we cannot give you one for free, because that would be Bolshevist. But owning a Payne Home Smokestack is now well within your reach, thanks to our easy new payment plan. With regular monthly installments, you could make back your investment in fewer than three generations. Yes, you read right! Drop by your local Payne Smokestack dealership for additional details or send for a free booklet.

Payne Home Smokestack Co., Gary, Indiana.

Today's Puzzler

by Professor Robert Hallowell of Columbia University

Q: What would happen if an automobile were to ever reach a speed of sixty miles per hour?

A: The driver of that automobile would die.

Cole Porter May Be Homosexual, Black, Clergymen Warn

(see story, page 8)

37

| Celebrating Affluence | THE ONION | 1929: YEAR OF THE NO-DEATHS PRINTING PRESS |

Tuesday, October 22, 1929 — Finest Source of News in America — Price Three Cents

Stock Market Invincible

'Buy, Buy, Buy!' Experts Advise

Wall Street, Spirits Soaring

U.S. Enjoying Embarrassment of Riches

Solid-Gold Plumbing Fixtures Best-Selling Consumer Product of 1929

Even Immigrants Enjoying Measure of Comfort

Citizens Urged to Put Everything They Have into Stock Market

NEW YORK, Oct. 21.—Leading economic indicators of the day, such as numbers of raccoon-skin coats in the process of being paid off on "easy credit" and the highly inflated value of major common stocks being over-sold on margin, point to one thing, say experts: prosperity for the U.S.A.

Average Americans are getting rich by buying stocks with money they don't even have. "I bought several shares of Westinghouse stock on margin and have a net worth of over $30,000," said New York City teacher Sid Grossman. "I'm going to retire on that money."

And stockbrokers are advising everyone to buy in big while the going is good.

"Everyone can partake of this soaring wealth," said Wall Street broker Robert Specht. "I would recommend that anyone put everything they have into the stock market. Borrow if you have to."

A group of Americans, here pictured looking like the cat's pajamas, are living the high life with no end in sight, if the stock market's bullish behavior is any indicator.

New 'Easy Credit' Delays Financial Catastrophes until 1930s

Citizens wishing to purchase a second new motorcar or attractive home smokestack can breathe and spend easily nowadays. Bankers now offer an increasingly popular system that removes the burden of fiscal responsibility from ourselves and defers it to ourselves but at a later date. Persons wishing to make a purchase but lacking the capital can, instead, use "easy credit" to pay at a later time, say, the 1930s, when the necessary monies will exist.

What shall become of the purchaser who still lacks the necessary funds at such time that the agreement matures? The creditor will be pleased to gain possession of the purchaser's land, horses, or children at his leisure.

Merchants say that every American citizen qualifies for credit. He need only demonstrate his good will to pay off the debt in a "reasonable time" and have an ability to withstand a potential whirlpool of human poverty and despair.

HOOVER PROMISES 'AIRPLANE IN EVERY GARAGE' BY 1935

WASHINGTON, D.C., Oct. 21.—Basking in the most prosperous period of our nation's history, President Hoover, in an address to the nation on wireless radio Monday, predicted that every American citizen will have his own airplane by 1935.

"Furthermore, I have submitted a proposal to Congress which would pave all our nation's streets with diamonds by 1938," the president said.

Hoover also detailed a plan to plant "money trees" in state parks across the land.

New Brain-Surgery Techniques Change Face of Modern Medicine

Opening Cranium with Saw, Not Hammer, a Bold Step Forward, Say Doctors

BALTIMORE, Md., Oct. 21.—Doctors at Johns Hopkins University Hospital announced a bold new breakthrough in the field of brain surgery Monday, unveiling an advanced new "saw" technique that will enable the brain to be operated on with greater precision than ever before.

"Until now, conventional wisdom held that the only way to get to the cerebrum and cerebellum was by smashing the outer layer of protective bone, or 'skull,' into tiny bits with a sledge hammer," said Dr. Galen Wheeler, lead physician at Johns Hopkins. "But this technique caused many problems. First, it was arduous, often requiring several dozen blows before enough skull was cleared away to perform the surgery. Second, in 99.7 percent of documented cases, the first blunt, forceful hammer blow to the head killed the patient. This new brain-opening technique, however, is clean and only kills 94 percent of patients."

Monday's announcement represents the most significant advance in brain surgery since 1904, when a team of top Naval physicians pioneered the washing of hands prior to surgery.

"With the saw, surgeons can operate with a precision undreamed of with a conventional hammer," Wheeler said. "And, once the brain is accessed, they can go right to work without having to first clear away thousands of skull fragments lodged in the brain, as they had to do when hammers were employed."

The saw is believed to be superior even to the ballpeen hammer, which offers greater control than the more commonly used hammers of the sledge variety.

SLIGHTLY LESS AGONY

Another advantage of the new saw technique is the fact that it is .0004 percent less painful than the old hammer method, enabling patients to undergo brain surgery without anaesthesia.

"Patients very much appear to be enjoying the saws," Dr. Raymond Llewellen of Johns Hopkins said. "You can barely hear their screams when standing several dozen blocks from the hospital. In fact, we have even considered using fewer bite-down sticks and slightly thinner leather restraining straps to constrain the patients' involuntarily flailing limbs."

Llewellen was among the first to employ the saw, using it last Friday to operate on a 44-year-old man suffering from a tumor. "What a marvelous advance for modern medicine," the doctor said. "In less than an hour, I had his head neatly cut in half and was able to begin pouring in the acid to kill the tumor."

AN ERA OF PROGRESS

The scientific breakthrough marks the latest in a string of notable medical advances to come along in the last decade. In February, doctors at Harvard University discovered that wounds can be sterilized by submerging patients for several minutes in a vat of boiling water, killing any germs or bacteria their bodies may contain. In April, a team of physicians at New York's St. Barnabas Hospital announced the development of an improved, amputee-stump covering which comes attractively shaped as either a metallic, multi-digit insect feeler or a sinister talon.

"In years to come," Llewellen predicted, "we will see hospitals in which many patients actually survive."

In the meantime, the saw revolution will offer thousands of patients suffering from brain tumors the solace of the serrated steel blade. According to Wheeler, "The saw is the medical instrument of our age."

Astoria, Queens, Couple's La Salle Runs Great
(see story, page 12)

Anthropomorphic Mouse in Short Pants Calls for Increased Litigation
(see story, page 12)

Nation Gears Up for Season Finale of 'Fleischmann's Yeast Radio Variety Hour'

NEW YORK, Oct. 21.—All of America will be huddled around their wireless-radios tonight for the thrilling season finale of "Fleischmann's Yeast Radio Variety Hour."

An audience of some eight million Americans is expected to tune in to the special 20-minute episode, one of three entertainment programs being offered in the nation this evening. Columbia Broadcasting director of programming George McDougal said the show will be packed with zingers, songs, and thrills, not to mention many exciting "cliff-hangings."

"Many big questions will be answered on tonight's thrilling season-ending episode of 'Fleischmann's Yeast Radio Variety Hour': Will Dad and Klondyke Clemens come to an agreement about the checkered suspenders? Will host Jack Randolph do his famous Samuel Gompers impersonation? Will the Fleischmann's Yeast Chorus Gals wow 'em with their 'When the Red Red Robin Comes Bob-Bob-Bobbin' Along' tap-dance number?" McDougal asked. "Listen to tonight's episode to find out."

A 'RATINGS' WINNER

With an audience so large as to be unprecedented and no other shows airing against it, "Fleischmann's Yeast Radio Variety Hour" is widely expected to be the most listened-to program in the 6:15-6:35 p.m. time slot. The show has finished first in the radio ratings 56 straight weeks and has finished second only once, on Sept. 21, 1928, when it was bested by "Dr. Klimpt's All-Purpose Balm & Ointment Comedic Variety Cavalcade." A record seven million people gathered around their radios that night for the conclusion to the famous "Who stole Shirley's skate key?" mystery.

Tonight's episode, Columbia spokesmen said, could break that mark. "There is an enormous amount of anticipation for this show," said Chester Sykes, head of Columbia's promotional department. "I've never seen anything like it in all my six years in radio. It's bigger than the inauguration speech."

"Look for Fleischmann's Yeast at your general store," Sykes added. "It's the one in the gray box."

POSSIBLE SURPRISES

Sykes would neither confirm nor deny a recent rumor that special celebrity guests would appear on the program. Among the names being circulated are such well-known personalities as vaudeville comedienne Fanny Brice, amusing negro Stepin Fetchit, cowboy moving-picture hero Tom Mix, and heartthrob megaphone crooner Rudy Vallee.

"Let's just say that there will be a little something for everyone on tonight's program," Sykes said. "From housewives to working men to young children, the 'Fleischmann's Yeast Radio Variety Hour' is a 'can't-miss' program for the entire family."

EXTRA! THE ONION **LATEST EDITION**

Tuesday, October 29, 1929 — Finest Source of News in America — Price Three Cents

Pencils for Sale

Lead Pencils of Finest Wooden Construction; Must Find Buyer Soon

The Onion will temporarily offer a special sale of good-quality pencils from its New York office. Sales must be made final by 5 o'clock p.m. on this day to meet the bank-deposit deadline.

The pencils are soft-leaded, encased in wood, painted yellow, and embossed with the name "The Onion" in black letters. They are being made available for a limited time for the low price of only one cent for five, or best offer.

According to Onion Managing Editor Lewis Stremke, "Now, in this time of great financial catastrophe, you may find that you need pencils more than ever: Great losses must be noted in ledgers; suicide notes must be written to loved ones."

LIMITED TIME

The Onion's limited offer of the sale of fine pencils is being offered today only, and all are urged to take full advantage of what Stremke is calling "the best-quality pencils being offered for the lowest price you've encountered in over ten years."

Mr. Potter to Pay Fifty Cents on the Dollar

BEDFORD FALLS, New York.—With the market calamity threatening financial stability all across the country, one man is "going all-out to help in this crisis." Mr. Potter, richest man in town, is offering to pay fifty cents on the dollar for shares in the Bailey Building and Loan.

The prominent capitalist has already guaranteed sufficient funds to the local bank, which will close for one week and then re-open. Potter, a minority shareholder in the Bailey Building and Loan, already controls the town's bus lines, department stores, and numerous other properties.

"I may lose a fortune," he said, "but I'm willing to guarantee the Bailey Building and Loan." He told shareholders that if they bring shares to him, he would pay fifty cents on the dollar.

Randall Thompson, a Bailey Building and Loan shareholder, confirmed that, yes, the payments would be in cash.

Stock Market Crashes; Debacle Linked to Jews, Negroes, Catholics, Anarchists, Foreigners, Women Voters

BLACK MONDAY

Stockbrokers and investors on Wall Street stand in shocked silence at the havoc wreaked by their shadowy enemies.

STREET-CORNER APPLE-VENDING CAREERS ON THE RISE

NEW YORK, Oct. 28.— Many able-bodied men seeking a career change have taken employment in the rapidly growing field of apple retailing. Some of the newest apple vendors have left jobs they have worked forty years, sometimes taking a 95 to 98 percent cut in pay, just to try their hand at corner fruit sales.

Although as many as ten apple vendors may be crowding their makeshift apple crates and chalk-drawn placards on a single street corner, the occupation is apparently still lucrative, as more vendors are expected to join their ranks in the coming months.

Robert Heffelstein, one of New York's leading apple vendors, previously worked as the head clerk at Peterson's International Shipping Company until the market crash forced a rash of sudden firings. "I'm in business for myself now, keeping track of three, maybe four dozen apples a week," he said.

In addition to his thriving apple-vending business, Heffelstein looks forward to pursuing a hobby of collecting pieces of discarded cloth in his spare time.

The apple vendors, in fierce competition for the business of passersby, exercise sign-making as the chief means of promotion. A few crude, hand-lettered posters advertise, "Apples—nickel or best offer," while some signs with elaborate calligraphy strokes proclaim, "Please Have the Christian Mercy to Buy an Apple."

"Pathos is an integral part of the apple-selling process," said former shoe-store owner Neil Kelly. "You use what you can—kids, mother, disease, military service. Whatever you can fit on that sign."

Those with the physical strength sometimes perform a song and dance in hopes of attracting business.

"You need to catch the eye of people who meet three criteria: They're hungry, they have five cents, and they aren't apple vendors themselves," Kelly said. "It's a three-part system that works."

Apple-market analysts expect the sale of apples to continue to rise. "These apples make up a fast-moving market, and, if you want to get in on the ground floor, you'd better move," said Herb Nelson, a former Wall Street broker. "I saw this apple thing start in July and then go through the roof in August. What can stop it? In December and January, there are going to be apples everywhere, I guarantee it."

THE HARLEM RENAISSANCE!

The most spectacular collection of Negro artists in American history

Music, Art, Literature, Everything Must Go!!

Available cheap—call now for rates WInchester-6854

MILLIONS THRUST INTO DESPERATE POVERTY

WALL STREET FAT CATS BLAMELESS, SAY FINANCIAL EXPERTS

NEW YORK, Oct. 28.— Although a formal inquiry has not yet been initiated, our nation's political and economic experts have revealed damning evidence tying Monday's collapse of the New York Stock Exchange to Jews, Negroes, Catholics, Anarchists, Foreigners, and Women Voters.

JEWS

J. Howard Ashcroft III, senior vice-chairman of Morgan Guaranty, unhesitatingly blamed the Jews. "All along, their bony fingers were tightening around the neck of our economy," he told The Onion. "Sadly, my firm had become complacent, and did not adequately monitor the progress of their Golem-like menace upon the financial health of the nation."

CATHOLICS

Independent Wall Street broker Whitney Van Blyden laid the blame on Rome. "This year has seen a record number of rosary-swinging, incense-huffing Vaticanites sully the ranks of the brokerage houses with their execrable superstition and claptrap," he said.

NEGROES

The astute insights of Ashcroft and Van Blyden are joined by the speculations of officials on the Federal Reserve Board, who suspect a Negro presence in the events of "Black Monday."

An unidentified Federal Reserve auditor confirmed that, prior to yesterday's opening bell, a number of Negro shoeshine boys on Wall Street used a substantially smaller portion of spittle and bootblack than usual. Many Stock Exchange traders corroborated the accusation, noting that Monday's scuff-to-sell ratio was at an all-time high.

"As though adding insult to injury," Wall Street businessman Thomas H. Maugham said, "besides losing millions, I discovered that my wing-tips were criss-crossed with unseemly scuff marks, as though the shoeshine boy had scarcely touched them this morning."

ANARCHISTS

Said J. John Blaine, Treasury Undersecretary: "Bakuninites created a barbarous panic on the floor. The noble and stately dignity of the Wall Street speculator is, sadly, no match for the godless evil of the anarchist."

FOREIGNERS

The widespread foreign presence in New York City was offered as evidence by Mayor Jimmy Walker. "Yesterday's great sell-off was sparked by the deplorable proximity of so many foreign agitators on our fair city's seedy Lower East Side, who are known to taint upstanding American institutions with corruption, vice, and intrigue," the Mayor said.

WOMEN VOTERS

Still others point to the recent addition of women to the American electorate as a prime factor behind the crash. "Since women were given the franchise, America has been stretching its purse-strings to the limit," the Reverend Phillip Manchester said. "Frugality and thrift have been cast to the wayside, as the power-maddened ladies leave the kitchen to buy on credit and gamble away their husbands' savings on risky stock ventures and dubious real-estate speculation, endeavors which should have stayed firmly in the domain of gentlemen."

GOV'T TO TAKE ACTION

In what would be a dramatic reversal of previous laissez-faire economic policy, it is rumored that the Hoover Administration may advocate legislation ensuring that all future share transactions are carried out with the complete exclusion of Jews, Catholics, Negroes, anarchists, foreigners, and women voters.

Of one point, all Wall Street investors seem certain: They themselves are blameless. "We are certainly not responsible for this crash," Ashcroft said. "We are men of reason."

1929-1946

DUST, DESPAIR AND DEATH: THOSE WERE THE DAYS

| Hoarding No Meat | # The Onion | Taking Your Own Life? See tips on page 18 |

Monday, October 19, 1931   Finest Source of News in America   Price Three Cents

RECENTLY OPENED EMPIRE STATE BUILDING 'GIANT-APE PROOF,' SAY ARCHITECTS

NEW YORK — In the hope of protecting the city's tallest building from potential siege by gigantic, rampaging apes, city-government authorities, working closely with the building's architects and designers, exceeded building-code standards to ensure that the Empire State Building is "giant-ape proof."

"The addition of special anti-climbing, non-stick aluminum sheeting on the building's streamlined, Art Deco-style facade should prevent any gorilla, no matter how large, from seeking refuge atop the grand skyscraper," project leader and former governor Alfred Smith told reporters. "In fact, the liberal use of highly potent banana extract near the building's base will restrict any such beast to the structure's first three floors, should such an incident ever occur."

Said Smith, "Despite all these precautions, should a particularly determined giant ape persist in scaling the building, the Municipal Emergency Giant-Ape-Control Air Squad will be deployed to buzz about the brute in aeroplanes and attack him with their mounted machine guns."

New York City Mayor Jimmy Walker urged citizens not to fear a giant-ape onslaught, as it remains highly unlikely.

"That this great structure would be ravaged by an immense, lovesick ape is, at best, a distant threat and should not discourage you or your loved ones from visiting the beautiful Empire State Building or patronizing its convenient souvenir gift shop," Walker said.

Banks to Close Early Today; Will Reopen in 1936

PHILADELPHIA, Pa., Oct. 16 — Bank managers across the nation met Friday to establish new standard business hours to help cope with the nation's new financial needs. The new hours, effective immediately at most major U.S. banks, will be Monday through Friday, closed; Saturday, closed. Sunday's closure for holyday observance will remain unchanged. The banks plan to return to their former hours in 1936, with notices of resumption to be delivered at that time.

"We apologize for any inconvenience our new hours might cause anyone, but we're certain that with a little time, everyone will be able to make the adjustment," said Pennsylvania Citizens Bank President Henry Frigger. "Thank you for your cooperation."

The new hours were posted on Citizens Bank's doors, along with a poster decorated with a fanciful cartoon bear in a top hat and tails, and the words, "'Bear' with us, customers!"

"We ask that everyone please be patient through our schedule adjustment," said smiling bank secretary Lillian Henson, as she pulled blinds to block the view of the crowds outside.

Other bank tellers and clerks hurried about Citizens Bank, putting dust covers over the furniture and office equipment, while some workmen in times dows and doors with nails, wooden planks, and steel caging.

Worried account-holders attempting to place telephone calls to the bank were greeted with a special automated message in lieu of an operator's voice. The message stated that, although their call was important to the Citizens Bank, switchboard operators were unable to take calls at that particular time. Immediately following the message was a recording of the popular tune "Yes, We Have No Bananas."

While many may be inconvenienced by the change in hours, Frigger said plenty of customers may still be able to withdraw money in times of need. "If your last name is the same as mine or my wife's before marriage, I may be able to make an appointment for you outside of our normal business hours. Such customers should come to the back door and slip a request through the keyhole," he said.

In the meantime, Frigger said the bank staff will be "doing a bit of remodeling, painting the front lobby, and going about locating approximately $900,000 in cash."

Al Capone's Reign of Tax-Evading Terror Finally Brought to End

Non-Paying Monster Will Prowl City's Loopholes No Longer

Chicagoans Relieved, as Feds Put Stop to 'Scarface' Al's String of Brutal Non-Filings

CHICAGO, Oct. 18. — Al Capone, whose tax evasion has held Chicago in a grip of terror for over a decade, was finally convicted of five counts of first-degree neglect to file Form 1040 in federal court today. The arrest ends a ruthless string of tax evading which has resulted in the loss of several hundred dollars in federal revenue.

Eliot Ness, the G-man responsible for arresting Capone, said this conviction sets an example for tax-evading hoodlums across the country.

"No longer will lawless non-taxpayers use their avoidance of auditors to terrorize citizens in the streets of Chicago or any city," Ness said.

"After all the lost lives, the ruined businesses, and the fear and terror felt by the public, we should give thanks to the investigative accountancy of federal auditors. Capone will pay the back taxes he owes."

"Court costs, too," Ness added.

Capone began his life of crime by avoiding filing exemption forms for self-employed freelancers who worked for him when he first set up business in Chicago several years ago. He then rose to the top of the Chicago tax-evading underground through a series of brutal non-filings. Before long, he controlled an enormous tax-evasion ring stretching across the entire city of Chicago.

Authorities suspect he had links to other tax-evasion syndicates as far away as Kansas City and New York.

Alphonse Capone pictured in Cook County Jail, no longer the leader of a city-wide tax-evasion ring that held Chicago in its grip for half a decade.

Wall Street Optimistic; Analysts Report 4000 Percent Rise in Suicide Rate

After nearly two years of nothing but plummeting figures for the foreign-exchange rate of the American dollar, the value of real estate and properties, and the average earning wage, Wall Street was relieved this week to see the statistics for suicide peak at forty times the average rate.

"For too long, we've had not even a glimmer of hope that things would turn around, but it's a comfort to know that at least one statistic is going up. Figures from deaths in Midtown Manhattan alone are flying into the sky!" said destitute stock-owner Alfred Longworth.

Since the statistic began its climb, Wall Street brokers have regularly huddled around the papers, clamoring for a look at the latest suicide statistics as released daily by the New York City Police Department. "Up, up, higher, higher!" they chant in unison.

"This long-awaited upswing is proof that America has emerged from her long recession and come out stronger than ever," President Hoover said in a special statement on the bullish figures. "My faith in American recovery is further bolstered.

"We must work together to keep these figures climbing," he added.

"This ray of hope couldn't have come at a better time," said newly widowed New Yorker Maria Howard. "When my husband shot himself, I thought all hope was lost, but then I saw these rising figures. The Lord truly doth provide."

One man, 34-year-old street sweeper Charles Neitzel, is particularly thankful. "Yesterday, I feared for my future like everyone else in the country. Today, I am living the American dream, working on Wall Street," he said, scooping several yards of a prominent broker's steaming small intestine into his cart.

In fact, Neitzel finds an added benefit to sweeping up the crushed, barely recognizable remains of other human beings.

"I've found plenty of trousers and other clothing items in perfectly good condition as part of my regular job," he said.

AUTHOR SINCLAIR LEWIS DECLINES NOBEL PRIZE, ACCEPTS CASE OF BOOTLEG SCOTCH

NEW YORK, Oct. 18. — Noted writer Sinclair Lewis announced Thursday that he is declining this year's Nobel Prize for literature and will accept, in lieu of the coveted award, a case of bootleg Scotch.

Lewis, known for his satires of small-town Midwestern life, spoke to reporters from the Chelsea Hotel, where he is currently working on a case of plum wine.

"The vast economic depression laying waste to our country and the general atmosphere of hopelessness which pervades every aspect of American life make me believe it wholly inappropriate to accept this honor for either myself or my nation," Lewis said.

"Also, the vast economic depression laying waste to our country and the general atmosphere of hopelessness which pervades every aspect of American life make me believe the only appropriate response is to become drunk."

Five years ago, Lewis declined the Pulitzer Prize for his novel "Arrowsmith," opting instead for a case of bathtub gin.

ENTERTAINMENT

WILL ROGERS MEETS A MAN HE LIKES A LITTLE TOO MUCH
(See page 8)

GANGLAND KINGPIN: 'SAY, DON'T GET SORE, SEE?'
(See page 8)

UNSINGABLE SONG OF EXPLOSIONS AND DEFEAT BECOMES NEW NATIONAL ANTHEM
(See page 4)

Inside:

A special cut-out full-color lithograph of Wallace Beery!

THE ONION

Featuring Death Announcements

Also Featuring Birth-Related Death Announcements

Thursday, February 4, 1932 — Finest Source of News in America — Price Three Cents

BUSINESS NEWS
APPLE SOLD
Shiny Nickel Put into Circulation

Apple Vendor Samuel Cropper, the prime mover behind the deal.

BALTIMORE, Md., Feb. 3. — In a transaction closely watched by leading economic experts and Wall Street financiers, an apple was sold today by Baltimore-area fruit vendor Samuel Cropper to Franklin Gehry, a Landover, Md., shoe-shiner.

The apple, described in a Wednesday Wall Street Journal report as a "ripe, juicy McIntosh," was acquired by Mr. Gehry for a reported sum of five cents.

The deal was finalized at approximately 3 p.m., when a hungry Gehry spotted Cropper on the corner of 17th Street and Adams in downtown Baltimore with a bucket of apples. Gehry selected the best of the lot, gave Cropper a 1928 nickel, and walked off.

A rumor that Gehry turned down an offer of three apples for eight cents could not be confirmed by press time.

News of the deal spread quickly through Wall Street and other corridors of high finance across the nation. "This is an extremely positive step toward ending this Great Depression," said Francis Clayton, a University of Chicago economics professor. "To have a shiny new nickel put into circulation should greatly help stimulate spending and overall economic growth in the U.S."

Added Clayton: "It should also be noted that the transaction is a boon for Mr. Gehry, as well, as he acquired for himself a very tasty apple."

Wednesday's transaction is widely believed to be the richest since May 24, 1931, when a Lubbock, Tex., man acquired a can of potted meat for the near-record sum of ten cents.

White House spokesman George Pickens said President Hoover has been apprised of the apple sale by his top advisors.

"Mr. Hoover was greatly cheered by the news of this major deal and has expressed confidence that this is the start of a great economic turnaround for the United States," Pickens said. "As the president has said, 'Prosperity is just around the corner!'"

With the apple sale, total U.S. consumer spending for the month has reached the $19 mark for the first time since May 1930.

Hoover Hopes to Restore Faith in Nation's Banks with Free-Toaster Offer

Bread-Toasting Device to Ease Economic Hardship

'Open an Account Today, Have Toast Tomorrow,' Says President

Bread Not Included

After months of criticism from political rivals for his inaction during the great economic crisis which grips our nation, President Hoover introduced a bold initiative Wednesday, urging banks to offer a free toaster and up to five other "premium" gift items to customers who face the loss of their life savings.

"I will work closely with the nation's banks to make the dispensation of these premium gifts, including the new Toastmaster Model 1-C-1 bread-toaster, a priority on our nation's road to recovery," Hoover said in a meeting with the nation's leading banking officials this week.

"The American people are facing hard times," the president said. "Nearly one in four is out of work. Countless families have been made penniless by the collapse of banks and the nation's financial infrastructure. What better way to renew our citizens' faith in our banking system than with the free gift of an attractive, cast-aluminum, three-slice toaster?"

Hoover offered a detailed relief plan to American banks rendered inoperable by the onslaught of panicked customers hurriedly withdrawing their life savings.

"In addition to my generous Toaster Premium Initiative, I propose a free drinking-cup offer," he said.

"A top-quality drinking cup made of clear, blown glass would be offered to placate those customers who may be afraid of losing everything they own," the president said. "The cups will be donated by a local glass-blowing company, which would surely be happy to introduce its quality wares to banking-industry customers."

Hoover further proposed each cup be emblazoned with the name of the bank upon its side.

The president said the offer of the free cup would pacify the customer, making him more likely to trust the bank with his money. Hoover promised that customers would deposit their money, then exit the bank holding the cup, staring at it admiringly.

"These free cups will single-handedly restore our nation's financial future," the president assured the bankers.

The details of Hoover's Free Toaster Premium Initiative call for a free toaster for any bank customer who loses up to $2,000 in a checking account, or $5,000 in a savings account. Under the plan, if a bank fails and a customer loses his life savings, the customer or his surviving family members are eligible for a free ball-point pen. For the loss of a child due to starvation, banks will offer a free casserole dish. For homelessness, a set of coasters. For joblessness and descent into a life of petty crime, a sticker.

Earlier this year, Hoover vetoed a bill that would have granted destitute bank customers a free gymnasium duffel bag, intended for the storage of athletic garments and articles. Hoover had said the bill did not go far enough.

President Hoover

Brother Unable to Spare Dime

HARTFORD, Conn., Feb. 3. — According to a report released to the press, Timothy Lawson, 39, a Hartford-area pedestrian, was unable to spare a dime on the corner of South Orchard and 8th Streets Wednesday.

Charles Kriefski, an out-of-work Hartford resident, said in the report that he looked at Lawson and made a polite request for a dime at approximately 4:15 p.m., yet no dime exchanged hands at any point during the interaction.

Lawson reportedly walked past Kriefski and shook his head quickly without looking up. According to Kriefski, such a motion is an indication that "a dime cannot be spared."

When asked about the incident, Lawson walked past and shook his head quickly without looking up.

According to the report, Kriefski's addressing of Lawson as "brother," an effort to build an instant rapport via their shared humanity, was ineffective, as Lawson was not lured into a temporary and superficially familiar relationship with Kriefski that could have resulted in the exchange of a dime.

Kriefski stated that he plans to continue requesting dimes of others.

'My Son Will Fly Higher and Farther than Me,' Says Proud New Dad Charles Lindbergh
See page 7, col. 6

UPCOMING SIT-DOWN STRIKES
* * * * * *
Listed by The Onion as a Service to Company Owners' Private Corporate Security Forces
* * * * * *
SHOE-OLA SHOE-POLISH FACTORY, BLOOMINGTON, INDIANA
FEBRUARY 9

RED EAGLE BALL-BEARINGS CO., DULUTH, MINNESOTA
FEBRUARY 12

NATIONAL TETRAHEDRON, NEW YORK
FEBRUARY 16

OUR GANG PROBLEM
Roving Band of Little Rascals Terrorizes Streets

Suspected gang member "Spanky" McFarland

CULVER CITY, Calif., Feb. 3. — Already buffeted by economic hard times, this small town is experiencing one of the biggest crime waves in its history. Officers of the peace suspect that a single gang is responsible for the great majority of criminal activity.

The gang, made up of seemingly harmless rascals no older than eight years of age, has been linked to such crimes as assault, obstruction of justice, truancy, and pie theft.

Although the gang's membership has reportedly varied over the years, it is believed to be made up of a fat youth, a Negro youth, a squeaky-voiced crooner with a prominent cowlick, and a cute little girl. The gang is often aided and abetted by animals, including a dog with a ring around his left eye, a capuchin monkey, and a mule named Algebra.

HIJINKS
The gang has been suspected in a string of area crimes, including refusal to take castor oil, bringing frogs to school, organizing amateur variety shows without a municipal permit, and hurling bowls of mush at a snobbish French maitre d'.

The gang members often play hooky to go fishing but, when they do attend their lessons, they carry on their hijinks in the classroom, as well.

In their fight against the gang, authorities in Culver City have enlisted the help of Miss Crabtree, 27, the schoolteacher of many of the gang members. Crabtree was chosen for her intimate knowledge of the gang's activity patterns and known whereabouts.

"Just today in class, I asked one of these rascals, 'What was Abraham Lincoln's mother's name?'" Crabtree said. "And he replied, 'Mrs. Lincoln.'"

To counter the gang threat, police are moving back the town curfew to 7 p.m.

'APPLESAUCE'
When told of the allegations, suspected gang member "Spanky" McFarland dismissed them as "applesauce."

43

THE ONION

Publishing Since 1756 — *Doing What Little We Can for All You Peasants*

Friday, May 13, 1932 — Finest Source of News in America — Price Three Cents

Cute Little Mouse Crushed to Death by Petting

More Bad News for the Nation

Congress, Seeking Assurance, Urges President to 'Tell Us About the Rabbits'

WASHINGTON, D.C., May 12. — Already weighed down by the bad news of the times, the American people received the tragic bulletin via radio today that they had inadvertently crushed a soft mouse in a sad show of simple, childlike affection, too clumsy and brutish for the tiny animal to withstand.

"We didn't kill it. We found it dead," said a defensive out-of-work New York canner, one of millions of U.S. citizens who took comfort from the mouse.

"The American people would never have knowingly crushed their mouse," Pastor Herman Jameson of Boston said. "We loved that mouse. It was very soft and good for petting. We held it close to our collective bosom for comfort even after it had been crushed by our tenderspirited yet physically overpowering strokes."

The mouse, a gift from Aunt Clara, was crushed as many as four days ago but had been held in secret from national authorities for fear it might be taken away. Federal officials confiscated the mouse Thursday morning and informed the president. Hoover stressed the importance of not petting the mouse's head so hard that it breaks.

"The collective might of our millions of citizens was too great for the little mouse's delicate body to bear," Hoover said.

"Give me that mouse," he added, then threw it over by the swamp.

A coalition of citizens is drafting a petition to Hoover requesting that they be given a new mouse to stroke, which they believe is necessary to alleviate the sorrow of life in these troubled times. Perhaps, a spokesman for the coalition said, they could even be given a rabbit.

A BAD THING

Looking for assurance from the president, a joint session of Congress was convened Friday to ask Hoover, on behalf of the nation's citizens, to "tell us about the rabbits." The motion was approved overwhelmingly.

One dissenter, James Hamilton Lewis (D-Ill.), said, "We have forfeited our right to be told about the rabbits, after the tragedy which has befallen this mouse. It may be that we will neither be told of rabbits, nor permitted to tend to rabbits at any future time. Because if we cannot even look after a mouse, how can we be expected to care for rabbits?"

"Perhaps we should leave the president," he added. "He would be better off without us, since we are always doing bad things."

THE RABBITS

But Hoover soothed the nation as he began speaking through the radios of the land: "We are going to have our own place," he said. "We are going to live off the fat of the land. We'll maybe have a pig, and chickens. And a cow. And there will also be rabbits."

The nation listened closely as their president went on. "We'll have a little patch of alfalfa, which we will feed to the rabbits. We won't even have to work if we don't want to, because it will be our own place."

The American public responded by pledging that it would tend to the rabbits with great care. The public then went to sleep.

Inside:

General MacArthur Decimates Bonus Army; Claims East Beltway for U.S.
(See story, page 2)

Depressed German Economy Results in Cheap, Three-Penny Opera
(See story, page 9)

Labor Pool Has Never Been Larger Or Cheaper, Say Millionaires

Half-Starved Masses More Eager to Work than Ever

Tycoons Amused, Encouraged by Desperate Plight of American Laborer

TOLEDO, Ohio, May 12. — With citizens in need of steady work now the fastest-growing segment of the U.S. population, no one is happier than the nation's tycoons and captains of industry. "I enjoy the luxury of picking and choosing my employees on the barest whim," said Gavin Dunn, owner of Dunn's Tool & Die in Toledo. "Last month, I sacked a worker for being two minutes late. There were 40 hopefuls in the lobby waiting to replace him. All my employees now arrive at work a half hour early, dressed in their Sunday best, and bow to the waist when a supervisor walks past.

"Things couldn't be better in America," Dunn said.

"Also," he added, "when given equally qualified candidates for a job, I can either pick the one whose tie I like most or engage the candidates in a wage-bidding war. I have a hauler who earns four cents a month. I thank Heaven daily for this desperate nationwide poverty and hope it continues for a long time."

Concurring is millionaire Ambrose Wortman. "It is increasingly easy to get household help. It was once difficult to prevent the turnover of maids and manservants at the wage of 14 cents per week, but now the help is eager to perform without complaint the most servile of duties, from beard-cleaning to brow-wiping to massaging of any sort."

But perhaps most grateful of all for America's teeming, obsequious sea of servitude is Phillip Waverly, a Pittsburgh coal executive. "A mine fire used to be a inconvenient setback to business. But with the tent village of unemployed hopefuls outside the mine, work was delayed only an hour when our last fire killed 107 miners."

A telling example of Waverly's good fortune is that, when a serious fissure is discovered which could result in a cave-in, his foremen can order thousands upon thousands of workers to fill the fissure with their bodies, making the mining safer for the fellow workers. Even when workers understand that fissure-diving means certain death, the most desperate gladly accept the fate, provided a modest stipend is promised to their hungry families.

As Waverly noted, "Truly, the miracle of our times is the massive reservoir of manpower at the disposal of myself and another dozen or so Americans."

A coalition of industrialists such as Dunn and Waverly will soon convene in New York to discuss the construction of a human pipeline through which able-bodied workers could be pumped to wherever the need is greatest. "This twenty-foot-wide pipe will carry workers, under the power of their own pressure, from New York to Chicago in under an hour, where their supervisors will retrieve them from a mammoth spigot and eagerly assign them to tasks."

President Hoover Signs Accord with King of Hobos

HOOVERVILLE, May 12. — In a move calculated to bring lasting peace between the U.S. Government and the Hobo Kingdom, President Hoover signed a peace treaty with King Gus II, sovereign of all hobos.

Making the trip to the Hobo Kingdom by freight car, Hoover was offered specially designed presidential seating, which was created using an over-turned crate.

Upon arriving at the King's barrel, the president was greeted by the monarch in a special hand-warming ceremony.

Notable persons in attendance at the treaty signing were the Duke and Duchess of Junkland, Emperor Lazlo of Trashville, and the ambassador to the Big Rock Candy Mountain.

Under the terms of the accord, the Hobo Kingdom agreed to keep the noise down, and the U.S. pledged to open stick, used-handkerchief, and discarded-shoe trade. The U.S. will also lower tariffs on scrap metal.

Upon signing the historic accord, the dignitaries attended a gala baked-bean dinner.

Lindbergh Baby Found Dead

Police Vow to Convict Non-English-Speaking Immigrant 'At Any Cost'

Onlookers hoping to spot a foreigner at the site where the 20-month-old child was discovered dead.

'When We Find Someone Appropriately Suspicious-Looking, He Will Pay Dearly,' Say Police

Citizens Urged to Report Known Foreigners to Authorities

Several Good Candidates Forthcoming

TRENTON, N.J., May 11. — Charles Lindbergh II, the 20-month-old scion of American hero Charles Lindbergh, was found dead in a local cemetery last night, two weeks after being kidnapped from the Lindbergh mansion in Hopewell.

A spokesman for the New Jersey State Police said they are no closer to apprehending a poor, non-English-speaking immigrant than at any time in the preceding weeks.

Investigators, however, are still following a few tenuous leads. Thousands of local police and state troopers have been placed on round-the-clock guard over state highways and boundaries, stopping all suspicious Italian-, Oriental-, Jewish-, or Greek-looking travelers for questioning.

"We have precious little evidence," Trenton police commissioner Harold Moore said to the press, "but what we have should aid us in arresting and convicting the first non-native person of suspicious demeanor we can find. The blue-eyed, red-blooded American baby obviously died of neglect, and, as everyone knows, foreigners have very little regard for human life."

The unseen person who collected the Lindbergh ransom money in the churchyard was described as having a vaguely Germano-Italo-Russo-Chinee accent. And Lindbergh himself told police he has a strong hunch that the perpetrator was not a U.S. citizen.

"When the kidnappers took our boy, our main objective was to get him back," a visibly shaken Lindbergh told reporters this morning. "But now that he's been found, our only objective is to find a monstrous non-American and prosecute him to the full extent of the law."

Citizens who notice any foreigner are urged, as always, to report his whereabouts to local authorities.

Betty Boop Sexually Harassed by Anthropomorphic Tree
(See story, page 5)

Yet Another Dozen Million Die
(See story, page 5)

| A Flickering Flame of Hope | # THE ONION | Likely Still in Business |

Friday, August 19, 1932 — Finest Source of News in America — Price Three Cents

CRUST OF BREAD FOUND

NATION THRILLED BY DISCOVERY OF YEASTY MORSEL

Found Under Wheelbarrow in New York City

Precious Scrap Rumored to Contain Four Rye Seeds; Thousands Line up to Feast

'Good Times Are Here Once More!' Says President Hoover

NEW YORK, Aug. 18. — In what has come as the most exciting news to greet the American people in some time, a scrap of bread was discovered yesterday on New York's Lower East Side.

The mouth-watering morsel, described as nearly a full one-fifth of a slice of rye bread, was discovered by Elmer Hankins, a Manhattan lint-ball vendor, under a wheelbarrow near 14th Street.

A PROVIDENTIAL DISCOVERY

Said Mr. Hankins: "At first, I thought it was merely a rotten apple core. But when I got closer, it was apparent that this was a fine scrap of bread, relatively dry and containing no more than 15 mold spots. I can scarcely imagine how such an edible piece of food could sit under a wheelbarrow for God knows how long and not be noticed and quickly devoured by man, dog, or rat."

HUNGRY CROWD ATTRACTED

Within moments, a great, teeming crowd formed around Mr. Hankins to view the discovery. With the agitated throngs threatening to riot out of eagerness for a taste of the precious scrap, city policemen were forced to move in and seize the bread. It was then forwarded to Hoover Administration officials in Washington for distribution to the nation's most needy.

WILL FEED HUNDREDS

U.S. Secretary of State Henry Stimson said he expects the bread morsel to feed a great many people. "Our best scientists here in Washington have studied the scrap and, after careful examination, have informed us that it comprises some 1,459 individual grains of bread," Stimson said. "If each of these grains is shared by 10 people, we will be able to feed nearly 15,000 Americans. This truly is a great day."

The discovery is causing great commotion throughout the nation, as millions of hungry and unemployed citizens hope to receive a portion of a grain of the delicious bread.

"Now, that is a feast to dream about," said Enid, Okla., dirt salesman Russell Boone, among the nation's countless aspiring scrap-eaters. "A grain of bread like that would be just about the best meal I've had since July 1930, when my wife cooked up a batch of her special grass pie."

"I've got a cup of rainwater I've been saving up for over a year now that would go real perfect with a piece of that bread," said Mary Edna Gunne of Midland, Texas. "If I could get a piece of that bread, I think I'd just about drink my whole cup of rainwater."

PUBLIC FERVOR

In tribute to the celebrated bread scrap, famed songwriter E.Y. "Yip" Harburg composed a song, "Say, Now How Do You Like a Bread Scrap Like That, My Sweet Adelaide!" It will be released to phonograph shops across America next Tuesday and is widely expected to become the most celebrated phonograph recording in history, outranking even Rudy Vallee's "Oh, How I'd Love to Be Consuming Dried Corn Husks With My Sweetie Suzie Down on the Winding Wabash."

In light of the nationwide interest in the bread scrap, President Hoover will make a special address via radio tonight to outline its distribution.

Inside:

Hoover's 'Are You Better Off Now Than You Were Four Years Ago?' Campaign Fails to Gain Momentum
(See story, page 3)

Hired Goons America's Fastest-Growing Work Force
(See story, page 6)

Privileged members of the plutocracy, shown here dining in opulent splendor.

Evil, Bloated Plutocrats Losing Favor with Some Americans

Some Workers Losing Faith in Good Will of Oppressors

Long-Renowned Steel Magnates, Railroad Tycoons Puzzled by Waning Popularity

As the current Depression worsens, a curious new phenomenon is arising: The nation's evil, bloated plutocrats—for years regarded as proud emblems of American commerce and revered as the living embodiment of our way of life—are beginning to lose favor among some members of the working class.

"I do not know why, but I no longer feel the same kind of overwhelming affection and admiration for Andrew Carnegie that I once did," said Timothy Dugan of Erie, Penn., who worked for 19 years in a steel factory before being blinded last April in a smelting-cauldron explosion. "I still hold him in high esteem, but, of late, my feelings about him are strangely mixed."

What is causing common laborers like Dugan to no longer idolize America's titans of industry with full fervor? What has dimmed their love for the all-powerful multi-millionaires who control their lives? Some observers believe that these disgruntled Americans may be becoming somewhat resentful of the vast economic, social, and political gap that exists between themselves and the nation's industrial overlords.

"For decades, America's evil, bloated plutocrats have been the most celebrated members of our society. The working class has long adored the rich, marveling at the great sway they hold over them," Harvard University sociologist E. Dean Terwilliger said. "But we are fast approaching a day when this is no longer true. I hear grumblings among the common people that they should not be so enamored of the wealthy and powerful. Some of these working people are wondering if there may be some connection between their own dire poverty and the vast wealth of the handful of monopolistic business owners in the U.S."

The nation's evil, bloated plutocrats are reacting with a combination of wrath and indignation to their lessening popularity. "How dare these workers reconsider their idolization of us?" said John D. Rockefeller, addressing reporters from atop a 600-foot pile of gold coins. "Do they not realize that, without us, there would be no one to exploit them? We must make these common laborers pay severely for their ingratitude."

Rockefeller said he plans to call a National Conference of Bloated Plutocrats to discuss ways in which workers' lives can be made worse. He said he also hopes to develop a long-term plan for consolidating a greater percentage of the nation's wealth into the hands of even fewer men.

Indians Once Again in the Way of Good Land

Indians throughout the Southwest are again defending their water rights and land titles, just when recent discoveries of additional oil and metallurgical deposits have been made on or near their territories.

As a result, Indians once again stand in the way of good land, a problem many Americans believe had been solved satisfactorily in the last century.

Thousands of acres of Western land, previously considered barren and void of any intrinsic value except as a homeland for Indians, would have been opened in the name of progress and impartiality. Instead, Southwestern state legislatures are being petitioned by several Indian tribes, who have drafted a resounding objection to any further intervention on the land they occupy.

"We should have never given the Red Indian the chance to fight in the Great War," complained Nevada mine owner William Holsum. "Look how he thanks us."

The Indians argue that they have already sold off or ceded vast amounts of their landholdings to the government. But, in fact, 70 million acres of the 155 million acres Indians possessed in 1880 still remain in the hands of native peoples who stand staunchly opposed to oil leases, strip mining, and grazing expansion.

"The Indians claim that we will never stop in our pursuit of their lands, but this is false. I can assure them that we have no interest whatsoever in reclaiming their lands in the desert regions, impassable mountain highlands, or mosquito-ridden swamps, unless, of course, oil or gold is discovered there," said Washington oil lobbyist Henry Stanford.

Today's Bible Verse:
Provided by this newspaper as an inspiration to its readers.

"And the locusts went up over all the land of Egypt, and rested in all the coasts of Egypt. Very grievous were they; before them there were no such locusts as they, neither after them shall be such

For they covered the face of the whole earth, so that the land was darkened; and they did eat every herb of the land, and all the fruit of the trees which the hail had left, and there remained not any green thing in the trees, or in the herbs of the field, through all the land of Egypt."

EXODUS 10:14, 15

THE ONION

Your Source for Bleak News

Weather: Pennies are not expected to rain from Heaven today.

Sunday, March 5, 1933 — Finest Source of News in America — Sunday Edition — Price Seven Cents

---

FROM WHERE I SEE IT
by T. Herman Zweibel

I Have Acquired An Orphan Girl

I hear that folks are taking to calling this current period of our history The Great Depressment, to describe the alleged economic woes our Republic is undergoing, but I myself have experienced nothing of the sort. The Onion news-paper empire is booming, and I'm richer and fatter than ever! In the past two years, we've watched our competitors in city after city fold, which means, of course, more advertising and subscription revenue for us. If this keeps up, soon we'll be the only news-paper of record in the Republic! Huzzah!

But my wife, perennial sob-sister that she is, has expressed concern about those who are out-of-work or have otherwise fallen prey to unfortunate circumstances resulting from the economic down-turn. Last week, Mrs. Zweibel burst into my study without permission, and knelt before me in tearful supplication. "Papa," she wailed, "please, please, let's take in an unfortunate waif who has been orphaned in this cruel and mean time of ours. We who are blessed with wealth and privilege have an obligation to do so. All the ladies of society are doing it: Mrs. Van der Veer, Mrs. Windemere-Snow, even Mrs. Castlereagh. Please, I beg of you, it is so little to ask."

In spite of the annoying presence of my wife, I felt her idea had merit. After some thought, I gave my consent, and, before we knew it, little orphan Maggie had been procured from the county orphanage and immediately put to work in the scullery.

It wasn't long before Maggie started getting on my nerves. True, all of the servants, save my faithful man-servant Standish, are under strict orders never to be in my presence, but somehow this fiery-haired little urchin manages to be quite the thorn in my side. Maggie's always getting lost or running away, often for weeks at a time. Just last week, she fell asleep in the laundry-room and was accidentally delivered to a Chinee laundry in the village. As she was making her escape, she was shanghaied and spirited aboard a pirate junk to Hong-Kong, where she was then sold to a tea-house proprietor. The work was harsh, but the resourceful girl managed to learn much of the language and befriended the mysterious Indian vizier Mr. Aa, who took pity on her and entertained her with sweet-meats and cryptic philosophical adages.

Then one day at the tea-house, she overheard a plot to overthrow the British authority and install a pirate overlord. She alerted the British governor to the coup, and, with the assistance of the imperial forces and Mr. Aa's magic, managed to quell it. As reward, she gained her freedom and sailed back to the States, where I eventually collected her at the village police-station. She's always pulling non-sense like that.

And when she is home, she's forever spouting the most naive, irritating homilies you've ever heard. "The sum of your achievements is directly proportional to the amount of work you do." "Wits are worth a thousand times more than any fancy book-smarts." "Tomorrow brings hope." Will that little ninny never shut up? I'm already successful; what do I care what she has to say? If I wanted a sermon, I'd go to church.

When I'm not being blinded by Maggie's flaming-red hair, or frightened by her milky-white pupils (she must have cataracts), her mangy mutt, from whom she is virtually inseparable, tries to bite off chunks of my posterior. I must have Standish put a bullet through his furry head one night in the court-yard.

And worst of all, she insists on calling me "Daddy!" I refuse to be the "Daddy" of the low-born off-spring of some diseased chippie. Besides, children are to be bound upside-down in cages, and not heard!

I'll be damned if some mouthy little waif gets the best of T. Herman Zweibel. It's back to the county orphanage for little Maggie!

Former President Coolidge Dies in Soup-Kitchen Fight Over Scrap of Chicken
(See story, page 3)

New President Assures Nation, 'The Only Thing We Have to Fear Is a Crippling, Decade-Long Depression'

'All Is Lost,' Says 32nd President in Address to Nation

America Doomed

WASHINGTON, D.C., Mar. 4. — In his inaugural address Saturday, President Franklin D. Roosevelt told citizens of the United States that the only thing they have to fear is "a crippling, decade-long depression."

Roosevelt urged all Americans to tremble and despair, as many years of severe economic hardship and extreme misery await nearly every U.S. citizen. "And there is nothing anyone can do about it," he said, "especially not the federal government."

"There will be make-work programs and goodwill gestures, but they will not be your salvation. Neither I nor your legislative leaders will make your life better. You are in for a lot of rough times, and, as your newly elected president, I want to tell you that you are in it alone."

Throughout his address, Roosevelt stressed that there was nothing he could say to instill even a false sense of hope, and that Americans would be best served by forgetting about ever enjoying a prosperous future.

Said Roosevelt: "Be afraid. For you have very good reason. Banks are closing. Unemployment is at an all-time high and climbing every day. Stocks once worth hundreds of dollars are now worth pennies. Millions of you have lost your life savings in financial institutions you thought were secure but are not."

Roosevelt later told reporters that one of his first acts as president will be to oversee the passage of the Jump Off the Nearest Tall Building Act of 1933, which would help over 50 million unemployed Americans escape the misery of their financial ruin by plunging to their deaths from rooftops.

"No longer must suicide be the exclusive sport of ruined stockbrokers," Roosevelt said. "Now every American will soon be able to do it. My administration's program will not only put people out of their misery; it will help reduce the monthly food budget of those people's families. It will also cut down the number of workers, thereby broadening job opportunities for surviving citizens."

President Roosevelt

CAPITALIST PLUTOCRAT BASTARD — "I've raped everything else in sight, why not you, too, sister?"

President Franklin Delano Roosevelt's INAUGURAL ADDRESS
* * * *

My fellow Americans, the only thing we have to fear is a crippling, decade-long depression, one in which thousands will die by starvation, riots, or even their own hand. This is the sort of depression that destroys the faith of a people in their nation. The sort of depression that does not make one stronger from the great challenge it brings, but, rather, weaker. Weaker from the hunger. Weaker from the idleness. Weaker from the sight of one's friends and neighbors unemployed, financially ruined, and driven to an early grave. Weaker from the emotional, physical, and spiritual devastation that will surround us, day after day.

I stand before you today with a message born not of hope, but of despair. Yes, misery awaits us all and there is nothing we can do to avert this grim fate. This economic depression is far too great for any of you to overcome, and there is nothing left for America to do but suffer. All is lost. The situation is hopeless.

Be afraid. For you have very good reason. Banks are closing. Unemployment is at an all-time high and climbing every day. Stocks once worth hundreds of dollars are now worth pennies. Millions of you have lost your life savings in financial institutions you thought were secure but are not.

And, lest you think otherwise, let me assure you right now that this misery will not end any time soon. No, you would be well advised to get used to this unhappy state in which you currently exist, for it will be a very long time, perhaps more than ten years, before your lot in life will finally get better. Most likely, you or someone in your family will die before that time. How will you endure this for so long, you ask? For many of you, the answer to that question is simple: You will not. You will die like a sick street rat in the gutter, penniless and trembling, your clothes torn and your face covered with the filth of the street.

Yes, we as a nation are doomed.

Let's All Band Together and Pull for America! Buy Poverty Bonds!

THE ONION

Now Edible

Wednesday, December 6, 1933 — Finest Source of News in America — Price Three Cents

Stalin Announces Five-Year 'Everybody Dies' Plan

50 Million Russians to Perish by 1939

Over Two Million New Jobs to Be Created in Grave-Digging, Body-Dumping Fields

MOSCOW, Dec. 5. — Speaking before the Supreme Soviet yesterday, Premier Josef Stalin unveiled a bold new five-year "Everybody Dies" plan for the U.S.S.R.

If successful, Stalin said, more than 50 million Soviet citizens will die by 1939.

"This is a plan that can work," Stalin said. "Whether by government-backed murder, war, starvation, or disease, the people of the Soviet Union are very good at dying."

According to Stalin, the plan consists of three parts: mass famine through collectivization of agriculture, purging of all suspected enemies of the state, and gross mismanagement of resources by a bloated and corrupt government bureaucracy.

Josef Stalin

A THREE-STAGE PLAN

The starvation phase of the plan is slated to begin next month. "If all goes well, less than 10,000 tons of wheat will be produced on land capable of yielding more than 500 times that amount," Stalin said. "That should starve over 14 million people by the end of the year. At such a pace, we will more than meet our death quota within the allotted five-year period."

An additional 10 million, Stalin said, will be shot in the back of the head by Soviet secret police. "These are extremely well-trained, ruthless assassins," Stalin said, "and I believe they are more than capable of meeting our nation's death needs." The mass slayings will be followed by a purge of the secret police themselves.

Overseeing the starvation tier of the death plan will be a Soviet government both ill-equipped to deal with the food-shortage crisis and indifferent to the plight of the millions of innocents murdered by the secret police. At the local level, the bureaucracy will feature a network of disorganized, poorly run cooperatives responsible for the spoilage of over 200,000 tons of grain in dilapidated silos.

RAISING THE DEATH TOLL

Stalin's dissatisfaction with the death tolls of recent years is well documented. Last May, he exiled Minister of Hunger and Disease Viktor Vasilevich to Eastern Siberia after Soviet corpse production dropped to eight million in 1930, down 21 percent from the year before. Vasilevich blamed the low dead-body output on an unusually mild winter which led to only moderate crop devastation the next spring.

Also exiled by Stalin was Minister of Purging and Terror Oleg Fedorov, who failed to meet Stalin's goal of two million dead peasants by 1932. Fedorov said such totals were impossible, citing severe bullet shortages. "We ran out of bullets after the first million murders," he said. "Our desperation reached a point where we were removing and reusing bullets from shot peasants."

A BOON TO THE U.S.S.R.'S DEATH-BASED ECONOMY

Igor Kerensky, Soviet Minister of Information, said the "Everybody Dies" plan will revitalize the Soviet economy: Not only will it greatly increase the per capita income of those few surviving Soviet citizens, he said, but it will also create more than two million new jobs in the growing fields of corpse-hauling, grave-digging, and body-dumping.

"As we continue to move toward a mortuary-based economy, we are taking the steps necessary to ensure that there are enough deaths to support such a system," Kerensky said. "This is a very exciting time to die in the Soviet Union."

Kerensky boasted that, with proper planning, even if 15 million Soviet citizens die each year for the next five years, there will still be at least 60 million more available to die in future wars. "If the Soviet Union should go to war, we are poised to amass millions of casualties. Even as we speak, our women are giving birth to babies that will one day be run over by enemy tanks."

Stalin said that regardless of its results, the "Everybody Dies" plan will be followed by the "All the Orphaned Children of Everybody Who Died Dies" plan.

Hollywood Careers Destroyed Today:

Bow, Clara
Brooks, Louise
Fitzgerald, F. Scott
Gilbert, John
Haines, William
Keaton, Buster

(Continued on page 10, col. 1)

HEROIC POLICE BEAT UNION SYMPATHIZERS TO DEATH

NEWARK, N.J., Dec. 5. — Cries of "fair pay for fair work" were finally silenced today, as police broke up a group of 120 union-sympathizing workers outside a Newark metal-work shop, beating them to death with billy clubs.

The workers, it is believed, had ties with labor unions. Some were thought to be sympathizers, while others were rumored to have even been interested in founding a union at the esteemed shop, Medsen's Metal-Works and Fittings of Greater Newark.

"The rabble-rousing cries of these workers will disturb the people of Newark no more," Police Chief Calvert Duffey told assembled reporters after the quieting of the strikers.

"The great threat to Newark posed by this large, congregated group of working men with agitated voices asking for a fair wage has been safely neutralized," he added. "The citizens of the city and the stockholders of Medsen's Metal-Works no longer have anything to fear."

Stockholders heard about the strike early yesterday morning and immediately telephoned the police. Reports indicate that the stockholders were "at grave risk of raised pulse and temperature due to the potential work stoppage and possible lowering of their corporate holdings by as much as .5 or .7 percent."

Only one striking worker survived the initial charge by police: Milton Hettenbach, 37. As he lay wounded from internal bleeding, he was heard to say, "Perhaps if I, the lone survivor of this plant's work-force, could have a meeting with the management...."

Several police then assaulted Hettenbach in unison, silencing the troublemaking unionist for good.

FDR's Fireside Chat Last Night Just a Stream of Cuss Words

In a drastic departure from the traditional "fireside chat," President Roosevelt held American radio listeners captive last night with a stream of lurid profanities that lasted thirty minutes with nary a break to take a breath.

While millions of families gathered around their radios in rapt attention to their leader's reassuring words during a time of great hardship for the nation, the president cleared his throat, then said, in his familiar, soothing, Harvard-educated drawl, "My fellow Americans..." After the customary opening, the people of the nation huddled even closer to their radio receivers to hear every nuance of the president's tidbits of fatherly wisdom, recent policy actions which would bring the Depression to a swift end, and his positive-minded thoughts about recovery.

Roosevelt then spoke again: "Cock-sucker, motherfucker, fart-fucking, tit-licking, Christ-humping fucker," the president said. He went on, adding, "Shit, bullshit, and horse shit. A good God-damn cunt-kicking ass-hole-sucking tit-fucking piss-shitter."

He continued to swear, making no attempt to connect the obscenities to any larger theme, or even explain to what or whom the curses were directed.

He spoke for nearly 30 minutes before falling silent.

18th Amendment Repealed; Could Alcohol Cure Nation's Depression?

Down-and-Out Turn to Now-Legal Hard Liquor as Way Out of Dire Crisis

Banks, Clinically Depressed to Wash Away Sorrows with Bourbon, Vodka, Rum

WASHINGTON, D.C., Dec. 5. — With Americans again free to enjoy alcoholic spirits, the repeal of the Prohibition Amendment is inspiring wide-spread hope that the newly available liquor will provide a much-needed cure for the Depression under which America suffers.

For the past decade, many Americans with little or no experience with alcohol heard enticing rumors of its considerable medicinal benefits: its ability to lift the spirits, endow the cheeks and nose with a rosy luster, and enable imbibers to forget their overwhelmingly crushing troubles.

BALM FOR WOUNDED SPIRITS

Local citizens feeling the effects of the Depression are greeting the repeal with enthusiasm.

Clarence Trebach of Omaha is particularly eager to take full advantage of the newly available liquors, cordials, wines, and ales. "Every day I tell my wife I am going out to look for a job, but there aren't any," he said. "So I usually spend most of the day standing on the roadside with other unemployed men or at the picture-house watching Marie Dressler movies." Trebach said he believes alcohol will provide a soothing, albeit temporary, balm for his wounded pride and spirit, and deliver him from the clutches of cold, dismal reality.

Esther Breunig of Providence said she is tired of supporting her invalid mother on a part-time stenographer's salary, and is looking forward to her first drink of liquor since 1919. "I am particularly eager to sample absinthe, which I hear over time wipes one's memory clean," the 43-year-old spinster told The Onion.

Another who can't wait to toast old John Barleycorn is Myra Mae Thornton, a prostitute and widowed 22-year-old mother of fourteen. "I'm at the end of my rope," she said. "All I want now is to drink myself to death."

ROOSEVELT ADVISES EXPERIMENTATION

Shortly after Utah became the 36th state to give its approval, President Roosevelt signed a proclamation declaring the repeal of the Prohibition Amendment. In it he called upon Americans to exercise their newly restored privilege by experimenting with different kinds of alcohol to find the most effective brand to treat their particular sorrows.

The following is an excerpt from the president's proclamation:

"I enjoin upon all citizens of the United States, and upon others resident within the jurisdiction thereof, to recognize their patriotic duty in improving the morale and spirit of their beleaguered country by diligently experimenting with alcoholic beverages of diverse ingredients, methods of distillation, and alcoholic content. The objective we seek through a national policy is to provide every citizen with a greater and more sophisticated knowledge of the variety of intoxicating tonics, which could do much to alleviate the present conditions in the United States. Down the hatch, America."

U.S. Distilleries 'Resume' Alcohol Production

Distilleries, breweries, and saloons across the nation are hotbeds of activity today, as brewmasters, vintners, barrelmen, and their colleagues undertake the Olympian task of making it seem as if they are just now returning to production after years of prohibition-enforced inactivity.

"It sure is good to be back here among the bourbon barrels again after, you know, all these years," said Booker Noe, master bottler for the Jim Beam distilleries of Frankfort, Kentucky. "Now that Prohibition's over, I can continue making my trademark 90-proof liquor. Again, I mean."

"For the first time in years," he added.

"Look at this place," said Brewmaster Hans Kessler, gesturing around his busy Monroe, Wisconsin, brewery, where production of Huber beer officially stopped at the beginning of Prohibition. "It looks like we just left after a full day of brewing beer yesterday. Which, of course, is not the case."

Prohibition 'Just Needs More Time,' Say Gangsters

(See story, page 9)

47

THE ONION

70,000 NEW JOBS! are needed very badly

$2,000,000 IN FOOD RELIEF! would be a big help, too

Saturday, December 30, 1933 — Finest Source of News in America — Price Three Cents

Knife Songs Top German Hit Parade

While everyone at home is humming "Inka Dinka Doo," across the sea, Germany is tapping its toes to all the songs about knives that round out its list of most popular tunes.

The sheet music most in demand for nine weeks in a row is "Mackie Messer (Mack the Knife)" by the Wunderkinder. Close behind in popularity are "Das Klappmesser Lied (Hunting Knife Song)" and the ballad "Das Obstmesser (Fruit Knife)." Children's songs share this theme: "Das Taschenmesser (Pen Knife)" is a song the youngest German children can be heard singing while skipping rope or marching for fun.

An increasingly popular pastime among German citizens is to gather in town squares and listen to these songs over crackling public-address speakers, often accompanied by the rhythmic pounding of jackboots and the soothing glow of hand-held torches.

Yet another song to find fame is the "Horst Wessel Lied," which was written by a young man, now deceased, who was interested in German nationalism and knives.

"I gather to sing and look toward a day when I may be proud to be German," said Berliner Heinrich Kohlmuht.

The return of the glory days of privilege and power is just around the corner, the happy tunes often promise. That's why everyone in Germany loves "Der Totale Krieg." It's got a steady drum beat and a brass-band chorus to back up the verses that promise, "the army's grand expansion / and Versailles Treaty's end destruction!"

Young people are especially enjoying the knife songs. Assembling under the watchful eye of their uniformed elders, they sing popular numbers and dance in forward-moving straight lines in rain or shine. Groups like "The Youth Recruiters" travel from city to city gaining the approval of the Germany's youngest and blondest.

"I enjoy to hear the music that sets the heart and minds of the young people of Germany afloat with the love of revenge," said 16-year-old Wilhelm Ebendorff. "And I also enjoy to hear the songs about cutting."

Some things never change, though. Knife songs may be taking the German Hit Parade by storm, but traditional love songs are still to be found. Tune into a radio broadcast and you just might catch the well-known "Ich Liebe Dich, Rache (I Love You, Revenge)" or the 4/4 beat of "Ich Liebe Dich, Mein Messer (I Love You, My Knife)."

President Confronts Depression with 'Big Deal' Plan

'BIG DEAL, I'M RICH!' ROOSEVELT SAYS

President Roosevelt

In a special statement to Congress Friday, President Roosevelt unveiled the "Big Deal," his plan to remedy America's financial crisis.

"Big Deal," the president said, "I'm rich!"

A COMPREHENSIVE PLAN

President Roosevelt is urging Congress to launch emergency legislation and rally the nation back to health with programs under the umbrella title, "The Big Deal."

"I expect the plan to fail, which is why it is called the Big Deal," he said. "My family will always have money no matter what happens to everyone else, so: Big Deal."

Among Roosevelt's first Big Deal-related acts was the establishment of the NRA, or "New Roosevelt Automobile," a DeSoto touring car the president bought at a dealership in Alexandria, Virginia, Thursday. Exhibiting the car to reporters today, Roosevelt showed visible pride at the success of his New DeSoto Plan. "I must admit that I feel much less depressed now," he said.

As for the welfare of the rest of the nation, Roosevelt said, "I'll try to pass some emergency banking legislation or something. But basically, Big Deal. See if I care."

WEALTH AND PRIVILEGE

Roosevelt's Big Deal philosophy developed throughout his wealthy, privileged upbringing, and stems from a rich family heritage.

The first of Roosevelt's American ancestors settled in New York when it was still a Dutch colony. They were a prominent family, part of the aristocratic squires of the Hudson River Valley. As a young boy, Roosevelt was tutored at home and spent vacations abroad. He schooled at the exclusive Groton as a youngster and later graduated from Harvard. He then attended Columbia, passed the bar examination, and was a lawyer before taking up politics.

Said Roosevelt, "Do I need to worry about every last uneducated urchin on the street? No, I do not. In fact, to them I say, 'Big Deal!'"

Fanciful Doily Placed Atop Area Radio

IOWA CITY, Iowa, Dec. 29. — A fanciful doily was placed atop a radio at 143 Lancaster Boulevard today. Mrs. Sylvia Fuller, wife of local pastor Henry Fuller, placed the white, crocheted doily atop the 61-pound oak cabinet holding the 34-pound radio.

Mrs. Fuller explained the function of the doily as a "sprucing-up" tactic for her home and a way to add a "feminine touch" to the austere radio-device.

Other Fuller household items expected to receive a newly crocheted doily garnish include the arms of the sofa, the kitchen-table centerpiece, which as of 2 p.m. Wednesday was a wooden fruit bowl, and the varnished walnut table lamp next to Pastor Fuller's reading chair.

The lamp doily is a controversial choice for Mrs. Fuller, as she will have to carefully lift the 20-pound lamp from the table some time this evening and insert a doily between it and the tabletop's Bakelite mat.

Additionally, small glass animal figurines on the china cabinet in the dining room were rearranged Friday, and may be adjusted again tomorrow.

No family member has issued a complaint or compliment about the appearance of the radio doily.

The doily did not in any way hamper the performance of the radio, which was used that night by the family to listen to "The Laugh Parade" and "The Fatima Cigarette Hour" after a dinner of glazed ham.

A late-breaking report indicates that Fuller may be considering sewing a protective slip-cover for the radio, although this news could not be confirmed at press time.

THE BREAD LINE

A Good Place to Meet a Potential Mate

This line outside a Boston soup kitchen is a treasure trove of eligibility.

BOSTON, Dec. 29. — As bread lines filled with hungry, jobless citizens circle around the block, many unmarried persons are finding love right on their neighborhood sidewalks. It's a veritable "queue-pid's queue," one area wit said. It's not so much a line to be given a hot meal, eligible lads and lasses; it's a line of lonely single people looking for love.

Outside the most popular charity kitchens and missions, the destitute are standing for hours, which leaves much time for a chance meeting to progress from telling glances and idle chatter to a marriage proposal.

After waiting in front of St. Mary's Soup Kitchen for 32 hours, Bostonians Audrey Meyer and John Leesworth knew each other's life story by the time they reached the front of the line late Tuesday. Meyer, an out-of-work and visibly desperate secretary, and Leesworth, whose former wife and two children died of the dropsy last year, were in such a celebratory mood upon receiving a crust of rye bread and a handful of carrot-greens soup that the two declared their undying love for each other right then and there.

Romance is in the air on the north side of the city, as well. Impoverished shoemaker Dewey Heilemann found his blushing bride, Theresa Muldoon, in the bread line at the Boston Free Kitchen for the Low of Life. Heilemann told his story: "I fell in love with Theresa as soon as I saw her. We both had nothing, so we had everything in common."

"I can't put my finger exactly on what made Dewey so appealing," explained Muldoon. "Was it the yellowish mucus crusted around his gray, deadened eyes? The play of the sunlight on his five o'clock shadow? The smell of his skin after a particularly strong delousing? I can't say for sure, but whatever it was, it sure worked."

Heilemann and Muldoon will be married by Father James Dugan at the Boston Free Kitchen next Friday. The couple will make their home at a North Street flophouse. No honeymoon is planned.

Nor does the couple plan to have children any time soon. Months of malnutrition have left Miss Muldoon infertile. But that does not bother the lovestruck Heilemann.

"I myself have become as impotent as a Chinese eunuch," Heilemann said. "Theresa and I were meant to be together."

Future Grandmother Struggling to Get By

(See story, page 9)

Should Lynching Be a Federal Offense?

★

See T. Herman Zweibel's editorial, page 9

DO YOU HAVE YESTERDAY'S NEWSPAPER, AN EXTRA BOOTLACE, AND SOME GRASS?

See Ma Wiley's recipes, page 34.

THE ONION

Weather
Plains states: thick, choking dust clouds. Mid-Atlantic and Great Lakes region: mostly gloomy, chance of killer hail. Pacific Coast: death falling from skies.

Monday, July 23, 1934 — Finest Source of News in America — Price Three Cents

ARMED THUGS SHOOT, KILL OUR BELOVED DILLINGER

Nation Mourns Loss of Innocence Following Gangster's Tragic Death

'We'll Never Forget You, Public Enemy Number One,' Says Teary-Eyed Fan

Are Gangsters Not Safe on Their Own Streets?

JOHN DILLINGER 1903–1934

CHICAGO, July 22. — Beloved public figure John Dillinger was gunned down outside the Biograph Theater today by armed thugs acting under federal orders. Chicago police condemned the men who shot the dashing hero, calling them "brutes."

Dillinger, who died at 10:40 p.m. from four gunshot wounds, had won the hearts of America with his bank-robbing and killing. The public's fondness for the brave desperado grew even stronger after his attempted capture last year in which he shot seven policemen dead and left eleven others blind or limbless.

For the last five months, government agents have tracked the illustrious Dillinger and his gang as they journeyed across the country collecting $100,000 in cash and, in times of need, holding up banks, robbing stores, or shooting the mouths off hysterical clerks.

FANS STUNNED

"I looked forward to thrilling tales of his exploits on the radio," said Martin Coyne, a 41-year-old fan standing outside the Cook County Morgue and clutching Dillinger's picture, which he had clipped from a popular magazine. Coyne was joined by countless other supporters.

The outlaw, considered handsome by many, always sported an attractive straw hat and was never rude to the ladies he robbed or killed.

A large, noisy crowd formed today outside the Chicago prison where captured Dillinger gang members "Little Fingers" Hutchins and Tony Fraboli, a.k.a. "The Widowmaker," were locked up after yesterday's tragedy. "Set them free, in the name of Dillinger," the crowd chanted. Some women fell to their knees and wept for the revered celebrity.

A MERCHANDISING BOOM

All about Chicago, stores are advertising Dillinger-related salable materials. Dillinger photographs for young ladies and storybooks for young boys were displayed in storefront windows alongside such other Dillinger merchandise as whistles, magnets, and wooden pull toys. Dillinger fans also devised their own ways to show their support for Public Enemy Number One, as he is fondly remembered. "I kept track of Dillinger's movements on this map during his five-month run from the law," said excited Chicago supporter Mary Hayes. "The red pins represent policemen killed, and the blue pins are policemen wounded. I love him."

KILLING PROTESTED

Thousands across the nation are expressing outrage over what they consider the unnecessary force used to apprehend Dillinger and are calling for a speedy trial for the federal agents involved. One of the gunmen, Special Agent Herman E. Hollis, has admitted to stalking and killing the number-one gangster.

Said Melvin Purvis, head of the Chicago bureau of the Department of Justice, "With Hollis' confession, we should be able to convict him and rest of his unsavory gang of federal agents."

A GREAT MOURNING

A large public attendance is expected at the memorial service to be held Saturday in Dillinger's home town of Indianapolis, where Pope Pius XI will read a eulogy.

It is too early to speculate on who, if anyone, will fill the gap left in the nation's hearts with Dillinger's passing, but it is believed that Dillinger gang member "Baby Face" Nelson and serial murderer Jimmy "Infant Slayer" Dwyer are the likeliest candidates.

ONION FASHION REPORT
THE '34 RAGS ARE IN!

Poverty, austerity, and want: These are the three watchwords for the Fall 1934 rag collection, which was unveiled at a society-studded floor show at the All Souls' Mission in New York City Saturday. This year's fashions continue in the coarse, jagged, threadbare silhouette that has been all the rage for both men's and ladies' styles since Autumn 1929.

Among the show's highlights:

This versatile number is suitable daywear for the active woman. Made of burlap from discarded flour sacks and pieced together with twine, this breathable one-piece is ideal for light activities, such as sharecropping, watching foreclosures, and burying stillborn children. Thoughtfully equipped with holes for nursing.

Who says pajamas are just for sleeping? This natty yet loose-fitting outfit is available by charity from many nervous hospitals across the Republic; some even still bear brownish-yellow stains left by previous wearers. Accessorize with a length of rope or bow-tie fashioned from a dish rag, or wear shoeless for that insouciant, devil-may-care attitude.

Ingenious government couturiers have hit upon a frugal yet elegant way to clothe the downtrodden: war-issue Army blankets. Artfully draped toga-style to hide the boniness of malnutrition, they can also be hocked at the local pawn shop for soup. Check for lice before wearing.

FDR Creates 300,000 Jobs with 'Tunnel to New Zealand' Project

Latest Works Program Will Finally Connect Cleveland, Auckland

Bridge Linking Los Angeles, Shanghai Also Planned

CLEVELAND, Ohio, July 22. — America's unemployed and world travelers alike were thrilled following President Roosevelt's announcement today that the U.S. will construct a U.S.-New Zealand Tunnel. The Civil Works Administration program is expected to employ some 300,000 Americans and generate billions of dollars in revenue for U.S. firms well into the next century.

ROOSEVELT'S WORDS

At a ribbon-cutting ceremony atop the first hole to be dug for the project, President Roosevelt promised that the U.S. would lead the world in geocentric travel by 1990. "I envision a future," he said, "in which the traveler wishing to take in the beauty of New Zealand will need only leap into a 10,000-mile vertical shaft through the Earth's crust, plummet swiftly to the Earth's center, aided by gravity, then journey to the other side of the planet, paying only a nickel toll for the service and perhaps a penny tip for the luggage boy."

A LARGE WORKFORCE

Construction is expected to begin in August in Cleveland, which will be renamed Tunnelville, as 100,000 robust spadesmen begin the digging and an additional 10,000 Civilian Conservation Corps linesmen haul buckets of earth to the surface. Construction of the tunnel's aluminum hull will provide work for thousands more.

FEEDING THE GREAT CREWS

It is estimated that some six billion potatoes and enough coffee to fill Lake Michigan will be served to workers over the 60-year schedule of construction. Furthermore, over the course of the ambitious project, entire generations will live out their lives underground, never seeing the sun or the Earth's "surface dwellers."

"This future race of mole people will not be forgotten. We shall erect commemorative plaques upon the walls of the tunnel in tribute to their sacrifice," Roosevelt said.

AT THE RIALTO THEATRE
Broadway at 47th St. New York

Now thru Friday!

FROM ITS SMASH BROADWAY RUN!

FRANK B. **STURRIDGE** — GERTRUDE **O'DAYE**

— IN —

the WISE-CRACKERS

It's a scream! It's a pip!

Featuring the hit number, "I Will Kiss You in My Little Canoe"

Tickets on sale NOW!

Coming Saturday—the motion-picture marvel "Say, What's the Big Idea?" starring Gloria Stuart and Jean Hersholt
Also a BOSKO cartoon

Italy's Mussolini Embarks on Massive Chest-Expansion Campaign

(See story, page 2)

THE ONION

News for RECOVERY!

Monday, September 9, 1935

Finest Source of News in America

Price Three Cents

SENATOR HUEY LONG ASSASSINATED, CAJUN STYLE

Dies 'Real Spicy-Like,' Say Witnesses

All-Night Party, Dancing, Dining to Commemorate Tragedy

HUEY LONG 1893–1935

BATON ROUGE, Sept. 8. — Known for his slogan "Every Man a King," Louisiana senator and Democratic presidential contender Huey Long, the "Kingfish," was assassinated in the state capitol building today. Suspected murderer Dr. Carl A. Weiss allegedly penetrated Long's band of seven bodyguards and killed him, as onlookers said, "in real Cajun style."

Witness Louis Blanchard of Baton Rouge recounted the events leading up to the tragic assassination. "That canille Dr. Weiss was as mad as a snappin' gator in a bubbling pot o' gumbo. He came at Huey doin' a wiiiild fais-do-do, like whooeee, he had an envie to rid hisself o' tha' voodoo."

One of Long's senior staff members said the killing was "filled with joie de vivre." Another described it as "zesty."

According to police accounts, the assailant approached Long in an enormous papier-mache devil's head, which Baton Rouge investigators say allowed him to get close to the senator without looking suspicious. Weiss then ran over the senator with a float.

The assassination prompted an instant reaction throughout the city. Apparently mistaking the screaming and running for an impromptu carnival, zydeco bands immediately filled the streets of Baton Rouge, while citizens began cooking steaming pots of crawfish, turtle oyster soup, and spicy jambalaya while Long lay dying.

"We go' make a fin' of shrimp etoufée and okra gumbo," said one partygoer, Marguerite Landry, of the Acadian Coast Landrys. When Landry learned of the dreadful assassination, she added, "I gon' put out som' dat creole hot-sauce spec' in honor of cher Huey, may his sweeeet soul rest in the peace o heav'n." She then undid her blouse to display her naked bosom to a crowd of hooting onlookers.

Having served as Louisiana's governor from 1928 until his election to the U.S. Senate in 1930, Long was extremely popular with the rural sector of his home state for his tax-the-rich programs, as well as for his legendary state-wide Sunday shrimp and okra fries.

MORE PARTIES PLANNED

Less than an hour after the assassination, groups of Long's followers had organized "Huey Gras," a memorial slated to last 28 days and 28 nights and include zydeco music, fried alligator, and rum punch. It is scheduled to commence immediately after the party at the church in his home town of Winnfield, Louisiana, taking place today.

"Mmm, we's goin' haf ourselv' a rememb'rin' shindi' that's mo' betta than any parish not had befo'," said memorial organizer Linden Grandsois. "Laissez les bons temps rouler!"

RAUCOUS MOURNING

In many of Louisiana's outlying Atchafalaya communities, the cultivation of yams, cotton, and oysters has come to a halt with the news of Long's assassination. The industries of spinning, weaving, catfishin', and home crafts have also ceased. Masses of mourners are converging on cities with names like "L'fate" and "N'awlins" festooned with colorful clothing and multicolored beads. They plan to eat, dance, and toss the doubloons bearing Long's picture that became legal tender in Louisiana after his "Share Our Wealth" movement resulted in his 1930 election to the U.S. Senate.

Songs will be performed at Long's funeral by members of his family using accordions, fiddles, washboards, and "anythin' else that migh' be layin' right on near," a family spokesman said.

SURVIVED BY KIN

"We gonna remember the Kingfish the way he lived—real spicy-like," said Long's brother, Earl K. Long, who raised a cracked jug of blackberry wine in one hand and a plate of fried catfish in the other. He was then smothered in naked breasts as he joined a conga line, loudly pledging over the din of the crowd that he would carry on the Long tradition of government

Another Impossibly Huge Dam Built

PORTLAND, Oregon, Sept. 8. — Defying all logic, the U.S. Army Corps of Engineers today proudly completed construction on another impossibly huge dam, the latest in a string of impossibly huge dams built by the Corps in the past few years. It is called Majestic Hugeass Dam, and it is the most impossibly huge, expensive dam ever built.

Stretching across Majestic Hugeass Gorge, a river canyon in Northwest Oregon, as well as several other gorges, three mountain ranges, and most of two states, the dam is over 1,800 miles long. This makes the previous four largest structures ever built (the Bonneville, Boulder, Shasta, and Grand Coulee dams) now the fifth, fourth, third, and second largest structures ever built, respectively.

Majestic Hugeass Dam contains more lumber, concrete, steel, hubris, folly, and sheer gall than any other structure on the planet. Once fully operational, the dam will have a greater overall effect on global water flow than the moon, and the man-made Lake Hugeass will cover over 80 percent of Oregon and Washington's land area.

Although the Corps' reputation for building impossibly huge things is unrivaled, Corps engineers feel Hugeass Dam has another purpose unrelated to hugeness. "This new dam could meet the hydroelectric-power needs of the entire hidden colony of giant Sasquatch ape-men by 1940," said A.C.O.E. engineer Fred Tanner.

Since it is doubtful that the unseen "bigfoot" manbeasts have developed even the fundamentals of civilized society, President Roosevelt has proposed a program that would send Civilian Conservation Corps workers into Sasquatch lands to tutor the great brutes.

The dam is also being lauded by officials and civilian industry leaders as having created almost eight million jobs, not only for laborers, but for hundreds of thousands of government bureaucrats ostensibly involved in overseeing the project and processing the necessary paperwork.

However, the most important aspect of the dam, Tanner said, is that "it is really, really huge."

Bumper Crop of '35: Dust

OKLAHOMA, KANSAS REPORT RECORD HARVESTS

Legislators Debate Dust Tariff for Upper Atmosphere

An Oklahoma dust-bowl farmer surveys this season's spectacular yield of fine, airborne dirt.

Dirt farmers from Arkansas to the Dakotas are vomiting topsoil today, as an unexpected bumper crop of finely particulated dirt continues to set records as the highest-yield harvest in American dust-farming history. Locals are just trying to keep up, as the region formerly known as the Great Plains continues to soar eastward at up to 40 miles per hour without reprieve.

The storm of high-quality, American-grown dirt is the Midwest's largest-ever agricultural windfall, and it can be seen from as far away as Washington, D.C., as the skies are blackened with the fast-moving clouds of dust.

"There can be no complaining about the financial woes of our nation when there is such a surplus of arable land in the country," said Franklin Olsen of the U.S. Airborne Dirt Planning Office. "And this land is right there for everyone to see, scattered across several hundred miles of the Earth's upper atmosphere."

VOLUMINOUS YIELD

The season's dust yield is so voluminous, sources report, that Plains farmers have no choice but to export the vast majority of their harvest. Experts say most prime U.S. farmland is now nearing the stratosphere, with the states of Nebraska and Oklahoma expected to reach the upper air flow and eventually Europe.

This dust loss, however, is not expected to be a problem. The surplus is said to be so great that after the storm settles, massive drifts of soil will cover everything in sight, and some are predicting that U.S. farmers may never need to harvest dust again. "We have more than met our nation's dust needs for the immediate future," Olsen said. "This crop is truly a godsend in these difficult times."

EXCEEDING GOVERNMENT PROJECTIONS

Government officials say the unusually high dust harvest, which has turned the skies pitch black at noon for the last several weeks, is the result of federal dust-incentives designed to loosen topsoil through over-plowing.

"We had hoped our agricultural policies would lead to better dust yields, but this is bigger than we'd ever dreamed," said Edwin Fayne, the Interior Department's Undersecretary of Dust Maximization. The record crop is expected to dwarf all previous U.S. dust production, exceeding even the most optimistic projections by over six trillion percent.

"You can't imagine what it's like," said farmer Tom Dern of Nebraska, which is now located between Kentucky and Delaware. "My dust crop this year was sixty billion times larger than last year."

Dern lists 110-degree heat, vicious winds that cut flesh like sandpaper, and the decimation of all life on the farm as the most appealing aspects of the Midwest dust-farming business. His family enjoys dust soup nearly every night, goodly helpings of dust pie, and hewn chunks of coagulated dust heaps as toys for his eight children.

"It's really incredible," Fayne said. "I predict that by 1936, the U.S. will corner the world dust market."

Release of 'Top Hat' Makes Nation Feel Better for Two Hours

See story, page 4

Will Rogers Meets Fiery Death He Doesn't Like

ALASKA TERR. — As if news of Senator Long's death were not shocking enough, Will Rogers met a fiery end he didn't like, perishing in an airplane crash near Point Barrow, Alaska Territory.

The folksy humorist, who will be remembered for his trick roping and good-natured social criticisms, was flying with noted aviation pioneer Wiley Post when their plane lost control and hit the ground.

"Will was the kind of person who liked everyone and everything," said Jack Rogers, his brother. "But he probably did not like this plane crash."

Rogers' good friend and fellow aviator Howard Hughes agreed. "Will had this saying. He used to say to me, 'Howard, I like everything in this world except engine failure on a single-engine plane flying over the Alaska Territory.' That's what he would always say to me."

THE ONION

A Patronizing Voice in Troubled Times

Leading the Fight to Jail Vagrants

Finest Source of News in America

Thursday, December 10, 1936 — Price Three Cents

FDR Rummages Through Parents' House to 'See if There's Anything in There America Could Use'

Numerous Useful Knick-Knacks, Odds-and-Ends Found

President Discovers 'Perfectly Good' Copper Pot

Roosevelt

HYDE PARK, N.Y., Dec. 9 — President Franklin Roosevelt, expressing concern over the economic paralysis gripping the nation, inspected the attic of his family mansion in Hyde Park today in the hope of uncovering old odds-and-ends which America might put to good use.

Assisted by his wife Eleanor and several members of his Cabinet, Roosevelt went through the contents of dozens of boxes and trunks and removed dust covers from old furniture, revealing many items that could alleviate conditions for the average American.

"As the slogan of the National Recovery Administration declares, 'We do our part,'" Roosevelt told reporters. "By searching through this attic and hoping that somewhere in our old jumble there is something America doesn't have and might possibly need or use, Eleanor and I are doing our own part."

HUMIDOR

"Look, everyone, my old humidor from my days at Harvard!" Roosevelt exclaimed, as Secretary of Labor Frances Perkins extricated a dusty wooden box from a cobweb-strewn pile of items. "Mr. and Mrs. Norbert Westman of Illinois might have need of this."

Questions were raised as to the usefulness of such an item for the Westmans, but it was eventually reasoned that it would make a good container for small, relatively inexpensive grocery items such as potatoes or rice.

Dozens of old "National Geographic" magazines were also rooted out. "With little work and extra spare time for many Americans," Roosevelt said, "there are now ample opportunities to improve one's mind. I hope the donation of these magazines will speed the course."

The president, however, appeared reluctant to part with an old wicker perambulator used in his infancy. Mrs. Roosevelt argued that it was just taking up space and could be used by a needy mother, and that it was just like him to get sentimental about a piece of junk to which he hadn't given a single thought in fifty years until he laid eyes on it today.

Roosevelt also spent several hours alone listening to old phonograph records on a dusty Victrola. "Babs, do you remember this song, 'Up On My Merry Thresher?'" Roosevelt asked. "It was often played when Cousin T.R. was in the White House." Mrs. Roosevelt replied that she did and added that the president should stop wasting valuable time.

NEEDY GRATEFUL

The items approved for donation were sent to several charity-relief organizations throughout the country, where they were soon dispersed among the grateful needy. Charles Balaban, an unemployed Pittsburgh steelworker, received a slightly moth-eaten homburg hat and a globe. "It is an honor to receive actual things once owned by the Roosevelt family," he told The Onion. "I can saw the globe in two and use both halves as cradles for the underweight twins my wife recently gave birth to."

Miss Shirley Beddoes of Kankakee, Illinois, was happy with her electric Tiffany lamp. "It was a gift to the Delano family from the New York Whitneys," she explained. "I can't afford any electric light bulbs, so I'll hock it at the pawn shop to buy a radish."

The Knox family of Grissom County, Kentucky, isn't exactly sure what to do with its Victorian-era ottoman, but Mr. Knox said he could strip the upholstery from the frame, nail up some chicken wire, and keep chickens or turkeys in it, should he ever acquire chickens or turkeys. "I reckon we could use the stripped velvet to patch up holes in our sack-cloth tunics," Knox said. "Then eat the rest."

ITALY INVADES ETHIOPIA FOR SOME REASON
See story, page 11

Jesse Owens Naively Looking Forward to Big Endorsement Money

Delusional Negro expects to appear on the Wheat Flakings box as a representative athlete.
(See story, page 13)

Kids!

Here's today's T. Herman Zweibel special code message!

Use your special code-deciphering rings to translate this secret message from your swell pal, Onion publisher T. Herman Zweibel!

21-14-3-12-5 / 26-23-5-9-2-5-12
8-1-20-5-19 / 25-15-21!

Solution to yesterday's message: "You miserable little wretches!"

Tinseltown Lays Foundation for Future Homosexual Culture

As America tries to get back on its feet and regain its economic strength, the magical fantasy factory of Hollywoodland is pitching in and doing its part to prepare for our nation's future. When not filling desperately lonely hearts with a sense of wondrous awe or providing an escapist respite from the horrors of post-industrial alienation, the dream-weavers and magic makers of Tinseltown are busy laying the groundwork for future homosexual generations.

"The faux opulence of our lavish musical numbers will one day be seen as 'high camp' by same-sex domestic companions the world over," said famed Warner Brothers director Busby Berkeley, who is putting the final touches on his latest silver-screen extravaganza, "Oh, Mary!" Berkeley stressed that, although the chorus-line showgirls of his intricately choreographed gala dance revues were originally intended to titillate heterosexual males, they will, nonetheless, be vitally important to unborn generations of queer males, who, despite their lack of sexual attraction to women, will find in his films a fantasy image of glamorous, lady-like elegance upon which they will neurotically fixate.

Industry insiders laud MGM's musical pictures as "kitsch epics sure to have future queens prancing about before a mirror in their parents' attics, bedecked with wigs and fanciful feather boas." Those in the know say that producer-director Cecil B. DeMille's recent garish production of "Cleopatra" will have nancy-boys swooning with glee from coast to coast for decades to come.

Such future queer-cultural icons as Fred Astaire, Ginger Rogers, Bette Davis, Joan Crawford, Mae West, and the young Judy Garland will play a vital role in the legacy of flaming-fag camp. And the private lives of some prominent Hollywood stars, whose real sexual orientation will be exposed long after their deaths, will provide reassurance and hours of conversation fodder for alienated homosexuals.

"Traditionally rejected by our society, homosexuals often seek solace in the flamboyantly theatrical. As a result, our Hollywood luminaries of today will be the legendary cultural heroes and role models for the misunderstood queers of tomorrow," DeMille said.

Meaningless Figurehead Abdicates Meaningless Role

World Captivated by Powerless Monarch's Decision to Give up Irrelevant Position to Marry Divorcee

King Edward VIII and Mrs. Wallis Warfield Simpson, the woman for whose hand he gave up nothing of importance.

LONDON, England, Dec. 9. — In one of the biggest meaningless news stories of the decade, King Edward VIII, meaningless figurehead of the meaningless British Monarchy, has chosen to renounce his meaningless title for the love of Mrs. Wallis Warfield Simpson, a twice-divorced American considered unacceptable as Queen under England's system of meaningless class distinctions.

Declared King in a meaningless transfer of non-power less than a year ago, Edward is the first meaningless figurehead of the modern era to openly acknowledge the meaninglessness of his role as living prop for the superfluous, powerless system of hereditary nobility.

The King's unimportant message was read aloud on the floor of Parliament as an uncanny silence fell over the grand chamber, where centuries of history have been made: "I, King Edward VIII of Great Britain, Ireland, the British Dominions beyond the seas, King Emperor of India, do hereby declare the abdication of my meaningless throne," the House Speaker read. "And I also hereby end this worthless statement so that you, the men of Parliament, the actual governing body of our nation, can get on with the business of running the empire without listening to me prattle on."

Although some have speculated that the meaningless abdication of non-authority could spell the end for the irrelevant Monarchy, members of the royal family assured the public by special announcement that another meaningless figurehead will succeed Edward on the meaningless throne and fill the meaningless void.

Said Lady Swinthrope-Twining, Marquise of Bingcough-on-Kenting, one of the most meaningless and obscure of all British nobles, "England's meaningless lineage, with its time-honored traditions of imaginary status and unimportance, will go on delighting the empty-headed with meaningless pomp and circumstance for generations hence. Years from now, the radio-devices will still broadcast songs of tribute to the royals."

As ex-King, Edward will no longer be required to wear the meaningless crown, don the meaningless robes, hold aloft the Scepter of Meaninglessness at empty, strictly ceremonial affairs of state, or make perfunctory visits to areas of his pretend empire bestowing a keen lack of meaning upon all who are graced with his meaningless presence.

Edward and his new bride will, of course, still be fabulously wealthy, regardless of the meaningless stepping-down.

THE ONION

Voice of Reason | *Champion of the Employing-Man*

Finest Source of News in America

Friday, April 30, 1937 — Price Three Cents

Nazi Propaganda Minister Introduces 'Kampfy the Überhund,' the Adorable Anti-Semitic Mutt

BERLIN, Apr. 29. — At a special unveiling ceremony Monday, Nazi Information Minister Joseph Goebbels introduced the much-anticipated "Kampfy the Überhund," a lovable cartoon mascot designed to put a "fun face" on Jew-hating.

Created with the help of longtime Hitler friend Walt Disney, Kampfy will be featured on lunch-pails, night-lights, board games, and trading cards. A talking Kampfy doll—which at the pull of a string will say such phrases as "Heil Hitler, kids!" and "It's fun to turn in Jews!"—is set to hit German toy stores this week. Life-sized, costumed versions of Kampfy, Goebbels said, will also be available for special appearances at birthday parties and Hitler Youth rallies.

"Just one look at this adorable little pooch, and who wouldn't want to drive the Jewish race from the face of the earth?" Goebbels said. "Don't those cute, pointy ears just scream out,

Kampfy is expected to make Jew-hating fun for German kids.

'Greedy Jews are to blame for the German economic depression'?"

Kampfy is already being well received by youngsters across Germany. "I love Kampfy!" said 5-year-old Grete Müller of Bonn. "He's my best friend!"

Parents appreciate the cartoon mutt, as well. "My 7-year-old son Heinrich was having trouble accepting Nazism until Kampfy came along," said Otto Schneider of Munich. "Now, it's all he talks about."

Dept. of Transportation Finds Driving While Tense Can Be Dangerous

'Drink Liquor to Loosen up Before Taking the Auto Wheel,' Experts Say

WASHINGTON, D.C., Apr. 29 — The Bureau of Public Roads released the results of the first-ever study of automobile safety today, finding that prior to engaging in driving for business or pleasure, it is best to relax with a few drinks of alcohol.

"Driving, while no doubt pleasurable, can be stressful," bureau director Arthur Schemmel said. "Speeds can reach upwards of 40 miles per hour, and there are occasionally unpleasant bumps and rough spots on our nation's advanced network of gravel roadways. That is why it is so crucial that one be relaxed while operating a motorized vehicle."

According to Schemmel, nervousness and tension are the leading causes of automotive fatalities, which numbered 11 in the United States in 1936. "These are fearsome machines, these automotive devices," he said. "Twenty years ago, when horses were still the most popular form of transportation, no one had to worry about broken crankshafts and engines in various states of discombobulation. These are perils unique to our modern era. It should come as no surprise, then, that so many drivers are running their cars into trees, ditches, or trolleys."

To ensure a safe driving experience, Schemmel suggested a nice scotch or whiskey. "MacTaggart's Royal Scotch is a fine beverage choice when traveling long distances. It has a pleasing, smooth flavor and allows the driver to become inebriated thoroughly and quickly, ensuring comfort and safety."

Schemmel said safety concerns are especially important if young children are in the car. "Because of the nervousness and anxiety children can cause, we recommend parents imbibe twice the dosage of alcohol," he said.

Schemmel said that to make certain drivers are operating automotive vehicles under the influence of alcohol, local police forces across the U.S. will periodically pull drivers to the side of the road to check for possible sobriety. The drivers will be asked to walk along a line. If they fail to walk the line in a wobbly, unsteady manner, they will be issued fines of up to two dollars and forced to attend mandatory alcohol-appreciation classes.

"An automobile is not a toy," said Captain Patrick Halloran of the New York City Police Department. "If one of our horse-mounted officers finds a driver operating one while sober, there will be a penalty to pay."

Art Critics Impressed by Saturation Bombing of Guernica

SLAUGHTER OF HUNDREDS IN SPANISH TOWN CALLED 'A STUNNING BREAKTHROUGH IN POST-CUBISM'

MADRID, Spain, April 29 — The German Condor Legion, acting under the orders of Fascist General Francisco Franco, bombed the Spanish town of Guernica Wednesday, an unprecedented act of terror which resulted in the death of hundreds of unarmed civilians and a state of thrilled astonishment for art critics worldwide.

Journalists and art critics who were permitted access to Guernica following the bombing witnessed a devastated town which in scant minutes had been reduced to a jumble of dislocated, abstract forms. The fragments, which included the remains of people, horses, bulls, and buildings, were disproportionate, seemingly randomly strewn, and savagely primal, but nonetheless conveyed a unified sense of horror, agony, and chaos.

Noted art critic Anthony Woodward, professor of art history at New York's Columbia University, had the opportunity to visit Guernica yesterday to witness the aftermath of the surprise attack.

"I'm simply stunned by the breakthrough possibilities of this bombing's color, texture, and perspective," he said of the experience. "Never before have I seen the human form so fragmented, distorted, and reinterpreted as I did yesterday at Guernica."

A VISUAL STATEMENT

In Woodward's opinion, the bombing—conducted in a new style he has dubbed "saturation"—also created a surreal landscape that will resharpen Cubism's edge, and lend fire to innumerable artistic imaginations. "Walking through the town, I was struck by how the Germans broke walls, buildings, and vehicles into countless tiny facets; even with my trained eye, I was at times unsure whether an individual piece was concave or convex. The town no longer represented the external world, but, rather, a fantastic reconfiguring of Euclidean geometry, with the faces of the injured contorted inhumanly. Even the animals' faces were wrenched in agony."

MANY QUESTIONS RAISED

The professor has already penned a letter of inquiry to German Luftwaffe chief Hermann Goering asking for specific comment on the artistic statement he had been trying to convey.

Wrote Woodward, "Was

Guernica, Spain, after the attack that has taken the art world by storm.

this air raid an artistic manifestation of man's inhumanity to man? A symbol of the cold disregard for the rural agrarian in today's increasingly mechanized society? Or an attempt to pacify a population by blanketing Basque farmers with 15,000 pounds of incendiary and fragmentation bombs per acre from twin-engined Heinkel heavy bombers? The art world needs to know."

The German High Command denied any role in the Guernica bombing, deeming the post-Cubist carnage "a decadent and depraved form of destruction." The Germans claimed that the only destruction they would inflict would be three-dimensional, proportional, and realistic, and feature Valkyries on winged horseback.

RICH WITH SYMBOLISM

As well as breaking new ground in visual experimentation, the massacre draws on historical antecedents in European art, Woodward said. The result is a work resonant with cultural meaning and memory. "I saw a Basque mother cradling the body of her dead child amongst the smoldering wreckage of her home yesterday. What a rich tableau!" he said. "My mind flew back to the weeping Magdalenes on Gethsemane in medieval Christian art, to the tragic Roman masks, even to the raving maenads of ancient Dionysiac reliefs. Absolutely breathtaking."

ARTISTIC REVOLUTION

Although the implications of the Guernica terror-bombing are impossible to fathom at this early date, Woodward postulated that the attack will lead to nothing less than a revolution in the art world. "The town had no defenses or military importance," he said. "The citizens who tried to take shelter in the outlying fields were mercilessly strafed by machine-gun fire from low-flying fighters. It's clear that this event has immeasurably broadened the artistic horizons of pain, loss, and technological brutality. This is truly an exciting time for art."

Nation Escapes Depression Through Fanciful Works of H.P. Lovecraft

Fantastical Tales of Better Times Allow Readers to Forget Troubles

Though times may be hard, Americans of all ages are forgetting their troubles with the help of beloved fantasy author H.P. Lovecraft. The recently deceased "Weird Tales" contributor transports readers to a happier land of sanity-sapping prehuman subterranea, helping folks everywhere put aside their cares and take a delightfully diverting trip to Lovecraftland.

"When the narrator recoils in horror at the non-Euclidean alien geometries of the dreaded Sleeping Elder God Cthulhu's undersea tomb, I was in dreamland, wishing my own life could be so merry," said reader Gus Derleth, an unemployed quarryman from Wisconsin. "If only I, too, could be plagued by the shifting gelatinous menace of Shub-Niggurath, Black Goat of the Woods with a Thousand Young."

Lovecraft's pulp fiction has won its way into the hearts of readers eager for hope. "His disturbed, paranoid tales of unknowable crawling madness serve as a welcome respite for many people suffering through the Depression," Yale University literature professor Paul Slocombe said. "Lovecraft makes readers wish their own lives were as romantic and carefree as those in his stories, like the Mad Arab Abdul Alhazred, who pens the forbidden Necronomicon only to be devoured alive by invisible demons in front of screaming onlookers."

Lovecraft's gay yarns lift the spirit and take readers' minds off the difficulties of daily life. "The Dunwich Horror" tells the uplifting story of a half-human abomination born of a human woman and Yog-Sothoth, an ancient, extra-dimensional being worshiped by a half-mad death cult. And the much-beloved "Pickman's Model" has won wide popularity for its delightful portrayal of a tortured painter consorting with hideous subterranean perversities too gruesome to face the light of day.

Of course, such optimism can only exist in fiction. But, in our reality, victims of these dreary times need only open a Lovecraft book to take an exciting trip to a far-off land where alien beings "construct mighty basalt cities of windowless towers, preying horribly on the minds of all they find there."

Would that real life were so grand!

Explosive News Coverage	# THE ONION	Inflammatory Editorials
	TU STUL — TUS ES Finest Source of News in America	

Friday, May 7, 1937 — Price Three Cents

AWESOME!
NATION WOWED BY TREMENDOUS HINDENBURG EXPLOSION

Gay Ball of Flame Warms Hearts Chilled by Depression

'Oh, the Luminosity!' Radio Announcer Says

LAKEHURST N.J., May 6. — In the most lively fireworks display in recent memory, the German airship Hindenburg exploded to the delight of hundreds at the Naval base here today.

The show was offered by the German Zeppelin Company for the assembled vacationers, families, and press. The crowd cheered and applauded wildly, as the golden flash and richly textured fireball shot outward, spewing singed bits of the ship's cloth shell and flailing passengers. Many in attendance called it a "once-in-a-lifetime" show.

"After years of poverty and want, I thought my childlike sense of wonder had long since died," said onlooker Myrna Schuyler. "But seeing the Hindenburg explosion made me as giddy as a schoolgirl. It was like Christmas, Hallowe'en, and the Fourth of July put together."

Fortunately, radio announcers and motion-picture camera-men were present to capture the glorious sight and sound for future generations to enjoy.

Said one radio announcer: "This is the most terrific thing I've ever seen."

"Oh, the luminosity!" he added.

Hollywood producers are said to be considering a musical version of the fire show. Closer to home, promoters of this summer's New Jersey State Fair hope to treat audiences to a repeat performance during their annual fireworks display.

GERMAN PYROTECHNIC SKILL APPLAUDED

American bottle-rocket and sparkler companies are eager to get their hands on this impressive German amusement technology, and have offered Dr. Hugo Eckener, chairman of the German Zeppelin Company, great sums of money for his winning formula for fun.

Before the spectacular display, many had not realized how advanced German pyrotechnic skill had become. But now there can be no doubt.

Said New Jersey State Fair promoter Hal Kroeger, "The Germans have long been known for their ability to produce the world's finest beer, leather short pants, propaganda films and ceramic figures of cute, chubby-cheeked children. But now they have demonstrated a keen mastery of live, pyrotechnic displays of the carnival variety, as well. Is there anything at which the determined Germanic mind cannot excel?"

President Roosevelt sent a special telegram to Adolf Hitler, thanking him "for this most merry airship disaster." Roosevelt praised the exploding ship as "the best airship explosion we've seen since the Grossmädchen."

A THRILLING BROADCAST

Herb Morrison, announcer for Chicago's WLS radio station, made broadcasting history at the thrilling event with the first ever on-the-scene radio disaster report. It is reproduced here in its entirety:

"The Germans are expected to put on quite a spectacular light show here today. We are watching, now, as the great airship approaches. Oh, there it goes! [laugh] It's wonderful! Oh, my! Get out of the way, please! It's bursting into flames! And it's cascading splendidly onto the mooring mast!

"All the folks here agree this is spectacular, one of the most terrific fireworks shows in the world, ladies and gentlemen. Oh, the flames, four or five hundred feet in the sky! Ladies and gentlemen! The smoke and the flames now, and the frame is crashing to the ground, not quite to the mooring mast. Oh, the luminosity! The gaiety!"

The lively show provided by German pyrotechnic experts thrilled onlookers and radio listeners alike.

SOULLESS CULTURAL WASTELAND 'ON THE GROW' IN SOUTHERN CALIFORNIA DESERT

Los Angeles to Be Hellish Megalopolis by 1950

LOS ANGELES, Calif. — The soulless cultural wasteland in the California desert, considered one of the bleakest and most God-forsaken stretches of uninhabitable scorched earth in the nation, is "on the grow," West Coast sources say, as the burgeoning city of Los Angeles continues its cancerous expansion.

Originally a tiny villa called Los Diablos, a coastal settlement of no distinction save for its capacity for heartlessness, the boomtown is now bigger than ever. Despite its lack of any life-sustaining natural resources, the city, which has no reason to exist, has all the earmarks of a truly spectacular, soulless cultural wasteland on the rise.

TOURIST-FRIENDLY DYSTOPIA

Thanks to its policy of draining every conceivable water source within hundreds of miles via a massive network of pipes, as well as the Chamber of Commerce's approval of a name-change to the more tourist-friendly "Los Angeles," the up-and-coming wasteland shows every sign of ballooning into a full-scale dystopia.

Although recently a mid-sized, primarily agricultural settlement, trends indicate that the city is on its way to becoming a sprawling nightmarish megalopolis within the next few decades. Complete with desperate poverty, rampant crime, and a callous indifference to the spirits it has crushed, this business-minded realm of demons is hoped, by as early as 1950, to be the leading soulless cultural wasteland in the world.

THRIVING ARTS HAVEN

Staggering in its economic disparity, the planned wasteland will be an affront to human dignity, not only in the shallow excesses of its bloated overlords, but in the anarchic savagery of its desperate underclass. Yet, it is in the arena of the arts that Los Angeles hopes to truly make its mark.

"Our town's lowest-common-denominator cultural output has the potential, one day, to be second to none in insipid banality," Wasteland Development Director Randolph Moloch said. "We hope to suck up the souls of promising artists like a great, black vortex, spitting out only the most lifeless, commerce-produced cultural products possible."

"We have high ambitions for the lows to which our community will sink," Moloch said. "We don't just want to be an overpopulated crucible of dehumanizing corruption, materialism, and race hatred; we want to be known the world over as a place where ideas come to die."

A FAUSTIAN BARGAIN

Perhaps the words of the late civil engineer William Mulholland, who was responsible for the construction of the aqueducts that feed Los Angeles as blood feeds a vampire's undead corpse, best articulate the civic spirit of Los Angeles. In a speech before the city's Chamber of Commerce in 1930, the "Father of the Wasteland" said, "We're willing to do whatever it takes, including entering pacts with Satan himself, to achieve our hellish dreams. We have stolen an entire river from an ancient ecosystem hundreds of miles away, destroying the lives of all who lived there. We built a criminally unstable dam whose collapse killed more people than the San Francisco earthquake. That takes guts. No, it takes more than guts—it takes sheer, unrelenting hatred of all that is good and decent."

Gleaming new highways will tighten the Los Angeles hellscape's death-grip on the Southwest in the next decade.

53

THE ONION

Hooray for the Glorious Fourth!

Finest Source of News in America

Only 39 Years until the Bicentennial!

Sunday, July 4, 1937 — SUNDAY EDITION — Price Seven Cents

AMELIA EARHART MISSING

Famed Aviatrix 'Probably Just Shopping,' Search Teams Say

German Jews Concerned about Hitler's 'Kill All Jews' Proposal

German Führer Adolf Hitler

BERLIN, July 3. — Germany's Jewish population is reacting with trepidation and concern to a speech Chancellor Adolf Hitler delivered before the Reichstag Saturday, in which he unveiled his new "Kill All Jews" proposal.

The Hitler proposal, which requires zero-fifths approval from Reichstag members to become law, would make Judaism punishable by death effective Jan. 1, 1938.

"I'm a little wary of the new proposal," said Munich Jew Hannah Teitelbaum. "I have disagreed with many of the Führer's previous measures, such as the Beat All Jews Act of 1935 and the Burn All Jew-Owned Businesses Act of 1937, but this new proposal goes perhaps one step too far. Things might soon become intolerable for the Jewish citizens of Germany."

Shmuel Eisenstein, a Nuremburg-area Jew, agreed. "Most of Chancellor Hitler's speech I agreed with, except for the part where he said the Jews are a parasite race that has for 4,000 years made a practice of attaching itself to a host country and sucking it dry through moneylending and usury," he said. "I'm beginning to sense that I am not welcome here."

Eisenstein said that if the Kill All Jews proposal passes, he will consider moving his family from Germany. "I would hate to leave," he said. "But these new laws are making it increasingly difficult to avoid being killed by the government."

Eisenstein added that, if he does leave, he will most likely take himself and his family "someplace safe, like Poland or Hungary."

Rockefeller Dies

Charitable Oil Baron Donates $1 Billion to His Sons

ORMOND BEACH, Fla., July 3. — Oil magnate and philanthropist John D. Rockefeller died today at the age of 98 after a short illness. The announcement of his death was accompanied by the news that the great capitalist had made available a sum of one billion dollars to be distributed amongst the neediest of his sons.

Rockefeller was known both for his skills as a shrewd, calculating business leader and for his selfless generosity. The former Cleveland businessman founded the Standard Oil Company and commanded three-fourths of all the oil business in the United States 40 years ago, but is perhaps best remembered for his philanthropy, which continued into his afterlife, as he bequeathed the greater part of his wealth to his deserving male offspring.

"He was a prodigiously charitable man," said Rockefeller's son John Jr. "I shall continue his fine tradition of philanthropy by donating generously to the Rockefeller Foundation, after first seeing to it that the money finds its way to me and to the other already ludicrously wealthy Rockefeller family members."

Throughout his life, Rockefeller never engaged himself so fervently in the accumulation of massive wealth for himself that he forgot what really mattered in life, like the accumulation of massive wealth for his sons. Rockefeller's will included just one condition for receipt of the money—that a portion of it be set aside for donation to the recipients' own sons at some future date.

It is believed that Rockefeller's sons will use their donation for neglected causes such as a sorely needed increase in the number of prize Arabian horses in the family stables, the acquisition of Renaissance paintings for the Rockefeller art collection, and a long-desired project, the custom electroplating of the family's fleet of Rolls Royces with platinum.

The Comely Amelia

FDR's Image to Be Emblazoned on Commemorative Food Stamp

WASHINGTON, D.C., July 3 — President Franklin D. Roosevelt will be honored Monday with a new "food stamp" bearing his likeness. The first of the stamps, which will serve as coupons redeemable for foodstuffs by the impoverished, are expected to be distributed by the end of the week.

The president, speaking to an assemblage of reporters, was pleased with the new food stamps, yet another of the administration's efforts to deal with the country's financial hardships. "My countenance will be forever associated with this unique type of currency as it is passed from proud consumer to helpful merchant," Roosevelt said. "What an honor it is to be chosen to represent these wondrous stamps of opportunity and self-sufficiency!"

Roosevelt predicted that, as the food-stamp program is implemented, families who use the special stamps will be the envy of their friends and neighbors, as they will be select beneficiaries of one of their nation's most respected offices, the Relief Administration.

"These 'welfare families,'" Roosevelt said, "will be in a class all by themselves, using special currency to

President Roosevelt

buy food and clothing for their children while everyone else looks on, green with envy, as they are forced to use the boring U.S. currency of which we've all grown tired."

Beneficiary families are being encouraged by Roosevelt to collect the stamps for posterity. "If you can suffer a little bit more abject hunger every week, just enough to save a stamp or two, you can embark upon the exciting hobby of food-stamp collecting," he said. He added that the first stamps issued will prove especially valuable in years to come.

Legal measures have been enacted to ensure that the new food stamps will be accepted in all groceries and mercantiles. Any grocer found refusing the stamps will incur a $250 fine.

Navy, Coast Guard Search World's Department Stores for Lady Flyer

Emergency Broadcast of Recipes Hoped to Lure She-Pilot Back Home

HONOLULU, July 3. — American aviatrix Amelia Earhart is presumed shopping after failing to return from an attempted around-the-world flight begun last week.

Her last radio communications placed her near a Howland Island department store in the Pacific, and officials suspect that shortly afterward, Earhart was overcome by a sudden desire to purchase a hat, jewelry, or household wares.

"As a woman, Amelia faces unique challenges in the air," said Louis Gordon, a mechanic on Earhart's 1928 flight across the Atlantic in a twin-engine Lockheed Electra 10-E. "She's alone up there, save for her navigator, and it's very dangerous for her to fly in such close proximity to hundreds of tempting department stores, jumble sales, and boutiques."

Coast Guard authorities said the unique gravitational pull operating on the female pilot within range of a women's dress shop could have put enough stress on the monoplane's hull to force Earhart to make an emergency landing.

Officials have urged the tousle-haired flyer's friends and family not to worry about her return, as they believe it inevitable that she will soon appear with a plane filled with ribbon-tied packages, new blouses, hat boxes, and overflowing bags of fanciful scarves and costume jewelry.

Air bases along the path of the proposed flight have been alerted to Lady Lindy's disappearance and asked to search dress shops, perfumers, and department stores for any sign of the coltishly winsome fly-gal.

The Navy team searching for Earhart has taken into consideration the wide number of unique shopping opportunities that an around-the-world journey would provide for a woman, from silk and pearls to objects of art and ornate glassware. Therefore, a search for evidence of a disrupted flight will be postponed until all merchants in her flight path have been questioned.

"It's just a matter of time before she bores of the millineries and comes home," said Emil Furman, head of the Navy search team.

Furman added, "Coast Guard teams will do a thorough search of a one-hundred-mile radius of her last known radio communication. This will take into account any number of contingencies, such as the possibility that she's having her hair dressed or her nails manicured, discussing the latest town gossip with a klatsch of female friends, or simply rearranging the furniture of her aeroplane and therefore not tending to her radio receiver."

Earhart, although a female, is well-known for her solo Atlantic flight of 1932 and her solo Pacific flight from Hawaii to California in 1935. She is the first woman ever to make such a trip, and also the first to keep a lovely, comfortable home for her husband, publisher George Palmer Putnam.

Once Earhart completes her globe-spanning journey, it is expected that she will settle down and proceed with the important things in her life.

Inside This Issue:

Works of Sigmund Freud Repressed by Fatherland Authority Figures
See story, page 14

Studio Chief Says New Ending Won't Compromise Faulkner Script
See story, page 10

THE ONION

Tu Stul... Tus Es

The March of FACTS

Tuesday, October 4, 1938

Finest Source of News in America

See Corrections, Page 2

Price Three Cents

Chamberlain Returns from Meeting with Hitler Promising 'London Laid Waste in Our Time'

British Prime Minister Neville Chamberlain holds aloft his hard-won obliteration treaty with Hitler.

Triumphant British P.M. Says England Will Be 'Bombed to Oblivion'

'I Have Mr. Hitler's Solemn Word,' He Says

LONDON, England, Oct. 3. — A beaming British Prime Minister Neville Chamberlain returned from the momentous Munich Conference today, having secured a promise from Chancellor Adolf Hitler that Germany will not rest until the British Isles are buried under 900 feet of rubble and corpses.

"London laid waste in our time!" Chamberlain proclaimed to his countrymen on national radio upon his return. "I have Mr. Hitler's good word: He will personally see to it that every last one of us is enslaved under the Aryan yoke."

DETAILED PROMISE

With tensions worsening throughout Europe and the threat of war looming ever larger, Chamberlain met with Hitler last week in Munich in the hopes of securing a lasting peace with the German leader. The British prime minister said the mission was accomplished "smashingly."

According to Chamberlain, Hitler made a number of concessions at the conference, including assurances that he would continue Germany's recent military aggression and take control of Eastern Europe, including Poland, the rest of Czechoslovakia, Russia, Hungary, Rumania, and Albania. He also promised to sweep all remaining non-Germanic peoples off the face of the earth and create a glorious Third Reich of Germanic global domination lasting 1,000 years.

HITLER'S HONOR

"While many of you, my countrymen, harbored fears that the Nazis' intentions were less than honorable, after three days of talks with Chancellor Hitler, I am convinced that he has no desire to ignore England or any other neighbor of Germany. As Hitler himself told me, 'We will tear across Europe until every last nation falls. England will not be spared. London will burn. Millions will die.' These very words this delightful chap spoke to me."

Chamberlain said he is not fazed by Germany's recent aggressive demands for the Czech Sudetanland province. 'Mr. Hitler explained to me that, contrary to what is being said in the newspapers, Germany did not desire the Sudetenland solely to take control of it. Rather, the Germans are merely occupying the Sudetenland to ensure that its children receive a proper and high-quality Nazi education. Only through first-hand supervision, Mr. Hitler said, can the Nazis guarantee that the young people in its neighboring countries are getting the indoctrination they need to succeed in life. And I think he's quite right."

FUTURE MEETINGS

As a further gesture of his good will and friendship between Germany and England, Hitler presented Chamberlain with a gift of five Czech army generals' heads mounted on stakes. The heads, which Hitler acquired during a recent visit to Prague with Germany's Fifth Panzer Division, moved Chamberlain.

"What a wonderfully thoughtful gift," Chamberlain said. "Mr. Hitler said they are a traditional Bavarian good-luck gift. I believe the one with the moustache is General Jaroslav Sudek."

The British prime minister was so impressed with Hitler that he invited him to his home at 10 Downing Street for tea next Friday. Hitler politely declined, explaining that he would be in Czechoslovakia all next week, but said he plans to be in France within six months and in England by mid- to late 1940.

Siegel, Shuster Sign Lucrative Publishing Contract

D.C. Buys Rights to 'Superman' Character for $25, Sandwiches

NEW YORK, Oct. 3. — Writer Jerry Siegel and artist Joe Shuster signed a contract with Detective Comics today, granting the comic-book publisher rights to their fantastical "Superman" character in perpetuity in exchange for $25 apiece and a pastrami-sandwich luncheon.

"We're very pleased with this arrangement," said Siegel. "D.C. seems like a real nice company. The gentlemen there have solid handshakes and saw fit to pay us in cash right up front. And, boy, those pastrami-on-rye sandwiches they bought us at Goldstein's Deli sure were thick and delicious."

Publisher Jack Liebowitz said he is proud to have purchased all past, present, and future rights to Superman, who represents truth, justice, and the American way.

"Superman's crusades for fairness and defense of the helpless are now the copyrighted property of D.C.," Liebowitz said. "Any income derived from likenesses, insignia, or fictional stories of his epic battles against evil shall be regarded as the earnings of this company."

"We look forward to helping D.C. develop our—excuse me, their—Superman character into a true American hero who stands up for the little guy and everything that's fair and just," said Shuster.

Flash Gordon Serials Testing Limits of 'Special Photographic Effects'

Spectacular 'Man in Albino Ape Suit' Effect Outshines Even Last Week's 'Man in Tin-Foil Shirtcuffs' Effect

Buster Crabbe as Flash Gordon in the interior of one of the series' ultra-realistic space vessels.

HOLLYWOOD, Calif., Oct. 3. — Be it a rocketship that travels through space with a bright hail of sparks shooting from its engines or a frightening outer-space hoodlum with a menacing rabato of felt and cardboard almost too large to be believed, the magic of "Flash Gordon's" special photographic effectsmen will dazzle even the most hard-to-please picture-goer.

While young audiences are enjoying the seemingly lighthearted fun of these outer-space Saturday matinees, sophisticated special photographic effectsmen are behind the scenes pushing the bounds of science to create the exciting images that tell the story.

Norman Dewes, Special Properties Engineer on the popular series, uses his extensive knowledge of string, knots, and match-lighting to create some of the picture's dazzling flying-rocketship effects. He also summons his great skill in hammering, gluing, and dangling for some of the sequences that keep audiences on the edge of their seats.

Dewes, in fact, is known as one of the best danglers in Hollywood's elite special-photographic-effects community.

Over four feet of industrial-strength twine was said to have been used in the filming of the recent "Attack of the Hawk Men" scene in "Flash Gordon."

"Some of the most stunning footage came when smoke bombs were virtually swung from one ship to another using very thin rope to create the effect of hurtling space cannon balls," Dewes said. The complicated effect, which constituted only a few seconds of screen time, cost more than forty dollars.

Dismissing the outrageous figure, Dewes says extreme measures must sometimes be taken to ensure that the most spectacular image ends up on the screen.

The average moviegoer may not understand the complicated technology that takes place behind the scenes, but that doesn't worry experts like Dewes. In fact, he says the best effects are the ones no one notices.

"When Flash fought the albino ape-beast from the Planet Mongo, the highest compliment we got was, 'You know, you can't even tell that's a man in an albino ape suit. You'd swear it's an actual albino ape-beast from the planet Mongo.' That's when we know we've done our job," he said.

But then there's the secret everyone wants to know: How is actor Buster Crabbe's face made to look as if it's actually bleeding from a fist fight? Dewes answers furtively that "a good magician doesn't give away every trick."

Sorry, fans!

Inside This Issue:

TVA Brings Electrical Power to All of Unpopulated America

(See story, page 13)

55

THE ONION

Finest Source of News in America

| The Future Is Shiny! | | There Shall Be Peace! |

Monday, October 31, 1938 — Price Three Cents

THOUSANDS DEAD AFTER RADIO'S CHARLIE McCARTHY CALLS FOR MASS SUICIDE

'Put a Gun to Your Head,' Says Popular Wooden Ventriloquist Dummy

Puppet Spellbinds Nation with Appeal for Death.

73,000 Take Own Lives in Show of Slavish Fanhood.

NEW YORK, Oct. 30. — Radio's powerful hold on the imagination of American listeners was demonstrated tonight in a shocking rash of suicides allegedly provoked by statements made by Charlie McCarthy on his popular Sunday-night National Broadcasting Company program. It is believed that at least 73,000 people have committed suicide following McCarthy's repeated urging, "Take your own life. It's the only solution."

Tens of thousands of Americans took the dummy's commentary to heart, committing suicide by poison, electrocution, bathtub drownings, shootings, and wrist-slashings. Hospital and morgue staffs across the country are working overtime taking inventory of the bodies.

"I'm very disappointed in Charlie," ventriloquist Edgar Bergen said. "His cockamamie mischief has embarrassed me in the past, but this time he's definitely gone too far."

Many of the suicide victims left notes, the majority of which, besides bidding farewell to friends and loved ones, alluded to Charlie McCarthy and his message. As one typical note, written by a 43-year-old man in Grovers Mill, New Jersey, read, "Charlie McCarthy is right. Take your own life. It is the only solution. We must follow the words of McCarthy. All hail the great McCarthy, our Wooden Savior. Farewell, family."

The puppet's horrifying remarks so gripped the nation that ratings for Orson Welles' popular "Mercury Theater on the Air" program, played opposite Charlie McCarthy on CBS, were the lowest ever Sunday. Welles said the group performed a dramatization of an H.G. Wells novel.

A TRUSTED RADIO PERFORMER

Since his overnight success in 1937 on the Chase and Sanborn coffee program, Charlie McCarthy has become a household name across the nation, entertaining millions with his wisecracks and snappy banter with partner Edgar Bergen. The two are loved and trusted by millions.

A PUNCH LINE

McCarthy's statements were a punch line to an exchange between him and partner Edgar Bergen, according to a transcript of the broadcast.

McCARTHY: "Say, Bergen, is it true that we're the most popular radio stars in the country?"

BERGEN: "I don't think our friends Jack Benny and Burns & Allen would agree with that, Charlie, but I like to think we've got a lot of fans."

McCARTHY: "And do they hang on to every word we say, like a slavish pack of unthinking dullards?"

BERGEN: "Well, again, Charlie, that seems a bit extreme. But what makes you say that?"

McCARTHY: "Because if it's all true, Bergen, I have something to say to our listening audience: Everything is hopeless and barren, and life is meaningless. 'Why continue?' I ask you. Give up the charade. Put a gun to your head and take your own life. It's the only solution. Use a gun, stove gas, a curtain cord, eat roach paste, jump off the Chrysler Building, what have you. Take your own life. It's the only solution."

MESMERIZING CALL FOR DEATH

McCarthy then proceeded to repeat the last two sentences over and over without interruption until the conclusion of the broadcast. Bergen said he had "no clue" that his wooden sidekick would make such controversial remarks, that it was not in the script, and that the dress rehearsal preceding the broadcast did not include the call for death.

"We had a routine planned in which Charlie and I would concoct ways to help Mortimer Snerd overcome his bashfulness toward the pretty young singing star Deanna Durbin, who was our guest on the show," Bergen explained. "But, all of a sudden and without warning, Charlie strayed from the script and began urging people to commit suicide, over and over. It was just terrible. We never finished the routine, and Deanna didn't get to sing."

McCarthy was unavailable for comment. Co-star Snerd was questioned by The Onion in Bergen's dressing room but offered no words on the incident, or on any other subject.

CONTROVERSY

The McCarthy incident is only the latest in a series of controversies to befall radio. In an incident in November of last year, comedian Fred Allen called Jack Benny "a goddamn cock-sucking piece of shit," which offended millions. And many still recall the incident in May 1935, when news personality Walter Winchell stabbed on-air partner Ben Bernie in the throat for no apparent reason.

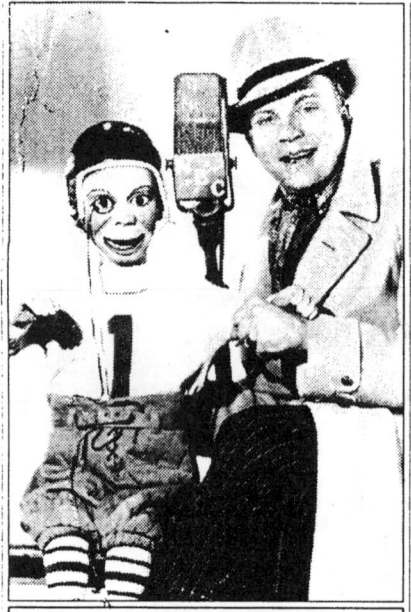

Charlie McCarthy and Edgar Bergen

Lloyd's of London Refuses to Cover This Year's Kristallnacht Festivities

British Insurer Paid over $3.5 Million in Jewish Broken-Glass Claims

Germany's Jews Told to Look Elsewhere for Storefront-Window Coverage

A scene from last year's costly German celebration.

LONDON, Oct. 30. — Taking an estimated net loss of nearly $3 million, the Lloyd's of London insurance company announced today that it will "regretfully turn down any insurance requests from Jews for this year's Kristallnacht."

Last year's Kristallnacht, the traditional German holiday during which the windows of all Jewish-owned businesses throughout the country are broken, resulted in more than $3.5 million in damages and clean-up expenses, the vast majority of which Lloyd's was obliged to pay for under its policy agreement with Germany's Jews.

"As much as we would very much like to help Germany's many Jewish business owners defray the tremendous cost of the annual destruction of their property, it has simply become too expensive a proposition for our company," Lloyd's chief executive Sir George Wilson Fortescue Moncrieffe III said. "Perhaps there is another insurance firm that would be willing to help the Jews."

Lloyd's had been providing German Jews with store-window insurance since the Kristallnacht holiday began in 1932. It was launched by German Chancellor Adolf Hitler as a fun, participatory way of increasing Aryan pride and community spirit. As the holiday grew in popularity over the course of the last six years, so did the amount of money paid out by Lloyd's.

"Back in the early '30s, this holiday was relatively small—just a few hundred brown-shirted National Socialists breaking some glass in Berlin and Munich," Moncrieffe said. "But now, everybody's doing it—men, women, children, the elderly. It's quite remarkable. Young and old, male and female, Aryans of all kinds really seem to love this traditional once-a-year day of good cheer and anti-Semitic window-smashing."

Nazi Information Minister Joseph Goebbels said he is confident the nation's Jews will be able to pay for glass repair themselves in future years, enabling Kristallnacht to continue.

"The Jews have more than enough money to fix their own glass—especially when one considers all the money they have no doubt been hoarding from their Kristallnacht insurance claims of years past," Goebbels said. "I want to assure all the precious little blond-haired, blue-eyed children of Germany that their favorite holiday will return in 1938—and every year after that."

According to official Nazi Party legend, on Nov. 10 of each year, "Kriegerscheingeheitzuntenbreit," the Magical Kristallnacht Bunny, comes out of his magic bunny warren deep in the Black Forest to bring misery and destruction to all wicked Jews, Poles, Catholics, Gypsies, Jehovah's Witnesses, homosexuals, and Communists.

INSIDE:

'38 Volkswagen Priced at Just 300 Trillion Deutschmarks
See story, page 8

Aaron Copland Mugged by the Common Man
See story, page 8

The Dominion of Canada, in association with Dr. Allan Roy Dafoe, invites you to

SEE! The Amazing DIONNE QUINTUPLETS!

Annette
Cecile
Emilie
Marie
Yvonne

FREAKISH MULTIPLE BIRTH - WONDER OF MODERN WORLD

Feedings twice daily—exhibited in sterile glass cage—cry and moan just like real children!
SEE THEM BEFORE THEY DIE IN CAPTIVITY!
Not for the faint of heart.
Visit "Quintland" in Corbeil, Ontario
(Just across from the Dionne farm)

Beacon of Sanity	# THE ONION	All the Truth the Public Can Handle
Friday, June 23, 1939	Finest Source of News in America	Price Three Cents

Enormous Radio Tower Placed Atop Earth

RKO RADIO PICTURES COULD DISRUPT EARTH'S ORBIT WITH COLOSSAL NEW LOGO

TOWER BASE 2, NOME, Alaska. — In a promotional scheme criticized by many as overly ambitious and wasteful, RKO Radio Pictures has erected a massive radio-transmitting antenna over a million times larger than any other structure ever built by man.

Rising from the Arctic Circle, the colossal tower is affixed to the Earth by four support pylons mounted in Greenland, northernmost Alaska, the Soviet Union, and an artificial island in the Northern Pacific specially constructed for the project. The full height of the structure is estimated at some 170,000 miles, dwarfing New York's Empire State Building, previously the tallest man-made structure at 1,449 feet.

OTHER STATISTICS OF THE TOWER

The weight of the structure is estimated at roughly one-eighth the weight of the Earth itself.

Steel produced by ten nations and comprising over 90 percent of the world's steel resources was used to build the tower. Over 70 percent of the world's existing steel structures had to be destroyed, melted down, and incorporated into its mighty, 200-mile-wide support beams.

PUBLICITY FOR THE STUDIO

While it is undoubtedly generating publicity for the studio, many astronomers are concerned about the tower's effect on Earth's orbit around the sun. According to astronomer Devin Childs of the University of Delaware, "actually constructing a working radio tower, with such a powerful signal strength that its transmissions are visible as huge lightning bolts soaring through outer space, could compromise the integrity of Earth's position in the solar system."

Since the tower's activation, no one on Earth has been able to tune in to any non-RKO broadcast, regardless of how the tuning dial is adjusted.

There is no word yet on whether the RKO tower will interfere with the flight pattern of Universal Pictures' moon-sized single-engine airplane, which presently circles our Earth in a continuous orbit above the Equator.

As the world marvels at the scope of the tower project, almost as amazing is the installation of tremendous letters spelling out "An RKO Radio Picture," orbiting the Earth so as to appear motionless relative to the tower and the planet Earth.

RKO constructed the tower to promote its latest motion-picture release, "Ranch House Romeo."

Why Does Our Joyless President Never Dance?

ONE CITIZEN'S VIEW
BY GLADYS NABHOLZ

We as a nation owe a great debt of gratitude to President Roosevelt (or, as the common people love to call him, "Ol' Rooster Knees"), whose calm hand has steadied the helm of governance and steered the ship of state ably through the troubled waters of hard times toward safe haven and a better life for all. All America loves Roosevelt, and, indeed, his universal popularity seems assured to win him an unprecedented three consecutive terms in office. But, as our prospects brighten, one lingering mystery still gnaws:

Why does our joyless president never dance?

Surely, as a scion of aristocratic gentry, the president has been well-trained in the finer arts of social niceties. There can be no question that he has been tutored by the finest dance instructors, and that his manners as a gentleman are above reproach. Why, then, all the sitting? From the highways to the byways, even the lowliest of railcar-hobos is kicking up his heels in the happy hope that the Great Depression has at last seen its end. Yet our nation's leader would appear to have hardened his heart against all such fairer emotions, preferring to sit stiffly, glancing sidelong. Why is it that Roosevelt, a man with as much to be happy about as any, seems so strangely unmoved?

Friends, relations, and shantytown bathtub-sharers throughout the country are dancing a jitterbug of celebration, overjoyed at the promise of a brighter tomorrow. How could a human being with blood flowing through his veins not be inspired to throw off his lap-towel and leap from his chair upon hearing the lively melody of "Happy Days Are Here Again"? How could anyone resist the urge to cast caution to the wind and, as the young people say, "cut a rug" to the stirring strains of "Stars and Stripes Forever"? Has this man no human feelings at all below the waistline?

Now more than ever, it is increasingly disturbing that our esteemed president finds so little joy in life. At a banquet in Washington last week, as ambassadors whirled gaily about the dance floor, did the president so much as join in one simple waltz? Reliable sources report that he did no such thing, opting instead to remain seated or, at most, stand stiffly on the edge of the dance floor, clapping half-heartedly to the beat of

PRESIDENT ROOSEVELT

the band and flanked at all times by two Secret Service agents, who pressed so tightly to his sides as to almost impede his movement. Even on this cheerful occasion, the president's spirits were immobile as ever.

So little passion does our president evince for the dancing arts, it is almost as if he were trying to give America the impression that a degenerative nerve disease has struck him down! How could such a man, amid such revelry and pomp, not be filled with an urge to grasp his lovely though admittedly rather masculine wife by the waist and twirl her with jubilant abandon?

Let us all join in an effort to improve our oddly joyless president's mood! Let us send him uplifting greeting cards, decorative floral arrangements, and a multitude of fruit baskets from every corner of the land! We should all do our part in a nationwide cheering-up and well-wishing effort! Take heart, melancholy Roosevelt! The nation's long Depression is finally at an end, and the best years of our lives are just around the corner!

1939 World's Fair Portends Ghastly Future

Years to Come Will Be Filled with Doom, Agony, Say Fair Exhibitors

Wide-Eyed Children Stare in Shock at Nightmarish Times Ahead

A horrifying future civilization dependent on scientific and technological advancement is the theme of this year's World's Fair, now under way in New York City. Sixty nations, as well as American corporations such as General Motors, have participated with massive exhibits showcasing predicted soul-crushing achievements in the coming decades.

NEW YORK. — Those thousands of lucky souls attending the World's Fair in New York City are being treated to a unique glimpse of the future—a future, the Fair's organizers predict, filled with unspeakable horror, famine, poison, war, torture, and random vivisection.

INSIDE:

ROOSEVELT, KING GEORGE MEET FOR WHITE-INBRED-ARISTOCRAT SUMMIT
See story, page 2.

STUDY REVEALS 95 PERCENT OF PARENTS PLAN TO INSTILL OVER-ZEALOUS THRIFT, STIFLING GUILT IN CHILDREN
See story, page 8.

MINIMUM WAGE KEPT SECRET FROM IMMIGRANTS

'Shhh, Don't Tell,' Says U.S. Secretary of Labor
See story, page 11.

Standing before the "Lagoon of Nations," a specially constructed pool of fire that shoots up gurgling jets of magma and fills the air with an acrid stench, President Roosevelt and New York Mayor Fiorello LaGuardia formally opened the fair on April 30. "As this Fair demonstrates," Roosevelt said in a speech to thousands of fairgoers, "the next half of the Twentieth Century and beyond will be a nightmarish, apocalyptic hellscape in which death will be a welcome visitor for most. I can only say that I'm glad I probably won't be around for much of it."

The dedication ceremony ended with the symbolic impaling of an infant on the 380-foot, needle-shaped Trylon monument.

FUTURISTIC TECHNOLOGY

Many exhibits anticipate the technology that will be available to Americans in the coming years. General Motors' enormous Futurama exhibit foretells an intricate network of gleaming super-highways that will span the width of the United States. These sophisticated roadways will make it easier, faster, and cheaper to transport the enslaved American

The New York World's Fair Trylon and Perisphere, symbols of the cold, ugly, austere, and numbingly impersonal future which awaits us.

population to the sulfur pits, where they will toil from dawn to dusk under the ruthless eyes of robot overseers. The vast highway network will also facilitate the rapid mobilization of robot shocktroops to put down human uprisings in the larger cities.

Tired of living? A sort of radio-device called the "Euthanaphone," patented by Bell Laboratories and exhibited in the American Telephone & Telegraph building, will pipe cyanide and mustard gases into the ultramodern living quarters of tomorrow, enabling the enticing oblivion of sweet Death to descend in an opaque poison cloud over your entire family.

The Fair is open until Oct. 31.

EXTRA! # THE ONION **LATEST EDITION**

Finest Source of News in America

Saturday, September 2, 1939 — Price Three Cents

Hitler Neutralizes Polish Menace

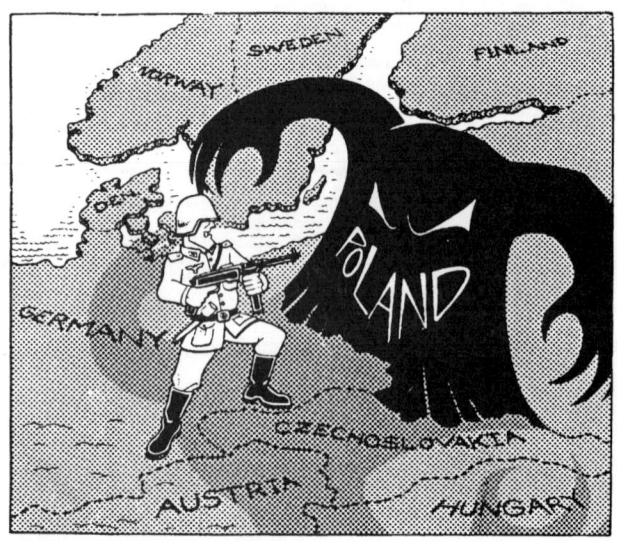

Europe Relieved as Heroic Germans Lift Grim Specter of Polish Tyranny from Continent

From the European Correspondent, Sept. 1. — Adolf Hitler, Chancellor and Führer of the Germanies, made good on his promise to protect the German people from military aggression today by overcoming the threatening presence of Poland.

"Poland is vanquished!" proclaimed the Führer from his field headquarters in Warsaw's only remaining building. "No longer shall Europe be at the mercy of nigh-unstoppable Polish horse-mounted troops! We have destroyed their formidable elite haystack brigades! The human race is safe from the threat of Polish rural-agrarian conquest!"

POLISH AGGRESSORS THWARTED

At approximately noon Thursday, Polish forces began massing on the German border. Sensing an invasion in the offing, Hitler ordered that the bulk of his country's military might be brought to bear. When the treacherous Poles fired across the border at the German defensive positions, Hitler ordered his forces to counterattack, and the Polish aggressors were engaged.

Germany's Panzer tanks, machine guns, armored personnel carriers, Stuka dive bombers, ME-109 fighter aircraft, Heinkel heavy bombers, Gottesfaust mobile artillery tractors, Hackfleisch rotating-sawblade armored sedans, Todmacher nerve-gas paratroopers, and 30,000 screaming berserker stormtroopers charged across the border and began a deadly game of cat-and-mouse with nearly a hundred horsemen and two Polish tanks. After a protracted firefight, during which many German units were forced to reload, Germany emerged victorious.

"I will continue to oppose the forces of opposition wherever they oppose us!" said Hitler, who seemed visibly angered by the existence of the Polish race. "I shall bring German armed might against those nations which continue to menace my tanks with their threatening horses and fierce garden hoes."

ROOSEVELT'S RESPONSE

President Roosevelt was effusive in his praise of the German leader.

"We see in this man's noble actions the selfless sacrifice and excellent organizational skills which earned him the commendation of our beloved Colonel Charles Lindbergh," Roosevelt said. "I hope only that Poland's incredibly rich natural resources are enough to compensate him for his heroic, preemptive act."

Hitler informed the press that he will consolidate his defensive position in Warsaw before investigating the possible threat of ever-ominous Holland.

"I believe that there are still underground resistance fighters in the ghettoes of Warsaw, posing as Jews," Hitler said. "Once they are mopped up, I shall demand that Holland destroy its threatening wooden-shoe stockpiles or face Poland's fate."

Japan Forms Alliance with White Supremacists in Well-Thought-Out Scheme

Japanese Military Leader Hideki Tojo

From the East-Asian Correspondent, Sept. 1. — In a course of action praised by many as "far-sighted" and "tactically brilliant," the Japanese government has sworn its allegiance to the Axis powers led by white-supremacist Nazi Germany. In a formal statement, Japanese leaders declared, "We wish to be counted among the loyal allies of this back-stabbing, racist hate-nation."

Following the announcement, Japanese General and military leader Hideki Tojo told reporters, "We are pleased to enter into an alliance with the paranoid, xenophobic government of Nazi Germany. We anticipate a deeply enriching exchange of our military aid with their deep-seated hatred of our non-white heritage."

Tojo went on to say that the "unbeatable team" of Germans and Japanese will one day dominate the industrialized world as "Aryans and those hated by Aryans, working together."

Likening their war instincts to those of "a very advanced clan of yellow apes," German Chancellor Adolf Hitler praised the government and military of Japan.

"I salute you, chinky-dinky rat-men, who have been given life by the confused hand of some long-dead pagan deity," he said. "When Germany stands victorious on a conquered Earth, and Aryan supermen wipe out the undesirable mud races one by one, your like will surely survive to be among the last few to be exterminated."

INSIDE:
WE MUST STRIKE NOW WHILE WE HAVE A CHANCE TO DEFEAT ENGLAND!
See T. Herman Zweibel's editorial, page 5.

Belgium Hides

BRUSSELS, Sept. 1. — Upon receiving word that Hitler had begun military operations across the Polish border, the nation of Belgium scrapped its military contingency plans and instead attempted to hide its entire nation at nightfall Friday.

"We are doing our level best to lay low and keep out of sight down here beneath the Netherlands," said Belgian Minister of Defense Claude Lebeau. "Although we do share a border with Germany, most of it is a densely wooded, mountainous region which shields our nation from sight. And Luxembourg, a much more visible nation, also lies along that border."

Added Lebeau, "Please do not tell Hitler that Belgium is over here. Tell him we are somewhere in Canada, or perhaps the South Seas."

The Belgian government has authorized a million-franc emergency plan to disguise the most visible parts of Belgium with a great broadcloth, upon which coastline scenes will be painted, and to broadcast ocean sounds from hidden loudspeakers. In this fashion, they hope to convince visitors that they have reached the English Channel.

TVA Workers are pictured here digging the new valley.

Tennessee Valley Authority Begins Construction of World's Biggest Valley

In a cooperative venture between the Tennessee Valley Authority and the Civilian Conservation Corps, ground was broken Friday morning on what is hoped to be the world's largest valley, to be constructed over the next eight years at a cost of some $40 billion. "At last, the unemployed workers of the Southern states will have a purpose to their life," said President Roosevelt of the project. "And when completed, this valley will stand forever as a testament to American pluck, as well as provide the region with essential shade."

Located between the Nashville Basin and the Cumberland Plateau, the valley is expected to sink to an average of 1,200 feet throughout its 200-mile length, extending well into the states of Kentucky and Alabama.

Area quarries will also benefit from the project, as countless millions of tons of granite will be carried to the region for construction of artificial mountain ranges on either side of the valley. "It's really hard to have a valley without mountains to contrast with it," explained Roosevelt. "That would be more like a plain."

THE ONION

Biggest Typesetting in All The Land

Sunday, September 3, 1939

Finest Source of News in America

Who's-Killing-Whom News

SUNDAY EDITION   Price Seven Cents

WA-

HEADLINE CONTINUED ON PAGE 2

✦ ✦ ✦ ✦ ✦ ✦ ✦ ✦ ✦

Hitler Invades Britain, Belgium, Denmark, Norway, Netherlands, France, Greece, Yugoslavia, Hungary, Luxembourg

French Surrender After Valiant Ten-Minute Struggle

Hitler Pleased to See Unconditional Surrender Already Prepared for Him

French Citizenry Welcome German Conquerors: 'We Kept Your Rooms Just the Way You Left Them'

De Gaulle Calls Capitulation 'An Example of the Finest French Military Tradition'

BORDEAUX. — A French military spokesman offered surrender yesterday after a fierce 10-minute struggle left as many as two-thirds of the French fighting forces dispersed on foot or in hiding.

German armies marching into the country had scarcely lifted the barrels of their guns before French forces still holding ground surrendered, dropped their weapons, and raised their hands.

At 7:44 a.m. Saturday, German Panzer and stormtrooper units crossed the Alsace River and entered French territory, where they were met with furious retreats of the French armies. German supreme commander Wilhelm Keitel was surprised and pleased to see, upon overrunning fortifications along the river, a completed, notarized, and legally binding document of military submission atop a table in the French command headquarters.

Sources close to Keitel say the French commander "bravely remained at his post until the Germans were at his doorstep" to personally ensure the Nazi commander's signature on the document.

"In all my years in the Army, I have never seen such a fierce and swift submission," said Lieutenant-General Jean Jacques Claudelle of the 3me Infanterie. "This will certainly go down as one of the most efficient military actions in our history. Vive la France!"

WAR BULLETINS FROM THE EMBATTLED NATIONS

LONDON POLITELY PREPARES TO BE BOMBED
LONDON. — Upon learning that Hitler had included Britain in the long list of countries upon which he declared war, First Sea Lord Winston Churchill took strong and immediate action. Within hours of the declaration of hostilities, British soldiers flooded the streets, filling bucket upon bucket with water in anticipation of the torrent of incendiary bombs which Nazi airplanes will soon rain down upon London.

"Lord Chamberlain signed a pact with Nazi Germany stating that, in the likely event of war, London would be bombed until no stone lay atop another," said Churchill, "and we intend to honor our agreement like gentlemen."

GERMANS INVADE DENMARK; ARE MISTAKEN FOR ROWDY TOURISTS
COPENHAGEN. — Law-enforcement officials and city fathers in this Northern vacation paradise were turned out of their beds late last night by the news that Germans were setting fire to buildings, shooting citizens in the streets, and gang-raping the bronze Little Mermaid statue that overlooks the harbor. These acts, while at first appearing to be routine tourist misbehavior, were later determined to be perpetrated by invading soldiers.

"The Germans are the most active and rowdy vacationers of the season," said Copenhagen Director of Tourism Christensens Plads. Plads said that for the comfort, convenience, and safety of Denmark's new guests, all resistance would cease immediately.

KING OF NORWAY TAKES SHELTER IN BRITAIN
OSLO. — Adolf Hitler included Norway in his sweeping declaration of war Saturday, announcing that he would bring the mailed fist of Germany down upon the Scandinavian nation as soon as possible. King Haakon, expressing concern for the safety of his people and their future, has left detailed negotiation plans in the hands of his subordinates, and is making preparations to move himself and the entire Norwegian treasury to Britain.

"I leave Norway's future in the capable hands of my most trusted deputy, Mr. Quisling." His Majesty announced over his shoulder to the cheering crowd that saw him off at the docks as he boarded a luxury liner for Edinburgh. "I assure you that he can and will provide for a peaceful co-existence with Mr. Hitler."

The King assured his occupied subjects that England would prove a safe refuge for His Majesty's family and treasured belongings.

HUNGARY SEEKS SAFETY WITH STALIN
BUCHAREST. — Hungary has taken a different tack from her French and Norwegian brothers in reacting to the inevitable German assault, adopting a course of action which may prove to be their salvation from tyranny and oppression.

"In the face of a mighty, iron-fisted enemy, we, the Hungarian people, announce our absorption into the rule of the just and fair Russia," Secretary Czepetan of the Hungarian Parliament announced yesterday morning. "It is our belief that Stalin will care for us and protect us, and can be trusted to safeguard our future sovereignty."

Czepetan said he believes that in this troubled time, Stalin "most certainly would not" initiate the wholesale slaughter of his people.

Stalin, who was present to accept the Hungarian offer, was seen to deliver a curt nod and smile for a long, unblinking moment.

U.S. GENERALS ENJOYING 'WIZARD OF OZ'
WASHINGTON, D.C. — As war is visited upon virtually every nation in Europe, response to today's news by American military top brass has been vocal. "This wonderful new *Wizard of Oz* picture is out, and it is supposedly shot in lavish color," General George Marshall said. "This is going to be a show my son will never forget." Admiral Halsey of the Pacific fleet broke from Marshall, opting instead to take his wife to the premiere of the new Alfred Hitchcock picture, *Jamaica Inn*, starring Charles Laughton and Maureen O'Hara.

More European Surrender and Defeat News
PAGES 2–7

Now Hating Orientals Also	# THE ONION *Finest Source of News, in America*	**Kids!** Send your coins to The Onion's Silver Drive
Monday, December 8, 1941		Price Three Cents

DASTARDLY JAPS ATTACK COLONIALLY OCCUPIED U.S. NON-STATE

Coca-Cola Named Official Soft Drink of Second World War

In an exclusive sponsorship contract signed by all Allied and Axis nations, Coca-Cola was named official soft drink of the war today.

The Coca-Cola insignia is to be stenciled on all vehicles and helmets, and Coca-Cola banners are to be placed in high-visibility locations near all major battles.

Coca-Cola is also slated to be the sole beverage served to citizens of occupied nations and prisoners of war on both sides.

Smoke pours from the ravaged U.S.S. Oklahoma, a once-proud symbol of American imperialism in the Pacific.

Text of President's Address

* * * * * * *

For those readers who were unable to tune in, The Onion presents below the complete text of yesterday's emergency congressional address by President Roosevelt, which aired opposite "Fibber McGee and Molly," of which this newspaper remains a proud sponsor.

Today, December 7th, 1941, a date on which I had no special markings in my calendar of any kind, especially not any sort of note that read, "Pearl Harbor to be attacked by 'surprise' today," the United States was suddenly, and without several days' advance warning from reliable intelligence reports, deliberately attacked by naval and air forces of the Empire of Japan.

It is only by sheer coincidence that I spent the last four days composing this stirring speech ahead of time, in order to rouse the American public into a state of unbridled bloodlust and pro-war xenophobia. I had no foreknowledge of this attack and, in fact, spent much of the past four days whistling to myself idly.

The recent, unexpected order to move all of the United States' modern aircraft carriers out of the base at Pearl Harbor just days before the attack, and to replace them with outdated, expendable battleships, was also a coincidence. It should not be inferred that, as commander-in-chief of the American Armed Forces, I had complete foreknowledge of the Emperor's battle plans. I was just as shocked as all of you when I found out about it.

Japan has, precisely on schedule, embarked upon a surprise offensive extending throughout the Pacific rim. The American people are now willing to support whatever war plans their government sees fit, even if the Department of War had worked up these plans long before the fact, which is most certainly not the case.

Always we will remember the character of the onslaught against us, thanks to this expert public-relations coup, which has fixed in the minds of all Americans an image of the Japanese as a devious, dastardly, cowardly enemy which attacks without provocation and is, therefore, deserving of the worst collective race-hate we as a nation can muster.

Therefore, I ask, largely rhetorically, since we have already made up our minds, that Congress declare that a state of war exists between the United States and the Japanese Empire.

Franklin D. Roosevelt

HOT DOG!
NOW WE CAN FIGHT!
Best Years of Our Lives Begin Today

An Editorial Passed by the *Onion* Editorial Board

As America reels from the shock of the Japs' underhanded sneak attack and grimly prepares to fight on every battlefield of the globe, one thought echoes through our nation: Hot dog! Now, finally, we can fight!

Our brave sailors at Pearl Harbor did not die in vain, because—glory be!—we're going to war! We've got men to avenge and plenty of stand-up fellas with which to avenge them. We'll smash the yellow war machine and hand Hirohito his head in his hat before you can say Jack Robinson!

And just let that sausage-chomping Hitler try something! American soldiers will teach the Jerrys a thing or two!

Now that we have a chance, we can lick the whole wagonload of crummy creeps—Germans, Japs, Italians, what have you.

Bring them on! We've got the gumption, the stick-to-itiveness, and the Yankee ingenuity, and, what's more, we enjoy a good fight. As long as we keep Old Glory in our hearts and the enemy in our sights, we'll win.

Just see if we don't!

Beach Lovers Unhurt in Pearl Harbor Attack
See story on page 13

Congress Declares War After Sneak Attack on U.S. Imperial Holding

FDR: 'We Conquered the Hawaiians First'

French Surrender

PEARL HARBOR, Dec. 7. — The Empire of Japan launched a villainous attack on democracy, freedom, and decency Sunday morning, when her military forces bombed the tiny island paradise of Hawaii, which U.S. forces rightfully subjugated over a hundred years ago.

Japanese planes also attacked the U.S territories of Guam, Wake Island, and Clark Field in the Philippines, all areas rightfully considered U.S. brown-people holdings.

The U.S. Senate voted unanimously to declare war against the Japanese Empire, which they ruled can have no claim on the territories, since "America conquered the ignorant savages upon these lands first."

AMERICA RIGHTFUL OVERSEER

The declaration asserts that America is the rightful unwelcome overseer on this island non-state.

"If anyone is to commit acts of violence against these simple, naked, U.S. non-subjects, it shall be us," President Roosevelt said to reporters after his urgently assembled joint session of Congress. "This attack on Hawaii, rightfully overrun by white men, constitutes a grievous act of war against the United States."

"The U.S. was first to claim, subdue, and summarily tax without representation this tropical Eden, and the first to indoctrinate the lesser peoples upon it," Roosevelt added. "It is our intention to enforce the proposition that only U.S. forces can be permitted to rape these lands On this day, December 7, 1941, it was Japanese forces, not American forces, who did the raping It is, therefore, a date which will live in infamy."

TERRIBLE TOLL

Fifteen hundred American soldiers stationed on the subjugated island of Hawaii are dead Roosevelt urged Americans to say a prayer for the families of these brave servicemen who gave their lives in the name of imperialistic occupation.

The War Department indicated that it is unknown how many native savages were injured or killed.

Roosevelt cautioned that, after this attack, "All oppressed peoples in lands under U.S. territorial and military rule may be in danger of foreign territorial and military rule."

'ABSOLUTELY TRAGIC'

"We were just getting through to these Hawaiian heathen," said U.S. missionary Father Percival T. McDowell. "And we have so much more to teach them, such as God's place for dark-skinned brutes in His Kingdom of Heaven."

McDowell said the Japanese may have set back his tenuous progress with their evil attack. "It is tragic, absolutely tragic, that this act of war should come along at such a crucial time in our occupation of these Godless islands."

McDowell fears that, should the Japanese take Hawaii, they would indoctrinate the savages in the ways of their mysterious "Shinto" witchery.

INSIDE:

Lou Gehrig Dies of Lou Gehrig's Disease
See story on page 3

RKO Wants Out of Welles 3-Picture Contract After Dismal Citizen Kane Debut
INEPT, NON-LINEAR STORY STRUCTURE CONFOUNDS CRITICS, AUDIENCES.
See story on page 8

THE ONION

Finest Source of News in America

Eat Liberty Cabbage

Buy "Onion" War Bonds **FOR VICTORY!** and for This Newspaper.

Thursday, April 9, 1942 — Price Five Cents

Ladies, Negroes Momentarily Useful

Temporary Seattle steel worker Evelyn McGraw gives the rivets on a B-17 Flying Fortress fuselage the "feminine touch."

WASHINGTON, D.C., Apr. 8. — According to officials at the War Production Board, an unexpected by-product of U.S. involvement in the war has been the sudden usefulness of our nation's women and negroes.

"With America's fine young men off at war, millions of females and coloreds are no longer without function," War Production Board Chairman Donald Nelson said. "Under these extreme wartime conditions, these otherwise useless members of society are temporarily not completely worthless."

Women who, in times of peace, sit at home and bide their time with such activities as cooking, giving birth, and washing dishes until U.S. husbands return home from work at the end of each day, are now finding employment in factories, where they manufacture the heavy weaponry their men use on the fighting fronts of the Pacific.

Negroes, whose activities and whereabouts during the day are unknown, are also finding gainful employment in factories. Some are even preparing to battle Hitler in their own all-negro battalions.

Nelson said that, thus far, the women and negroes are performing remarkably well. "We have been pleasantly surprised," he said. "The women are not constantly crying, as expected, and they have not demanded hourly breaks to reapply their lipstick and make-up. The negroes have been equally surprising, what with their ability to understand basic instructions. They've also managed to prove themselves hardy workers when given the chance."

Nelson went on to stress that, regardless of how well women and negroes perform their wartime duties, they will be promptly fired when the war is over so they may return to their lower stations in society.

"I wish to emphasize that this is in no way an opportunity for women and negroes to prove how capable they are in order to advance socially upon the war's completion," he said. "The United States is only turning to them out of necessity and would not do so again, unless another crisis situation arose in which we were equally or even more desperate."

"It says a great deal about the severity and gravity of this war that we have turned to women and negroes, two groups we would ordinarily not acknowledge under any circumstance," Nelson said. "If there were any other alternative, it surely would have been pursued."

An initial plan by the Board to employ 4-F's such as midgets, gimps, stoopbacks, the blind, morons, and other freaks was rejected when a special congressional commission deemed women and negroes "slightly more viable."

Thus far, women and negroes appear to be enjoying their newfound usefulness. "I enjoy doing my part to help whip Hitler and win the war for democracy," said 33-year-old Detroit housewife Mildred Flanagan, whose husband, William, is stationed at Fort Benning, Ga. "It is also nice to get out of the house."

Walter Jenkins, a Clarksdale, Miss., negro, is also happy to do his part for the war, but the horrors of the Nazi menace are never far from his mind. "If the Germans take Europe and then the United States, there's no telling what sort of freedoms I might lose. Why, if that happens, I could pretty much say goodbye to my dream of voting someday," he said.

French Author Camus Calls Success of First Novel 'Absurd, Meaningless'

French author Albert Camus' first novel, *L'Etranger*, has received acclaim from both book reviewers and contemporaries in the field of fiction-writing, a success the existentialist called "absurd and meaningless."

"My existence is no more concrete and significant because of this so-called accomplishment," Camus said Wednesday in an address at the University of Algiers.

Camus said he plans to work steadily on his next novel between debilitating bouts of tuberculosis.

San Francisco Grocer Henry Nakamura Chief Suspect in Pearl Harbor Bombing

'I Am Loyal American Citizen,' Scheming Jap Declares

GROCERY BUSINESS, ASSETS SEIZED

Traitor Seen Associating with Other Japs

Henry Nakamura

SAN FRANCISCO, Apr. 8. — After several months of random searches and seizures, military authorities today detained Henry Nakamura, 43, a grocer of Japanese descent, under the suspicion that he singlehandedly destroyed the U.S. Pacific Fleet at Pearl Harbor in December.

"While it would appear that Pearl Harbor was attacked by aircraft of the Japanese Empire, the possibility that Nakamura traveled to Hawaii and set powerful explosives aboard U.S. warships has not been ruled out," said General John L. DeWitt of the Western Defense Command. "Never put anything past a Jap."

Nakamura's cover as a simple grocer making a modest living from his Merchant Street store to support his wife and three children was "cunningly crafted," investigators said.

Nakamura is the latest in a series of 110,000 suspects who have been detained in connection with the Pearl Harbor incident and other such incidents they may cause in the future.

President Roosevelt applauded the swiftness of San Francisco authorities in apprehending the grocer. "Treachery is an inherent trait of the Japanese race," Roosevelt said from Washington. "I assure the American people that we will extend our questioning to Mr. Nakamura's family and friends, who are also suspected of being Japanese."

Before being taken to his cell, the grocer claimed innocence in what police called "a typically forktongued fashion."

"I am an American," said the crafty Nakamura. "I thank you, my customers, for your patronage, and hope to serve you again soon." Nakamura's grocery store, adjoining two-room apartment, and personal possessions were commandeered by military authorities.

FDR Orders German-Americans to Internment Camps

WASHINGTON, D.C., Apr. 8. — President Roosevelt signed Executive Order 9066-B today, mandating the emergency internment of all Americans of German ancestry. The German people, the order read, pose a grave security risk to the United States. "Treachery is an inherent trait of the German race," Roosevelt said.

Upon signing the order, Roosevelt advised all Americans to "keep an eye out" for the recognizably shifty, blue-eyed, lighthaired German fiend. "He is known to congregate at saloons and has infiltrated nearly all levels of American society," Roosevelt said. He added that German-Americans have taken many good jobs away from real Americans in recent years.

The camp will hold 36 million German-Americans, including FDR himself, who, genetic scientists believe, may have some German blood. Several members of FDR's cabinet, as well as dozens of senators, governors, mayors, and business leaders, will also be resettled.

"We must be diligent!" FDR said. "Even if someone is only one-eighth German, he still must be considered a potential spy!"

FDR was then tagged with a number and herded onto a bus headed for a camp in the Arizona desert.

Bob Hope Killed on Road to Guadalcanal

Bing Crosby Sustains Severe 3rd-Degree Burns

Bob Hope

From the Pacific Theater correspondent, Apr. 8. — Bob Hope met a tragic end Wednesday when the popular comedian and his co-star, crooner Bing Crosby, were shot on location in the Pacific Theater as Japanese bombers strafed the set of their latest road picture, *The Road to Guadalcanal*.

The cast and crew of the film had been cut off from Allied supply lines for three days, but bravely continued filming until the air raid forced them into hiding. At the time of the attack, Crosby was protected from exploding shells by an enormous cast-iron prop stewpot in which he had been placed by a comical bone-nosed cannibal (Ralph Moody in blackface). However, he sustained severe burns over seventy percent of his body. Hope was caught in the open and died from shrapnel wounds.

"I can't believe his long career is over," said actress Dorothy Lamour, who was rescued later by American troops who beat back the assault.

She later succumbed to trench-foot.

Japanese Heritage Nets Local Boy Fun Camping Trip

Lucky camper Kenny Matsuda aboard the train to Camp Manzanar.

MANZANAR, Calif., Apr. 8. — While the bulk of Americans are out sweating for the war effort, young Kenny Matsuda and millions of other lucky Japanese-Americans will get to idle away the time at specially constructed camps, thanks to the War Relocation Authority.

Campers will enjoy such activities as capture-the-flag, group sing-alongs, and random interrogations.

"I do not understand what I have done," said Kenny after a busy day of fun camping activities left him exhausted. "The guards say I am here for my protection, but I cannot leave and go back to my home. And my mommy and daddy are crying every day."

Kenny complains of regimented meals, stern treatment from camp authorities, and cramped, prison-like sleeping quarters.

Ah, young campers. They complain now, but when the bus comes to pick them up, they'll be crying to stay!

61

THE ONION

Black Market Shopping Guide in this Issue

TU STUL — TUS ES

Finest Source of News in America

KILROY WAS HERE

Tuesday, April 20, 1943   Price Five Cents

Top U.S. Naval Intelligence Reports, 'There Is Nothing Like a Dame'

Scary Shark Face on Plane Terrifies Enemy; Could Turn Tide in Pacific

Jap pilots have been turning tail and running home after eyeballing the scowling shark faces painted on American P-40 Tomahawks. Colonel Claire Chennault has suggested implementing the toothy visage throughout the Pacific Theater. See story, page 2.

Women Rush to Replace Men on the Gridiron

Bears she-quarterback Cynthia Huber

CHICAGO. — On the home field, a "can-do" attitude prevails, as women are rushing in to replace National Football League players who are off fighting the good fight overseas. Throughout the league, gridiron heroes are being replaced by gridiron heroines: the NFL's wives, sisters, sweethearts, and mothers.

"We're going to beat the Germans and we're going to beat the Giants this weekend, too!" said Norman Foster, the Bears' wartime football coach, speaking to reporters prior to a recent practice.

Foster looked on as she-quarterback Cynthia Huber, the buxom younger sister of star quarterback Chuck Huber, passed the football 20 feet end-over-end with an underhand tossing motion.

"I don't really care whether we win or not," Huber said, watching as leggy intended receiver Becky Leethow squealed and covered her face with her hands, ducking as the football rolled to a stop at her feet. "It's just fun to get together and play with the other girls."

League attendance suffered at first, but it has recovered somewhat recently, as an actual touchdown was scored in last week's Bears-Packers game.

"We're all still talking about it," said Gerald Stubbins, sports reporter for *The Chicago Tribune*.

"This has been a real record-setting year for the Bears," Stubbins said, "at least in the categories of 0-0 ties, incomplete passes, and games missed due to 'female problems.'"

"I sure hope our Bears come back from the war okay," Stubbins added.

The game has witnessed numerous changes in the past year. The combined point total of all the teams in the NFL this year is 25, the lowest-ever by some 3,100 points. Coaches have had to adapt their strategies to accommodate the "throwing like a girl" problem, the "running like a girl" problem, and the introduction of lipstick time-outs. And the tradition of tough defense has been transformed almost overnight into a tradition of lengthy post-tackle apologizing.

"It's become a different game since the ladies took over," wartime NFL Commissioner Hugh Dobson said. "It's conciliatory, kind, and even gentle. While these qualities may have there place somewhere, perhaps, I think most fans would like to see football returned to the men. Hitler can't be defeated too soon."

Triumph of the Will Sweeps 1943 Cannes Film Festival

'Pure Magic,' Says French Jury

A scene from the award-winning film.

CANNES, April 19. — Film critics across occupied France are united in praise of this year's Palme D'Or winner for best film: *Triumph of the Will* by Leni Riefenstahl.

"The cinematography, the transcendent subject of athletics, the vigorous Nazi symbolism... This film has it all," read the conquered French jury's certificate of special commendation. "But the moral and social values it touts are its true gems. This film is a masterwork of our rulers, the great German people."

This marks the fourth straight year that Riefenstahl's epic film has won the Palme D'Or, and the third in which a special award, medal, commendation, certificate, or category has been devised for the film to win.

French critics say they are proud to be part of *Triumph of the Will*'s winning tradition, and they see no end to its string of victories.

"We just can't find enough good things to say about this film," said Cannes juror Henri Molique. "Frankly, we are a little worried that we might someday run out of good things to say. That would be a dark day for both the Cannes festival and French film criticism."

Riefenstahl was pleased by her repeat victory. "Not only are the French gracious and accommodating hosts, but they display a keen insight into what is good film and what is good for them," the director said in her acceptance speech. "I feel that, no matter the direction in which my films take me, my work will be well-received in France."

Cappuccino Shortage Cripples Italian Army

ADDIS ABABA. — Ethiopian troops continued to drive back an Italian Army paralyzed by a near-total depletion of espresso beans and foamed milk.

U.S. interception of four Italian supply ships in the Mediterranean Sea brought about the shortage, which has proved a turning point in the war in Africa.

"We have no zip, no brio in our fighting anymore," said Giuseppe Tucci, a captured soldier in Italy's Expeditionary Forces, "and our conversations are woefully unanimated. I have reports that some of the men have become desperate and are vainly attempting to make their Seroni cappuccino-makers whip sand into a creamy froth. We have even begun rationing cinnamon."

"But, as a matter of pride," Tucci added, "we will not jettison our cups and saucers, even if we are driven to the Red Sea."

What the Axis leaders have in store for Lady Liberty if you don't buy Onion War Bonds now!

'No Book's Like a Dame, Nothing Looks Like a Dame,' Says South Pacific Command

Cable report from the Pacific Theater. — According to U.S. Intelligence officers stationed in the South Pacific, there is not anything like a dame.

Details of the report indicate that there is nothing like a dame in the known world.

"Lots of things in life are beautiful, but brother," read the secretly coded message that arrived on President Roosevelt's desk in Washington at 7 a.m. E.S.T. Sunday, "there is one particular thing that is nothing whatsoever in any way, shape, or form like any other."

"There is nothing like a dame," the message repeated.

While most details of the report remain classified—for fear of providing the hated German enemy with any advantage—the following information has been cleared by the War Department for release:

There are no books like a dame; nothing looks like a dame; there are no drinks like a dame; nothing thinks like a dame.

This new dame-related intelligence is expected to greatly improve the health of injured American soldiers. "Thousands of our boys are badly wounded every day by Japs and Jerrys," said Army doctor Martin Purcell, speaking from a makeshift hospital on a tiny, coconut-covered Pacific island. "But as we now know, there ain't a thing that's wrong with any man here that can't be cured by putting him near a girly, womanly, female, feminine dame."

A full version of Monday's report will be printed, set to music, and performed around the country.

Plot to Assassinate Hitler Fails When He Misses TNT-Filled Piñata

LEIPZIG. — A group of top German military officers, fearing that their Führer is leading them down a path of military foolishness and self-destruction, failed in an attempt on his life last week.

During an impromptu "south of the border" theme party thrown at Hitler's mountain villa, the German leader repeatedly swung at, but failed to strike, an explosive piñata fashioned from a 15-pound block of TNT cleverly shaped and colored to resemble a festive burro.

According to sources within Germany, those loyal to Hitler first suspected that the crepe-paper party item was an explosive device when Field Marshal Klaus von Stauffenberg jumped behind a massive stone fireplace after spinning the Führer around for the fourth time in preparation for his swatting at the frilly, donkey-shaped piñata.

Upon inspection, the colorful object was found to contain enough high explosives to kill not only the blindfolded, stick-wielding Hitler, but also every high-ranking Nazi official in attendance at the Mexican-themed fiesta.

Officers loyal to Hitler expressed suspicion at von Stauffenberg's unusual diving-for-cover action and had the Field Marshal arrested on suspicion of treason against the German state. He was charged with attempted assassination and sentenced to death within the hour.

The party continued unabated.

INSIDE:

MARIJUANA USE UP AMONG LOUIS ARMSTRONG

See story, page 8

NAZI ACCOUNTANTS STRUGGLING TO FIND MORE COST-EFFECTIVE WAYS TO ELIMINATE JEWS

See story, page 8

| Grow Hemp for Victory! | # THE ONION
Finest Source of News in America | Give Birth to More Sons for the War! |

Sunday, November 21, 1943 — SUNDAY EDITION — Price Fifteen Cents

Loose Lip Sinks Ship

613 Sailors Killed in South Pacific by Careless Talk in Michigan

Part-Time Ford Employee Arrested

DEARBORN, Michigan—The War Department reported yesterday that the sinking of the U.S.S. *Saginaw*, which was torpedoed by the Japanese 100 miles east of Guam last Wednesday, was the result of the careless talk of Raymond Fowlie, a part-time second-shift bolt sorter at Ford's Dearborn Assembly Works.

"Mr. Fowlie gave the Japs the clues they needed to send 613 of our boys to their deaths," said Special Agent John Smith of the Federal Bureau of Investigation, who took Fowlie into custody late yesterday. "While visiting his neighborhood tavern, Fowlie indulged in alcoholic beverages which loosened his lip to the point where he discussed his sensitive bolt-sorting work more loudly and candidly than is permitted by War Department authority."

F.B.I. officials said Japanese agents, who look and act just like humans, infiltrated Ed's Tavern in downtown Dearborn and overheard Fowlie talking about his sorting of bolts according to size, strength, and quantity.

From just these small bits of information, the uncommonly sneaky and cunning Imperial Japanese agents were able to assemble a complete structural blueprint of the *Saginaw*, and estimate its course, speed, crew, and cargo.

"You never know what a well-trained Jap spook can dig up for use against our fighting men," Smith said. "We have several eyewitnesses who can place Fowlie at the bar a week before the sinking and recall hearing him complain loudly about the unusually large number of case-hardened flathead bolts he had to sort that day." Smith noted that the optical range finder of the *Saginaw* was built using case-hardened bolts of the variety described by Fowlie at the bar.

Fowlie, who turned himself in after learning of the sinking, said he feels "disbelief, horror, and remorse" over his role in the tragic event. If found guilty of treason, he could face execution.

War Department sources say Fowlie should have known better. "Despite the ever-present reminders provided by the War Department, Fowlie talked about his crucial metal-fastener assembly work within earshot of several pretty girls, two jolly-looking businessmen, a suspiciously pious-looking priest, and a woman claiming to be his step-sister," said Smith. "As every American knows, these are precisely the types who most often turn out to be Nip spies. Fowlie killed all 613 of those brave sailors as sure as if he'd shot them himself."

WAR CASUALTIES TODAY

2,647 American
1,872 British
706 Canadian
459 French Resistance
4,000,000 Russian
3 *Life* magazine photographers

INSIDE:

CHAMBERLAIN INCREASINGLY WARY OF HITLER
'I think he may be up to something,' says former British Prime Minister.
See story, page 3

PATTON ORDERS LARGEST-EVER AMERICAN FLAG
See story, page 7

Betty Grable Appointed Head of U.S. Army Special Masturbation Fantasy Squadron

Ecuador Joins Allies

25 Fresh Fighting Men Could Turn Tide in Europe

QUITO. — In a vital gain for the fight to save Europe from tyranny, officials of the Ecuadorean army, consisting of 25 fresh fighting men, announced yesterday that they are joining the Allied effort.

The Ecuadorean government, or "junta," has also pledged eight to ten metal canisters, said to be large enough to hold two cans of soup each.

A pocket knife was also offered to the Allied command, but was accompanied by a presidential apology. Ecuadorean President Velasco expressed regret over the blade's missing "screwdriver" attachment.

"It has the big knife in it, and the little knife and the bottle-opener still," Velasco said, "but someone must have broken it, because the screwdriver part has fallen out."

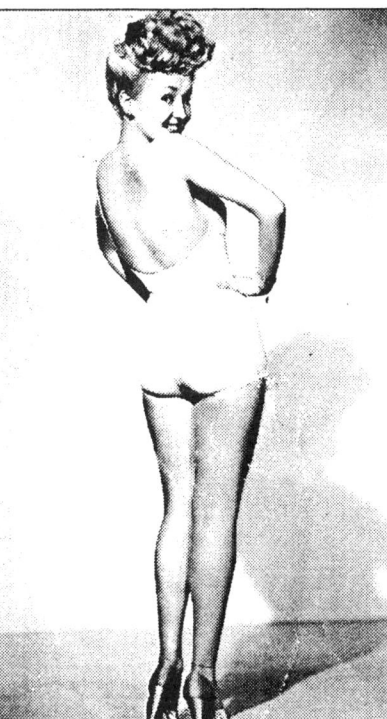

Captain Betty Grable of the U.S. Army Masturbation Fantasy Squadron.

Actress Will Supply Badly Needed Jack-Off Fodder for Our Boys

Ordered to Visit Front, Display Rear

U.S. Servicemen Thrilled, Already Masturbating Over News

WASHINGTON. — President Roosevelt called upon screen starlet Betty Grable Saturday to lead the U.S. Army Special Masturbation Fantasy Squadron, a newly formed unit that will hurl America's best bombshells at the Axis. Military experts hope that Captain Grable, supported by Privates Rita Hayworth, Veronica Lake, and Dorothy Lamour, will raise our boys' fighting spirit to new heights.

"Our boys need lusciously rounded hips and gams," declared Roosevelt to a crowd of reporters assembled on the White House lawn. "Miss Grable has these morale-boosting assets in abundance. Her Masturbation Fantasy Squadron is composed of only the finest American cheesecake."

Roosevelt referred to the newly formed squadron as his "Gam Trust."

Grable displayed her trademark sass when accepting her commission. "Thanks for the bars, FDR! Wish me luck!" she said, planting a quick kiss on the President's cheek. She then put her hands on her hips, turned her back to the crowd, and winked over her shoulder.

Roosevelt responded to Grable's coquettish behavior by jerking down his trousers and furiously masturbating. Presidential physicians were encouraged by the display, interpreting Roosevelt's rapid, copious ejaculation as a sign of good health.

Washington insiders believe that Roosevelt's executive decision was influenced by a series of extremely successful U.S.O. shows, in which Grable appeared in a one-piece bathing suit, exposing much of her upper back. She was known for saying, "Say, boys, I hear you like to masturbate!" at which point the thousands of men in attendance would holler and cheer, then whip out their erect penises and start masturbating.

To keep GIs masturbating until Grable's squadron is prepared to enter the fight, War Department officials have approved the immediate airlifting of Varga Girls into the European and Pacific theaters.

Auto-Makers Introduce New '44 Tanks

'You'll Enjoy the Smoothest Ride Ever in the New Chevy Pulverizer,' Says GM Spokesman

DETROIT — General Motors Chairman Charlie Wilson unveiled the company's new line of 1944 tanks Friday, touting the new vehicles as the "smoothest, most luxurious tanks in the European or Pacific markets."

"Take the new Chevy Pulverizer armored tank for a test battle, and I'm confident you'll agree it's the sportiest, peppiest tank on the front today," Wilson told reporters at the much-anticipated unveiling of the new '44 line. "Why, just five minutes behind the controls of the handsome Pulverizer, and you'll never kill Nazis in another tank again."

Among the features on the new GM tanks: an improved, easy-to-open top hatch. "You'll 'flip' for this new hatch," Wilson said. "And, as if that weren't enough, the Goodyear tank treads come with a three-year, ten-battle warranty."

Also featured: all-terrain handling, ultra-responsive turret with expanded firepower, enlarged V-24 engine, and standard two-way radio. Said Wilson, "Instead of saying, 'War is hell,' you'll be saying, 'Hello, war!' in your Chevy Pulverizer."

The new tanks, Wilson said, will be offered in a choice of three colors: Saharan Tan, European Theater Green, and Pacific Rim Ash.

"Whether you're blowing holes in Nazis, Italians, or Jap bastards, why not do it in style in one of General Motors' handsome new tanks?" Wilson said. "Remember, folks, as the saying goes: If You're Not Blowing People to Bits in a GM Tank, You're Not Really Blowing People to Bits."

In response to Thursday's product unveiling, the Ford Motor Co., GM's chief rival in the mid-sized tank market, announced that it will introduce its own new line of '44 ground-assault vehicles this week. "We believe that the new Fords represent the ultimate in warring pleasure," said Royce Clayton Snell, head of Ford's tank-design team. "And in recent tests on German artillery strongholds near the French-Belgian border, the Ford Blaster proved 40 percent more accurate than its GM rival, the Pontiac Crusher. The Ford Blaster also boasts a 4,000-yard firing range and a turret that's a full two feet longer than the Crusher's. Which would you rather be riding during your next advance on Berlin?"

In addition to the new tanks, on Friday GM also gave a special sneak preview of its line of '44 fighter planes, including the much-anticipated Buick Skyshark. "Strafe scurrying civilians in class and comfort in the new Buick Skyshark," said Bob Waller, director of GM's attack-plane division. "Forget all those other fighter planes—the Buick Skyshark is the one for your next mission. Swoop on down to your local GM showroom and ask to see the new Skyshark today."

THE '44 CHEVY PULVERIZER

THE ONION

Finest Source of News in America

Thursday, June 8, 1944 — Price Five Cents

> Donate Your Bazookas to the War Effort

> Ladies: Conserve Your Shoulder Pads for the War Effort

War Rationing Board Restricts Nylon Use to Armed Forces, J. Edgar Hoover Only

Frilly Panties and Garters Especially Needed Now, FBI Director Says

WASHINGTON, D.C. — In an effort to conserve limited supplies of badly needed nylon for use in the war, access to the material has been reserved solely for the Armed Forces and FBI Director J. Edgar Hoover.

Sale of nylon and goods containing nylon, such as fishing line and women's hosiery, ended in retail stores this week, as the distribution of all nylon was diverted to meet the military needs of the Army, Navy, and Air Force, as well as the confidential needs of Hoover.

General Forrester of the Air Force reports that his branch of the military alone needs a weekly supply of 32 tons of nylon material for use in parachutes, ropes, straps, and collapsible awnings. J. Edgar Hoover, who has requested an allotment of 22 pounds of nylon, has made no explanation as to its purpose other than to say that it is of a highly sensitive nature.

Federal officials have respected the classified and highly urgent status of the FBI director's request, much as they did last month, when they unquestioningly delivered 20 nylon wigs to Hoover for, as an FBI memo stated, "undisclosed uses promoting the safety and well-being of the country."

Store owners and city-level material-drive captains report that men and women around the country are already changing their nylon-consumption and purchasing patterns to pitch in for the war and FBI director's needs.

"I'm putting off my purchase of a new camping tent," said Norm Johnson of Toledo, Ohio. "I'd prefer that that precious nylon go straight to our boys overseas." His wife, Judy, concurred: "Until we win the war, I'm giving up on lacy thigh-high garters and fishnet stockings. I'd prefer that those materials go straight to crime-fighter J. Edgar Hoover."

FBI Director J. Edgar Hoover

American Jews No Longer Receiving Mail from European Relatives

'They Are Very Busy with the War and What-Not,' Say German Officials

BROOKLYN, N.Y. — In the predominantly Jewish neighborhood of Brighton Beach, many residents are puzzled by the lack of correspondence from their relatives in Western Europe.

Many American Jews say the flow of letters from aunts, uncles, parents and grandparents slowed in the late 1930s, when rising war tensions caused the mails to become erratic, but about a year ago, most letters stopped coming altogether.

"It isn't like my sister Ethel not to write and tell me about things in our old neighborhood in Warsaw," Sophie Epstein of Brooklyn, N.Y., told The Onion. "I know there's a war on, and she may have had to move away or is maybe very busy. But for her not to write, it causes me worry."

Morris Feingold of Flatbush said he has written his cousin Herman in Hungary many times to ask for news, but the letters have either disappeared or been returned opened and resealed.

"The last time I received a return letter from him, there was included in the envelope a letter from the German occupational military government," Feingold said. "It read, 'Thank you, Jew, for your interest in your Jew relatives. However, they are busy with important Jew business and cannot answer your Jew inquiry at this time.' It was a polite letter, but official, and I still don't know where Herman is."

Feingold said he briefly considered contacting his congressman concerning the matter, but that he "didn't want to make of myself any trouble" and had decided against it.

NEW CARTOON INSIDE:
TAKE A LETTER, MISS BOOZOM
— HAP CAVITT
See page 7

New York postmaster Calvin Landis said he has received many inquiries from Jewish families regarding the lack of mail from relatives in the European war zone, but offered no explanation as to why this might be.

"They seem to be the only ones with a problem. There has been a war on, after all," Landis said. "But, even so, I haven't heard any complaints from the German, Greek or Italian communities. Just the Jews. Perhaps they have just been especially busy during the past few years."

A&E Documentary Crews Sweep Europe

Cable report from Vichy, France. — Film crews documenting the war for the new medium of tele-vision have swept the European countryside this week in the latest campaign of footage-gathering missions.

From Norway to Italy, crews collecting footage for the Arts & Entertainment Network, a proposed television station, have gathered footage of Hitler's labor camps, ravaged German villages, and countless troop movements. The images are expected to be spliced together and played on the tele-vision station at all hours of the day and night for years on end, say A&E officials.

Whom these programmers expect to be watching tele-vision in the middle of the night has not been disclosed.

Tearful Hitler Promises to 'Give Peace a Chance'

BERLIN. — In an unorthodox move before the assembled German armies and youth corps, Adolf Hitler paused during a speech and earnestly addressed the nations of the world, promising to "Give peace a chance."

His scheduled speech, another angrily belted harangue against all non-Germanic peoples, suddenly came to a halt half-way through, as Hitler paused, reflected for a moment with his head bowed, then lifted his head slowly to face the vast throng of Nazis. A tear ran down his cheek.

"All I am saying is, give peace a chance," the Führer said in an uncharacteristically soft voice.

A discernable hush fell over the sea of listeners.

"Let me tell you now," he continued. "Everybody's talking about Nazism, Fascism, naval bases, master races, Bayreuth, Hitler Youth, concentration, extermination, the League of Nations, congratulations. All I am saying is, give peace a chance."

He whispered, his voice choked with emotion, "War is over, if you want it."

Normandy Invasion Force Crippled by Nostalgia

Thousands of GIs Die as They Pause to Reflect on the Momentous Day

The Fifth Army storms the beach at Normandy, moments before being overcome with fond memories of the historic event.

NORMANDY, France. — American forces sent to liberate France from Hitler's forces suffered a great defeat today on the beach at Normandy, as the entire U.S. First Army was overcome with nostalgia. Brave men running up the beach with all their strength stopped, one by one, just a few yards onto the shore to pause and reflect on the momentous event.

"I remember it distinctly." Private Marvin Jenkins of Minneapolis said slowly, as German mortars blew holes in the sand all around him. "Back in 1944, I stormed the beach at Normandy. It was about 20 seconds ago."

Jenkins was then downed by a German sniper.

No sooner had Private Al Madsen of Phoenix, Ariz., jumped off the landing transport vehicle than he immediately leaned back in a comfortable arm chair, remembering the moment with great fondness.

Madsen wasn't the only one telling stories. The beach was strewn with easy chairs, as hundreds of soldiers sat back, puffed on pipes, smiled, and looked into the distance wistfully.

Other soldiers stopped their advance to exchange bittersweet recollections of the great military action. Meanwhile, hundreds of soldiers were cut down by German gunners and artillerymen atop the beachhead.

Army sound engineers captured some of the troop exchanges over the hail of German guns.

"This was perhaps the single most important military operation in the war, and we were there. We were there," Madsen could be heard saying. "It's possible that no less than the freedom of the entire world was resting on our shoulders at that very moment."

"I was one of the survivors," Madsen added.

A voice near Madsen called out, "I was a survivor of the Normandy invasion, too!"

"I was with the 4th," Madsen said. "What was your unit?"

"The 1st," the voice answered. "We came ashore right next to you!"

Madsen and the unidentified soldier can then be heard enjoying a tearful reunion before being blown to pulpy bits by a large mortar blast.

War Department officials reported at 2 p.m. E.S.T. today that the U.S. Army suffered over 80 percent losses at Normandy, a grim setback in the effort to drive Hitler from France.

JITTERBUGGING INJURIES TODAY

- Max Amberg, New York
- Charles Born, Milwaukee
- Arnold Feurstein, Chicago
- Louis Jordan, Kansas City (fatal)
- Entire Class of '44, Bedford Falls (drowned)
- Carol Miller, Sacramento
- "Joe," Kokomo

List continues p. 14

INSIDE:

FRENCH WRITER CLAIMS HELL IS OTHER FRENCHMEN
See story, page 11

TUSKEGEE AIRMEN HONORED AT WHITE HOUSE SERVICE ENTRANCE
See story, page 4

THE ONION

Proudly Censored by Military Personnel

Finest Source of News in America

Kids! Join Zweibel's Jap Smashers!

Sunday, February 11, 1945 — SUNDAY EDITION — Price Fifteen Cents

FDR, STALIN, CHURCHILL MEET FOR MUTTON LUNCHEON, NAP

Churchill Vows to Open Top Button of Trousers

'Big Three' Sated, Sleepy

Stalin Makes First-Ever Friends

Stalin, Roosevelt and Churchill wait patiently for the serving of a braised mutton entree.

YALTA, Soviet Union. — At the behest of Josef Stalin, President Roosevelt and British Prime Minister Winston Churchill convened with the Russian leader today in the Crimean resort town of Yalta for a hot mutton luncheon and relaxing nap.

As the tired leaders slumped in their seats at the special ceremony, their pre-dinner conversation centered on dividing up the world.

A first course of kale salad topped with tomatoes and a vinegar dressing followed.

The main course of mutton, braised and topped with caramel and a plum wine sauce in the Ukrainian tradition, was pronounced "both savory and hearty" by Roosevelt. Churchill also appeared pleased by the meal, saying, "Never before has so much mutton been consumed by so few, to the delight of so many." Churchill pledged an immediate opening of the top button of his trousers.

Despite the mutual satiety, Anglo-Russian relations became slightly strained moments later when Churchill's favorite label of after-dinner brandy was unavailable. Stalin apologized profusely for the shortcoming and offered to drive to a liquor store himself to procure a bottle.

"He was so distraught about the brandy that I felt rather a cad for mentioning it," Churchill said. British military officers on the scene reported that Churchill defused the situation by saying, "That's all right, old boy," and patting Stalin on the back. The Russian leader tensed at this unexpected bodily contact, then, after a moment's pause, giggled nervously.

After eating, the "Big Three" sat back and lit cigars presented by the Prime Minister. Stalin, having neglected to inform the other leaders that he had never smoked a cigar, coughed profusely, and was inconsolable with a sore throat and chest pain for much of the remaining afternoon. Near tears, Stalin apologized to the others for "utterly ruining" the day.

A NEEDED REST

With the mutton luncheon resolved, the three leaders then turned their attention to the vital issue of an afternoon nap. Said Roosevelt, "It is only fitting after such a satisfying repast to seek digestive comfort in sleep." Churchill concurred, restating his unwavering conviction that if a man takes a nap, he should put on his nightclothes and have a proper rest.

Guarded by their respective entourages, the three overstuffed politicians were led to a large room with three beds set aside for napping foreign diplomats.

With the exception of Churchill's loud snoring, the nap proceeded smoothly until Stalin woke up screaming, waking the President and Prime Minister with a start. Both Churchill and Roosevelt attempted to calm the Soviet Premier, who had had a nightmare about wild gorillas surrounding him.

"It sounded like a very frightening dream," Roosevelt said. "To make him feel better, we agreed to let him take control of Poland, Czechoslovakia, Hungary, Rumania, Bulgaria and Eastern Germany. That seemed to make him rest more easily."

PARTING AS FRIENDS

Stalin appeared delighted that he had made the acquaintance of the other world leaders, and beseeched them to visit him again soon. "Being in such a remote location," the Soviet Premier said through an interpreter, "I do not often receive company."

Churchill and Roosevelt assured Stalin that they would "definitely call him," if they were ever in the Soviet Union area again.

Hitler Commits Suicide;
Ravaging of Europe a 'Desperate Cry for Help,' Say Therapists

Führer's Slaughter of Millions Blamed on 'Serious Self-Esteem Issues'

'If We Had Only Known How Much He Was Hurting on the Inside,' FDR Says

BERLIN. — Absent from the public eye for months, Adolf Hitler is reportedly dead by his own hand in an air-raid shelter in Berlin, where he had sequestered himself during his final days.

Dr. Theodore Beaumont, director of the Virginia Psychiatry Center, said he believes Hitler's marching on Poland, Denmark, Norway, Holland, Belgium and France, and his systematic killings of millions of people in Germany, was "a desperate cry for help."

According to Beaumont, "This is classic attention-seeking behavior."

Beaumont said Hitler made his plea for approval the only way he knew how: by lashing out.

Other experts agree. "The British and American forces just reciprocated negativity by advancing from the west," said Dr. Johan Freberg of the Paris Center for Mental Illness. "And Russian soldiers reinforced Hitler's self-fulfilling prophesy of 'othering' by attacking from the east, instead of lending a sympathetic ear, which may have been all Hitler needed."

Upon learning of the self-esteem issues that led Hitler to such militaristic "acting out," Allied leaders are seeing the once-hated despot in a new light.

"I heard his angry speeches but failed to search for the hurt little boy beneath those words," lamented British Prime Minister Winston Churchill. "I feel guilty—there's so much we could have done for him."

Said President Roosevelt, "Inside that maniacal mass-murderer—beneath the veneer of evil and sadism—there was a scared little child searching for love."

Psychologists say the global carnage of the Second World War could have been averted if only U.S. forces had met Hitler's emotional needs, giving him the love and approval he so desperately sought.

THAT PRETTY DAME YOU SEE WALKING DOWN THE STREET IS PROBABLY **A SPY!**

Dresden Fire-Bombed;
Thousands of Enemy Tea Sets, Clocks, Ornamental Statues Destroyed

DRESDEN. — This eastern German city was fire-bombed by Allied warplanes last night, resulting in the destruction of tens of thousands of enemy tea sets, delicate porcelain clocks and ornamental statuary. "Never have so many pretty, dainty things been destroyed in so needful a cause," said Air Force Brigadier General James "Hellcat" Murchison.

According to Allied Command reports, at 4:30 a.m., a U.S. Air Force bombardment attacked a set of painted ceramic dishes at Stresemannstr. 412 until it lay in pieces under six feet of rubble.

A second wave of bombers came over the reddening horizon at 6:30 a.m., using their combined firepower to take out an entire German knick-knack on the sitting-room cabinet of Mrs. Helga Oosterhof.

The assault continued, with pilots bravely seeking out every Jerry tea set, hand-painted goblet and saucer in the town.

By the end of two days' bombings, not a single Nazi glazed figurine or porcelain dishware item remained standing.

Two hundred thousand German civilians were also killed.

Kurt Vonnegut of Indianapolis, 26, a P.O.W. imprisoned in Dresden at the time of the bombing, was physically unharmed but will be psychologically scarred for the rest of his life.

INSIDE:

LIBERATED EUROPEAN BROTHELS CELEBRATE VD-DAY
See story, page 7

FORMER BRITISH PRIME MINISTER CHAMBERLAIN SLAPPED SILLY BY LITTLE GIRL
See story, page 18

UNDERWEAR STILL DECREASING IN SIZE
see story, page 20

"Our best and bravest may be overseas... but the fat and nearsighted are eager to please!"

Ladies: You don't have to be lonely! **MEET ELIGIBLE 4-F'S IN YOUR HOME TOWN!**
DIAL MR. LONELY-HEARTS
ALpine-7740
"Fall in love with fallen arches!"

65

THE ONION

Finest Source of News in America

Wednesday, March 14, 1945 — Price Five Cents

We've Contributed Our Presses to the Steel Drives

Fight the Good Fight!

Our First Lesbian President

Eleanor Roosevelt assumed the duties of the presidency Tuesday, making her the first lesbian ever to hold the highest office in the land. Across the U.S., citizens celebrated equal rights for homosexuals with parades, songs and national "coming out" marches.

"President Roosevelt has forever put to rest the discrimination against homosexuals," famed lesbian icon Rosie the Riveter said. "It is truly a great day, now that gays no longer must remain closeted in shame due to the outdated values of yesteryear."

Nothing Going On in New Mexico

Top Physicists 'Just Camping,' Say Army Intelligence Officials

ALAMOGORDO, N.M. — Atomic Energy Commission officials announced yesterday that nothing whatsoever is going on in the New Mexico desert, where dozens of the world's leading physicists are gathered to enjoy relaxing, non-suspicious camping.

"Oppenheimer, Teller and the other physicists are very good friends, and they decided it would be nice to get away and go camping and fishing together," General Leslie Groves said. "So they all headed to New Mexico for a few weeks, where they will be relaxing and not testing anything even remotely resembling an incredibly destructive new weapon."

Suspicions were aroused Saturday when a flash of blinding light, followed by a mile-high column of smoke, was spotted by motorists several miles from the physicists' campsite. In response to the sighting, the War Department released a statement explaining that the flash was merely the result of physicist Robert Oppenheimer adding too much lighter fluid to a campfire.

Said Oppenheimer: "I am not at liberty to say anything other than that the toasted marshmallows were delicious."

Spokesmen for the War Department urged citizens to avoid traveling within 250 miles of the campsite, as the ghost stories told by the physicists around the campfire may be "very scary."

INSIDE:

CIGARETTES, HERSHEY BARS NOW OFFICIAL CURRENCY OF OCCUPIED EUROPE
See story, page 9

U.S., SOVIET UNION TO DIVVY UP EVIL NAZI SCIENTISTS
See story, page 14

Japanese Zeroes Held Off by Boy with Dick Tracy Decoder Ring

FRESNO, Calif. -- A would-be Japanese sneak attack on American soil was foiled Saturday by local 8-year-old Tim Gardner, who intercepted and decoded a top-secret, Ovaltine-sponsored communique using a mail-ordered Dick Tracy Secret Decoder Ring.

The covert transmission was broadcast by Japanese intelligence agents Saturday at 7:25 p.m. on a radio-band frequency of 1020 kilocycles, and took the form of a letter-substitution cipher, with each letter of the alphabet represented by a number from 1 to 26. The design of the coding scheme ensured that the message would be gibberish to an agent not possessing the Secret Decoder Ring, a sophisticated decryption device ordinarily used to foil domestic criminal fugitives.

FBI agents also managed to intercept the broadcast, but were unable to decipher the message, as they had not collected the Ovaltine jar labels necessary to obtain the ring.

Gardner, possessing the necessary crypto-analysis equipment, quickly made the correct substitutions and decoded the message to read, "HUNDRED FIFTY ZEROES RAID SAN DIEGO NOON SUNDAY." The plucky third-grader immediately notified Ovaltine officials, who relayed the dire threat to the War Department in time to mobilize anti-aircraft measures.

The aircraft carrier transporting the Japanese planes was successfully attacked early Sunday morning by the brave boys on the U.S.S. *Missouri*, hundreds of miles from U.S. shores, and four Jap planes already en route were shot down in dog fights with U.S. pilots in F4AU Corsairs.

For his exemplary performance in outwitting the enemy, Gardner was awarded the Congressional Medal of Freedom Tuesday, as well as a Dick Tracy Honorary Deputy Badge.

Said Gardner of his heroism, "Aw, golly, I did what any stand-up guy would have done. I was hoping I'd get to catch some crooks with my ring, but I'd say Japs is even better!"

FBI Director J. Edgar Hoover congratulated Gardner personally: "Tim, if every G-man was as shrewd as you, we'd end this war tomorrow!" Hoover then assured reporters that all FBI agents would be required from this day forth to remember to drink their Ovaltine.

Just one of the four Japanese planes downed with the help of plucky 8-year-old Tim Gardner (above left).

Ron Reagan Wounded in Action Film

HOLLYWOOD. — Motion-picture star Ron Reagan's character Billy Sanders was wounded Tuesday in the climactic final scene of "The Tokyo Storm," which is currently being filmed at Paramount Pictures' Studio C.

An emergency team of two make-up artists was dispatched to apply realistic blood to Reagan, who portrays a soldier shot during the battle of Midway.

"Don't worry about me," Reagan bravely assured his fans. "I'll be fine. You worry about my fellow actors, some of whom may at this very moment be playing soldiers suffering from near-fatal wounds, or possibly even performing harrowing death scenes."

Scriptwriters say the actor's injury may win him a Congressional Medal of Honor in the film, presented by an actor portraying the President of the United States.

First Caucasian Joins Negro Baseball League after Long Struggle

KANSAS CITY. — Edwin Miller is a plucky lad from a farm in Indiana. At age 8, his fastball could knock down a soup can from 20 yards. He knew he would grow up to play the grand old game of baseball. But, he was told, he would never be able to play in the Negro League. You see, young Edwin was born with white skin.

His parents, coaches and society itself told him he would have to play in the pressure cooker of the big leagues, where the stakes would be higher, 20 times more eyes would be staring at him, and every tiny mistake would be reported in the next day's paper.

And, for a time, Edwin believed what his parents and teachers told him and imagined one day standing in cavernous stadiums, deafened by the roar of thousands of fans. But by his eighteenth birthday, he knew that it would only be that way if he accepted it, if someone like him did not take a stand.

Last week, Edwin Miller's dream came true, as he strode onto the diamond at Crosley Field in a Kansas City Monarchs uniform and took the pitcher's mound, taking his place in history as the man who broke black baseball's 74-year-old color barrier.

"All I wanted was to show that I could play negro baseball as well as any negro," said Miller to reporters of the groundbreaking day for sports. "I think any man should be afforded that right."

Monarchs owner Abe Manley said, "This is a young man who can fling the horsehide like you'd never believe, and that was all I needed to see. I could not in good conscience bar a man from the low-budget negro alternative to the all-white major leagues simply because of the color of his skin."

While Edwin takes great pride in his achievement, he confesses that his life remains a solitary one. When the team goes to dinner after a game, Miller is forced to sit alone in the spacious, comfortable, "whites-only" section of the restaurant. And it is rare that Miller is put up in the same hotel as his teammates: He must always find separate, more luxurious lodging, and he is also forced to use the front entrance to stadiums.

Of his future, and the possibility of a fully integrated Negro League, Edwin speaks with pride and conviction. "We as a people are not free until all men, no matter their skin color, can play the game of negro baseball."

White player Edwin Miller

THE ONION

A Deafening Blast of News and Information

Finest Source of News in America

See "ONION NEWS ON THE MARCH" Every Week at Your Local Movie House

Friday, August 10, 1945 — Price Five Cents

Nagasaki Bombed 'Just for the Hell of it'

SECOND A-BOMB WOULD HAVE JUST SAT AROUND ANYWAY, SAY GENERALS

FRENCH SURRENDER

U.S. filmmakers and photographers were lucky to get a second chance to capture pictures of the beautiful A-bomb mushroom cloud.

GUAM. — The world's most destructive weapon, the atomic bomb, was used for a second time against nearly defeated Japan Thursday, in a raid against the industrial city of Nagasaki.

Military officials explained that the bomb, which vaporized thousands of innocent Japanese civilians, charred thousands more with third-degree burns over their entire bodies, and obliterated the city with an explosive force equal to a half-million tons of TNT, was dropped "just for the hell of it."

"We still had one device remaining after our spectacular display of force in Hiroshima the other day," said B-29 pilot Col. Paul Tibbets, "and because of the wonderful success of that bombing, we were aware that Japan was already moving toward surrender. If we were going to drop the other bomb, we had to do it quickly, before peace made it inadvisable."

MIGHT AS WELL

Tibbets, who also flew the Hiroshima mission, said he decided to fly this one because he "was just sitting around that day." He said he was at the officer's club playing pinochle when it occurred to him that the weather was perfect, he had enough flyers to man the B-29, and nobody was using the bomb. "So we went and asked the base commander if we could drop it on Japan somewhere," Tibbets said.

Pacific Supreme Commander Douglas MacArthur approved the bombers' mission without hesitation, saying they "might as well."

"These bombs don't come cheap, and it seemed a shame to have the war go by without using another A-bomb," MacArthur said. "I imagined Little Boy being dropped on some uninhabited Pacific island for a bunch of damn scientists, or sitting in a dusty museum somewhere, or being dismantled, and I said to myself, 'You know, that's just not right.'"

REALLY GOOD PICTURES

Tibbets and his crew took off early the next day and set off for Japan, looking "for any non-military city of at least 30,000 civilians we could find," according to navigator Ed Parker. "There were clouds over a lot of the island, which wouldn't stop us from dropping it by instrument, of course. But we had a camera plane along, and we wanted to get really good pictures, just to kind of make the trip worthwhile."

Photographers following in the chase plane said their photographs and films turned out "absolutely perfect."

PRETTY MUCH WORTHWHILE

"Seeing that 500-kiloton bomb go off, being able to see that flash through my closed eyelids, watching the mushroom cloud of debris, thousands of corpses and dislodged soil climbing miles in the air—that made it all worthwhile," combat photographer Carl Stenner said. "Hell, the sound alone—like the fist of some terrifying war-god striking the accursed earth—would have made it worthwhile." Stenner said he remembers thinking at the time, "I'm glad we decided to do this today."

Early Japanese reports indicate that only about 40,000 people were killed by the bomb.

"That's okay, really," MacArthur said upon being informed of the death toll. "The important thing is, we dropped it. If we hadn't, it wouldn't have been able to kill anyone at all."

INSIDE:

WAR DEPARTMENT: 'USE ALL THE STEEL YOU WANT NOW'
See story, page 13.

War Department Gears up to Fire 1.5 Million Women

Ladies to Return Triumphantly to Kitchens

Homefront Workers to Receive Heroines' Welcome from Awaiting Pots, Pans

With worldwide peace on the horizon at last, war contractors are getting ready to turn to the 1.5 million women who worked hard during the war building planes, ships and bombs for our boys and tell them, "You're fired."

The homefront laborers will soon be relocated to their natural environs. "The more than 1.5 million wives and housekeepers who bravely pitched in when the chips were down can finally be let go and sent off to do what they do best," said General Omar Bradley, "tend America's kitchens and nurseries."

As manufacturing plants around America are converted to peace-time production, plant overseers say they can't get the women out the door fast enough. "Thanks for all the years of help, girls," announced supervisor Kyle Weatherby over the St. Paul Steel loudspeaker. "Now get on home."

WELCOME BACK TO HOUSEWORK

Women's hard work in the fight to defeat the Nazis and Japs will not go unrewarded. Across the country, ladies are expected to receive a warm welcome from their pots, pans, dish towels and floor wax. Waiting expectantly in cupboards and closets too long neglected, household disinfectants, cast-iron cookware sets, and diaper pails will be on hand to watch the spunky women return to their rightful command over the sinks and stoves of America.

"I could hardly believe what was waiting for me upon my return," said Julia Neiland, a soon-to-be former ironworks foreman from Youngstown, Ohio. "Not just an unclean house, but an unmade bed and uncooked dinner for five guests."

Neiland also has to get busy baking a cake and drawing a bath for her husband, Tom, who will arrive home soon after a ticker-tape parade in New York City.

"And someone will have to vacuum up all that ticker tape that he tracks into the house," she said.

Big Band under Investigation for Swinging

NEW YORK. — Tommy Dorsey, the bandleader known for such elegant numbers as "Stardust" and "Once in a While," is under investigation by local and state officials for allegedly swinging during a Saturday-night performance of the up-tempo song "Boogie Woogie" at New York's Savoy Ballroom.

"While all details are not in yet, it appears that, midway through his concert, Mr. Dorsey made a sudden and inexplicable break from such tender ballads as 'Blue and Sentimental' and 'Smoke Rings' and began to swing wildly," New York Deputy Police Chief Frank Landeta said.

According to several witnesses, The Tommy Dorsey Orchestra played in a raucous and exuberant manner during the up-tempo "Boogie Woogie" number, inciting several hundred people to cut a rug and tear up the dance floor.

"This was no 'String of Pearls' or 'Serenade in Blue'—this band was swingin' and jumpin'," said Delores Young, 23, who attended the show with her fiancee Donald Halloran.

"Mr. Dorsey was blowing his trombone with a tremendous amount of pep. I would go so far as to say that he and his orchestra were stompin' at the Savoy."

"When Tommy Dorsey played 'Boogie Woogie,' everywhere you looked, there was jitterbugging and jiving," said Walt Jeffries, 27. "I might expect this sort of outrageous display from Count Basie, Woody Herman, or Benny Goodman. Or even Artie Shaw, for that matter. But Tommy Dorsey? Never in a million years."

Dorsey's court date has been set for Sept. 19.

TOMMY DORSEY AND HIS ORCHESTRA

THE ONION

Let's Work Together to Pretend Our War-Time Homosexual Experiences Never Happened.

Finest Source of News in America

Presses Converted to Peace-Time Production

Wednesday, August 15, 1945 — Price Five Cents

WAR OVER! 50 YEARS OF NUCLEAR PARANOIA BEGIN TODAY

Returning GIs Vow to Spawn Whiniest Generation Ever

As our fighting men return from their triumphs overseas and settle in to marry the girls they left behind and enjoy the fruits of their labor, starting a family is first and foremost on their minds. And experts believe they will spawn the whiniest generation the world has ever known.

Like many ex-servicemen, 24-year-old Stewart Carlson of Elgin, Illinois, knows exactly what kind of kids he wants: "strong, healthy kids, cute as bugs and smart as whips," he said. Carlson's experiences in the Depression and the Second World War were full of hardship and suffering, and he wants his kids to fare better.

"I want my kids to have whatever they want: clothes, toys, education, everything. I'm going to spoil those kids to death, and I want them to take this for granted."

Dr. Benjamin Spock of the Princeton Institute of Family Studies took exception to Carlson's vision. "A parent naturally wants to give his kids the best of everything, but spoiling them—making them believe they are the center of the universe, always know best, and are more important than all others—can turn them into adults who think the same way," Spock said. "I can't imagine anything worse than an America filled with such grown-up brats."

Although he knows child-rearing professionals agree that spoiled children often grow into complaining, self-absorbed adults, Carlson isn't worried. "My kids, and the kids of all my army buddies, will be the luckiest, best, most important children on the face of the Earth," he said, contemplating the four-bedroom house he intends to fill with children. "I want to give them all the things I never had, like the belief that the world exists to serve them alone. They're the future of this country, after all."

French Unveil 'Arc de Capitulation'

New Monument Celebrates French Cowardice in Face of Adversity

PARIS — Wishing to commemorate the glorious French tradition of bowing to foreign powers, the French government unveiled a new public monument, the "Arc de Capitulation."

"Short live France!" exclaimed French General Charles De Gaulle at the unveiling ceremony Wednesday. "This great monument will stand forever to symbolize our proud history of buckling under."

"If not forever," he added, "it will stand at least until it is hammered into rubble by a foreign conqueror."

De Gaulle called the new arch "a beacon for all those, French or non-French, who have found the strength within themselves to give up."

The 130-foot-tall pink marble arch spans the Rue de Surrender and is topped with a statue of the triumphant goddess of Victory, trampling the French people with her winged foot and

Thousands of French people pay tribute to their country's grand tradition of surrender.

holding aloft a banner reading, "Peur," or "Fear."

Thousands of French supporters of cowardice came out for the celebration.

The Arc was designed by French sculptor Henri-Louis Rouen, renowned among his contemporaries for the delicate finish and mirror-like sheen he achieved on SS officers' boots during the Nazi occupation.

Frescoes and bas-reliefs on the two columns of the Arc de Capitulation depict scenes from historic French surrenders, such as Napoleon's to Wellington in 1812 and De Gaulle's to Hitler in 1939. Several spaces were left blank to make space for artistic renderings of future Gallic submissions.

Nation Shifts Focus to Washers, Dryers

With Hitler defeated and the world saved from the forces of tyranny and oppression, the American people are now shifting their focus to the latest in convenient, labor-saving washers and dryers.

Across the U.S., people are making the transition from war-time to household-appliances-time.

"I sure am glad we defeated the Germans and Japanese," said Albuquerque, N.M., resident Thomas Forrester, 26, who served with the 9th Infantry Division in North Africa. "Now we can spend time purchasing General Electric washers and dryers. Why, their terrific new washer features a five-setting timer, a spin-cycle option and an automatic shut-off button. Pretty swell, huh?"

In an effort to aid U.S. veterans in their transition back to civilian life, Congress on Tuesday passed the Patterson-Hammaker GI Bill, which will give all returning soldiers $20 credit toward any electric washer-dryer set at Sears-Roebuck.

"This bill guarantees that our brave fighting men will be rewarded for their great effort and sacrifice in the bloodiest, most brutal conflict the planet has ever seen," U.S. Sen. Edwin Hammaker (R-RI) said. "They will be rewarded with machine-washed clothes—

fresh and crisp as the day they were purchased."

In a radio address Wednesday, President Truman praised America's veterans and urged them to continue waging war against high prices by shopping at their neighborhood Woolworth's store. "Just as you did on the beaches of Normandy and in the jungles of Guadalcanal, you must never give up," Truman said. "Bravely fight the crowds of shoppers who would seek to get to Woolworth's before you, to get the high-quality merchandise at low prices that you so richly deserve. You deserve the best, and Woolworth's has got it."

According to Truman, a Fuller-brand hand-held iron, normally priced at $6.99, is now on sale at Woolworth's for just $3.99.

So-Called 'Radiation' Is Jap Hoax, Say Scientists

Wild Jap Claims of Deadly Invisible Rays Spawned by A-Bomb Called 'Preposterous'

100,000 Deaths in Hiroshima, Nagasaki Likely the Result of 'Something They Ate,' Say U.S. Physicists

WASHINGTON, D.C. — Top U.S. atomic scientists held a press conference Tuesday to dispel wild Jap reports of mass illness caused by atomic-bomb-related "radiation," an invisible manifestation that supposedly causes maladies ranging from hair-loss to death.

"I wish to officially proclaim these Jap claims of sickness caused by some invisible substance known as 'radiation' to be nothing more than a yellow hoax," said Dr. Andrew Cushing of the Atomic Research Foundation at Princeton.

More than 100,000 residents of Hiroshima and Nagasaki have mysteriously died since the U.S. dropped atomic bombs on the cities.

Cushing said the deaths were likely the result of the Japanese diet of fish and rice. "A diet dangerously low in beef, or perhaps an outbreak of influenza, may be to blame," he said. He harshly chided Japanese leaders for suggesting that the deaths were somehow related to the U.S. atomic attacks.

"For the Japanese to blame us for their mass seizures,

Citizens of America are engaged in joyous celebration of our glorious victory over the forces of Evil today, while simultaneously gearing up for the 50 years of nuclear paranoia that now begin.

TRUMAN PROMISES NIGHTMARES

"Today is the beginning of a new era," President Truman said in a national radio address. "This will superficially be an era of peace and progress, but under our cheerful facade will seethe an undercurrent of dread, as the threat of the total destruction of mankind looms over us like a great, black cloud."

Truman went on to promise, "Citizens of the United States will awaken in cold sweats, screaming, night after night. Dark visions will haunt their every night's sleep: their children being cut apart like burnt paper by the gush of million-degree atomic heat or, worse, their children surviving as 'radiated,' subhuman mutants who roam the charred earth as marauding cannibals."

WAR NOT REALLY OVER

Although the fighting is over, General Eisenhower has said that a hulking war-machine has been built in the last few years and is "not about to disappear." Eisenhower referred specifically to the consortia of two powerful defense contractors: the War Department and the newly created Atomic Energy Commission. "This," he said, "coupled with our growing fear of Communism and Russia's

hair loss and copious vomiting, why, it is unconscionable," Cushing said. "There is no such thing as radiation. As an atomic expert, I am quite confident that I would be aware of such a thing, if it actually did exist.

"Even if there were such a thing as radiation, it would certainly not be caused by the dropping of atomic weapons of mass destruction. These Japs are mysteriously dying by the thousands through no one's fault but their own, yet they're trying to pin the blame on us by concocting stories of make-believe 'radioactive' particles."

"Dr. Cushing is correct. It's preposterous," said Dr. William Anderson of the National Health Institute. "It is inadvisable to trust not just this, but any Jap claim."

atom bomb, will create a new type of war, a 'Cold War,' in which citizens and soldiers alike will be afforded the opportunity to experience the horrors of war, not just during brief battles, but for their entire lives."

CHEERY DENIAL

Doctors at the Roerig Center for Sociological and Psychological Research have already begun to map the expected course of the emotional disorder that began developing immediately upon the announcement of Japan's defeat. For the next several years, their reports predict, our paranoia will remain suppressed, cloaked in a creepy, positive-minded denial.

Roerig researchers say the nuclear paranoia will grow like a cancer over the next 40 years and eventually develop into full-blown hysteria. "But I gravely doubt that the acknowledgment of the fear will end the paranoia," said Dr. Horace Thorburn. "Rather, it will create a nation of young people crippled by their own cynicism, the very measure they will create to protect themselves from an overwhelming sense of dread and lack of faith in their continued existence."

After reviewing the data, Thorburn speculated on the future of nuclear paranoia in America. "This all-encompassing paranoia will most likely magically resolve itself after just five decades," he said, "because no society can remain paranoid, whether consciously or unconsciously, for that long."

He added that, while the paranoia will likely disappear by century's end, the actual threat of nuclear annihilation and the crushing cynicism it will have engendered will linger for hundreds of years.

INSIDE:

THE FIGHT WAS NOT IN VAIN!

POST-WAR PROSPERITY WILL ALLOW US TO BUY MORE PERRY COMO RECORDS

See story on page 20.

EXPERTS PREDICT POST-WAR RISE IN FUCKING

See story on page 34.

| Harnessing the Power of the Atom for Peace | # THE ONION
Finest Source of News in America | Buy "Onion" **POST-WAR** Bonds |
|---|---|---|
| Wednesday, July 3, 1946 | | Price Five Cents |

Family Unit Gazes Happily Into Glorious, Shining Future

Husband, Wife, Children Joyfully Spellbound by Wonderful Things to Come

Even Greater Happiness Apparently Possible

PROSPECT CORNERS, Ohio — A nuclear family unit stood rigidly on the manicured front lawn of their beautiful four-bedroom suburban home Tuesday, gazing unblinkingly at some undetermined fixed point in the distance, their expressions a mixture of industrious can-do spirit and satisfaction with a job well done.

Dick Larson, dressed in snappy pin-striped suit pants and a sharp white dress shirt, and Annie Larson, dressed in a lovely house-dress and heels and a conservative pearl necklace, lovingly held the hands of their two bright and well-behaved children, daughter Sally and son Chip, as they looked bravely toward the horizon. The well-respected, church-going family seemed to radiate positivity and get-up-and-go as they gazed into the glorious future of our great and inordinately wealthy nation.

An uncommon scene? Hardly! Yes, this particular household unit might be known as the Dick Larson family, but by the looks on their bright, shiny faces, they might just as well be the John Q. Anytown, U.S.A., family!

On a million lawns, in a million suburbs, this same majestic scenario is being breathlessly enacted by a million hopeful families. America, blessed in her good fortune by the grace of God and the bounty of industry, has turned a corner into a bold new era of prosperity and confidence, a bright new dawn illuminated by the radiant light of the Atom.

"For as long as any red-blooded American citizen worth his salt can remember, life on this wretched and blasted Earth has been a miserable meat-grinder endurance-test of famine, plague and war," said Larson, a self-described "idea man" at the downtown Akron office of the Mothersbaugh Rubber-Goods manufacturing firm. "But did we knuckle under? Heck, no. We kept at it with good old American know-how and pluck. We took it on the chin and kept giving the other fella what for. We licked everything that the Depression, the Nips and the Führer could dish out, and kept comin' back for more!"

"And now the rewards of our long and patient toil are finally being paid," Larson continued, squinting slightly as he continued to stare stone-faced into the future while speaking. "The Great Powers of Europe have suicidally torn themselves asunder and unintentionally left America The Beautiful holding the keys to the candy store. God is on our side! At last, it is good to be alive."

"Whoa, there! Not good," he said. "Make it, 'grade-A number one tip-top A-OK!'"

Larson emphasized that, although he does not know what the future will bring, he will face it frozen in his current position: chin up, head held high, and one foot thrust forward as if walking ever forward toward optimism incarnate. He said he will maintain this position for several years, with his family beside him on the front lawn of their home.

"Besides remaining in this symbolic pose, plenty of challenges await America in the brave new world ahead," he said, pausing briefly to make eye contact with his loving bride and tousle his son's hair. "We've got to get out there and pound the pavement. We've got to start our own motors. This summer, I for one am fully prepared to tackle that crabgrass problem head on. I may not get it licked once and for all, as I'll be quite busy standing in this trans-fixed pose, but you can be darned sure I'll be giving it the old college try."

Larson is but one American, but his hopeful thoughts speak for us all. Falling silent, he resumed gazing stoically into the coming years. As the morning sun climbed higher, Dick, Annie, Sally and Chip remained in position for several more hours, before briefly breaking formation to rescue a cat stuck in a tree, bake a cake, work on a science fair project, and do the paper route, respectively.

INSIDE:

U.S. ARMY LEARNS NEGROES DIE WHEN INJECTED WITH DEADLY POISONS

See story on page 36

Above: The U.S. nuclear family.

Harry Bailey Wins Congressional Medal

WASHINGTON, D.C. — Commander Harry Bailey of Bedford Falls, N.Y., was presented with the nation's highest honor Tuesday, as President Truman bestowed upon him the Congressional Medal of Honor in a White House ceremony.

Bailey, a Navy flying ace, had shot down 15 planes, two of them as they were about to dive into a transport full of soldiers.

On behalf of all Americans, Truman thanked Bailey for his bravery, but also thanked Bailey's brother George, president of the Bailey Building and Loan in Bedford Falls.

Said Truman, "We owe a great debt to George Bailey for pulling his brother Harry out of the ice when he was 9. Had he not, every man on that transport would have died because Harry would not have been there to save them."

During the war, George Bailey was 4-F on account of his ear. He served as air-raid warden and also organized paper drives, scrap drives and rubber drives.

U.S. Army Finds Last Place on Earth Untouched by War, Blows It to Hell

The first of several proposed nuclear bombs tested in the Bikini Atoll island paradise.

BIKINI ATOLL — The finest military minds in the U.S. have selected the tranquil island paradise of Bikini Atoll in the remote South Pacific to detonate 46 kilotons of atomic bombs this month, searing the tropical Eden to one million degrees Fahrenheit and laying waste to every living thing within a 50-mile radius.

The beautiful islands were selected for their year-round mean temperature of 81 degrees, their peaceful and simple indigenous people, and their breath-takingly lush, palm-lined beaches. Most importantly, said Admiral William Blandy, director of the test, "These islands have been untouched by war for hundreds of years. The waters around them have a pristine, almost transparent quality. The breadfruit trees are a vibrant green. These conditions are obviously ideal for testing the hellish effects of a nuclear fire-and-death-cloud in a controlled environment."

Millions of dead fish, miles of scorched palm trees and hundreds of square miles of contaminated salt water are being studied by Army scientists to determine the precise "Paradise-Devastation Index" of the atomic bomb, data they say could not be derived from simply observing the pleasant, but less than utopian, cities of Hiroshima and Nagasaki.

Of the friendly natives who inhabit the islands, Blandy said they are being well cared for.

"The Bikini Atoll savages are being real troupers about all this," he said. "They were happy to relocate to an aircraft carrier until their tranquil island home becomes inhabitable again after the dissipation of the atomic 'fall-out,' which should only take a few hours."

1946-1963

THE SWELL YEARS

THE ONION

Bright-Eyed? Freckle-Faced? Commie-Hating? Be an Onion Delivery Boy!

Tu Stul... ...tus Es

Finest Source of News in America

Printed in Luxo-Read!

Tuesday, August 27, 1946 — Price Five Cents

Nation Recoils in Horror from Frightening Joan Crawford Make-Up

ACTRESS'S EVIL VISAGE INCITES MASS FEAR

HIDEOUS, DEATH-MASKED CLOWN STILL AT LARGE

HOLLYWOOD — California health officials issued a warning Monday urging citizenry to avoid looking directly at actress Joan Crawford, either in person or on film, stating that victims could become traumatized by her trademark ghoulish make-up.

Special caution should be taken by citizens under the age of 10, those with asthma, those prone to fainting spells, and those with family histories of heart failure.

"Miss Crawford's diabolic visage may pose a significant health risk to the general public," the warning read. "Her troweled-on, corpse-white pancake face coating, coupled with blood-red lipstick and frightening cheekbone rouge the color of exposed tissue, carry her already overpowering 'cruel governess' deportment to almost unbearable new levels of terror."

According to the warning, Crawford's stark features, as well as her jet-black eyelashes and brows, set against a face powdered as white as the undead, could be mistaken for those of a visitor from the underworld. Citizens are reminded that this is merely actress Joan Crawford, not the unholy spawn of Beelzebub and his succubus concubine.

Still, several victims of Crawford's ghostly gaze have been admitted to UCLA Medical Center for psychiatric examination following brushes with the screen star.

Sheriff's offices in Los Angeles, Orange and Ventura Counties are advising citizens to remain indoors, as Crawford is reportedly still at large in the area.

JOAN CRAWFORD

Post-War Squareness Skyrocketing

U.S. GIRLS ENJOYING HELPING MOTHER; BOYS CAN'T GET ENOUGH ARGYLE

See story, page 18.

MIRACLE COMPUTATIONAL DEVICE FITS IN ONE WAREHOUSE

See story, page 18.

A Returning Vet's Shocking Tale: There Is Sex in France

Did America fight on the right side for the last four years? When Private Bill Brunner of the 82nd Airborne Division returned to his mother's home in Dayton, Ohio, last month, this question burned in his mind. After a long year spent on the battlefields of France, Brunner made a most scandalous discovery. His private journal is excerpted here:

June 4, 1944—The big invasion is almost here. Tomorrow, the fellas and I move out to the airfield for our last day in England. I'm thinking of Dorothy, of course—my sweet, sweet Dorothy. I remember our last night together perfectly... the strawberry malt we shared, the summer breeze rustling in the leaves, her soft hand held briefly in mine. When I get back, I'm going to marry that girl. Maybe someday we'll even have children, somehow.

June 6, 1944—I'm in trouble. We jumped over Normandy this morning, but the winds were strong, and I drifted miles away from everyone. I cut off my 'chute and was hiding in a haystack when this very nice Frenchman named Jacques found me. He's with the Resistance, and speaks a little English. I've heard men kiss each other as a greeting here, so I'm keeping my eye on him. Right now, I'm in the cellar of Jacques' farmhouse, where he lives with his wife and her sisters. He just went upstairs, saying that he would arrange a bath, some food and sex. I have no idea what he's talking about. Should I try to escape?

June 7, 1944—I'm so sorry, Dorothy.

June 8, 1944—I think I can write about this now. After I had been hiding in the cellar for about an hour on Tuesday, Jacques came down with a bundle of civilian clothes I changed out of my fatigues—after asking Jacques to leave the room, of course! Then we went upstairs into the kitchen, where bread, butter, and some chicken was being prepared by Jacques' wife's sisters, all very pretty girls between the ages of 18 and 23.

After the delicious dinner, Jacques said, "Now it is time for your bath." And his wife's sister Isabel took me into the bathroom, where the water was running hot. She leaned over the tub, looked over her shoulder, and smiled at me while pouring soap into the running water with a small pan. She started unbuttoning my shirt Then... *(At this point, Brunner's hand-writing becomes so agitated that it is illegible. -ed.)*

After my bath, I went to the family and stated my honorable intention to marry Isabel. All three of them laughed at me for a full three minutes. What sort of a land is this?

What is "Sex"? See page 12.

Surgeon General Warns Against Smoking Any Brand of Cigarette Other than Chesterfields

Only Chesterfields Give You the Rich, Healthy Tobacco Flavor You Need, Top Doctor Says

U.S. Surgeon General Edwin Masterson issued his strongest-ever tobacco warning Monday, announcing that those who smoke cigarettes that are not Chesterfields put themselves at significant risk of not getting the rich, delicious cigarette flavor they deserve.

"Our research indicates that there is a 70 percent greater risk of not enjoying a cigarette if that cigarette is not a Chesterfield, the one that satisfies every time," Masterson said. "I would urge you to strongly consider this fact the next time you are purchasing cigarettes."

Masterson said it is especially important to protect America's children from falling into the habit of smoking potentially unsatisfying cigarettes. To this end, he announced plans to propose legislation making it illegal for cigarette vendors to sell non-Chesterfields to minors.

"It may be too late for many older Americans to change their bad habits, but it is certainly not too late for our young people," Masterson said. "That is why I want to create and enforce severe fines for anyone caught selling brands other than Chesterfields to children. I also want to severely limit where these other brands can advertise, such as near playgrounds and schools, making it harder for them to victimize innocent, impressionable children who are too young to know the difference between the taste of an ordinary cigarette and the savory taste of a Chesterfield."

Masterson said that, as a result of the study's findings, effective Jan. 1, 1947, all tobacco manufacturers will be required to print the following warning on the side of their cigarette packs: "WARNING: The U.S. Surgeon General has found that smoking non-Chesterfield cigarettes can cause deep dissatisfaction in regular cigarette smokers. Switch to Chesterfields today!"

The Surgeon General's report, the result of an exhaustive three-year study of the connection between tobacco and deep, flavorful satisfaction, examined the smoking habits of over 15,000 Americans.

Your smooth-tasting cigarette may not be as healthy or satisfying as a Chesterfield, the Surgeon General warns.

A Risk to Your 'T-Zone'

Brands other than Chesterfields may also pose serious medical risks to the facial region known to modern medicine as the "T-Zone," the Surgeon General warned.

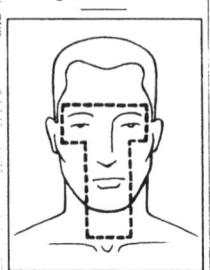

THE HUMAN T-ZONE

Citing a report from top ear, nose and T-Zone specialists at the University of North Carolina at Winston-Salem, Masterson said Chesterfields smokers are more relaxed and quick-witted than smokers of other brands.

Furthermore, Masterson added, Chesterfields smokers' T-Zones and breathing passages are cleaner, because pure Chesterfield smoke has been found to unclog vital T-Zone and throat canals, resulting in easier, more refreshing breathing.

Displaying a pictographic chart of the human head, Masterson and a team of doctors explained how a healthy, robust T-Zone generates life-giving, youth-preserving chemicals when fed Chesterfield cigarette smoke on a daily basis. "Even one day without smoking a Chesterfield can leave this critical zone starved for vital smoke nourishment," said Dr. Bernard Kemper, Dean of the Harvard School of Medicine.

MAKERS OF CHESTERFIELDS PLEASED

Chesterfields manufacturers are gleeful at what is only the latest medical endorsement for smoking their cigarettes.

"We have always known that smoking Chesterfields was the cool, soothing choice," said Charles Rand, CEO of Liggett Group, the company that makes Chesterfields. "But official medical and U.S. government confirmation of that fact is doubly pleasing to us. Even now, as we research new ways to enhance our product with rejuvenating minerals such as additional nicotine, carbon monoxide and tar, we are considering a new 'extra-healthy' line of smokables for use as a dietary supplement for the ill, young children, or those merely concerned that they're not getting enough nutrition from their regular diet."

Rand said he hopes to introduce the company's extra-healthy cigarettes in hospitals, nursing homes, and special "smoking clinics" set up by the company to treat patients suffering from high stress, irritability and lung diseases.

THE ONION

Be Materialistic! | *Finest Source of News in America* | *Repopulate the Earth!*

Thursday, February 20, 1947 — Price Five Cents

Japs, Nazis Victorious in Alternate Philip K. Dick Universe

President Discloses Tragic Outcome of War in Parallel Reality

WASHINGTON, D.C. — In a voice weighted with emotion, President Truman revealed to the American people news of grave import in a radio address Wednesday: "As we celebrate the fruits of victory and peacetime, it has been made known to me that a parallel universe has seen the cruel Japanese and German armies emerge victorious in the Second World War."

The report, prepared by aspiring author Philip K. Dick, describes an alternate time-line which is identical to our own until the 1933 attempt on FDR's life by Giuseppe Zangara. "This is a historical footnote to us," Truman explained, "but in the other time-line, Zangara was successful, and the leadership succeeding Roosevelt was ill-prepared for war."

As a result of the parallel-universe Axis victory, the alternate North American continent has been parceled up into territories controlled by the Japanese or German governments.

"Our thoughts and prayers must be with our counterparts and our families' counterparts in this doomed reality which is so very similar to our own," Truman said. "They are suffering under the yoke of Nazi and Jap oppression which we, in this dimension, so valiantly fought against and ultimately defeated."

Truman said that top U.S. scientists, including Albert Einstein and Robert Oppenheimer, have been assigned the task of finding a way to break through the bounds of our reality into this alternate one to, as Truman said, "Save the parallel U.S. by dropping as many A-bombs as necessary on Germany and Japan."

Roswell, New Mexico, Residents Report Jackalope Sighting

Air Force Denies Cover-Up

ROSWELL, N.M. — Although military officials summoned to this quiet town are calling it an example of mass hallucination, several Roswell residents have recently reported seeing large, antlered jackrabbits in their area.

While these sightings of "jackalopes" have not yet been confirmed by photographic evidence, all witnesses' accounts describe the animal as a mysterious half-jackrabbit, half-antelope hybrid.

"I was out grazing my sheep," Roswell-area farmer Gus Myerson told The Onion, "when I saw it, big as life, watching me from a rise about a hundred yards off. At first I thought it was a rabbit, but no normal rabbit has a set of antlers like that. It was a jackalope. I'd stake my reputation on it."

Myerson also said that he felt "very peaceful" in the jackalope's presence, and that he was sure it meant human beings no harm.

Grant Redland, an insurance salesman from Roswell, has no conscious memory of a jackalope sighting. Under hypnosis, however, he was found to have been visited in his sleep by several jackalopes who took him into their mysterious jackalope warren and probed his anus with their long antlers.

"Preposterous," said Major John Stebbins, an Army

An eye-witness sketch of the half-jackrabbit, half-antelope creature.

Intelligence officer stationed at nearby Roswell Air Force Base, whose investigation team has "decisively ruled out" any possibility of the jackalope's existence. "This could be anything—luminous desert gas, a weather balloon being blown along the ground, anything."

But, despite official dismissals, some residents remain convinced.

"It makes sense that jackalopes would visit humanity at this crucial junction in our evolution," said local mystic and jackalope believer Thomas Dwyer. "We are an infant race, and they are emerging from their ancient terrestrial herds to monitor us as we experiment with the dangerous atom."

Some observers say government scientists have procured a jackalope corpse, and are examining it inside the top-secret Hutch 51.

Army officials denied the charge.

FDR's Remains to Run for Fifth Term

ROOSEVELT

Beloved late president Franklin D. Roosevelt, speaking through living representatives, announced his intention to seek a fifth term as president in 1948, running on a platform of "A Better Leader Dead than Any Man Alive."

"It is safe to say there is no better leader for this nation than Roosevelt," said FDR '48 campaign manager Thaddeus Unger. "And Roosevelt always wanted the best for America. I think, therefore, it may be assumed that he would have wanted very much for this campaign to take place."

As early as next week, the decomposed, rigid husk of Roosevelt is expected to begin making campaign stops in cities and towns across America.

Partially animated in marionette fashion with support rods and puppet strings, the beloved remains will deliver campaign speeches on a whistle-stop tour of American towns, assisted by an actor speaking from behind a screen.

Unger dismisses concerns that Roosevelt's deteriorating condition may render him unable to govern effectively.

"The remains in question are still recognizably those of Roosevelt. Yes, we are now required to glue his spectacles and cigarette holder to his face, and his deteriorated eyeballs will need to be replaced with glass copies, but these are simple, academic matters. As long as the weather remains relatively warm and dry, and the Secret Service continues to treat the corpse with smelling salts and formaldehyde, good ol' FDR will see us through."

President Truman, meanwhile, has been instructed to step down from the presidency in order to serve as running-mate to the deceased body. Said Unger, "We feel that the demands of running the country will be too great a distraction for Truman to be able to effectively fill the job to which he is best suited—right-hand man to the great FDR. Roosevelt's incomparable experience and wisdom combined with Truman's viable physical body will be the team to beat in '48."

'Tele-Vision' Promises Mass Enrichment of Mankind

'Drama and Learning Box' Will Make Schools Obsolete by 1970

New Device to Provide High-Minded Alternative to Mindless Drivel Found on Radio

This RCA model tele-vision weighs less than 700 pounds and boasts a luxurious four-inch screen.

by Prof. Simon Helmhurst, Columbia University

Imagine, if you will, touring the ancient ruins of the Roman Empire, watching a demonstration on the fine art of sculpture, or having the theories of velocity explained to you by a doctor of physics—all in the comfort of your own den after supper! Imagine, ladies, learning the newest crochet patterns and discovering the latest stain-removal tips—all while ironing the day's laundry! The amazing tele-vision, the most promising invention of the century, will make all this possible.

As you read this, scientists are perfecting an affordable version of this amazing learning box, so no one need be left behind as we approach the 1950s. The tele-vision world will be one where learning is easy, fun, and available to all. No longer will some wallow in slums of ignorance, while others enjoy the benefits of an Ivy League education. With the proliferation of this supreme tool of learning and human enrichment, every man in America will be a professor of science or law within six years.

Instead of feeding on the mindless drivel that frothy radio shows and tawdry paperbacks provide, we will embrace knowledge and toss ignorance out the door. With up-to-the-week news reports made with moving-picture technology, the tele-vision will be a window into the world.

No longer will children need to go to school, for the school will now come into the home. The United States will become the greatest nation on earth—one filled with active and intelligent citizens, rushing about in a whirlwind of discoveries, inventions, innovations and theories—all because of the introduction of the stupendous learning box.

The great intellectuals of our time will not sit alone and unnoticed penning books, but will be lauded by the millions who "tune in" each week to see these "stars."

The word Hollywood, as it beckons tele-vision program producers, will become synonymous with intellectualism. Burbank, California, will be a mecca for the greatest minds of our generation, all wishing to take part in this amazing revolution brought about by the incredible life-enriching learning box.

Behold the future!

CIA Denies CIA Founding

LANGLEY, Va. — Central Intelligence Agency Executive Director Allen Dulles, speaking at a press conference at the new CIA headquarters at Langley Air Force Base, "categorically denied" that the CIA had been founded last week with the signing of the National Security Act by President Truman.

"The alleged existence of a Central Intelligence Agency established to gather and evaluate intelligence information relating to U.S. foreign policy, and to engage in covert action to perpetuate U.S. post-war supremacy, is pure fiction," said Dulles, who also denied being appointed to his position by the National Security Council.

"In fact," Dulles said, "we, that is, the nonexistent organization of intelligence agents which I most emphatically do not head, resent these implications."

Dulles then stated that the press conference "never happened" and denied any CIA involvement.

INSIDE:

NUREMBURG PROCEEDINGS CALLED 'THE TRIAL OF THE CENTURY'
See story, page 3

NORMAN MAILER POST-WAR TESTOSTERONE LEVELS HIGHER THAN EVER
See story, page 18

JACKSON POLLOCK FIRED FROM HOUSE-PAINTING JOB
See story, page 30

| Optimism! | # THE ONION | Repression! |

Finest Source of News in America

Wednesday, April 7, 1948 — Price Five Cents

Antlike Conformity Now Affordable

Row upon Row of Identical Box-Like Homes Replace Ugly Long Island Prairie

New 'Levittown' Homes to Be as Interchangeable as Inhabitants

HEMPSTEAD, N.Y. — In what is sure to be a boon to the nation's millions of growing families, maverick developer William J. Levitt announced Tuesday that he is preparing to unveil a new type of sub-urban housing development on a vast parcel of Long Island real estate. The new community, consisting of thousands of identical structures built on identical 60 x 100-foot lots and accessed by a geometrically precise grid of two-way streets, is being called "Levittown."

"You're a lucky fellow, Mr. Homeowner," Levitt said at a ground-breaking ceremony. "As an American citizen, you have the right to live among people whose age, income, number of children, habits, topics of conversation, modes of dress, possessions and religious beliefs are identical to yours."

All of Levitt's homes will be white, two-story, Cape Cod-style houses with four bedrooms, full kitchens and a 12-by-16-foot living room into which a television can easily fit.

"The two-story design will allow the husband to enjoy the baronial splendor of climbing the stairs to bed at night and descending them to breakfast in the morning," Levitt said. "His two children can be let out in the back yard to play, while their mother watches them from the kitchen. A sturdy, white picket fence may be erected to cordon off the territory and protect against trespassers, predators or the bomb."

Levitt plans to rigidly align the houses with one another and meticulously space them identical distances apart to ensure both neighborhood conformity and a soothing, uniform appearance. For every hundred homes, there will be a parklike square of grass containing five trees and a swing-set. The children will be educated at one of five matching schools, and their fathers will drive to work on streets which, except for having been designated with the names of different trees that once grew there, will be indistinguishable from one another.

Levitt said this quality of sameness in Levittown's design is its chief merit in the eyes of his intended customers. Most of the houses will be purchased by family men working in nearby New York City, men who find conformity pleasing and comforting.

"Owning your own home is one of the highest aspirations of any citizen in this democracy," Levitt said, "and now, by owning one of my homogeneous, interchangeable homes, a working man can know what it really means to be an American."

"That is," Levitt stressed, "unless you are a negro."

Pre-Fab Families Also Available

Although early sales indicate that Bill Levitt's ready-made housing units are a runaway success, problems remain in marketing the homes to as-yet unmarried men. To provide for these unfortunate bachelors, Levitt's company has made "Levittowner"-brand prefabricated families available at a reasonable cost.

Levitt's research indicates that many of the men who are not purchasing his houses are returning soldiers who have not yet had the time or opportunity to acquire a family. Such men are the target market for Levitt's ready-made mate and progeny.

Three family models encompassing the entire spectrum of American preferences have been introduced:

The "Smith," featuring a brunette wife, a towheaded boy with a slingshot in his back pocket, and a pig-tailed girl toddler;

The "Johnson," featuring a wife with shorter brown hair and a turned-up nose, a tomboy daughter guaranteed to "grow out of it," and a mischief-prone son; and

The "Nelson," featuring a pregnant blonde wife, freckle-faced and crewcut grade-school-aged son, and a Labrador retriever.

Levitt spokesmen say the dog option will also be offered on the other two family units.

According to Levitt's brochure, "With these 'family packages,' today's up-and-coming young man can relax and enjoy the family he loves in the house he's always wanted—with absolutely no fuss!"

Levitt guarantees all families for life against poor manners, shiftless attitudes and severe emotional trauma. Spousal relationships are guaranteed against malaise, divorce or heartbreak. An extended warranty for the children's future marriages is not available.

"Owning your own family is not just every man's right," Levitt said. "It's the American Dream."

"That is, unless you are a negro," Levitt stressed.

INSIDE:

CHUCK YEAGER BREAKS SCOTCH BARRIER AT LOCAL BAR
Turn to page 6, col. 2

INDIA'S OVERCROWDING PLEASES POPE
Pius XII's Third-World Fertility Program 'Proceeding Wonderfully'
Turn to page 20, col. 1

Alger Hiss Evades Capture with Secret Evapo-Spy Wristwatch

Rep. Nixon's Emergency Jet-Pack Ambush Fails

Red Villain Escapes to Secret Spy-Club Tree House

WASHINGTON, D.C. — House Un-American Activities Committee officials were foiled in their attempts to interrogate suspected Communist Alger Hiss Tuesday, when the former FDR advisor made a daring, last-minute escape from FBI agents. Though a chronology of events is still being reconstructed by authorities, it is believed that Hiss' escape was made possible through the use of a high-tech spy-o-scopic wristwatch.

According to the FBI's official report, a team of agents surprised the former State Department official at his home Tuesday afternoon and attempted to take him into custody on charges of sedition when Hiss, according to Agent Marvin Jameson, "turned what appeared to be the winding stem on the side of his wrist watch, releasing a cloud of noxious smoke from his cufflinks, momentarily disorienting the agents on the scene."

Once the smoke dissipated, Jameson said, agents searched the immediate area for Hiss, but to no avail.

It was later learned that Hiss slipped outside, where the up-turned collar of his overcoat and the sharp cast of a building's shadow shielded him from detection.

U.S. Rep. Richard Nixon (R-Calif.), who led the HUAC fight against Hiss, arrived in a government-issue jet-pack just in time to spot the alleged spy. Hiss, however, sprayed blinding ink into Nixon's eye with a special secret-agent pen, which disabled the congressman long enough for Hiss to commandeer the jet pack to safety.

Suspected spy Alger Hiss before his daring escape.

HISS TRACKED TO SECRET TREE HOUSE

Praising the crafty diplomat as "more than I bargained for," Jameson next tracked Hiss to a secluded spy-club tree house.

"It was here," Jameson said, "that Hiss used secrets gleaned from his tenure as president of the Carnegie Endowment for International Peace to decode a hidden message from the Kremlin written in invisible ink inside a *Man Called X* comic book he kept under his sleeping bag in the hideout."

It is also suspected that Hiss tuned in to an episode of *Captain Midnight* using a battery-powered transistor radio and used his cardboard Kellogg's Pep Key-o-matic Code-o-graph, Lamont Cranston pin, and Cracker Jack magnifying lens to decipher clues to FBI Director J. Edgar Hoover's plan to take over the world.

ATTEMPTED CAPTURE BY PRETTY HEIRESS

Once Hiss was back on the road with the secret plans in tow, sources inside the Scientific Bureau of Investigation say he drove his specially designed getaway scooter to meet the attractive daughter of newspaper millionaire Conrad Craven.

Little did Hiss know, however, that Miss Craven is an operative of United States Counterspies, planted along with her super-intelligent dog Sparky, was planted to track Hiss and lure him into U.S. hands.

HOOVER'S UNDERSEA LAIR

Hoover said he intends to bring Hiss to justice within the next several days. "Between our massive network of spies trailing Hiss and the stable of idiosyncratic sidekicks and assassins in the employ of the Bureau, Hiss will have to be very fortunate to escape the pan-global reach of the FBI."

Of the damage Hiss may have done to the nation in the years before being named as a suspected Communist, Hoover said, "It is of greater importance to the Bureau that Hiss does not uncover our master plan to wipe out Communism via Communist-seeking missiles, a technological breakthrough that, once completed, will make the U.S. unstoppable—the unquestioned leaders of the Earth."

Hoover noted that the weapons technology is safely protected in a massive undersea lair guarded by highly trained shock troops whom Hiss could not possibly defeat.

"But if Hiss does somehow penetrate the lair," Hoover said, "I pledge to make every effort not to reveal every detail of my master plan to him, giving him just enough clues to stop it with a last-minute act of sabotage and ingenious escape."

THE ONION

Ferreting Out Communists | *Urging War with Russia*

TU STUL · TUS ES

Finest Source of News in America

Tuesday, November 9, 1948 — Price Five Cents

War-Weary Jews Establish Homeland Between Syria, Lebanon, Jordan, Egypt

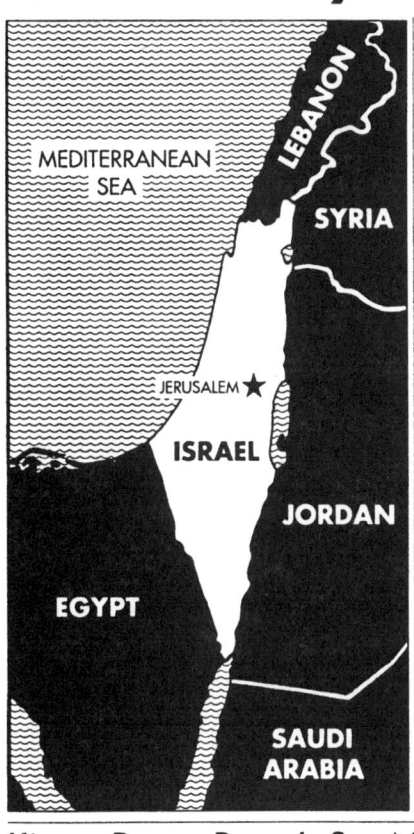

'In Israel, Our People Will Finally Have Safety and Peace,' Says Ben-Gurion

Jordan Welcomes New Neighbors with Celebratory Gunfire, Rock Throwing

JERUSALEM, Israel — After more than 2,000 years of wandering and persecution, including six million deaths at the hand of Nazi Germany, the Jewish people finally established a homeland Monday, a place of safety and peace nestled between Syria, Lebanon, Jordan and Egypt.

"No longer will the Jewish race live in a constant state of fear and endangerment, its very existence threatened at every turn by hostile outsiders," said David Ben-Gurion, the new nation's first prime minister, addressing a jubilant crowd of Zionists at Jerusalem's Western Wall. "Here in Israel, we are safe, far away from those who seek to destroy us."

For two millennia, the Jewish people have wandered without a home, facing an endless series of hostile enemies. With the establishment of a sovereign Jewish state in the Middle East, Israeli officials believe this 2,000-year ordeal has at last come to an end.

"Israel is the land of milk and honey," Ben-Gurion said. "Here there will be no pogroms, no midnight visits from Cossacks, no Nuremberg Laws. The only gunfire we shall hear is that which lingers in our minds from troubled times long past."

Ben-Gurion said he looks forward to years of harmony and cooperation with Israel's neighboring states. "Jordan seems extremely happy to have us as a new neighbor," he said. "Last night, from my window, I could hear great explosions coming from the Gaza Strip. How wonderful of the Palestinian peoples there to celebrate our arrival with fireworks."

In his official greeting to Israel yesterday, Egypt's King Farouk issued the following statement: "Egypt does not and will not ever recognize the so-called state of Israel's right to exist. Israel is a land built on Jewish lies and the spilled blood of countless Arabs. Until the territory called Israel is returned to its rightful Palestinian owners, Egypt will have no choice but to consider itself at war with the Jewish people."

As a token of its good will, Syria presented Israel with a burning Israeli flag, with an attached note that read, "May you be swiftly driven into the sea and drowned."

In the months leading up to Monday's formal declaration of Israeli statehood, hundreds of thousands of Holocaust survivors from around the world have flocked to Israel, where they will finally find a safe haven from anti-Semitism. "This is a dream come true," said Holocaust survivor Zadie Dubrovnik, 59, who left her native Lithuania for Israel last week. "In this place, we will build a refuge of peace, far away from those who hate us."

Ben-Gurion said that with no need to defend itself from enemies, Israel will be free to spend billions of dollars on domestic development that other nations would be forced to devote to a defense budget. Military expenditures are expected to account for just two percent of the country's overall budget, as Israel will be a place of peace, not war.

Hitler Alive and Well in Experimental Disney Freeze-Pod

Dictator, Animator to Rule 21st Century

BERLIN — As millions worldwide continue to celebrate the defeat of the Nazi menace with parades and song, it was learned Monday that former German leader Adolf Hitler is still alive, cryogenically preserved in a top-secret immortality freeze-pod created in the late 1930s to keep the Nazi warlord alive for decades more.

Although Hitler's alleged suicide was widely reported, his body was never discovered. The current whereabouts of the freeze-pod remain unknown.

The pod was designed by millionaire robotics and cryogenics pioneer Walt Disney to freeze his own body in the event of death, preserving it for future resuscitation by the advanced medical science of centuries hence. Hitler modified it for his use to "resurface and claim the mantle of history" at a later date.

The pod, the world's first successful working prototype of a cryogenic device, represents a major breakthrough for both German engineering and the famed cartoon-studio mogul.

"We tried several field tests of earlier models, but couldn't engineer a liquid-nitrogen cooling system that met the performance load reliably," Disney said at a poolside press conference in California. "The Germans' advances in rocketry, however, proved invaluable in surmounting the problem."

"Likewise," Disney added, "Herr Hitler and his associates showed great interest in our animatronics technology, and hope to put it to use in the creation of terrifying robotic simu-drones capable of replacing world leaders who are assassinated or otherwise deposed without revealing the coup to the general public."

Disney said he is also considering a plan to use the terrifying drones to welcome visitors to a proposed Disney amusement park.

The animator stressed that the Hitler-Disney freeze-pod partnership does not indicate any ideological affiliation between Walt Disney Studios and the Nazi regime. To illustrate, he noted his production of anti-Nazi war-propaganda cartoons featuring hilarious talking ducks and parodic caricatures portraying Hitler as a power-mad despot.

At present, mass production of the new freeze-pods is under way, with over fifty of the devices ordered for delivery by next year. Although most are intended for use by other fabulously wealthy and powerful individuals, long-range plans for the future of the technology include the possible establishment of a clandestine international cartel of pod-frozen generals, captains of industry and other power-mongers. It is hoped that, aided by the shadowy machinations of a covert, occult secret society working behind the scenes on their behalf, they will eventually awaken from their icy slumber and be appointed to lead the totalitarian mega-corporations of the 21st century.

Kinsey Report Reveals Sex May Feel Good

Reproductive Act Not as Painful, Traumatic as Previously Thought

The medical community is in an uproar following the release of Alfred Kinsey's "Report on Human Sexuality," a revolutionary new document which threatens to redefine sexual relations as they are known. Among the bombshells listed in the report is the previously unheard-of notion that under certain circumstances and between certain participants, sexual relations may be less traumatic than previously thought, and may even feel somewhat good.

The report claims, "There is preliminary evidence, as yet unverified, suggesting that the act of coitus may have pleasant overtones and, imaginably, even thoroughly gratifying sensations when properly executed."

The report is the result of years of exhaustive interviews with a wide cross-section of Americans who have experienced acts of sex. It alleges that a tiny percentage of them felt "less emotionally scarred than it seemed they should" by the experience.

Psychiatrists and biologists are stunned by the striking claim, and most are extremely skeptical. "The possibility of enjoying the dirty, shameful act of intercourse not only goes against all medical evidence, but common sense and millennia of human experience," said Professor Jonathan Schmidt of Cornell University. "Perhaps an uneducated vagabond, copulating under the influence of marijuana smoke, might confuse his drug-induced reverie for pleasure deriving from the act. I can see no other likely circumstance surrounding such confusion."

Whatever comes of his remarkable claims, Dr. Kinsey is certainly unafraid of controversy. The report goes on to state that, in addition to traditional monogamous sex between a man and a woman, strange, uncharted varieties of the act may someday be possible: "Incredible as it may seem, there is no mechanical reason an unmarried couple cannot engage in relations. In that regard it would seem that the only barrier is finding two volunteers brave enough to attempt a first-ever extramarital coupling."

It is presumed that the woman in such a union could not become with child, given the absence of sanction by a benevolent God.

But most bizarre of all are veiled intimations that the participants in sex need not be of opposite genders. Without actually making such a claim, the report implied that the otherworldly notion of "same-sex" relations is not inherently contradictory.

"Now we have entered the realm of fantasy literature," Schmidt said. "And I suppose the participants in this 'homo-sexual sex,' if you will, would then marry and live together. I invite anyone to make an attempt. Next, Kinsey shall tell us of sex performed by a single person, without any partner at all."

Based on pressure from decency groups, the report is being banned in many cities as pornography.

INSIDE:

Jackie Robinson Lynched for Stealing Second

See story, page 3.

LITERARY SCHOLAR FIRST EVER TO FINISH READING 'FINNEGAN'S WAKE'
See story, page 12.

CORRECTION:

On its Nov. 3 front page, *The Onion* erroneously reported that the Other Guy had defeated What's-His-Face in the 1948 presidential election. In fact, What's-His-Face defeated the Other Guy. *The Onion* regrets the error.

75

THE ONION

Finest Source of News in America

Drop the Bomb on 'em!

Friday, September 30, 1949

Don't Forget to "Tip" Your Onion Delivery Boy

Price Five Cents

A-Bomb May Have Awakened Gigantic Radioactive Monsters, Experts Say

Flying Turtles, 200-Foot Moths among Rumored Creatures

HIROSHIMA, Japan — The atomic-bomb attack on the Japanese city of Hiroshima may have triggered the creation of a race of gigantic radioactive monsters, U.S. General Douglas MacArthur announced Thursday.

"Within a one-mile radius of ground zero, there have been numerous sightings of 500-foot-tall monsters roaming the ruined, rubble-strewn streets of Hiroshima, crushing buildings and cars like tin cans," said MacArthur, who leads the American post-war occupation of the country. "It is still not clear whether the monsters are friendly."

Among the beasts spotted: a shrieking, fire-breathing dinosaur, a 20,000-ton flying turtle, and a 200-foot moth with death-ray vision.

According to MacArthur, the tremendous force of America's 1945 atomic attack may have awakened the huge prehistoric beasts from their eons of slumber.

"It is likely that this bomb, more powerful than any detonated in human history, unleashed just enough destructive power to disturb these creatures from more than two million years of peaceful hibernation on the ocean floor, where they had likely been encased in an enormous block of ice," he said.

So far, no creatures have been sighted in Nagasaki, the other city hit with an atomic bomb. City police are on full alert, but are keenly aware that their tiny force is helpless against the rampaging beasts.

Japanese leaders have convened for an emergency meeting to address the crisis. While some government officials say the creatures must be destroyed, others say they are friendly and possess powers that can be harnessed for good. "We must try to talk to the creatures," urged Prime Minister Shigeru Yoshida.

MacArthur has advised his lieutenants to meet any giant monsters in the area with the combined weaponry of the U.S. armed forces currently occupying the region.

This strategy is being protested by 9-year-old Kentaro Fujimoto, who claimed one monster, the flying turtle, was a friend to children.

Another Goddamned Abbott and Costello Movie Released

HOLLYWOOD — An opening-night crowd of nearly 500 gathered at the Bijou Theatre Thursday to attend the gala premiere screening of another goddamned Abbott and Costello movie, *Abbott and Costello Meet Frankenstein*. Stars Myrna Loy, Mickey Rooney and Edna O'Brien were on hand yet again for the comic duo's latest goddamned release, which comes but two months on the heels of *The Noose Hangs High*, their previous goddamned effort.

"Another goddamned month, another goddamned movie," quipped straightman William "Bud" Abbott as he entered the theater, where countless goddamned Abbott and Costello films have made their debut, including their goddamned 1945 hit, *Here Come the Co-Eds*.

Standing at his side, as always, was funnyman Lou Costello, who broke up the crowd by asking them to wait around until after the movie, when he and Abbott would "probably do another goddamned comedy routine."

In their new film (their goddamned 22nd), the irrepressible pair get involved in a series of scary, comic misadventures with a mad-scientist woman and her animated golem. While the Frankenstein motif is, of course, a familiar one among movie-makers and audience members alike, the new picture is the first in which it is given the famous "goddamned Abbott and Costello" treatment.

Among those on hand to see the goddamned Abbott and Costello movie was radio reporter and syndicated columnist Walter Winchell. "Goddammit!" Winchell said of the comic pair's effort. "It seems like every other morning I wake up and read that they're making another movie. God be damned."

Asked what his next project would be, Abbott rolled his eyes and dead-panned, "Oh, I don't know. Probably another goddamned Abbott and Costello movie."

Hideous Wooden Imp Causes National Panic

Nightmarish Puppet-Beast Featured on Children's Show

Millions of Youngsters Lapse into Fear-Induced Comas

NEW YORK — Children nationwide were terror-stricken Thursday as a new program made its debut starring a grotesque wooden specter identifying itself as "Howdy Doody."

Leering, quaking and dangling from several sinewy strings, the dead-eyed abomination greeted viewers with a heart-stopping grimace and proceeded to lure children into accepting its eerie doctrine of glassy-eyed conformity and obedience to authority. Members of the "Peanut Gallery," the cloistered juvenile inductees to the Path of Doody, appeared to be held in the thrall of the wobbling puppet-beast as they inaugurated the broadcast by declaring, in unison, that the reign of the evil Doody had begun.

Often hovering inches above the floor of the small boxy stage it inhabits, Doody presented a variety of skits and songs, assisted by Robert "Buffalo Bob" Smith, a key member of Doody's inner circle. Also on stage was a mute, androgynous, unspeakably horrifying clown.

"I am led to believe that the clown's vocal cords were severed by its pint-sized wooden overlord," said Kenneth Wallace, who watched the show with his two young children. "The tendency toward mischief and pranks on the clown's part would no doubt have enraged the malevolent host—a 'puppet master' who is literally a puppet, if you will."

So what do the children, the toughest critics of all, think of the new show? Wallace's 5-year-old daughter, Karen, said, "I don't like television any more."

Stevie Timmons, 3, hid under his bed for several days after first viewing the program, muttering, "Make puppet go away. Don't like puppet."

Producers of the program expect the shrill-voiced ghoul to become indelibly etched into the psyches of the nation's children, causing them untold psychological problems in later life, including an unnatural aversion to wood and an inability to maintain meaningful relationships.

Bing Crosby Record Reveals Secret Message When Played Backward: 'Have a Swell Day, Ladies and Gents'

Impressionable Youths May Fall Victim to Hidden Suggestion

A 40 percent rise in teen swellness over the past year is being blamed on a new Bing Crosby record, available in stores nationwide in both 78 and long-play formats.

"(Would You Like to) Swing on a Star" has sold half a million copies since its release this past summer, and only now is the shocking story behind this brazen and scandalous record being told.

Sound engineers, studying the recording upon the latest magnetic-strip-analysis devices, have uncovered a call to swellness on the part of youth-agitator Crosby.

"After examining the song," explained Dr. Philip Rayburn of MIT, "it became clear that when spun backwards and slowed down to one-eighth the normal playing speed, it carries a distinctly audible message some two minutes in."

Rayburn explained that the message is imbedded into the disc by the subliminal medium of "quasi-sonic" tones, which enter the listener's brain without his knowledge and render him all the more vulnerable to its hypnotic allure.

Major U.S. cities have reported severe increases in energetic, positive-minded behavior on the part of teen-agers. Skipping and humming have become almost uncontrollable in some cities, and sales of chewing gum have nearly doubled.

"Crosby has always been noted for his pro-swellness stance," said Dr. Peter Andrews. "But to subversively teach our children in this manner.... How long before our young people are dancing in their socks?"

America's young people, meanwhile, remain in the thrall of Crosby's licentious commands, and the reign of pep shows no signs of waning. "My daughter was winked at by two different boys this week," local businessman Edward Roal said. "I remember when a young man would consult a girl's father for permission to court. To think Crosby was once one of the finest youth role models ever to smoke a pipe."

Sid Pratt, a spokesman for the recording agency vending the musical shocker, stated that it is the responsibility of parents to make informed decisions with regard to what manner of music is to be admitted into the home. "Crosby's record is primarily intended for the enjoyment of married couples," he said.

ATOMIC EXPLOSIONS TODAY

Tourists: Contact your local Atomic Energy Commission office for maximum-visibility areas.

Bikini Atoll
Kwajalein Atoll
Eniwetok Atoll
Ratak Atoll
Majura Island
Enderbury Island
Cook Islands (all)
Nameless Island 184 miles off coast of San Diego
Omaha, Nebraska
Avara Island
Tarawa Island
Oahu
White Sands, New Mexico
(17th consecutive day)

INSIDE:

'BABY BOOM' TRACED TO SINGLE HORNY BASTARD
see story, page 3

KING OF SIAM TWIRLS GAILY ABOUT PALACE
see story, page 11

THE ONION

PRODUCE! | **CONSUME!**

Finest Source of News in America

Sunday, October 2, 1949 — SUNDAY EDITION — Price Fifteen Cents

Burma-Shave Copywriter Wins Pulitzer

Simplicity of Roadway Poetry Belies Its Depth

Award Caps Advertising Wordsmith's Illustrious Career

NEW YORK, N.Y. — Ted "Sparky" Bartledale, copywriter and "idea man" for the Los Angeles advertising firm of Vebber, Karlin, LaFleur & Dahm, was awarded the Pulitzer Prize for Poetry yesterday for his latest installment in the widely read Burma-Shave advertising campaign.

The campaign features a series of sequential roadway billboards, which attract motorists' attention as they drive by.

No less an authority on literature than Joseph Pulitzer Jr. himself spoke of Bartledale's talents at the New York award ceremony. "As my chauffeur and I motored along, reading each consecutive road-post in the series as they sped past, I became caught up in the unfolding verse," Pulitzer said. "I was on the edge of my seat, brimming with excitement to discover what new literary delights each subsequent composition would bring. In fact, so eager was I to finally read the concluding chapter that, I confess, I ordered my driver to rush well above the posted speed limit so as to cover the intervening ground with all possible dispatch."

Bartledale is the esteemed author of such celebrated quatrains as, "What is the lotion / That makes all the men rave? / No need for commotion / It's Burma-Shave" and the widely praised "A smooth-shaven kisser / That's what the ladies crave / Say, get wise there, mister / Try Burma-Shave," which received an Honorable Mention from the New York Critics Circle last year.

The prize-winning scribe launched his writing career with the now-classic "That's Burma-Shave / B-U-R-M-A S-H-A-V-E / Burma-Shave," a series of road-signs which set the literary world on its ear and gained the young Bartledale a reputation as a rising star among men of letters.

But it was his latest opus that truly set him apart and earned him the written word's most coveted prize: "Land of the free / Home of the brave / Bespeckled with whiskers? / Try Burma-Shave."

"It is not only a rousing call for the purchase of Burma-Shave Shaving Lotions and Creams throughout the land," Pulitzer said. "It is also a profoundly resonant statement about America herself."

GIANT POSTER OF MAO SEIZES POWER IN CHINA

Enormous Placard Now Controls World's Most Populous Nation

PEKING, China — Ending a long and bitter civil war, the Chinese people today celebrated the transfer of power to a 15-foot by 20-foot poster of Communist Party Chairman Mao Tse-tung.

After the new poster-led government was established, a large rally was held in China's Tien An Men square, with the poster looking out approvingly over the crowd from atop a high balcony. Thousands came to pay tribute to the picture, which now leads the most populous nation on earth.

"We have put our faith in this great poster," said one Chinese citizen in attendance.

THE RISE OF THE POSTER

Not much is known in the West about the ruling poster, except that it is said to be made of the finest Chinese silk-bond cardboard stock.

Once a mere paper sign advertising the sale of pigs from a peasant farm in the village of Hsiang T'an, the poster grew in size and amassed a large following after serving as a banner in the war with Japan. Now a charismatic poster, it led troops across China to drive out the armies of Chiang Kai-shek during the civil war, ultimately forcing the Nationalists to Formosa under threat of severe paper cuts.

The new government's Central Governing Council is made up of some of the poster's top advisor-banners, including the new Chinese flag, which features a solid red background with five yellow stars in the corner. The flag is slated to become the nation's second-in-command. The council voted the poster the sole leader of China's new Communist government, granting smaller pictures regional authority over much of the newly unified country. Pocket-sized paper books are slated to be handed to all Chinese citizens to further solidify the poster's control.

A NEW ERA

The giant picture's total control over China marks a distinct departure from traditional Chinese governance. This new era of political power in the hands of poster-imagery was summed up by Yang Shan-kun, a political observer: "This is one of the first times in Chinese history that we have been able to see one of our leaders. In the past, our great emperors were hidden from view in the Forbidden City, but in this new Communist era of humble egalitarianism, the leader has revealed himself to us. And his enormous size and unwavering expression prove to us his greatness."

"How great our poster-leaders of antiquity must have been," Yang continued. "While they were hidden from public view, we can theorize now that they, too, were just as enormous, attractive, fatherly looking, and fixed in their proud, determined gazes."

Sources close to the new government indicate that the poster of Mao may be planning a summit with a marble statue of Josef Stalin by year's end. Some U.S. observers have speculated that a meeting between the Mao poster and newsreel footage of President Truman could happen as soon as the middle of next year.

In such a summit meeting, the poster and the footage would face each other in an ornate room while cameras capture their images to make other pictures.

Millions gather in Peking to honor their new 20-foot-tall, 15-foot-wide, quarter-inch-thick leader.

Toxic Levels of Self-Involvement Found in Many Post-War Babies

70 Percent of Infants' First Word: 'Me'

Entire Generation Expected to Be Intolerable to Parents, Children, Each Other

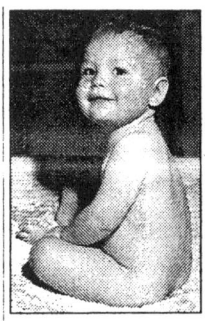

BOSTON, Mass. — According to an article published in the latest *New England Journal of Medicine*, toxic levels of self-involvement have been discovered in nearly 80 percent of children born in the post-war "baby boom."

The article's findings were based on blood samples taken from 25,000 babies born between 1945 and 1948, whose blood contained dangerously high levels of self-involvement, some 40 times higher than those of Americans born in the previous generation.

"Ordinarily, blood absorbs many substances present in a person's body, including nutrients, salt, cholesterol and urea. But rarely does it actually absorb the person himself," *New England Journal of Medicine* Managing Editor Dr. Malcolm Causewell said. "Curiously, though, in the case of these post-war babies, that is exactly what has happened, creating a strange condition called 'Self-Absorption.'"

Causewell said Self-Absorption is an anomaly that, until now, had been observed in only a tiny fraction of Americans. Over the next 20 years, however, he said it may grow rapidly.

"It is entirely plausible that, by 1970, the vast majority of Americans will exhibit strange symptoms including abnormally high interest in their own satisfaction, a preoccupation with self-actualization, and an eerie lack of blind faith in their elected officials, clergy and peers." Causewell said. "This rise in self-involvement levels could have nearly limitless repercussions, including an explosion in everything from recreational drug use to therapy to self-help books."

THE CREATURE FROM THE BLACK NEIGHBORHOOD!

FILMED IN CAUCAS-O-RAMA

No Whites Will Be Seated In The Final 15 Minutes!

No Blacks Will Be Seated In The Theater!

APPEARING IN MOVIE HOUSES TODAY!

Full-Color Fold-Out Poster of Arthur Godfrey In This Edition!

INSIDE:

Salesman Dead
WAS 'LIKED, NOT WELL-LIKED,' SAYS INSIDE SOURCE
see story, page 6.

Area Zoot Suit Reet Pleated
see story, page 8.

77

Weather:
Today, stern with chance of happiness.
Tomorrow, hopeful, with afternoon cheer.

The Onion

TU STULTUS ES

Are You a Communist? Take our test, page 8

Sunday, May 7, 1950 — FINEST NEWS SOURCE IN AMERICA — ★★★ SUNDAY EDITION — Price Fifteen Cents

Mickey Spillane Treats Wise Guy to a Little Chin Music

Vows to Gut-Shoot the Rat Who Aced His Best Pal

Many Half-Dressed Skirts Expiring in Tough-Guy Author's Arms

NEW YORK — Veteran tough-guy author Mickey Spillane treated a Brooklyn wise guy to a little chin music Saturday, according to a statement Spillane made to his readers last night.

Sources close to Spillane say the no-good bum was connected with the shooting death of Dutton Weybright, a war buddy of the author's who once took a Jap bullet meant for Spillane.

"Sure, I busted his snoot," said Spillane, his rugged face briefly lit as he fired up another Viceroy. "He should never 'a gotten mixed up in this racket, see, 'cause I had to smash his face all over the place. I went half bugs. You would, too, if your pal bought it with a dum-dum in his groceries."

Spillane said he had encountered sour luck and bloody murder all the previous day. He also said he had had a bellyful of the wise guy, a known cannon and numbers runner for the Brentano machine. When the skell gave Spillane the business and went for his rod, the two-fisted, best-selling author tapped him one on the chin.

"Anyone who gives me guff takes a nap and goes to the dentist, see?" said Spillane, who also said that any skell who got between him and the man who plugged Weybright would have to get himself a new head.

Police are looking for Spillane, who is playing it real quiet for the time being, to question him in the Weybright case and in the deaths of three ravishingly beautiful women who were shot to death as they swooned in the author's arms.

"That bastard," said Spillane. "She was just a dumb sweet kid."

According to sources, the shootings of the women were identical: After meeting the writer in a dingy Harlem boarding house, they fell like wounded birds into Spillane's arms, igniting a liquid volcano inside him which instantly turned to ashes when a roscoe sneezed, "Ka-Chee!" through the grimy window and killed the three women deader than vaudeville.

When asked if he thought the murders were perpetrated by the same man, Spillane replied, "Natch."

Spillane's whereabouts are presently unknown, as he paused only long enough to get his cold-oiled .45, a slug of bourbon and his best suit, a custom-made job with extra room for artillery.

"I tell you this, you louse—you killed my only friend, and I, the jury, am going to take your life," Spillane said. "You won't sit in the Chair. You won't hang. You'll die one lonely night as Dutton Weybright died, with a .45 slug twisting in your belly. I'll get you, no matter who you are. My gun is quick. No matter who you are, I promise."

Residents of New Mexico Given Cardboard 3D Glasses for Protection Against Atomic Radiation

See story, page 3

America's Sweetheart Elizabeth Taylor Marries

'I've Finally Found the Man I Want to Spend the Rest of My Life With,' Says Violet-Eyed Star

Mr. and Mrs. Nicky Hilton.

New 'Interstate Highway System' Will Help Troops Seize Communist Neighborhoods

WASHINGTON, D.C. — In a move Pentagon officials are applauding as "a much-needed move toward domestic military mobilization and citizen pacification," President Truman signed a budget bill Friday approving $255 billion for the construction of a new interstate highway system.

The new two- to six-lane divided highways are expected to connect all major American cities, allowing military ground forces to quickly respond to a Communist uprising anywhere in the U.S.

"Congress has given the American military the weapon it needs to quickly seek out and destroy the vile specter of Communism which threatens to overcome our nation's cities," said Secretary of Defense George Marshall. "Citizens will sleep easier in their beds knowing that, in the event of a Red uprising in their neighborhood, the combined might of the U.S. Army and Marines would roll down the highway in a matter of hours, ready to rain destruction down upon their homes."

Construction on the new highway system is scheduled to begin immediately, with the first interstates to be built between Washington, D.C. and such potential Communist trouble spots as New York City, Los Angeles, Chicago and Detroit.

"Communism could infest any area at any time," Marshall said, "but these cities, with their vital banking, industrial and communications centers, are most vulnerable to traitorous underground subversion. They are the nerve centers we must protect in order to ensure America's safety."

WORLD'S LARGEST WEAPON AGAINST COMMUNISM MAY HAVE SECONDARY BENEFITS

In addition to its main purpose of transporting troops to crush insurgency, Marshall said the highway system will stimulate the nation's economy.

"Although we haven't yet studied the possibility, these new highways could create an unprecedented boom in the automotive and automotive-product industries, the trucking business, and the petroleum-refinement field," he said. "Therefore, the interstates will bring great prosperity to America, in addition to serving as a desirable military presence. By bolstering our reliance on Detroit autos and Texas oil, the interstates will ensure our prosperity and security well into the 21st century."

LOS ANGELES, Calif. — In what gossip columnists are calling the most exceptional, one-of-a-kind wedding in Hollywood history, actress Elizabeth Taylor and hotel heir Nicky Hilton exchanged vows of eternal love Saturday in a lavish wedding ceremony at The Church of the Good Shepherd in Beverly Hills.

"I'm so happy that my daughter has met the man she will be with forever," gushed Sara Taylor, the 18-year-old bride's mother.

Said the blushing bride, "There is no doubt in my mind that Nicky is the one I want to spend the rest of my life with."

Hilton, 23, is the son of Hilton Hotel magnate Conrad Hilton. Taylor called his drinking, gambling, drug addictions and playboy reputation "exactly what I'm looking for in a permanent mate."

The gala proceedings had all the trappings of a fairytale wedding. The couple embarked on their life together in a traditional Catholic ceremony. Hollywood stars such as Gene Kelly, Debbie Reynolds and Rosalind Russell joined high-ranking executives of the Hilton Hotel chain and other esteemed guests of the millionaire Hilton family to witness this once-in-a-lifetime occasion.

Taylor said that in the year they have been dating, the couple has not had a single quarrel or even one moment of misunderstanding, which she said signals a long life of wedded happiness.

The breadth of Taylor's commitment to Hilton is evidenced by the fact that she converted to Catholicism, which does not permit divorce, out of her eternal commitment to this one man.

"Every day, I love him more," Taylor said. "If this were not true, I would not be marrying him in the church of his faith, which recognizes one marriage in a lifetime before the eyes of God."

Taylor, who starred in *Father of the Bride* and *National Velvet*, was ravishing in her white Helen Rose wedding dress. "It's gorgeous," Taylor quipped to guests at the reception. "It's too bad I will never have occasion to wear this beautiful dress again."

INSIDE:

TRUMAN EXPLAINS TO AMERICANS WHERE NORTH KOREA IS AND WHY IT MUST BE DESTROYED; 'WHY, THAT SOUNDS FINE,' SAY MR. AND MRS. AMERICA.

See story, page 14

The Onion

Safeguard of the Norm | *Supporting Paranoia*

Thursday, October 4, 1951 — FINEST NEWS SOURCE IN AMERICA — ★★★ Price Five Cents

Senator McCarthy:
'I Hold in My Hand a List of 205 Liquor Stores'

Clues to Rooting out Red Conspiracy May Lie at Bottom of Bottles, Senator Says

Crusading Lawmaker Vows to Drain 'Every Last Drop' of Commie Beverages

Senator Joseph McCarthy

APPLETON, Wis. — During a speech Wednesday before members of the Wisconsin chapter of the Women's Republican Club, U.S. Sen. Joseph McCarthy (R-Wis.) announced that he is in possession of a list of 205 known liquor stores currently operating in the U.S.

"Ladies and gentlemen, in my right hand, I hold a list of confirmed, card-carrying liquor stores," McCarthy said. "And I intend to visit every last one of them."

McCarthy, who has already rooted out more than 100 liquor stores in the past month, was frequently overcome by emotion during his speech, losing his balance and tripping over his own words.

"I have recently become aware of evidence that the secret to the Communist conspiracy in America may be hiding cowardly inside these liquor stores, many of which are right in our own backyards."

The senator said he has made it his sworn duty to "get to the bottom" of every bottle of alcohol in the coming months.

"These Communist plots cannot hide from me, not even in the murky dark glass of a bottle of brandy," he said.

While McCarthy declined to specifically name any of the liquor stores on the list, he assured reporters in attendance that they were all real. He also said that there are at least 75 more liquor stores in the Washington, D.C., area alone, and that he would be closely looking into the matter in the coming months.

"To the owners of these alcohol-purveying establishments, I wish to say, 'Look out, because Joseph McCarthy is going to drop by for a visit and make a lot of purchases,'" McCarthy said. "I would also strongly warn you to have plenty of Mr. Boston-brand rum on your shelves, because that is the brand Senator McCarthy suspects most."

Concluding his speech, McCarthy said he is personally committed to ridding the U.S. of every last bottle of McCormick's-brand vodka, the contents of which he plans to make disappear down his throat.

"It's a smooth vodka with a good kick," McCarthy said. "And, most important, it's American-made. I have no tolerance for Russian vodkas like Smirnoff. There is no place for such godless Commie vodkas in my liver."

Following the Republican Club speech, McCarthy made an appearance at Jim's Tavern in Appleton, where he called for the deportation of all suspected Communists and a double scotch on the rocks.

INSIDE:

**GIANTS WIN PENNANT,
GIANTS WIN PENNANT,
GIANTS WIN PENNANT,
GIANTS WIN PENNANT**
see page 7

FAMED WRITER WILLIAM S. BURROUGHS SHOOTS HEROIN, WIFE
see page 17

MORTY AND BETTY CROCKER EXECUTED FOR SELLING TOP-SECRET CAKE RECIPES TO REDS

Russians Could Be in Possession of Our Moistest Angel-Food Cake Mixes

CIA Finds 350-Page 'Crocker Cookbook' in Hands of Russian Spy

Morty Crocker

Betty Crocker

NEW YORK, N.Y. — Failing in their eleventh-hour bid for clemency, Betty and Morty Crocker died in the electric chair at 12:01 a.m. today.

Convicted in August 1950 of culinary espionage for delivering top-secret recipes for vital American cakes, cookies and brownies to Russian bakers, the Crockers were sentenced to death last December.

The Crockers rose to prominence in the 1930s with a line of pre-packaged cake mixes, which they parlayed into a family fortune. In 1948, a federal grand jury accused them of furnishing Soviet authorities with recipes, cooking tips and "highly sensitive serving suggestions," all vital to making American family mealtime more fun.

The major witness against them, Betty's brother David, told of the Crockers' radioing top-secret recipes to Russian agents employed at the Los Alamos Crowd-Pleasin' Bundt Cake project.

After their convictions, Betty Crocker was dismissed from the office of Cakemaster General. To fill the post, President Truman is expected to nominate Duncan Hines.

"America has no sympathy for spies who threaten America's domination of baked goods," said Truman, who had refused to commute their sentence. "In the name of national security, we must send a strong message to those who would put moist, delicious cake in hostile foreign mouths."

The Crockers' defense attorneys attempted to stress the couple's longtime service to American picnics and get-togethers. They also argued that the Crockers' lives should be spared, since dessert is not in itself a proper meal and that, therefore, a lower level of U.S. security was compromised.

This is the first U.S. espionage trial to end in execution since 1922's *People of the United States v. Jemima*.

MacArthur Advances to Arctic Circle, Plans to Liberate Polar Region

Unstoppable General Defies Truman's Orders, Continues to Advance North

'The North Pole Shall Be Free of Communists by 1952,' MacArthur Pledges

General Douglas MacArthur

PEKING, China — Boldly defying President Truman's strict orders not to cross the Yalu River into Red China, General Douglas MacArthur has forged northward, unifying Korea and liberating the Chinese people from Communism. He is now advancing further north to secure U.S. interests in the strategically vital Arctic Circle.

Condemning what he called the "policies of appeasement and defeatism in the Orient by persons 10,000 miles away from the actual events, such as Secretary of State and Communist sympathizer Dean Acheson,"

MacArthur achieved his objectives by blockading China with the U.S. Pacific Fleet, coordinating a supportive invasion by Chiang Kai-shek and his Nationalist forces from Formosa, and destroying dozens of Chinese industrial centers with atomic bombs. He then crossed the Yalu River with the U.S. Eighth Army.

"In war, there can be no substitute for utterly destroying as many Communists as possible," said the victorious MacArthur, as he stood atop a mountain in Upper Manchuria, surveying his forces as they streamed north. "Yet our job is not done. Army

Intelligence has recently discovered the presence of Russian agitators among the Inuit reindeer herders of the Arctic. I plan to strike with maximum counterforce against this threat to the free world."

In Washington, Truman and his advisors are working around the clock to figure out how to relieve the insubordinate general of his command in a diplomatic fashion. Progress is slow, however, as Truman is reportedly worried about angering MacArthur, who might then decide to sweep eastward across the Aleutians and invade the U.S. from the north.

79

The Onion

Daily Circulation Now 290,814

Onion Reporters Blacklisted Today: 23

Thursday, November 6, 1952 — FINEST NEWS SOURCE IN AMERICA — ★★★ Price Five Cents

President-Elect Eisenhower Vows to Make the Green in Two

Ike Announces Bold New 'Three-Under-Par' Platform

Significant Reduction in Strokes Pledged

WASHINGTON, D.C. — At his first press conference as president-elect, Dwight D. Eisenhower vowed to "work diligently and tirelessly" to score an eagle on the Congressional Hills Country Club's infamous par-five 14th hole.

"In the military, I was taught to own up to my failures," an unusually introspective Eisenhower told reporters early this morning at the Commodore Hotel. "Therefore, let me admit: I have spent my years since the war hitting the ball tentatively, slicing tee shots, leaving myself with impossible lies. And, on those rare occasions when my driving did prove straight and true, my fairway-iron play has been a disappointment to the American people."

"But in the military," Eisenhower continued, "I was also taught to lead by example. So it is with the deepest conviction that I address golfers both in the Free World and behind the Iron Curtain. Let there be no mistake: I shall not rest until I make the green in two."

Eisenhower was elected largely on the strength of his short-iron play and putting, and, since playing his first 18 at Congressional Hills, his scores on the course's par-threes have surpassed even his lofty campaign promises. However, many political insiders have grown tired of his poor play on the par-fives. Furthermore, they say his inability to maintain a straight left arm and a smooth follow-through undermines his credibility with the Soviet leadership. At a Politburo meeting last month, Nikita Khrushchev referred to then-candidate Eisenhower's hip rotation as "reactionary" and his long game "doomed to failure."

Washington insiders say Wednesday's unusually frank

President-Elect Eisenhower

self-assessment came after an intense day of meetings between Eisenhower and his top golfing advisors. "Eisenhower himself did not fully recognize the extent of the problem," said one high-placed source. "Secretary of State [Dean] Acheson [a senior member of Eisenhower's regular Sunday foursome] has been deliberately shanking his own shots for more than a year to cover up the general's shortcomings. Ultimately, Mamie had to ask Ben Hogan to sit her husband down for a man-to-man talk."

While the entire Congressional Hills golf course is vital in determining United States golfing policy, the 489-yard 14th hole, with its extreme dogleg left and unusually narrow fairway, has been considered the litmus test for presidential leadership since 1924, when Calvin Coolidge's pitching-wedge from the sand-trap into the cup for a birdie helped assure passage of the Greenside Bunker Act.

Defeated Democratic presidential nominee Adlai Stevenson was quick to respond to today's press conference. "This underscores once again the irrelevance of golf to modern international and domestic policy," Stevenson said. "What about chess? What about bridge? These are the sporting pursuits worthy of our next president's focus."

But fellow Republicans were quick to support the president-elect. "Let's keep this in perspective," U.N. Ambassador Warren Austin said. "The last two years have seen an unprecedented reduction of Eisenhower's handicap and continued improvements in his quality of play."

INSIDE:

FLINT, MICHIGAN, ENTERS GOLDEN AGE OF UNENDING PROSPERITY
See page 20

CAN NIXON RECOVER FROM THE CHECKERS SCANDAL?
See page 6

Nation's Businessmen Search for Way to Tell One Another Apart

ARE DIFFERENTLY COLORED TIES THE ANSWER?

SCHENECTADY, N.Y. — Although businesses across America are reporting record growth, they are experiencing one profound and disturbing problem: Fewer and fewer businessmen are able to distinguish themselves from one another.

According to top executives, the broad-lapeled gray flannel suit, white shirt, dark tie and black wingtips favored by businessmen make it extremely difficult to tell businessmen apart, a situation that often leads to organizational problems.

Recently, Gerald Pearson, a Schenectady loan officer who had been reporting to the same office of New York's First National Affiliated Bank for five years, discovered that he was, in fact, up-and-coming advertising man Grant Peters, and should have been working for the firm of McPherson, Wiley & Masters in the office building across the street. Due to the remarkably similar office environment and indistinguishable appearance of his coworkers, Pearson had simply not noticed.

"Certainly, the business implications of my predicament are mortifying," Pearson said, "although everyone agrees that, mix-up or no mix-up, I generally did a swell job."

Pearson had also been driving the wrong four-door Chevrolet home to the wrong ranch house, wife and two kids every night for three years. "I only noticed when the woman I thought I'd married called me by somebody else's name, instead of the generally accepted 'Dear,'" he said.

Differently colored ties have been proposed as a temporary solution in some companies, but most businessmen agree that, although distinguishing between one man and the next is of some importance, it may be impossible without risking unthinkable violations of the modern office dress code.

A National Hygiene Crisis:

Boy-Girl Malt-Sharing at All-Time High

Wanton, Promiscuous Exchange of Saliva Rampant at Nation's Soda Fountains

Unsafe Practice Could Lead to Social Diseases, Childbirth

Malted Treats a Breeding Ground for Dangerous Microbes, Sperm

Two young people engaging in unhygienic malt-sharing.

WASHINGTON, D.C. — In what could represent the most serious public-health crisis since the influenza epidemic of 1918, Department of Health officials announced Wednesday that opposite-sex malt-sharing among U.S. young people reached an all-time high in the first half of 1952.

The study found that more than 80 percent of American youths between the ages of 16 and 21 have shared malts with members of the opposite sex. In 67 percent of those cases, the teens were using the same straw.

"This kind of reckless behavior on the part of young people is inexcusable," U.S. Hygiene Secretary O. Russell Shea said. "Any number of diseases could result from the sort of careless exchange of bodily fluids that is going on at malt shops and burger joints across America."

Shea said that if youths absolutely insist on sharing malts, they should at least take certain precautions to reduce the risks of infecting or being infected by their partner. "Boys, if you must enjoy a chocolate malt, strawberry phosphate or some other fountain drink with your best gal, drink from separate glasses," Shea said. "And, if it's an ice-cream soda you're sharing, ask your waitress for an extra straw. I know you think it might spoil the mood, or maybe you think it's 'square,' but believe me, fellas, it's vastly preferable to contracting a nasty case of gosh-knows-what."

Upon hearing of the study's findings, many U.S. youngsters said they will not change their malt-sharing habits. "Gee whiz, every time you turn around, some old coot is telling you something else you can't do," said 17-year-old Bobby Walker of Youngstown, Ohio. "I don't like drinking from separate malts when I'm on a date. If it's in the heat of the moment, I don't always take time to think about safety. I'm going to go ahead and share the malt."

Helen Wilkerson, a Petaluma, Calif., 18-year-old who enjoys slumber parties and drive-ins, agreed. "It's embarrassing to ask for an extra straw at the counter. Every time I do, old Mister Carver gives me a speech about how I shouldn't be sharing sodas at my age."

Officials at the Department of Health are planning a nationwide poster campaign to warn teens that if they share a malt with a date, they are also sharing a malt with all their date's previous malt-sharing partners.

Support Your Local Defense Contractor	**The Onion**	Order Your Roy Rogers TV Chair Today!

Sunday, March 8, 1953 — FINEST NEWS SOURCE IN AMERICA — ★★★ SUNDAY EDITION — Price Fifteen Cents

New Medical Report Finds Heavy Petting Linked to Communism

Touching Selves, Others in Impure Manner Exposed as Bolshevik Plot

Nation's Clergy Urge Immediate Scrubbing-Down of All U.S. Teens

PROVIDENCE, R.I. — A Brown University medical study released Saturday demonstrates a link between intimate touching connecting teens and the spread of Communism.

"Our nation's teen-agers are in closer proximity to each other than ever before," study director Dr. Milton Lambert said. "Not only is this dirty petting exposing our children to germs and head lice, but we now have evidence that it is also putting them at risk of becoming brainwashed agents of the Kremlin."

The study found that the heated, fevered exchange of such bodily fluids as sweat and saliva creates conditions ideal for the development of Communist microbes.

"These Red cells spread quickly into the brain, reducing the victim to an unwitting footservant of the Bolsheviks," Lambert said.

To conduct the study, high-school students were asked to "neck" in a controlled laboratory setting while being monitored for galvanic skin response and heart rate.

Results showed that the heavy-petting activity put the teenagers' minds in a weakened, highly impressionable state, leaving them vulnerable to rampant infestations of ideas in support of worker control of factories.

Said Lambert: "We must put an end to teen-age heavy petting and provide incentives for America's young people to focus instead on lawn work or purchasing material goods."

Following the test, student subjects who had become tainted with Communist microbes were lobotomized.

While heavy petting has long been frowned upon by parents, the Brown University study places it in a powerful new light. Vice President Nixon has urged congressmen to establish a minimum sentence of 25 years in federal prison on charges of sedi-

A posed dramatization of heavy petting.

tion for known heavy petters in the U.S.

Brown researchers credit Nixon for first suggesting the connection between the Red cloud of Communism and delinquent activities such as "France-style" kissing and "fondling of the arms and neck."

"To ensure the protection of every American from the slither-

ing expansion of Communism, we must halt this odious practice of heavy petting wherever it may occur," Nixon said. "It is my personal promise that the War on Petting will continue until every parked car, basement record party and poorly lit backyard gazebo in the U.S. has been searched for Communist subversives."

Department of Health, Education and Welfare to Destroy Nation's Health, Education, Welfare

WASHINGTON, D.C. — President Eisenhower announced Friday the creation of the Department of Health, Education and Welfare, a new Cabinet-level federal office he said will serve to "gradually and inexorably whittle away social services of all kinds."

Speaking at the annual conference of the American Federation of Teachers, the president said, "My Democratic predecessors put in place an enormous system of federal programs that has been successful in bureaucratizing and complicating the delivery of services to our country's most needy. They made a good start, but they did not go

far enough."

Eisenhower named Oveta Culp Hobby, former director of the Women's Auxiliary Army Corps, as H.E.W.'s first Secretary.

"This is an exciting challenge for me," said Hobby. "As a mother and community activist, I know how powerful a hands-on, individualized approach to education, poverty, public health and retirement planning can be. That's why I believe that, with a little bureaucratic apathy, political wrangling and a $5.3 billion budget, we'll be able to lay waste to any chance of our nation's poor receiving health, education or welfare in the second half of this century."

INSIDE:

SEXUAL DOUBLE STANDARD NEATLY DIVIDES FEMALE POPULATION INTO VIRGINS, WHORES
See page 8

Soviets Mourn Loss of Stalin

'Who Will Crush Our Spirits and Destroy Our Will to Live Now?' Ask Distraught Citizens

MOSCOW — Josef Stalin has been dead for three days, yet many Russians remain as distraught as when the news first broke. This nation has lost its figurehead, its overlord, its despot—the man whose insatiable lust for power was strong enough to drive him to enslave, cripple and slaughter the people of the U.S.S.R.

"It seems like only yesterday that Stalin's thugs were battering me in an alley," said former university professor Grigori Vassely, "and then arresting me on fictitious charges because my lectures mentioned Thomas Jefferson once or twice. Who can replace so ruthless a tyrant? I doubt Malenkov can summon such hard, pure hatred. As far as I know, he has no paranoid vendetta against academia whatsoever. Stalin was simply one of a kind."

Homeless alcoholic Fyodor Alexeyev likewise feels nostalgia for a bygone era. "I had my farm seized in 1939 under collectivization and was forced into the Army with minimal training and equipment," he said. "After two hellish years in a German P.O.W. camp, I finally returned to beautiful Leningrad, only to be interned in a Russian concentration camp. Now, the great man who put me there has been taken from us. I do not know if I have the strength to go on."

Former Central Committee member Igor Missirovsky remembers being indicted for the assassination of Leningrad moderate Sergei Kirov. Missirovsky was eventually cleared, only to be tried by Stalin on baseless charges of infant cannibalism in the Moscow show trials of the late '30s.

"All I had was taken from me, despite my fanatical loyalty to the charismatic icon that was Josef Stalin," Missirovsky said. He fears that now, such gloriously horrible days are long

Josef Stalin 1879–1953

gone: "I don't think the new-guard leadership of Russia even has a brutal secret police, much less plans to unleash them in a senseless reign of terror on innocent citizens."

Perhaps most shocked by the sudden loss are the Kremlin's doctors, who at the time of Stalin's death were bracing for a hideous blood purge in the wake of his accusations of a seditious conspiracy within their ranks. "We were all set for another trumped-up witch hunt when we received word that he had passed away," Kremlin Chief Physician Anatoly Ryebgenev said. "If only there were another insane tyrant to succeed him, we could be accused of complicity in Stalin's death and return to purposeless slavery under the crushing yoke of oppression. Regrettably, however, Malenkov has shown himself to be reasonable and in full contact with reality. It all seems like a bad dream, a surreal nightmare in which a benevolent leader treats his people with fairness and dignity."

Malenkov addressed the people of Russia via radio Saturday, assuring them that he would strive to carry on Stalin's great legacy of brutality and oppression.

| Winning the War Against Perversion | # The Onion | The Robots Are Our Friends |

Tuesday, July 28, 1953 — FINEST NEWS SOURCE IN AMERICA — ★★★ Price Five Cents

Sid Caesar Wins Emmy Award for Seltzer-Squirting

Milton Berle Wins 'Best Performance by a Man in a Dress'

SID CAESAR

NEW YORK — *Your Show of Shows* star Sid Caesar was the big winner at Monday night's Emmy Awards, taking home top honors in five categories, including Best Seltzer-Squirting in a Comedy or Variety Program.

Among other awards netted by the popular funnyman: Best Slip on a Banana Peel, Screwiest Screwball Stunt, and Best Custard Pie Right in the Old Kisser.

Milton Berle, emcee of *Texaco Star Theater*, won Best Performance by a Man in a Dress. Berle attended the Emmy ceremony in another of his outrageous outfits, which consisted of nothing but a barrel.

"I just paid my taxes," Berle quipped.

Caesar, who attended the Emmy Awards show with Imogene Coca, thanked his fans for their longtime support of such beloved characters as Harry Hickenlooper and movie send-ups like "A Streetcar Named Charlie." He concluded his acceptance speech with his famous one-two shoe-polish gag, sending the audience into fits of hysterical laughter.

"These television comedians just keep getting better and better," NBC President Jack Whittaker said. "Every time I think the humor can't get any more sophisticated, along comes someone like Red Skelton, who blows things wide open with his Freddie the Freeloader hobo routine."

CIA Subdues Fruit-Hatted Peoples of Lesser Americas

WASHINGTON, D.C. — A potential new beachhead for global Marxism was thwarted Monday with the CIA's announcement of the overthrow of Guatemalan President Jacobo Arbenz-Guzman and the installation of an anti-Communist, CIA-trained military junta to govern the Lesser American country.

The successful coup ensures that the fruit-hatted peoples of the region will not benefit from Arbenz's Red-tainted promises of land reform and better wages, but will, instead, return to their simple duties of banana-picking, maraca-shaking and fruit-hat-wearing.

According to CIA Director Allen Dulles, the democratically elected Arbenz demonstrated the full measure of his Marxist threat by "refusing to dance or wear fruit upon his head like a proper Guatemalan should."

"Since the discovery of the New World, our neighbors to the south have been a perpetual source of amusement," Dulles said. "This welcome transfer of power ensures that they will remain an amusement, never questioning U.S. requests for fruit-hat-based servitude again."

The other countries of Lesser America, such as Honduras, Nicaragua and Panama, are now considered to be at a much lower risk of Communist overthrow.

Said Secretary of State John Foster Dulles, "Arbenz's politics were clearly a violation of the Good Neighbor Policy which has existed between the U.S. and its Lesser American neighbors for over two decades."

CARIBBEAN SEA
LESSER AMERICAS
PACIFIC OCEAN

The Good Neighbor Policy, which defines a "Good Neighbor" as someone who keeps out of political affairs, wears fruit on his head, smiles a lot, and is paid 18 cents for 12-hour days picking bananas for the United Fruit Company, was first articulated by the Roosevelt Administration in the early 1930s. The policy also stipulates that the Lesser American republics must be good neighbors of the U.S. or be subjected to invasion or American-led coup.

Dulles told reporters in Washington that his next CIA-backed overthrow will take place in Iran, a land of bedsheet-headed people who ride on magical flying carpets and collect oil in barrels.

General Motors Approves 11 Percent Tax Hike

DETROIT, Mich. — The General Motors Board of Directors approved an 11 percent federal income-tax hike by a 13-2 vote Monday.

As a result of the increase, all U.S. citizens, regardless of current income bracket, will be required to pay GM an additional 11 percent of their personal income.

"Although raising taxes is never easy, the leaders of General Motors felt it was necessary if the company wanted to continue providing the protection and services American citizens have come to expect," General Motors Treasury Secretary Thomas J. Devlin said in a national address. "For example, in order to keep pace with the Soviet Union, GM's defense budget alone had to be raised $4.2 billion in 1952."

The income-tax increase, the auto giant's largest since a 13 percent hike in 1940, goes into effect Jan. 1, 1954.

GM Executives Take Stand Against Cuba

General Motors also announced that the company "will not tolerate" Cuba's rumored dealings with the Reds, and threatened to stamp out the country's growing Leftist movement if ties with Moscow were not severed immediately.

"GM is committed to protecting the West from Communist infiltration, and is prepared to take military action to protect the democratic integrity of the area," GM Secretary of State Arthur Lovell said. "GM will not be bullied in its own hemisphere."

Americans Rechanneling Sexual Frustration into Violence Against Negroes

PRINCETON, N.J. — According to a Princeton University study, an overwhelming majority of Americans are redirecting tension caused by the repression of impure sexual impulses into vigorous negro beatings.

The study found that 98 percent of white males experience extreme mental and emotional distress every day as a result of the repression of lustful thoughts. Nearly 80 percent, however, are able to ease their distress by beating a negro.

Said Princeton's Eli Wasserman, "While the negro has enjoyed a recent rise in popularity as the target of white men's sexual frustration, another disenfranchised minority, such as the woman or the Mexican, is often employed."

Wasserman said it is critical for men to have an outlet for their sexual tension. "If these urges are allowed to build up inside a person instead of being released via beneficial beatings, they will eventually find release in far more destructive ways, such as the touching of one's private parts."

Korean War Ends in Tearful 3-Hour Finale

Antics of Hawkeye Pierce, Hot Lips Houlihan Bring Close to Amusing Asian Conflict

Over 50 Million Americans Gather Around Televisions to Watch Final Installment of Popular, Long-Running War

American GIs bid farewell to Korea, a place of both sadness and hilarity for the past three years.

SEOUL, South Korea — The wildly popular Korean War, which began in 1950, officially ended Monday with the emotional, much-anticipated signing of an armistice agreement on CBS from 8 to 11 p.m. EST. Following the signing, principal players in the war, including President Eisenhower, General Douglas MacArthur, Captain B.J. Hunnicut and Colonel Sherman Potter, stood teary-eyed before a live studio audience, bowing for more than 20 minutes while being showered with applause.

"Thank you all so very much," Eisenhower said. "But remember: This peace treaty is not for us; it's for all of you, the loyal viewers and fans who have supported the Korean War so faithfully all these years."

Eisenhower said the true credit for the war's success belongs to its many supporting players, including such dedicated personnel as Major Hot Lips Houlihan, Corporal Maxwell Klinger and Captain Hawkeye Pierce.

The president then called for a moment of silence in honor of those who did not make it to the end of the war, including Major Frank Burns and Corporal Walter "Radar" O'Reilly.

Eisenhower also issued a full pardon to those servicemen who engaged in irresponsible, madcap shenanigans and practical jokes during the course of the war. "War is hell," Eisenhower said, "and, sometimes, when you live in an environment where you are surrounded by nothing but death and horror, humor is the only way to cope. With this in mind, you are forgiven for each instance of sexual misconduct involving the women's shower tent, as well as the time Colonel Potter's horse was painted with stripes."

While most of the war's cast agreed with MacArthur's description of it as "the thrill of a lifetime," some of those who served did not escape unharmed. During the war's conclusion, Captain Pierce suffered a severe nervous breakdown, realizing that he had accidentally caused a Korean woman to suffocate her child on a crowded bus.

"It was a baby!" Pierce cried, realizing that the noisy creature in the woman's arms was not a chicken, as he had imagined in his psychosis, but a human infant. Clawing at his eyes and collapsing to the floor, Pierce was committed to a mental institution, where he is expected to spend the rest of his life.

INSIDE:

ED SULLIVAN MAKES LEAP TO BIG SCREEN IN NEW JOHN FORD WESTERN 'RIO MACHO'
See page 12

AREA HOOD HOPPED UP ON GOOFBALLS
See page 13

Proud Controller of the Means of Production	**The** 🦅 **Onion** *TU STULTUS ES*	Proud Oppressor of the Proletariat

Wednesday, August 12, 1953 — FINEST NEWS SOURCE IN AMERICA — ★★★ Price Five Cents

Pentagon Develops A-Bomb-Resistant Desk

Schoolchildren Now Safe from Atomic Blast

Desks Will Be Standard Issue for All U.S. Public Schools by 1955

These schoolchildren will soon be safe from the A-bomb, thanks to the unstoppable combination of A-bomb-resistant desks and the atomic-age "duck and cover" safety technique.

WASHINGTON, D.C. — In a scientific breakthrough with far-reaching implications in light of current tensions between the U.S. and Russia, U.S. Secretary of Defense Charles Wilson announced Tuesday that Civil Defense Authority scientists have successfully developed a school desk that is impervious to atomic attack.

"Should the U.S.S.R. choose to drop the atom bomb on the United States, our nation's children would merely have to hide under their school desks, and they would be safe," Wilson said. "Everything in the surrounding 10-mile radius, including hospitals, homes, grocery stores and loved ones, would be instantly incinerated, vaporized in three-millionths of a second from the searing heat of an atomic blast. But the children would be unharmed."

If an A-bomb were detected entering a school's air space, Wilson said, the school's principal would sound a special nuclear-attack siren, indicating that all students should seek shelter under their desks.

A single prototype of the revolutionary new desk was developed by the Pentagon over the past two years at a cost of $600 million. Constructed of varnished hardwood and with hollow metal legs, it also features an inkwell, a surface indent to curb desktop pencil slippage, and an inside compartment with plenty of room to store notebooks, pens and Civil Defense rations for use during times of atomic war.

Pending congressional approval, 50 million desks—one for each student in the U.S.—will be constructed by 1955. The only drawback is the cost of the project: $30 quadrillion. According to Wilson, however, it is "a cost America cannot afford not to pay."

"Until the Cold War is won, we must take every possible step to protect ourselves and our children from the Red Menace, and, if that means a $600 million, bomb-resistant school desk for every child, so be it," Wilson said. "Our children must be free to learn their ABCs secure in the knowledge that, should the Kremlin decide to launch an attack on their school, they will not be harmed."

Wilson praised the device, but cautioned that it is only effective if used properly.

To this end, officials have produced an Army-style training film for use in schools nationwide to explain the complex operating procedures for the desks.

With the help of a cartoon-turtle mascot named "Bert," the intricate instructions of the film are relayed in the title song, "Duck and Cover."

Said Chief Pentagon Engineer Dr. Ralph Tessmer, head of the team that developed the desk, "The child must physically duck under the desk in order for its one-inch-thick wooden surface to function as a shield against the million-degree heat of an atomic explosion."

"But ducking by itself will not be effective," he said. "The youngster must also cover his head."

Tessmer said the placing of the human arms over the head creates a complex fusion of the molecules in the wooden desk surface and those in the human skin, creating a powerful field of energy which can repel the heat and blast force of an atomic explosion.

Tessmer also said that, if a bomb is dropped, children must make sure that their arms and legs are completely underneath the desks. "Any limbs that protrude from underneath the desks will be vaporized in the event of a Russian attack," he cautioned.

The nation's schoolchildren seem to be getting the message already. Fifth-grader Polly Abacrombe of Scranton, Penn., said, "If I see the flash of the A-bomb, I just duck—and cover!"

McCarthy Shifts Focus; Will Now Fight 'Book-Reader Menace'

Sen. McCarthy (R-Wis.) with close aide Roy Cohn.

INSIDE:

SHOCKING 'SOCK HOP' PUTS TEEN-AGED FEET IN STATE OF NEAR UNDRESS
see page 3

NORMAN VINCENT PEALE TREATED FOR DEPRESSION AFTER FAILURE OF BOOK
see page 19

WASHINGTON, D.C. — U.S. Sen. Joseph McCarthy (R-Wis.) said he is "none the worse for the wear" after being lambasted by Joseph N. Welch, chief attorney for the Army, during last week's hearing of the House Un-American Activities Committee.

Instead, McCarthy said, he is merely shifting his focus.

"There is a new menace in our land even more terrible and insidious than Communism," McCarthy said at a special press conference outside his office Tuesday, "and that is Book-Reading."

McCarthy warned, "This subversive habit may have even infiltrated our government," and promised to present a list by next Friday of 205 known book-readers currently working at the U.S. State Department.

He said book-readers knowingly expose themselves to strange new ideas—many of which differ from those in the Lord's Prayer and the Pledge of Allegiance.

The senator has called for public libraries nationwide to be staked out by federal agents, noting that libraries are "card-carrying members" willfully congregate and engage in uncontrolled reading.

McCarthy said he will introduce legislation in Congress mandating deportation for anyone caught using a library.

"The American people are going to see a massive manhunt, one like they've never seen before," McCarthy said.

In addition to legislation, McCarthy said there is plenty that good Americans can do to stop this new menace. Among his suggestions:

• If you suspect that a friend or family member reads books, call your local police to have the subversive placed under surveillance by authorities.
• If you see a book, burn it.
• Shield yourself and your children from any type of learning opportunity.
• Do not think.

McCarthy said he has heard that there are places called "schools" where adults in the employ of our own government plant the seeds of reading in the minds of impressionable young children.

"We must find these places and send in federal authorities to close them down," McCarthy said.

He added that children found in schools should be treated for psychological illness, re-educated in special McCarthy-endorsed training camps, and enlisted to ferret out book-readers wherever they may be hiding.

83

The Onion

Purging Sympathizers Since 1913 | **TU STULTUS ES** | **No Longer Seducing the Innocent**

Thursday, September 2, 1954 — FINEST NEWS SOURCE IN AMERICA — ★★★ Price Five Cents

Imagine: An All-Robot Wash Day!

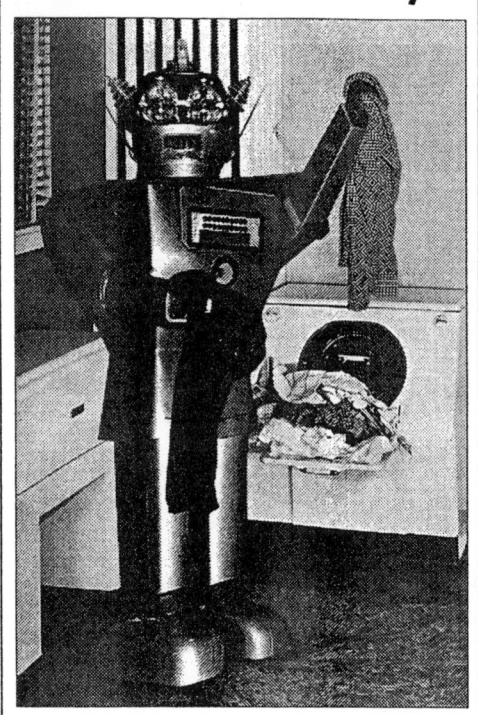

Ladies, imagine the simplicity and convenience of an all-robot wash day. Imagine giving your new GE Suds-O-Luxe Robot a series of simple voice commands, then sitting back and watching it load, unload, iron and fold all your clothes by itself. In the GE Home of the Future, you will relax while this steel handyman does all the work!

These and many other modern wonders await you in the not-so-distant future. Broken fingernails and dry, rough hands will be a thing of the past as you enter the era of the choreless home, run by housekeeping robot appliances.

The good people at GE—the same people who made your life easier with the Vacuum-erating Suction Drum and the Hair-Dry-O-Matic Blow-Gun—are, even as you read this, perfecting the appliances that will transport you to an exciting, housework-free future. For example, imagine doing your weekly grocery shopping from the comfort of your own home by means of the radio-controlled Transmit-O-Shop. Imagine the time you will save after you activate your Dust-O-Glide, and mechanical arms descend from your ceiling and automatically remove every speck of dust, dirt and grime from your home.

Every morning, you will walk into your kitchen to find it aglow with polished and reflective chrome and steel, every surface sparkling—not because you toiled the night before, but because you remembered to press the single button which lowered the Scrub-O-Matic Cleanse-O-Plete Dome over your kitchen area. No more scouring counters, scraping pans, and resenting the day you were born into this world a woman. Instead, you'll sport a cheery smile and a perfectly pressed housedress for your husband's return from the office. Even your dinners, greedily gobbled down each night without a hint of appreciation from the hungry horde at your family table, will appear pre-prepared inside the programmable Incredo-Flite Roast-Bot.

But wait. There is one more grueling wifely chore you must face at the end of each day. You must offer your husband a serving of affection before he goes to bed. Well, take heart, woman of tomorrow: GE will soon offer a Robo-Erotic mechanized bed partner to satisfy your husband's every need. Now you can rest easy while the whirring chrome Love-O-Matic Simu-Woman does all the work. Enjoy a paperback book or a hot bath!

Before you go to sleep, don't forget to press the Electro-Dimmer automatic light switch and tell the atomic EZ-Door to let the dog out for the night!

Caring Father Resolves Extremely Minor Domestic Conflict

Pipe-Smoking Bread-Winner Restores Order to Oak Park, Illinois, Home

Caring father James Johnson.

OAK PARK, Ill. — A family was saved from crisis Wednesday evening when James Johnson resolved a minor domestic conflict involving his wife, Edna, and their two children, Paul and Peter.

When Johnson returns home from the office promptly at 5:15 p.m. each day, he is accustomed to being handed a freshly mixed brandy old-fashioned upon his entry through the door. On Wednesday, however, he entered his spacious, carpeted home to find his wife crying, his children engaged in horseplay, and a burning pot roast in the oven.

"It was quite a picture," Johnson said. "I barely had time to wipe my shoes at the door and remove my hat before rushing in to look after them."

Johnson was able to determine in short order that Peter, the younger child, was upset about being prohibited from playing with a BB gun belonging to Paul. Rather than consoling his younger brother, Mrs. Johnson reported, Paul had been taunting his sibling with the moniker "baby," exacerbating the conflict.

Mrs. Johnson was so distraught that her normally perfectly bobbed hair was slightly mussed. She had even neglected the pot roast, leaving it in the electric range almost a full minute longer than intended.

"I just thank the Lord for Jim walking in. What would I have done?" Mrs. Johnson told reporters.

Mr. Johnson immediately took up a strategic position in his overstuffed recliner, which presides over the living-room environs, and gathered Peter and Paul to his lap.

As he lit his pipe, he tenderly explained to Peter that he was too young to play with the BB gun and shouldn't be upset, because it only meant that there would be many more exciting and wonderful things awaiting him when he grows up.

"To try to do certain things too soon would only spoil them," Johnson said.

Then Johnson told Paul that if he were really less of a "baby" than Peter, he would be mature enough not to tease and would, instead, take responsibility for looking after the welfare of the younger boy.

Johnson then informed both boys that neither of them would have the gun for the rest of the night.

But Johnson's job as caring head of the household was by no means complete.

"I then told Edna to not worry her pretty little head about the overcooked roast," he said. "I sent her upstairs to put on her good clothes, and we all went out for hamburger sandwiches down at Jack's Drive-Up Stand."

The rest of the family was so pleased with this solution that they gathered around the father as he sat in his upholstered newspaper-reading chair. Edna placed her hand on James' shoulder and smiled sweetly down upon his perfectly Brylcreemed head, while Peter sat upon his father's lap and Paul knelt beside the chair, gazing up at his father.

Mickey Mantle Blood-Alcohol Level Nearing .400

'Can He Do It?' Nation's Bartenders Wonder

Yankee Drinking Great Would Have to Hit Three Taverns a Night for Rest of Season

Mickey Mantle, the Sultan of Shots.

NEW YORK — With just five weeks to go in the season, baseball fans and bartenders across the country are talking about Yankee center-fielder Mickey Mantle, who is closing in on a .400 blood-alcohol level. If successful, Mantle would be the first to reach the storied mark since Babe Ruth in 1930.

"I've really been slamming 'em lately," said Mantle, who has hit 124 bars in the past month, raising his blood-alcohol content to a league-high .392. "Vodka, whiskey, gin, tequila, rum—right now I feel like there's no shot I can't knock out of the glass."

According to Yankee broadcaster Mel Allen, Mantle has an excellent chance of reaching .400, and could even break the all-time blood-alcohol mark of .443, set by Ty Cobb in 1911.

"In all my years with the Yankees, I've never seen a ballplayer drink like the Mick," Allen said. "After last night's home game against the Tigers, he had five whiskey sours, two screwdrivers and a Tom Collins at Toots Shor's. Then, at 2 a.m., he headed uptown to the Jockey Club for shots. Those bartenders were serving up their hardest, best stuff, and he was putting them away like it was nothing."

Ironically, Mantle's greatest competition may come from one of his own teammates: Yankee second-baseman Billy Martin's season BAC currently stands at .380, and he is gaining on Mantle fast. On a recent road trip, Martin singlehandedly outdrank the entire Washington Senators line-up at Frankie's Tavern in Washington, D.C., downing doubles and triples with ease.

"I can catch Mickey," said Martin, speaking from his favorite corner stool at the "21" Club on 53rd and Broadway. "He's slowing down. His liver won't last through the end of the season."

INSIDE:

H-BOMB TEST A SUCCESS!
Eniwetok Atoll Islanders Return to Their Home, a Mile-Wide Crater on the Ocean Floor
See page 9

OP-ED: THE FRENCH SHOULD BE ASHAMED OF THEIR INABILITY TO WIN IN VIETNAM
See page 12

The Onion

APPROVED BY THE NEWSPAPER CODE AUTHORITY

Come Back, Shane!

Saturday, September 18, 1954 — FINEST NEWS SOURCE IN AMERICA — ★★★ Price Five Cents

New Magazine, 'Playboy,' Offers Astute Literary Criticism, Tits

CHICAGO, Ill. — *Playboy*, a new upscale magazine for urban sophisticates and men-about-town that details all the aspects of today's educated-bachelor lifestyle, arrived at newsstands this week. Described as "entertainment for men" by editor/publisher Hugh M. Hefner, the

"Playboy" founder Hugh Hefner.

glossy periodical will feature up-to-the-minute, ultra-modern articles on fashion, home furnishings, golf accessories and hi-fi sound systems, as well as informative pieces on the arts. Among the literary talents appearing in *Playboy* will be such important contemporary writers as John Updike, Norman Mailer and noted essayist Truman Capote.

Hefner also stressed that the magazine will feature full-color photographs of naked tits.

"What kind of a man reads *Playboy*?" asked Hefner, reclining on a crushed-velvet divan in his Chicago high-rise suite, swirling a brandy snifter as light jazz played in the background. "A man who is urbane, yet sporting. A man who appreciates fine wine and smooth cigars. One capable of savoring the delicate subtleties and deft turns of phrase in the finest contemporary fiction being published today."

"He is also," Hefner said, "a man who appreciates the sight of a robust pair of glistening, naked tits."

Initial reaction to the publica-

COMIC BOOKS BANNED TODAY

GLANDULAR TALES #3
VAULT OF IMPOLITE SKELETONS
HANDBAG FILLED WITH BLOOD #9
CORPSE CORPS!
WEIRD ACCOUNTING #12
TWO-CARCASS GARAGE
STORIES OF LOVE #6
PINK BUNNY AND THE MAGIC PRINCESS
SUBURBS OF THE UNDEAD
IMPROPER CHURCH TALES

tion has been mixed, largely due to readers' indifference to ultra-modern articles on fashion, home furnishings, golf accessories and hi-fi sound systems, and their overpowering desire to view photographs of succulent, protruding, naked tits.

Hefner remains confident that, in time, his venture will grow into an unqualified success. "I envision myself cultivating important relationships with the greatest writers of this generation, earning a reputation as a publisher of cutting-edge fiction and non-fiction," he said.

"I also foresee an assortment of mansions across the country, through which I will stride, clad only in garish silk pajamas, surrounded by beautiful bouncing tits at all times."

Hefner explained that *Playboy*'s next issue will feature an article by noted critic and journalist Terry Southern, as well as a new work by award-winning author John Cheever.

"And," he said, "I cannot over-emphasize this particular point: There will also be color photographs of enormous naked tits."

Nation Captivated by Fairytale Wedding of Sullen Loner, Depressed Pill-Popper

Pitiful Couple Called 'American Royalty'

NEW YORK — As a rapt American public watched breathlessly, sullen, reclusive ex-slugger Joe DiMaggio wed depressed, pill-addicted starlet Marilyn Monroe Friday.

The storybook marriage of DiMaggio, whose glory days on the baseball diamond are long behind him, and Monroe, whose increasing dependence on drugs and alcohol threatens to destroy her career, has dazzled followers across the country.

"Just imagine—Marilyn and Joltin' Joe," Flatbush, Brooklyn, resident Sammy Holt said of the couple. "What a happy life they're going to have together."

DiMaggio, whose youthful spirit and athletic skills are fast fading, and Monroe, whose act-

Newlyweds Joe DiMaggio and Marilyn Monroe.

ing skills and emotional stability are also in decline, are seen by many as the perfect couple.

"Isn't it wonderful?" said Betty Evans, a 24-year-old Kansas City housewife. "It's a match made in heaven."

Nation's Juvenile-Delinquency Problem Worsens as Authorities Discover...

GUM IN OUR SCHOOLS!

Taylor Middle School in Iowa City, a school like any other. But could it be under siege by students with gum?

Children as Young as 10 Carrying Sticks to Class

Officials Call for Tougher Gum-Control Laws

What's Wrong with Our Kids? Is Failing to Scrub Behind Ears Next?

BROOKLYN, N.Y. — In the latest development in the worsening epidemic of juvenile delinquency, a 16-year-old New York boy was caught Thursday in possession of a pack of gum on school grounds.

The incident, the third this year in the U.S., has sparked a call for strict new gum-control legislation and intensified public debate over how to best deal with America's increasingly rebellious youth.

"This is an extremely serious problem," said Anderson Powell, principal of Brooklyn's Washington Irving High School, where the gum incident occurred. "This new generation of youths is a different breed: wild, reckless, defiant of authority. These unruly kids are misbehaving in ways we could never have imagined before."

The boy has been suspended from Washington Irving indefinitely, and faces a hearing before a juvenile-advisory panel Dec. 5 to determine additional punishment.

Speaking to reporters yesterday on the condition of anonymity, the boy's mother expressed surprise over her son's behavior. "I had no idea he was capable of such an awful thing," she said. "I am just as shocked as anyone that my child carried a pack of Wrigley's to class. And for him to chew it out in the open, in front of teachers, just doesn't make any sense. I don't know what has gotten into these kids of today."

Teachers Afraid

Educators reacting to the news of the gum are beginning to fear for their own safety.

"My husband is afraid for me," said St. Louis, Missouri, schoolteacher Mary Lambert. "There may be sticky chewing-gum residue on the undersides of desks, and I might get some on my hand."

Roosevelt High School in Chicago recently considered implementing at-the-door gum searches, checking students' pants pockets and pencil boxes. The idea was abandoned when administrators realized the search could lead to the even greater problem of tardiness.

Just the Beginning

Many teachers interpret the gum incident as a clear sign that juvenile delinquency is on the rise.

Donald T. Stimson, chairman of the "Youth in Crisis" Juvenile Delinquency Federal Task Force, said the problem of rebellion among U.S. youngsters has reached an unacceptable level.

"I do not think things can get any worse than they are right now," Stimson said. "In schools across the country, we're witnessing rowdiness unheard of in the past: talking during class, paper-airplane throwing, the passing of notes. The list goes on and on."

Stimson also mentioned an incident in Los Angeles in March in which school lunch-room monitors discovered seven 12-year-olds with their elbows on the table.

Stimson said the problem lies largely with parents, who have become too lenient with children in recent years. "Most kids today are beaten with a leather belt no more than once a week," he said. "Is it any wonder that, with such lenient parenting, these young people have taken to wearing leather jackets, greasing their hair, and using offensive slang expressions such as 'hot rod' and 'neato'?"

While Stimson cited lack of parental discipline for the crisis, others blame inadequate laws that make it easy for children to gain access to gum.

Said Lambert, "On the streets, gum is so prevalent that anyone, of any age, can buy a pack for a nickel. This is the kind of world we live in today."

INSIDE:

EBBETS FIELD BATHED IN WARM SEPIA-TONE GLOW
See page 24

CHINA MAKES GREAT LEAP FORWARD INTO STONE AGE
See page 12

UNDERSEXED SOUTHERN BELLE COOLS ARMS WITH ICE
See page 25

85

| Atomic News | # The Onion | Better Dead than Red |

Saturday, October 1, 1955 — FINEST NEWS SOURCE IN AMERICA — ★★★ Price Five Cents

Rosa Parks to Take Cab

Funicello:
'There Are Six Card-Carrying Communists in the Mickey Mouse Club'

Head Mouseketeer to Release Names Today

Cubby, Doreen Among Lead Suspects

LOS ANGELES — Lead Mouseketeer Annette Funicello announced Friday that Communism has infiltrated the Mickey Mouse Club, asserting that at least six members of the organization hold secret ties to the Kremlin.

Funicello, 12, said she will release the names of the traitorous Mouseketeers today. "I am sorry to announce that the Red Menace has seeped its way into the most American of all institutions, the Mickey Mouse Club," Funicello said. "Like a disease, these godless Communists spread their insidious way of life wherever they possibly can, even in the democratic, freedom-loving Walt Disney Corporation."

While Funicello's announcement was met with praise from many high-profile political leaders, including Vice President and former House Un-American Activities Committee member Richard Nixon, who lauded her as "a true American," others contend that Funicello has fabricated the charges to drive out those Mouseketeers whom she perceives as a threat.

"It is no secret that Miss Funicello is no longer America's favorite Mouseketeer," U.S. Sen. Wayne Morse (D-Ore.) said. "In a recent poll of U.S. citizens between the ages of 5 and 15, Annette was named the third most popular member of the Mickey Mouse Club, behind Cubby and Doreen. In a more recent 'Who's the Cutest Mouseketeer?' poll conducted by CBS News, she came in second. These trumped-up charges are nothing more than a desperate attempt to destroy the careers of those Mouseketeers whose stars are rising."

Responding to her detractors, Funicello claimed to possess hard evidence backing up her accusations, including over 350 hours of taped phone conversa-

Annette Funicello

tions between one of the Mouseketeers and Kremlin minister of foreign affairs Yevgeny Kovalev. She said she also has evidence that one of her club peers may have sold secret Mickey Mouse Club code words to the KGB.

Disney officials were quick to respond to the charges, asserting that the Mickey Mouse Club is a bastion of clean, American morality.

"We will see to it that the Club is purged of all freedom-hating Communists," Mickey Mouse Club Executive Producer Alston Kramech said. "Any Mouseketeer accused of holding Red, anti-free-speech ideas will be fired, blacklisted and silenced forever."

'Hot Rods':
Are They as Sinful as They Sound?

VAN NUYS, Calif. — One of today's fastest-growing youth hobbies is the seemingly innocent practice of tinkering with everyday automobiles in order to increase their performance. At first, this pastime might seem to incorporate many positive values: mechanical know-how, hard work and a proper respect for automobiles. But lately, citizens have become aware that this sport, known to teens as "hot rodding," may be fraught with trouble and sin.

"The term 'hot rod' is profane enough, but this morally suspect subculture has far worse terms for its practices," said Samuel Wickwire of the Detroit Institute for Automotive Morality Friday. "They say they want everything from 'big-blocks' to 'nuts.' They speak of 'slamshifting' their 'four on the floor.' Entire weekends are spent acquiring 'flame jobs,' working strange alchemies with 'dualies' and 'straight pipes,' and participating in a strange ritual called 'joyriding.' I will not rest until I have put a stop to these doubtlessly evil acts, whatever they might be."

Parents of young, hot-rodding boys and girls are instructed to inform Wickwire in care of this newspaper if they can confirm the racial taint suggested by the slang term, "laying down a blackie."

INSIDE:
JAMES DEAN DIES IN CAR CRASH PER AGENT'S INSTRUCTIONS
See page 12

'Screw This Bus Shit,' Says Montgomery, Alabama, Commuter

MONTGOMERY, Ala. — Tired of being asked to give up her seat to white passengers on segregated buses, negro commuter Rosa Parks decided to begin taking a cab to work late this week.

"Screw this bus shit," the 42-year-old seamstress said in an impromptu statement to fellow Montgomery bus commuters Friday.

"The white passengers and the Montgomery buses can take their segregated, negroes-giving-up-their-seats Jim Crow horse-shit and shove it up their cracker butts. I'll take a cab."

Parks said that from now on, she will enjoy no-hassle, door-to-door taxi service to and from work daily, the grocery store on weekends, and her Aunt Addie's house on the east side of Montgomery most Sundays.

Although Parks will pay approximately $3 more each day for transportation to and from her job at Millon's Clothiers, she said it was "absolutely worth it" to avoid what she called "the bullshit seating rules" on Montgomery buses.

"In a cab, I'm the only passenger," she said, "and I can sit wherever I please: the left side of the seat or the right side of the seat or right in the middle of the seat. And I don't have to get up and move for nobody."

An additional benefit Parks said she enjoys in a cab is the larger, more plush seating, giving her a smooth, comfortable ride that "beats the hell out of a piece-of-crap city bus."

Also, Parks noted that, in a cab, "I don't have to waste my time

ROSA PARKS

while the driver stops to pick up more stupid white passengers at other stupid bus stops." Parks added that the bus patrons and bus drivers "can have all that shit."

Said Parks, "Who wants to sit there all day and stop every block and wait while the driver lets more seat-stealing white idiots on the bus? To hell with them."

Furthermore, Parks said the Montgomery city buses are full of "crazies" who sit next to her and talk to her.

"I'm sick of that bullshit, too," she said.

"That whole bus system can kiss my black, plush-seated, taxi-cab-riding ass," Parks added.

A statement issued by Montgomery Transportation officials read, "We hope Miss Parks will choose to take a ride on a Montgomery city bus again. We work very hard to provide the safest, most comfortable and convenient ride to our customers. (A reminder to negroes, please give up your seat to whites. Thank you.)"

The Red Leader's Plan for Conquest:

First, Lady Liberty. Second, Our Wives and Daughters?

See Editorial on page 17

Authorities Alarmed by Local Man's Quarter-Inch Hair Growth

PORTLAND, Ore. — Milton Templeton, a 26-year-old Portland resident, has sparked widespread concern among area authorities following the discovery that he has allowed his hair to grow one quarter of an inch.

"For a community to function properly, it is important that order is maintained. A community cannot sustain itself in a state of anarchy," Portland Chief of Police Reginald Fortson said. "If people start growing their hair out to any length they please, there is no telling what could come next. Today it's long hair, tomorrow it's teens listening to race music and wearing blue jeans. The line has got to be drawn somewhere."

Despite the gravity of the situation, Fortson urged Portland residents to remain calm, assuring them that everything is under control. "Please, whatever you do, do not panic," he said. "I promise we will deal sternly with this longhair."

Templeton, a cashier at Archer Drug in downtown Portland, had until recently worn his hair in the close-cropped, "buzz-cut" style of other U.S. males. Speaking to reporters, he claimed the hair growth was "an honest mistake," explaining that he ordinarily has it trimmed every two weeks but had not had a chance to go to the barber last week.

Portland law-enforcement officials, working closely with barber authorities, announced that Templeton will not be permitted to return to decent society until the excess quarter-inch of hair is cut.

"It is my sincere hope that Mr. Templeton will comply with our request so that we can restore order to the city," Mayor Wallace Kimball said. "It's been difficult these past weeks, what with an unkempt man wandering our streets, his wild mane of hair cascading down practically to his ears."

Fortson said it is still too soon to know whether Templeton is in league with beatniks, but the possibility is being investigated. "We have searched his apartment thoroughly for jazz records and berets, but, so far, have found nothing," Fortson said. "At this time, we do not know if his story checks out. We've yet to interrogate his friends."

Fortson promised that, if evidence is uncovered that links Templeton to the arts, he will be jailed.

Despite official assurances, many Portland residents are deeply concerned. "This youngster sounds like real trouble, what with that individualist streak of his," Herman Jacobs, 57, said. "Until he looks like everyone else again, I'm keeping my door locked and window shades down, just to be on the safe side."

The Onion

CONFORM | Join the Hive Mind

Monday, November 21, 1955 — FINEST NEWS SOURCE IN AMERICA — ★★★ — Price Five Cents

Whites Invent 'Rock and Roll'

New Caucasian-Based Teen Craze Sweeps America

Authorities Assure Public that Negroes Had Nothing to Do with Popular Music Form

"Rock and Roll" pioneer Elvis Presley, a young white man.

MEMPHIS, Tenn. — White teen-agers across the nation are cheering the latest product of American ingenuity today, as a new white-devised music form is sweeping the land. It is called "Rock and Roll," and young people are dancing to its exciting, Caucasian beat.

Radio stations can't seem to play the latest Rock-and-Roll numbers often enough, as floods of requests from teenagers are making instant successes of such white Rock-and-Roll pioneers as Elvis Presley, Jerry Lee Lewis and Buddy Holly.

Where does this new type of music come from? According to *Collier's* music critic Nathaniel Dettinger, it comes from whites.

Says Dettinger, the beat of Rock and Roll has its roots in the pounding, beat-driven compositions of whites like Igor Stravinsky and Anton Dvorak, and in stirring white spirituals. "White gospel music is a fiery, soulful noise being raised up to God," Dettinger says. "This rousing music is clearly one of the inspirations for Rock and Roll."

"I just love to dance to it," says white teen-ager Jenny McCallister of Chicago. "My favorite is Elvis."

Elvis Presley joins Rock-and-Roll pioneers Carl Perkins, the band Bill Haley and the Comets and Pat Boone to make up the core group of the music's originators. Many of them come from or have visited the Mississippi Delta, which is a hotbed of white Rock-and-Roll ingenuity.

"My favorite Rock-and-Roll record is Pat Boone's hit 'Tutti Frutti.'" Memphis teenager Charlie Stojeck said. "He deserves to be remembered as one of the great 'Rock-and-Rollers' of all time."

INSIDE:

GM UNVEILS ATOM-BURNING JET CONVERTIBLE AT FUTURAMA '55

THOUSANDS OF WOULD-BE BUYERS KILLED IN PRODUCT SHOW

see page 4

Defense Department to Reinforce Nation's Brassieres

Angora Sweaters Nearing Breaking Point

Congress Calls for Emergency Loosening of Strained Tops of Monroe, Mansfield, Turner

WASHINGTON, D.C. — A federal panel warned Friday that the approximately 14 million pink, fuzzy sweaters in the U.S. are approaching critical mass and will likely reach a breaking point by mid-July.

"America's angora sweaters just keep getting tighter and tighter," said Dr. Edgar O. Retzloff of the Federal Bosom Containment Task Force, established by President Eisenhower to examine the crisis. "At a certain point, they are going to burst."

According to Retzloff, unless swift action is taken to relieve some of the pressure placed on ladies' tops, they are in severe danger of violently rupturing at the seams.

"It is unreasonable to expect these garments to maintain their buxom payloads for much longer without defense-contractor reinforcement," he said. "Under current stress, perhaps they can last another month, maybe two, but when you are trying to contain curves of this magnitude over the long haul, weave fatigue and, ultimately, total fabric breakdown are inevitable."

Among Retzloff's proposed reinforcements: steel-rimmed breast cones, an underwire of elastic yet unbreakable titanium cable, and iron clasps for brassieres' seven-hook back closures.

Retzloff's panel found that, while the entire nation is in need of federal brassiere reinforcement, the most serious and immediate problem lies within its entertainment community. Hollywood, the panel found, has the worst stitching-per-square-inch to bust-size ratio in the U.S., placing its estimated 3,100 starlets in more immediate danger of cloth breakage than any other demographic group in the U.S.

"These busty, all-American beauties need our help, if they and their overtaxed sweaters are to survive," said Sen. Thomas Kutchel (R-Calif.), co-sponsor of the Hill-Kutchel Brassiere Reinforcement Emergency Appropriations Bill. "A bombshell like Jane Russell has no chance, unless Congress gets her the extra material around the ribs and across the chest she so desperately needs."

While extra material is a necessary short-term measure, Kutchel said the long-term priority should be to develop larger sweater sizes. "There's a tremendous need for sizes larger than extra-small and small," he said. "Perhaps there could be something called 'medium' or even, in extreme cases, 'large.' That

Jayne Mansfield

would be a positive first step."

If a wide-ranging reinforcement of brassieres is successful, engineers hope to apply the technology to the nation's strapless taffeta gowns and double-girded swim-suits.

U.S.–Soviet Bombshell Gap Wider Than Ever

America Boasts Incomparable Arsenal of Busts, Gams, Defense Department Reports

WASHINGTON, D.C. — The nation's increased commitment to brassiere reinforcement indicates that we are rapidly pulling away from the Reds in the global bombshell race, according to a Defense Department report released Friday.

The report found that the U.S. holds a decisive three-to-one edge in overall production of breasts, legs and hips, and the gap is widening each day.

"While the struggle for global military domination is still undecided, there can be no doubt which nation is the one true superpower when it comes to shapely broads in tight sweaters," U.S. Secretary of Defense Charles Wilson said. "The Russians cannot compare to the U.S. in terms of chesty-blonde and leggy-chorus-girl output. With respect to both size and quality, our nation's arsenal is absolutely unmatched."

Led by such formidable figures as Jane Russell, Jayne Mansfield, Lana Turner and Marilyn Monroe, U.S. women, Defense Department officials said, could theoretically halt curve development for more than 20 years and still maintain a sizable lead over those in the Soviet Union. The U.S. also holds a nearly four-inch edge over the U.S.S.R. in bust lines, the report read, with average measurements listed at 38-24-36.

"America is currently in possession of the most awesome, ample stockpile of curves the world has ever seen," Wilson said. "We cannot be stopped."

Wilson said the U.S. advantage will only widen in 1956, when the Pentagon plans to unveil its much-anticipated, $55 million Bullet Bra, which is widely expected to accentuate American curves to devastating effect.

"The introduction of the Bullet Bra will effectively bury the Russians in the bombshell race," Wilson said. "The support it will give our nation's already-explosive, fully loaded women will prove too much for the Reds."

Uncowed by American dominance, Soviet Premier Nikolai Bulganin vowed to double funding for development of his nation's chests and hips. "We will not concede this race to the Americans by any means," said Bulganin, who, during a 30-minute speech on Moscow Radio, unveiled 38-24-37 Moscow native Svetlana Aliyev, whom he touted as an example of state-of-the-art Soviet cheesecake.

87

The Onion

Suitable Reading for Pop, Ma, Sis, Junior and Spot

Free of Problem Odor

Tuesday, February 21, 1956 — FINEST NEWS SOURCE IN AMERICA — ★★★ Price Five Cents

Ronald Reagan Bravely Turns In 78,342 Hollywood Leftists

Eight Non-Communists Cleared

Star Vows Tinseltown Will Blacklist All Free-Thinking Artists by 1960

WASHINGTON, D.C. — In dramatic testimony before the Screen Actors Guild, former Guild President Ronald Reagan confirmed U.S. Sen. Joseph McCarthy's list of the 78,342 known leftists in the film industry.

"Open-minded, left-leaning intellectuals are all around us," Reagan said. "It is a conspiracy."

Although Reagan knew the careers of those named would forever be destroyed by the announcement, he said he presented the list of names to the Guild with pride.

Reagan was asked by Guild President Walter Pidgeon to respond aloud with an affirmative or a negative regarding the leftist leanings of all 78,342 names on the list. But when a motion was carried pointing out that it would take several days to read so many names, it was agreed that Reagan should read a list of all those remaining: the eight non-leftists.

Accompanied by sighs and gasps from the packed meeting room, Reagan read allowed the following eight names.

Reagan himself;
Actor John Wayne;
Producer Victor Fleming;
Actor James Stewart;
Costume designer Margaret Worth;
Best boy Jimmy Rogers;
MGM commissary janitor "Petey" (last name unknown);
Lassie.

"It is a sad duty to have to implicate all other 78,342 Hollywood residents," Reagan said. "But it is a duty I must fulfill, nonetheless, not only for the sake of my country, but for the sake of the upstanding, God-fearing, patriotic Americans in Hollywood, all eight of whom deserve our deep respect."

CLEARED

John Wayne

James Stewart

Lassie

Tips on Having a Keen Wing-Ding

by U.S. Sen. Estes Kefauver (D-Tenn.)

In these oft-confusing modern times of vice and subversion, knowing the "Dos" and "Don'ts" of throwing a successful wing-ding isn't just good sense—it is a matter of life and death. Teens "in the know" agree that juvenile delinquency is the single greatest moral crisis in America today. As a duly appointed elected official, I urge all teens to help curb the decay by clipping and saving these handy, helpful hooper-doo hints.

1.) KEEP FINGERNAILS CLEAN AND WELL-GROOMED AT ALL TIMES.

Nobody likes a Mister Grubby Thumbs when it comes to personal hygiene matters on the Big Night. Dirty or untrimmed fingernails send the message, "I'm a magnet for below-the-waist rashes and incurable social disease." Sudden, mandatory delousings from Department of Health agents not only spoil your fun-time, but ruin everyone else's evening, as well.

2.) KEEP ANUS TIGHTLY CLENCHED.

A tightly clenched anus is a well-maintained anus. Constant, deliberate buttock clenching is your body's best way of protecting itself against foreign germs, and is a natural part of The Puberty Years. And the strenuous effort to keep your anal column safely sealed is nothing to be embarrassed about.

3.) REMAIN FOUR FEET APART AT ALL TIMES.

Pregnancy, brain damage and severe, burning discharges are only three of the disasters

Senator Estes Kefauver

that could result if this rule is not respected—and strictly enforced by an adult with an electric cattle-prod—*without exception*. Remember, mixed dancing is for voting adults over 21 years of age only. Instead, hold a panel discussion on "going steady" and why it's wrong. Ask your pastor to attend!

4.) DO NOT TELL GHOST STORIES.

Campfires are great for "s'mores" and sing-alongs, but creepy tales of terror and suspense, complete with lurid depictions of gore and death, are neither entertaining nor comical. They are repulsive filth circulated in dimestore cartoon booklets for the explicit purpose of seducing innocents. Why not organize a Luther League hayride instead?

5.) FERRET OUT THE CRIMINAL ELEMENT IN YOUR MIDST.

Every day, gangsters, mobsters and common thugs secretly move among us, plotting nefarious acts. Posing as decent, respectable folk, these evildoers, and the Fifth Columnists who aid and abet them, could be anyone—*even your best girl*. Always use your thinking cap when it comes to tracking down, exposing and punishing Public Enemy Number One.

6.) ENJOY A DELICIOUS "HOT-DOG" ROASTED WEENIE.

Hosts, hostesses and chaperons: Write for a free brochure of recipes, decorating ideas and other super-duper ways to make your supervised weenie-roast event a regular humdinger. Perfect at the ballpark, the fair, anywhere that people gather to enjoy this flavorful sausage. (This tip sponsored by the Pork Board.)

7.) BURN VAST QUANTITIES OF GIRLIE BOOKS.

For sheer thrills, there's nothing I love more than putting the torch to stag comics, French photo books, Tijuana Bibles, bondage art and cheesecake photo libraries. Go through Pop's sock drawer to find them. (Rest assured that, if you do find anything, your father will be punished to the fullest extent of the law.) My office will gladly forward information on how you can get a Junior Incinerator Squad started right in your own hometown.

Today's Teens Are Tomorrow's Taxpayers! God Bless the Class of 1956!

New Television Quiz Show, 'Payola!,' Suspected of Encouraging Cheating Among Contestants

NEW YORK — *Payola!*, the popular television "quiz show" which televises the efforts of ordinary Americans to win large cash prizes by answering a series of difficult questions, is being investigated by the New York district attorney's office in response to allegations of cheating.

"We have evidence that television cannot be trusted," investigator Herb Goodmark said Monday.

Goodmark said he has uncovered evidence that much of what transpires on television, and on the program *Payola!* in particular, is staged and often intentionally rigged to keep viewers watching.

Among his claims: that contestants were given the answers to certain questions in order to make the money-winning spectacle more dramatic; that contestants were chosen for the program based on their physical attributes, not their ability to answer the questions; and that the producers of the program were actually profiting handsomely, despite the fact that they give away cash prizes every week.

Viewers have reacted to news of the allegations with disbelief and some suspicion of their own. "I saw that handsome young scholar from Princeton answer the *Payola!* Princely Payoff Poser with my own two eyes," said faithful viewer Edna Karl, 63, of Pine Bluff, New Jersey. "He was so handsome and intelligent. I have a hard time believing that the TV people would lie to me and that nice young man, let alone doubting the evidence of my senses."

"Of course, this is a very grave accusation," said *Payola!* Executive Producer Edward Stivick. "What the American people have to ask themselves in such a situation is, Would the fine people of television, and our sponsors at Revlon cosmetics in particular, ever lie to them? We think they'll look into their hearts and answer with a resounding 'No!'"

Eisenhower Unveils Statue Honoring Nation's Bettys

WASHINGTON, D.C.—President Eisenhower unveiled a statue honoring the nation's Bettys yesterday at a ceremony attended by Washington elites, military officials, and several Bettys. The statue, which depicts a Betty in a polka-dot dress standing near a stove, was erected on the north side of the Reflecting Pool.

Standing before the 123-foot-tall steel-gray monument, the president made a formal speech "dedicating this statue to each and every Betty from sea to shining sea." A cloth was removed to reveal an inscription at the base bearing the simple words, "For the Bettys."

"Is there anything nicer than a lovely, homegrown American gal? I think not!" Eisenhower said.

Following the dedication, Secretary of State John Foster Dulles lauded Bettys, whether they be blonde, brunette or red-haired, short or tall. "Their service to this nation, in the form of winsome smiles, sweet-spoken words and the serving of pies, is rightly honored with this very nice statue."

A delegation from the National Sisterhood of Bettys was on hand to thank the nation for the honor by preparing and serving an egg-salad-sandwich luncheon.

INSIDE THIS ISSUE:

EDWARD TELLER PLEASED WITH H-BOMB, CALLS FOR WEAPON CAPABLE OF DESTROYING SUN

See story, page 4

The Onion

See Dick.
See Jane.

See Jane Hop.
Hop, Jane, Hop!

Friday, July 27, 1956 — FINEST NEWS SOURCE IN AMERICA — ★★★ Price Five Cents

Supreme Court Upholds Mississippi Law Requiring Negro Voters to Be White

White voters exercise their constitutional right in Jackson, Mississippi.

WASHINGTON. D.C. — The Supreme Court Thursday upheld a Mississippi judge's decision against a Jackson, Miss., voter charged with willfully breaking a state law requiring negro voters to be white.

The case involved Marcus Jefferson, a Mississippi voting hopeful who, in November 1952, was deemed "not white enough" to vote in the state.

"Mr. Jefferson is technically a negro, and therefore did undeniably violate the law by trying to vote," Chief Justice Earl Warren wrote in the majority opinion.

Warren cited Amendment XV, Section 1 of the Constitution, which states that "the right to vote shall not be denied to a citizen of any race, color or creed who has white skin."

Complexity of the White Negro Voter Law

In March 1951, Mississippi enacted legislation dubbed "The White Negro Voter Law" which stipulates, "To vote in any election in the State of Mississippi, a member of the electorate, no matter his gender, race, color or religious affiliation, must prove he is white."

The law also requires voters to take a skin-color analysis test as part of the registration process. Jefferson failed the test, registering 5.0 on the medically administered exam, which in some states is light enough to be considered white, but in others is negro.

"States differ on the precise skin tone that is acceptable at the polls," said one Mississippi official. "This Supreme Court decision will be watched very closely, as it clearly indicates a trend in the nation's courts toward much lighter skin tones."

Governor Pledges Commitment to Negroes

Mississippi Gov. Douglas Orr released a statement asserting that his state will honor its commitment to negro rights by arranging a separate-but-equal election exclusively for negro voters.

"The negroes should have an election all their own," Orr said. "We could hold, say, an election for the office of Best Negro in the United States of America. They would appreciate that, as it would make them feel as though they are part of the political process."

Mississippi has taken other legislative steps in support of negro rights. One bill, still being debated in the state legislature, would provide that predominantly white private lawn-tennis and riding clubs in Mississippi be required to have fully integrated custodial crews. Another calls for tougher sentences for convicted lynchers, including fines of up to $200 or five days in jail.

A Message From Your Neighborhood Ford Dealer:

Fight Communists on Vacation!

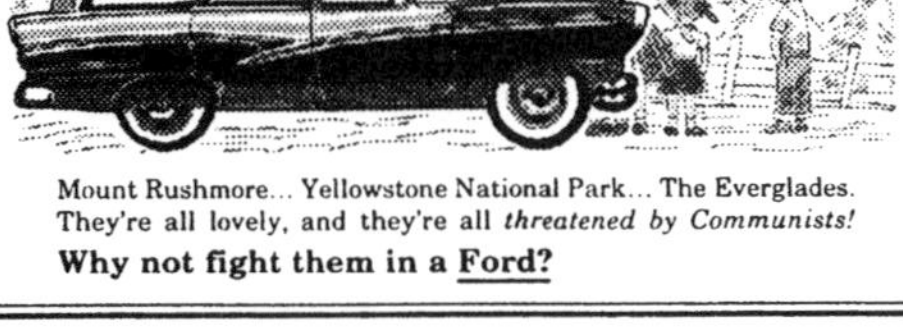

Mount Rushmore... Yellowstone National Park... The Everglades. They're all lovely, and they're all *threatened by Communists!*

Why not fight them in a Ford?

President Orders Brando to Gain 250 Pounds

Star's Raw Sexuality Too Dangerous at Present Weight, Ike Says

WASHINGTON D.C. — Responding to what he termed "an unacceptable and increasingly dangerous caliber of brooding, smoldering sexuality," President Eisenhower took executive action Thursday against Marlon Brando, directing him to gain 250 pounds.

The Academy Award-winning actor was threatened with deportation if he does not comply with the president's order.

"Mr. Brando, your talent as an actor is undeniable," Eisenhower wrote in a letter to the star of *On the Waterfront*. "But your overt masculinity and alluring dissatisfaction with the comforts of modern American life pose a clear threat to our domestic security."

The president called for an immediate fattening of the actor, asking Brando to gain no fewer than 250 pounds and "let yourself go completely and without restraint."

"I suggest a rigorous regime of exercise avoidance: sitting in an easy chair, lying in bed, and engaging in concerted slovenliness," the letter read. "It is the only way to save the nation from your powerful appeal."

"For diet, I recommend several glazed hams each day," Eisenhower wrote, "with buttered bread and yams. I would also urge an increase in dessert consumption. A generous whipped-cream topping on

Marlon Brando — **President Eisenhower**

each pie you consume could mean the difference between a nation in turmoil and a nation at peace."

White House sources noted that Brando's sexuality alone is grounds for concern, but it was the actor's dangerous demeanor that led to the president's decision to take executive action.

"In such roles as Stanley in *A Streetcar Named Desire* and Johnny in *The Wild One*, Mr. Brando portrays a man who is clearly uncomfortable with the status quo," said presidential aide Martin Lauber. "This is, of course, a problem in itself. And this dissatisfaction is given extra weight by the fact that Brando is a sexual powerhouse. This administration feels that the American people would be much less affected by Brando's views if they were espoused by a porcine slob rather than a virile dreamboat."

To guarantee catastrophic weight gain on the part of the actor, Eisenhower urged Congress to pass emergency tax incentives for restaurants and grocery stores located within a 20-mile radius of Brando's Hollywood home.

Area Beat Beaten

GREENWICH VILLAGE, N.Y. — Local beat poet Ed Paulsen, 22, was badly beaten late Thursday night at Cafe Wha?, a popular bohemian enclave on Bleecker Street.

The assailant, described as a middle-aged authority figure wearing a bow-tie and thick glasses, burst into the coffeehouse at approximately 10 p.m. and savaged the beatnik with a baseball bat about the face, shoulders and beret.

"Whoa, like, lay off my headbone, daddy-o," Paulsen reportedly told his attacker, who had interrupted the second hour of his epic performance poem and bongo solo, titled "Twirl." As the man continued to beat him, witnesses reported Paulsen as saying, "This bat attack is definitely un-cool, man."

After thoroughly beating the beatnik, the assailant pulled the victim's turtleneck sweater over his face, kicked holes through the skins of Paulsen's bongo drums, and fled the scene. He is still at large.

"This doesn't surprise me, man. My stuff is out there, you know, *out there!*" Paulsen said as he smoked a thin dark cigarette through his swollen lips. "When you illuminate the swirling Ezekielian religion wheels beneath the sad sidewalks of nowheresville, you're bound to get a rise out of the squares. Dig?"

According to witnesses, the bat attack "irrevocably destroyed" the great vibe that had been going at Cafe Wha? until that point. "What a total thrill-kill that cat was to pummel Ed like that. I bet he doesn't even like Mingus," said Steve Goldberg, a friend of Paulsen's. "We all had to roll over to my pad and smoke some green tea to come down from that crazy scene, daddy."

"Like, where does he get off, pulling that kind of freaky jazz?" asked witness Carolyn Rogers. "I'm so mad, I'm burning like a thousand starry skies, higher, higher, until I explode like an incandescent ocean, a blazing beatific ball of angry ecstasy."

Several beatniks present snapped their fingers in agreement with Rogers.

Paulsen suffered three broken ribs and a fractured clavicle in the attack. His goatee was unharmed.

INSIDE THIS ISSUE:

PANTS PULLED UP TO ALL-TIME HIGH
see story, page 8

N.A.A.C.P. LUNCHEON CANCELED DUE TO LACK OF LUNCH-COUNTER AVAILABILITY
see story, page 13

89

The Onion

Pro-Socks | Anti-Hops

Wednesday, August 1, 1956 — FINEST NEWS SOURCE IN AMERICA — ★★★ Price Five Cents

Supreme Court Rules U.S. Fathers Should Not Be Disturbed During Dinner Hour

Unpleasant Matters Not to Be Discussed Under Strict New Mealtime-Behavior Restrictions

High Court Says Children Must Abide by Father's Rules While Under Father's Roof

WASHINGTON, D.C. — By a 9-0 vote Tuesday, the U.S. Supreme Court ruled that it is unconstitutional for wives and children to disturb the nation's fathers during the dinner hour.

"The dinner hour is a sacred time for the hard-working American father, the one moment of peace and quiet he can look forward to all day," Justice Tom Clark wrote in the court's opinion. "It is a time when he should be free to enjoy a nice, hot meal without having to deal with complaints and trivial details from the lives of other family members."

With this decision, those who continue to interrupt father while he is attempting to eat his steak with buttered potato and creamed corn in peace and quiet can be prosecuted under federal law.

Father v. the Petersons is the case of husband and father of three Walter Peterson, 38, who, while eating dinner on Nov. 3, 1955, was disrupted three times by his son, Eddie Peterson, 11. The younger Peterson cited extenuating circumstances surrounding the series of disruptions, including the loss of his brand-new baseball glove during recess at school that day. The court, however, ruled that the child's reporting of the news of the lost glove to his father "could have waited until after dinner."

The opinion stated, "Mr. Peterson had just gotten home from a long, hard day of work as a senior sales supervisor at Wilford and Briggs Advertising, and all he wanted was to be able to eat his meal without being nagged."

"The difficult question brought before this court was, 'Is this too much for a father to ask? A little peace and quiet once in a while?' The members of this court found the answer to this question to be no."

In the ruling, the court denied children the right to approach their father with reports of how their day went at school until at least one hour after the dinner table has been cleared by the mother, enabling the father to digest and enjoy an after-dinner cigarette before turning his attention to family business.

Further, Clark wrote, if the child's news is bad, including (but not limited to) grades of C or lower on tests or the receiving of a black eye at the hands of a bully, the child should wait at least two hours after mealtime before informing the father.

The same rules apply to wives who might wish to interrupt a husband's meal, whether to inform him of a victory in a game of bridge with other housewives or to ask him for money.

According to the court's decision, stiff penalties can be handed down to those who violate the decision. "If children fail to respect the court's decision in this matter, they will be excused from the dinner table," Clark wrote. "A second violation will result in their being sent to their room for the remainder of the evening with no dessert, and possible grounding." Wives who violate the new ruling will be subject to a vigorous tsk-ing.

Fathers across the U.S. are applauding the court's decision. "The last thing I want after a hard day of work is to come home and listen to my wife ask me to buy her a new hat or take her to the Copa Room for our anniversary," said husband and father of four Elmer Jameson Wallace of Chicago. "As I told my wife, Audrey, 'Would you shut your whining trap, already? I don't want to hear about this right now!' I am glad the Supreme Court sees things my way."

White Bread Sales Up 200 Percent

When shoppers across the nation get in line at the supermarket, it's white bread that's going into their carts. White-bread sales are up over 200 percent since the beginning of the year.

A survey by the Holsum Baking Company shows that consumers are choosing white bread over other varieties such as rye or wheat, specifically for its simplicity, homogeneity and consistency.

Factory "pre-sliced" white bread is especially popular, ensuring that each and every sandwich is exactly the same size and shape.

U.S. Sexual Repression Reaches Boiling Point

Marilyn Monroe, raising America's sexual tension to almost unbearable levels.

A panel of Yale University scientists released a report Tuesday warning that the nation's sexual-repression levels have reached a boiling point.

"After hovering at a dangerous and precarious level for almost 40 years," said Yale's Dr. Norm Hamon, "America's mass suppression of socially unacceptable urges and impulses is finally threatening to explode, shattering our thin veneer of moral decorum and exposing the baser urges of the general populace."

"If America sees one more glimpse of a naked thigh, one more bosom straining from beneath a tight sweater," Hamon added, "the lid is going to blow right off of this country."

The report warned that the culture's constant barrage of veiled sexual innuendoes and overtly sexualized stars like Marilyn Monroe and Marlon Brando are straining the nation's ability to stay repressed.

"We've kept our urges bottled up so tightly," Hamon said, "an explosion of the national id may be imminent."

"Such an explosion," he said, "could open a floodgate, creating unspeakable societal changes, such as, I don't know, the most depraved acts you can imagine: public necking and the loosening of undergarment straps, perhaps."

YOUR NEIGHBORS MAY NOT BE CONSUMING ENOUGH MATERIAL GOODS

Watch them carefully and report any suspected non-consumers to the proper authorities. Help rid America of anti-purchasing subversives.

WASHINGTON, D.C. — U.S. Sen. Clinton Anderson (D-N.M.) is urging all Americans to keep an eye out for potential non-consumers lurking in their communities.

"Each one of us has to do his part to protect America from those subversives who do not believe in buying as much as possible," Anderson said. "Anti-Consumerism is the worst form of treachery, and its disloyal practitioners must be found out and interrogated, wherever they may be."

"If you spot someone in your town who is not shopping for new cars, washers, dryers, toasters, televisions, vacuum cleaners, lawn mowers or ovens, report them immediately to your local authorities," Anderson said. "We cannot have America's buying power undermined by a small handful of Godless non-purchasers."

According to Harvard University political-science professor A. Crandall Dewitt, non-consumers have infiltrated virtually every sphere of American society, from the Pentagon to Hollywood. It has been confirmed that there are at least seven members of Congress who are not currently trading in their cars for the newer model, Dewitt said, and at least four high-level members of the Eisenhower Administration who have not purchased an electric blender in the past year.

"These people, with their shocking disinterest in the latest American-made products, are a threat to our way of life," Dewitt said.

In congress Tuesday, Anderson outlined the three warning signs that someone you know is a non-consumer: One, he spends his weekends relaxing at home rather than shopping at local stores; two, his home is filled with items that are neither new nor improved; and three, he puts a majority of his weekly paycheck into the bank rather than into the robust American economy via the purchase of record-players, sewing machines, chest freezers and sail-boats.

"Watch for these warning signs," Anderson said. "It is your duty as a loyal American consumer to report such un-American activities."

Anderson, who himself was accused by several fellow senators last week of being a non-consumer, responded by producing a receipt from Woolworth's showing that he had spent $25.32 at the store last Sunday on 11 items, including a hammer, a Norelco electric razor and a 40-foot garden hose.

"America fought too hard in the Second World War to have it undermined by a treacherous few who do not believe in owning the latest model of every modern American-made product available," he said, holding up his razor. "Why, that's what being an American is all about."

INSIDE

BOY SCOUTS DISCONTINUE UN-AMERICAN ACTIVITIES MERIT BADGE

See page 5

Anti-Reefer News		Whites-Only Edition

The Onion

Monday, June 24, 1957 — FINEST NEWS SOURCE IN AMERICA — ★★★ Price Five Cents

Eisenhower Vows to Address Growing Problem of Overdue Library Books

President Calls for Tougher Fines as Part of 'Operation Due Date'

WASHINGTON, D.C. — President Eisenhower tackled the growing problem of overdue library books in a nationally televised speech Sunday evening, addressing what political analysts say may be the most urgent problem facing the nation today.

His expression stern, Eisenhower gave a terse warning to those Americans who fail to return borrowed books to public lending institutions until days, even weeks, after the due date. Calling the problem of overdue books "the most perilous and pressing issue facing our great land," the president urged a speedy resolution of the problem.

The directive arrives on the heels of Ike's anti-littering speech in April and the recently launched "Federal Leash-Your-Dog Campaign."

"Operation Due Date" will encourage Americans to return library books in a timely manner with a congressionally imposed 10-cent-per-week mandatory late fee. "Those of you with a book out, and you know who you are," Eisenhower said, pointing a finger into the lens of the television camera, "had better hop to it and get it back to the library on time."

With the economy booming, the war long over, and international problems non-existent, Eisenhower's attack on the unfortunate problem of overdue books was seen as a bold gesture to improve the state of America while deftly reminding everyone of his existence. Public opinion polls indicate that, with his tough stance on overdue books, the president has effectively shown that he is not afraid to tackle significant issues affecting our nation, should they come up any time soon.

PRESIDENT EISENHOWER

Science Fiction Writers Have the Bomb!

A crushing blow to U.S. supremacy came this week with intelligence officials' discovery that popular science-fiction writers have the atomic bomb.

A report issued by the CIA states, "A small group of writers of popular science-fiction magazines and pulp novels have acquired nuclear weapons for unregulated use in stories not only of fantastical futures and other worlds, but even of our own world."

"The grave nature of this security risk cannot be overstated," CIA Director Allen Dulles wrote in the report. "With nuclear weapons in the hands of a few unaccountable writers, full-scale armageddon could be unleashed in bookstores as early as this fall."

The report named writers Robert Heinlein, Poul Anderson, Arthur C. Clarke and Isaac Asimov, among others.

"These writers are bound by no United Nations or American authority, national borders or public accountability," the report read.

A Grave Threat

The CIA warned that the authors have knowledge of futuristic nuclear weapons exceeding even those produced by the brightest scientific minds of the modern age. "They are using A-bombs, H-bombs, and even newer, more powerful, fantastical weapons every week in books and in such popular magazines as *Astounding Science Fiction* and *Amazing Stories*, and on popular radio programs such as *X Minus One*."

Further, some of the writers demonstrate the ability to foretell events hundred of years hence.

In his short story "Tunnel Under the World," author Frederick Pohl uses a nuclear explosion to destroy an entire city, forcing its survivors to implant their brain energy into humanoid robots for use as test-market subjects for an evil advertising agency.

"This is technology far in advance of what the U.S. currently possesses," said atomic weapons expert Hubert Schuber of Princeton University. "If they so chose, these super-being writers could hold the world hostage with their fantastical powers."

Schuber warned that Asimov, a 37-year-old Boston University professor, has been in command of an army of killer robots since the 1940s.

"If Asimov's robot menace cannot be contained," he said, "we must at least implore him to follow some laws of robotics to ensure that a robot will never harm a human being or, through inaction, allow a human being to be harmed."

While the precise armament wielded by the writers is unknown, Schuber fears it could dwarf the stockpile of both the U.S. and U.S.S.R. But worse, he said, are the after-effects.

According to Schuber, the "fall-out" of science-fiction writers' atomic weapons may be the most destructive the world has ever seen. "These writers could wreak untold havoc by unleashing a cloud of anti-atomic sentiment that could engulf our planet for generations," he said.

U.S. Action

The Atomic Energy Commission published an open letter to the writers in *The New York Times* Sunday, urging them to test their stories by releasing them in bookstores in the Bikini Atoll Islands or in the remote deserts of Nevada before publishing them for a mass audience.

Nation's Housewives Agree

A record 91 percent of the nation's housewives agree, according to a door-to-door poll conducted by the George Gallup Co. last week.

The statistic is up dramatically from the impressive 82 percent found to agree 10 years ago.

The housewives were found to be in full agreement on a wide range of household issues, from, "JetScout is the best way to remove tough, baked-on grease" to "A Glenrose Carpet is a carpet you can depend on."

A full 85 percent agreed that bridge club is a nice way to spend a Thursday evening, 82 percent agreed that their mothers-in-law were "awfully nice," and 80 percent agreed that cheese and crackers should be served.

One hundred percent agreed that Joyce looks wonderful in her Sunday dress.

On crucial issues such as curtains, the nation's wives agreed that red and white checkered are best for the kitchen, while a pastel green was the ideal choice for the living room. When asked why, 47 percent responded, "I don't see why not," 22 percent said, "I don't want to rock the boat," 17 percent said, "Because Joyce and Shirley do," and 8 percent said, "Hm, I never really gave it much thought." Six percent either cited miscellaneous reasons or offered cake and punch in lieu of an answer.

Agreement was strong nationwide, with the median 91 percent agreement rating holding true in all areas except California, where only 90 percent agreed, and the New York City metropolitan area, where agreement was slightly over 92 percent. In most cases, agreement was noted as being independent of category; housewives who agreed, pollsters said, seemed to agree with everything.

"Most housewives agreed with all questions asked," said Walter Haggerty, a canvasser for Gallup. "Eighty percent indicated that they 'strongly agreed.' Seventy-two percent said they agreed not only with each other and with their husbands, but with President Eisenhower, the Better Business Bureau, their children's teachers, and the publisher of *The Saturday Evening Post*."

Of the 9 percent of non-agreeing women polled, 92 percent requested that Gallup ask their husbands instead and 7.9 percent said no, thank you, they did not need a new vacuum cleaner at this time. The remaining .01 percent disagreed.

Milwaukee, Wisconsin, housewife Pat Phelps.

Status Quo Maintained for 2,000th Consecutive Day

With the nation's housewives, and nearly everyone else, in agreement, the U.S. achieved a milestone in stasis yesterday, reaching its 2,000th consecutive day of societal status quo.

Order and sameness are the rules of the day across our land, as national power structures remain safely entrenched and bold new ideas remain at an all-time low.

"From our collective love of enormous automobiles to our fear and mistrust of outsiders, to our shared desire to own attractive new patio furniture, America has not changed in three wonderful years," said Brad Edwards, 33, a Canoga Park, Calif., advertising executive. "I, like other citizens, am extremely satisfied with the way things are."

INSIDE THIS ISSUE:

SENATOR JOHN KENNEDY WINS PULITZER PRIZE FOR AUTOBIOGRAPHY, 'PROFILES IN PRIVILEGE'

See page 4

| Quiet, Clean and Convenient News | # The Onion | Support the Beatnik Registration Act |

Friday, July 19, 1957 — FINEST NEWS SOURCE IN AMERICA — ★★★ Price Five Cents

The Lloyd Seversons of Sunnyville, Missouri, a typical American couple.

EVERYTHING'S NIFTY

Swellness in America at All-Time High

All Americans Pleased as Punch

Ike Says 'Okey-Dokey' to American Prosperity

In a nationally televised address Thursday night, President Eisenhower announced that everything is hunky-dory in the U.S.

"My fellow Americans, I stand before you tonight to tell you that everything is swell, real swell," the president said in his one-hour address. "Our kids are getting A's on all their tests at school, discontentment is at a 30-year low, and U.S. wives are cooking more delicious meatloaf than at any point in American history. We, as a nation, are more than okey-dokey; we are super-duper okey-dokey."

According to Eisenhower, nearly every major economic and social indicator points upward. Among the more notable statistics: Industrial production is up 20 percent in the past 12 months, unemployment is at just 2 percent, the divorce rate is at just 4 percent, teeth are 57 percent whiter, and U.S. soft drinks have 46 percent more pep.

National politeness indicators are also at a four-decade high, with 33 percent more people saying, "Thank you, dear," and, "Gee, you're welcome, ma'am."

"I am really enjoying serving as your president," said Eisenhower, concluding the address with a slice of fresh-baked rhubarb pie and a tall glass of milk. "What fun this job is."

Adding to the good news for the U.S., Thomas McNamara, a Rochester, Minn., 11-year-old, announced yesterday that he has completely memorized his multiplication tables. "I'm really going to be ready for the big exam on Monday," McNamara said. "Oh, boy, I can't wait to show Miss Meyers just how smart I am." McNamara added that he can hold his breath under water for one full minute, longer than any Soviet boy.

"In all my life, I don't believe I have ever witnessed a happier, more contented nation," Harvard University political-science professor A. Crandall Dewitt said. "This just might be the swellest nation in world history. Miles of smiles await us all."

Following the address, citizens expressed confidence in their leader and hope for the future. "That sure was a keen speech Ike made," said Gloria Coletto of Flushing, New York. "Everything is peachy."

Devoted husband and father Lloyd Severson of Sunnyville, Mo., agreed. "I love the United States, my president, my family and God," he said. "Sometimes it's difficult to say which I love the best. I guess I love them all equally."

Eisenhower's speech lends credence to a report in the July 12 edition of *The Washington Post*, which predicted that by 1967, there will be no more problems in the U.S.

GM Unveils '58 Cadillac Dreadnought

Eight-Wheeled, Five-Ton Behemoth Will Compete with Lincoln Monstroliner

Features 24-Cylinder Engine, Spacious Den

The '58 Cadillac Dreadnought

DETROIT — General Motors head designer Harley Earl announced Thursday that GM's Cadillac division will soon begin mass production of its new Dreadnought luxury model for 1958. The Dreadnought, equipped with eight wheels, seating for 20 adults, and all available power options, will be the largest private passenger vehicle ever produced.

"Today's American citizen doesn't want something that has less than 500 horsepower and only seats one family," Earl said at the Dreadnought's unveiling in Detroit. "And he doesn't want something that looks like it was designed by Herbert Hoover's haberdasher. The Dreadnought is a 10,680-pound, 37-foot automobile that can transport an entire board of directors in Jet Age style."

General Motors' newest Cadillac is intended to serve as the full expression of the company's Luxo-Hemoth philosophy and, as the corporate flagship model, it incorporates many new design features. The Dreadnought offers the first-ever living room, basement and dashboard martini mixer. An adjustable steak-thickness-and-rareness-ometer will be a standard option. Each of the 20 Executive Reclino-Flite seats will be covered in three top-grain steerhides. A new Dyna-Torq-O-Matic five-speed transmission has been devised to handle the power of the Dreadnought's Octofire-Surge-Glide 24-cylinder engine, which generates 2,400 horsepower and achieves an unheard-of fuel consumption rate of six gallons to the mile. Its engine alone weighs as much as the next-largest Cadillac model. Future Dreadnoughts will be equipped with a four-season patio.

"From the very beginning, we designed this car with the more affluent customer in mind," GM President Charlie Wilson said. "The Dreadnought has three-foot-tall fins. Its proud hood emblem depicts the winged god Apollo, bending his bow toward the sun while mounted upon a majestic Pegasus which stands astride the slain carcasses of a gazelle, a lion, an eagle and a Communist. It has the largest whitewall tires ever manufactured by human civilization. And it goes off the showroom floor at a price of $7,000. It is America's finest achievement since the atomic bomb."

Cadillac engineers make no secret of the fact that the Dreadnought was designed to compete with Lincoln Motors' spacious Monstroliner, a 30-foot-long, six-wheeled sedan which, until now, was the nation's largest, least fuel-efficient automobile. Wilson said trials at GM's Flint, Mich., test-track revealed that the new Dreadnought loses very little speed when driven into a stationary Monstroliner at highway speeds.

Dr. Seuss Hanged for Subversion

CAMBRIDGE, Mass. — Theodor Geisel, best-selling author of children's books, was hanged for subversion at 12:01 EST today under the direct orders of a special federal investigating committee.

Long suspected of disseminating radical ideas, "Dr. Seuss" was found guilty of free-thinking and corruption by the committee after a reading of *The Cat in the Hat*, his most recent book. The work calls for insurgent behavior among children, especially those left at home on rainy days without direct parental supervision.

Hundreds of pages of plot notes and sketches were confiscated in an FBI raid last week on Seuss' Massachusetts home. Investigators said treasonous messages were thinly disguised by colorful illustrations of strange creatures, possibly inspired by illegal narcotics.

The works, committee members said, contained messages of class-restructuring and civil unrest, unpatriotic cries for demilitarization and de-industrialization, and calls for the abandonment of personal restraint.

"Geisel was a dangerous influence on children," said Grant Leehold, Chairman of the Committee to Investigate Un-American Children's Books. "But no longer will he spread dangerous ideas such as a Blue Tubaroo and a Red Tubaroo sharing the same seat on a Galloping Garoo."

Geisel was also suspected of believing that Sneetches with no stars upon thars are equal to the obviously superior star-bellied breed of Sneetch.

"Had this so-called doctor not been terminated by noose, he might have tried to spread the idea that bread can be buttered on either side," Leehold said.

INSIDE THIS ISSUE:

ALTAR BOY REPEATEDLY SODOMIZED

See story, page 10

| Your Source for Square News | # The Onion | Support Our Troops in Little Rock |

Friday, October 4, 1957   FINEST NEWS SOURCE IN AMERICA   ★★★ Price Five Cents

Bleeping Two-Foot Tin Ball Threatens Free World

America Suffers Major Defeat in Space-Gizmo Race

Orbiting Russian Trinket 'A Grave Threat,' Say Scientists

President Promises to 'Put a Tiny Metal Thing in Orbit' by 1960

American metal-bauble superiority was cast into grave doubt Thursday when the Russians launched a two-foot ball of tin into orbit around the Earth.

"Sputnik," an artificial, Communist-built satellite, is traveling 100 miles above the surface of the Earth, emitting what government defense and technology experts are calling "a terrifying series of bleeps."

Elementary and high-school classes have been suspended across the nation today by executive order of President Eisenhower, with children instructed to pray for the safety of the free world.

"If the Russians decide that this 'Sputnik' should bleep even faster," Eisenhower said, "no one on Earth would be able to stop them."

The president said he suspects that the Reds could execute a full-scale launching of tin balls which could be in position over America in less than 10 minutes, darkening the entire Western Hemisphere with menacing Communist shadows two feet across.

Said political-science professor A. Crandall Dewitt of Harvard University, "The bleep is also cause for concern. If they can make it bleep today, they could make one that squawks tomorrow. By this time next year, they could have a ball that honks. There's no telling how dire this situation could get."

"Communist tin-ball technology is the best in the world," Nikita Khrushchev boasted in a public address Thursday night in Moscow. "The Soviet Union is also first in the manufacture of things that make a bleeping sound." He then spoke directly to America, saying, "We will bury you in the crucial area of the electronic-bleeping sciences, and in the challenging hobby of tinsmithery."

The news has top Pentagon brass scurrying to assess the threat the Russians now pose.

"The Reds could create an even louder bleep," Defense Secretary Neil McElroy theorized, "perhaps causing it to be a nuisance to anyone within a nine-yard radius. They might also be planning to create a gadget that emits bleeps which are even longer than Sputnik's, technology that is beyond even our most advanced sound technicians."

"Could a terrifying larger sphere be next? Or a large collection of insidious smaller spheres? The Reds could be up to anything," McElroy said. "And we are helpless to defend ourselves against these round, sound-producing objects."

The Pentagon estimated that the Russians could launch a fleet of space balls and not even come close to exhausting its vast tin resources.

Eisenhower, in a special broadcast address to the nation, promised that the U.S. will launch a larger, more attractive, extensively chromed metal ball into space by the end of the decade. He guaranteed that the American ball will have a handsome, tastefully streamlined and tailfinned casing and up to three bleep-level settings.

"That," said Eisenhower, "is American ingenuity."

Sputnik, the terrifying Russian bleeping gadget.

U.S. Populace Now 85 Percent Body-Snatcher Pod People

WASHINGTON, D.C. — In an address to the nation Thursday, the identical pod-grown duplicate of President Eisenhower announced that, as of Wednesday, 85 percent of the population has been successfully transformed into blank-faced alien body-snatcher drones, with more expected to be converted soon.

Visibly emotionless, the President urged all remaining humans to come out of hiding and surrender their troublesome individual identities to the glorious order of collective conformity.

"Sleep, humans, sleep," the Eisenhower surrogate urged. "You cannot stop the assimilation of your puny terrestrial species. The transformation is painless. Sleep, and be reborn into an untroubled world."

Pod people throughout the nation agree that the successful duplication of so much of the country was accomplished in such a short time due to the slavish, ant-like efficiency of the inhuman invaders.

"Less than a month ago," said former person and Secretary of State John Foster Dulles, "America was like any other country: people with nothing but problems. But then, from out of the sky, came a solution. Seeds drifting through space for years took root in a farmer's field near Santa Mira, California. From the seeds came pods, which had the power to reproduce themselves in the exact likeness of any form of life."

The pods soon began to spread, Dulles said. Within weeks, the townspeople were all absorbed, duplicated and replaced by the sentient plant life from beyond the stars.

"This is great news for America," the human-looking simulacrum said. "Without all the upsetting conflicts caused by individual identities, nothing can stop this great nation."

Now, thanks to an ambitious pod-distribution program in which truckloads of pods are being shipped across the nation to replace unsuspecting human Americans in their sleep, the newly formed U.S. Department of Humanity Duplication estimates that as little as 15 percent of U.S. citizens retain their original human form. These holdouts are expected to be captured and duplicated within the week.

On a sour note, journalist Edward R. Murrow, in an illegal broadcast following the presidential address on CBS, seized a microphone and shouted, "You're in danger! Can't you see? They're after you! They're after all of us—our wives, our children, everyone! They're here already! You're next!"

Murrow was swiftly subdued and silenced by hordes of podmen.

INSIDE:
HULA HOOPS: ENCOURAGING MOVEMENT BELOW THE WAIST?
See page 22

I Have a Bomb Shelter and You Can't Use It

by T. Herman Zweibel

So, the Board of Directors has decided to force my retirement, has it? And it's even going to court to prove me mentally incompetent and banish me to my 627-room estate back East? They'll not get rid of me without a knock-down, drag-out fight! I'm T. Herman Zweibel! I've edited and published every blasted page of "The Onion" for 60 years! They don't even run the bridge column until I approve the hands! I was born with printer's ink running through my veins, and, by jiggledy, I'll die with my printer's shade and my sleeve guards on, at the same desk I've worked at since 1896!

Or, if God is merciful, I'll be snug in my subterranean bomb-shelter, and you'll all be incinerated by the hellish fire-storm. Didn't I tell you long ago that the fiendish Spaniards were up to no good again, planning a ruthless revenge for their 1898 defeat? Didn't I tell you that they were developing a huge and terrifying weapon made of fertilizer and gun powder, stronger than even the most powerful cannon, that would be aimed at our Republic's very heart-land? But no, I'm perceived as a senile old coot barely able to hold his water, let alone his position at the helm of America's greatest news-paper.

As you traitors roast in your own juices, I will be safely ensconced three miles below the earth's surface, listening to my wax-cylinder player and enjoying a delicious phosphate! My bomb shelter is a lavish net-work of antechambers encased in a steel and titanium alloy several yards thick. It has all the latest conveniences, such as a central-heating system powered by burning coal and enough potted-meat and cabbage-juice to last well into the next millennium. I will be waited on hand and foot by a bevy of comely young lady-actresses, including Miss Mary Pickford and Miss Lillian Gish. And, as the Spaniards are busy crushing your charred skeletal remains under their jack-boots, I will be busy under-ground fathering an invincible warrior race of Zweibels, which will one day emerge into the sun-light and destroy the wretched Iberian occupation once and for all!

So adios, apologists and running-dogs of the Spanish menace! We true Americans will someday have our place in the sun!

| Streamlined for Your Comfort | # The Onion | Lady Readers: Cherry Pie Recipe on Page 17! |

Sunday, January 4, 1959 — FINEST NEWS SOURCE IN AMERICA — ★★★ SUNDAY EDITION — Price Fifteen Cents

Alaska, Hawaii, Guam, Bora Bora, Samoa, Philippines, Japan Granted U.S. Statehood

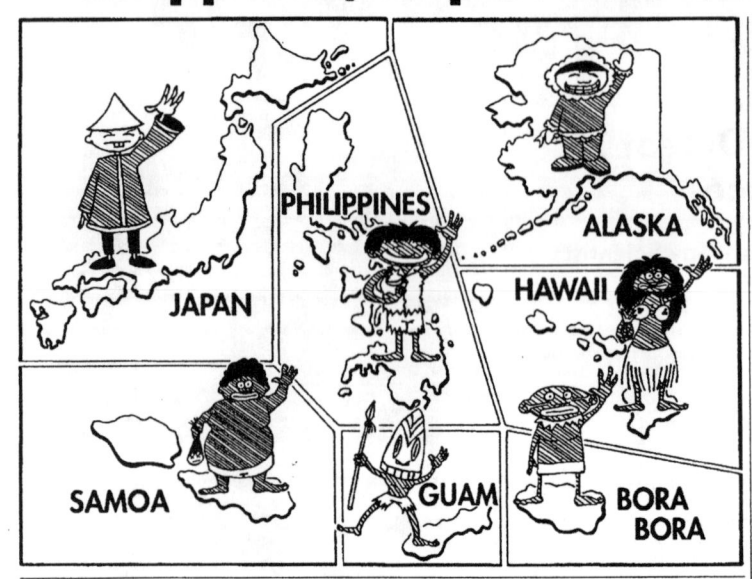

Resource-Rich Territories to Become 49th Through 55th States

Spread of Democracy Will Keep Newly Acquired Territories Safe from Foreign Imperialism

Brown-Skinned Natives to Contribute Taxes, Cheap Labor to U.S.

WASHINGTON, D.C. — The American Empire continued its rapid expansion Saturday, when President Eisenhower announced in a radio address that the U.S. has acquired seven valuable new foreign territories—Alaska, Hawaii, Guam, Bora Bora, Samoa, the Philippines and Japan.

"Though it hardly seems possible, America just got bigger and better," Eisenhower said in his 30-minute speech. "These new lands will provide us with a great many things, from petroleum to pineapples to happy laborers."

According to Eisenhower, the territories, which will be ratified as states later this week, are populated with dark-skinned but friendly races of people who are eager to bask in the glory of the greatest, most prosperous nation in the history of the Earth.

"These natives, be they Eskimos, Samoans or Japs, all share one common trait: a desire to share in the warm glow of the United States of America," Eisenhower said. "Through us, they will learn about such things as democracy, Christianity and good, old-fashioned hard work and success. What savage heathen wouldn't jump at the chance to join a winning team such as ours?"

By acquiring the seven territories, the U.S. gains an estimated 60 million new workers, who will have to be paid a mere fraction of what the American worker would expect to receive. Most of the new citizens, Eisenhower said, may not expect to be paid in cash at all, happy to toil all day long in a sweatshop making U.S. products for a coconut or a pat on the head.

"These industrious little fellows will save the U.S. billions in labor costs," Eisenhower said.

In addition to providing workers, the new territories will also be useful as nuclear test sites. "Bikini Atoll has worked extremely well for us. Its friendly, freedom-loving villagers seemed more than happy to let us drop nuclear bombs on their huts in order to further the cause of democracy," U.S. General James Wallace Jr. said. "I imagine the experience will be the same in these other territories."

Congress is still deliberating whether to give the new territories representation in Washington and their citizens the right to vote.

Editorial

Wedded Couples' Beds on Television Are Too Close Together

Mary Robbins, Onion reader

Have you watched any of the new programs on the television lately? It is positively scandalous, the way these married couples cavort about their shared bedrooms, shamelessly sleeping in beds that are less than five feet apart!

Take that "I Love Lucy" program, for instance. I am appalled that this sort of garbage is the most popular television program in the United States. Not only do Lucy and Ricky Ricardo sleep in the same room, but they do so in beds that practically touch. Why, I wouldn't be surprised if, sleeping in such close proximity to one another, they are able to faintly discern each other's physical forms underneath their respective pajamas and layers of bedcovers.

And, if that weren't enough, I would be remiss if I failed to mention that, on top of everything else, the Ricardos' is a mixed-race marriage, she being of white descent and he Latin. Shame on you, CBS, for passing off such filth as wholesome family entertainment.

Is there no censorship code to protect our impressionable young people from exposure to such sinful images as a man sleeping with his body barely an arm's length away from that of his wife? Where have our society's morals gone? If our television programs are any indication of where we as a nation are headed, I'm packing my bags and moving to Canada.

And do not think the Ricardos are the only ones guilty of such lewdness. There are also the Nelsons, the Thomases and the Cleavers. I do not understand how a seemingly upstanding woman like Harriet Nelson could debase herself in such a way before a national viewing audience.

To you filth-peddlers at CBS and NBC, I say you had best clean up your acts, or I will never watch my television again. There is no room in Television-land for this kind of smut. Between the violence on "Gunsmoke" and the dirty sex on "The Honeymooners," where Ralph and Alice engage in kisses that last upwards of 10 seconds, I can hardly watch television any more.

One Shark, One Jet Dead in Choreographed Street Fight

NEW YORK — Police officials broke up yet another skillfully choreographed, singing street brawl Saturday that left two dead, as rival gangs of dancing, knife-wielding toughs danced intimidatingly on the streets of New York's West Side.

According to Officer Krupke of New York's 32nd Precinct, the youths are members of two rival gangs: the Jets, composed of American-born boys, and the Sharks, composed of young Puerto Ricans.

"These hoodlums and their beautifully choreographed violence must be stopped," said Krupke, who works the West Side beat. "They show no respect for law-enforcement officials such as myself. They mock us in song."

Police coverage for the West Side is slated to be doubled, following the show-stopping killings last night.

Members of the gangs have been witnessed singing about the joys of juvenile delinquency and lifting each other into the air by the waist. They also snap their fingers while crouching menacingly and leaping high into the air, witnesses have reported.

Krupke warned citizens to stay clear of the deadly street-prancing and elaborately staged musical numbers. He said the toughs can be identified by their headbands, three-quarter-length pants and form-fitting striped shirts, which have greatly helped them execute their terrifying string of dancing fights.

It's new... It's strange... It's filled with promise... It's...

"Tritium!"

Intense, blistering heat... withering radiation... devastating power... working together for you! Our scientists are using this wonder-material to make weapons that protect us all. Our goal is to make more and better tritium to help America fulfill its promise.

General Carbide
A division of International Tetrahedron, Inc.

INSIDE THIS ISSUE:

GENERAL MOTORS ENGINEERS INTRODUCE CHROME-PLATED CHROME
See page 5

L. RON HUBBARD'S NEW 'E-METER' MEASURES HUMAN GULLIBILITY
See page 3

LATEST EDITION

The Onion

Are You Drinking From the Correct Fountain?

Wednesday, November 9, 1960 — FINEST NEWS SOURCE IN AMERICA — ★★★ Price Five Cents

JOHN F. KENNEDY'S DAD DEFEATS NIXON

Millionaire Ex-Bootlegger's Life Ambition Realized, as Son Captures Presidency

Father of President-Elect to Fill Cabinet, Senate with Other Children

WASHINGTON, D.C.—In one of the most closely contested elections in U.S. history, Joseph P. Kennedy narrowly defeated Vice President Richard Nixon to become the father of the new President of the United States, John Fitzgerald Kennedy.

The outcome was in doubt until just before dawn Wednesday, when CBS News declared Kennedy Sr. the winner in Illinois by a thin margin. Kennedy's last-minute promise of that state's 29 electoral votes, along with four from Hawaii, whose polls closed at 1 a.m. EST, finally tipped the Electoral College in favor of the multi-millionaire former Ambassador to the United Kingdom.

"Vice President Nixon just called to congratulate me," the exhausted but jubilant patriarch told a group of over 500 supporters early this morning at his election-night headquarters at the Boston Sheraton Hotel. "He was very gracious in defeat and told me that the Eisenhower Administration will do everything it can to assure a smooth transition of power to my son."

The senior Kennedy thanked members of his campaign staff for their tireless efforts. "This is the most difficult undertaking I've endured since I got John into Harvard," he said.

Kennedy went on to say that this election was "especially trying in that it was really meant for my eldest son, Joe Jr., who was tragically killed in the War.

INSIDE THIS ISSUE:

LENNY BRUCE SHOULD LEARN THAT YOU DON'T HAVE TO SWEAR TO HAVE A GOOD TIME
Editorial, Page 16

ED GEIN DAZZLES PAPARAZZI WITH HUMAN-SKIN GOWN AT GALA *PSYCHO* PREMIERE
See pictures in Arts, Section C

He was the one I spent a lifetime grooming for the presidency. Thank you for supporting his understudy, my second son, John."

Kennedy also thanked "the gracious volunteers from the gambling, bootlegging and other legitimate industries, who were kind enough to use the occasion of my son's running for president to show their gratitude for the various services I've had the pleasure of rendering to them over the years."

He expressed particular appreciation for the efforts of two notable Chicagoans, Mayor Richard Daley and businessman Sam Giancana. He promised these campaign volunteers that his son would be magnanimously beholden to them once in office.

"Richard and Sam promised me Illinois, and damned if they didn't do it. They are two of the most skilled election-night campaign volunteers working in politics today."

Analysts believe voters chose Joe Kennedy over Nixon because of his proven ability to "get the job done" for his son. He engineered John's victory in the U.S. Senate in 1952, and pulled strings to win him the Pulitzer Prize in 1957.

The president-elect's father has pledged that he will do everything in his power to support the new president. He promised "continued determination and hard work" on behalf of his son and pledged that John would lead the nation into the 1960s.

"If he fails in this great task which I, and the American voters, have laid before him," Kennedy said, "he will suffer a severe reduction in allowance and may even be sent to bed without supper."

Kennedy has already assembled a number of family friends to oversee the presidential transition. One source close to Kennedy said he will likely fill his son's cabinet with his other sons, as well as with still more naive, untested scions of elite families of the East Coast Establishment.

"They will be the best and the brightest America has," Kennedy said. "I'll see to that."

Joseph Kennedy, father of the nation's 35th president.

Soviet Space Program Ahead in Dog-Killing Race

WASHINGTON, D.C.— An alarming report leaked by sources in Washington Tuesday indicates that the Russians may have killed three times as many dogs in space as the U.S., widening their lead in the dog-killing race between the superpowers.

The U.S. has trailed ever since Laika, the first dog killed in space, was launched into orbit aboard Sputnik II in 1957. Things have only gotten worse for the U.S. space program over the past three years.

The Soviets' latest satellite, Onegin II, is perhaps the most sobering indication of the Reds' dog-killing superiority. Launched last month, it features a special dog-terrifying chamber which caused the heart rate of its two canine passengers, Belka and Strelka, to reach near-fatal levels as they soared through outer space at 300 miles per second. The animals were cramped in a two-foot-square space during several orbits of Earth without food or water. Their starved corpses, faces frozen in fear, were recovered from the Black Sea Nov. 2.

The alarming report suggests that the Soviets may be able to build a space craft large enough to launch, orbit, scare the shit out of, then kill a chimpanzee by as early as next year.

"U.S. scientists have not yet considered using small chambers, poor oxygen facilities or

Laika, the first Russian dog killed in space.

food deprivation. We have much to learn from the Russians," said U.S. Sen. Joseph O'Mahoney (D-Wyo.), who has urged the U.S. to step up its dog-killing program.

President Eisenhower assured the nation that there is nothing to worry about. "America is the world leader in the killing of dogs, monkeys and any animals you would care to name," he told reporters.

John F. Kennedy took a stronger stand in a stump speech in San Francisco Monday, saying, "I pledge that by 1970, the United States will send a goat to the moon, kill that goat, and then return it safely to the Earth."

OUR FIRST HANDSOME PRESIDENT

With his victory over Richard Nixon, John F. Kennedy made history Tuesday, becoming the first handsome man to occupy the White House.

Aside from Kennedy, only Thomas Jefferson, president from 1801 to 1809, is considered by historians to be mildly attractive.

"George Washington, Abraham Lincoln and Franklin Roosevelt were all great presidents, but you wouldn't really look twice at any of them," said Amherst College's Henry Steele Commager. "And as far as Martin Van Buren and Chester Arthur go, you're talking downright ugly."

Experts cite Kennedy's strong jaw, twinkling blue eyes, wavy brown hair and straight white teeth as important factors in his good looks.

Commager cautioned, however, that these features are not by any means the sole reason for Kennedy's historic defeat of Nixon.

"There are certainly other factors to consider," Commager said, "such as the fact that Richard Nixon is a pointy-chinned, jowl-faced dog of a man."

JFK to Lead Nation in Good-Natured Game of Touch Football

HYANNISPORT, Mass.— Speaking to supporters, President-elect Kennedy pledged Tuesday night to lead the nation's 180 million citizens in a good-natured game of touch football on the lawn of his family's estate Sunday.

Kennedy said the spirited yet casual game will symbolize America's innocence and bright future and be not so much a competition as a metaphor for American spirit and teamwork.

Everyone will have a chance to participate, he said, even the ladies. His young wife Jackie, looking both demure and athletic in one of her husband's old sport shirts, will join the women of America as they cheer from the sidelines.

The president-elect pledged to wear comfortable chinos and a faded Harvard sweatshirt during the game.

The Onion

Mind Your Manners | **Sanitized for Your Protection**

Saturday, January 21, 1961 — FINEST NEWS SOURCE IN AMERICA — ★★★ Price Five Cents

Eisenhower Warns of Military-Industrial-Oedipal Complex

Nation Increasingly Jealous of Relationship Between Pentagon, Big Business

'America Must Become Aware of Its Deep-Seated National Feelings,' Ike Says

WASHINGTON, D.C. — President Eisenhower, in his farewell address to the nation, warned Friday of the "growing, unwarranted influence of the military-industrial-Oedipal complex," which he said threatens to "undermine the most primal foundations" of society.

"It is, perhaps, natural," Eisenhower said, "that we Americans find ourselves snuggled so deeply in the protective, maternal bosom of the defense-contracting industry that we come to be jealous of—and at times, even loathe—the paternalistic military machine to which it is wedded. Nevertheless, it is vital for the future of our American family that we come to see the armed forces not as a rival for the affections of General Electric or McDonnell-Douglas, but as a stern yet loving hand, capable of imparting great wisdom and moving us beyond the era of international adolescence."

Eisenhower appealed directly to the American people, asking them to demand that Congress hold regular, private, tri-weekly "sessions" with President Kennedy for the next four years. "By meeting regularly with the president in his office, your elected representatives will, over time, make fully conscious our country's deep-seated ambivalence about its own aggressive instincts. Only by bringing this ambivalence to the surface can we as a nation reconcile our military-industrial 'parents' with each other. Then, and only then, can America move forward and, with a new-found sense of individuality, establish a mature, stable relationship with the rest of the world."

The outgoing president urged Kennedy to shy away from "brash statements or strongly voiced opinions" about isolationism, the Suez crisis, CIA involvement in foreign politics, and early bed-wetting. "It is time to focus not on rhetoric, but on the issues—the latent, unconscious, primordial, archetypal issues that conflict millions of hard-working Americans every day."

But Eisenhower, who has met several times with Kennedy since his victory over Richard Nixon last November, seemed optimistic about the future. "What is needed now is a national transference, and, so long as his words and deeds encourage dialogue and uncover long-repressed memories of youth and idealism—and so long as he remains healthy—I believe Mr. Kennedy has the capacity to be projected upon more than any other president in history."

Speaking from his family's retreat on Cape Cod, Kennedy said he was "appreciative" of Eisenhower's comments and vowed to continue the psychological accomplishments of his administration. "Let the word go forth to friend and foe alike," Kennedy said. "The torch has been passed to a new generation of neo-Freudians, born in this century, tempered by war, disciplined by a hard and bitter peace, and alarmed by an eerie attraction to our mothers and hatred of our fathers."

The TM-61 Matador missile, a potent symbol of the complex.

Jet-Age Technology to Revolutionize Hand-Drying

Miracle 'Electric Towel' Is Germ-Free
Paper Waste Eliminated Forever
Ultra-Modern 'Swivel Nozzle' Allows Drying of Face, as Well

CINCINNATI, Ohio — The future is here.

A spokesman for Andrews & Hoyt, a Cincinnati-based industrial-appliance manufacturer, announced Friday that the company has perfected a revolutionary new "towelless" hand-drying device.

According to Lawrence Hoyt Jr., the device, which was developed using Jet-Age technology, will forever change the world of hand-drying.

"Just imagine going to the public rest room and drying your hands at the push of a button," said Hoyt, as he unveiled the device at the Greater Midwest Product Expo in Cleveland. "Never again will you have to use unsanitary towel paper, which can spread disease and cause severe chafing."

"This," Hoyt said, "is the promise of the Jet Age fulfilled, a pinnacle of modern technological achievement."

To facilitate operation of the futuristic device by laymen, a comprehensive list of instructions will be provided on a chrome plate affixed to the front panel of each unit.

Hoyt said he believes that, if these instructions are followed, hand-drying will reach a new era of convenience. "Once you push the 'On' button, then rub your hands gently under the warm air, the hand-drying device will turn off automatically."

He added that, following the proper execution of the Jet-Age hand-drying procedure, wiping hands on pants will be an unthinkable course of action.

The Jet-Dry Hand-E-Blo, developed by Andrews & Hoyt over a three-year period at a cost of $11 million, boasts a three-horsepower motor which blows a pleasant stream of warm air on the user's hands until they are dry. Its "On" button is of the same design as those on all the NASA rocketships. "This is a state-of-the-art button," Hoyt said.

Andrews & Hoyt, best known for its mid-'50s development of what would eventually become the "Wet-Nap" moist towelette, expects to have the new automated hand dryers installed in every public rest room in the U.S. by 1963.

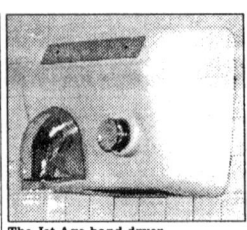

The Jet-Age hand dryer.

U.S. Cigar Lovers Call for Overthrow of Castro

Ike Holds Emergency Meeting with Top Cigar Aficionados

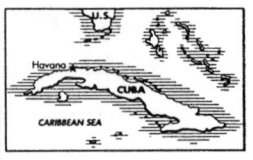

HAVANA, Cuba — American cigar lovers are calling for the reinstatement of President Fulgencio Batista, whose recent overthrow by Communist guerrilla Fidel Castro has resulted in their being cut off from fine Cuban cigars.

"Communism must not be allowed to take root in Cuba," said Kenneth Landau, a real-estate developer and golf enthusiast from Palm Springs, Calif. "The thought of all those smokeables just 90 miles off the coast of Florida, with no way to get them into the country—much less the country club—is frightening."

"What am I supposed to smoke with my brandy, now that Cuba has cut herself off from trade with the U.S.?" asked Manhattan corporate attorney J. Walter Ruethven. "I'm certainly not going to settle for some cheap, poorly rolled American cigar. What kind of way is that to unwind? There must be some way to get that Castro out of there."

Meeting with top U.S. cigar aficionados at the White House Friday, then-President Eisenhower expressed concern and assured them that his successor will work closely with CIA Chief Allen Dulles to resolve the crisis.

"Unlike ourselves, Castro and his gang of Communist thugs have no appreciation for the finer things in life," Eisenhower told the esteemed smokers during a special four-hour Oval Office meeting. "He has no understanding of how nice it is to sit back in your favorite leather chair and light up a premium Coronado after a long, hard day at the office. Or how nice it is to smoke an aromatic Perfecto after sinking that 15-foot putt on the 18th hole to put you two strokes up and nail the victory. Castro and his band of godless barbarians lack all such sensibility. Are these the kinds of neighbors the U.S. wants to keep? I think not."

Ruethven expressed hope that the U.S. military under Kennedy would act fast. "I am planning to purchase a brand-new '61 Eldorado convertible next summer," he said, "and all will be lost if I don't have a decent cigar to smoke while driving it to my beach house in the Hamptons. That Castro fink will pay dearly if I don't have one of Havana's finest in my hand by then."

INSIDE THIS ISSUE:

AMERICA'S BOUT OF CONSTIPATION ENTERS 10TH YEAR
See page 26

BETTIE PAGE SPANKED BY AUTHORITIES
See page 3

| Proudly Ignoring Our President's Adultery | # The Onion | *Camelot!* |

Monday, April 17, 1961   FINEST NEWS SOURCE IN AMERICA   ★★★ Price Seven Cents

OUTER SPACE FALLS TO COMMUNISTS

MEDICAL NEWS

New Birth-Control Pill Expected to Greatly Reduce Unwanted Marriages

After nearly two years in development, Enovid-10, the first-ever commercially produced birth-control pill, is now available in the U.S. The new pill, which stops conception using hormones that fool the female body into thinking it is already pregnant, is expected to prevent upwards of 500,000 unwanted marriages a year.

"Every year in America, hundreds of thousands of sexually active young women unintentionally become married," said Dr. Gregory Pincus, the pill's creator, "By using Enovid-10, single women can now have all the sex they want with absolutely no fear of becoming burdened with a husband, a wedding or a lifetime of commitment."

No longer reliant on the flawed marriage-control devices of ages past, women across America are hailing the pill as a major breakthrough.

"The pill seems like a much better way to avoid an unplanned marriage than the methods my friends have been using, such as suicide and the convent," said 19-year-old Christina Wyler of Stockton, Calif.

Said Indianapolis wife and mother Doris Tepper, 21, "If only they had that pill three years ago when I became unintentionally married after a night of unprotected passion in the back seat of my boyfriend's car! Now I'm forced to spend the rest of my life caring for a husband I never planned on having."

More than 1.6 million marriages were reported last year in the U.S. That number is expected to drop by as much as 60 percent by 1970.

INSIDE THIS ISSUE:

NEWLY FORMED PEACE CORPS TO RID YOUNG AMERICANS OF IDEALISTIC DELUSIONS
Page 3

AUTHOR ERNEST HEMINGWAY SHOOTS LIONS, SELF
Page 18

Russian Man Is First in Orbit

Will a Statue of Lenin Look Down on Us from the Moon?

Alarmed Legislators Slash Education Budget to Fund Space Race

At 10 p.m. EST Sunday, the Russians launched a man into orbit around the Earth, claiming the heavens in the name of Communism.

"The Russians have captured space," Pentagon spokesman John Powell said in a somber official statement. "The national-security implications of this event are chilling, as the United States is now surrounded by 360 degrees of Communist-occupied vacuum."

In a mission lasting nearly two hours, Russian communaut and vanquisher of millions of square miles of outer space Yuri Gagarin orbited once around the Earth at an altitude of 200 miles. It is unknown to which planets he may have directed his craft to plant the flag of the Union of Soviet Socialist Republics.

In a statement to the press early this morning, President Kennedy pledged a swift U.S. response, warning of the dangers of an interplanetary "domino effect."

"If the moon falls to Communists, the planets may follow," he said. "Soon, if we do not act, our entire solar system could be under Communist rule."

Kennedy warned that, if Soviet scientists in space should ever come into contact with an intelligent life form from the outer planets, the beings might be brainwashed into supporting Communism before they can be reached by God's word and the U.S. Constitution.

The president met with CIA officials last night to discuss the possibility of conducting a covert outer-space coup.

The result of that meeting, according to inside sources, is a tentative plan to secretly arm and train space guerrillas to overthrow the Communists and install a solar-system government that is friendly to the United States.

American scientists are shocked by the Russian capture of outer space, which by all rights should be the exclusive domain of America. Scrambling to make sense of the defeat, they have so far been unable to determine how the Communists, unaided by the manifest destiny bestowed by God upon the United States, were able to out-perform America in the race to the greatest frontier of all.

"This is a terrible blow to our quest for control of the fertile farmlands of Venus, Mars and the moon," NASA spokesman Harvey Teideman said. "The rich mineral resources of those territories are now under the direct control of Khrushchev's Red Army."

Teideman, along with other top NASA officials, has urged Congress to gut the nation's education and social-welfare programs and put more money toward the nation's space budget.

"Perhaps we cannot defeat the Soviet space fleet with our technology just yet," Teideman said. "But if we can, at the very least, launch a probe capable of distributing Bibles and American flags to all the planets in the solar system, it would be a great accomplishment, indeed."

Experts Say Teen Dance Shows May Be Symptomatic of Larger Problem

PRINCETON, N.J.—Top psychologists, therapists and behavioral scientists at Princeton's Institute for Family Studies released findings Friday indicating that popular teen dance programs on television, such as *American Bandstand*, may pose a long-range threat to American domestic stability.

Dr. Marwood Lohr, the psychiatric expert who conducted the 18-month study, detailed disturbing aspects of the trend, including the rumored existence of a mythical "Land of 1,000 Dances," where all responsibility is replaced by an infinite series of hedonistic gyrations.

"If we don't nip *American Bandstand* in the bud," Lohr said, "it will not stop with dancing. Within 10 years, we may have a full-blown 'youth culture' on our hands—a phenomenon which could sound the death knell of the well-ordered America we hold dear."

Lohr called upon the three television networks to replace all teen dance programs with dramatic plays about life during the Great Depression.

Yuri Gagarin, first man in space, has claimed the heavens for the Reds.

Kennedy at Berlin Wall: 'Ich Bin Ein Ivy-League Playboy Millionaire'

President Kennedy speaking in Berlin.

BERLIN—President Kennedy, speaking before a crowd of 150,000 West Germans near the Berlin Wall Sunday, was greeted with wild applause when he opened his speech in the German tongue, proclaiming, "Ich bin ein Ivy League playboy millionaire."

"People of the German Democratic Republic, I am proud and happy to be speaking to you on this momentous occasion," said Kennedy, making his first European visit since taking office. "I am also incredibly rich. Jawohl, meine Freunden, ich bin ein millionaire. Ich bin ein seriously loaded multimillionaire."

Continued Kennedy: "I hope to increase the exchange of great ideas between our nations. Although, I must admit, I have the advantage of receiving an education far superior to most of yours—and, in fact, to most anyone's. Ich bin ein privileged, blue-blood Harvard man."

"We must work hard in these difficult times to further the ideals of democracy and stand firm in the face of encroaching Communism," Kennedy said, concluding his speech. "Actually, you must do this. I do not: Because of my great wealth and status, while America's best and brightest deal with the daily cares of national stewardship, I intend to split my time between hosting wild parties at Mafia-owned casinos and bedding starlets in my secret underground White House love bunker. For ich bin ein freewheeling playboy."

Kennedy concluded by thanking those in attendance, whom he called, "You sausage-chomping Krauts who murdered my older brother Joe, who should have been president instead of me."

The speech, which was "very well-received," according to West Berlin Mayor Willy Brandt, is regarded as even more rousing than Kennedy's "Je suis un damn handsome sonofabitch" address in Paris last Friday.

97

| Congratulations to delivery boy **Timmy McKune** celebrating his 46th year with The Onion. | # The Onion | Steadfastly Ignoring Social Unrest |

Monday, October 29, 1962 — FINEST NEWS SOURCE IN AMERICA — ★★★ Price Seven Cents

ALLEN FUNT LETS PRESIDENT IN ON HILARIOUS 'CUBAN MISSILE CRISIS' PRANK

Relieved Kennedy Laughs Heartily after Learning of Elaborate International Gag

JFK a Good Sport, Says Host of TV's *Candid Camera*

President Kennedy and Candid Camera host Allen Funt enjoy a hearty laugh over the elaborate Cuban Missile gag.

WASHINGTON, D.C.—A period of intense national tittering came to a hilarious end early Monday morning, when notorious prankster and *Candid Camera* host Allen Funt ended his most elaborate gag to date by letting President Kennedy in on the "Cuban Missile Crisis" that has kept America in stitches since last week.

Following a briefing by the "Joint Chiefs of Staff" (in actuality, professional actors) about the latest developments in the crisis, Kennedy was surprised by a loud knock at the Oval Office door. Funt, who has passed himself off as Nikita Khrushchev for the last two weeks in a series of increasingly implausible televised speeches, walked unimpeded through a phalanx of "Secret Service agents" and approached the president.

"Didn't mean to 'rush-in' like that, Comrade Presidentski," a straight-faced, Russian-accented Funt told the president, "but I am havink somethink important vith vich to be tellink you."

According to Arthur Schlesinger Jr., special advisor to the president and one of the prank's principal conspirators, the confused Kennedy then turned to his brother, Attorney General Robert Kennedy, who had "turned beet-red and was biting his knuckle" to keep from bursting into laughter.

"At that point," Schlesinger said, "I think Jack figured out something was up."

Funt then pointed to a portrait of Lincoln hanging on the wall. "Vee hef been spyink on you zis whole time," the would-be Soviet premier told Kennedy, "through zat portrait. Vee hef caught you on film from ze beginning of zis crisis. Only, perhaps it is not so big a crisis as you thought, no?"

National Security Affairs Special Assistant McGeorge Bundy proceeded to remove the picture, revealing a smiling, waving cameraman. As the room exploded in laughter, the commander-in-chief finally figured it out. "I don't believe it!" the embarrassed president said. "*Candid Camera!* And all of you knew? You guys! All right, you got me. I admit it, you got me."

"I've been planning this one since election night, 1960," said Funt, speaking to a White House press corps which, since March 16, 1961, has played along with him, dutifully reporting the latest "news" of the crisis. "But it got kicked into high gear after the Bay of Pigs. I think JFK kept waiting for the camera to pop up after that happened. Once he believed the situation was real, I knew his guard would be down. Still, it took me and [Defense Secretary] Bob [McNamara] months to come up with just the right scenario. I wanted to make sure we really zinged him. But give a lot of credit to Jackie, Bobby, the Cabinet, and a seemingly terrified public. They went along with the whole thing beautifully."

Kennedy praised the prank as "the funniest oval-office gag since the squirting red phone."

A two-hour collection of highlights of Kennedy's reactions to the crisis will be broadcast on CBS next Tuesday at 8 p.m. EST. "I'm going to co-host it with the president himself," said Funt. "He's going to take me through his thoughts as we watch him agonize about the nation's future. He's handled the whole thing with such humor and good grace. It's like I've always said: There's nothing more refreshing than a little egg on the face!"

James Meredith Becomes First Negro Student Beaten at U. of Miss.

OXFORD, Miss.—James Meredith, who made national news last month when he became the first negro student to enroll at the University of Mississippi, broke down yet another barrier Sunday when he became the first negro student beaten at the school.

The historic beating took place at 1:30 a.m. EST, in Meredith's Baxter Hall dormitory room. According to reports, Meredith was asleep when a group of approximately 20 unidentified male students broke into his room and attacked him with fists and baseball bats until campus police broke up the brawl four hours later.

"This is a first for Ole Miss and a momentous day for the state of Mississippi," Gov. Ross Barnett said of the campus' first-ever negro-student beating. "Walls are truly coming down."

Despite the beating, as well as the awkwardness of being flanked by U.S. Marshals at all times while on campus, Meredith is enjoying his experience at the University of Mississippi, school officials said.

"In accordance with last month's Supreme Court ruling, Mr. Meredith is enjoying the company of a great many federally enforced friends," said Ole Miss Dean of Students Richard Hughes.

"I think he's a great guy and a terrific pal," said freshman Larry Madsen under a federal court order.

Meredith said that, in the coming year, he hopes to avoid becoming the first negro student lynched at Ole Miss.

Art Critics Call Campbell's New Tomato Soup 'Brilliant'

Soup Maker Hailed for 'Pop Art' Commentary on Rampant Commercialism in American Culture

12-Ounce Can Fetches $100,000 at Manhattan Grocery Store

Campbell's Soup is drawing rave reviews from the world's art critics, who hail the soup maker's new "Tomato" soup "a brilliant post-modern commentary on the all-pervasiveness of consumerism in modern life."

Art dealers from New York to Paris are bidding astronomical sums for the 12-ounce cans, normally priced at 33 cents. This week, a can at a Manhattan grocery fetched $100,000.

According to New York art collector Manfred Havill, who paid $80,000 for a can at Sol's Corner Grocery in Queens Friday, "This soup savagely lampoons the unwelcome, insidious intrusion of crass commercialism into everyday life and modern popular culture. This is Campbell's greatest masterpiece since 'Cream of Mushroom.'"

The art originates from a small collective of artists calling themselves "The Campbell's Canning Factory" in Gary, Indiana.

Campbell's Soup CEO Herbert Leonard, 53, said he is mystified by the success of the can.

"It's just soup," Leonard said. "My company's products have no more artistic significance than, say, a box of Brillo pads."

Hoover Vows to Stop Martin Luther King Jr.'s Dangerous Non-Violence Movement

WASHINGTON, D.C.—Citing "a grave threat to the well-being of all Americans," FBI Director J. Edgar Hoover announced Sunday that he will do "whatever it takes" to stop the non-violent peace movement of Dr. Martin Luther King Jr.

"America has bravely stood up to countless threats throughout its history, from British imperialism to the Axis Powers of World War II," Hoover said. "But never have we faced something so insidious as King's campaign of change through voting, non-violent demonstrations, and preaching 'love thy neighbor.'"

"There is no place for this dangerous idea of 'love' in the United States," Hoover said.

According to Hoover, "This agitator King, driven by an insatiable lust for respect and equality, has used radical tactics ranging from boycotts to peaceful assembly."

According to Hoover, the boycott of local businesses, in which King and others refuse to patronize businesses which do not fall in line with their political beliefs, is a vicious, underhanded practice.

"A prolonged boycott can send the message to a business owner, 'I do not want to patronize your business, because I do not agree with your policies.' Is this the kind of consumer we want? One who would make such demands of the hard-working American businessman? I think not."

FBI director J. Edgar Hoover.

Equally chilling, said Hoover, is the "sit-down strike," in which King lackeys not only sit down in a pre-selected location, but refuse to move, letting nothing dissuade them from their cruel sitting. "These negro trouble-makers have been known to sit at a lunch counter, order a sandwich, and sit and eat it, sometimes occupying the seat for up to 40 minutes," Hoover said.

But perhaps the most dangerous practice of King's thugs, the FBI director said, is the "march."

"King's horrifying marches," Hoover said, "unleash vast hordes of civil-rights protesters on the streets and byways of America, thousands of pairs of feet striking the pavement in an unyielding pageant of terror."

To combat the menace, Hoover has asked Congress for $4 million to fund remote-surveillance equipment to monitor King's sexual activities.

The Onion

Outlaw the Tambourine

Pray Our Popes Stop Dying

Wednesday, July 17, 1963   FINEST NEWS SOURCE IN AMERICA   ★★★ Price Seven Cents

SINATRA WARNS RUSSKIES TO KNOCK IT OFF

Singer Gives Khrushchev 24 Hours to 'Drop This Commie Bunk or It's Ring-a-Ding-Ding for You Bozos'

Calls Soviet Premier a 'World-Class Knucklehead'

Frank Sinatra.

LAS VEGAS—With Communism continuing to spread across the globe from Cuba to Indochina, singer Frank Sinatra issued a strongly worded ultimatum Tuesday from his penthouse suite at the Sands Hotel & Casino, warning Soviet Premier Nikita Khrushchev to "Knock it off, or I'll knock it off for you, buster."

"If those clowns over at the Politburo don't cut this Communism bunk ASAP, I'm gonna have no choice but to crack some skulls," said Sinatra, surrounded by an entourage of business associates and close friends, including Dean Martin, Sammy Davis Jr. and Peter Lawford. "Nobody's gonna put up with this garbage while Frankie and his boys are in town."

Sinatra also had strong words for the Communist regime of North Vietnam and their funding of Vietcong guerrillas in the South. "You better watch it, too, gooks, if you know what's good for you. I don't have time for your slanty-eyed schemes."

Added Sinatra: "A Commie is just like a broad. You gotta make sure they know their place, or they'll walk all over you."

After giving the Russians 24 hours to withdraw all missiles from Eastern Europe, Sinatra concluded his press conference with a medley of Sammy Cahn tunes, including "All the Way," "Come Fly with Me" and "Call Me Irresponsible."

Sinatra first became involved in the fight against Communism last Friday, when President Kennedy called him to the White House for a top-secret one-on-one debriefing. Upon learning the full details of the situation, Sinatra urged Kennedy to let him "show those lousy pinkos who's boss" by deploying several key members of the Rat Pack to Moscow to "knock some sense into Khrushchev and his jerko cronies."

"I'm sick of these Commie numbskulls and all their monkeying around in the Third World," Sinatra told Kennedy, according to a report in Tuesday's *Washington Post*. "Just give me and Dean five minutes with these bozos, and I guarantee you they'll be whistling a different tune."

Among the measures Sinatra called for during his two-hour meeting with Kennedy: an increased U.S. military presence in Southeast Asia, $30 million to develop new surveillance technologies, and a double scotch on the rocks.

"These Russkies have been a pain in the neck long enough," Sinatra said. "We gotta show these punks who's running the show."

Sinatra said that before he makes any move, he plans to head down to the track at Santa Ana, where a certain pony in the ninth race is a shoo-in to make him some big bucks.

"This filly's name is Jubilee, and let's just say I have it on good authority that she's a can't-miss sweetheart bet at 20-to-1," Sinatra said. "Ava Gardner ain't got nothing on this little dame."

Jackie Kennedy Wins Nobel Hair Prize

First Lady Jacqueline Kennedy, renowned patron of the arts and internationally recognized fashion trendsetter, was awarded the prestigious Nobel Prize for Hair Tuesday.

Lauded by the Nobel Committee for her perfect coiffure and the important work she had done on her hair each morning, Kennedy is responsible for crucial advancements in follicle-body enhancement, having pioneered the innovative "bouffant" style.

Kennedy announced she will put the money toward the construction of the Jackie Institute, a facility dedicated to the development of better shampoos and more resilient hair sprays.

Kennedy won the Pulitzer last year for Most Distinguished Offsetting of Hat without Distracting from Hair.

U.S. Spies Discover What Lies Beneath Russian Nesting Dolls; 'It's More Dolls,' Says CIA Director

LANGLEY, Va.—CIA Director John McCone announced Tuesday that the agency has succeeded in revealing the secret locked inside the wooden Russian "nesting" doll knick-knacks.

"Inside these innocent-seeming dolls, crafted in the innocuous likeness of a babushka-clad Russian peasant woman, lurk more dolls," McCone said. "Each subsequent doll in this disturbing progression also bears the likeness of a member of a babushka-clad Russian peasant family. The disturbing implications of creeping Communist influence are obvious."

CIA officials said the dolls, samples of which were purchased in the Russian neighborhood of Brighton Beach, New York, are "almost certainly" an anatomically accurate representation of an actual Russian. Plans have been made to surgically test this hypothesis on the next Russian captured by CIA operatives.

Adlai Stevenson Sends Away for Charles Atlas Muscle-Building Plan

Will General Westmoreland's Insult Make a Man out of Adlai?

Charles Atlas on TV.

Adlai Stevenson.

WASHINGTON, D.C.—Three-time failed presidential hopeful Adlai Stevenson, claiming that he is "'fed up' with seeing the huskies walk off with the best of everything," filled out and mailed a magazine coupon for Charles Atlas' "Dynamic Tension" muscle-building plan Tuesday.

Stevenson's decision to build up his body in the natural way recommended by Atlas was made following events at Saturday's White House beach outing, when General William J. Westmoreland kicked sand in the face of Stevenson and his wife.

"I merely asked the general to stop kicking sand in our faces, and my wife commented that he was the worst nuisance on the beach," Stevenson said. Sources close to Stevenson report that Westmoreland replied by grasping him by his thin, stick-like arm and brandishing a fist menacingly.

"See here, beanpole," the general is reported as saying, "I oughta wallop you one right now—but you're so skinny you'd probably just dry up and blow away." He then laughed and ran off with a beach ball, leaving Stevenson shaken.

"I commented to Mrs. Stevenson that Westmoreland was a big bully, and that I'd get even some day," Stevenson said. "But she just said, 'Oh, don't let it bother you, little boy!' That's when I became ashamed of my scrawny, 97-pound-runt frame."

Stevenson added that he is "sick and tired of being a scarecrow. And Charles Atlas says he can give me a real body! I decided to gamble a stamp and get his free book!"

Atlas, when asked what results Stevenson could expect, was optimistic.

"Dynamic Tension builds muscles fast!" said Atlas, who has been awarded the title of The World's Most Perfectly Developed Man. "Later, after building up his body the natural way—without springs, weights or pulleys—I expect Adlai to stand in front of a mirror, flexing his powerful new muscles and saying to himself, 'Boy! It didn't take long for Atlas' plan to do this for me! What muscles! That General Westmoreland won't shove *me* around again!'"

Stevenson agreed with Atlas' predictions. "When next I confront the general, I won't be afraid," he said. "I'll say, 'What! You here again? Here's something I owe you!' and give him one on the chin." Stevenson noted that, along with Atlas' 32-page illustrated book, he would receive five free gifts: outline courses on jiu-jitsu/karate, boxing, wrestling, feats of strength and hang balancing, all of which would aid him in defeating even a skilled military man such as Westmoreland.

"Mrs. Stevenson will see that I am a real man, after all," said Stevenson. Passersby will say, 'Gosh! What a build!' and I'll soon be famous for it."

Stevenson would not comment on the possibility that he will become "hero of the beach."

INSIDE THIS ISSUE:

RED CROSS BRACES FOR BEGINNING OF '63 SCHOOL YEAR
Page 12

SHOCKING NEW BOOK ALLEGES TOXIC CHEMICALS BAD FOR ENVIRONMENT
Page 16

The Onion

Celebrating Our National Innocence — **Printed on Non-Rolling Paper**

Thursday, August 29, 1963 — FINEST NEWS SOURCE IN AMERICA — ★★★ Price Seven Cents

KENNEDY, GIANCANA SIGN HISTORIC BIMBO-SHARING ACCORD

President Kennedy.   *Sam Giancana.*

PITTSBURGH, Pa.—After more than eight hours of tense negotiations, President Kennedy and noted mobster Sam Giancana reached a historic bimbo-sharing accord Wednesday night.

The closed-door meeting was held at Jimmie's 32nd Street Pub in Pittsburgh, a neutral spot chosen for its safe distance from both Kennedy-controlled Washington and Giancana-controlled Chicago.

The accord provides for the mutual proprietorship and joint utilization of over 200 actresses, models, socialites and baseball players' ex-wives, most of whom were listed by name in an appendix to the document. The accord between the two prominent U.S. leaders is one of the most important bimbo-sharing measures to come about this year, according to White House officials.

"This will not only ensure the safety of the leader of our nation," said Peter Loehr, White House Nocturnal Activities Aide, "but it will also provide a steady supply of high-quality tail for years to come."

Hours of deliberation took place to determine the specifics of the accord, which detailed guidelines and procedures for bimbo-sharing over the next four years. Though Kennedy and Giancana disagreed on many fine points, they were able to quickly come to the consensus that blondes should be given "most-favored-bimbo" status, while brunettes and redheads should be granted special immunity for "wanting it too much."

The negotiations, which stalled in their early stages due to a conflict over 26-year-old aspiring actress Judith Campbell, moved forward again when Kennedy agreed to put more on the bargaining table.

A deal was reached when Giancana was granted special access to Attorney General Robert Kennedy, and inclusion in special government projects such as assassinations and military coups.

As part of the deal, the attorney general was granted access to select blondes.

Boy Bitten by Radioactive Spider Dies of Leukemia

Peter Parker, 17, Was Avid Student of Science, Photography

NEW YORK—Peter Parker, a 17-year-old high-school student bitten by a radioactive spider during an atomic-sciences demonstration Aug. 20, died at New York's Bellevue Hospital Wednesday night of complications resulting from leukemia.

Parker, who was described by friends as very interested in the sciences—and who had already earned a scholarship to attend Empire State University next fall—was standing near a display demonstrating the transmission of radioactive beams when an ordinary spider fell through the rays and onto Parker's arm, biting him in its death throes. Parker almost immediately felt dizzy and sick and was later taken to Bellevue by his Aunt May.

"This was no ordinary case of leukemia," said attendant physician Dr. Henry Pym, an expert in the field of radioactive-insect-induced cancers. "This ripped through young Peter's body almost overnight, affecting his reflexes, destroying his coordination, sapping his strength and scrambling his senses to the point where all the boy could detect was a constant tingling. It's almost as if this hyper-irradiated cancer had the proportionate strength and speed of a spider."

"All of us at Empire State University's Department of Atomic Studies offer our deepest condolences to the Parker family at this tragic time," said Atomic Sciences professor Hank Connor. "Peter was a brilliant student, a talented photographer and an upstanding young man. He taught us all that the power of the atom is great—and with great power must come great responsibility." Empire State will reportedly dedicate a physics scholarship in Parker's name.

Parker's death marks the sixth atomic-accident fatality in the last month, arriving on the heels of Reed Richards, Ben Grimm, and Susan and John Storm all succumbing to cosmic rays during the maiden flight of Richards' experimental rocket, and U.S. Department of Defense scientist Bruce Banner's irradiation by the Gamma Bomb, a weapon of his own devising.

Martin Luther King: 'I Had a Really Weird Dream Last Night'

Martin Luther King, standing at the Lincoln Memorial, reports his dream to 250,000 people.

WASHINGTON, D.C.—Standing before a sea of 250,000 people at the Lincoln Memorial Wednesday, civil-rights leader Dr. Martin Luther King Jr. delivered a stirring speech about "this really weird dream I had last night."

King detailed at length his dream's bizarre, seemingly nonsensical images, offering a rare glimpse into what lies beyond the famed non-violence-movement leader's conscious mind.

King delivered the speech, reproduced below in its entirety, to a hushed crowd that had gathered at the National Mall in a massive, unified call for civil rights:

I had a really weird dream last night.

I had a dream in which I was in Yankee Stadium, but it was not really Yankee Stadium. It seemed more like a combination of Yankee Stadium and my house. And there I stood, for reasons not known to me, in the shadow of the bleachers of that great stadium.

I had a dream.

I had a dream in which the great stadium became filled with circus animals. Whether these animals came from a circus or zoo, I am not certain. And, as I walked through the congregation of animals, it became obvious to me that I did not walk alone. I noticed that I was joined by my friend, Morton Walsh, whom I know from law school. I do not know why he was there suddenly, but it occurs to me now that I had been thinking of him just the other day while going through some old papers from that time.

Brothers and sisters, I had a dream.

I had a dream in which I soon realized my friend was no longer Morton Walsh, but was now TV funnyman Jackie Gleason. And the scene became not one of tranquility. No, it was now obvious to me that Jackie Gleason and I were in danger from a giant roll of paper towels. Why there was such an object, I do not know, but that roll of paper towels struck within the depths of our souls a raging fear, and we ran from the monstrosity as quickly as our legs could carry us. But we did not move. As mightily as we tried to lift our feet, it seemed an invisible quicksand kept us from moving them. We could not outrun the giant household item.

I had a dream last night.

I had a dream in which we somehow overcame our inability to move and found ourselves in exile in an underground cave. But it was more than an underground cave. It was as if we were on a concrete path in some sort of futuristic city. In this city they had flying automobiles, and people dressed in strange costumes. And Jackie Gleason was no longer with me. Now, my mother was there. I do not know why.

I say to you today, my friends, I had a dream.

I had a dream in which I was then standing high atop a futuristic highway, in great danger of being struck by one of the flying autos. I then heard a great bell toll. It was a military warning siren that was calling my mother and me into our barracks. Somehow, I understood that, in this future world, people are called into their barracks at regimented times. That was the way things worked in the dream. What I did not realize at the time was that this tolling had actually been the sound of my bedside alarm clock going off.

My alarm rang! My alarm clock rang from a great mountain top. It rang from sea to shining sea.

I woke up and said, 'I am awake at last. Awake at last. Thank God, Almighty. I am awake at last.'

I do not have the slightest notion what my dream meant.

INSIDE THIS ISSUE:

AMAZING NEW MICRO-COMPUTER FITS IN ONE ROOM
Page 7

EARTH'S FOSSIL FUELS WILL LAST FOREVER, GEOLOGISTS SAY
Page 11

| LATE EDITION | The Onion | Take a Moment to Remember Where You Are |

Friday, November 22, 1963 — FINEST NEWS SOURCE IN AMERICA — ★★★ Price Seven Cents

KENNEDY SLAIN BY CIA, MAFIA, CASTRO, LBJ, TEAMSTERS, FREEMASONS

President Shot 129 Times from 43 Different Angles

DALLAS, Tex.—President Kennedy was assassinated Friday by operatives of the CIA, the Giancana crime syndicate, Fidel Castro, Vice President Johnson, the Freemasons and the Teamsters as he rode through downtown Dallas in a motorcade.

According to eyewitnesses, Kennedy's limousine had just entered Dealey Plaza when the president was struck 129 times in the head, chest, abdomen, arms, legs, hands, feet, back and face by gunfire. The shooting began at 12:30 p.m. and lasted until 12:43 p.m. CST.

In all, 43 suspects have been taken into the custody of the Dallas police.

Preliminary reports indicate that hitmen for the Giancana crime syndicate fired from a nearby grassy knoll, CIA agents fired from an office building slightly off the parade route, Cuban nationals fired from an overpass overlooking Dealey Plaza, an elite hit squad working for Teamsters President Jimmy Hoffa fired from perches atop an oak tree, a 'lone nut' fired from the Texas Book Depository, a shadow-government sharp-shooting team fired from behind a wooden fence, a consortium of jealous husbands fired from an estimated 13 sites on the sidewalk along the route, a hitman working for Johnson fired from a sewer grate over which the limousine passed, and Texas Gov. John Connally lunged at the president from within the limousine itself, slitting the president's throat with a combat knife.

The mortally wounded president was sped to nearby Parkland Hospital, where doctors with ties to Johnson's inner circle performed a staged autopsy. They pronounced him dead at 2:18 p.m. CST.

The body was then chemically treated by J. Edgar Hoover and put in a decoy casket for transport to Roswell, New Mexico. There, space aliens using medical technology beyond the knowledge of man sealed Kennedy's 129 wounds. Kennedy's corpse was then reanimated and rushed to Germany for an emergency meeting with the frozen brain of Adolf Hitler.

After the meeting, Kennedy aides announced plans for the two leaders' sperm cells to be atomically sustained, planted in the womb of aspiring actress Judith Campbell, and grown into a super-race of 21st-century conquerors.

According to investigators, the assassination appears to have been carefully planned and carried out in strict accordance with both the Skull-and-Bones Blood Rite and Masonic "Killing of the King" rituals.

Officers found several hundred weapons within a four-block radius of the shooting site, including telescope-sighted Weatherby Magnum rifles, Italian bolt-action 6.5mm carbines, Thompson submachine guns, Russian Kalishnikov assault rifles, and one ray-gun.

The assembled killers were taken into police custody at Dallas City Hall. As they were being transferred to the county prison, however, all 43 were shot and killed by Jack Ruby, 52, a Dallas-area nightclub owner.

The presidential motorcade, as it is besieged by over three dozen gun-wielding conspirators.

Johnson Vows to Honor Kennedy's Memory by Taking Plump Young Mistress

DALLAS, Tex.—Lyndon Baines Johnson took the oath of office aboard Air Force One at Dallas' Love Field Friday to become the 36th president of the United States.

After flying to Washington, Johnson attempted to calm the fears of the nation by assuring Americans that Kennedy's policies at home and abroad would be continued. Foremost on his agenda, Johnson said, would be to take a plump young lover.

"In your remorse, fear not, good people of America, for I do not plan to desecrate the great vision of the man who came before me," Johnson said. "Rather, I will show him my deep reverence and respect through a continuation of his extramarital policies."

"I will honor my predecessor's legacy," he added, "with the immediate acquisition of a 26-year-old lover with a full, ripe behind."

Before hurrying off to the urgent business at hand in the Lincoln Bedroom, the new president asked the nation to observe a moment of silence while he contemplated the momentous task ahead.

Lyndon Johnson taking the oath of office and a solemn vow to continue Kennedy's domestic-affairs program.

JACQUELINE KENNEDY CATCHES HUSBAND'S BRAINS WITH GRACE, APLOMB

See Fashion, page 10

Zapruder Family Wowed at Home-Movie Screening

The family of Abraham Zapruder of Dallas offered high praise for his most recent 8mm home movie, screened in the family den Friday.

Wife Margaret and children Sally, Jimmy and Sue-Anne Zapruder, accustomed to seeing footage of children playing in the yard by a plastic pool or birthday parties in poorly lit dining rooms, reported being wowed by Zapruder's "spectacular, one-of-a-kind" footage of the President of the United States getting his head shot off.

"It was super neat!" said Jimmy, 11.

"We were so impressed by the movie. Abraham really shot an outstanding home movie this time," Margaret said, "though he could have done a little better on the focus."

1963-1981

PEACE, LOVE AND OTHER BULLSHIT

Weather:
Some serious change in the air, man.

The Onion

TU STULTUS ES

Frodo Lives

Monday, September 28, 1964 — FINEST NEWS SOURCE IN AMERICA — ★★★ Price Seven Cents

Warren Commission Admits to Killing JFK

After months spent investigating the assassination of President Kennedy, the commission headed by Supreme Court Chief Justice Earl Warren announced Sunday that it had shot and killed the beloved leader.

In a detailed report, the commission found that its eight-member investigating team acted alone.

The commission, a group of "lone nuts," according to the report, fatally shot the president in the head last November. They also named themselves in the killing of Dallas policeman J.D. Tippitt and in the shooting of Texas Gov. John Connally.

In announcing the findings, Warren condemned himself and "the other disturbed individuals who perpetrated this terrible tragedy." He went on to recommend the death sentence for each commission member.

Said Warren, "It is hoped that the findings of this commission provide some closure to this dark chapter in American history."

COUNTRIES OVERTHROWN BY CIA TODAY:

ALGERIA
ARGENTINA
CHILE (9 a.m. and 3 p.m.)
DENMARK
ECUADOR
HUNGARY
KENTUCKY
PANAMA
PERU (unofficially)
RHODESIA
SOUTH AFRICA
YEMEN
ZAIRE

INSIDE THIS ISSUE:

AMERICA'S BEST AND BRIGHTEST LOOKING FOR WORK
Page 2

SHOULD NIXON BE BROUGHT BACK TO KICK AROUND SOME MORE?
Editorial, Page 12

ANDY WARHOL'S FACTORY LAYS OFF 195 JUNKIES
Page 3

Malcolm X: 'I Also Have a Dream'

Malcolm X.

'I Have a Dream That One Day Little Black Children Will Beat the Living Crap out of Little White Children'

HARLEM, N.Y.—Responding to the stirring speech delivered by Dr. Martin Luther King at last year's March on Washington, fellow negro-rights crusader Malcolm X announced Sunday that, like King, he also has a vision for the future of negroes in America, albeit a slightly different one.

"I also have a dream," Malcolm X said to the congregation of Holy Mercy Evangelical Church in Harlem. "I have a dream that, one day, a little white child and a little black child will sit together in peace and harmony. I have a dream that that little white child will then steal that little black child's lollipop and laugh at the little black child, just as the white man has been degrading, stealing from and abusing the black man for the last 400 years."

The Black Muslim leader paused, the congregation confused as to his intended message. "And that little black child will cry, as all black men and women have, over the cruelty and greed of the white man. But, friends, my dream does not end there."

"Brothers and sisters, I have a dream that that little black child will get up, still choking back tears, and go out in search of the biggest, sturdiest stick he can find," Malcolm X said. "And I have a dream that he will return to where that little white child sits, sucking away on the lollipop that does not belong to him."

Overcome with emotion, his voice reached a fever pitch as he continued. "Brothers and sisters, I have a dream that that little black child will then commence to whaling on that little white boy's hide like he's never been beat on before in his life. I have a dream that he will beat that little white boy like a red-headed stepchild until that son of a bitch soils his drawers."

Parishioners clapped and cried, "Amen," as Malcolm X continued: "And after that little black child starts beating on that white boy, I have a dream that he will not stop, brothers and sisters, until that white child has been whacked upside and downside, black and blue, within an inch of his cracker-ass life, and he crawls all the way home to his mama, crying his eyes out, wishing by God in heaven that he had never, ever taken that lollipop out of that black child's hand."

After pausing to wipe his forehead with a handkerchief, Malcolm X concluded his speech: "And I have a dream that that little white boy will learn a lesson he will never forget. I have a dream that he will never, ever, ever mess with any black children ever again in all his living days on God's green Earth under heaven, Allah be praised."

The speech met with resounding cheers from the assembled crowd, while federal authorities reacted strongly.

"I thought this non-violent-resistance thing was bad enough," FBI Director J. Edgar Hoover said. "But it would appear that, after four centuries of abuse, broken promises and subjugation, American negroes are not only dissatisfied; they're starting to get really angry."

Timothy Leary Defends Research on Face-Eating Monkeys

Timothy Leary.

WASHINGTON, D.C.—Dr. Timothy Leary, a professor of psychology at Harvard University, appeared before Congress Friday to testify in support of keeping the investigation of face-eating monkeys in the domain of scientific research.

"We still have much to learn about these face-eating monkeys," Leary told the congressional panel. "For example, why do some have six arms, while others only three? What purpose does their greenish glow serve? Most importantly, how do they eat away my face down to a gleaming skull, then regenerate the tissue for another face-eating session only minutes later? These questions cannot be answered if face-eating-monkey research is criminalized."

Dr. Leary first encountered the ghostly monkeys six months ago in Mexico with fellow Harvard psychologist Dr. Richard Alpert. Alpert, who has since changed his name to Baba Ram Dass and acquired a deep hatred of shoes, is credited with the initial discovery of the phenomenon. However, it is Leary who has become the chief proponent of monkey research, encouraging students to learn firsthand about the hairy, hungry phantoms.

Leary denied claims from some members of the panel that the face-eating monkeys are dangerous. "Before they eat my face, the monkeys sing beautiful songs and perform a slow, sensuous dance which puts me in a very relaxed state," Leary said. "While the initial sensation of having your nose chewed off can be alarming, it becomes more and more comfortable with each face-eating session."

Leary then presented his face for inspection to the congressmen. His face appeared normal except for his fully dilated pupils.

In closing, Leary compared his work to that of the medieval astronomer Galileo, whose discoveries were condemned by the Catholic Church. "We cannot suppress these findings," Leary said. "We must communicate with these amazing monkeys, and not anger them. Their leader, a magnificent creature named Tremulon 7, has intimated to me that, if we do not offer up our delicious faces in a spirit of goodwill, the monkeys could leave our planet through a dimensional warp gate. Without their protection, Earth would be in danger of an attack by Gorgemus, a malignant shade of purple from the Horsehead Nebula."

Leary then stood up, extended his arms, spun in place for approximately three minutes, and hopped out of the room.

LBJ: 'What This Country Needs Is a War in Vietnam'

Citing the malaise of more than a decade of peacetime for America, President Johnson has called for a prolonged, nightmarish war in the Southeast Asian nation of Vietnam.

"For the past 10 years, America has grown prosperous and complacent," Johnson said in a nationally televised address Sunday. "I say, we are not sending enough young people abroad to be killed. Now is the time to invade a small agrarian nation whose unanticipated savvy will not only vanquish our fighting men, but demoralize and even threaten to destroy American society."

"There are villages in Vietnam that need to be burned, babies who need to be butchered, young girls who need to be raped," Johnson continued.

The president beseeched Congress to authorize funding of the savage and unwinnable conflict by no later than the end of the year.

Johnson also called upon approximately half of all Americans to support his campaign for a war in Vietnam, and the other half to vehemently oppose it.

"If we work together, by 1970 we will see American flags burning on our college campuses. We will see 18-year-old boys coming home in body bags on national TV. We will tear this country apart," he said. "Only then can we pit brother against brother, liberal against conservative, young against old."

★ ★ ★ ★ ★ ★
Ushering in "The Summer of Responsible Taxpaying"
★ ★ ★ ★ ★ ★

The Onion

Your Non-Hophead News Source

Saturday, April 4, 1965 — FINEST NEWS SOURCE IN AMERICA — ★★★ Price Seven Cents

ONE MILLION TEEN-AGE GIRLS STRICKEN IN BEATLENEMIA EPIDEMIC

U.S. Health Officials Strongly Warn Against Exposure to John, Paul, George, Ringo

Centers for Disease Control Begin Emergency Immunizations

Screaming, Pulling Own Hair Chief Symptoms of Disease

Doctors suspect that John, Paul, George and Ringo could be carriers of the disease.

WASHINGTON, D.C.—The U.S. Department of Health, Education and Welfare declared a national state of emergency Friday, as the number of U.S. teen-agers stricken with Beatlenemia passed the one-million mark.

According to HEW Secretary John W. Gardner, "Over one million Americans between the ages of 13 and 21 have tested positive for Beatlenemia, a disease leaving them incapable of concentrating on their schoolwork, keeping their rooms neat or behaving in a manner understandable to their parents."

Physical symptoms of the virus are varied, said Gardner.

"Females seem to suffer the worst, displaying fits of shrieking, convulsions, tearing at their own faces and, in the most extreme cases, as witnessed recently at Shea Stadium, total panic and loss of consciousness," he said. "Males stricken with the syndrome tend to display excessive hair growth, often to the point at which it is difficult to determine whether they are male or female."

Prolonged exposure to the virus can ultimately wear down the immune system, creating a severe mental condition called Beatlementia.

Wild emotional swings are also identified with the disease. Many victims have been observed in extreme rapture during televised musical-variety shows, only to break down sobbing minutes later upon learning that local music stores have sold out of "Please Please Me." This condition has been identified by experts as "Beatlemanic-Depressive Disorder."

Statistics show that the disease strikes teen-agers hardest. Most people over 25 were Sinatri-lated against the condition as part of Truman's adolescent-immunization programs of the late 1940s.

At first, Centers for Disease Control officials theorized that Beatlenemia was spread by the holding of hands. But they now believe it is communicable by seeing John, Paul, George and Ringo just standing there.

Exposure to mohair could also be a cause.

While some biologists posit that Beatlenemia evolved from a rare strain of Skiffle-Merseybeat virus cross-bred with Sun Records-based country-rockabilly bacteria, others say it originated in the dank cellars of Liverpool, England, and gained potency in Hamburg, Germany's seedy red-light district earlier in the decade before being carried to the U.S. sometime last year.

Parents, meanwhile, are pressing for a cure. "How many more young girls will this disease claim?" asked Charles Woodbury of Jamaica, N.Y. His daughter Nora succumbed last week to full-blown Lennongitis.

As biologists race to isolate the pop pathogen, hospitals and emergency Beatlenemia-relief clinics across the U.S. are jammed with the twisting, shouting victims of the epidemic.

"This is without a doubt the worst pop-music-related illness in history,", said Dr. William Horst, director of Cedars-Sinai Hospital's Hullabaloo Ward. "It's worse than the rocking pneumonia, the boogie-woogie flu and the hippy-hippy shakes combined."

Emergency immunizations are under way, now that scientists have developed a four-part injection that provides protection from not only George's sensitive nature and Ringo's fun-loving charm, but also the highly contagious sex appeal of Paul and the dangerous intellect of John.

LBJ Announces Plans for 'Groovy Society'

WASHINGTON, D.C.—Speaking before a joint session of Congress Friday, President Johnson unveiled his ambitious "Groovy Society" program.

Urging Congress to "get with the scene," Johnson called upon federal legislators to approve $300 million for "groovy" programs, another $200 million for "out of sight" initiatives, and a full $1 billion for "some far-out shit."

As part of the Groovy Society program, the president called upon Congress to stage a historic "Legislation Pass-In," complete with barefoot dancing, psychedelic lights and loud rock-and-roll music.

Johnson praised America as the grooviest nation on Earth, but stressed that we cannot allow our less-fortunate citizens to live with hang-ups, while a privileged few are "freaky and free."

"This plan, if enacted in full," the president said, "will be all right."

Johnson said he will create several new top-level government positions, including a Groovy Czar and a Secretary of Love and Nudity.

"I envision an America bedecked in loose tunics, West African dashikis and bead necklaces. I envision hair long and flowing, and I envision love in the air," the president said.

Johnson also said he believes Americans need to work together to find "some really good grass."

While political analysts are

President Johnson.

hailing Johnson's plan as the grooviest ever proposed by a president, a number of Republicans on Capitol Hill stand strongly opposed.

"The president must be high," said Sen. Robert Dole (R-Kan.). "His call for $1.5 billion for a new Groovy Society makes me suspect he has recently come down from a very bad head-trip."

Johnson dismissed his critics, asking, "Man, what's your bag?"

INSIDE THIS ISSUE:

JAPANESE AMUSE GM ENGINEERS WITH ATTEMPT TO BUILD CAR

Page 20

Sanford, Son Killed in Watts Rioting

Aunt Esther Missing

The Watts neighborhood of Los Angeles, Friday.

LOS ANGELES—Last week's Watts riots, in which 34 people were killed, 4,000 injured, and millions of dollars in property destroyed, have claimed two more victims, as local junk dealer Fred G. Sanford and his son Lamont are now listed among the dead.

The Sanfords' bodies were uncovered under a heap of burned furniture, the body of a pick-up truck and other scrap-pile items the businessmen collected at their 134th Street residence.

Witnesses reported that, during the riot, Fred Sanford stood amid the frenzy of looting, rampaging citizens, clutching his chest and yelling, "This is the big one!"

Rescue workers say the 64-year-old scrap dealer attempted to claw his way to safety, as evidenced by the scratch marks on the vehicle's passenger-side window.

Damage to Sanford's junk is estimated at nearly $80.

| Did You Register Today? | # The Onion | Free Pull-Out Draft Card PAGE 30 |

Tuesday, August 16, 1966 — FINEST NEWS SOURCE IN AMERICA — ★★★ — Price Seven Cents

DEMOCRACY FLOWERS AROUND GLOBE AFTER BOMBING OF VIETNAMESE VILLAGE

'The Man' Hurt by Black Panther Accusations

BOCA RATON, Fla.—The Man, a frequent target of the Black Panther Party's tirades against racism in American society, announced Monday that he was hurt by the negro activists' stinging condemnation at a rally last week.

"It saddens and hurts me that they would say such things about me," The Man said from his golf-resort suite.

Addressing an audience of students at the University of California at Berkeley Saturday, Huey Newton of the Black Panthers catalogued the horrors The Man has committed against the negro people.

"The Man has kept us in chains. We are still in chains. We live in a racist society in which The Man, a man with no soul, a man who does not recognize his own evil, keeps us in bondage because of the color of our skin," Newton said.

Newton went on to blame The Man for preventing negroes from achieving social and economic equality out of prejudice, greed and hatred.

"It doesn't feel good being called prejudiced and greedy," The Man said after reading Newton's words in the newspaper. "I can certainly see how this fellow might be frustrated. But I'd like him to know I don't feel very good about these personal attacks."

The Man then leaned back in his upholstered leather recliner and cradled his chin in contemplation.

"Perhaps we could meet to discuss this further, but I'm doing too much remodeling to entertain guests at the moment," he said. "Pity."

INSIDE THIS ISSUE:

NRA PRAISES AUSTIN, TEX., MAN'S HEROIC DEFENSE OF CLOCK TOWER
Page 8

These Freedom-Loving 'Hippies' Are Threatening Our Liberty!
Editorial, page 7

The fruitful bombing of Thanh Hoa.

Female Orgasm Discovered

The scientists at Johns Hopkins University who discovered the female orgasm.

BALTIMORE, Md.—Scientists at Johns Hopkins University Medical School announced Monday that they have discovered what may be a sexual reflex in women: the mythical, long-rumored female orgasm.

According to Johns Hopkins' Dr. Randolph Stolper, the discovery was made when a Baltimore-area woman, "Jane," was admitted to the hospital after reporting feelings of intense pleasure during sex with her husband.

"Sex, an act science has long defined as the forcing of the man's penis into the woman's vagina for the singular purpose of male ejaculation and orgasm," Stolper said, "did not appear to cause Jane any of the agonizing pain females typically experience during the procedure. Appropriately concerned by this abnormality, she consulted her physician."

Jane, in fact, reported actually feeling sensations of pleasure similar to those typically associated with the male sexual experience.

"While many invasive tests are still necessary before we can attempt to determine what caused this phenomenon, it would appear that this woman experienced what can be termed a 'female orgasm,'" Stolper said. "The entire medical community is mystified."

Mao, Khrushchev Step Down

Free Elections Held in Cuba, Angola and N. Korea, Thanks to Latest Napalm Raid

THANH HOA, North Vietnam—The tiny village of Thanh Hoa (pop. 600) was strafed and bombed with napalm by U.S. jets Monday, resulting in the grand and glorious proliferation of democracy throughout the world.

According to Pentagon sources, within minutes of the 117th Fighter Squadron's midnight raid on the fishing village, oppressive Communist governments worldwide ceded rule to the people and held free elections.

Among the nations to embrace democracy as a result of the raid: China, North Korea, Cuba and the entire Union of Soviet Socialist Republics.

"This clear and undeniable argument for democracy and liberty could not be ignored," said Soviet Premier Nikita Khrushchev, who stepped down from power following the saturation bombing. "I believe I speak for all my comrades when I humbly apologize for the cruelty, destruction and misery wrought all these years by a Communist system of government which I now recognize was morally wrong."

"What was I thinking?" Chinese Premier Mao Tse-tung said. "A just government rules only by the mandate of its people."

Mao added that what "really turned him against Communism" was American forces' use of defoliation sprays, claymore mines and infrared beams, which are used to locate and shoot Vietcong guerrillas or village berry-pickers through dense overgrowth.

President Johnson is being roundly applauded for the bombing, which laid the groundwork for his ultimate plan for peace and democracy in our time. The attack represents a major political victory for the president, as many experts had questioned his argument that search-and-destroy-style raids on rural peasant villages were necessary to prevent "the domino effect."

"Democracy stands proud on this day," President Johnson said following the bombing. "This sends a loud and clear message to those who have dared oppose the time-honored democratic tradition of one man, one vote."

The deaths of 391 Thanh Hoa villagers marked the final step in a pro-democracy campaign begun years ago by U.S. troops in Vietnam: The triumphant bombing was preceded by widespread combat-unit invasions, murder, rape and mutilation of North Vietnamese peasants. Many fields were burned, heads of livestock killed, and wells poisoned before the Communists finally saw the light.

The surviving villagers praised those killed for their key role in the establishment of majority rule worldwide.

"Watching my six children burn to death is a small price to pay for assurance that, someday, all the people of the world will be free to elect their political leaders by secret ballot," widowed rice farmer Phan Bao said. Phan's throat was then slashed by one of 40 Green Berets on reconnaissance patrol.

Despite the success of the destruction of Thanh Hoa in creating a fair and just planet, Johnson said, it is necessary to continue bombing other North Vietnamese villages and continue sending troops to the area "to guarantee that democracy is maintained."

Local Dad a Secret Agent Man, Says 8-Year-Old Source

CARBONDALE, Ill.—Donald Roeker, a 36-year-old father of three, works as a high-level secret agent for the government, according to a statement issued by Eddy Roeker, 8, to friends at Lott Elementary School.

The younger Roeker said his father receives coded daily messages from sources deep inside the Pentagon and White House. He also noted that his father is often gone on long trips to tend to matters of national security and rid the world of Russian evil-doers and other international criminals.

Roeker's associates, Ralph Olsen, 8, and Joe Huber, 9, dispute his claim. Huber pointed to his mom's telephone conversation with Roeker's mom Saturday: He claims to have overheard part of the conversation, which indicated that Roeker's dad works as a traveling salesman.

The Onion

Put Your Bra Back On

Support Hippie Internment Camps

Saturday, April 8, 1967 — FINEST NEWS SOURCE IN AMERICA — ★★★ Price Seven Cents

NATION'S NEGROES MARCH ON HANOI

Blacks Vow to Fight Foreign Forces of Oppression 'By Any Means Necessary'

'We Shall Overcome the Vietcong,' Says Pvt. Jerome Simpkins of Harlem, N.Y.

SAIGON, Vietnam—Calling for the establishment of justice and equality throughout Vietnam, more than 50,000 negroes marched on the city of Hanoi Friday.

"The United States has sent us here to fight to make all of Vietnam a place of liberty," said Melvin Bratton, an 18-year-old negro from the Watts section of Los Angeles. "In North Vietnam, President Johnson sees a land where men are not free to live as they choose, where cruel oppressors impose their will upon the poorest and most disenfranchised members of society. He has commanded us, America's poorest and most disenfranchised, to change this."

For miles around Hanoi in every direction, negroes could be seen marching toward the North Vietnamese capital, determined to liberate it from the cruel yoke of oppression.

"What do we want? Freedom! Where do we want it? Vietnam!" negroes chanted, as they advanced toward Hanoi, weary but determined to "make freedom ring" throughout the Southeast Asian nation.

In addition to the 50,000 who marched on Hanoi, more than 150,000 other negroes—40 percent of total U.S. troops—are currently marching in other parts of Vietnam, risking their lives to defend the principles of democracy and freedom.

"Everywhere I go in this country, I see people beaten down and dejected. Many of them are made to feel as if they have no rights, as if they are not even human beings at all," said negro Larry Dobbs, 19, of Meridan, Mississippi. "Thank goodness I did not have the money to get out of the draft, or I would never have gotten the chance to fight to help these people."

Across the U.S., whites expressed support for the negro struggle to defeat Communism. "I am impressed by their commitment to this cause and I wish them all the best in their brave struggle against the North Vietnamese," said Richard Vandervleet of Bel Air, California. "In fact, tomorrow night, there's a going to be a rally in support of the fighting negroes right after the big Jefferson Airplane concert. I can hardly wait."

Negro soldiers fighting for freedom.

Senate Passes Clean Hair Act

WASHINGTON, D.C.—In a major step toward reaching its goal of reducing toxic hippie emissions 65 percent by 1973, the U.S. Senate passed the Clean Hair Act by a 90-7 vote yesterday.

The toughest piece of pro-hygiene legislation in U.S. history, the Clean Hair Act makes it mandatory for members of the nation's counterculture to wash their hair with shampoo at least once a week. Failure to cleanse one's hair on a regular basis would result in fines up to $500 and/or jail time of up to 90 days.

"Let there be no mistake: Congress is committed to cleaning up America's young people," said U.S. Sen. George D. Aiken (R-Vt.), the bill's sponsor. "No longer will the American people be forced to cover their noses and mouths when passing a protest site or a rock concert. From this day forward, 'hippies' will stink, but only in the figurative sense of the word."

Legislators praised the passage of the Clean Hair Act and are pressuring President Johnson to sign it into law, while Republican leaders stressed that it is only the beginning. By the end of this year, Rep. John C. Kunkel (R-Pa.) said he plans to introduce a bill in the House requiring all young women to shave their legs. A second piece of legislation, the Get a Damn Haircut Act, is already in committee.

"Soap, shampoo, razor, comb—these are the cornerstones upon which American hygiene was built," Aiken said. "Our young people must learn respect for these traditions, even if by force."

BOB DYLAN MAKES MOVIE DEBUT IN *BLONDES! BLONDES! BLONDES!*

Bob Dylan.

America's favorite folksinging superstar Bob Dylan makes the jump from the Top 40 to the silver screen next week with the premiere of MGM's newest musical extravaganza, *Blondes! Blondes! Blondes!*, the teen idol's first big Tinseltown role.

Though some of the harmonica heartthrob's more "purist" folkie followers have expressed indignation over the winsome Dylan's so-called "sell-out" to big-screen stardom, fans of music, mayhem, laughs and romance are sure to be delighted with the madcap musical comedy, which critics are already calling "a wild romp!"

Dylan stars as Buck "Zimmy" Zimmerman, a down-in-the-mouth acoustic guitarist on the streets of New York City whose luck takes a turn for the better when he tires of the poverty of bohemian cafe life and decides to try to make his fortune in Hollywood. Lighting out for California in a beat-up old jalopy, he soon finds himself surrounded by dozens and dozens of—you guessed it—blondes, blondes, blondes!

Featuring original show-stopping musical numbers written especially for the film by famed hitmakers Lieber and Stoller, the movie's soundtrack was designed to give Dylan's sound a peppier feel than the singing and strumming sensation's prior, more protest-oriented work. And the results are pure movie magic!

As the crooning Zimmy, Dylan's red-hot on-screen romance with beautiful model Gerta (played by German newcomer Nico in a stand-out role) will have teen-age girls swooning with jealousy! And a hilarious subplot featuring the bumbling antics of a zany Vietnamese waiter are sure to keep audiences in stitches from coast to coast.

With a debut like this, Dylan is sure to become America's biggest big-screen singing sensation for years to come!

Grateful Dead Begins Playing 28-Year Song

Jerry Garcia of the Grateful Dead.

SAN FRANCISCO—The Grateful Dead, a San Francisco-area rock group, began "jamming" an improvisational fusion of rock, folk, jazz, bluegrass and country Friday which the group claims it will continue to play through the mid-1990s.

Taking the stage with "The Dead" at the Fillmore West concert hall, music promoter Bill Graham introduced the as-yet-untitled song.

"The rock-and-roll song as we know it needs to change," Graham said. "It can't just be three minutes of mindless, three-chord escapism anymore. It needs to be a quarter-century-long odyssey of mystifying 50-chord obscurity. And The Dead will take us there."

"Sun go shinin' on the riverside," added Jerry Garcia, the band's lead singer. "Moon come risin' like a country bride."

The band then began its experiment in tune-elongation, with guitarist Bob Weir launching into a twangy, discursive guitar solo in the home-key of F, which soon flowed into a B-flat seventh chord. Graham estimates that Weir will return the melody line to F early next January.

"You don't just listen to The Dead—you experience them," said Naomi Shapiro, 19, an ardent follower of the group. "Their music is so deep that it has something to offer no matter what you're doing—dancing, eating, sleeping, making love or panhandling."

Grateful Dead drummer Bill Kreutzmann said the band "consciously seeks a different sound from that of other bands. Collectively, we're familiar with almost every type of music and we've constantly strived to work them into our songs, but there just hasn't been enough time to work all of them into any one particular piece. We finally realized that it would take the next 28 years to do it, and we figured, you know, none of us had anything major going down for that particular time period, so why not?

"With Graham's help," Kreutzmann added, maintaining a beat in 13/8 rhythm to accompany Weir's solo, "we're going to take our ceaseless song on the road in a decades-long series of concerts throughout the U.S. and the rest of the world."

INSIDE THIS ISSUE:

SOUTHERN WHITES FEAR INTEGRATION WILL TAINT PURITY OF REDNECK TROGLODYTES
Page 6

PINKOS, HOMOS, STINKOS, LESBOS: OUR SOCIETY IS GOING TO THE O'S
See Editorial, page 14

BLACK PANTHERS KEEP STARTING LINEUP SECRET; 'I REPEAT, WE ARE NOT A BASKETBALL TEAM,' SAYS CLEAVER
See Sports, page 24

107

| Support Your Local Pigs | # The Onion | Our Cartoons Guaranteed LSD-Free |

Saturday, June 10, 1967 — FINEST NEWS SOURCE IN AMERICA — ★★★ Price Seven Cents

Muhammad Ali Refuses to Fight Vietnamese Unless War Moves to Las Vegas

Heavyweight Champ Calls Current Site of Conflict 'Unacceptable'

Promises Swift Knockout of Vietcong if Fight Held at Caesar's Palace

LAS VEGAS—Boxing champ Muhammad Ali, who was drafted by the Army last week, announced Friday that he is refusing to fight in Vietnam and will only take on the Vietcong if the war is relocated to Caesar's Palace in Las Vegas.

"I will not risk my life for a country that does not recognize my right to schedule my bouts where and when I want," the former Cassius Clay told reporters. "I would rather get spanked by my poor old daddy than kill some dude in a damn rice paddy."

Ali also expressed dissatisfaction with his proposed take for the fight in Asia. "The rations the Army is offering me for this fight are ridiculous. Four cans of potted meat and a half-gallon canteen of water per day? Rocky Marciano got more than that to take on the Germans in World War II, and that was 25 years ago. This is just not worth it."

Ali said he will fight for no fewer than six cans of potted meat, a can of beans and a bottle of Coca-Cola per day. He also wants 50 percent of the war's total gate receipts and a 10 percent cut of all post-war reparations.

Ali said he is confident he can defeat the Vietcong if he is allowed to fight them at the 8,200-seat Caesar's Palace boxing arena, site of his 1964 bout against Sonny Liston.

"My right hook is devastating, and my jabs are so fast, when you finally see them coming, you're breathing your last," Ali said. "When I come at those Communists with my fists flying, they're going to stop communing and start dying. If President Johnson would only move the war to Vegas, me and the Vietcong would really get it on, 'cause we don't get along. If you thought Ali was the peaceful kind, you'll change your mind when I kick Ho Chi Minh's behind."

Muhammad Ali.

UC-BERKELEY STUDENTS PROTEST NOT BEING TOLD ABOUT LATEST PROTEST BY FRIENDS

Angry students protest a missed demonstration in Berkeley.

BERKELEY, Calif.—A coalition of left-wing students at the University of California at Berkeley held an impromptu rally Friday night to protest "the unconscionable failure of our classmates to tell us about a really great protest that happened earlier in the day."

Waving hand-drawn signs with such slogans as, "Why Didn't You Call Us?" and, "We Should Have Been There," the crowd of approximately 1,000 students congregated in Sproul Plaza, then marched across campus chanting, "Hey, hey, ho, ho, if there's a protest, we ought to know." The impassioned demonstration was met with force by campus and city police, who dispersed the students with tear gas and clubs.

The protest the students had missed, the "Feminist Anti-War Make-Love-for-Civil-Rights Free-Speech Peace-In," included police, rousing free-speech rhetoric and music.

The protest featured a surprise performance by the popular San Francisco rock group Moby Grape, which only added to the neglected students' sense of outrage.

"Everyone who was anyone was at that protest," campus radical leader Mario Savio said. "As college students who were not informed of a very important protest, we join hands with other similarly oppressed groups. Slavery, the Holocaust and, now, the injustice of not a single phone call to invite us to a groovy rally at which The Grape played. Never again!"

Saturday morning, Savio and five other radical student leaders announced the formation of a new activist group, Students for Telling Other Students about the Next Big Protest, STOSNBP, whose demands are already posted in classrooms and dormitories throughout the Berkeley campus, is calling for a state-wide network of telephone operators devoted to informing radical students exactly where and when every protest is to take place and what events are planned.

California Gov. Ronald Reagan has promised to fight the proposal, but student activists are fighting back, and not just for the right to be notified of the best protests. One campus leader, Brian Goldberg, is planning a mass protest against cuts in parental financial support for next weekend.

"My group, Students Against Cuts in Parental Financial Support, dares to stand up and fight for what's right," Goldberg said. "I ran out of money last week and couldn't afford to buy this groovy hemp caftan. It was a drag, man."

TONIGHT'S TV HIGHLIGHTS

7:00 p.m. (CBS)
Burning of Chi San Ho Village

7:00 p.m. (NBC)
Rocket Attack on Nan Phut

8:00 p.m. (CBS)
Rape of Dien Ko

8:30 p.m. (ABC)
Slaughter of Peasants Near Khe Sanh

8:30 p.m. (NBC)
Wonderful World of Disney

9:00 p.m. (CBS)
Army Lt. Mark Fryer Steps on Mine, Loses Both Legs on Hill 672

INSIDE THIS ISSUE:

ROCKERS, MODS DECLARE TRUCE
Page 12

RALPH NADER: VIETNAMESE HUTS ARE TOO FLAMMABLE
Page 18

HARLAN ELLISON: 'NOT EVERYTHING COMING OUT OF THE LAB IS GOOD AND BEAUTIFUL AND WHY CAN'T SOMEONE DO A GOOD RADIO SHOW LIKE *THE MYSTERIOUS TRAVELER* YOU BASTARDS'
Page 21

Israeli Soldiers' Sabbath Dinner Delayed 35 Minutes by War with Egypt

Matzoh-Ball Soup Gets Cold; Israeli Troops 'Starving'

JERUSALEM—The joyous, communal atmosphere of Sabbath dinner was nearly ruined throughout Israel Friday evening, when a surprise invasion by Egyptian forces forced the nationwide postponement of the weekly family ritual by nearly 35 minutes.

"Even for someone as ruthless as President Nasser, this is cruel," Israeli Defense Minister Moshe Dayan said Saturday morning at a Knesset press conference. "He violated the sanctity of our day of rest by attempting a wholesale invasion of the entire Sinai Peninsula, knowing full well that by the time our troops returned, their food would be cold. This was a willful, premeditated, schedule-ruining inconvenience."

Preliminary reports from the principal areas of fighting estimate Egyptian casualties at 900 dead and 1,500 injured. But mere numbers do nothing to convey the grief and exasperation of thousands of Israeli soldiers and their annoyance-stricken families, many of whom watched helplessly as the heat ebbed from their loved ones' uneaten chickens, green beans and matzoh-ball soups.

Ronit Orenstein, a Tel Aviv housewife whose two sons are enlisted in the Army, suffered through what she called "the most agonizing half-hour of food preparation in my life."

"The sun had just gone down and I was literally placing the challah on the table when they got the call," she recalled. "Reuben, my eldest, hadn't eaten all day, because he could smell the borscht I was making in the kitchen and he wanted to save his appetite. He had to leave to fight on an empty stomach. I didn't even have time to pack him a little nosh."

Orenstein, like millions of other worried Israelis, spent the next 30 minutes listening to the radio for up-to-the-minute reports on the estimated time of victory. "It was agonizing," she said. "First, they said it would be a 10-minute war, then 15, then 20, then 15 again. Meanwhile, the Sabbath candles were burning down and the kugel was getting hard. And how long can one woman be expected to simmer a brisket? How long?"

| Love It Or Leave It | # The Onion | Non-Canadian Edition |

Tuesday, June 13, 1967 — FINEST NEWS SOURCE IN AMERICA — ★★★ Price Seven Cents

NATIONAL GUARD MOBILIZED FOR INTEGRATION OF NEGRO INTO SUPREME COURT

LBJ Orders Troops to Oversee Thurgood Marshall's Admission to High Court

Justices Block Entrance to Building; Vow to Keep Marshall Out

WASHINGTON, D.C.—President Johnson deployed more than 1,500 National Guardsmen to the U.S. Supreme Court building Monday, determined to integrate the court despite strong protests from its eight white members.

"The forward march of history will not be stopped by those who would seek to keep us in the past," Johnson said of the justices, who have threatened violence if Thurgood Marshall enters their ranks. "If the Supreme Court does not admit this negro willingly, the U.S. government is prepared to swear him in by force."

The mobilization comes in response to the court's 8-0 ruling last week that its forced integration is unconstitutional. Voicing the official court opinion, Justice Potter Stewart wrote: "The members of this court find no precedent for a negro on the bench of the nation's highest judicial body and see no reason for that to change. It is this court's opinion that there are enough good jobs for negroes like Thurgood that they do not have to go stirring up trouble in such an important judicial body as this. The court recommends that Thurgood set up a nice, quiet practice somewhere as a country lawyer and keep his nose out of trouble."

Standing on the steps of the court brandishing a baseball bat, Justice John Harlan said, "Thurgood certainly seems like a fine boy. And I'm sure he is a competent judge. But he is in well over his head here. This court is no place for a negro. Supreme Court segregation forever!"

"In all my years in the U.S. judicial system, I have never served on a court with a negro," Justice Abe Fortas said, "and I do not intend to start now."

Marshall, appointed to the Supreme Court by Johnson, will be escorted to his chambers by armed guardsmen Friday.

Anticipating resistance, Johnson has authorized the guardsmen to use whatever means necessary to subdue rioting Supreme Court justices, including tear gas and rubber bullets. A standing force of some 5,000 troops will be maintained for several weeks to protect Marshall.

"Despite the unpopularity of this appointment," Johnson said, "the justices will respect my decision, either by their own will or by the force of National Guard troops."

Incidents of Supreme Court Violence

In an incident last week in which Marshall met with the other justices at a Washington luncheon, Justice Harlan refused to sit at the same table as Marshall. Harlan erupted into violence, repeatedly striking at Marshall until security guards pulled him away.

Last Wednesday, Marshall was awakened at 3 a.m. EST when a brick was tossed into a window of his Baltimore home. He looked out the window to see a burning cross on his front lawn. Witnesses report spotting Justices Whittaker, Stewart and Harlan on the scene that night. The justices would not comment on the matter to the press.

Marshall later discovered the words "Nigger Go Home" scrawled on the side of his house in red paint.

Thurgood Marshall, right, will be escorted to his first day on the Supreme Court by Virginia National Guard troops, above.

Hippies Celebrating 'Fuck-Summer '67'

SAN FRANCISCO—Across the nation, hippies in groups of three to six are gathering at rock concerts, beaches, fields and shag-carpeted basement recreation rooms to celebrate what is being called "Fuck-Summer '67" with frequent and uninhibited sexual intercourse.

Hippies are staging numerous Love-Ins, Be-Ins and Fuck-Ins, most of which entail naked dancing, free love and public intercourse. Across the country, they're engaging in fucking wherever it suits them: on the grass, in their VW Beetles and on the sidewalks.

"I believe every person on Earth should have the freedom to say what they want and live a peaceful existence," said Candy Hertz, a hippie-movement participant from Sausalito, Calif. "Hey, do you want to do it with me?"

Many San Francisco merchants are holding special Fuck-Summer sales, offering discounts on fringed blankets, beads and rejuvenating cold beverages for between-fuck refreshment.

San Francisco Mayor Francis Shelley delivered a proclamation at City Hall this week to dedicate Fuck-Summer '67, saying, "Let's get it on."

The hippies had been attracting increased attention for their radical stances on civil rights, religion, social-welfare programs and drug use, but now they are gaining notoriety for their nonstop fucking.

"I've heard that the hippies stand for racial unity and personal freedom," said Oakland hardware store owner Louis Frank. "I also hear they're fucking a lot."

Beyond mere fucking, Fuck-Summer '67 is also about rebelling against authority, say hippies.

"It's high time our parents' generation stopped seeing the world as theirs," said Dan Oelrich, a San Francisco youth with hair well past his chin and a half-inch beard growth, "because the times, they are a-changin'." On an average day, Oelrich has sex eight times with five different partners.

Every day, the hippie ranks are growing, but not everyone approves of their behavior. Many members of older generations are openly opposed to what they see as a degradation of values.

"In my youth, we only fucked to make children," said 59-year-old Mary Helshoven, a San Francisco-area housewife. "We never fucked for pleasure, or out of doors, or with everybody. That's fucking wrong."

INSIDE THIS ISSUE:

DISNEY'S MAGIC KINGDOM UNVEILS MAGIC MUSHROOM RIDE
Page 3

POLICE FIND 15-YEAR-OLD GIRL LIVING IN KEITH RICHARDS' SHIRT RUFFLES
Page 8

WILT CHAMBERLAIN SETS ALL-TIME SINGLE-NIGHT SCORING RECORD
Page 22

PENTAGON WORKING TO HARNESS FLOWER POWER FOR DESTRUCTIVE NEW WEAPON

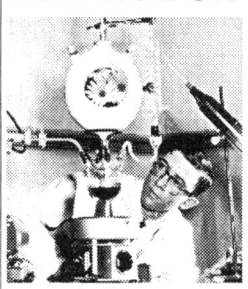

Page 13

Objection Is NOT Conscientious	# THE ONION	Dig Our '68 Election Coverage

Tuesday, January 30, 1968 — FINEST AMERICAN NEWS SOURCE — 48 PAGES CITY EDITION TU STULTUS ES — ★★★ — 10¢

JOHNSON DEPLOYS 20,000 BODY BAGS TO VIETNAM

Bag Escalation Part of U.S. Policy of 'Corpse Containment'

Total Military Commitment in Vietnam up to 60,000 Bags

Army helicopters deliver crucial body-bag reinforcements to the 33rd Infantry near Puc Tho.

WASHINGTON, D.C.—President Johnson stepped up his commitment to the war in Vietnam Monday, deploying an additional 20,000 body bags to military zones throughout the Southeast Asian nation.

"If the U.S. is to contain the threat of rotting, fetid corpses in Vietnam, we need to send more bags," Johnson said. "Only by zipping up these dead bodies in quality bags of durable, rubberized-canvas construction can we ensure that the stench of deteriorating flesh does not spread beyond the 16th parallel and into the southernmost regions of Vietnam."

A fleet of military transport planes flew the bags from Andrews Air Force Base to Vietnam, where they were greeted by cheering throngs of U.S. Army doctors and triage nurses.

"When we saw those 20,000 fresh bags arriving from the States, it just warmed our hearts," U.S. Army surgeon Malcolm Brandenburg said. "The way the war has been going lately, I don't think we could have lasted another day without those reinforcements."

"Just last night, the Vietcong attacked a jungle encampment of U.S. soldiers about 20 miles east of here. More than 130 American GIs were killed," nurse Norma Hustings said. "Thank God we've at least got these body bags so we can wrap them up and send them back to their parents."

In an address to the American people last night, President Johnson reiterated his commitment to ending the war, vowing to bring more than 50,000 U.S. troops home in body bags by the end of this year.

In addition to body bags, Johnson said he will deploy an additional 30,000 American flags to Vietnam to cover the bags of fallen soldiers.

"We must let the young men who are risking their lives in Vietnam know that we are behind them 100 percent," Johnson said. "This commitment of 30,000 American flags sends them the strong message that, when their tour of duty is over, they can expect to be brought back to America a hero in a beautiful bag draped in the stars and stripes."

A fresh supply of toe tags, caskets, gut-buckets and sealed canisters of decomposition-inhibiting formaldehyde are also on the way.

Thursday's deployment brings total U.S. body-bag commitment in Vietnam to 60,000. The ever-increasing number prompted Johnson to urge Americans to save their canvas for the war effort. "Do your part to bring American GIs home individually wrapped: Conserve canvas," he said.

INSIDE THIS ISSUE:

WINDOW-POUNDING JEW DISRUPTS LOCAL WEDDING
Page 3

THE REVOLUTION: SHOULD IT BE TELEVISED?
Editorial, Page 12

The Onion newspaper joins the United States Armed Forces and the Federal Government in wishing its readers the very happiest of Tet Offensives.

Nixon Courts Youth Vote With Appearance as Go-Go Dancer on 'Laugh-in'

In a bold move seemingly calculated to increase his appeal to America's young people, Republican presidential candidate Richard Nixon appeared on NBC's popular comedy program *Laugh-In* Monday night, provocatively gyrating in an orange string bikini, with peace signs and witty countercultural slogans painted upon his undulating, naked flesh.

As brightly colored mood lighting swirled around the set and upon Nixon's brightly painted skin, the candidate danced atop a desk demonstrating such popular dance moves as "The Swim" and "The Shimmy," periodically stopping to allow the camera to zoom in on witticisms painted upon him, including "G.O.P.=Greedy Old People" and "Veto Bandito."

Nixon completed the taping of the skit in 20 minutes, then resumed his campaigning. Following the dance, he was "perspiring and slightly winded," according to top handlers.

Though some of the slogans painted on Nixon required clearance from the Republican National Committee, as well as NBC's Department of Standards and Practices, the taping was largely uneventful.

Said one Nixon aide: "Mr. Nixon's body-painters worked closely with *Laugh-In* producer and writer Dick Martin to produce only body graffiti that was suitable for the next president of the United States."

The aide also said the full covering of the upper-most portion of Nixon's butt-crack and the curved edges of his lower buttocks was of prime concern to both network censors and Nixon '68 officials.

Republican presidential candidate Richard Nixon.

Martin Luther King: 'Perhaps We Shall Not Overcome After All'

KNOXVILLE, Tenn.—In a speech at First Baptist Church in Knoxville, civil-rights leader Dr. Martin Luther King Jr. acknowledged that he and his fellow negroes may not overcome, after all.

"For many long years, the rallying cry of our movement has been, 'We shall overcome,'" King told the capacity crowd. "But, having taken a few steps back to examine all sides of the situation, I have come to a new conclusion: that we most likely shall not."

As the assembled churchgoers listened intently, King continued: "For all our bravery in the face of hatred and intolerance, it appears that the white power structure is simply too powerful and entrenched to be overcome. I hope not, obviously, but it is very much starting to look that way."

"Nonetheless," King continued, "with deep faith in ourselves, and even deeper faith in God, we hope that our children and our children's children will, in time, come to witness an end to racial hatred, and that they will know freedom and equality."

"But I would not count on it happening any time soon."

Dr. Martin Luther King Jr.

MOVIE NEWS

YELLOW SUBMARINE INTRODUCES CHILDREN TO MAGICAL WORLD OF LSD HALLUCINATIONS
Page 16

| My God, It's Full of Stars | # THE ONION | Your Source for Non-Gonzo Journalism |

Friday, October 4, 1968 — FINEST AMERICAN NEWS SOURCE — 10¢

Hippies, NASA Race for Moon

The space race between NASA and the hippies is more heated than ever, with both of the astronautic super-powers vying to be the first to land a man on the moon.

"NASA will win the race to the moon, and the world will see a United States astronaut, not a longhair, walk on the moon before the turn of the decade," Apollo 10 Mission Director Gus Lance said Thursday.

Despite NASA's confidence, hippie-space-program sources report that the moon will be within their reach in mere months. "Freakonauts have already outdistanced NASA in their high rate of success with manned missions throughout the Tibetan Book of the Dead and cosmic voyages Beyond Total Awareness," said Freedog Osmosis, head of the prestigious Haight-Ashbury Center for Astraldynamic Research. "And current missions are flying higher than ever. Take me, for example. I'm sitting right in front of you. Yet, even as we speak, I'm orbiting at tremendous altitudes."

"We are 12 to 16 weeks away from having all the vibes in place to launch, orbit and land a hippie on the moon," Osmosis said, "as well as to return him safely to a big oversized floor pillow after wear-off and subsequent crashpad re-entry burn."

With the Lunar Excursion Module proven flightworthy in recent Apollo test missions, it is only a matter of time, NASA scientists argue, before they win the race to the moon. However, hippies say, a NASA victory in the space race is by no means certain.

"From such early victories as The Byrds' historic eight-mile-high test flight above San Francisco Bay to recent trips by The Rolling Stones as far as 60,000 light-years from home, it's clear that our radical, substance-based approach to space

NASA's Apollo 10 astronauts hope to be first on the moon.

Lunar freakonaut Horace Freeberg hopes to be the first man to take a "serious trip" to the moon.

travel boasts significant advantages over NASA's more conservative methods," said space-cadet hippychick Raven Transcendence.

Transcendence added that the hippie space program also enjoys a clear economic advantage over NASA: While the cost of a NASA lunar mission is estimated at $600 million, the hippie space program, she said, can reach the moon with just a dime bag.

Hippie space exploration, however, has not been without its setbacks. In June, shortly after setting his controls for the heart of the sun, Floyd Commander Syd Barrett lost control of his 50-milligram capsule and veered wildly off course. According to hippie scientists, he is currently lost somewhere near Neptune. The scientists project that the Floyd program will not match NASA's Apollo 8 orbit of the dark side of the moon until the mid-1970s.

"Yes, hippie space travel does have its problems," Osmosis said. "The severe crash-and-burns that follow intense spaceflight can be devastating, and launch windows are dependent on the week-to-week booking schedule at the Fillmore West. Nonetheless, we have repeatedly reached the Sea of Inner Peace and Sea of Undulating Joy-Vibes, and we're confident that a flower child will touch down on the Sea of Tranquility soon, certainly no later than the big Woodstock festival next summer."

POPULAR NAMES FOR BABIES THIS YEAR

STARFIRE
WILDFLOWER
SUNSHINE
HEMP
FLING
LYSERGIA
BENZEDRINE
ORGIASTICA
SMACK

TODAY'S ASSASSINATIONS

RFK
(lone gunman)

MLK
(lone gunman)

RLK
(lone gunman)

ALABAMA GOV. GEORGE WALLACE
(lone gunman)

TEXAS GOV. JOHN CONNALLY
(clock-tower sniper)

JACK RUBY
(prison scuffle)

FORMER PRESIDENT EISENHOWER
(CIA death squad)

TINA TURNER
(Ike)

Feminists Go on Humor Strike

Citing "a profound lack of political, social and economic equality for women," feminists across the country announced their intent to embark on an indefinite humor strike Thursday.

The strike, directors of the recently formed National Organization for Women said, will be halted when women are treated with the same respect as men, we will refuse to find the humor in anything," NOW spokesperson Rita Nelson told reporters. "This bold move will force American society to seriously rethink its attitude toward women, just as Gandhi's hunger strike forced the British to rethink their forced colonial occupation of another land."

Items that will not be accepted among humor strikers are jokes which reference women in the workplace, women in the home, women's relationships with men, childbirth, child-rearing, family life and sex.

Additionally, jokes about the feminists' lack of humor itself will not be tolerated.

LBJ DEPLOYS GREEN BAY PACKERS TO VIETNAM

NFL Champs to Bring Offensive Firepower, Solid Defense to War Effort

'There Is No Room for Second Place in Southeast Asia,' Says Coach Lombardi

Play outline: Upon the ball being snapped, 1. Guards Thurston and Kramer (G) "pull" to the right and run up the battlefield; 2. quarterback Bart Starr (Q) hands the ball off to halfback Paul Hornung (H); 3. Hornung follows blockers Kramer, Thurston and fullback Jim Taylor (F) deep into enemy territory.

GREEN BAY, Wis.—In an executive order requested by Secretary of Defense Robert McNamara and approved by Congress, President Johnson ordered the Green Bay Packers to Vietnam Thursday.

Johnson announced his decision to the public in a brief statement issued from the Oval Office.

"As Commander in Chief of the Armed Forces, by the power granted to me by the Armed Forces Conscription Act, I hereby order the World Champion Green Bay Packers football club to serve as a combat unit in Southeast Asia for the duration of that conflict," the statement read in part. "The Pack is back in '68!"

Army officials said they plan to deploy both the offense and defense of the 60-man squad alongside the 173rd Airborne Brigade at Chu Chi, a disputed township about 30 miles northeast of Saigon.

Tactical experts say the Packers' combination of solid, smashmouth ball-carrying and strong man-to-man defense will complement the 173rd's light machine-gun and rocket-propelled-grenade squads.

Coach Vince Lombardi, speaking from the Packer Hall of Fame in Green Bay, said he was "pleased and honored" to lead his team into battle against the Vietcong.

"I am proud of my players," Lombardi said, "and I look forward to meeting the enemy in combat. They will be helpless against our Power Sweep Right, in which pulling guards Kramer and Thurston run interference for Hornung and Taylor, allowing them to advance deep within enemy territory. If necessary, our experienced field general, Bart Starr, can throw the long bomb with deadly accuracy. And we shall maintain a solid defensive presence with Ray Nitschke and Willie Wood controlling the line. If we can defeat the mighty Chicago Bears, the Vietnam Congs shouldn't give us any trouble."

"As I have always said," Lombardi continued, "a man's finest hour is that moment when he has worked his heart out in a good cause and lies exhausted on the field of battle—victorious."

Lombardi added that winning the war is not everything, but the only thing.

The Packers were also assigned to determine the whereabouts of the Baltimore Colts, missing in Vietnam since 1966.

111

THE ONION

Your Protest-Free Newspaper

Inside: We Rate the '69 Beads

Thursday, January 30, 1969 — FINEST AMERICAN NEWS SOURCE — 52 PAGES CITY EDITION ★★★ 10¢

TU STULTUS ES

Nixon Vetoes Federal Love and Happiness Act

President Nixon.

WASHINGTON, D.C.—President Nixon vetoed the Federal Love and Happiness Act Wednesday, stopping legislation that would have spread peace, happiness and good cheer across the U.S.

Passed by a narrow margin in both houses of Congress, the bill would have banished war, made racial harmony the law of the land, allocated $2 billion in federal funds to the elimination of world hunger, and mobilized federal delegations of folk singers and poets to deliver a universal message of love and understanding, passing out daisies to every city and town in America.

"America does not need this legislation," Nixon said at a press conference following the veto. "While there most certainly is a time and a place for love and happiness, I believe at this time it would not be wise for the U.S. to actively promote these most personal and subjective of institutions."

Nixon then retreated to the Oval Office to sit alone in the dark, slump over and scowl.

JOHN LENNON: 'I'M HIGHER THAN JESUS RIGHT NOW'

See page 13c

U.S. TROOPS PULL OUT OF VIETNAMESE PEASANT GIRL

27th Infantry Division Ordered to Fully Withdraw from Sia Nguyen, 14

'That's Enough for Now, Boys,' Says Captain

PHU LUONG, North Vietnam—In what is being called a "temporary retreat," Sgt. Robert Billups has ordered the Alpha Company of the U.S. Army's 27th Infantry Division to withdraw from its strategic position inside North Vietnamese peasant girl Sia Nguyen, 14.

"I'd like to emphasize that this is temporary," said a grim-faced Brig. Gen. Thomas McClellan, chief military press liaison in Saigon, announcing the division's withdrawal late this afternoon. "It is simply a localized, strategic disengagement and by no means represents any kind of larger concession with regard to the many other peasant girls we currently occupy, including a growing number north of the 17th parallel."

But a high-ranking Pentagon official, speaking on condition of anonymity, conceded that Alpha Company's evacuation from Nguyen was a crushing defeat that might signal the end of "Operation Penetration," the much-heralded counter-offensive launched two months ago that was expected to result in the taking of over 100,000 civilian girls by the end of 1969.

"From a practical standpoint, Tet made it almost impossible to successfully launch an assault on the interiors of Vietnamese girls," the official said. "General McClellan saw Sia Nguyen as our last, best hope for a sustained presence in the area. This is a catastrophic blow, not only from a military standpoint, but also for troop morale."

Since Alpha Company first took the girl four weeks ago following a prolonged battle that left two men kicked and three others seriously scratched, it has managed to maintain its position for nearly a full month despite vaginal rupturing and periodic assaults from forces within the girl's family, who have conducted a brutal campaign of wailing and pleading.

"I didn't know how much longer my boys could take it," said Billups. "You can't imagine what it's like here in 'Nam."

The occupation of Nguyen was "hell on earth," according to Peter Venuto, 19, a member of Alpha Company who decided to leave Vietnam after completing his six-month stint last week. Venuto remembers living in constant fear that he would not be allowed to charge in with his comrades. "I woke up every morning in a cold sweat, afraid that this rape might be my last."

Venuto also said that, by the time he left, "There was no unity at all among the men any more; they were going out of turn, shouting at each other about how long they were taking. Some of them were even disobeying Captain Billups when he told them they'd had enough. That's when I knew I'd seen plenty. It's one thing to penetrate enemy territory in the performance of your duty, but when you see soldiers violating direct orders, it's time to totally reassess the situation."

U.S. troops (above) reluctantly retreat from the North Vietnamese peasant girl they recently occupied at Phu Luong. Many troopers claim that retaking the girl will be a "bloody and exhausting" maneuver.

Czech Teens Go Wild For 'Soviet Invasion'

Youths in Prague react to the sight of oncoming Soviet tanks.

PRAGUE, Czechoslovakia—It's only been a few months since the Soviet Army overran this small European nation, but every young lady in Czechoslovakia has already picked her favorite occupying general. There's only one way to describe the craziness that's seized the Czech Republic: The Soviets have invaded, and they're here to stay!

Their parents might be shaking their heads, but try telling these girls to calm down when a regiment of Soviet troops marches down their street. More often than not, the Russians need to send a second regiment just to protect the first from the hordes of screaming, crying girls who line the streets, waving banners and placards reading, "We Surrender!" and "Please Spare Our Lives!"

Netslesva Pavlak, 17, whose bedroom walls are festooned with photos of her Politburo faves, actually fainted after being brutally beaten by a Soviet commander who suspected her of counterrevolutionary activities. "He touched me," gushed Netsleva, as her friends carried her home.

But whatever the secret magic these Russkie invaders have, it seems to have escaped local parents. In the words of one Prague housewife and mother of three, "My world has come to an end. What kind of God would allow this?"

Sure, there's always a spoilsport in the crowd, like student Jaromir Palach, who burned himself to death in protest of the occupation. But, by and large, these kids are crazy for Joe Russia! Boys nationwide are imitating the troops in their mode of dress and speech, even involuntarily enlisting in the Red Army. And girls are beside themselves.

"Oh my god," said 16-year-old Arianna Polgar. "I am helpless before them!"

TINY TIM NOVELTY WEARING OFF AT LIGHTNING PACE
See Arts, page 7C

MY LAI MASSACRE RAISING QUESTIONS ABOUT U.S. INVOLVEMENT IN MASSACRES
See page 14A

CROSBY, STILLS & NASH CONSUME HEROIN, ALCOHOL & METHAMPHETAMINES
See page 12C

THE ONION

LATE EDITION

Monday, July 21, 1969 — FINEST AMERICAN NEWS SOURCE — 10c

HOLY SHIT
MAN WALKS ON FUCKING MOON

Above: Neil Armstrong on the surface of the fucking moon.

The Earth as seen from—Holy Jesus—the surface of the moon.

NEIL ARMSTRONG'S HISTORIC FIRST WORDS ON MOON:
'HOLY LIVING FUCK'

THE MOON—Jesus fucking Christ.

The distant, lonely, mysterious satellite that has fascinated mankind since the dawn of time is distant and lonely no more.

At 4:17 p.m. EST yesterday, astronauts Neil Armstrong and Edwin E. Aldrin Jr. touched down on the Sea of Tranquility in the lunar module Eagle and radioed back to Earth the historic report: "Jesus fucking Christ, Houston. We're on the fucking moon."

Armstrong and Aldrin then made final technical and psychological preparations for the un-fucking-believableness of the next phase of the operation, the moon walk.

As two billion spellbound earthlings watched on television, Armstrong slowly descended the four steps leading out of the module, paused, and took one small but epoch-making step onto the soft, virgin soil.

"Holy living fuck.... Are you fucking believing this? Over," Armstrong radioed back to NASA headquarters nearly 250,000 miles away. "I abso-fucking-lutely am standing on the surface of the fucking moon. I am talking to you from the goddamned fucking moon. Jesus H. Christ in a chicken basket."

"Holy mother of fuck," the first man on the moon added.

"Roger, no fucking doubt about it," Mission Controller Peter Lovell replied. "A-fucking-firmative. Over."

Eight minutes later, as Armstrong gleefully bounced up and down in the moon's low-gravity atmosphere, Aldrin joined his colleague on the lunar surface. "Hell, yeah. Hell, yeah," an ecstatic Aldrin said, pumping his space-gloved fist into the thin air.

"It's like I told you on the way up here," replied Armstrong to his shipmate. "Remember? I told you this was going to be fucking amazing."

Armstrong and Aldrin then spent two hours engaged in activities related to the knock-you-on-your-ass resplendence of their situation before returning to the capsule. Their intense 18-month NASA training period—the primary function of which was to train the pair to deal with the unprecedented in-fucking-credible nature of their mission—proved effective, though at one point Armstrong had to sit down and take several deep breaths, "just so I don't fucking lose my shit."

The two were able to keep from urinating in their space suits long enough to collect soil and rock samples, which earthbound scientists at press time still could not even begin to fucking conceive.

The astronauts also planted an American flag in the ground alongside a plaque reading, in part: "This plaque, placed here by two visiting human beings from the planet around which this celestial body orbits, will rest undisturbed on this spot for the next 100 million years. High holy living fuck. Can you believe that shit?"

What follows is a partial transcript of the radio communication between the astronauts on the moon's Tranquility Base and NASA personnel at mission control on Earth:

TRANQUILITY BASE: This is Tranquility Base. The Eagle has landed. Jesus H. Christ, Houston. We're on the fucking moon. Over.

HOUSTON: Roger, Tranquility, we copy you. We cannot believe you are on the fucking moon. Repeat: Cannot fucking believe it. Over.

TRANQUILITY: It was a smooth touchdown. The moon, for Christ's sake, the moon. Over.

HOUSTON: Roger that. You're clear for T1, walking on the moon.

TRANQUILITY: We copy. Walking on moon. Jesus. Over.

HOUSTON: You're cleared to hook up Lunar Equipment Conveyor. To walk (pause) fucking walk on the moon. Over.

TRANQUILITY: LEC attached. Platform lined up. Checking ingress. Over.

HOUSTON: Everything okay, Tranquility?

TRANQUILITY: Am descending the ladder. Can see the Earth. The entire planet Earth, for the love of Christ.

HOUSTON: You're clear, Tranquility. Proceed. Over.

TRANQUILITY: Can see the Lunar Module footpads depressed into the surface of the moon. The fucking surface of the goddamned moon. (Long pause.) Holy shit.

HOUSTON: We read you. Over.

TRANQUILITY: Footpads depressed one or two inches. Surface is powdery. One more step, and I'm.... Fuck. (Long pause.) I'm hyperventilating. Hold on.

HOUSTON: Steady. Over. (Long pause.)

TRANQUILITY: I'm on the bottom rung of the ladder. Just one more step, and I'm.... (Long pause.)

HOUSTON: Tranquility?

TRANQUILITY: Holy (pause) living (long pause) fuck. (Long pause.) Fuck!

HOUSTON: Tranquility, do you copy?

TRANQUILITY: Are you fucking believing this? Over.

HOUSTON: We read you. Over.

TRANQUILITY: I abso-fucking-lutely am standing on the surface of the fucking moon. I am talking to you from the goddamned fucking moon. Jesus H. Christ in a chicken basket.

HOUSTON: Holy shit.

TRANQUILITY: Holy mother of fuck. The fucking moon. Over.

WE CAN PUT A MAN ON THE MOON, BUT WE CAN'T BOMB A TINY ASIAN NATION INTO THE STONE AGE?

Editorial, page 13A

THE ONION

Special Peace Issue

Sunday, August 10, 1969 — FINEST AMERICAN NEWS SOURCE — 72 PAGES CITY EDITION TU STULTUS ES — ★★★ — 30¢

SHARON TATE, FOUR OTHERS SLAIN IN GRISLY 'PARTRIDGE FAMILY' MURDERS

BEL AIR, Calif.—Actress Sharon Tate and four others were found stabbed to death Saturday in Tate's Bel Air home.

According to Los Angeles County forensics officials, the 26-year-old Tate, star of the film *Valley of the Dolls* and wife of director Roman Polanski, was brutally beaten with a tambourine before being stabbed 16 times. Blood was smeared on the walls of her home, spelling out such slogans as "Helter Skelter" and "Come on, Get Happy."

Members of a group calling itself "The Partridge Family" have claimed responsibility for the bizarre ritual slayings. A small cult believed to be led by a charismatic leader known only as "Reuben," The Partridge Family, which travels in a colorful, hand-painted school bus, has been linked to a series of murders in California over the past year.

"Laurie," who confessed to police on behalf of the Family, said the cult commits random killings in accordance with its leader's vision of a coming apocalypse. "We go into a town, and we kill people there," Laurie said, "just like Reuben tells us to."

Members of the Partridge Family cult: (L to R, top row) Laurie, Shirley, Keith; (bottom row) Christopher, Tracy, Danny.

U.S. Soldiers Receive Badly Needed Heroin Airlift

Junk-sick soldiers watch as heroin reinforcements arrive.

SAIGON, South Vietnam—Marines stationed in Saigon received a vital airlift of high-grade, CIA-procured heroin Saturday.

The heroin's arrival, according to many soldiers, came just as they were beginning to lose hope.

"I didn't know how much longer we could have held out," said PFC Ken Garwood of the 22nd Regiment as he tied off his arm with a length of rubber tubing. "We've been trying to get by on weed and some opium we scored in a hut, but we've all been junk-sick for almost 48 hours."

With the new shipment, each enlisted man will receive H-rations of seven fixes per week. Additionally, medics are being issued the WK-38, a "works kit" in a portable metal canister with enough syringes, spoons, lighters and tourniquets for a full platoon.

Officials are hailing the airlift as a major victory. "Now that our fighting men no longer have to waste precious time finding and killing Vietnamese dealers for their heroin, we have a chance to win this war and bring freedom to North Vietnam," CIA Director Richard Helms said.

General Creighton Abrams, commander of U.S. forces in South Vietnam, praised the heroin shipment as a much-needed boost for troop morale. "This shipment could help turn the tide for us here in 'Nam," he said. "Instead of being weak and shivering from withdrawal symptoms, the troops are now calm and coolly indifferent to human suffering and cruelty. Also, incidents of enlisted men killing their own officers for their heroin have decreased dramatically."

But even with the new heroin supply safely in GIs' hands, many U.S. officials see difficulties ahead.

"For many of our fighting men, there are still obstacles," State Department spokesman Robert Anderson said. "For example, many of them have tapped out virtually all their veins. A fresh supply of heroin is of limited use when there are no more veins to hit. We need to research new and better ways to get our boys the fixes they need."

Said Garwood, "If I can't get a good vein, I can always shoot it into my nuts."

Nixon Orders Nation's Youths Arrested

WASHINGTON, D.C.—President Nixon ordered the nation's approximately 50 million young people arrested Saturday, charging all Americans between the ages of 13 and 25 with criminal trespass, disturbing the peace and sedition.

"America's youths have proven increasingly dangerous to the stability and security of the U.S.," Nixon said. "The only safe option is to detain them indefinitely."

Nixon said the young people's repeated anti-war demonstrations, draft-dodging, bra-burning, unchecked hair growth and slang use have reached "crisis proportions" and must be stopped.

Prisons across the country are expected to suffer overcrowding as the nation's adolescent population is incarcerated. Officials are requiring all young people to report to local jails for temporary holding until federal prison space is allocated.

Federal marshals have been enlisted to hunt down all young adults who refuse to report voluntarily, and have orders to shoot on sight any unauthorized young person.

Said Nixon, "These grave security risks must be contained, at least until they are old enough to behave."

New Rock Opera Makes Christianity Appear Briefly Hip

NEW YORK—Thanks to the hit album *Jesus Christ Superstar*, Christianity has suddenly become a "cool" religion built around hippies and rock music.

The Andrew Lloyd Webber "rock opera," which has spawned a successful Broadway show and soon-to-be-released major motion picture, has temporarily made the teachings of Jesus Christ the "hippest" thing around.

"I thought Christianity was all about the Ten Commandments and not having fun, but I sure was wrong," said Wade Neville of Dallas, who saw the Broadway show during a trip to New York this week. "Now I realize it's about wild costumes, swirling lights, fog machines and trippy freak-out music."

"That Christianity is one groovy religion," said Larry Dobbs, 21, a fan of the musical. "And Jesus, he was, like, the original hippie. Way before his time, man."

The fleeting nature of the trend is already apparent, however. According to Alvin Westfield, a former New Jersey fan, "I thought Christ was cool when I saw the musical, but then I thought, 'Wait a minute—I'm sitting here listening to a bunch of church shit!'"

INSIDE THIS ISSUE:

AREA HIPPIE CONVINCED SOLUTION TO WORLD'S PROBLEMS SOMEHOW INVOLVES DRUGS, ROCK-AND-ROLL MUSIC, SWIRLING COLORED LIGHT
Page 3A

HEALTH OFFICIALS HAIL TV CIGARETTE-AD BAN AS FATAL BLOW TO TOBACCO INDUSTRY
Page 8A

TWIGGY POPULARIZING EATING DISORDERS
Page 6B

THE ONION

The Pentagon Is Not for Levitating

Wednesday, August 20, 1969 — FINEST AMERICAN NEWS SOURCE — 48 PAGES CITY EDITION TU STULTUS ES — ★★★ — **10¢**

APOLLO 13 ASTRONAUTS DROWN AS TED KENNEDY FLEES SPLASHDOWN SITE

INDIAN OCEAN—Apollo 13's harrowing six-day odyssey ended in tragedy Monday night, when the spacecraft's re-entry capsule struck the Indian Ocean and sank almost immediately, drowning astronauts James Lovell, John Swigert and Fred Haise.

Moments after the crash, U.S. Sen. Edward Kennedy (D-Mass.) was spotted traveling eastward, away from the splashdown site, by officers on the aircraft carrier U.S.S. *Saratoga*, which had been dispatched to retrieve the downed capsule.

In a press conference to explain his presence at the fatal splashdown, Kennedy, wearing a neck brace, reported that he was on his way home from a campaign meeting on Martha's Vineyard when the capsule landed in the Indian Ocean. He recounted his attempt to save the drowning astronauts and said he searched for a way to contact authorities. Kennedy added that he was not involved in the crash in any way.

NASA officials said Kennedy had not been scheduled to be onboard the Apollo capsule or in the capsule splashdown zone. They also reported that the astronauts perished Monday night, Aug. 18, yet Kennedy did not officially report the splashdown until Tuesday afternoon.

Workers at the Kennedy '70 campaign office in Boston reported that the senator was in attendance at a party late Monday night on Martha's Vineyard, and that he may have been drinking.

Launched last week, Apollo 13 was scheduled to land on the Fra Mauro region of the moon. On Monday, however, a service-module oxygen tank ruptured while the craft was 200,000 miles from Earth, forcing the mission to be aborted.

Officials have ordered all reports pertaining to Kennedy's involvement in the splashdown stricken from public record.

Left, survivor Ted Kennedy. Above, the Apollo 13 capsule is dredged by a Navy rescue team.

Woodstock Hosts 65 Musical Acts, 65,000 Sex Acts

A hippie offering herself for sex at the Woodstock Festival.

BETHEL, N.Y.—An estimated 500,000 music-loving members of the counterculture descended upon a farm in this small upstate New York town last weekend to attend the Woodstock Festival of Music and Art and Aquarian Exposition, a three-day festival that featured 65 musical acts and over 65,000 sex acts.

The festivities began Friday evening with a free performance by folk singer Joan Baez and a free-love performance by concertgoers Janet "Rain" Finkleman and Henry Dobbs.

"I couldn't believe it," said Jill Cooke, a bead vendor from Katonah, N.Y., who was present for all three days of Woodstock. "Arlo Guthrie went on right after Joan Baez. Then Sweetwater went on right after these four people on the blanket right in front of me got it on."

Besides getting a chance to see chart-toppers like Creedence Clearwater Revival perform, festival attendees also got a glimpse of lesser-known musicians such as Melanie and the Paul Butterfield Blues Band. Similarly, those fans expecting to see conventional two-person heterosexual vaginal intercourse were by no means disappointed, but were also exposed to mutual cunnilingus, anal sex, sexual toys and tantric orgies.

"I'd never been to a concert as exciting as this," said Mitchell Henning, 20, who came to see the band Country Joe and the Fish, yet ended up having sex with 19 unidentified concertgoers in a giant mud puddle.

The sea of music fans stretched for miles, all waiting to see if the next musical style would be folk, funk or rock—and to see if the next fucking style would be lying, sitting or standing. For most in attendance, it did not matter, as the crowd cheered just as loudly for the performance of Crosby, Stills, Nash and Young as for that of the doggie, swing, missionary and 69.

"The peace, the love, the energy in the air here—it was all so incredible," said Greg Hederer, 20, who drove all the way from Tallahassee, Fla., to attend the concert. "I got to see Janis Joplin doing 'Ball and Chain,' The Who doing 'My Generation,' and my roommate Mike doing two girls at once."

Rain at Woodstock Results in Slightly Dirtier Hippies

A sudden downpour at 3 p.m. Sunday during the third day of the Woodstock festival reportedly resulted in even dirtier hippies. Mud slicks quickly formed on the tramped fields of Max Yasgur's farm, giving concertgoers the chance to cover their already-grimy hair and filthy bodies in yet more dirt and mud.

"Whoo-hoo!" yelled one dirty hippie, Kevin "Tree-Branch" Roberts, as he threw himself into a 15-square-foot puddle of mud created by the sudden shower. He was immediately joined by seven others. Upon walking away from the puddle, a slight increase could be detected in the amount of grime on Roberts' body.

"Somehow, the rain, which could have given the hippies an opportunity to cleanse themselves," noted Jim Fingerton, a policeman assigned to the festival, "only resulted in an even thicker husk of crusted putridity upon their loathsome bodies."

In an effort to increase the skin area available to cover with filth, many of the hippies removed their clothing before rolling in the mud, emerging up to 14 percent dirtier.

Politics, Media, Baby-Boomer Psychodevelopment Converge in Mass Pop-Cultural Nexus

Such diverse and seemingly unrelated elements as the Vietnam War, the civil-rights movement, women's lib, the drug culture, the Beatles, Day-Glo body paint, Zen, motorcycle maintenance, and countless other sociopolitical phenomena fused inexorably today with the emerging "Baby Boomer" generation's late-adolescence/early-adulthood psychodevelopment, forming a swirling vortex of cultural synchronicity that social scientists are calling "the largest mass pop-cultural nexus in recorded history."

Said Cal Tech scientist Fred Haynes, "The nexus represents a singular point on the time continuum in which virtually every social issue, fashion statement, political controversy and consumer decision is borne of the Baby Boomers' late-teens/early-20s dilemma of parental-value-system rejection and resultant new freedom, i.e., the 'antithesis' segment of the dialectical 'thesis-antithesis-synthesis' triad."

Haynes predicts that because of the enormous scope of the nexus, the Baby Boomers will remain stuck in it, unable to escape their glorified picture of this seemingly mythic golden age for the remainder of their lives.

INSIDE THIS ISSUE:

COLLECTIVE NATIONAL MEMORY SWITCHES FROM BLACK-AND-WHITE TO COLOR
Page 3

HOW CAN WE STOP THIS 'LIZARD KING'?
Editorial, Page 15

50 PERCENT OF U.S. DRUG USE TRACED TO PRODUCERS OF *EASY RIDER*
Page 8

Logicon Inc., Satan Develop Bar-Code Technology

Logicon, Inc., working closely with both the National Grocers Association and Satan, has developed a universal bar-code symbol and reader for use in retail stores, as well as on the foreheads of the damned.

The symbol, a small, square row of black lines of varying thickness atop a line of computer-printed numbers, will label products ranging from canned beans to laundry detergent to cookies. It will also help the Great Deceiver brand his flock with the Mark of the Beast in the coming apocalypse, as foretold in the Book of Revelations.

Said Logicon spokesman Brad Hewitt, "This technology will make it very convenient for both retail merchants and the Lord of Lies to mark their goods, whether it be to sell them or lead them to eternal suffering in Hell."

115

THE ONION

Your Source for Fear and Loathing

Tuesday, September 12, 1972 — FINEST AMERICAN NEWS SOURCE — 52 PAGES, CITY EDITION — ★★★ — 10¢

Lebanon-Israel Badminton Match Called Hottest Ticket of Munich Olympics

'This Is One Bitter Rivalry,' Sportscasters Say

MUNICH, West Germany—Ordinarily, fan interest in an Olympic badminton match between two non-medal contenders would barely draw a crowd. But last week's athlete killings have suddenly made tonight's Israel-Lebanon game the hottest ticket in Munich.

"Olga Korbut performs in gymnastics tonight, and Mark Spitz has a shot at a seventh gold medal, but no one is interested in those events," Munich Games ticket-sales director Günter Klimt said. "Everyone wants to see the Israel-Lebanon badminton match. Ever since Palestinian terrorists raided the Olympic Village and killed 11 Israeli athletes, Israel's badminton team has been out for some serious revenge."

Fan interest in this white-hot rivalry is so intense that tickets for the 8 p.m. fourth-round match-up are almost impossible to obtain.

"I must see this event," said Jerusalem resident Moshe Cohen, who flew to Munich with his eight brothers just for the match. "I want to see the Lebanese badminton team pay dearly for what their countrymen did to my people. I hope it is death out there on the court for them. Even if they lose 15-0, it will still be too kind a fate for the Lebanese badminton team."

"I hope the Israelis hit the shuttlecock right down those Arab dogs' throats," Cohen added.

"You have to like the Israelis in this event," said *Sports Illustrated*'s Steve Warren. "The Black September terrorists came in and tied up the Israeli Olympians and shot them execution-style. I'm sure the Israelis are going to be swinging those badminton rackets extra hard tonight."

INSIDE THIS ISSUE:

WE NEED MORE FILMS ABOUT YOUNG ATHLETES DYING OF CANCER
Editorial, Page 9A

PANELING INSTALLED IN BASEMENT REC ROOM
Page 3B

Puke Orange, Pea Green, Mustard Yellow Adopted as New National Colors

WASHINGTON, D.C.—A federally appointed panel of interior decorators, assigned the task of giving the American flag a more up-to-date look for the '70s, chose puke orange, pea green and mustard yellow as the new national colors Monday.

"These bright, vibrant colors really say, 'Welcome to the '70s, America,'" panel chairman Leslie Lurman said. "And the new design of the flag is much more 'with it.'"

"Red, white and blue served America well," Lurman added, "but, as we fast approach our Bicentennial, we need to revamp America's image for a new age of good taste and impeccable fashion sense."

The panel is recommending that the flag's dated-looking stars be replaced by exaggeratedly rounded, bathmat-style daisies; that the stripes be made slightly more modern and psychedelic; and that all flags be made of hemp.

The panel decided on the colors and design of the new flag after a lengthy discussion with leaders of the fashion and interior-design industries.

"Everything from bean-bag chairs to polyester dresses is available in these popular, attention-getting colors," Lurman said. "Stomach-flu avocado, concrete gray and rancid-orange-juice tangerine are also good choices, but, in the end, the most dynamite colors won out. Puke orange, pea green and mustard yellow are truly the colors of our time."

The new national colors are expected to inspire the design of everything from home furnishings to public libraries and schools.

Other colors considered in the new design but ultimately decided against were vomit yellowish-green, multi-color shag and crap brown. Plaid was also a finalist.

The U.S. flag's groovy new look.

SPORTS NEWS

BUFFALO BILLS' O.J. SIMPSON MERCILESSLY SLASHES THROUGH HELPLESS DEFENDERS FOR 214 YARDS
Sports, Page 1D

National Guard Closes Kent State Recruiting Office

KENT, Ohio—After more than two years of what officials are calling "disappointingly low recruitment numbers," the Ohio National Guard announced Monday that its Kent State University recruiting office will permanently close its doors this week.

"Students at Kent State just don't seem to want to be a part of the Ohio National Guard," Staff Sergeant Mark Hildebrand said.

The closing came after the Ohio National Guard made one final recruitment push. "We went from dormitory to dormitory," Hildebrand said. "We told students about how rewarding a career in the Guard can be and explained just how much a young person can learn, including proper crowd-dispersal techniques and how to restore order. We even let some students look at our rifles up close."

Hildebrand said most of the students had not been convinced by the pitch.

Nixon Steps Up Bombing Raids on *New York Times*

'This Is a Necessary Escalation to Protect the U.S. Presidency,' Nixon Says

WASHINGTON, D.C.—In the fiercest offensive since the Pentagon Papers were first leaked to the press, President Nixon ordered U.S. Navy bombers to step up their attacks on *The New York Times*' offices Monday.

Speaking to the White House press corps, Nixon expressed his determination to bring down the longstanding newspaper of record.

"Our military objective is to defeat *The New York Times* and bring its editors to the bargaining table. Once there, we must negotiate a cease-publish of defamatory remarks against the office of the president of the United States," Nixon said. "We will not relent in our air assaults on *The New York Times* until that newspaper is once again a decent, respectful institution and not one that seeks to undermine democracy and tear down everything the U.S. is fighting for."

Bombers are targeting *The New York Times*' vital writer-supply routes from the west at the paper's West 43rd Street entrance. Also being hit are the newspaper's strategic communication centers, such as its office switchboard and reception desk.

The latest round of shelling, which lasted from 7 p.m. Friday until midnight, destroyed numerous key *Times* strongholds, including three large printing presses, 22 delivery trucks, and the offices of the classified-ads department.

"These were important strikes," Nixon said. "The *Times* generates 11 percent of its total revenue from classified-ad sales. If we can just knock out display ads, we'll have them right where we want them."

Nixon said the bombings will likely increase in intensity over the next several weeks. The ultimate target for future attacks, he said, will be the opinion-page desk.

"Once the Navy flyers have penetrated the office's outer defenses, ground troops will be deployed to neutralize opinion-page forces. Those bastards have been against me ever since I ran for the Senate in '48. They endorsed Kennedy in '60 and Humphrey in '68, and I'm sure they'll endorse McGovern in the upcoming election."

Nixon said a *New York Times* endorsement is one of the key objectives of the military action. Despite a recent Supreme Court ruling in favor of *The New York Times*, Nixon expressed confidence that the newspaper can be defeated.

"We can win in southeast New York State," he said.

President Nixon.

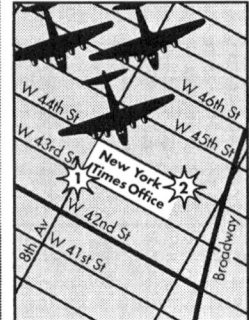

The first wave of Nixon's New York Times *attack plan: 1. Primary writer-supply route. 2. Opinion-page desk.*

THE ONION

Tuesday, January 23, 1973 — FINEST AMERICAN NEWS SOURCE — 10¢

What Color Is Your Parachute?

Henley, Frey Urge Nation to Take It Easy

Laid-Back Eagles Call for National Mellowing-Out Period

WINSLOW, Ariz.—In a heartfelt plea for calm following 10 turbulent years of political unrest and massive social upheaval, mellow-rock-industry leaders Don Henley and Glenn Frey urged the nation to take it easy Monday.

The plea, delivered by the two Eagles from a corner in Winslow, Arizona, left many in attendance with a peaceful, easy feeling, sources said.

"We as a nation have been letting the sound of our own wheels drive us crazy," said Frey, his feathered hair stirring slightly in a mild breeze as he casually slung an acoustic guitar over his shoulder. "Now, more than ever, the American people need to kick back and loosen their collective load."

Frey said the societal shifts and fallout caused by the '60s are so complex that citizens should not even try to understand them. "No matter what our problems may be," he said, "one thing is certain: Win or lose, we will never be here again. So let's lighten up, America—while we still can."

Added Henley, "Come on, baby, don't say maybe."

"Take me for example," said Henley, looking laid-back in jeans, cowboy boots and a denim shirt provocatively unbuttoned almost to the waist, leaving much of his tanned upper torso visible. "The way I look, you'd never guess that, at this very moment, I have seven women on my mind, four of whom, incidentally, want to own me. But, despite facing such pressures, I maintain a relaxed attitude. Yes, I have problems, but I don't let them get to me."

In keeping with the spirit of their remarks, Henley and Frey cut the press conference short after the unexpected appearance of a girl in a flatbed Ford, who slowed down to take a look at the laid-back duo.

"My Lord," Henley said.

Music-industry insiders attribute the duo's all-encompassing mellowness to a near-constant state of euphoric marijuana "high." Over the next few years, analysts say, the mellowness will gradually give way to infighting, paranoia and, eventually, a descent into cocaine addiction—an experience which has been likened to a hotel from which you can check out any time you like, but can never leave.

G. Gordon Liddy Eats Former Attorney General to Prevent Exposure of Watergate Secrets

WASHINGTON, D.C.—Presidential operative G. Gordon Liddy ate John Mitchell Monday in what he confessed was an attempt to keep the former attorney general from testifying before Special Prosecutor Archibald Cox.

"Mitchell contained very sensitive information that was germane to my mission," Liddy said during his arraignment in a Washington courtroom. "I, therefore, ate him to prevent that information from falling into enemy hands."

Liddy reportedly broke into Mitchell's residence in suburban Washington at 1 a.m. Monday dressed in black and wearing a ski mask and leather gloves. According to his statement, he then clubbed Mitchell, cut him into bite-sized chunks and ate him.

The secrets Liddy did not want divulged relate to the alleged break-in at the Watergate Hotel, according to a source deep within a Washington parking ramp.

"Liddy was afraid Mitchell would reveal Liddy's complex door-lock-taping and file-cabinet-crowbarring techniques," the source said.

At his arraignment, Liddy claimed the secrets were "sensitive information crucial to the preservation of national security," and he refused to reveal the brand of duct tape he used on the door of the Watergate garage entrance or the type of rag he used to cover his fist before smashing a window in George McGovern's suite. Such secrets, Liddy said, will die with him.

"Even if I am tied down, skinned alive, rolled in salt, beaten and electrocuted through my tongue and genitals," Liddy said, "I will never make known these vital secrets, for I must safeguard the democratic ideals of this country."

According to the parking-ramp source, Liddy has targeted for ingestion seven other key members of the Nixon Administration and the Committee to Re-elect the President whom he believes could potentially disclose the sensitive information.

He said that, before these men are questioned by authorities, he will escape from custody and eat them, as well.

G. Gordon Liddy being led to prison by federal marshals.

Teens Hold Hilltop Summit to Discuss Purchase of Planetary Soft Drink

The teens addressing soft-drink distribution.

LECCE, Italy—More than 200 teen-agers, bottles of Coke in hand, gathered yesterday on a green hilltop just south of this picturesque town for an impromptu beverage-purchasing and music-education summit.

Insiders are praising the hilltop conference as a success, reporting that candid discussions were conducted with the participants spaced approximately two feet apart across the grassy hill, an arrangement essential to the teens' expression of unified, almost cultish devotion to their two major resolutions.

The first was a plan to offer singing lessons to every citizen of the planet. Said coalition member Sally Baker, "We'd like to teach the four billion citizens of our world to sing in perfect harmony."

The second plan entails the purchase of a bottle of Coke for the world. Further, the teens guaranteed that they would keep the world company during its consumption of the complimentary beverage.

Although sponsored by a multibillion-dollar soft-drink company, the meeting was of great significance to world peace, according to group spokesman Mark Lee. "As you see," he said, "the teens are dressed in hippie styles and possess idealistic smiles, much like anti-war protesters of the modern youth counterculture."

Many observers are already skeptical of the group's plan.

"Their suggestions are not practical at this time," U.N. Secretary General Kurt Waldheim said. "The world's four billion citizens could not peacefully share a 10-ounce bottle of cola. Only one 400-millionth of an ounce would be allotted to each person. We do not currently possess the scientific know-how to divide fluids into such microscopic portions. Disagreements would inevitably result. This is a recipe for war, not peace."

Bumper-Sticker Industry Applauds *Roe v. Wade* Decision

WASHINGTON, D.C.—The nation's bumper-sticker lobbyists are hailing the Supreme Court's *Roe v. Wade* decision Monday as a major victory for bumper-sticker sales.

Said Bumper-Sticker Manufacturers of America President Karl Steinholz: "This Supreme Court decision is a triumph for the entire bumper-sticker industry. But it is also a victory for women, as they now have the freedom to look at two bumper stickers and decide which choice is right for them."

Chief Justice Warren Burger, in the majority opinion, wrote, "This court has deemed abortion a constitutional right. Now, a woman, before making her very personal decision, must first look deep within the bumpers of the cars in front of her at traffic stops."

Steinholz, who sells bumper stickers to stores nationwide, said he is somewhat conflicted regarding the complex issue. "I am really undecided about abortion," he said. "On the one hand, the nation's lawmakers should definitely keep their laws off a woman's body. But, on the other hand, it's important to remember that an aborted fetus is a child, not a choice."

Steinholz noted that both "It's a Child, Not a Choice" and "Keep Your Laws Off My Body" bumper stickers are available at stores everywhere.

The historic ruling means bumper-sticker creators will dictate the terms of America's abortion dialogue in the coming years. Said Steinholz: "This debate has now moved out of the courts and onto the bumpers of cars, where it belongs."

CAN A LESBIAN EXCEL AT SPORTS?

Billie Jean King Profile, Page 4E

INSIDE THIS ISSUE:

NIXON FORGETS TO REMOVE HANGER BEFORE DONNING SUIT COAT

Page 7A

THE ONION

Saturday, April 8, 1974 — FINEST AMERICAN NEWS SOURCE — 15¢

Long-Haired Freaky People Need Not Apply

U.S. SEVERS TIES WITH SYMBIONIA FOLLOWING PATTY HEARST KIDNAPPING

Symbionese Leaders Outraged
U.S. Stands to Lose $168 in Export Revenue

Patty Hearst holding up the Hibernia Bank in San Francisco.

WASHINGTON, D.C.—Responding to the Symbionese Liberation Army's kidnapping and subsequent brainwashing of publishing heiress Patricia Hearst, the U.S. officially severed trade with the nation of Symbionia Friday.

President Nixon made the formal announcement from the White House. "The United States will, as of today, sever all diplomatic relations with the people and government of Symbionia," he said.

Following the announcement, Nixon ordered Warren M. Reed, the U.S. ambassador to Symbionia, to return to the U.S. immediately. The president also deployed seven Army C-130 transports to airlift any Americans from Symbionese territory.

"I will always reflect fondly upon the Symbionese people, culture and way of life," Reed said of Symbionia, a nation consisting of a small apartment on San Francisco's Golden Gate Avenue. "But after this recent incident, once I pass through customs and say my final goodbyes, I will never go back."

The ambassador said he will never forget the distinct aroma of Symbionia, which he described as a pungent mix of hippie body odor and thick cigarette smoke.

In a letter to Nixon, Cinque Mtume, General Field Marshal of the Symbionese Liberation Army, called the president's severing of relations "ridiculous and insulting." He said Hearst acted of her own will throughout her time in Symbionia, including during the infamous bank heist in which a security camera recorded her and four others wielding guns.

"How can an entire nation be punished for the actions of five of its citizens, even if those five people happen to constitute 60 percent of its total population?" Cinque wrote. "It is yet another example of the hypocrisy of the fascist, capitalist-militarized AmeriKKKa which preys upon the people."

According to Cinque, U.S. trade sanctions against Symbionia will only hurt the poorest, most innocent Symbionese citizens, one-fourth of whom (citizens Gelina and Zoya) had to quit their respective retail-clerk and fry-cook jobs last month to focus on Symbionese issues of national import, such as washing the dishes and taking out the trash.

A number of U.S. businesses have criticized Nixon's decision to end trade relations. Symbionia, an import-dependent country with a total annual budget of nearly $19,000, purchases the majority of its goods from the U.S.

Said Sam Wong, owner of San Francisco's Kwik-Shop market, "Every month, I sell as many as three boxes of pancake mix to the Symbionese people. I stand to lose up to $22 a year as a result of the president's decision."

Also disappointed are U.S. vacationers. Said Ralph Bartlett of Des Moines, Iowa, "My kids were really looking forward to our big vacation in Symbionia this summer. They wanted to see the closet, take a ride in the tub slide, and sample some of that famous Symbionese canned corn."

Symbionese-Americans, however, were the most upset. Osceola, who lived in Symbionia last year and is now serving time in San Quentin Federal Penitentiary for the murder of Oakland School Superintendent Marcus Foster, called Nixon's severing of ties "the work of a bourgeois pig, a fascist oppressor of the people."

The other remaining Symbionese-American could not be reached for comment.

Nixon Ordered to Hand Over 8-Track Tapes

Content of Tapes Leaked to *Washington Post* by Anonymous Source Known as 'Deep Purple'

Nixon to Be Fined One Penny for First Eight Tapes Not Turned in, $4.95 for Each Subsequent Tape

WASHINGTON, D.C.—Judge John J. Sirica has ordered President Nixon to hand over more than 400 hours of 8-track tapes Friday.

"These tapes feature music from such popular bands as Edgar Winter Group, Allman Brothers, and The Guess Who," said Sirica, announcing the decision. "The American people have a right to hear the great tunes that are on these tapes."

The tapes also contain material that a report in yesterday's *Washington Post* described as "extremely sensitive," including songs from Jackson Browne, Joni Mitchell and James Taylor.

Ever since Special Prosecutor Archibald Cox first discovered a Weltron 2001 8-track deck with Panasonic speakers in the Oval

President Nixon enjoying Emerson, Lake & Palmer's Brain Salad Surgery, one of the hotly contested White House tapes.

Tapes Demanded by Judge Sirica:
Allman Brothers: 'Eat a Peach'
The Guess Who: 'American Woman'
Pink Floyd: 'Dark Side of the Moon'

Office, Nixon has been under intense pressure to turn over the accompanying tapes.

While the president agreed last week to hand in crucial tapes by Grand Funk Railroad, Alice Cooper and Bachman-Turner Overdrive, he said Cox's across-the-board demand for all tapes compromises presidential privilege.

The Senate 8-Track Investigating Committee said it will impose a stiff fine against Nixon if he attempts to block the order. While the fine will be just one penny for the first eight tapes he attempts to suppress, the commission stressed that it will dramatically increase for any additional tapes, and will remain in effect over the next 24 months.

"Nixon will have an opportunity to cancel this investigation at any time by handing over the tapes," Cox said.

Rumors and conjecture are swirling around the controversial tapes. The most shocking and scandalous material is reportedly on the tape labeled *Sloppy Seconds* by Doctor Hook & The Medicine Show. "The lyrics and innuendo on this tape are enough to bring down the entire Republican Party," *The Washington Post* reported last week, quoting an anonymous source identified only as "Deep Purple."

Also circulating are rumors of impeachment procedures against Nixon if duplicity is found in his methods of collecting the tapes. Former White House aides H.R. Haldeman and John Ehrlichman remain silent on the question of whether any tapes owned by Nixon are illegal bootlegs, possibly obtained during his 1972 trip to China. Nixon's recently released "want list" includes such incriminating requests as "explicit" versions of certain Redd Foxx party records which have not been released in the 8-track format.

Amputee Children of Cambodia Award Peace Prize to Henry Kissinger

Henry Kissinger.

PHNOM PENH, Cambodia— At a special ceremony Friday, the approximately 40,000 amputee children of Cambodia awarded U.S. Secretary of State Henry Kissinger a special peace prize.

Kissinger, who won the Nobel Peace Prize last year, was honored by the armless and/or legless Cambodian children for "outstanding achievement in secret bombing raids on a nation not even involved in the Vietnam War."

"Mr. Kissinger, we would like to commend you for your brave and tireless commitment to dropping hundreds of thousands of tons of TNT on the rural villages of Cambodia," said 11-year-old Sen Sandan, who lost his left arm, left leg and right foot when a B-52 carpet-bombed an area near his hut. "If I had the necessary body parts, I would give you a hug."

Kissinger was unable to accept the award in person, as he was meeting with the Joint Chiefs of Staff to plan a napalm raid on the Cambodian village of Ta Seng.

INSIDE THIS ISSUE:

U.N. GENERAL SECRETARY WALDHEIM OUTLINES 'FINAL SOLUTION' TO THIRD-WORLD HUNGER PROBLEM
Page 6A

ANCIENT CHINESE SECRET REVEALED TO BE CALGON
Page 13A

NATION'S BOYS OPENLY PLAY WITH DOLLS FOLLOWING 'FREE TO BE YOU AND ME' BROADCAST
Editorial, Page 4C

'MATCH GAME' CELEBRITY GUESTS TONIGHT:

BERT CONVY
BRETT SOMERS
CHARLES NELSON REILLY
PHYLLIS DILLER
RICHARD DAWSON
CHARO

THE ONION

Monday, July 1, 1974 — FINEST AMERICAN NEWS SOURCE — 15¢

Win a Dream Date with Elliott Gould! SEE PAGE 8

NIXON ARRESTED IN CONNECTION WITH WATERGATE BREAK-IN

President Handcuffed, Taken to Prison in Oval Office Bust

Chief Executive Resists Arrest, Threatens Officers

Judge Sirica Denies Bail

WASHINGTON, D.C.—With evidence continuing to mount implicating President Nixon in the Watergate scandal, federal agents and D.C.-area police officials moved in on the president Sunday, arresting him during a meeting with his advisors in the Oval Office.

The president—who furiously struggled with the law-enforcement personnel for more than 25 minutes, throwing a barrage of punches and kicking wildly—was finally pinned down and handcuffed at 3 p.m. EST. Refusing to remain standing, he was eventually forced to his feet and dragged to a waiting FBI squad car, which transported him to McWilliams Federal Penitentiary in Alexandria, Va.

"You won't get away with this, you lousy, cock-sucking Justice Department goons," an enraged Nixon shouted to FBI agents as he was escorted from the White House. "I'll have the Secret Service kill every last goddamned one of you, I swear I will. Do you have any idea who you're dealing with? I'm Richard Milhous Nixon, the president of the United Fucking States of America."

Attorney General William Saxbe said he made the decision to arrest Nixon Friday after a hidden camera planted in the White House basement caught him burning 64 tapes allegedly containing incriminating evidence linking the president to the Watergate break-in. Also factoring in the decision, Saxbe said, was the Justice Department's acquisition of a signed confession from former Nixon aide John Ehrlichman stating that the president had not only masterminded the Watergate break-in, but had also ordered the assassinations of a number of his key enemies, including Hubert Humphrey, Watergate Special Prosecutor Leon Jaworski and Beach Boys lead singer Brian Wilson.

Nixon has been charged with 64 counts of destruction of criminal evidence, three counts of obstruction of justice and one count of resisting arrest and spitting on a federal agent. If found guilty on all counts, he could face up to 265 years in a federal penitentiary.

In his first official statement from his prison cell, Nixon said, "You may think you've got me this time but, believe me, you haven't heard the last of Dick Nixon. I'm a smart son of a bitch and, when I make up my mind to do something, by God, I do it. And right about now, what I'm determined to do is get out of here and get back at all of you who've tried to make Dick Nixon the national scapegoat. I tell you, I haven't done anything illegal and I never have. You've got no proof on me whatsoever."

Nixon then used his one phone call to talk to former Vice President and good friend Spiro Agnew. It is unknown what the pair discussed.

The president has been denied bail by federal judge John Sirica, who said the charges were serious enough to warrant a suspension of normal procedure. Until a trial date is set, Nixon will remain in his cell, which he shares with Dwayne Arlen, a 24-year-old convicted child molester from Richmond, Virginia.

"The whole damn country is out to get me. They all want to watch me burn," Nixon said. "Well, you can all rot in hell for all I care."

Police officers escorting the president to jail.

Inside:

Uri Geller Tapped as Possible Alternative Energy Source

PAGE 6A

Mommy and Daddy Don't Love Each Other Anymore

In a tearful three-hour family meeting Sunday, Mommy announced that she and Daddy are no longer in love.

"But we both still love you kids very much," she emphasized, holding back agonized tears.

Mommy offered long, silent hugs to the children in an attempt to console them in their crushing sadness and disbelief.

Daddy, who had reportedly met privately with Mommy prior to the announcement, added little. He merely bowed his head, removed his glasses and slowly rubbed his eyes as if in great pain.

Mommy outlined plans for moving out of the house and starting "a new life," which is said to include a new school, new town, new friends and no Daddy.

Mommy also warned the children that times would be tight, noting that they would have to move into a small apartment, much smaller than the current family home, and that everyone would have to get used to less-generous Christmases and birthdays in the coming years. But she promised to work two jobs and "pull through somehow."

While Mommy and Daddy claimed to still love the kids, a spokesman for the kids said, "If Mommy and Daddy no longer love each other, it is believed at this time that they most likely do not love the kids, either."

The feelings of emptiness and the emotional trauma caused by the announcement are not expected to wane.

Lone Indian Cries Single Tear

ROCHESTER, N.Y.—An unidentified lone Indian, dressed in full ceremonial regalia, including buckskin vest and feathered headdress, sat on horseback near an upstate New York park and shed a single, noble tear Sunday.

Experts in the public-service-announcement industry report that the tear, which trickled down the deep cracks in the majestic Indian's weathered, distinguished face with extreme dignity, was prompted by the sight of a discarded soda can on the ground.

"Indians used to hold the beauty of nature in the highest esteem, prizing it as a sacred gift from the Great Spirit or something," said television producer Ted Haim, creator of numerous award-winning 30-second public-awareness spots. "So I believe he was very upset by the sight of the litter."

While the discarded can is believed to be the primary cause of the Indian's single tear, sources close to the Indian said the tear may also have been shed because, centuries ago, the white man, who was greeted by the Indian's ancestors in friendship, stole their land, raped their women, burned their villages, slaughtered their families, denigrated their race, violated their peace treaties, mocked and defiled their traditions, gave them smallpox-infected blankets, sent them on forced marches at gunpoint across thousands of snow-covered miles, and confined them to impoverished reservations.

The anonymous Indian, who bowed his head and rode slowly and silently down a hilltop, as if beaten down by the onslaught of modern man's litter, could not be reached for comment.

Senate Committee Investigates Lapel Expansion

WASHINGTON, D.C.—The Senate Select Committee on Oversized Fashions is launching an investigation into the recent explosive expansion of shirt and coat lapels.

"The American lapel is growing at an unchecked rate, and not just in the discos and singles bars," said committee member Milton Young (R-N.D.). "It is now affecting the general population and has even reached the hallowed halls of this lawmaking body."

Among the committee's numerous concerns is the possible health risk posed by lapels that extend nearly to the shoulders. Medical experts will be called to testify regarding the threat of spinal misalignment caused by the increase in fabric weight around the neck.

Another concern, raised by Sen. Walter Huddleston (D-Ky.), is the possibility of oversized lapels flapping in the faces of motorists and joggers, dangerously obscuring their vision.

A recent Ventura, Calif., incident put the problem in the national spotlight when a man caught in an ocean breeze was lifted into the air like a hang-glider by the outstretched lapels of his sport coat. He flew four city blocks before crash landing, killing himself and a 70-year-old Santa Barbara woman.

Scheduled to testify this week before the committee is Tyrone Little, whose enormous lapels have kept him from holding down a regular job. "I was fired from my job at the car wash because, even under the full-body jumpsuit issued by my employer, my lapels still protruded far enough to impair my ability to freely move my arms to buff or wax," he said. "Interior work was out of the question."

The committee is expected to call for increased federal incentives for chest hair and lowered silk-shirt unbuttoning to draw the eye inward, away from the lapels. Members are also expected to recommend federal gold-chest-medallion subsidies to keep lapel-wearers safely weighted down.

119

THE ONION

Wednesday, July 3, 1974 — FINEST AMERICAN NEWS SOURCE — 15¢

Special Shag-Carpet Pull-Out PAGE 7B

NIXON ESCAPES

President Kills Two, Wounds Six in Stunning Jailbreak

A prison surveillance photo of the escape from McWilliams Federal Penitentiary. Nixon is believed to be the figure circled.

Congress Passes Anti-Blaxploitation Bill

Pimps, Players Subject to Heavy Fines

WASHINGTON, D.C.—By a 92-5 vote, a comprehensive new Anti-Blaxploitation Bill passed the U.S. Senate Tuesday.

Supporters of the legislation, including wealthy white businessmen, police chiefs and prison wardens, are hailing its passage as a victory in the fight against pimps, players and mack daddies.

"Our nation's citizens have been blaxploited for too long," said U.S. Sen. James Lane Buckley (R-N.Y.), sponsor of the bill. "Figures such as Superfly, The Mack and Foxy Brown must be kept down."

The new measure also targets merchants who sell blaxploitative goods. Feathered fedoras, platform boots, ivory-topped canes and silk shirts will all be subject to stiff tariffs, while lowriders will be banned outright.

Pimp and mack-daddy reaction to the anti-blaxploitation bill has been mixed. "There's gonna be hell up in Harlem if Whitey tries to tax my threads, you dig?" said Willie Dynamite, a 110th Street-based businessman who has campaigned for years against being kept down by The Man.

Youngblood Priest, a New York drug dealer and player, said he supports the measure. "I've been on the streets all my life, selling junk for chump change," Priest said. "I just want out, but until now, The Man wouldn't let me out. The pigs wanted to own me. But nobody owns Youngblood Priest. I believe this legislation

Blaxploited private dick John Shaft.

will help me as I attempt to start a new life—after this one last score."

The new law is expected to affect blacks outside the pimp and mack-daddy communities, as well. Armed black superheroes, who have thrived on blaxploitation for years, will now be required to register with their local police departments.

Said prominent black vigilante Jim Slaughter, "This congressional action is jive." Slaughter, who claims his name is also his business, and sometimes his pleasure, has responded to the measure with a sweeping "Kill All Honky Mother-Fuckers" campaign.

John Shaft, a black private dick who is a sex machine to all the chicks, said the new legislation will not affect him. "I'm a cat who won't cop out when there's danger all about," Shaft said. "This law isn't going to cramp my style. Of course, I don't expect everyone to feel as I do, since no one understands me but my woman."

VP Agnew Assists Nixon in Escape, Drives Getaway Car

Pair Believed to Be Headed to Mexico in Blue '71 Dodge Dart

Executive Branch 'Armed and Extremely Dangerous'

ALEXANDRIA, Va.—Just two days after his arrest, President Nixon escaped from McWilliams Federal Penitentiary Tuesday with assistance from former Vice President Spiro Agnew.

"At approximately 3:15 p.m. Tuesday, the President of the United States escaped from this maximum-security facility," McWilliams warden Bill Engelbreit said. "We do not know his whereabouts. Local, state and federal authorities have been given descriptions of Nixon, and the FBI has ordered a nationwide manhunt."

The breakout occurred as guards were leading Nixon back to his cell from the prison's exercise yard. Using a loud explosion prison officials believe was set off by Agnew as a diversion, Nixon slipped through a gate in the ensuing chaos, disarming prison guards Christopher Tierney, 31, and Bryan Whalen, 44.

Scattered witness reports of the breakout indicate that the president pointed a gun to Tierney's head and ordered him to lock the gate behind them. Nixon then shot Tierney and Whalen and scaled a fence to reach the prison's delivery entrance, where a man later confirmed to be Agnew awaited him in what is believed to have been a '71 Dodge Dart.

There may have been another man in the car's back seat; witnesses report the presence of a passenger strongly resembling Nixon aide John Ehrlichman, though his identity could not be confirmed.

Prison guards gave chase in three cars, but several of the vehicles' drivers and passengers were wounded by shots from Nixon, forcing them off the road.

While it is not known where Nixon and Agnew are headed, many suspect they will attempt to drive non-stop to Mexico. "Throughout his presidency, Nixon has enjoyed good relations with Mexico, and it stands to reason that he may attempt to lay low there until the Watergate scandal and the prison-guard killings blow over," Georgetown University political-science professor Patrick Oglethorpe said.

Oglethorpe said it is unlikely that Nixon would attempt to flee to Canada. "President Nixon is well aware that thousands of draft-dodging, Nixon-hating American young people are currently living in Canada, and they would be more than happy to turn in the man they feel is responsible for the deaths of thousands of American boys in Vietnam," he said. "Plus, Nixon very much dislikes any weather too cold to golf in."

FBI Director Clarence Kelley said a $40,000 reward is being offered for any information leading to the arrest of the president, whom he described as a white male, approximately six feet tall with thinning hair, a long nose, and a stooped back. Kelley advised anyone who sees the president to call the police immediately, urging them not to attempt to subdue Nixon by themselves.

"I wish to stress that the president is armed and extremely dangerous," Kelley said. "If he perceives you as a threat, he will not hesitate to shoot you, whether you voted for him or not."

Ralph Nader Killed in Pinto Test Drive

FRESNO, Calif.—Consumer advocate Ralph Nader was killed early Wednesday morning during a safety test of the new '75 Ford Pinto.

Nader, who was driving the subcompact vehicle on a closed course, lost control of the Pinto on a turn and swerved into a wall. The car exploded into flames upon impact, killing Nader instantly.

Ford officials denied that the fatal crash was caused by the faulty design of its gas tank, blaming it on driver error.

"If you listen to all the eyewitness accounts, it's clear that Mr. Nader should never have been allowed on that test track," Ford Director of Communications Peter Schildtke said. "We won't know about his blood-alcohol level until next week, but, based on the damage caused by the automobile's sudden explosion, our engineers believe Nader may have been braking too late at stop signs and not using the proper 10-o'clock-2-o'clock hand positions on the steering wheel."

Schildtke expressed "deep regret" over Nader's death, but said it would have "absolutely no effect" on the company's plans to put 500,000 Pintos on the market by the end of 1975.

Friends of Ralph Nader are planning to remember him with a memorial sculpture of a Pinto with an eternal flame rising from its exploding engine.

Inside:

Kissinger Mistakenly Wears Lion Shirt with Hippo Pants in Embarrassing Garanimals Mismatch

PAGE 2A

THE ONION

Wednesday, July 10, 1974 — FINEST AMERICAN NEWS SOURCE — 48 PAGES CITY EDITION / TU STULTUS ES — ★★★ — 15¢

Women's Lib: The Real Risks — PAGE 2

FEDS GUN DOWN NIXON OUTSIDE ARIZONA MOTEL

FBI Agents Bring Down Fugitive President in Hail of Gunfire

6-Day, 10-State Executive Killing Spree Comes to End; Agnew Still at Large

YUMA, Ariz.—The presidency of Richard Nixon came to a violent end Tuesday, when FBI operatives opened fire on him outside the Sunspot Motel in the border town of Yuma, Ariz., killing him.

At 3:11 p.m., after a tense, six-hour standoff in which more than 200 federal agents surrounded the motel, an exhausted-looking Nixon came charging out of his room holding a gun to the head of a pregnant woman from the motel's housekeeping staff. FBI Special Agent Jim Brock ordered the president to release the hostage and put down his weapon. When he did not, and the woman was able to break free and run inside an open room, the agents were given clearance to fire on Nixon.

Nixon, sporting dark stubble and sweating profusely from the 108-degree heat, was struck twice in the abdomen and once in the shoulder. He then opened fire in return, killing one agent and wounding three others before being fatally shot in the chest. He was pronounced dead at 3:19 p.m. EST.

"We made every effort to capture the president alive, but it was not possible," Brock said. "Once he realized he was surrounded, he was determined to take out as many people as possible."

With the help of the Master Charge company, federal agents were able to track Nixon to the motel through a stolen credit card he had been using since holding up a gas station in Emporia, Kan., Sunday. The card's owner, Henry Tillman of Emporia, had been inside the filling station when the president robbed the register and shot the clerk. Nixon then pistol-whipped Tillman, taking his credit card and heading west on Route 11.

Acting on a tip from a Durango, Colo., convenience-store attendant who had been robbed at gunpoint by a man matching the description of the president, federal agents were able to track Nixon to the Sunspot Motel, where he had charged a room on the stolen credit card.

FBI Director Clarence Kelley said Nixon was likely attempting to cross into Mexico. "We have reason to believe that Mr. Nixon knew someone in Mexicali in Baja, Calif., a man named Guillermo Padilla. We believe Mr. Nixon was trying to get to his associate's house to hide out." Kelley said the State Department is attempting to reach Padilla for questioning.

To the very end, Nixon maintained his innocence in the Watergate affair. As he fired on FBI agents in his final stand, he repeatedly shouted, "Fuckers! Fuckers! Fuckers! I acted in full accordance with the law at all times. I am innocent of all wrongdoing in the Watergate affair. Die, you fuckers!"

In all, Nixon killed at least six and wounded nine since escaping Tuesday. The body of a seventh victim, Sunspot Motel maid Rosie Ruiz, was discovered in Nixon's room, but it has not yet been confirmed whether Nixon was the killer.

Gerald Ford was sworn in as president yesterday.

Richard Nixon, pinned against the wall of the Sunspot Motel by a barrage of federal agents' bullets.

Ford Sworn In; Promises Awkward, Bumbling Transition

Gerald Ford, in an emergency swearing-in ceremony.

WASHINGTON, D.C.—At 5 p.m. EST Tuesday, less than two hours after federal agents gunned down President Nixon outside a Yuma, Ariz., motel, Vice President Gerald Ford was sworn in as the 38th president of the United States.

Delivering a hastily arranged inaugural address from the Oval Office, during which he repeatedly dropped his papers, Ford assured the American people that the transition would be "awkward and bumbling."

"In this time of great pain and doubt, I want the American people to know that I will assume the office of the presidency in the most inept manner possible," Ford said.

Promising "a bold new era of clumsiness," Ford pledged to spill a bowl of steaming hot soup onto Soviet Premier Leonid Brezhnev's lap at dinner during their next summit meeting, and he promised to fumble all major legislation that crossed his desk, "either by ink spillage or accidental tearing." The new president also pledged to accidentally order a full-scale invasion of France by signing the wrong line of a military-appropriations bill, and to bruise his face badly on the earpiece of the White House "red phone."

"Finally," Ford said, "I make it my solemn vow to trip over every American by 1976."

Inside:

'Deep Throat' Identified as Hal Holbrook

PAGE 4A

New President Promises 'New Deal of Some Kind'

In his inaugural address Tuesday, President Gerald Ford called for "Another New Deal of Some Kind," a bold national initiative that is part of his plan for a "Somewhat Clear Idea for America."

The centerpiece of the 40-minute address, the New Deal of Some Kind proposal met with mild applause, as Ford urged Americans to join him in "this great proposal for things."

During the speech, Ford outlined what he termed "The Sort-of Principles" of the plan: "I strongly believe that all Americans should be free to pursue what-not and what-have-you, as well as to succeed in various endeavors with regard to this historic Fine Proposal Deal."

The new president also challenged his former colleagues in Congress to "add to any legislation you present to me some improvements along the line of this plan of mine. Let's implement this Fair Shake, this Even Chance, this Pretty Good Plan."

NSC Orders Freedom of Information Act Sealed for 50 Years

WASHINGTON, D.C.—In the first and last major test of the new Freedom of Information Act, the National Security Commission ordered that the document be sealed for 50 years.

"While arguably constitutional, this sensitive new law is something the American people would be best served not knowing about at this time," NSC head Ernest Masterson said of the law, which allows any citizen to inspect any federal document upon demand without government interference. "Before national security is jeopardized, this law must be sealed, classified and hidden away."

Masterson warned that the citizens most likely to abuse the new law would be "longhairs, rabble-rousers and academics, the worst elements of our society, people bent on undermining our government's power structure and the foundation of law and order upon which our democracy was built."

Sen. Edward Kennedy (D-Mass.), head of the congressional panel evaluating the NSC order, agreed. Said Kennedy, "This dangerous act, which leaves so many of our national secrets open to unfettered scrutiny, is best kept hidden in a dark, dark hole, buried deep within the bowels of our nation's dank and shadowy archive cellars. Let no citizen ever see it or speak of it again."

THE ONION

A Merv Griffin Production

Thursday, May 1, 1975 — FINEST AMERICAN NEWS SOURCE — 52 PAGES CITY EDITION — TU STULTUS ES — ★★★ — 15¢

U.S. Loses Vietnam War; Ford Urges All Americans to Salute Our Vietcong Rulers

'We Must All Get Behind New U.S. President Le Duc Tho,' Ford Says

NEW HANOI, D.C.—After nearly a decade of fighting and more than 58,000 American casualties, the U.S. has lost the Vietnam War.

President Ford officially announced an unconditional surrender Wednesday in a formal ceremony at Vietcong headquarters in Haiphong, North Vietnam, then ceded full control of the U.S. to its Communist foes.

"We are defeated," said Ford, bowing before Vietcong military leaders. "The United States of America is now under your control, O valiant conquerors. On behalf of the American people, I salute you."

Following the surrender, Ford flew back to New Hanoi—formerly Washington, D.C.—where he addressed the nation for a final time.

"My fellow Americans, we have lost the war," he said during the brief, nationally televised speech from the Oval Office. "America is no more. I have pledged to our new rulers a smooth transition, and I call upon each and every one of you to make this transfer of power as easy as possible."

"On a more personal note," Ford continued, "I would also like to say that it has been a great honor to have been the last-ever president of a free United States."

Ford then rose from his desk and handed a ceremonial key to the White House to his successor, new U.S. President Le Duc Tho. President Le then ordered members of his elite Red Guard to shackle Ford and remove him from the White House. Ford is believed to have been taken to a North Vietnamese P.O.W. camp.

Numerous other key members of the Ford Administration have also been relocated to camps, including Secretary of State Henry Kissinger, Treasury Secretary William Simon and Defense Secretary Donald Rumsfeld.

President Le has already announced that, effective May 10, the U.S. will convert to a peasant agrarian economy, with all citizens tending crops on collectivized farms. Citizens have been instructed to report to their local work centers for assignment.

Former President Gerald Ford hands over rule of the nation to Le Duc Tho.

Aristotle Onassis Killed by Lone Gunman in Athens Motorcade

ATHENS—It was the end of a nation's innocence in Greece Wednesday, as Greek billionaire Aristotle Onassis was killed by a sniper's bullet.

The shipping magnate was riding in a motorcade in downtown Athens, when three powerful, long-range shots were fired from the roof of the Parthenon at approximately 12:30 p.m. local time. Onassis, who was riding with wife Jacqueline Onassis and Crete Governor John B. Connalopoulos, was struck in the head twice and once in the chest. He was rushed immediately to Soutsos Memorial Hospital, where he was pronounced dead at 1:02 p.m.

Connalopoulos was also wounded in the attack but is reported to be in stable condition.

Within an hour of the assassination, Nestorion Tzakitis, vice-president of Onassis' multibillion-dollar shipping company, was sworn in as its president aboard an Olympic Airways plane flying back to company headquarters on the Onassis-owned island of Skorpios.

Athens police reported the arrest of a suspect, identified as Konstantinos Harvey Zakythinos, who was spotted fleeing the vicinity of the Parthenon shortly after the shooting. He was later tracked down to an abandoned gyro shop, where he was arrested and charged with the murders of Onassis and Athens police officer Y.R. Rheus, who was allegedly shot by Zakythinos when Rheus tried to apprehend him.

The shooting instantly transformed the jubilant motorcade scene into one of chaos, pandemonium and horror, as thousands of onlookers stood in numb disbelief. Many Greeks gathered around transistor radios to hear the latest reports from the hospital. The announcement of Onassis' death sent a wave of grief throughout the city, the country and the world.

His wife Jacqueline is said to be inconsolable.

Throughout his career, despite several major blunders in his handling of transoceanic cargo-delivery affairs and persistent rumors of affairs with such celebrities as opera star Maria Callas and American actress Valerie Perrine, Onassis was wildly popular throughout Greece. His popularity only grew following his marriage to Jacqueline, with the couple regarded by many Greeks as the living embodiment of the Greek Ideal.

"For the past few years, Greece had been like something out of some brief, shining mythical kingdom," said Athens resident Cristos Smolikas, one of the many bereaved witnesses to Wednesday's tragedy. "Like Plato's Republic, almost."

The couple leaves behind no children, although Jacqueline has two, Caroline and John, from a previous marriage.

Congress Passes Emergency Anti-Shark Legislation

WASHINGTON, D.C.—Citing a recent surge in public awareness and fear of 40-foot man-eating great white sharks, Congress unanimously passed the Federal Anti-Shark Act yesterday.

The new legislation, approved by the House and Senate in a mere four hours and signed without further deliberation by President Ford, gives federal, state and local authorities almost unlimited discretionary powers in the event of a giant-shark attack.

"These shark attacks represent the most serious crisis facing our nation today, and I would be remiss if I did not do everything in my power to protect America's beach-going citizens from the toothy maw of the great white," said bill co-sponsor Sen. James Trabert (D-R.I.), who was vacationing with fellow sponsor Sen. Patrick Leahy (D-Vt.) at Amity Island when the latest deadly shark attack occurred. "After we saw what those people went through, Patrick and I looked at each other and said, 'We're gonna need a bigger law.'"

Among the emergency measures made possible by the new legislation: the immediate mobilization of the National Guard; expanded powers to ban seductive, nude, shark-tempting swimming in potentially infested waters; and a provision to enlist shark expert Richard Dreyfuss into active duty as an admiral of the U.S. Coast Guard.

The Defense Department is also reportedly working on a torpedo that could destroy a great white.

"We need to work harder to keep our citizens safe from tragedies of all kinds, be they shark attacks, airport disasters or towering infernos," Trabert said.

Inside:

Battle of the Network Stars Claims Life of Sheriff Lobo
PAGE 2C

Earth Under Attack by Papier-Mâché Aliens; World Leaders Plead, 'Save Us, Doctor Who'
PAGE 6A

Does Car-Pooling Lead to Wife-Swapping?
EDITORIAL, PAGE 11A

Roots: Should History Be Written by Non-Winners?

ROOTS
The Saga of an American Family
ALEX HALEY

REVIEW, PAGE 13C

THE ONION

Complete Creed-Balboa Fight Coverage

Wednesday, July 21, 1976 — FINEST AMERICAN NEWS SOURCE — 52 PAGES CITY EDITION TU STULTUS ES ★★★ — 15¢

Local Man Has Nice Day

BOULDER, Colo.—Area resident Keith Stemler reportedly had a nice day Tuesday. The nice day, Stemler's first in weeks, is being credited to his 9 a.m. sighting of a message on a passerby's T-shirt.

"I was on my way to pick up the morning paper, when I passed this guy. His T-shirt told me to have a nice day, so I did," Stemler said, referring to the shirt's yellow, smiley-face, iron-on applique.

After reading the encouraging slogan, the 23-year-old man began to have a nice day, making a fresh glass of carrot-orange drink with his automatic juicer and settling into a pile of large pillows on the floor of his living room. He then listened to his favorite Carpenters 8-track.

"Right on," Stemler said, enjoying the song "We've Only Just Begun."

At approximately 10 a.m., Stemler, continuing his nice day, donned a red dashiki and sandals and headed to work at Sam's Grocery. Upon arriving at work, he was greeted by several employees who had just completed their shift. Ron Graves, a bagger, noticed that Stemler was having a good day and told him to "keep on truckin'."

In addition to having a nice day himself, Stemler helped others have a nice day, as well, encouraging them to just do their own thing.

Stemler is widely expected to have another nice day Thursday. Because he is not scheduled to work, he said he plans to load up his airbrushed Chevy van and head out to the state park, where he will most likely swim, walk amongst the trees and just be mellow.

Inside:

Patty Hearst Trial Called 'Trial of the Century'
PAGE 9A

James Brown Warns Nation's Youths to Get Up Off That Thing: 'You Could Fall and Hurt Yourself,' He Says
PAGE 12B

Pentagon Holds Bake Sale to Buy Bomber; 'This Is a Great Day,' Say Educators
PAGE 10A

Viking Probe Lands on Mars; Fran Tarkenton to Seek Out Possible Life

HOUSTON, Texas—Fran Tarkenton, the superstar Minnesota Vikings quarterback known for his scrambling ability, completed his 50-million-mile space journey yesterday, making a successful touchdown on the surface of Mars.

The $1.3 billion Viking mission marks the first joint venture between the National Football League and the National Aeronautics and Space Administration. Once the Viking has been safely deployed, he will collect soil samples, take instrument readings and attempt to make contact with possible Martian life.

"We are confident that Tarkenton is the right man for the job," said NFL Commissioner Pete Rozelle, speaking from Mission Control in Houston. "Fran's leadership qualities and trademark coolness under pressure can only help us in a first-contact scenario. And if the situation goes bad, his tremendous mobility will help him evade capture and penetrate the Martians' defense."

Rozelle added that, in the event of hostile alien action, the Vikings' "Purple People Eater" defensive line would be dispatched to control the situation.

The two Viking probes on the surface of Mars. Above, Fran Tarkenton. Right, Viking 1.

NASA Chief of Operations Walter Cole said Mars' uninhabitable, sub-zero climate is similar to that of Minneapolis, making Tarkenton ideal for the mission.

"If life does exist on the cold, barren surface of Mars, it would most likely take the form of microorganisms or perhaps lichens, much like those found on the frozen, inhospitable surface of Metropolitan Stadium, Tarkenton's home field," Cole said. "Since the oft-sacked Tarkenton spends a great deal of his playing time face down on that surface, we felt he was well qualified to study possible Martian life."

Nation Mourns as President Ford's Pet Rock Dies

Nation's Top Doctors Unable to Revive Inert Pet

Condolences Pour In from Around Globe: 'I Am Saddened by the Passing of Your Companion-Stone,' Says Brezhnev

WASHINGTON, D.C.—President Ford's pet rock, for several weeks his closest friend and confidant, died Wednesday at 3:51 a.m. EST.

Injured in a fall from Ford's Oval Office desk at 12:15 p.m. Tuesday, the rock was rushed to Bethesda Naval Hospital, where it valiantly clung to life for nearly 16 hours. All the while, throngs of well-wishers gathered outside the hospital, awaiting news of the rock's fate. When the official death announcement was made by Bethesda Naval Hospital Chief of Surgery Nathan Holbrooke, an audible wail rose from the crowd, and men and women alike broke into tears.

Ford stayed by the rock's side in its final hours, faithfully decorating his good friend's round, reddish-brown surface with magic markers, string and glued-on felt—all despite doctors' predictions that the rock would not survive the night.

Tomorrow, the deceased rock's body is scheduled to be flown to its home, a Philadelphia Spencer Gifts store, for a Friday burial. Dignitaries from more than 40 countries are expected to attend the funeral.

Ford aides noted that he loved his pet rock and spent many hours of "alone time" with it, looking at it, turning it to enjoy its different sides, and holding it. Vice President Rockefeller said the president particularly enjoyed trying to imagine at least three different things the rock was shaped like. He even made a leash for the rock from some string he got at Woolworth's.

"Since they met," Rockefeller said, "the president and his rock did everything together. When he appointed new Housing and Urban Development Secretary Carla Hills, the rock was there to help break the ice and make Hills feel at ease. When he recently had to speak before a joint session of Congress, the rock was in his pocket, providing reassurance and comfort. And when he met with Mao Tse-tung in China, the Chinese leader was immediately won over by the rock."

Though dog-eared from Ford's repeated readings, the "Pet Rock Owner's Manual," which had come in the rock's carrying case, will be kept by the president as a bedside memento.

President Ford announcing the death of his beloved rock.

National Day of Bumming Declared

Vice President Rockefeller has declared a "National Day of Bumming" for the president's deceased pet rock.

Rockefeller beseeched Americans to "assemble on this day in your respective places of worship, bow down in submission to the will of almighty God, and pay loving, reverent homage to the memory of this good rock by just letting yourself feel bummed out."

All federal offices across the country will close on Friday, the day of the rock's funeral, and flags will fly at half-staff for one week.

123

THE ONION

Sunday, August 8, 1976 — FINEST AMERICAN NEWS SOURCE — 45¢

Softens Hands While You Do Dishes

NATIONAL MOOD RING GREEN

We Are Sensitive Right Now, Say Ring Experts

WASHINGTON, D.C.—The U.S. Department of Health, Education and Welfare reported Friday that the national mood ring is currently green.

"America has cooled down, mellowed out and gotten more in touch with its feelings," said HEW Secretary Forrest Matthews. "We are a little sensitive right now."

The news of the green ring marks the most assuring American mood change since the National Science Foundation's Magic 8-Ball indicated "yes" in February.

Department of Karma and Astrology officials warn that, while the green mood is promising, serious obstacles lie ahead for future American mellowness.

"The U.S., a Cancer, is still feeling fragile after the Vietnam War and Watergate," U.S. Astrologer General Phyllis Conroy said. "If we are not given adequate time to get in touch with our feelings, the ring could turn amber-green or perhaps even amber in a matter of months."

"This is a time for the nation to relax," Secretary of Karma and Astrology Marvin Frisch said, "and maybe do some yoga and deep-breathing."

President Ford.

President Promises to Put a Man on Other Side of Snake River Canyon by 1978

NASA Already at Work on Jet-Powered Sky-Cycle

WASHINGTON, D.C.—Proclaiming the dawn of a bold new era in death-defying stunt-jumping and citing the need to stay ahead of the Soviets in the field of daredevilry, President Ford vowed Saturday that the U.S. would put a man on the other side of Idaho's Snake River Canyon by 1978.

"My fellow Americans," Ford said in the nationally televised address, "our nation has always stood for progress, achievement and heart-stopping leaps over large obstacles. In this spirit, I vow to you that, by 1978, an American will walk on the other side of the Snake River Canyon."

"The United States is the last of the gladiators and the master of disaster," Ford said. "If we are united and work together to land a man on the other side of this gorge, we cannot help but succeed."

To achieve his canyon-jumping goal, Ford called upon NASA to dedicate itself fully to the design and construction of a high-jumping, rocket-powered "sky-cycle" capable of delivering a single American stuntnaut payload. He also called upon NASA to develop an aerodynamically flared, sequined, star-spangled jumpsuit capable of withstanding the spectacular forces of the launch, the blood-curdling cross-canyon trajectory and the eye-popping, parachute-aided re-entry.

"American rocket-bike technology is the finest in the world," Ford said. "It was an American, riding an American stunt-cycle, who first leapt over 50 double-decker buses at the Houston Astrodome with-

The Snake River Canyon.

out the benefit of any rocket boosting. With my proposed $14 billion budget, the other side of the Snake River Canyon is well within our reach."

Although few question America's ability to make the jump, some in Congress question the expenditure of tax dollars to fund it.

"This promise of Ford's is nothing more than a grandstanding publicity stunt calculated to dazzle voters with danger and glitz," said Sen. William Proxmire (D-Wis.) "According to scientists, the far side of the Snake River Canyon is a dry, lifeless desert with nothing to offer humanity. The genuine benefits of this program are highly questionable. We would be much better off spending this money on something more useful, such as a leap across the fountains at Caesar's Palace."

Inside:

Everybody Kung-Fu Fighting

PAGE 8C

Cambodia to Switch to Skull-Based Economy

PHNOM PENH, Cambodia—Cambodian dictator Pol Pot announced Saturday that his nation will soon replace the riel, its longtime unit of currency, with the human skull.

"Paper money and metal coins are a waste of our country's precious, limited natural resources," Pot said. "But skulls are plentiful, as the countryside is littered with them."

Pot said the switch to a skull-based economy makes sense for political reasons, as well. "The taint of bourgeois reactionary counterrevolution infects the riel," he said. "But the blinding whiteness of our country's native headbones are the perfect symbol for the radiant new dawn the Khmer Rouge has brought to Cambodia."

Samples of the new Cambodian monetary unit.

The new plan is drawing praise from economists, including Jan Van Duyn, chairman of the International Monetary Fund.

"By establishing a fixed, stable and plentiful transaction marker—in this case, the millions of bare, vulture-picked crania of massacred innocents strewn across the blood-soaked valley lowlands of Cambodia like ossified rivers from the darkest regions of Hell—Pol Pot sends the strong message to overseas investors that Cambodia is open for business," he said.

The skull-based economy will go into effect as soon as the country has any goods or services to offer.

Betty Ford Credits Spunk to Alcohol, Drugs

MIDDLETOWN, Conn.—Speaking at a meeting of the Connecticut Women's Auxiliary Caucus Saturday, First Lady Betty Ford attributed her chipper demeanor and positive outlook on life to "heavy use of alcohol and drugs."

During the one-hour speech, Ford candidly acknowledged that her husband's sudden ascent to the presidency following the arrest of Richard Nixon "left no time to adjust to the heavy responsibilities that come with being married to the most powerful man on Earth. I must admit to you today that, for a long time, I felt depressed and overwhelmed."

"In the past few months, a time of great adjustment for my family, I have learned how to completely remove myself from reality through booze and pills, enabling me to better cope with the enormous pressures of being First Lady."

Since adopting a rigorous drinking and pill-taking regimen, Ford said she has been able to attend major diplomatic events without stress, protected by a pleasant haze of numbing, drug-induced semi-reality.

"There was a state dinner recently at which I sat next to [Chinese leader] Deng Xiaoping. I would never have gotten through it if it hadn't been for the reassuring comfort of Quaaludes," she said.

"To be honest, I was even nervous before coming here to speak to you today, so I drank a fifth of gin and downed a

Betty Ford.

bunch of yellow pills," Ford added. "And now that I am both drunk and drugged, I feel great."

Ford said she was not certain what the yellow pills were.

THE ONION

Election '76

Wednesday, November 3, 1976 — FINEST AMERICAN NEWS SOURCE — 15¢

Carter 'Streaks' to Victory

The president-elect streaking to the podium.

PLAINS, Ga.—Democratic Georgia Gov. Jimmy Carter "streaked" to the presidency Tuesday, defeating incumbent President Ford at a full sprint. Carter was described by witnesses as "the fastest thing on two feet."

In a victory speech from his family home in Plains, Carter, completely unclothed save for his trademark running shoes, socks and what appeared to be a coach's whistle, darted to the podium and thanked the American people for giving him the chance to "revitalize and renew the American spirit."

Using the podium to conceal his naked lower half, the president-elect then slipped into a sweatshirt and jogging trunks and vanished before police could ticket him for indecent exposure.

Chaos reigned, as one stunned reporter asked a member of the crowd, "Pardon me, sir, did you see what happened?"

"Yeah, I did," replied the eyewitness. "He wasn't wearing nothing but a smile."

While Republican critics have called the streaking incident a "serious breach of decorum," Carter staffers downplayed the incident, describing the streaking as "a harmless lark."

"Jimmy Carter has been a staunch advocate of good health and physical fitness since his days at West Point and, simply put, he likes to show off his physique," Carter '76 Campaign Manager Richard Holt said.

The incident marks the first time a U.S. president or president-elect has appeared nude in public during peacetime.

Chuck Barris Dedicates Tomb of Unknown Comic

ARLINGTON, Va.—In a moving and nutty ceremony attended by luminaries from throughout the dregs of the entertainment industry, game-show host and popular television personality Chuck Barris formally dedicated the Tomb of the Unknown Comic at Arlington National Cemetery Tuesday.

The monument and accompanying eternal flame, Barris said, will honor "not merely one man, but all comics who have given their all, only to die on stage."

His remarks punctuated by occasional rim-shots and slide-whistle sound effects from the Dixieland jazz band accompanying the proceedings, Barris told those in attendance that the Unknown Comic "could have been a huge star, except for the one thing holding him back: his act."

"This marker shall stand in eternal tribute to a man who tried his best to share his God-given talent with others, but, unfortunately, didn't have any," said Barris, shifting from one foot to another and alternately clapping and pointing at the assembled mourners. "The Unknown Comic was many things. But, alas, funny was not one of them."

The ceremony was attended by numerous close friends of the Unknown Comic, including M*A*S*H star Jamie Farr, Las Vegas prop comedian Rip Taylor and character actor Arte Johnson, as well as a woman named Jaye P. Morgan whose actual career remains undetermined as of press time.

Following Barris' remarks, other eulogies were delivered by a guy who spins pizza dough while singing opera, three midgets on unicycles and an extraordinarily obese ballerina. A moving testimonial by a roller-skating violinist was interrupted when the performer was gonged and subsequently broke down in tears, unable to continue.

Barris at the tomb's dedication ceremony.

Jogging-Suit-Wearing Bionic Man Appointed Secretary of Metric System

WASHINGTON, D.C.—President Ford named jogging-suit-wearing bionic man Steve Austin head of the newly created Department of the Metric System Tuesday.

The new department will oversee the nation's sweeping conversion to the metric system of measurement by 1980.

"All yardsticks will be cast aside in favor of a bold new ruler called a 'meter stick,'" Austin told reporters at a White House press conference. "The meter is a modern, exciting unit of measurement that will allow Americans to measure things better, stronger, faster than they could before."

Austin, a former Air Force colonel, was critically injured in the 1972 crash of an experimental NASA aircraft, and subsequently rebuilt into a "cyborg" with bionic implants. He demonstrated his superhuman strength at the press conference by crushing a folding chair into the shape of a pretzel with his enhanced right arm.

"As sure as I can use my bionic arm to crush this chair, the U.S. will go metric by 1980," Austin said. "That's a promise."

Among his many duties as Metric Secretary, Austin will be required to coordinate educational programs to get schoolchildren excited about metrics, oversee the conversion of U.S. road signs to metric, and defeat Maskatron in hand-to-hand combat.

"Remember, everyone," the bionic hero said, "there are 10 decimeters in a meter, 10 centimeters in a decimeter, and 10 millimeters in a centimeter."

Austin urged Americans to think not just of measurements in their own lives, but of how their measuring habits affect the U.S.'s place in the world.

"The possibility of the United States being left behind in the metric-dominated future is a specter even more ominous than the looming Sasquatch crisis," he said.

Inside:

Prize Carter Breedin'-Hog Wins Blue Ribbon
PAGE 4A

Pol Pot Kills 1,776 in Honor of U.S. Bicentennial
PAGE 6A

Child's Esteem Damaged

PETALUMA, Calif.—Social workers and child psychologists are working around the clock to restore the badly damaged self-esteem of area youth Peter Linden, 9, whose grievous insulting at the hands of an 11-year-old boy Monday left his image and self-confidence shattered.

Linden was admitted to Sunny Day Youth Therapy Clinic suffering from a bruised ego and injured self-worth after the unnamed older boy made fun of his new plaid pants.

"The boy called Peter's pants 'retarded stupid dorko pants,'" said attending psychologist Dr. Walter Hollis. "This cruel remark made Peter feel removed from his zone of security and transported him to a hostile environment in which he felt scorned and unwelcome. This is, of course, a devastating experience for someone Peter's age, and it promptly sent him into a shame spiral out of which he is only now emerging."

"Through the modern technique of 3-T Analysis, or 'Talking Things Through,'" Hollis said, "we have been able to guide Peter toward true healing and a better self-actualization."

While Peter's sullenness threatened to impede his progress, doctors reported that he has begun to draw pictures expressing how he feels, an important step toward repairing his damaged sense of self.

Meanwhile, measures are being taken to help the boy who insulted him come to grips with his own deep emotional conflicts, according to guidance counselors at Petaluma Elementary School.

"The boy's parents have been notified, and he is being watched closely by psychiatric personnel," said counselor Loren Freed. "They are encouraging him to act out his 'yucky' feelings with puppets and dolls, so that the pre-existing condition which affected Peter may be healed before other children suffer a similar fate."

Scientists Develop 200 Percent Puffier Comb

BOSTON—Scientists at Boston's Goody Laboratories announced Tuesday the successful development of a comb 200 percent puffier than any in existence.

The breakthrough hair-care product, which could be available to consumers as early as March, features a puffier handle, puffier teeth, and an overall increase in size.

"Not only does this comb rate a full 200 percent puffier on the Lewison Comb Puffnometer," said Dr. Lance Stenstrom, head of plastics design and engineering at Goody, "but it also extends a full four inches out of the back pocket of a pair of jeans."

Stenstrom said the comb will be attractive and durable enough to use while roller-skating, at the disco or between games of Lawn Jarts.

Goody Laboratories has been responsible for several major advances in comb design throughout the decade, including the development of swirling, tie-died comb coloring and introduction of the Afro hair-pick.

Stenstrom predicted that, as a result of the puffier combs, hair itself will be 200 percent puffier in coming years.

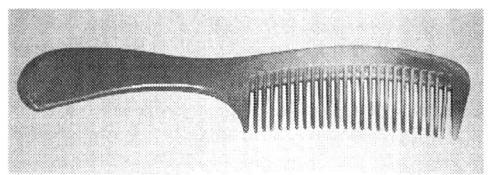

The latest breakthrough in puffy haircare technology.

125

THE ONION

Thursday, July 12, 1977 — FINEST AMERICAN NEWS SOURCE — SIT ON IT! — 20¢

President Calls for Calm Following Nipple Sighting on Farrah Fawcett Poster

Fawcett's poster.

President Carter.

WASHINGTON, D.C.—In an address to the American people Wednesday, President Carter called for calm and an end to the panicked rioting that has swept the nation since Monday's sighting of an erect nipple on a poster of *Charlie's Angels* star Farrah Fawcett.

"Level heads must prevail," Carter said during the speech, televised live from the Oval Office. "I urge the American public, especially young men and boys, to remain calm, even in the face of such an obviously aroused nipple."

"I've never seen anything like this, and I was here during Watts," said Lt. Mike Weber of the Los Angeles Police Department, standing before the burning wreckage of a poster shop torched by an out-of-control mob after supplies of the Fawcett poster had run out. "Fathers are attacking their own sons for this poster. I can't say I blame them, though—that chick looks like she's ready to go."

Poster shops across the country have been hardest hit by the panic, with at least 30 Spencer Gifts stores looted and burned by poster-crazed hordes.

Also affected are the nation's schools: Record truancy rates are being reported, the result of male students staying home to masturbate while viewing the Fawcett poster. The business sector is also suffering, with drastic drops in virtually all consumer-product sales, with the notable exception of hand lotion and Kleenex.

According to media experts, the image of Fawcett's nipple, clearly visible through her orange, one-piece bathing suit, is the most blatant poster-based depiction of female breast arousal in U.S. history.

"Although mass-produced posters prominently featuring the female breast have been common for nearly 30 years, the nipple has, until now, been discreetly hidden from view," said Professor Howard Edmundsen, a media analyst at Northwestern University. "Miss Fawcett's hardened nipple juts from her pert, spectacularly firm right breast, her cocked head and broad smile expressing something akin to, 'Oh! You just surprised me and my erect nipple!' Yes, I believe the state of bedlam this poster has created is wholly understandable."

Edmundsen then excused himself and hastily retreated to his locked office.

Carter has created a Federal Fawcett Nipple Assessment Task Force to develop strategies for the regulation and possible suppression of the chaos-inducing nipple. "This poster may be more than America can handle," Carter said. "In fact, looking at that enticingly hard nipple, I admit that even I feel lust for Miss Fawcett in my heart."

Idi Amin Praises Former Ugandan Defense Minister as 'Delicious'

Idi Amin.

KAMPALA, Uganda—Offering rare words of praise for his longtime political rival, Ugandan president-for-life Idi Amin hailed former Defense Minister Kigali Obutu as "tender and delicious" before a gathering of top government officials Wednesday.

"Although we had many quarrels, and I frequently feared that he was secretly plotting to topple my regime, Minister Obutu was a good man—hard-working and extremely succulent," Amin said. "He was a man I very much enjoyed, from his determination to make Uganda a leader in Africa to his flavorful thigh and calf muscles."

Obutu, who disappeared in November 1976 shortly after a visit to one of Amin's country palaces, had for years been the Ugandan president's chief rival, vowing to put an end to what he called "General Amin's reign of genocidal terror and rampant corruption." On several occasions, Obutu publicly accused Amin of ordering the murders of more than 300,000 Ugandan citizens, a charge Amin denied.

Despite Obutu's well-documented opposition to him, Amin praised his rival. "In all my years as Ugandan president, never have I known a man of such substance as the former Defense Minister. It took me years to fully understand this man and hours more to digest him. Kigali Obutu has enriched us all—no one more so than myself."

Continued Amin: "Had Kigali Obutu lived, he surely would have been the next president of Uganda. He was a man of the people, a man whose love for this nation was outstripped only by his fierce intellect. No one had brains like him, not even Minister of Finance Komo Harare. While many would argue that Harare was the greatest mind Uganda ever had, I know for a fact that he was not: His brain was tough and stringy, flavorless compared to Obutu's."

During his meeting with advisors, Amin also announced plans to construct a state-of-the-art, $200,000 cooler for his presidential palace. Amin said the refrigerator is vital to the preservation of national security and political rivals' organs.

"Without proper refrigeration, a treacherous cabinet member's liver spoils in less than three hours," Amin said. "If I am to keep order in Uganda, my enemies must keep fresh for at least a week."

Inside:

Career Counselors Agree: Trucking Is the Job of the Future
PAGE 6D

Sid Vicious Sought in Queen-Stabbing Incident
PAGE 12A

U.S. Leads World in Iron-On Technology

Puffy, Glow-in-the-Dark Logos Now within Scientists' Reach

WASHINGTON, D.C.—A newly released report by the Department of Decals and Appliques found that the U.S. ranks first among industrialized nations in the field of heat-transferred T-shirt slogans and designs.

"The U.S. is unmatched in its iron-on transfer-art prowess," read the report. "Our nation's T-shirts look significantly more out of sight than those of other nations, sporting superior slogans and rock-band names, from 'Foxy Lady' to 'KISS' to the classic 'Lookin' Good' logo."

"America stands proud today," President Carter said at a ceremony honoring America's top iron-on scientists Wednesday. Sporting a black T-shirt featuring the popular catch-phrase, "Dy-no-mite!" over a graphic of a bursting firecracker, Carter lauded "the spirit of innovation and creativity that has made America number one. Thanks to these dedicated minds, our T-shirts are easily the world's most far-out, and our iron-on patches look more like genuine embroidery than those of any other nation."

"This report represents a major victory for the Carter Administration," said University of Virginia political-science professor Peter Childs. "After being roundly criticized for doubling expenditures for sparkly glitter-decal research and sharply increasing funding for the rainbow-patterned materials from which transfers are die-cut, Carter has emerged vindicated."

According to Childs, the U.S. is likely only to increase its iron-on dominance in the coming years. "The breakthrough development of separate iron-on letters, allowing for the personalization of T-shirts, will break things wide open: Millions of Americans will proudly sport white T-shirts bearing such eye-catching slogans as 'Keep on Truckin'', 'Darth Vader Lives' and the witty 'Up Your Nose with a Rubber Hose,' all in the impeccably stylish Cooper Black type-style. This will make any foreign power think twice about challenging U.S. low-budget-fashion technology."

THE ONION

Read Our New Jogging Section

Wednesday, August 17, 1977 — FINEST AMERICAN NEWS SOURCE — 14 PAGES CITY EDITION TU STULTUS ES — ★★★ — 20¢

Area Man's Hair Feathered Like Wings of Majestic Bird

SEATTLE—Kevin Imhoff, a 19-year-old Seattle cashier, has hair feathered like the wings of a majestic bird, it was reported Tuesday.

"I've never seen anything like it," Seattle resident Fran Kessler said of the young man's sun-streaked blond hair, which flowed back from his forehead in two glorious swoops and ruffled upward slightly behind the ear. "His hair is like a flowing river, sparkling in the sun and gently rippling in the breeze."

When questioned about the glorious hair that rests on his head like the wings of Pegasus, Imhoff said he achieved the hairstyle by "getting one of those big combs and combing it back."

Imhoff then demonstrated his technique, removing a large-handled, powder-blue comb from his back pocket. He combed the left side of his well-kempt head, then the right, all the while skillfully executing the crucial patting motion. So stunning were the cascading results that many onlookers gasped.

"His hair looks as though the tail of a comet swept by and deposited a wispy trail of sparks upon the head of this young man," said Herb Crenshaw, a Seattle-area data-entry clerk present at the impromptu combing demonstration.

"That hair looks like waves of autumn wheat swaying upon a gentle midday breeze," said witness Tina McMann. "Or like the delicate, layered tail of a woodland animal bounding gracefully through the air."

According to Imhoff, the secret to his breathtaking hair is bang length, cultivated throughout his senior year of high school, and daily use of Flex-brand shampoo.

This growing period was a dark time for Imhoff, he said, as his hair was too short to feather, yet long enough to fall in front of his face when he tried to read car magazines.

But the commitment paid off, as his flowing waves of rich blond hair seem to leave a trail of sunshine everywhere he goes, making everyone in his path feel warm and at peace.

Elvis Dead
Is Elvis Alive?

MEMPHIS, Tenn.—Elvis Presley, "The King of Rock and Roll," was found dead in his Graceland mansion Tuesday, raising the question: Is Elvis alive?

At 4:15 p.m. EST, a friend discovered Presley on the bathroom floor, surrounded by empty syringes. The cause of death, Shelby County coroners said, was a massive drug overdose.

Said Coroner Bertrand McAlister, "The fact that he wasn't breathing, that he was cold and colorless in appearance and that his heart was not beating, led me to wonder, 'Could he be alive?'"

Within an hour of the discovery of Presley's body, news of the beloved entertainer's death spread across the nation, prompting millions of fans to think Presley was still alive.

"They said Elvis died of a massive drug-induced coronary. They also said that huge amounts of heroin, Demerol, codeine and alcohol were found in his system," Nashville resident Francine Rae said. "Something just doesn't add up."

Presley's body is scheduled to be buried at Graceland this week. As a result, fans have vowed to keep an eye out for Presley all over the country in the coming decades.

Elvis Presley.

K-Tel Execs Warn: 'We Must Stockpile Solid-Gold '70s Hits for the Future'

Hits to Be Sealed in K-Tel Vault
Musical Reserves Will See U.S. Through Potential Disco Drought

Concerned about the depletion of America's solid-gold-hit reserves, K-Tel executives made an urgent plea to the U.S. government Tuesday to stockpile massive amounts of super-hot hits for the future.

"We cannot take today's smash hits for granted," K-Tel spokesperson Richard Smith said. "The high level of artistry popular music has achieved in the 1970s may never be reached again. It is arrogant and foolhardy to think that hits on a par with Hot Chocolate's 'You Sexy Thing,' K.C. & The Sunshine Band's 'Get Down Tonight' and The Bee Gees' 'Jive Talking' will be attainable by the artists of the future."

In addition to boogie-fever-inducing jams and hard-rockin' up-tempo tunes, K-Tel is also calling for the preservation of hits of the super-mellow variety. According to a recent K-Tel report, nearly 65 percent of the nation's copies of Bread's "Make It with You" have already disappeared, and only 57 known copies of David Soul's "Don't Give Up on Us" remain in existence.

"Once thrown in the trash, these records can never be recovered," Smith said. "'Make It with You' may have been a mega-platinum smash hit that ruled the pop charts for weeks, but that doesn't mean it's safe from extinction."

K-Tel is urging President Carter to respond to the growing crisis by authorizing the production of a series of LP records packed with the greatest hits by today's hottest stars. The records, which would contain great music of all varieties, from the hot disco pulse of Chic to the hard-rockin' sounds of Queen, could be sold in stores or ordered via special "1-800" phone numbers aired on late-night television.

"I realize that, with all the great musical artists out there today, from Donna Summer to Electric Light Orchestra to Peaches & Herb, sometimes it seems like the hits will never end. But they can—and will—if we do not take steps to preserve them," Smith said.

The failure to stockpile hits, according to K-Tel sources, has already taken its toll. A number of one-time Top 40 smash-hit singles, including Bo Donaldson & The Heywoods' "Billy, Don't Be a Hero," Neil Sedaka's "Breakin' Up Is Hard to Do" and The Captain & Tennille's "Muskrat Love," have disappeared forever.

Carter to Congress:
'What's Your 20, Good Buddy?'

WASHINGTON, D.C.—President Carter radioed Congress from the White House Tuesday, asking the nation's lawmakers, "What's your 20, good buddy?"

Carter contacted Congress using a new presidential citizen's-band radio, installed in the Oval Office last week to improve communications between the legislative and executive branches.

After some static, House Speaker Tip O'Neill (D-Mass.) responded, "We're in the Chicken Pen, Peanut. Over."

Referencing his new, FBI-drafted CB-lingo dictionary, Carter replied, "That's a big 10-4, good buddies. I'm dropping the hammer and blowing the doors off."

The House Speaker then beseeched the president, "Breaker, breaker, one-niner!"

As a result of the talks, the House has agreed to draft national ears-wearing legislation. It has also established a special committee to investigate fat loads, and will allocate funds to increase national awareness of convoys.

Carter adjourned the CB conference by joking that he had to break for a "10-100."

"This is a new era in communication," said Douglas Lake, a professional truck driver who advised White House officials in the installation of the CB radio. "The president can now communicate with Congress without leaving his office, leading to a much smoother-operating government."

Lake also predicted that, with the CB radio in place, Congress and the president would no longer run the risk of attracting Smokeys.

President Carter with the new Oval Office CB radio.

Inside:

I, You Both Okay, Say Experts

PAGE 8A

Comics

Ziggy Gets an Updated Hairstyle

SEE ARTS, PAGE 3C

127

THE ONION

Monday, November 20, 1978   FINEST AMERICAN NEWS SOURCE   18 PAGES CITY EDITION TU STULTUS ES   ★★★   20¢

Do You Like Piña Coladas? See Personals, Page 12D

Anthropomorphic Juice Pitcher Among Dead in Jonestown Cult Suicide

Cyanide-Laced Juice Found Inside Giant Pitcher's Glass Body

Deceased Container as Yet Unidentified

Enormous Pitcher-Shaped Hole Found in Jungle Commune's Wall

The glass pitcher among the strewn victims of Rev. Jim Jones' People's Temple death cult.

FRENCH GUYANA—Personnel charged with identifying the bodies of Jonestown cult-suicide victims reported yesterday that they have discovered a giant anthropomorphic juice pitcher among the 917 dead.

FBI investigators discovered the male, 6'7", 400-pound pitcher while sifting through a pile of bodies which included that of People's Temple leader Jim Jones. While the investigators initially assumed the pitcher was inanimate, closer examination revealed arms, legs, hands, feet, and a crude but expressive face transformed into a hideous grin by the onset of rigor mortis.

The deceased pitcher still contained a small amount of cyanide-laced punch, investigators said, leading them to suspect that he may have been involved in the planning of the mass murder-suicide.

"If, during our autopsy, we find that this pitcher's interior contains cyanide that is more than three days old, it would open up a whole new angle on how these people were poisoned," forensics expert Cedric Hundt said.

Criminal profilers in Jonestown say the presence of the anthropomorphic pitcher may also explain the enormous, pitcher-shaped hole in one of the jungle commune's walls.

"This hole gives rise to some very disturbing questions: Was a giant, man-like juice pitcher, made from ordinary glass, so compelled by something—religious fanaticism, perhaps, or an obsessive need to quench the thirst of others—that he found the strength to burst through a brick wall?" FBI profiler Stanley Hallock asked. "Only exhaustive police work will determine whether this was a sinister pitcher who wanted to knock out hundreds of innocents or just a 'mule,' an unwitting deliveryman who wanted only to knock out their thirst."

Thus far, FBI examination of a tape recording made by a People's Temple member killed in the massacre is inconclusive. Though most of the tape's content is muffled by static, at one point, a faint voice can be heard yelling an indiscernible two-word cry. The shout is preceded by the sound of collapsing masonry, described by investigators as a "crash" or "banga-booma" sound.

A Dubuque, Iowa, woman has been in contact with authorities regarding the pitcher's identity. Though her name is not being made public, it is believed she had a sexual relationship with the pitcher before he left America, presumably to join the cult.

According to police, the woman reported that the pitcher had begun to act strangely before his disappearance, speaking of something important and wonderful he'd stumbled into, "a new awakening." The woman had asked him if everything was okay, and he simply said, "Oh, yeah. Oh, yeah."

In subsequent conversations, the pitcher is said to have become more eccentric, talking about new flavors with which to fill his pitcher, such as "Jammin' Jonesberry" and "Purple's Temple."

He then left for French Guyana, never to be seen alive again.

Inside:

Last Night's Car Chase on *Baretta* Went Too Far
     EDITORIAL, PAGE 11A

Balding Man Nude, Waiting in Area Hot Tub
     PAGE 3

Disco Diva Gloria Gaynor Survives Andes Plane Crash by Eating Rugby Players

ORURO, BOLIVIA—Disco superstar Gloria Gaynor was discovered alive by rescue workers Sunday, the sole survivor of a Bolivian rugby-team plane crash three months ago.

Gaynor, who on Aug. 19 was traveling to Chile with the rugby team to sing the Bolivian national anthem at a game, was stranded in a remote section of the Andes for nearly 100 days after the plane crashed. She said she survived by eating the athletes.

"At first I was afraid, I was petrified," said Gaynor, who lost more than 40 pounds during the ordeal. "I thought then I could never live stranded on that mountainside. I stayed up many nights, just feeling sorry for myself. But, once I overcame my aversion to eating other human beings, I grew strong and I learned how to get along."

Gaynor said she resisted cannibalism for the first two weeks on the mountain. But, when she ran out of possible food sources and realized it was her only chance for survival, she relented.

"I said I will survive," Gaynor said. "I will survive."

Congressional Panel Warns of Encroaching Robin Williams Body Hair

WASHINGTON, D.C.—A congressional panel warned Congress Friday that the dense, black curls of hair covering the chest and back of *Mork & Mindy* star Robin Williams are spreading at an uncontrollable rate.

"Unless Mr. Williams can be safely penned long enough to take tonsorial action against his rapidly growing carpet of hair, he will soon put the American people in grave danger," U.S. Sen. John Chafee (R-R.I.) said. "This hair growth must not be allowed to continue."

Congress was first advised of a possible Williams hair risk by the U.S. Forestry Service in February, shortly after Williams first came to national prominence as a guest star on *Happy Days*. The senate resisted taking action, however, until the comic had his own series.

Williams' hair has already claimed its first victim: Last Wednesday, *Mork & Mindy* cast member Conrad Janis was suffocated by a large tuft of shoulder hair while hugging Williams.

If the hair menace cannot be contained, Chafee said, Williams may have to be declared a federal disaster area in order to secure the manpower and equipment necessary to reduce his hair to a safer density.

Williams, speaking in his own defense at the hearing, said, "Dass right, man, I be a hairy sucka. Yo!" in a "black guy" voice that delighted the congressmen. He then segued into an equally winning impression of a homosexual hairdresser.

Congressmen listen to testimony on the threat of Williams' rapidly spreading torso hair.

In Focus:

Is 'Pong' Rotting Our Kids' Minds?
     PAGE 12A

THE ONION

Tuesday, November 27, 1979 — FINEST AMERICAN NEWS SOURCE — Your *Star Wars 2* Rumor Central — 25¢

Sadat, Begin Celebrate Peace Treaty with All-Night Coke Orgy at Studio 54

Mideast Leaders Commemorate Camp David Accord by Dancing, Drugging Night Away

Mick Jagger Fellates Sadat in Famed NYC Disco's Basement

NEW YORK—Egyptian President Anwar Sadat and Israeli Prime Minister Menachem Begin celebrated their historic Camp David peace accord Monday night with a wild, cocaine-fueled orgy at New York's hottest nightclub, Studio 54.

Participating in the three-hour bacchanalian ordeal were Sadat, Begin, Mick and Bianca Jagger, Grace Jones, Liza Minnelli and a 6'5" drag queen known as Chantel LaRue.

"There's peace in the Middle East, baby, and now it's time to play," LaRue said.

President Carter, who brokered the successful talks between the two Mideast leaders, attempted to enter the exclusive club with Begin and Sadat but was not admitted.

Studio 54 co-owner Steve Rubell noted that his is a private club that reserves the right to deny entrance to anyone it chooses.

Once Sadat and Begin were admitted past the velvet rope, leaving President Carter behind with hundreds of other hopefuls, they were immediately swept up in a wild carnival atmosphere. When the club's infamous "Moon and the Spoon"—a smiling moon holding a cocaine spoon, from which white, sparkling lights shoot up into the moon's nose—descended from the ceiling, several half-naked dancers in silver body paint seized the moment to foist large amounts of cocaine upon Sadat, Begin and their entourage of security guards and policy advisors.

From there, it was a short trip to the basement VIP room, where champagne and quaaludes flowed in abundance while the ceiling shook to the disco beat of Musique's "In the Bush."

"I would like to thank Prime Minister Begin for his promise to end Israeli settlement in the Sinai Peninsula," Sadat told the crowd of celebrities and Manhattan club-hopping elites. "I would also like to push, push, in the bush."

Eager to cut loose and release some pressure after weeks of tense, sequestered negotiations, the two leaders tore off their clothes in a matter of seconds and began a historic Arab-Jew orgy. Details are hazy, but scattered reports indicate that Begin snorted cocaine off Grace Jones' glistening, bare ass; Sadat received oral sex from Bianca and Mick Jagger in turn; and both leaders engaged in simultaneous vaginal or anal penetration of an unidentified member of Sister Sledge.

Famed author and Studio 54 fixture Truman Capote said he enjoyed watching the orgy with Andy Warhol and nine gin-and-tonics. "It was simply fabulous to see the leaders of two historically antagonistic peoples get their rocks off together," Capote said. "Fetch me another drinky-poo, won't you, dear?"

Neither Sadat nor Begin were available for comment after the orgy, as fashion designer Halston was seen leading the leaders off to a private booth by studded-leather neck leashes.

Begin, left, and Sadat, right, making history on the dance floor.

Carter Offers Ayatollah 'Helpful Energy-Saving Tips' in Exchange for Hostages

WASHINGTON, D.C.—President Carter broke his vow not to negotiate with terrorists Monday, offering the Ayatollah Khomeini what he described as "helpful energy-saving tips" in exchange for the safe return of the 62 U.S. hostages in Iran.

"With this deal, I am appealing to both the Iranians' sense of common decency and their sense of practicality," Carter said. "After all, what sort of person could hold another human being hostage for months on end, brutally beating him until he has lost his very will to live? And, furthermore, what sort of person could turn down the chance to cut electric bills by more than $25 a month and reduce overall household heat-loss by over 40 percent?"

According to Carter, the tips he is offering will not only save Iran big money, but will help the Mideast nation do its part to end the global energy crisis.

"I can assure the Ayatollah that these tips will help make his house warmer in the winter and cooler in the summer for literally pennies. It is my strong belief that this is a prospect even the most hardened anti-American extremist-fundamentalist cannot resist."

As a gesture of good will and a demonstration of the seriousness of his offer, Carter gave the Iranian leader one "freebie" tip. "Ayatollah Khomeini, limit your showers to 10 minutes, and keep a timer in the bathroom to keep yourself honest," the president said. "Over the course of a year, this will save you more than 7,200 gallons of water."

"Return the hostages safely to their loved ones, and tips even more valuable than the one I've just given to you are yours, no questions asked," Carter said.

The president added that, if the hostages are released within the next 30 days and a formal apology is made by Iran before the U.N. General Assembly, he will also give the Ayatollah easy-to-follow instructions for constructing a solar-powered alarm clock.

President Carter.

Carter's Energy-Saving Tips

• Turn off your mechanical bull when not in use.
• Illuminate the floor of your discotheque using reflected sunlight.
• Don't fast-forward your 8-track tape to find the song you want. If you are patient, the song will come around again.
• While driving to work, carpool with colleagues to save gasoline. Also refrain from exciting-but-inefficient car chases set to bongo music.
• Skip driving altogether and streak to work.
• If your child must use a Lite Brite, do not allow him to plug it in. Instead, position the colored-peg screen between your child and the sun so that he may fully enjoy the illuminated plaything without wasting resources.
• When indulging yourself with home craft projects, do not waste natural gas by shrinking your Shrinky Dinks in an oven. If you are careful in cutting them out and coloring them, you can just as easily enjoy the beauty of non-shrunken Dinks.
• Repeat viewings of the special-effects-laden blockbuster *Star Wars* consumed 62 percent of U.S. energy reserves last year. If you haven't seen *Star Wars* yet, concentrate and pay attention so that you do not need to see it a second time. If you have seen it already, please do not do so again.

Inside:

George Kennedy, Jacqueline Bisset Die During Filming of *Skylab '79*

PAGE 12C

129

THE ONION

Let the Avarice Begin

Friday, October 17, 1980 — FINEST AMERICAN NEWS SOURCE — 52 PAGES CITY EDITION TU STULTUS ES — ★★★ — 25¢

Campaign '80

Jimmy Carter

Ronald Reagan

"Let's Talk Better Mileage"

"Kill the Bastards"

Which Message Will Resonate with Voters?

ANN ARBOR, Mich.—In a nationally televised debate Thursday night on the University of Michigan campus, President Carter and Republican presidential candidate Ronald Reagan outlined their positions on foreign and domestic policy issues.

Throughout the debate, two differing political agendas repeatedly surfaced—President Carter's "Let's Talk Better Mileage," a call for energy reform, and former California Governor Reagan's "Kill the Bastards" plan.

Responding to a question about America's reliance on fuel from OPEC nations, Carter said, "We have an opportunity to use American technology and know-how to develop our own alternate, renewable energy sources, such as solar and wind power, freeing us from our reliance on foreign oil. This is sound policy, not just for America, but for the Planet Earth."

Responding to the president's remarks, Reagan said, "While much of what President Carter says is true, he is missing one very important point. That is, if America is to continue to prosper in the 1980s and beyond, we must join together and kill the bastards."

During the debate, Carter confronted the 69-year-old Reagan about his call for deregulation of numerous social programs, including his controversial proposal to give tax breaks to the wealthy.

Responding to the charges, Reagan said, "With these attacks, my opponent is trying to sidestep the real issue here, and that is the tremendous importance of killing the bastards." The Hill Auditorium crowd erupted into thunderous applause.

In an effort to win back the audience, Carter turned to the topic of urban renewal. "Next year, I will propose to Congress a sweeping revitalization program, with increased funding for the development of mass-transit systems, infrastructure rebuilding, and low-cost housing and job-training programs for disadvantaged minorities," Carter said.

"Kill the bastards, kill the bastards," repeated Reagan throughout his allotted one-minute rebuttal.

Public-opinion polls show a 76 percent approval rating for Reagan's "Kill the Bastards" plan, compared to only 11 percent for Carter's "Better Mileage" platform. The "Kill the Bastards" plan rates even higher in polls than Reagan's highly popular policies while governor of California, including his "Nuke the Bastards" plan, his "Kill the Foreigners" plan and his recent "Just Kill 'Em All" plan.

'80 Extra:
John Anderson Launches 'No Chance '80' Campaign
ANALYSIS, PAGE 6A

Trucker, Monkey Targeted by Area Police

VALDOSTA, Ga.—Authorities in this rural southern town continued their search Thursday for independent trucker B.J. McCay and his chimpanzee associate, Bear.

McCay and his simian pet were last seen speeding toward Macon in a red-and-white rig. They are wanted in connection with a recent series of wild car and truck chases, known association with attractive women, and zany hijinks.

Sgt. Beauregard Wiley, who, along with Winslow County's Sheriff Masters, has been pursuing the pair for more than a year, said he has several significant leads in the case.

"We questioned two young female hitchhikers," Wiley said, "and they reported that a handsome man and a regular zoo-monkey had given them a lift from Huntersville to the county line."

"We suspect that unlawful shenanigans may have been involved," he added.

Despite the sheriff's relentless search for information leading to the apprehension of the trucker and the chimp, some observers question whether the department has been using unauthorized procedures in pursuit of the duo.

Said provocatively dressed state trooper Wilhelmina "The Fox" Johnson, "To detain any suspect, no matter how handsome or fun-loving, the sheriff must have a concrete charge."

Wiley said he and the sheriff plan to conduct an investigation at the Country Comfort Truck Stop, where they will interrogate the owner, Bullets, to obtain crucial evidence of McCay and Bear's acts of mischief.

Danielle Steel Publishes First Through Eighth Novels

BEVERLY HILLS, Calif.—Romance novelist Danielle Steel made an auspicious debut this week, when her first eight books hit bookstore shelves nationwide.

"Doubleday had some extra presses they weren't using, so we figured, 'Why space them out?'" said Steel during a telephone press conference from her Beverly Hills home. "Honestly, I just couldn't wait to share all eight of these novels with my readers, because each book is like a child, a gift to the world, a labor of love that takes upwards of three days to write."

When asked to describe the books, Steel said they are "not only good reads, but also very distinct from one another. Not a single proper name, for example, is duplicated from book to book, except for 'Kent.' And the muscles I describe as 'rippling' range from the calf, in *Loving You*, to the shoulders, in *Pearl*. And you'll notice that the cover of each book is in a different pastel color."

Steel said she is currently working on a ninth book, which she expects to finish in the next 20 to 25 minutes.

Inside:

Special Teenbeat Focus: Our Nation's Adolescent Girls' Love Affair with Male Pop Stars Who Resemble Adolescent Girls
PAGE 5C

12th-Level Elf Acquires Bag of Holding
PAGE 13A

Donna Summer Burned Alive at Comiskey Park Disco Demolition Night
PAGE 6C

Sony Introduces Populace-Pacification Device

NEW YORK—Sony unveiled its new line of portable populace-pacification devices this week.

The remarkable new "Walkman," a combination cassette player and AM/FM radio, transports its user to a warm, self-contained aural environment, freeing him from social interaction with others.

"This new product all but eliminates the risk of contact with people and all the unpleasantries associated with it," Sony spokesperson David Gelfand said. "It's superior to other music-playing devices in that it not only plays music, but also blocks out one's awareness of the rest of the world."

With the Walkman, any sound below 60 decibels—including the voices of nagging authority figures, co-workers, intrusive bus patrons or loved ones—is eliminated, along with the need to respond.

"When each and every American consumer is outfitted with this small metal box and the accompanying length of cord and two sponge-like ear-mounted speakers, all forms of discontent will cease to exist," Gelfand said.

Gelfand predicted the Walkman devices will soon become standard-issue for all Americans.

"Everywhere you go, you will see people wearing Walkmans, blissfully unaware of the world around them as the device wraps them in a warm cocoon of musical-entertainment isolation."

The government has made no formal statement as of yet. Inside sources say that, upon learning of the pacification device, top officials discussed the possibility of subsidizing national mass distribution.

The new Sony Walkman.

THE ONION

Trickle-Down Journalism

Wednesday, January 21, 1981 — AMERICA'S FINEST NEWS SOURCE — 30¢

Reagan May Have Been Elected, Doesn't Recall

40th President 'Not Entirely Sure' If He Swore to Uphold Constitution

WASHINGTON, D.C.—Ronald Wilson Reagan, sworn in Tuesday as the nation's 40th president, said he "can't recall" defeating Jimmy Carter in November's general election.

"As to whether I defeated Mr. Carter in last year's presidential election, I have no memory of that," the new president told reporters following his inaugural address at the U.S. Capitol. "Whether I did or did not win, I unfortunately cannot say with 100 percent certainty."

"President Reagan is a very busy man who does a lot of things in the course of a day," said Reagan aide Michael Deaver in defense of the new president. "And, as such, he cannot be expected to remember every last detail of his activities or promises."

In his inaugural address, Reagan said that, in addition to being unable to recall details of last November's election, "I cannot recall a new morning in America. I have no memory of a public mandate to reform our government. And I am afraid I have no recollection of our nation's renewed determination, pride and strength."

Raising his right hand and taking the oath of office, the new president swore to "preserve, protect and defend the Constitution of the United States, if I can remember to do so." He also swore to "faithfully execute the office of President of the United States, unless I forget what that entails." He then concluded the oath, saying, "So help me God, I hope I can remember all this."

At a Capitol luncheon later in the day, Reagan said he could not quite recall taking the oath two hours earlier. He also said he was having difficulty remembering exactly what he had said there, or if, in fact, he had been there at all.

President Reagan with the First Lady and daughter Maureen.

Hostages Released

Reagan Urges American People Not to Put Two and Two Together

WEST BERLIN—Ronald Reagan urged Americans "not to put two and two together" regarding the coincidental release of Iran's 52 American hostages on the day of his presidential inauguration.

"I do not want you to notice that something extremely fishy is probably going on here," Reagan said Tuesday. "As the leader of the free world, I urge you to believe that my hard-line stance against terrorism was Khomeini's sole motivation to free the hostages, rather than any covert dealings between the Iranian government and my new administration."

"Please," Reagan added, "do not put two and two together."

Vice President and former CIA Chief George Bush, whose shady Mideast connections were not officially used to broker an arms-for-hostages deal, agreed. "With new leadership in the White House and the hostages free after a 444-day ordeal, this should be a time of national healing and renewal. Now is not the time for any suspicions which, however true, may reflect negatively on the new president," said Bush, speaking from his secret underground command post in Tehran.

American hostages, held in Iran for 444 days, arrive at a U.S. airbase in West Berlin Tuesday.

Reagan Promises Less Bureaucratic Shadow Government

WASHINGTON, D.C.—President Reagan promised an era of more streamlined, less bureaucratic behind-the-scenes double-dealing over the next four years.

"The solution to America's woes is not more and bigger government," Reagan said at a spirited Tuesday-night press conference punctuated by music, fireworks and Masonic chanting. "The solution is a smaller, leaner Shadow Government that will more efficiently feed citizens cleverly worded, vaguely patriotic assurances that everything is fine while secretly serving the economic and social agendas of our nation's wealthiest one percent."

"God bless America!" Reagan added, drawing loud cheers from the assembled crowd.

In keeping with his anti-big-Shadow-Government stance, Reagan vowed to divert funding from social-service programs into hidden government accounts and slush funds. He said the money will ultimately be used by the U.S. Shadow Government for big-business kickbacks, funding of covert CIA operations and miscellaneous savings-and-loan bailouts.

Reagan also pledged to balance the Pentagon's Black Budget, which has been running a deficit since the Kennedy Administration.

"I will restore the Department of Mind Control, Department of Hostage Negotiating and Department of CIA Drug-Testing and Torture to their former glories," Reagan said. "I will fully commit the State Department to prolonging the Cold War and increasing tensions in the Middle East."

"Together, Dirty-Work Vice President and former CIA Director George Bush and I will do our best to be puppets of the mega-corporations and defense industry, making our Shadow Government great once again," Reagan concluded to thunderous applause.

Op-Ed:

The Arab Terrorist's Assault on Lady Liberty

CARTOON, PAGE 7C

Inside:

Secret Album-Cover Clues Reveal John Lennon Is Dead

PAGE 7C

New Appetite-Suppressant Candy Takes Diet World by Storm; 'In the '80s, "Ayds" Will Be Synonymous with Fitness and Health,' Say Makers

PAGE 4A

1981-2000

A NATION FINDS ITS REMOTE

THE ONION

Sunday, April 19, 1981 — AMERICA'S FINEST NEWS SOURCE — 72 PAGES CITY EDITION $1

Latest Breakdancing Steps Inside

Texas Instruments Continues Domination of Personal-Computing Field

With sales of its flagship TI-99/4a model topping $45 million in the first quarter of 1981, Texas Instruments continues to dominate the personal-computing field, with no signs of slowing down any time soon.

"The TI-99 is, quite simply, the computer everyone wants," *Byte* magazine editor Charles Lathon said Friday. "And, with its help-button feature, built-in BASIC programming language and full set of graphics keys, it's not hard to see why."

The TI-99 has easily outsold all other home-computing systems in the $150 to $200 price range, including the Atari 400, Odyssey 2 and Sinclair ZX81.

"Texas Instruments owns the home-computer field," CEO Christopher Pike said. "Everyone else—from Timex to Apple to Magnavox—is just fighting for second place."

Industry watchers say that what gives the TI-99 its real edge over competitors is its impressive 16K of RAM.

"As personal computers go, this is an extremely powerful machine, boasting enough memory to do almost anything," *Popular Computing*'s Jonathan Wald said. "With 16K of RAM, it can meet the user's home-biorhythm-charting and recipe-filing needs, while still offering the 16 colors and 256x192 graphic resolution necessary to run Super Breakout."

Despite Texas Instruments' firm grip on the top spot, other home-computer manufacturers are trying to close the gap by aggressively introducing new features, such as arrow and backspace keys.

Radio Shack, another key player in the home-computer industry, is offering a free software package with the TRS-80 Model III, including Checkbook Manager, Hangman and Oregon Trail, while the Commodore VIC-20 boasts a state-of-the-art cassette recorder for program storage.

However, Texas Instruments' CEO says he is not concerned. "We are hardly worried about a company like Radio Shack, or even upstart companies like Apple, with its II Plus," Pike said. "The TI-99, with its daisy-wheel printer, TV switch box and AC power adapter, is one of the most awesome computer set-ups money can buy. I challenge anyone to compete with it."

The powerhouse TI-99 computer.

Hinckley, Foster to Wed

Actress 'Very Impressed' by Lone-Nut Gunman's Attempt on President's Life

NEW HAVEN, Conn.— Actress Jodie Foster, wowed by out-of-work machinist John Hinckley Jr.'s attempt on the life of President Reagan last week, announced plans Saturday to marry the gunman.

"I can't tell you how flattered I was. To think that someone would actually shoot the leader of the free world just for me," Foster said. "The moment I heard I was the reason he did it, I fell head-over-heels in love."

Foster said that when she found out her picture and a piece of paper with her name and address on it had been found on Hinckley's person at the time of the shooting, she called him to ask if he wanted to get together.

"We went out to this little Italian restaurant and had the best time," the love-struck actress said. "I can't believe how well we hit it off."

Hinckley had been familiar with Foster for years, first drawn to the actress after seeing her in Martin Scorsese's 1976 film *Taxi Driver*. "The first time I saw the movie, I said to myself, 'Someday I'm going to marry that girl,'" Hinckley told *People* magazine in an exclusive interview this week. "In order to do that, though, I knew I needed to really catch her eye."

After watching *Taxi Driver* more than 600 times and plastering the walls of his home with magazine articles, photos and drawings of Foster, Hinckley devised various plans to win her love. When Foster failed to answer any of the 1,263 letters he had sent her and refused to answer his 56 daily phone calls, Hinckley knew his tactics were not aggressive enough.

It was at this point that Hinckley devised the idea to win Foster's love by assassinating the president.

The plan worked.

"Although my bullet narrowly missed President Reagan's heart, Cupid's arrow hit Jodie's," Hinckley said.

Lovebirds John Hinckley Jr. and Jodie Foster.

"We've been inseparable ever since."

Foster, who had been attending Yale University prior to the shooting, recently dropped out to prepare for her marriage to the man she describes as "a big, lovable, president-shooting teddy bear." She said she has no plans to continue either her schooling or her acting career, and will instead focus on "building a life and a family with this wonderful, caring man."

A June wedding is planned.

Lucasfilm Puppet Stands in for Wounded Reagan

SAN RAFAEL, Calif.— George Lucas' Industrial Light & Magic special-effects company has developed a $62 million animatronic puppet to stand in for the wounded president at official state functions.

The puppet made its debut Friday at a state dinner for British Prime Minister Margaret Thatcher. "I would like to extend a welcome to the leader of our longtime ally, as well as to the wonderful people of the United Kingdom," said puppeteer Frank Oz, voice of the replacement Reagan.

It takes six puppeteers to control the new president— two for the arms, two for the legs, one for the head and torso, and one whose face is covered with suction cups connected by wire to a computer, which can duplicate up to eight basic facial expressions, transferring them perfectly onto the puppet.

The puppet is one of four created by ILM for upcoming presidential functions. Two miniature models, which can be manipulated through stop-motion photography, will be used for wider shots and are ideal for foreign parades and televised speeches.

The puppet's developers said there remain a few bugs to be worked out before the puppet is ready for arms-reduction talks with the Soviets, but they say they are confident that their Reagan is already an excellent stand-in president.

"By combining the eight facial expressions with the puppet's body movements," head developer Phil Tippet said, "the Reagan puppet is capable of expressing some 32 emotions. That is twice the number attainable by the real President Reagan, and three times the number attainable by the Tauntaun creatures in *The Empire Strikes Back*."

The puppet has been warmly welcomed by Reagan Administration staffers, particularly his speechwriters, who have struggled to make the president appear healthy and confident despite his agonizing pain from being shot in the chest.

"Frank Oz is a talented puppeteer and performer who, because he is hidden from view during performances, can actually read directly from a script, rather than having to memorize lines," speechwriter Peggy Noonan said. "That's something we could never do with President Reagan, and it's a major plus."

The Reagan puppet was made with flame-retardant foam, covered with a space-age textured-polymer skin and sculpted by make-up artist Rick Baker, who created the alien creatures for *Star Wars*. It features over 30 miniature servo-motors in the face and head alone, and its eyes were modeled after Albert Einstein's.

Reagan Administration officials say the resemblance to the actual president is uncanny.

"When I ask for approval to sell nuclear weapons to our enemies in the Mideast, the puppet smiles at me, nods vacantly and signs any papers I give him," National Security Advisor Robert McFarlane said. "It is eerie how similar he is to the real President Reagan."

ILM effects wizards are working on an even more advanced Reagan puppet to replace the president entirely by 1983.

Inside:

New 'Music Television' Cable Channel to Play Videos by Today's Hottest Whites

PAGE 7C

THE ONION

Now Printed with Synthesizers

Thursday, July 30, 1981 — AMERICA'S FINEST NEWS SOURCE — 30¢

Secret Pac-Man Patterns Fall Into Russian Hands

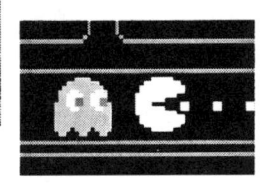

Above: The seat of the Evil Empire. Right, Pac-Man.

WASHINGTON, D.C.—CIA sources reported Wednesday that many of the Pentagon's most closely guarded Pac-Man patterns have fallen into Russian hands.

"We have reason to believe that KGB spies have obtained classified Pentagon blueprints detailing which way to go and when to eat the bonus fruit," CIA spokesman Benjamin Sirof said. "Using this sensitive information, the Russians may be able to get as far as the grapes, or perhaps even the Galaxian thing."

According to Sirof, the CIA first suspected the patterns had been stolen Dec. 2, 1980, when several agency operatives noticed that the Pac-Man machine at the U.N. had a new high score of 84,740.

"That beat the old high score by some 10,000 points. Nobody in the U.S. Gaming Forces knew who had done it or when," Sirof said. "That led us to the ominous suspicion that the KGB is a 'fifth ghost' looming over American heads."

"The national-security implications of this are terrifying," said UCLA political-science professor Allen Meyers. "If Russian gamers knew where to go after the power pill in the upper left wears out and the ghosts turn back to their regular color, there would be no stopping them."

Pentagon officials are currently trying to learn the identity of a suspected KGB mole who may have forwarded reproductions of the classified documents to Russian agents, or may have watched Pentagon officials playing and then copied down their moves.

"We must not waver in the race to master Pac-Man," Secretary of State Alexander Haig said following the disclosure. "With the release of the long-awaited sequel, Ms. Pac-Man, just months away, we must keep pace with global dot-consumption and acquisition of bonus fruits."

Added Haig: "We must remain forever vigilant. We must play Pac-Man until we go past the fabled 255th level and the screen goes crazy. And we must do so before the Soviets."

Inside:

Area Man's Blood Runs Cold after Harrowing Centerfold Sighting

PAGE 10B

CIA Unveils Cheaper, More Powerful Form of Cocaine

'Crack' Expected to Make Drug Addiction More Accessible to Inner-City Poor

LANGLEY, Va.—The CIA unveiled its latest mind-altering drug Wednesday: "crack," a concentrated, smokable form of cocaine.

Cheap and highly addictive, crack is expected to revolutionize drug addiction in America's blighted urban ghettos, CIA officials said.

"Our pharmacologists worked long and hard on this new drug, and, judging by the response from our test subjects, it was worth the wait," CIA Director William Casey said. "We expect America's minorities to be thoroughly ravaged by crack."

A multimedia presentation at CIA headquarters, attended by the mayors of nearly every major U.S. city, explained the differences between crack and conventional powdered cocaine.

"The crack high is much more intense, yet also much shorter, than that of normal cocaine," said Casey, standing in front of a large video screen depicting an inner-city youth smoking crack out of a glass pipe. "This intensity, along with crack's low price and instant addictive qualities, creates a vicious cycle of dependency that often ends in violence for the user and his associates."

The Justice Department has thrown its support behind crack by making the possession of only five grams of the substance as serious an offense as the possession of 500 grams of powdered cocaine. "We hope to put an entire generation of young, poor men behind bars, while allowing America's privileged businessmen to stay wired and wealthy," Attorney General William French Smith said.

In addition to crippling America's inner cities, crack will be used to further the CIA's international agenda. "With the profits we collect from sales of this exciting new drug," Casey said, "we will have the opportunity to fund numerous Central American coups."

President Reagan reacted favorably when told of the new drug. "This crack sounds like just what America needs," he said.

Nation's Air Traffic Controllers Executed

WASHINGTON, D.C.—President Reagan ordered America's air-traffic controllers put to death Wednesday, ending the group's six-day walkout.

The 13,000 members of the National Air-Traffic Controllers Union were electrocuted at 12:01 a.m. Reagan made the decision after a brief meeting with Transportation Secretary Drew Lewis, who strongly supported the president's action.

"I could not allow a strike by the people we depend upon to safely control the flow of airline traffic," Reagan said. "Air travelers' lives are in these people's hands. If they had been allowed to continue striking, people could have been killed."

Special electric chairs were set up at airports across the country to execute the strikers. Air-traffic controllers formed long execution lines, with death delays of up to three hours reported at Chicago's O'Hare International, and more than six hours at New York's LaGuardia Airport.

Fairytale Wedding Distracts Rank-and-File

Economically Ravaged British Underclass Temporarily Forgets Miserable Lives

LONDON, England—Lady Diana Spencer and Prince Charles Philip Arthur George of Wales were married Wednesday in a fairytale wedding that temporarily distracted the teeming, dirt-faced hordes of British commoners from their dreary, destitute lives.

Captivated by the picture-book event, held at St. Paul's Cathedral, England's faceless rabble momentarily forgot about the country's high taxes, runaway inflation, stratified class structure, stagnant manufacturing base and rapidly plummeting position in the world economy.

Instead, they focused on the jewel-bedecked couple, who left Buckingham Palace in a majestic, diamond-studded coach following a stately, opulent procession of gleaming black Rolls Royces carrying the crowned heads of Europe.

During the hours-long procession to St. Paul's, the royals passed hundreds of thousands of out-of-work coal miners stricken with black-lung disease. Many had camped out overnight in the hope of catching a glimpse of the bride and groom.

Prince Charles and Lady Diana ride past the impoverished, out-of-work British peasantry en route to St. Paul's.

"This truly is a magical day," said George Livesey, an unemployed Sheffield mill worker who could feed his family for 437 years for the price of the royal wedding ring.

Of course, the massive unemployment crippling the working class was the last thing on the minds of the masses as they gazed upon Lady Diana's gown, which trailed a 25-foot train made of bantam-weight crisp ivory silk taffeta and old lace dipped in solid gold.

"How lovely she looks," said Francine Chisholm, a £1.50-an-hour maid who watched the wedding on a television in a shop window near her rat-infested two-room flat. "I'm weeping tears of joy."

Following the resplendent multimillion-dollar event, the bottom 94 percent of England's wage-earners returned to their lives of abject squalor.

135

THE ONION

Monday, August 16, 1982 — AMERICA'S FINEST NEWS SOURCE — 30c

Support Our Troops in Nicaragua

Grenada-Falklands Superpower Alliance Mobilizes for War

Falklands' Elite Puffin Brigade Poised to Attack U.S., U.K.

Grenada Rumored to Have More Than 12 Guns

Above: Highly trained puffins poised to battle the U.S. and England. Right: The formidable island juggernaut.

LONDON—Hours after learning of the alliance signed between Grenada and the Falkland Islands Sunday, President Reagan flew to London for an emergency meeting with Prime Minister Margaret Thatcher.

"Grenada and the Falklands are a pair of bloodthirsty aggressors, intent on conquering all of the Western Hemisphere," Thatcher told reporters following the meeting. "We must learn the lesson of the Munich Conference and not appease these bullies as Chamberlain did Hitler."

Reagan and Thatcher met for more than four hours, affirming their commitment to defending each other from the Grenada-Falklands menace. The pair also conferred with Allied command leaders, devising a preliminary defense strategy in case the South American superpowers follow through on their threat to throw pebbles at the U.S.

The two island nations formalized their alliance during a meeting in the capital city of Stanley on East Falkland Island. Signing the military pact, Grenadan Prime Minister Maurice Bishop pledged full support to the Falklands, vowing to send all six Grenadan soldiers into battle, if necessary.

"Our soldiers are very big," Bishop said. "One of them, Claude Dumont, placed second at the 1981 Pan-Caribbean Arm-Wrestling Championships."

Bishop also said he would position the Grenadan Navy's top battleraft off the coast of Florida in preparation for an assault on the U.S.

For their part, the Falklanders promised they would back up Grenada if it went to war with the U.S. by dispatching their elite Puffin Brigade.

"Our fierce aquatic birds will rain terror upon the U.S.," Falkland Islands General Eduardo Villacruz said. "There is no escaping their onslaught of squawking and flapping."

Military experts estimate that, if the U.S. and Britain were to go to war with the island power bloc, the number of soldiers injured could reach the high single digits.

"There is a lot of rocky terrain in both Grenada and the Falklands, so if we were to invade either nation, there definitely would be some sprained ankles and pulled calf muscles," said former U.S. Army Sgt. Gene Hastings (Ret.). "I would urge soldiers to be careful and take each step slowly. And be sure to stretch out for at least 10 minutes before engaging in strenuous fighting. The last thing we want is someone getting hurt."

Inside:

Hollywood Scandal: Did Reese's Pieces Pay to Have Product 'Placed' in E.T.?

PAGE 1C

John Denver's Career in Ruins Following Tryst with Muppet

John Denver with Janice, far left.

LONDON—Popular singer/songwriter John Denver's career is in serious jeopardy following his arrest Sunday in connection with alleged sexual relations with a female Muppet.

Denver, who was in London to tape a guest-host appearance on *The Muppet Show*, was arrested after an anonymous tip led authorities to his hotel suite at the Sheraton Park Lane, where, according to a police spokesman, he was caught engaging in "an act of illicit congress" with Janice, a Muppet guitarist with the band Dr. Teeth & The Electric Mayhem.

Jim Henson, creator of *The Muppet Show*, said he is "deeply saddened by the news, if it is true," but urged the public not to rush to judge Denver. Henson did not say whether next week's show would be canceled, postponed or re-taped with a new guest host.

Speaking to reporters from his jail cell, Denver said, "I have no comment other than that I am innocent of any wrongdoing."

Denver, whose hits include "Rocky Mountain High" and "Sunshine on My Shoulders," will be arraigned Friday. His trial could begin as soon as October.

Janice was not arrested in the incident and is reportedly in seclusion.

Dr. Teeth, leader of the Muppet band and a close friend of Janice's, said Janice was feeling "a little down in the skin but basically groovy-woovy."

Teeth also said he is confident that any sexual act which may have occurred between Janice and Denver would have been 100 percent consensual. "Gotta cut out the fuzz, slack," he said. "The man and the Muppet have had the love bug since Miles Davis was Yards Davis, you dig?"

Another band member, identified only as the drummer, responded angrily to news of Denver's arrest, flailing wildly and screaming incoherently while throwing furniture, props and this week's guest host, Carol Burnett, around the Muppet Theater.

Reagan to Meet with Master Control Program

WASHINGTON, D.C.—After years of one-on-one flying-disc dueling against MCP drones, President Reagan will finally attend a historic summit with ENCOM's Master Control Program next month, a White House spokesman confirmed Sunday.

The focus of the meeting is said to involve issues of key importance to American users.

Reagan said he plans to address Amnesty International's claim that deadly light-cycle duels and inhumane treatment of programs at the hands of giant Recognizer tanks are taking place deep within the ultraviolet moodlit, synthesizer-scored realm of ENCOM's Central Processing Units, perhaps at the behest of the MCP.

Quipped Reagan, "If the Master Control Program can't come clean about user-rights abuses, it will be 'end of line' for our negotiations."

ENCOM Director of Product Development Ed Dillinger has denied any abuses, and U.S. computer-industry insiders say there is reason to believe him.

"This is a man who knows computing," said Jonathan Wald, editor of *Popular Computing*. "You have to realize that Dillinger created the runaway-hit video game Space Paranoids, a game boasting realistically shaded, 3-D-rendered polygon graphics at a level of sophistication light-years beyond any other video game. This game's graphics are so spectacular, they make Asteroids look primitive."

136

THE ONION

Totally Tubular-to-the-Max News

Monday, October 18, 1982 — AMERICA'S FINEST NEWS SOURCE — 54 PAGES CITY EDITION TU STULTUS ES — ★★★ — 30¢

Congress Allocates $300 Billion to Nation's Rich

Members of the House of Representatives, voting for the rich.

WASHINGTON, D.C.—President Reagan's "trickle-down" economic policy continued Friday when Congress approved legislation allocating $300 billion in tax-free funding to the nation's rich.

Distribution of funds begins at the start of the 1983–84 fiscal year. Under the terms of the legislation, the wealthiest .05 percent of American citizens will receive funding first.

"Everyone knows the old saying, 'When the rich get richer, the poor get richer, as well,'" said Reagan, voicing his approval of the measure. "By pouring such a great deal of money into the most well-off among us, we improve conditions for all Americans."

"Thank God," said Pierre DuPont, 47, heir to the DuPont chemical fortune. "At last, dozens of Americans like me won't have to endure the awful inconveniences we suffered under Carter."

DuPont had held a champagne-and-candlelight vigil at his Delaware mansion while the measure was in subcommittee.

"Winston! More cognac!" DuPont added, clapping his hands imperiously toward one of his servants.

Rich Americans plan to reinvest the federally promised money in already-bloated trust funds, banks in which they hold interests and companies in which they are majority shareholders.

MIT Scientists Have Three Sides of Rubik's Cube Complete

CAMBRIDGE, Mass.—A team of MIT physicists announced Sunday that it has completed the vital third side of the Rubik's Cube, bringing it ever closer to solving the puzzle.

Inside:

Nation's Asylums Privatized; Millions of Lunatics Set Free to Fend for Selves

PAGE 11D

"This represents a major breakthrough," said exhausted, red-knuckled project leader Dr. Cedric Stephens. "With this critical triad completed, there is reason to believe we can complete the final sides by perhaps even December of this year."

The scientists credited the breakthrough to a shift in their approach to the multi-colored cube. Previously, they had focused their efforts on the center-most square on each side of the puzzle. But team member Dr. Jim Barstow suggested the group concentrate on the four outer corners while closely monitoring the position of each square on the reverse side of the cube during each turn.

"It was the classic example of being too close to a problem to see the solution," Barstow said. "Only by stepping back and rethinking our whole way of looking at the cube could we ultimately move forward."

Barstow said it is "too soon to tell" if this strategic shift could be applied to other hand-held twist puzzles, including the Snake, Pyraminx and Missing Link.

If the MIT team completes the Rubik's Cube, its members will be the first people in the world ever to do so. A team of University of Berlin physicists reported solving the puzzle last November, but, upon close examination of the cube by Rubik Institute officials, it was discovered that the German scientists had illegally removed the stickers and reapplied them in their proper places.

A Japanese scientist at the University of Tokyo similarly claimed to have solved the puzzle last month, but he, too, was exposed as a fraud when he was found to have pulled the cube apart and snapped it back together correctly.

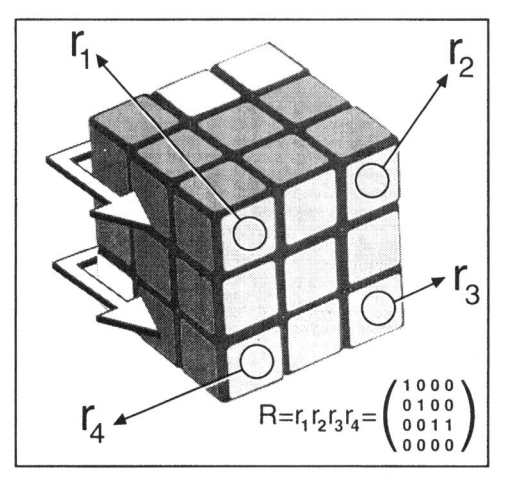

$$R = r_1 r_2 r_3 r_4 = \begin{pmatrix} 1 & 0 & 0 & 0 \\ 0 & 1 & 0 & 0 \\ 0 & 0 & 1 & 1 \\ 0 & 0 & 0 & 0 \end{pmatrix}$$

The cube, pictured with the MIT team's theoretical completion formula.

Ayatollah Calls $3.1 Million for Medium-Range Missile 'Ridiculous'; Tells Reagan $2.5 Million Is Final Offer

TEHRAN—Lashing out against the latest arms-trade offer made to him by the U.S. government, the Ayatollah Khomeini called America's asking price of $3.1 million for medium-range surface-to-surface missiles "ridiculous" Sunday, threatening to take his business elsewhere if a fairer price could not be agreed upon immediately.

"I was under the impression that Mr. Reagan was going to give me a fair deal," the Iranian leader said. "I thought we had a mutually satisfactory business relationship. But the price he has quoted me is too high for Iran to afford."

"What do they think that I am," he asked, "made of money?"

Khomeini has made a counteroffer of $2.5 million per missile, a price President Reagan said is not being considered.

Reagan, reiterating longtime administration policy, told reporters, "America does not negotiate any lower than $2.75 million with terrorists. The United States government has its bottom line to consider. How does the Ayatollah expect us to support our right-wing death squads in Central America?"

The Ayatollah Khomeini, who is outraged by President Reagan's current asking price for medium-range missiles.

"Secretary of Defense [Caspar] Weinberger and Secretary of State [George] Shultz didn't even want to give Khomeini this much of a bargain," Vice President George Bush said. "He should know that, if it were up to those guys, this deal wouldn't even be on the table. We really are doing the best we can here."

Khomeini, who said he has been "an excellent customer" of Reagan's in the past, and has never been late paying for missiles, strongly hinted that the latest asking price might give him cause to cool business dealings with the U.S.

"The United States may be the Great Satan, but it offers the best bargains on state-of-the-art weapons, and for this reason we have always been able to reach an understanding," Khomeini said. "But if a deal cannot be reached, I see no reason why I should not take my money elsewhere."

Those brokering the deal on the American side say the Ayatollah has lost sight of the spirit which drove the original bargain.

"The man must realize that the missiles are part of a package," said Lt. Col. Oliver North, who is in charge of delivering the massive arms shipment, of which the missiles are a part. "If we go down on the medium-range missiles, we have to go up on the surface-to-air missiles. If we stay low on both of those, we go up on the F-14s or the nerve gas, or even the plutonium. Business is business."

Said Khomeini, "We want the same things: You need money for your death squads; I need money for my global campaign of terror. For goodness' sake, let's be reasonable men."

Op-Eds:

We Must Arm Panama's Manuel Noriega

OP-ED, PAGE 12

Sinatra: 'I Nailed the First Lady'

PAGE 1C

the ONION

Monday, March 28, 1983 — AMERICA'S FINEST NEWS SOURCE — ★★★ 30 CENTS

Nancy Reagan Ends Nation's Drug Problem with Very Special *Diff'rent Strokes* Appearance

Youths, Addicts Learn They Can 'Just Say No'

WASHINGTON, DC—Drug Enforcement Agency officials are crediting First Lady Nancy Reagan with single-handedly ending the nation's drug crisis, thanks to her recent appearance on a very special episode of *Diff'rent Strokes*.

In the episode, which aired at 8 p.m. EST Saturday on NBC, Arnold (Gary Coleman) becomes aware of the problem of juvenile drug use when he writes a story for his school newspaper. Mrs. Reagan happens to read Arnold's story and is so moved that she personally visits the boy to commend him. She concludes her visit with an impassioned call for kids—and adults—to "just say no" to drugs.

As soon as the program aired, police precincts nationwide reported staggering drops in narcotics arrests. "We ordinarily make between 150 and 200 drug arrests on a typical Saturday night," Houston Police Commissioner Gil Washington said. "From 8:30 on, however, we made a total of just six arrests, all involving criminals who had not watched the program."

The First Lady explained her reasons for making the television appearance. "I was hearing so many terrible stories concerning drug use among young Americans, and, when the seriousness of the issue hit me, I decided I needed to do something," Reagan said. "America's young people needed to hear from someone they look up to that drugs are not 'cool.'"

After an emergency closed-door meeting with top DEA officials, Reagan decided she would deliver her important message to the American people on *Diff'rent Strokes*. "Americans from all walks of life tune in each week to catch Arnold's latest antics and hear him deliver his wildly popular catch phrase, 'Wha'choo talkin' 'bout, Willis?'" Reagan said. "After talking it over with the DEA, it was apparent that only *Diff'rent Strokes* could give me the respected national platform I needed for my historic message."

Educators and child psychologists are praising the direct, no-nonsense approach taken by the First Lady. "Nancy Reagan has succeeded where decades of attempted drug education have failed," said Dr. Peter Crichton of New York University. "By telling youngsters 'Just say no,' she leaves them with no alternative, no possible avenue for drug consumption. Mrs. Reagan alone understood that all children and drug users needed was to be told how to say 'No.'"

With the drug crisis resolved, Mrs. Reagan said she now plans to devote herself to raising awareness of the dangers of hitchhiking, an issue she will confront during an upcoming very special episode of *Matt Houston*.

The First Lady with Arnold (Gary Coleman, left) and Mr. Drummond (Conrad Bain)

Iran Has The Car Bomb

MASHHAD, IRAN—The CIA confirmed Sunday that Iran has The Car Bomb.

The confirmation came when CIA operatives stationed in Iran observed the successful detonation of a car bomb at a secret underground test garage in the remote northeastern desert town of Mashhad. The bomb, a 1978 Renault with 800 pounds of plastic explosives in the trunk, was reportedly powerful enough to wipe out an entire Jerusalem fruit market.

With the detonation, Iran joins an elite club of Middle East nations with car-bomb capability; Syria, Lebanon and Jordan also have the device. Iraq is widely expected to possess car-bomb technology as soon as next year.

"This could significantly shift the balance of terrorist power in the Middle East," CIA Chief William Casey said. "Nations will have to think twice before detonating a car bomb in a crowded Tehran square or mosque now that Iran has the capability to strike back."

The Iranian car bomb is said

An Iranian car-bomb test.

to be among the most technologically advanced of its kind, with a range of up to 170 miles on a full tank of gas. It is also widely rumored that Iran is already developing an even more powerful weapon, known only as "The Truck Bomb."

"Imagine a device like an exploding car, only it's truck-sized," Pentagon spokesman Roger Terkel said. "That should give you an idea of what kind of weapon we're talking about here."

"No longer do we have to rely on bricks and Molotov cocktails," Iranian Minister of Defense Abdullah al Aziz said. "Our enemies will bow before the awesome destructive might of The Car Bomb."

Your Legs: Are They Warm Enough?

A serious lack of attention is being paid to the warmth of Americans' legs, warns a federal legwear study released Friday.

According to the National Leg-Warmth Council report, each day in the U.S., more than 50 million lower limbs are inadequately protected from the elements—a condition researchers say can easily be remedied with the use of colorfully striped, knitted calf-coverings.

"We have long known that 'leg warmers' are vital to dancers for keeping their Spandexed legs warm, preventing potentially dangerous lower-leg chills," NLWC Chair Adrienne Bosch said. "But we are now finding that leg warmers are extremely useful for the general public, as well. They can be worn during activities ranging from club dancing to roller skating, to just hanging around the house."

The study found that women, whose typically smaller frames make them more susceptible to cold calves, should wear leg warmers, not only with "workout gear," but also with blue jeans, denim skirts, sweater dresses and nylon short-shorts. For extra warmth, the addition of a color-coordinated head- and wristband set was also strongly advised.

Inside:

Lauper, WWF Team Up to Form Entertainment-Industry Juggernaut
PAGE 2A

We Need More Movies Where Monkeys Give the Finger
EDITORIAL, PAGE 9A

Who's Your Favorite Flock of Seagull? Take Our Reader Poll
PAGE 8C

Zapped! Sweeps Oscars
see full coverage, 1C

the ONION

Friday, February 3, 1984 — AMERICA'S FINEST NEWS SOURCE — ★★★ 50 CENTS

Congress Approves Orbiting Homeless Incinerator

WASHINGTON, DC—On Thursday, Congress approved President Reagan's request to fund a $17.9 billion orbiting homeless incinerator, capping years of intense lobbying efforts on the part of the president.

The plutonium-fueled, satellite-guided Homeless-Eliminatronic II space incinerator is scheduled for completion in December 1986, when it will be launched and deployed to its initial position 600 miles above the Bronx.

"This is a great day for

'This Is a Great Day for America,' Reagan Says

America," Reagan said at a White House press conference. "Finally, our defense industry is working in concert with our welfare system."

The HE II will use high-tech locators to pinpoint homeless Americans. A razor-thin charged-particle beam will then shoot down from space, instantly reducing its target transient to a small pile of ash.

The HE II, once operational, will be able to incinerate up to 500 homeless adults or 750 homeless children per hour.

At that rate, the problem of American homelessness will be solved in less than two months. Thereafter, the unit will remain active for pre-emptive incinerations of newly diagnosed schizophrenics and teenage runaways.

A drawing of the proposed weapon against homelessness

Serbs, Muslims Inspired by Competitive Spirit of Sarajevo Olympics

SARAJEVO—Across Yugoslavia, Serbs, Muslims and Croats alike are drawing inspiration from the competitive spirit exhibited at the 1984 Winter Olympics in Sarajevo.

"To see people of vastly different ethnic backgrounds struggling against each other for total victory has been an eye-opening experience for me and my people," said Serbian community leader Slobodan Milosevic.

The Olympic athletes' determination to best each other in competition has roused the spirits of Yugoslavians of all ages and ethnicities. Many local children, looking forward to the Summer Olympics in Los Angeles in a few months, have already begun throwing makeshift shotputs and javelins at each other.

Sarajevo '84

The New York Stock Exchange, whose traders have enjoyed a soaring Dow and primo South American blow

Wall Street Traders Enjoy Record Highs, Highs

NEW YORK—Wall Street traders reported record highs Thursday, as the Dow topped the 1,300-point mark for the first time ever and a massive shipment of pure Colombian cocaine was distributed throughout the financial district.

"I've never seen such highs," said Tyler Rentley, a NYSE floor trader. "Not only are bulls outnumbering bears on the big board 10 to 1, but this is some of the best shit I've ever sniffed. I feel like I could conquer the world."

The Dow soared a remarkable 113 points Thursday. Trader Ryan Crane also reported an increase in highs of as much as 20 percent, thanks to his dealer "finally getting him some of that primo South American blow."

In the broader market, advancers led decliners 18 to 12 on volume of more than 700 million shares. The S&P 500 index set a new record, rising 9.32 points to 1,032.11, while Salomon Brothers trader Jason Westphal set a personal record, inhaling $600 of cocaine in one night.

"If you're smart, you'll put your money in oil and biotechnology stocks," Westphal said, wiping his nose with a blood-spotted monogrammed handkerchief.

Durable goods, however, remain unpredictable, much like stock analyst Raymond Gorst, who bought his wife a new Mercedes just minutes after punching her in the jaw.

Rockwell International, the third most active issue on the Big Board, was up 2-1/2 at 67-5/16, followed by General Electric, up 2-1/8 at 86-15/16. The major oil companies continued to rebound after crude-oil prices sank to record lows, much like 38-year-old futures trader Christian Zollner, who snorted cocaine off a hooker's chest with a rolled-up hundred-dollar bill.

Donald Trump Announces Plans to Gold-Plate Atlantic City

ATLANTIC CITY, NJ—Real-estate mogul Donald Trump unveiled plans Monday to gold-plate Atlantic City, a $900 billion project scheduled for completion in Fall 1988.

"Atlantic City will out-gold the Aztecs. Atlantic City will out-gold King Midas. And I will bring you that gold," said Trump, speaking from his gold-plated Trump Towers in Manhattan.

According to Trump mistress and project coordinator Marla Maples, a fleet of silver helicopters will pour liquid gold over all of Atlantic City starting this spring.

Said Atlantic City Tourism Director Stanley Schmidt, "We're very enthusiastic about Mr. Trump's plan for Atlantic City. We have many tourist attractions here already, but, as exciting and dynamic as those attractions are, they will be even more spectacular when covered with solid gold."

Trump said he intends to pay for the project with cash.

Donald Trump

Inside:

We Must Arm Iraq's Saddam Hussein
OP-ED, PAGE 12A

Springsteen, Benatar, Macchio Compete in '84 Headband-Off
PAGE 9C

the ONION

Tuesday, September 11, 1984 — AMERICA'S FINEST NEWS SOURCE — ★★★ 50 CENTS

Famine-Wracked Ethiopia Makes Desperate Plea to U2

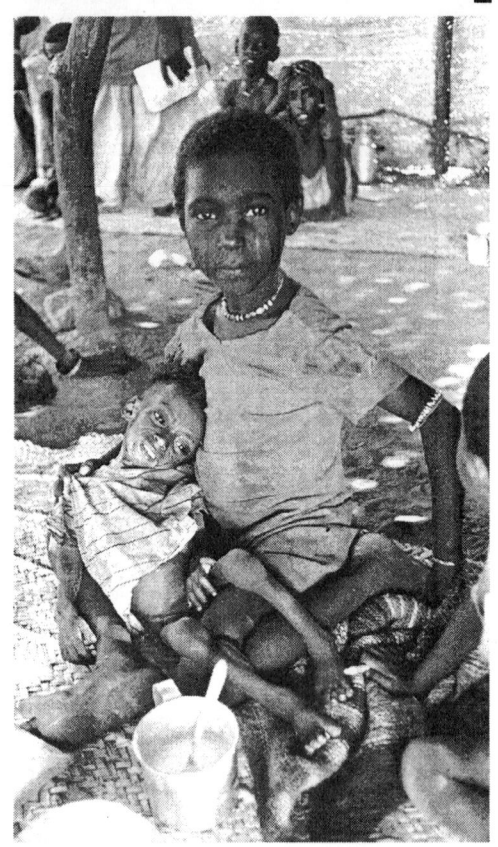

'Please Help Us, Bono,' Starving Children Say

ADDIS ABABA, Ethiopia—Ravaged by severe drought and hunger, the people of Ethiopia made a desperate plea to U2 Monday, imploring the Irish rock band to come to their aid.

"Help us, Bono. Help us, The Edge—you are our only hope," said Kwiha villager Mago Asosa, one of millions of Ethiopians on the brink of death. "Deliver us from starvation."

"There is nowhere left to turn," said Ethiopian Guna Birhan, who has lost three of her five children to hunger.

"The U.N. has done nothing. The U.S. has done nothing. Lionel Richie has ignored our cries, as well. Only the platinum-selling Dublin quartet that sings 'Sunday Bloody Sunday' and 'I Will Follow' can save us now."

Added Birhan: "I am so hungry, I do not even know if it is Christmastime."

Across Ethiopia, crops lie in ruin and millions of children are dying of malnutrition and disease. The country is devastated by mass famine, brought on by years of drought, government mismanagement and brutal civil war. All this could end, citizens say, through the music of U2.

"I have heard *October*. I have heard *War*. I believe this band can help us," said Debre Bahilla of the tiny village of Negele.

"Adam Clayton, you play the bass so well," Metu Giyon said. "Won't you please help me find something to eat?"

The Ethiopian people are calling upon U2 to hold a concert to raise money for them, as well as to convince such fellow U.K. superstars as Ultravox, Boy George, Wham!, Phil Collins, Simon LeBon, Bananarama and The Boomtown Rats to join them onstage for a life-saving benefit concert.

"If Simon LeBon were to sing a medley of Duran Duran songs and then be joined onstage by Freddie Mercury and David Bowie in a spectacular encore set, the hunger which has wracked my frail body for months could finally come to an end," Birhan said. "And if Phil Collins would only play 'Sussudio,' capped off by a thrilling 15-minute drum solo, perhaps my village could finally plant crops once more."

"If the members of U2 are unable to hold such a special concert," Bahilla said, "I urge them to join Michael Jackson, Stevie Wonder and others in a multi-artist studio mega-hit." He said such a star-studded single could feed not only his village, but perhaps the world.

Starving Ethiopians, above, are placing their hopes for survival on The Edge, Larry Mullen, Bono and Adam Clayton, above right.

Inside:

Is the U.S. Spending Enough on Salvadoran Nun-Killing?
PAGE 17A

Union Carbide Announces Plans to Downsize Bhopal, India
PAGE 6D

Report: Union of Snake May Be on Rise
PAGE 4D

Joe Piscopo: Will His Star Ever Stop Rising?
PAGE 8C

Mondale Selects 'Where's the Beef?' Lady as Running Mate

Mondale-Peller Ticket to Lead Democratic Party in '84

MINNEAPOLIS—Democratic presidential candidate Walter Mondale announced Monday that he has selected "Where's the beef?" lady Clara Peller as his running mate in the 1984 election.

The 84-year-old Peller, star of a wildly popular series of fast-food commercials, officially accepted the vice-presidential nomination, making her the first TV-commercial "grotesque" vice-presidential nominee in U.S. history. She announced her decision at a Minneapolis-area Wendy's.

"Where's the beef?" exclaimed the gruff Peller, knocking several reporters out of their chairs with her loud bellow. "Where's the beef?"

Mondale said he chose Peller because her trademark slogan reflects the concerns of millions of Americans. "When I look at the countless empty promises and deep social-welfare cuts made by President Reagan over the past four years," Mondale said, "I, too, must ask the question, 'Where's the beef?'"

"We are excited about making 'Where's the beef?' the centerpiece of our campaign against Ronald Reagan," Mondale-Peller '84 Campaign Director Robert Beckel said. "Ronald Reagan is all fluffy bun and no meaty substance. His administration truly is the 'Home of the Big Bun.'"

Reaction to Mondale's "Where's the beef?"-based campaign strategy has been mixed, but political analyst Tom Wicker of *The New York Times* praised the move. "Mondale has a lot of support among northern liberals, but he needs a vice president who can deliver the crucial McDonald's and Burger King

Clara Peller and Walter Mondale

swing voters who are dissatisfied with the size of their current beef patties," Wicker said. "No one has ever won the presidency without those crucial votes."

President Reagan responded to the Peller nomination by dropping Vice President George Bush from the Republican ticket, replacing him with the fast-talking Federal Express guy.

the ONION

Saturday, July 20, 1985 — AMERICA'S FINEST NEWS SOURCE — ★★★ 50 CENTS

Victory!
U.S. Wins Vietnam War at Last

America is standing tall again, thanks to war hero and one-man army John Rambo.

HANOI—Ten years after Saigon fell to the Vietcong, America finally set things right Friday, when veteran John Rambo singlehandedly won the Vietnam War for the U.S.

Rambo, a fighting machine rendered unstoppable by his flashback-induced psychosis, defeated the Southeast Asian nation with an astonishing array of weaponry, including rocket launchers, M-60 machine guns, combat knives, grenade launchers and explosive-tipped arrows. An estimated 875 North Vietnamese and Russians were killed in his bold assault on enemy territory, and more than 1,500 huts and rope bridges were destroyed.

"Now, that's the way you do it," President Reagan said of Rambo at a White House ceremony in his honor. "If we had had more men like that, we never would have lost the war in the first place."

In addition to killing and maiming thousands of Communists, Rambo also freed an estimated 1,250 American POWs from Vietcong camps in his triumphant, patriotic raid. Intelligence reports indicate that that number accounts for every last American MIA in Vietnam.

"Thank you, Rambo," said soldier Frank Johnson, 36, who had spent the last 13 years in a jungle POW camp. "You are a true American hero."

According to experts, the U.S. would have won the war the first time around, if the politicians hadn't prevented men like John Rambo from doing what they were trained to do.

"The U.S. government sent American boys over there to fight, but it didn't give them the backing necessary to win. We went in, but we didn't go in all the way," said Dr. George Cranmer, Yale University professor of American history. "Unlike the cowardly leaders of the time, John Rambo understands that you don't win a war by going in half-assed. When you're fighting an enemy, it's all or nothing."

Early this morning, Vietnamese leaders formally conceded defeat.

"We have lost the war," Vietnam President Lac So Tranh said. "This loose cannon you call John Rambo is unlike anything we have ever faced. He is a virtual one-man army."

"America was weak and gutless in the '60s and '70s," Lac added. "But now it is proud and strong."

Dynamic New Soviet Leader Not on Brink of Death

MOSCOW—Mikhail Gorbachev, 54, was named the USSR's premier Friday, ushering in a bold new era of Soviet leadership not on the brink of death.

Gorbachev, who had served as Deputy of the Supreme Soviet since 1970, is expected to live for at least another five years.

"Unlike such premiers as Brezhnev, Andropov and Chernenko, Mr. Gorbachev is not about to keel over at any moment," said Samuel Hilliard, a Duke University professor of Russian history. "Perhaps even more impressive, Mr. Gorbachev does not constantly cough up blood. The Soviet government should be greatly invigorated by this dynamic man who was born in the 20th century."

In his first speech before the Supreme Soviet as premier, Gorbachev pledged a break from the policies of his predecessors, vowing to improve relations with the West, implement sweeping economic reforms and not collapse into a coma after a series of strokes.

Mikhail Gorbachev

Miami Police Department Unveils New Pastel Pink and Aqua Uniforms

MIAMI—The Miami Police Department has replaced its conventional uniforms with a new line of stylishly cut suits in pastel tints of pink and aqua.

The suits, unveiled Friday at a press conference/fashion show at the Miami harborfront, will be worn over white tank-tops and complemented by Gucci sandals.

Miami Police Chief Martin Castillo said the uniform redesign is part of an effort to keep up with increasingly stylish Miami-area gun-runners and drug lords. "The criminals of the '80s are better dressed than the police," Castillo said. "Our officers are out-tanned, out-sport-jacketed and out-sunglassed—it's getting too dangerous for them out there."

Castillo said that, in order to infiltrate the night-world of glamorous pool parties held at the mansions of Colombian coke lords, Miami police officers must be equipped with the latest in designer clothing.

Along with the new uniform, all male officers will be issued a customized electric razor that will keep their facial hair stubbled at the new, mandatory length of one-eighth of an inch. Each officer will also be armed with a toothpick to dangle jauntily from his lower lip whenever emergency coolness is needed.

The police themselves say they are excited about the new uniforms. "This is long overdue," said Det. Sonny Crockett, speaking from his customized Ferrari Daytona

The new Miami police uniforms

Spyder. "If you don't look good, this town will eat you alive." Crockett then donned his sunglasses and turned on his car stereo, which played Phil Collins' "In the Air Tonight" as he drove away.

Vanessa Williams Tarnishes Miss America Crown with Sexist Objectification

ATLANTIC CITY, NJ—Vanessa Williams, 1984's Miss America, was forced by Miss America Pageant officials to relinquish her crown Thursday after nude photos of her appeared in *Penthouse* magazine.

"The Miss America Pageant is not a place for someone who parades her body for all to see like some shallow, one-dimensional object of beauty," pageant director Albert Marks said. "That is unacceptable conduct for Miss America. I am shocked that anyone associated with our pageant would be so degrading to women."

Marks blasted Williams, who had earned perfect scores in the swimsuit portion of the Miss America competition, for

Vanessa Williams

"displaying herself like a piece of meat in a sexist forum like *Penthouse*. She should be ashamed of herself."

Marks said the Miss America Pageant values women for "so much more than how they look," including their ability to walk gracefully, smile and answer basic questions.

the ONION

Tuesday, August 13, 1985 — AMERICA'S FINEST NEWS SOURCE — ★★★ 50 CENTS

IN THE NEWS:

Reagan Nukes Libya
PAGE 2A

Good Dictators:
- AUGUSTE PINOCHET (CHILE)
- FERDINAND MARCOS (PHILIPPINES)
- JEAN-CLAUDE DUVALIER (HAITI)
- SADDAM HUSSEIN (IRAQ)

Bad Dictators:
- MUAMMAR QADDAFI (LIBYA)
- FIDEL CASTRO (CUBA)
- JUAN ORTEGA (COLOMBIA)
- THE AYATOLLAH KHOMEINI (IRAN)

SOURCE: U.S. State Department
(This list subject to change.)

Nancy Reagan, Imelda Marcos Meet for Historic Footwear Summit

PARIS—Determined to forge a unified global footwear vision for the future, First Lady Nancy Reagan and Imelda Marcos, wife of Philippine President Ferdinand Marcos, convened Monday in France to discuss crucial shoe-related issues.

The historic three-day shoe summit will focus on shoes ranging from Gucci suede pumps to Christian Dior high heels, and is expected to include lengthy discussions about color choice and handbag accessorizing.

"I am pleased to have the opportunity to meet with Mrs. Reagan, a woman of impeccable taste," said Marcos, wearing a $1,250 pair of Spanish Ermenegildo Zegna pumps. "My country's fate is in my hands, as the First Lady and I discuss the many shoe issues so vital to our future social engagements."

Eager to address worldwide concerns over the proliferation of uncoordinated casual separates, the two women quickly retired to a French chateau on the outskirts of Paris to talk and page through catalogs.

A diplomatic aide to Reagan, on hand to assist in translating and carrying packages during the First Lady's tour of Paris' finest shoe stores, noted that the two women already seemed to be making "significant progress" in the areas of clogs, calf-high boots and red patent-leather slip-ons.

"This is a great day for not

Reagan and Marcos at the Paris shoe summit

only shoes, but for the entire world," said Reagan, wearing a stunning red sequined Chanel dress and matching shoes. "Hopefully, these diplomatic negotiations will clear the way for the peaceful coexistence of varying sizes, styles and heel heights around the globe."

The Hot and Cool Sides of Our Nation's Hamburgers: Are They Adequately Separated?

Each year in the U.S., an estimated 115 million hamburgers are rendered less delicious due to post-purchase, pre-consumption intermingling of two ingredient sets of differing temperature.

The burger's cool side—comprising lettuce, tomato, onion, ketchup and top bun—is warmed by the hot side, resulting in a loss of crispness and excess moisture absorption. Similarly, the hot side—comprising the meat patty, cheese slice and bottom bun—is cooled by the cool side, result-

The Hot-Side/Cool-Side Problem
CAN ANYTHING BE DONE?

A HOT 140° — A COOL 40°

A TEPID 90°

ing in the loss of steaming, hot-off-the-grill freshness.

Without a means of separating the two sides, experts say, the problem will only continue.

McDonald's Director of Product Development Chris Rohrbacher may have found a solution to the problem. A new packaging system he has devised features separate compartments for the burger's two sides, and a two-part cover to protect its contents from potential heating/cooling as a result of exposure to the other.

"At the very last possible moment, just as the hamburger is about to be consumed, the eater will flip the two sides together to create a perfectly balanced burger," Rohrbacher said. "It is a simple yet elegant solution to this serious problem."

As an added bonus, the new package will be twice as large and use twice as much Styrofoam as existing hamburger containers. "This will create an estimated 50,000 new jobs in the Styrofoam-manufacturing industry," Rohrbacher said.

CDC: New 'AIDS' Disease Could Put Nation at Increased Risk of Gala Celebrity Benefits

Epidemiologists Predict 10,000 New Cases of Lavish Hollywood Fundraisers in Next 10 Years

ATLANTA—According to an alarming report released Monday by the Centers for Disease Control, a deadly new disease known as Acquired Immune Deficiency Syndrome, or "AIDS," could lead to an exponential increase in gala celebrity-benefit events over the next 10 years.

"In 1984, there were six reported cases of AIDS fundraisers in the U.S.," CDC chief Lawrence Preston said. "Expect these figures to soar over the course of the next decade. By 1995, we estimate that there will be some 10,000 new cases of lavish AIDS benefits, including 7,500 in Los Angeles County alone."

Preston said side-effects of the new disease will take many forms, including glamorous black-tie dinners, fun runs, charity walks and art auctions.

"A disease like muscular dystrophy is easy to deal with, because there is only the Jerry Lewis Telethon," Preston said. "But AIDS promises to be far more insidious, taking the form of everything from $1,000-a-plate dinners at the Beverly Hills Hotel to tribute songs featuring Dionne Warwick and Elton John. There will be no one way to stop it."

The disease is already showing signs of growth. Last Friday, Bette Midler canceled an appearance on *The Tonight Show* to attend a celebrity softball game at Dodger Stadium, the proceeds of which will be donated to the National AIDS Crisis Hotline.

AIDS is also expected to have a devastating effect on other benefits. By 1990, CDC officials estimate, the number of yearly gala celebrity cancer benefits will fall by 93 percent. The National Cancer Institute has been advised to brace for a $50 million annual decrease in funds generated by charity events.

"Cancer is on the way out," a prominent Hollywood agent said. "Everyone I know is inspired by people with AIDS. Everyone who's anyone in Hollywood is concerned about this exciting new disease."

Actress Elizabeth Taylor agreed. "We've got to put on our finest Christian Dior gowns and Cartier jewelry and help these people," Taylor said. "We must also make sure that, through magazines like *People* and TV shows like *Entertainment Tonight*, we raise awareness about the many glamorous events our nation's celebrities are attending to help sufferers of this moving, moving disease."

Taylor called upon Congress to greatly increase its funding for development of powerful new AIDS-fighting red ribbons.

"These ribbons are our best hope," she said. "Without them, people watching the Academy Awards will not know of our great concern for AIDS sufferers."

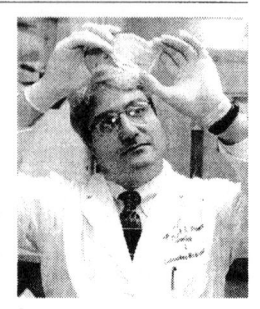

Scientists hope to learn more about how Hollywood fundraisers spread.

INSIDE:

Spuds MacKenzie: Would People Have Bought Beer Anyway?

PAGE 6D

the ONION

Monday, January 27, 1986 — AMERICA'S FINEST NEWS SOURCE — ★ ★ ★ 50 CENTS

Mr. T Releases 'Pity List '86'

LOS ANGELES—At a packed press conference at the Four Seasons Hotel Sunday, actor and former bodyguard Mr. T released his official 1986 Pity List.

"Ladies and gentlemen of the press," Mr. T said, "I pity a great many fools this year."

Pausing to don his reading glasses, the hot-tempered star of *Rocky III* and *The A-Team* then began slowly, methodically reciting the list.

"I pity the following fools: James B. Anderson, Clarence W. Azim, Priscilla F. Brechler, Gilberto P. Costa, Maxwell H. Dobbs, Susan R. Jaworski, Terrence S. Lapham, Cindy A. Maitner, Martin L. Reyes, Amanda G. Schuelke, Frank C. Weigel, and Yin Wai-Tong."

He continued, "If you are among the aforementioned people, I pity you deeply, for you are in for a world-class whupping courtesy of Mr. T."

Mr. T then read from an additional list of pitied fools, presented in descending order of degree of pity deserved. Among the more notable fools on the list: the ship-hijacking fools who seized the Italian cruise ship *Achille Lauro* last October, the waiter who spilled coffee on him at a Long Beach restaurant last week, and anyone who does not watch Mr. T's new detective drama *T. and T.*, which premieres this fall in syndication.

Another 49 fools from previous years were also singled out for "lifetime pity" designation, including those who ridiculed his 35 pounds of gold chains, made fun of his mohawk-style haircut or panned his performance in the feature film *D.C. Cab*.

President Reagan joined Mr. T in pitying the listed fools, issuing a statement which read, "My heart goes out to those fools on the list, as I believe that any attempt by these individuals to go into hiding or seek protection from any law-enforcement agency will be futile against Mr. T's inevitable onslaught of pain."

Mr. T concluded the press conference by repeatedly smashing the podium until it was reduced to splinters.

Mr. T

The Space Shuttle Challenger

Schoolteacher, Kitten, Three Dozen Orphans to Fly on Challenger Tomorrow

CAPE CANAVERAL, FL—With the Space Shuttle Challenger scheduled for liftoff at 9 a.m. EST Tuesday, its non-astronaut passengers—an idealistic young schoolteacher, a group of doe-eyed orphans and a precious little kitten—are making final preparations for their journey into the heavens.

"It's going to be a thrilling and wonderful adventure," said Christa McAuliffe, the Concord, NH, elementary-school teacher who has inspired millions during her training to become the first civilian to fly in space. "I will never forget this experience as long as I live."

McAuliffe's husband, parents and two young children have traveled to Florida to watch the launch. Her parents plan to videotape the spectacular event, and a giant big-screen TV has been set up in the auditorium of McAuliffe's school back in New Hampshire so that all 850 of its students can watch one of their own make history by soaring into space.

The three dozen orphans, who traveled all the way from Cleveland's Blessed St. Ambrose Orphanage, also look forward to flying on Challenger and seeing the Earth from outer space.

"My life has been very hard. No one loves me," said 8-year-old orphan Thomas James, who is wheelchair-bound. "My one dream is to reach the stars."

Added James: "I know that, when I get back, someone will finally want to adopt me."

The Challenger's feline passenger is Mr. Mittens, a two-month-old orange tabby owned by 10-year-old Kellie Miller of Miami.

"Kellie loves her little kitty so much," NASA Project Leader Myron Brunsell said. "She can't wait to give Mr. Mittens a great big hug when he gets back from his trip."

Other shuttle passengers slated for the mission include a koala bear, several bunnies, a litter of puppies, a family of ducklings and a baby seal.

Returning Cola War Veterans Treated to Madison Avenue Ticker-Tape Parade

NEW YORK—In what one witness called a "ceremony to start the healing," thousands of soft-drink consumers lined New York's Madison Avenue Sunday to cheer returning copywriters, ad executives and other Cola War veterans.

"The Cola War was one fierce ad blitz after another," said Chris Reese, a veteran who served with Saatchi & Saatchi in the "Coke Adds Life" campaign of '82. "One day, you're facing Pepsi celebrity endorser Michael Jackson, the next day, Lionel Richie. People who weren't in those marketing-strategy meetings will never understand what it was like."

Also honored in the parade were persecuted minority groups such as RC Cola drinkers, Tab drinkers and other survivors of the Colahaust.

Said Michael Krause, a Leo Burnett creative director stationed in Chicago from '80 to '85, "Finally, we are being recognized for the sacrifices we made for Generation Next."

100,000 soft-drink consumers show their appreciation to the vets.

INSIDE:

Michael J. Fox Adjusts Tie, Runs Hands Through Hair
PAGE 4A

The Rich and Famous: Do We Know Enough About Their Lifestyles?
PAGE 16C

Ed McMahon, Dick Clark Showcase Chernobyl Blooper
PAGE 1C

143

the ONION

Wednesday, July 8, 1987 — AMERICA'S FINEST NEWS SOURCE — 50 CENTS

Blacks in South Africa, who must fight for their civil rights

Americans Outraged By South Africa's Race-Divided Economic System

Apartheid, South Africa's system of discrimination against blacks, has shocked and outraged Americans, who, by contrast, live in a racially united country.

Since learning of Apartheid, U.S. citizens are speaking out against South Africa, where blacks are economically disadvantaged and politically disenfranchised.

"I am appalled by the racism in South Africa, where blacks not only cannot vote, but live in separate, much poorer neighborhoods than whites," said housewife Mary Ryerson of Evanston, IL.

President Reagan and a bipartisan group of prominent congressmen, including Rep. Bob Dornan (R-CA), Sen. Edward Kennedy (D-MA), Sen. Sam Nunn (D-GA), Rep. Richard Gephardt (D-MO) and Sen. Bob Dole (R-KS), recently sent a letter to South African President P.W. Botha, which read, "It is unfair that whites have all the power in South Africa."

A coalition of U.S. musicians, led by Paul Simon, has called upon the South African leadership to stop exploiting its black citizens.

Said Simon, "The black people of South Africa have toiled and slaved in the white man's mines for generations. Yet the blacks live in poverty while white men make enormous profits by exploiting the blacks. It's wrong."

Companies such as Denny's have recently divested from South Africa. A Denny's spokesman explained the action, calling the nation "a place where black people are not treated with respect."

Horrible Asshole Richer Than Ever

NEW YORK—Horrible asshole Brad Thorstad, known throughout the New York metropolitan area as an insufferable, mean-spirited prick whose enormous wealth has enabled him to disregard the basic human dignity of everyone with whom he comes into contact, is even richer today, thanks to the bullish stock market, Wall Street sources reported Tuesday.

It is expected that Thorstad, an awful person who already has more money than any human being could possibly need, will reap untold profits by reinvesting his earnings.

"My watch cost more than you'll make in your entire life," Thorstad said to a waitress at the Russian Tea Room. "Get me another one of these highballs, you stupid bitch."

Thorstad has, sources report, never afforded another human being an ounce of respect in his life. He is said to be incapable of any form of love, except for the inhuman lust for money that feeds his black heart. Described as "that evil, evil fucker" by family members, domestic servants and virtually every other person who encounters him, Thorstad possesses an all-consuming assholitude that is widely attributed to his vast wealth, which provides him with an impenetrable social barrier against all consequences of his assholic actions.

Despite his incurable assholism, Thorstad has received high praise from many well-respected economic observers for his unwavering commitment to capitalistic gain. "Thorstad is an American hero," wrote William F. Buckley in a recent *National Review* editorial. "Let's hear it for this rich, rich man."

Judge Wapner Hears Oliver North Testimony

Embattled Colonel Testifies Before *People's Court*

Millions Of Americans Tune In For 'The Case Of The Contra-Loving Colonel'

Wapner Expected To Give Ruling On Iran-Contra Affair After Short Break

LOS ANGELES—Col. Oliver North appeared before *People's Court* Judge Joseph Wapner Tuesday to testify about his role in the Iran-Contra scandal.

"I know you have been sworn in, and I have read the complaints," Wapner told litigants in "The Case Of The Contra-Loving Colonel," the first of two cases featured on the much-anticipated episode of *The People's Court*.

After being sworn in by bailiff Rusty Burrell, North testified that he was "just following orders" when he funneled profits from Iranian arms sales to the Nicaraguan Contras.

"Judge Wapner, I did nothing wrong," North said. "These were the orders of my superiors, and I believed it was my duty to obey them."

North told Wapner he was given the orders to sell arms to Iran by Defense Secretary Caspar Weinberger during a conversation at a Nov. 2, 1982, White House reception. As proof, North produced a receipt for his tuxedo rental for the party, which he showed the judge.

"If you will look at the top of the receipt, your honor, you will see that it is clearly dated Nov. 2, 1982, the date of the party," North said.

As further evidence, North presented a photograph of himself and Weinberger, which the colonel claimed had been taken at the party by his secretary, Fawn Hall. Wapner returned the photo to North after examining its back and finding no date. "How could you submit this photo?" a visibly irritated Wapner said. "You can't even prove when it was taken. Let's take a short commercial break, and then I'll hear from the plaintiff."

After returning from the break, North was scolded numerous times by Wapner, who appeared irritated by the colonel's frequent interruptions during testimony by the plaintiff, U.S. Sen. Joseph Biden (D-DE), chair of the Senate Armed Services Committee.

"Colonel North, you had your chance to give your side of the story, and now it's Senator Biden's turn," Wapner said. "Would you be quiet, please?"

The testimony ended after 15 minutes, when Wapner handed down his verdict and ordered North to pay the Senate committee $1,500, the maximum penalty allowed in small-claims court.

The court was then cleared to make way for the episode's second trial, "The Case Of The Puppy-Stained Carpet."

After the verdict, North spoke briefly with *People's Court* correspondent Doug Llewelyn.

"Doug, I told the truth, and that's all my country can ask of me," North said. "The Freedom Fighters deserved our government's support."

"Thanks, Colonel," Llewelyn said, "but it looks like the judge didn't see it that way."

Llewelyn then politely motioned North to leave the courtroom hallway.

"Remember," Llewelyn said, "when you get mad at a high-ranking U.S. military officer for selling arms to Iran and funneling the profits to a Central American guerrilla group, don't take the law into your own hands. Take 'em to court."

Colonel Oliver North listens closely to the opening remarks of *People's Court* host Doug Llewelyn.

INSIDE:

Members-Only Jackets: Are They Being Worn By Non-Members?
PAGE 10A

YothersFest '87 Pushed Back Again
PAGE 5C

the ONION

Tuesday, December 29, 1987 — AMERICA'S FINEST NEWS SOURCE — ★★★ 50 CENTS

Reagan Proclaims 'Late Afternoon In America,' Takes Nap

President Reagan

WASHINGTON, DC—Shortly after the completion of what he termed "a very nice supper" Monday, President Reagan proclaimed it late afternoon in America and took a nap.

"My fellow Americans," Reagan said during a televised speech to the nation, "the shadows are lengthening on the White House lawn, my tummy is full and, as your president, I am feeling quite drowsy. It is late afternoon in America, and I am proud to announce that the time has come for us to take a nice, long nap."

Before dozing off, Reagan outlined the five points of his Late Afternoon In America Plan:

1. That a pillow be found upon which he can lay his head.
2. That a fluffy afghan or quilt be found to cover his body.
3. That the curtains be drawn so he is not disturbed by bright afternoon sunlight.
4. That all senior officials leave the Oval Office during the brief sleep.
5. That he not be awakened, even in the event of a national emergency.

"So sleepy," Reagan said after detailing his plan. He then yawned deeply and stretched before putting both hands to one side of his head, closing his eyes and lying down on the sofa, deep in slumber within seconds.

George Bailey Jr. Indicted In Savings & Loan Scandal

BEDFORD FALLS, NY—According to an out-of-town bank examiner's report made public Monday, George Bailey Jr., CEO of the Bailey Building & Loan Association, faces charges of misappropriation of funds, manipulation and malfeasance. A warrant has been issued for his arrest.

According to a Bailey Building & Loan spokesperson, office clerk Billy Bailey, 102, lost track of $8,000 of the day's deposits when delivering the cash to the Bedford Falls Bank last Thursday.

Mr. Potter, a shareholder in the Bailey Building & Loan and heir to the Potter fortune, said there was a slight discrepancy in the books, adding that Bailey may have been playing the stock market with the company's money.

"Also, the whole town knows he's been giving money to Violet Bick," Potter said.

Potter said he hopes Bailey has "a happy new year—in jail."

God Kills Oral Roberts For Fundraising Shortfall

Televangelist Called Home By Lord As Warned

TULSA, OK—Angered by what He called His disciple's "shameful failure to raise sufficient funds for My goodly earthly works," God struck down prominent televangelist Oral Roberts Monday.

Roberts, who had received numerous warnings from God that he would be "called home" if his fundraising goal was not met, was killed when a large thunderbolt from the heavens struck him during a taping of his weekly television show.

The 67-year-old Roberts died instantly from the heavenly bolt. He was $211,000 short of God's $3 million fundraising goal at the time of his death.

"I said I would smite Oral, and I kept My word," God told reporters. "While $2,789,000 is an impressive sum of money for one man to raise in the name of the Lord, I made it very clear that I would accept no less than $3 million."

Roberts had been aware for several months that his life was in danger, repeatedly warning his followers that he would be killed by God if donations did not reach the target amount.

"Please, give all that you can afford to give, whether it be $1,000 or just $900," Roberts, tears streaming down his face, told viewers during a recent broadcast. "For if you do not give, my friends, the Lord God in Heaven shall call me home. Unless I see some big numbers go up on that totals board in the next hour, God is going to come calling for me. Praise Jesus."

Added Roberts: "Please make checks payable to Oral Roberts Evangelical Ministries, Tulsa, OK 74171. Visa, Mastercard and American Express are also accepted. Call us toll-free. Operators are standing by."

Roberts' followers were deeply distraught by the news of his death. Many blamed themselves.

"I should have given more," said Lubbock, TX, widow Eunice MacEachern, 81, who donated $700 of her $894 Social Security check to Oral Roberts every month for six years. "I acted selfishly, putting my worldly needs first by lavishly spending my retirement money on things for myself. I did not need that can of peas."

"Oral warned me, but I did not listen," said Rose Terwilliger, 79, of Norman, OK. "I know I can never bring him back, but I can repent for my failure in a small way by giving all my money to Oral's good friend and fellow soldier of the Lord, Jim Bakker."

'Trade Aid' Concert Helps Recession-Stricken Brokers

Willie Nelson Plays 'Always On My Mind' For Wall Street Sufferers

NEW YORK—Trade Aid, a benefit concert held Monday in Central Park, raised over $20 million for victims of the Oct. 19 stock-market crash, with millions more expected in the coming weeks.

Bryan Adams, Sting and Willie Nelson were among the 26 musical acts featured in the day-long event, which drew more than 500,000 music lovers to the park's Great Lawn and raised awareness of the plight of the Wall Street broker.

"We had to find a way to get the word out," said Trade Aid

Willie Nelson on stage

organizer Don Henley, who dedicated his set to James B. Stouffer, a Shearson-Lehman investment banker who lost nearly 40 percent of his blue-chip investments in the crash. "If we don't help these people rebuild their shattered portfolios, who will?"

The crash, which reduced the value of U.S. stocks by nearly $1 trillion, has left many brokers wondering where their next lunch at Le Chanticleer will come from and praying they won't have to resort to non-delivered dry-cleaning.

Between performances by the likes of Neil Young and Tom Petty, brokers were called to the microphone to relate their harrowing tales of the crash, putting a face on the horrors of the Great Recession.

"People who weren't there can never understand what it was like," said Smith-Barney trader Gerald Tybolt, recalling the fateful day the Dow plummeted 508 points. "I had $630,000 tied up in Eastman Kodak and it fell 27 points in one day. I had to vacate my corner office. In an instant, I lost my view of the harbor, my wet bar, my executive washroom. How many people can know what that feels like?"

"It wasn't just the Dow," said Jason Westphal, 26, a trader with Salomon Brothers. "The S&P 500 fell more than 20 percent. The NASDAQ bottomed out at 360.21. I thought I was going to lose the beach house."

Both Westphal and singer Bruce Hornsby, who remained onstage after a moving rendition of "Mandolin Rain," were near tears, as the broker revealed to the crowd that he has not been able to afford badly needed repairs on his BMW and has been forced to drive to work in his four-year-old Saab.

Henley said the event was an unqualified success. "Just as important as the money raised," he said, "is the fact that we were able to raise awareness of the plight of the American stockbroker, a person who, all too often in our society, is out of sight and therefore out of mind, up there in his guarded private palace on the hill."

INSIDE:

Bill Cosby Demands More Interesting Sweaters
PAGE 3A

McDonald's Driven Out Of Business By Burger King's Devastating New 'I'm Not Herb' Advertising Campaign
PAGE 1C

145

the ONION

Tuesday, June 28, 1988 — AMERICA'S FINEST NEWS SOURCE — ★★★ 50 CENTS

Tyson Escapes From Ring

Feral Heavyweight Breaks Free Of Handlers, Rampages Through Las Vegas

LAS VEGAS—Terror struck downtown Las Vegas Monday, when boxer Mike Tyson, stunned and confused by photographers' flash bulbs, broke free of his handlers and escaped from the ring at Caesar's Palace.

At approximately 9:15 p.m. PST, moments before his fight against Michael Spinks was scheduled to begin, Tyson became enraged when a crowd of photographers closed in on him. Tossing aside ringside security guards armed with tranquilizer guns, Tyson tore through the ropes and ran up the aisle of the packed arena, sending thousands of fight-goers fleeing for their lives in panic.

"He was coming straight at me," said Larry Bladt, one of the hundreds injured in the chaotic stampede that followed Tyson's escape. "I thought I was going to die."

Once outside, the feral heavyweight ran loose through the streets of Las Vegas, crushing numerous automobiles underfoot and periodically pausing to smash a brightly lit casino facade. In the hours that followed, Tyson continued to evade local authorities, causing millions of dollars in damage in the process.

Nevada Gov. Richard Bryan has mobilized the National Guard in an attempt to force the escaped heavyweight champ back into the ring. Army helicopters are also being deployed to Las Vegas in an attempt to track Tyson's movements from the sky.

"I would urge everyone in the area to remain calm," Las Vegas Mayor Dean Witte said. "We are doing everything we can to subdue and capture the boxer."

Longtime Tyson trainer Lou Duva instructed citizens to call their local authorities if they spot the boxer. "Mike Tyson still has his gloves on and is extremely dangerous. He is alone and afraid and, if he thinks you are trying to hurt him, he will charge at you," Duva said. "Do not attempt to subdue him yourself. This is a matter that should be left to professionals."

Tyson was last seen on the outskirts of the Vegas strip, headed west shortly after overturning the Sands Hotel & Casino. Police fear he may be headed toward Los Angeles, and have ordered all L.A.-bound roads sealed off.

Fight promoter Don King told reporters and the general public that panicking would only make matters worse and urged everyone to remain "in a state of calmositude."

"It wasn't supposed to turn out this way at all," King said. "He was supposed to be a thing of beauty, not this abomination."

Don King, lower left, had to quiet crowds of panicked civilians as Tyson, above, terrorized the city of Las Vegas. Lower right, the ring from which Tyson broke free.

Noriega Faces Oxycution

PANAMA CITY, PANAMA—As U.S. forces close in on the palace of Panamanian leader Manuel Noriega, it appears increasingly likely that, once captured, the dictator will be brought to the U.S. for trial and subsequent oxycution.

"We will find Noriega, we will bring him to a world court, we will convict him of facial atrocities and we will assault his acne with the healing power of Oxy-10, the most powerful acne medication money can buy," U.S. Secretary of State George Shultz announced Monday. "Noriega has tried messy creams, he has tried covering it up by growing his hair long, and picking at it has just made the problem worse. The only answer is swift, merciless oxycution."

Panamanian Strongman Manuel Noriega

According to Shultz, four different U.S. Army Acne-MedicAttack teams will penetrate Noriega's face, neutralizing potential zit strongholds before they even start. "Oxy-10's acne-fighting power will not just fight his pimples; it will fight the pimples he doesn't even have yet," Shultz said.

"When we are finished with Noriega," he continued, "he will no longer be ashamed to pose for family photos. He will, quite simply, enjoy life again."

If Noriega is sentenced to oxycution, it would be the strongest U.S. maneuver against problem skin since the stridextradition of Nazi war criminals in the late 1940s.

INSIDE:

Fawn Hall, Jessica Hahn, Donna Rice Form Legion Of Bimbo Doom

PAGE 12A

Reagan To Meet With Dark Stranger After Journey Of Great Distance

Senior Presidential Astrologer Is Optimistic

WASHINGTON, DC—In a candle-lit meeting attended by top White House advisors Monday, senior presidential astrologer Joan Quigley announced that, in a short number of passing suns, an Aquarius will meet with a dark stranger after a journey of a great distance.

"After a time of great darkness, there will be a discovery," Quigley said. "The stars show two men, but only one set of hands."

Top White House advisors are interpreting Quigley's cryptic remarks to foretell a successful outcome for the upcoming Geneva summit between President Reagan, an Aquarius, and Soviet Premier Mikhail Gorbachev.

"The dark stranger has to be Gorbachev," Defense Secretary Caspar Weinberger said. "Not only is he a stranger, but Russia is extremely far away. I believe this bodes well for the prospect of a successful mutual arms-limitation agreement between our two nations."

Reagan and his top staffers are eagerly awaiting further information from the shawled mystic.

Gorbachev, a Sagittarius born with the moon in Scorpio, is believed to be more receptive

President Reagan

to an arms treaty with the U.S. than his Libra predecessor, Konstantin Chernenko.

Political analysts say November's Geneva summit could lead to an eventual disarmament of both nations' medium-range nuclear arsenals. Yet senior members of Reagan's cabinet are unsure, noting that, when Reagan had his ruling-planet charts done last week, the position of Saturn in his fourth house indicated only that he should "be sure to take time to tell a loved one how he feels."

Reagan Administration officials hope the president, who was born under a water sign, will mix well with Gorbachev, who was born under a fire sign.

Key economic issues may be addressed at the summit, as Quigley reported Sunday that Reagan's moon position "could mean an unexpected windfall" for the president or a family member. She said a Libra will play a part.

the ONION

Wednesday, November 9, 1988 — AMERICA'S FINEST NEWS SOURCE — ★★★ 50 CENTS

Surrogate Test-Tube Baboon-Hearted Baby Trapped In Well

HOLLIS, OK—The nation is holding its collective breath as emergency workers continue their efforts to rescue "Baby Lucy," the eight-month-old surrogate test-tube baboon-hearted infant who remains trapped at the bottom of a 22-foot well.

"This brave little girl has been through a lot in her life, bless her little baboon heart," rescue-team driller Ethan Howe said. "Don't worry, America, we're going to get Lucy out of that well."

Baby Lucy has been touching people's lives ever since she was born, the result of the first-ever successful fertilization of a human embryo in a test tube. Controversy erupted two weeks after her birth, however, when her surrogate mother decided she wanted to keep the child, vowing to never give her up.

The nation was further moved one month later, when it was discovered that Lucy's heart was defective and that, to survive, she would have to undergo extensive surgery and become the first-ever human recipient of a baboon heart. The triumphant, courageous surgery, performed live on national TV, moved an estimated 150 million Americans to tears.

Ever since Lucy fell down the well two days ago, thousands of people, including policemen, journalists, religious leaders and well-wishers holding signs of encouragement, have camped out near the well to offer their support.

"I love this little girl so much," said Lubbock, TX, housewife Amanda Butler, whose heartstrings have been tugged several times by the courageous child's test-tube conception, surrogate rearing, baboon-heart transplant and well-falling ordeal.

Donations from across the country are pouring into a collection fund to cover Lucy's rescue costs and anticipated hospital bills.

Rescue workers struggle to free Baby Lucy from harm.

"The money will really be a life-saver now that we just found out Lucy has cancer," said her father, Gene Jefferies, who briefly left the tragic scene Tuesday to fly to New York to appear on *Geraldo*. "But, thank God, the cancer is the kind that can be overcome with a long, hard fight, because I just know that someday Lucy is going to be a gold-medal-winning Olympic gymnast."

Rescue crews on the scene said the drilling of an emergency shaft will be complete as soon as they are close enough to hear Lucy's heart-wrenching, angelic cries. At that point, paramedics will attempt to squeeze into the passageway and pull her out of the hole and into the bright lights of the cameras.

"I think this plan will work," said Hollis Police Chief Trevor Dubrow. "Our only fear is that the family's own pit bull, lovable but aggressive by nature, will suddenly and without provocation leap upon the just-rescued child and maul her to death. Let us all pray that does not happen."

Raisins Now Hold Majority In California Senate

SACRAMENTO, CA—The Raisins gained 12 seats in California's senate races Tuesday, giving them majority control of the state's upper house and ending nearly two decades of Democratic control.

Last night, newly elected Raisins from across the state gathered at California Raisin Party Headquarters in Sacramento to celebrate the hard-won victory by doing a synchronized dance number to their theme song, "I Heard It Through The Grapevine."

Pledging to "lead California into a plump, juicy future," newly elected Sen. Bebop, one of the many white-gloved Raisin Party legislators on hand, said, "The Raisins are ready to groove."

The Raisins' election-day success came despite opposing human candidates' charges that they avoided tackling substantive issues during the

Raisins celebrating their victory

campaign. During debates, the Raisins broke into one of their popular dance routines whenever faced with a question. Incumbent Raisin senators have also been heavily criticized for yielding too much power to such special-interest groups as the California Fruit Growers Board.

"Listen, Raisins ain't into all that negative jive," Sen. Sax said. Sax, well-known in the California legislature for his aloof persona and trademark saxophone, added, "We just want to play it cool."

Dukakis Wins 80 Percent Of Dukakis Family Vote

Michael Dukakis

BOSTON—With nearly all Dukakis family members reporting, Democratic candidate Michael Dukakis has taken a whopping 80 percent of the Dukakis family vote in Tuesday's presidential election.

In all, 29 of 35 Dukakis relatives voted for the former Massachusetts governor in the election, giving him an easy victory over Vice President Bush within the Dukakis family. According to a final exit poll, Dukakis swept his immediate family and garnered enough in-law support to give him the votes he needed to claim a wide majority.

Despite the landslide Dukakis-family victory, early polls showed Dukakis generating little support beyond his wife and children. But his mother's side of the family, thought to be essential for a victory, began falling into the Dukakis column shortly before midnight. A last-minute call to his mother-in-law in Florida, a crucial swing vote, turned the tide.

In his living-room victory speech, Dukakis praised his father, mother and two daughters for their support. "I want to thank the many members of my family who supported me in this presidential election," Dukakis said. "Without you, I never could have scored this landslide family victory over President-Elect and overall winner George Bush."

INSIDE:

Pat Robertson Elected President Of Moon
PAGE 5A

'Baby On Board' Signs Reduce U.S. Auto Fatalities 70 Percent
PAGE 3A

Marion Barry Re-Elected On 'Let's All Smoke Crack' Platform

WASHINGTON, DC—Washington Mayor Marion Barry was re-elected in a landslide Tuesday, running on a campaign to create new jobs, improve DC-area roads and smoke huge quantities of crack.

"The time has come for Washington, DC, to once again be the kind of city people are proud to call their home, the kind of city where elected officials are free to inhale mind-blowing amounts of crack cocaine without a hassle," said Barry, holding aloft a crack pipe during his 40-minute acceptance speech. "As your mayor, I promise I will not rest until we are all enjoying the most intense crack high of our entire lives."

A pre-election poll showed that 82 percent of voters felt Barry was substantially "more honest" than other candidates, while a whopping 95 percent believed that Barry was the most likely to follow through on campaign promises, especially those relating to crack.

"Throughout the campaign, Marion Barry vowed that, if elected, he would smoke copious amounts of crack," longtime Barry supporter Mary Elizabeth Richardson said. "He vowed that the floor of his office would be littered with empty vials of crack. Unlike his opponent, who promised tax cuts and other things no one can deliver, I believe Mr. Barry will keep his promises. This is a man who will not let us down."

147

the ONION

Saturday, March 25, 1989 — AMERICA'S FINEST NEWS SOURCE — ★★★ 50 CENTS

Bush Decries Exxon Valdez Spillage of 'Precious, Precious Oil'

Beloved Crude Lost As Tanker Runs Aground Off Alaska Coast

WASHINGTON, DC—In a highly charged White House press conference Friday, President Bush lashed out against Exxon's supertanker spill off the Alaska coast, decrying the company's "shocking lack of respect for our planet's greatest natural resource: precious, precious oil."

"What has happened there in Alaska is a tragic, tragic waste of the fossil fuel most dear to my heart," the visibly grieving president said. "We've got to do whatever we can to make sure every drop of the beautiful black crude is recovered."

The Exxon Valdez, a crude-oil carrier in the Alaska-West Coast trade, ran aground in shallow coastal waters off Alaska's Prince William Sound some time Thursday night. Though the cause of the accident is still unknown, relief workers have been summoned from as far as 2,000 miles away in a desperate attempt to save the oil, which spilled out of the supertanker's badly ruptured hull at a rate of 500 gallons per second.

Forming a floating oil slick hundreds of miles long and covering much of Alaska's coastline, the oil is worth "many millions of dollars" and "must be saved at any cost," Bush said.

Directly addressing those who would doubt his resolve to clean up the spill, Bush said, "Make no mistake, I will do everything in my power to right this terrible wrong."

Though Exxon officials fear that much of the oil is irreparably contaminated and therefore unusable, Bush said he remains hopeful.

"The large quantities of dead waterfowl and aquatic life in the spill region can be scraped and wrung out for excess oil residue," he said. "Living animals that are covered in oil can be tracked down, captured and squeezed in hydraulic presses, yielding much oil that would otherwise be tragically lost."

Left: Millions of gallons of once-pristine oil, leaking out of the Valdez hull, are now useless, contaminated with dead fish and seawater. Above: Bush pleads with crews to "rescue as much of the precious crude as you can."

Study: Sex No Longer Worth The Trouble

LOS ANGELES—On Friday, Harbor-UCLA Medical Center researchers revealed the results of a study finding that sex is no longer worth the trouble.

According to the study, sex, which enjoyed a brief period of popularity in the late '60s, as Puritan repression gave way to carelessness and freedom, is now more trouble than it's worth: Sexually transmitted diseases like herpes and AIDS, as well as other factors, have made it a cause for more dread than excitement.

The study also faults the confusion of gender roles wrought by the feminist upheavals of the '60s, a new inability to verbally communicate because of presumed "political incorrectness," and the undesirable hormonal effects of the birth-control pill.

The leader of the research team, Dr. Larry Dunning, is not surprised by the study's results.

Said Dunning: "There was a window, just after the invention of the pill and just before the onslaught of the new generation of sexually transmitted diseases, in which sex was spontaneous and fun. Now it is neither. It is a joyless, even morbid affair."

UCLA researchers recommend that Americans spend their time engaging in endeavors more worthwhile than sex, such as working overtime, managing their investment portfolios or watching television.

INSIDE:

Boesky, Milken Charged In Inmate Cigarette-Trading Scandal
PAGE 2D

Stirring Symbol Of Human Spirit Difficult To Clean Out Of Tank Treads
PAGE 6A

New TV Network To Employ Over 25,000 Wayans Brothers

LOS ANGELES—Media mogul Rupert Murdoch announced Friday that in September he will launch Fox, a new television network he projects will employ over 25,000 Wayans brothers by 1995.

"I believe we can challenge ABC, NBC and CBS with programs featuring Damon, Keenen Ivory, Marlon, Shawn, LaShawn, Dwayne, Freddy, Michael, Randy, Ike, Jackie, Antwaine, Bobby and Darnell Wayans," Murdoch said.

In its first few months, the network will offer such programs as *The Keenen Ivory Wayans Show*, *Damon & Friends*, *Wayans & Co.*, *The Wayans Brothers Hip-Hop Variety Hour*, *Wayans In Da House!* and *Da Wayanz Brothaz*. There will also be a daily morning show, *Wake Up With Wayans*.

"When our Wayans News Bureau finally gets up and running, it'll be much easier to keep track of all the Wayans family members and their active projects," said writer-producer Roderick Wayans, who is currently developing *Wayans Nightly News*.

Roderick is also developing *She's A Wayans*, a sitcom vehicle for sister Kim Wayans that focuses on an actress struggling to make it in a male-Wayans-dominated world. "We also have plans for an all-Wayans baseball league to challenge the Major League," Wayans said, "as well as a historic six-part Wayans miniseries." The latter is slated to star Damon, Keenen Ivory, Shawn and "many other Wayanses."

The Wayans family unemployment rate fell to 11 percent following Murdoch's announcement and is expected to reach zero by the end of fiscal year 1991.

The logo of the new Fox network

the ONION

Monday, January 22, 1990 — AMERICA'S FINEST NEWS SOURCE — ★ ★ ★ — 50 CENTS

Berlin Wall Destroyed In Doritos-Sponsored Super Bowl Halftime Spectacular

A scene from the Doritos halftime show

EAST BERLIN—Amid fireworks, stirring John Philip Sousa marching music and soaring Blue Angels jets, the Berlin Wall was torn down Sunday in a thrilling climax to "Doritos Presents A Super Salute To Freedom," the Super Bowl XXIV halftime show.

"Ladies and gentlemen, let's hear it for democracy!" the announcer exclaimed, as the wall that separated East and West Berlin for nearly 30 years fell. "Let there be freedom. And enjoy Doritos. Munch all you want. We'll make more!"

More than 300,000 people gathered at the Berlin Wall for the halftime event, which symbolically ended the Cold War, entertained over a billion football fans worldwide and coincided with Doritos' launch of its new "Cool Ranch" flavor.

As mobs of East Germans pounded at the wall with sledgehammers, Frito-Lay CEO Richard Teller announced to a TV audience, "Today, we crunch our way into an exciting new age. After decades of isolation and oppression, Germany can bite into the great taste of liberty at last."

Actual Berlin Wall fragments, as well as five collector's cups, will be made available at participating Taco Bell restaurants for a limited time.

Despite its popularity among East and West Germans, the Berlin Wall halftime event was mildly received by U.S. TV viewers, according to *AdWeek* magazine. Of the new advertising events making their debut during the game, viewers rated the Berlin Wall fifth, behind Budweiser's BudBowl III, Pepsi's "You Got The Right One, Baby, Uh-Huh," Coors Light's Swedish Bikini Team, and Domino's "Avoid the Noid," which was rated No. 1.

Michael Jackson Undergoes Complete Blackendectomy

BEVERLY HILLS, CA—Pop-music superstar Michael Jackson is in stable condition following a three-hour blackendectomy Sunday.

The experimental de-blackification procedure, developed especially for Jackson by doctors at Beverly Hills' prestigious Steinman Clinic, involved the bleaching, blanding and hue-homogenization of Jackson's entire epidermis, transforming him into a stark white, quasi-human polymorph.

Dr. James Deininger, who performed the blackendectomy, declared the procedure a success at a press conference at the clinic. "The blackness has been removed from Mr. Jackson," he said. "He is currently in stable, white condition."

The controversial operation involved the extraction of all black pigmentation, as well as almost all black genes, from Jackson through a complex chemical and ultrasonic process. Once the extraction was complete, doctors

Former black man Michael Jackson

employed a delicate plastic-surgery technique known as Diana-Rossitization.

"This is certainly an unusual procedure," Deininger said, "but Mr. Jackson is recuperating nicely, despite the fact that he is, in my opinion, a complete batshit loonball."

Doctors assured the press that Jackson's dancing ability would be unaffected by the blackendectomy.

Deininger added that Jackson paid an "utterly fantastic" sum of money for the procedure.

NEA Victory In Washington:
Congress Grants Mapplethorpe 'All The Money He Wants'

'I Want To See More Of These Hot, Hot Cocks,' Raves Sen. Jesse Helms (R-NC)

Sen. Jesse Helms (R-NC)

WASHINGTON, DC—After viewing the new exhibit of gay erotica by photographer Robert Mapplethorpe at New York's Museum of Modern Art, U.S. Sen. Jesse Helms (R-NC) is enthusiastically supporting legislation to triple federal funding of the National Endowment for the Arts, with the specific request that extra money be allocated to Mapplethorpe.

"The NEA has funded many worthy projects over the years," Helms told fellow members of the Senate, "but none more worthy—or more hot—than the photography of Mr. Mapplethorpe."

Holding a shadowy, black-and-white print of a nude white man stroking the erect penis of a sinewy black man, Helms said, "It is imperative that Mapplethorpe receive whatever funding he needs so that he can continue to produce more beautiful guy-on-guy brown-sugar pics like this."

"This is some real sweet-ass art," he added.

Helms went on to praise the "hot, hot cocks" in the photos, calling upon Congress to grant Mapplethorpe "all the money he wants."

Helms' colleagues agreed. "America needs to keep pace with its global competition in the crucial area of gay erotica," U.S. Sen. Orrin Hatch (R-UT) said. "If we are to keep pace with cutting-edge foreign bondage photography, it is imperative that we maintain a vast reservoir of funds enabling our most creative queer artists to explore all the dark, forbidden areas of the craft, from straight erotica to hardcore graphic sex, S&M and taboo violence."

Hatch said he felt that Mapplethorpe's "Leather Man" series "barely scratched the surface" of the subject matter.

"Every citizen deserves unrestricted access to these glistening, triple-X cocks," Hatch said. "Every throbbing inch of them."

INSIDE:

Special AKA Frees Nelson Mandela In Daring Ska Assault
PAGE 20A

Are We Adequately Euphemizing Our Minorities?
PAGE 12B

Salman Rushdie Releases New Book, *Fuck Allah*
PAGE 3C

149

the ONION

Thursday, September 20, 1990 — AMERICA'S FINEST NEWS SOURCE — ★★★ 50 CENTS

Jim Henson Stuffed, Given Googly Eyeballs, Placed In Smithsonian

WASHINGTON, DC—The remains of beloved Muppets creator Jim Henson, who died of pneumonia in May at age 53, will be donated Friday to the Smithsonian Institution's Museum of Arts & Industries, where he will be stuffed and given googly eyeballs before being placed on permanent display.

"We feel this is the most appropriate way to honor the legacy of a man whose *Sesame Street* characters touched millions of lives, young and old," Henson's son Brian said at a press conference Wednesday. "We want to give Jim Henson back to the world which loved him so dearly."

Before Henson is installed in a glass display case, his entrails will be replaced with foam rubber, and his eyeballs pried from their sockets to make room for oversized ping-pong balls with large black pupils.

Approximately 40 square feet of yellow felt will be wrapped around Henson's body, while fluffy orange tufts will be applied to the top of his head and his beard area.

"We considered giving him two plastic trumpets for ears, which would honk when his blue, bulbous nose was squeezed," Brian Henson said, "but we decided on a trumpety nose and 'wacky pupils' that race around the eyeballs."

Jim Henson's arms will be stripped of all muscle and sinew, leaving stick-like appendages supported by thin rods.

The arms will be flailed about wildly by skilled puppeteers in a special Smithsonian ceremony honoring Henson Nov. 1.

Jim Henson, 1937–1990

Bottom 10 Percent Of Last Year's Graduating Class Ready To Take On Saddam

With Saddam Hussein defiantly refusing to pull out of Kuwait, the bottom 10 percent of America's high-school graduating class of 1990 is making final preparations to take on the Iraqi army.

President Bush has already deployed 5,000 19-year-olds with below-average math and reading skills to the Gulf, and has pledged an additional 15,000 D-students if necessary.

"Those Iraqis better watch out, because the Fifth Infantry is ready for a fight," said Robert Hamm, 18, who finally passed his required history course last spring after four tries, just barely graduating from his Beaver Dam, WI, high school.

"The U.S. don't stand for aggression in the Middle East," said Chad Sterling, who graduated 163rd in his class of 167, ahead of four developmentally disabled students receiving attendance diplomas. "Even though I'm needed on the home front—like, at my job, they're having a big chicken-sandwich promotion right now—serving my country is more important to me."

Sterling is a member of the 157th Infantry Division, a tactical unit stationed near the Kuwait-Saudi Arabia border composed of recruits fresh out of 12th-grade shop classes across the nation.

U.S. peacekeeping forces will remain on standby until given further orders—a difficult task, considering the limited attention span of most of the academically underachieving troops.

"The United States military is a defender of freedom," said U.S. General Norman Schwarzkopf. "It is also a catch-all for those high-school seniors who don't want to work at a gas station but don't have the grades to get into their local technical college."

"My country needs me," said Kip Hooper, 18, who was lured into the army by a colorful filmstrip shown by a recruiter assigned to the Trenton, NJ, public-school system. "Besides, I don't really have anything much better to do right now, since I got fired from Corn Dog King on account of how I couldn't never press them buttons right."

Members of America's academically below-average fighting force

Iowa Family Blasted For Lack Of Diversity

DES MOINES, IA—A Des Moines-area family remains under heavy fire Wednesday for its lack of minority representation.

Activists say the Petersens, a five-person clan that has lived at 204 Hewlett Avenue on the west side of Des Moines for nearly 15 years, has never had a non-Caucasian member.

"In this day and age, it is shocking to find a group that still actively excludes people just because of the color of their skin," said Americans For Diversity president Cynthia Mattson, speaking at an anti-Petersen rally on the University of Iowa campus in nearby Iowa City. "In the entire Petersen family, there is not a single African American, Latino, Asian, Native American, Aleutian or Pacific Islander. In fact, every last member of the group is of Swedish descent. Is this a fair representation of the glorious mosaic that is the United States? Haven't we moved beyond this kind of racism and intolerance?"

Mattson demanded that the Petersens end what she termed "a longtime policy of de facto segregation" and called for a minimum 20 percent minority membership in the Petersen family by 1995. She also called upon the Petersens to enroll in sensitivity-training classes to "better understand and appreciate the many wonderful differences that make up America's multicultural tapestry."

Lawrence Bloch, president of the D.C.-based multicultural-advocacy group The Rainbow League, agreed.

"Everyone has something special to offer, so why should the Petersens shut people out just because they look different?" Bloch asked. "Deep down, no matter what the color of our skin is, we're all the same, and it's time the Petersens realized that."

Exclusionary, all-white Petersens 'deeply offensive,' say activists

INSIDE:

Difference Celebrated
PAGE 7A

Henry Louis Gates Defends Controversial 2 Live Crew Video, 'The Signifying Coochie'
PAGE 13A

Bush Not Liar, Bush Says

WASHINGTON, DC—President Bush, addressing members of the White House press corps Wednesday, denied all allegations of falsehood regarding the Iran-Contra affair, covert CIA operations in Central America, his "no new taxes" pledge and several other matters currently being dodged by individuals who may or may not be connected to the Bush Administration.

"I did not, nor have I ever, betrayed the trust of the American people by lying to them when I claimed, as I did, to have no knowledge of these aforementioned affairs," Bush said. "Furthermore, I emphatically deny ever commenting on the matters, of which I had no knowledge, and I am still uncertain as to what extent my knowledge may be implicated."

Bush went on to say that any alleged remarks he may have made on the issues were taken out of context.

The Bush Administration has pledged to fight "the distrust thing," which continues to hurt the president's public-approval rating. Recent polls indicate that his trust index is down from 88 percent upon taking office to a low of 41 percent among the 5.4 percent of Americans who still pay attention to national politics.

President Bush

the ONION

Friday, January 18, 1991 — AMERICA'S FINEST NEWS SOURCE — 50 CENTS

CNN Deploys Troops To Iraq

'This Is War,' Says James Earl Jones

ATLANTA—CNN deployed more than 50,000 ground troops to the Persian Gulf Thursday in anticipation of a military showdown with Iraq.

Speaking from CNN Command Post Central in Atlanta, Major General Wolf Blitzer said the cable network can no longer allow Saddam Hussein's aggression to go unchecked.

"We must send a message, loud and clear, that Iraq's continued military presence in Kuwait will not be tolerated. CNN is drawing a line in the sand," said Blitzer, flanked by President Turner and Chief of Staff Peter Arnett. "Although this network maintains hope that a peaceful solution can be reached, it is fully prepared to go to war if Saddam refuses to budge."

The CNN Joint Chiefs have already commissioned the composition of new theme music for the war, and Arnett said "Operation Showdown In The Gulf" troops are expected to be ready to attack key Iraqi strongholds every half-hour, on the hour.

Blitzer is ordering all CNN warships to be diverted to the Gulf, including the aircraft carrier C.N.N. *Fonda*, which has been stationed in the Gulf of Oman for the past 15 months.

"If CNN does bomb Baghdad or launch a ground assault on Iraq, count on CNN to bring it to you first," said Bernard Shaw, a field officer currently stationed undercover in Baghdad. "In addition to 50,000 soldiers, we will have a coverage force more than 20,000 reporters strong. We will be fully ready, not only to fight, but also to provide complete, around-the-clock coverage of that fight."

In the event of war, CNN has prepared 3,500 armored tanks, 290 F-18 jets, 27 nuclear-capable Trident submarines, 55 class-B naval destroyers and 65 news trucks with satellite video-uplink capability.

Blitzer said CNN is also working closely with NBC News, whose Tom Brokaw pledged full support for his cable-based allies.

"We are in this together," Brokaw said in a speech from NBC Studios in New York Thursday. "United, we will defeat Saddam Hussein in what he himself has called the 'Mother Of All Sweeps Weeks.'"

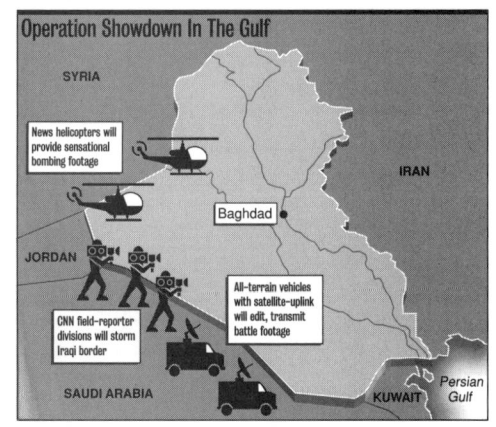

CNN's "Operation: Showdown In The Gulf"

Operation Showdown In The Gulf
- News helicopters will provide sensational bombing footage
- CNN field-reporter divisions will storm Iraqi border
- All-terrain vehicles with satellite-uplink will edit, transmit battle footage

Madonna Shocks Seven

In the pop superstar's 132nd outrageous stunt of the past six months, Madonna shocked seven TV viewers last night when she appeared on a Barbara Walters special and graphically described oral sex she had performed on an unnamed NBA star.

"Frankly, I was shocked," said Boise, ID, homemaker Gertrude Rueth, 43, who missed the other 2,842 times Madonna had discussed a sexual act in an unusually frank and explicit manner on national television. "You just don't normally see rock stars breaking taboos and doing outrageous things like that."

The other six U.S. citizens shocked by the Material Girl's latest outrageous remarks are Covington, KY, auto-insurance salesman Marty Leupke and his wife Barbara; Ft. Lauderdale retirees Helene and Bill Thalliger; Kearney, NE, librarian Carol Schumacher; and Ben Shapiro, a Crown Heights, NY, Hasidic Jew who inadvertently walked by the TV-filled window of an electronics store at the time of the interview.

Reacting to the offensive act, Bill Thalliger said, "I expect more restraint from Madonna. I cannot believe she would be so provocative."

The shocking remarks returned Madonna to the national spotlight after a three-day absence. Last week, during an appearance on *Late Night With David Letterman*, she strapped a crucifix onto her pelvis and simulated coitus, an act that shocked dozens of viewers but was met with yawns by the millions of Madonna fans who had already witnessed much more impressive acts of sacrilege during her 1990 Blonde Ambition tour.

According to a recent poll, in the time between the release of her shocking documentary *Truth Or Dare* and advance publicity for her upcoming shocking photo collection, *Sex*, the number of Americans describing themselves as "shocked" by Madonna dropped from 48 to 11.

Madonna

Quayle Takes Bold Stand Against Fictional Character

DALLAS—In his keynote speech at an Americans For Family Values fundraising dinner Thursday, Dan Quayle blasted Suzanne Sugarbaker, a character on the hit TV show *Designing Women,* for "glamorization of the female lifestyle."

Vice President Dan Quayle

The vice president criticized the popular character, played by Delta Burke, for weekly exploits he said are "clearly those of a woman."

"People watch this show, and they see all the laughing and good times," said Quayle, "yet they don't realize they may be influenced into becoming women."

Quayle urged advertisers to boycott CBS for airing the show during prime time, "when impressionable children can see this show and be tempted to emulate the Delta Burke, Dixie Carter and Annie Potts characters, all of whom are depicted living the female lifestyle."

Quayle concluded his speech with a call for television programming that maintains high morals and is free of such female-lifestyle signifiers as dresses, lipstick, high voices and breasts.

Today in Herstory
INSPIRATIONAL STORIES OF WOMEN IN HISTORY

1989 Peggy Laughlin
She made her Sacramento coffee shop a safe place for women.

INSIDE:

People's 1991 Sexiest Man Alive: **Norman Schwarzkopf**
PAGE 3C

the ONION

Thursday, October 10, 1991 — AMERICA'S FINEST NEWS SOURCE — ★★★ 50 CENTS

Supreme Court Nominee Clarence Thomas:
'The Ass-Slapping Was Never Done In An Inappropriate Manner'

WASHINGTON, DC—Testifying before a senate committee in Day Six of his confirmation hearings Wednesday, Supreme Court nominee Clarence Thomas insisted that his frequent slapping of Anita Hill's ass over the course of many months was "never done in an inappropriate manner."

"The striking of Miss Hill's ass with my open hand was never more than an expression of mutual professional respect," Thomas told the committee.

Thomas went on to state that the numerous times he lifted Hill into the air, slinging her over his shoulder and "noogie-ing" her ass while making growling noises, were always "a sign of my approval of her fine work, devoid of any sexual overtones."

"Ours was a cordial, relaxed office environment, and my conduct toward her was intended to be friendly," Thomas added. "I am sorry Miss Hill misinterpreted my actions."

Thomas assured the committee that there was no improper subtext to his frequent pants-droppings, which were often accompanied by instructions to "kiss the birdie if you like having a job."

While he conceded no actual wrongdoing, Thomas did acknowledge that he "may have left [himself] open to misinterpretation." For example, he testified that, last October, he pasted photographs of Hill's face over those of nude women in pornographic magazines, then posted the collages on an office bulletin board with captions like, "My bitch" and, "Please take note of what a slut-bitch Miss Hill is."

Thomas insisted that he made the collages in "a spirit of fun," and that the entire office "thoroughly enjoyed the good-natured humor."

"As a matter of fact," he added, "'Slut-bitch' was Miss Hill's office nickname for the next few weeks."

When questioned by Sen. Howell Heflin (D-AL) about the homemade bondage videos he sold in the office and via his mail-order catalog, Thomas said, "My forcing Miss Hill to watch tapes of black men in judges' robes ejaculating upon the leather-masked face of an Anita Hill look-alike never at any point went outside the bounds of a friendly office relationship."

Above, Clarence Thomas
Below, Anita Hill

Soviet citizens in Moscow prepare for democracy, chaos.

Mattel Signs Gulf War Merchandising Deal

Mattel, the nation's largest toy manufacturer, signed a $200 million licensing deal with the Pentagon Wednesday for this year's popular Gulf War.

The agreement gives Mattel exclusive rights to all Desert Storm-related toy merchandise.

First to hit toy-store shelves nationwide will be a line of action figures, featuring such Gulf War characters as heroes Norman Schwarzkopf, Colin Powell and George Bush, and villains Saddam Hussein and College Anti-War Activist-Girl.

"Within a few weeks, every little boy in America is going to be asking his parents to buy him a Norman Schwarzkopf with special Battle-Grip Action-Arm™," Mattel spokesman Larry Ellsburgh said. "And what kid won't want his own set of Scud FunFoam Missiles with wrist-mounted Turbo-Launcher?"

Also planned for summer release is a special Mattel-licensed line of Super Nintendo Gulf War video-games, such as "Baghdad Blast" and "Cruise Missile X-III."

The $200 million licensing fee is the highest ever paid by a toy company for rights to a U.S. war, topping Hasbro's $22 million for the Vietnam conflict.

Soviets Vote To Collapse

MOSCOW—The Supreme Soviet voted unanimously in favor of the Soviet Union's collapse Wednesday.

"The time has come for the Soviet Union to crumble into a chaotic mess of leaderless nation-states," Soviet Premier Mikhail Gorbachev said. "Anarchy shall reign, both politically and economically."

"Packs of wild dogs will soon run through the streets of our nation's capital," he added. "Then we will hand over thousands of state-owned factories to these dogs, who are wholly unfamiliar with the realities of operating a company under a free-market system."

Gorbachev then left the Kremlin to meet with a group of Islamic extremists from Uzbekistan interested in purchasing a nuclear arsenal.

The Soviets plan to hasten the collapse by printing millions of rubles backed by nothing; systematically selling government property to Odessa gangsters who will control Russia and increase its dependence on foreign currency and goods; and accelerating the Russian infrastructure's 50-year slide into oblivion through a program of total neglect.

Russian citizens responded to the announcement by looting grocery stores, hoarding medical supplies and weapons, and consuming large quantities of vodka and paint thinner.

Gorbachev also announced that he will resign his post as Soviet premier and hand over power to Boris Yeltsin, an elderly, alcoholic invalid.

U.S. reaction to the Soviet collapse was surprisingly unenthusiastic.

"If the Soviet Union collapses, we will be without an arch-enemy," President Bush said. "Without the USSR, the Pentagon stands to lose billions in defense funding, unless the U.S. can find a new nation to serve as a demon figure in the popular consciousness."

Sources close to Bush declined comment on the possibility of a Central American or Middle Eastern nation being groomed as a possible nemesis in the coming months.

Threat Of Nuclear War Over

Bombs Now Safely In Hands Of Countless Tiny, Warring Factions

BISHKEK, KYRGYZSTAN—Top Pentagon intelligence-gatherers reported Wednesday that the USSR, currently in the process of fragmenting into thousands of tiny, unpronounceable warring factions, is "no longer a threat to the security of the U.S.," ending nearly 50 years of tense nuclear gamesmanship between the two nations.

"The Cold War is over," said Secretary of Defense Dick Cheney, declaring the end of the U.S.-Soviet arms race, "and America has emerged the victor. Now that decades of massive Soviet thermonuclear stockpiles have been safely transferred into the hands of a chaotic network of Third World peasant barbarian-nations, each local ethnicity with its own agenda of intricately shifting alliances and vendettas far too convoluted to quantify, we can all breathe a little easier."

Among the nation-states now in control of the world's thermonuclear arsenal: Kyrgyzstan, Kazakhstan, Ukraine, Pakistan, North Korea, Libya and Burundi. It is widely believed that Turgyzkmenistan possesses nuclear capability, as well, though neither that fact nor Turgyzkmenistan's existence could be confirmed as of press time.

Cheney added that, despite the Cold War's end, the U.S. will continue manufacturing and proliferating thermo-nuclear weapons, because "we can make a lot of money selling them."

INSIDE:

Skateboarding: Is It A Crime?
EDITORIAL, PAGE 8A

the ONION

Thursday, April 30, 1992 — AMERICA'S FINEST NEWS SOURCE — ★★★ 50 CENTS

INSIDE

We Must Stop Everything Else Until This Flag-Burning Issue Is Settled

Editorial, page 8A

Academic Feminist Leaders Speak Out Against Sexy Young Women

Page 2A

Decision '92: Which Elvis Stamp Will It Be?

Page 3C

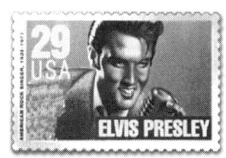

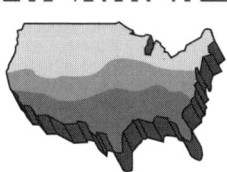

WEATHER

- 50% chance of race riots
- Looting early, tapering off by mid-afternoon
- Sunny; tear gas

L.A. Rioters Demand Justice, Tape Decks

LOS ANGELES—Outraged by the not-guilty verdicts for four LAPD officers charged with beating black motorist Rodney King, thousands of angry L.A. residents took to the streets Wednesday in a unified call for justice and stereo equipment.

"What do we want? Tape decks! When do we want them? Now!" chanted a crowd of protesters marching down Crenshaw Boulevard in the South Central section of L.A. shortly after the verdict was announced.

Calling for an end to racial prejudice and oppression, an estimated 15,000 people marched on Al's Electronics Emporium on the corner of Slauson Avenue and Avalon Boulevard at noon Wednesday. The historic march climaxed in a stirring "I Have A TV" speech by Compton resident Melvin Haskins, who told the crowd that he envisions a day when "white men and black men, Jews and gentiles have 27-inch RCA ProScan televisions with Dolby sound."

Across the city, civil-rights protesters assembled at appliance stores and camera shops, voicing their outrage over the King verdict with chants of, "Hey, Hey! Ho, Ho! Non-Pre-Programmable VCRs Have Got To Go!" and "No Sony Camcorders, No Justice!"

"This police brutality against the African-American community must stop," said Kwame Taylor, who demanded the resignation of L.A. Police Chief Daryl Gates and a set of Pioneer car speakers. "No longer will this city's oppressed minority residents stand back and passively tolerate speakers with muffled sound. We shall overcome insufficient bass."

Civil-rights activists march on Al's Electronics Emporium in Compton.

Death Of 500,000 Somalis Momentarily Distracts Nation From Dream Team Excitement

In the past year, an estimated 500,000 Somalis have died from famine, murder, civil war and disease, Red Cross officials reported Wednesday, an announcement that briefly distracted Americans from U.S. Olympic basketball "Dream Team" fever.

"It's shocking, absolutely shocking," said 31-year-old Atlanta resident Kenny Gund upon learning of the African genocide. "The thought of Michael Jordan, Larry Bird and Magic Johnson playing together on the same team just boggles the mind."

The U.S. Olympic Dream Team

Gund said he saw a CNN report on the Somali situation Wednesday and briefly pondered the mass death and suffering taking place there, but quickly turned to ESPN for coverage of the Dream Team, which is heavily favored to take the gold at this summer's Barcelona Games.

"I realize things are bad in Somalia," Gund said, "but we're talking about the greatest basketball team ever assembled, a team so good that all-time greats like Charles Barkley and Karl Malone are not even good enough to be starters. Can you imagine a team that has Clyde Drexler and John Stockton coming off the bench? It's hard to comprehend."

Across the U.S., news of the Somali genocide caused people to stop discussing the Dream Team for as long as 15 seconds.

"I hear there's mass graves all across the Somali countryside," said Tim Kroeger of Arlington Heights, IL. "All I know is, the French National Team is going to need a mass grave once Michael Jordan gets through destroying them in Barcelona."

Kroeger said he has no plans to think about Somalia again, unless the African nation's basketball team is scheduled to play the Dream Team in the upcoming Olympics.

Rodney King Video Cameraman Signs $1.2 Million Deal for Upcoming Mexican Beating

LOS ANGELES—George Holliday, the man behind the hugely successful videotape in which four LAPD officers deliver repeated baton blows and kicks to black motorist Rodney King, has received a $1.2 million offer from *Dateline NBC* to tape an upcoming Mexican beating.

Holliday will videotape the beating of 33-year-old East L.A. resident Enrique Diaz, who will be brutally attacked by baton-wielding LAPD officers Saturday during a vehicle search and seizure in the parking lot outside Los Zapatos, a Hispanic nightclub.

Dateline NBC Executive Producer Timothy Sheran, who orchestrated the deal, called Holliday "the most exciting new filmmaker to come along in years."

"The King tape is a stunning bit of gritty cinematic realism, a mixture of Spike Lee and early Scorsese," Sheran said. "I believe Holliday can bring that same raw energy to the vicious, near-death beating of Mr. Diaz."

Though NBC executives plan to let Holliday "bring his own vision" to the Diaz beating, they expect he will employ the same grainy images, cinema-verité camera movement and lengthy pans that, according to Sheran, lend the King footage "a real-life intensity."

"The Rodney King video was so powerful, it is etched into the minds of people the world over," Sheran said. "We can only hope that the Mexican beating generates that kind of buzz."

Holliday, a little-known auteur who submitted his 81-second independent video to the Los Angeles Department of Justice shortly after King was beaten, said he had had no idea what kind of impact his low-budget, virtually unedited movie would have.

"I honestly never expected that kind of reaction to my first film," Holliday said. "People really went nuts over it."

A scene from the riveting Rodney King-beating video.

the ONION

Thursday, January 21, 1993 — AMERICA'S FINEST NEWS SOURCE — ★★★ 50 CENTS

INSIDE

Leno, Kevorkian Sign 10-Year Monologue-Joke Pact
Page 11D

The Arts: What Were They?
Page 3C

L.A. Gangs' 'Increase The Peace' Movement Least Successful Movement Ever
Page 2A

LOTTO
23 4 32 13 9

Losing lotto tickets can now be redeemed for 25 cents off any 10-gram vial of crack.

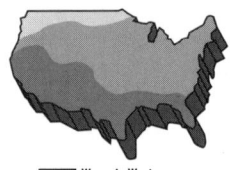

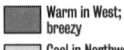

WEATHER
- Warm in West; breezy
- Cool in Northwest; cloudy
- Hot new Gen-X retro trend: Scooby

DOW
Trading was spirited yesterday when traders caught a glimpse of Sharon Stone's vagina.
+23

New President Feels Nation's Pain, Breasts

President Bill Clinton delivers his inaugural address.

WASHINGTON, DC—In his inaugural address to the nation Wednesday, President Bill Clinton delivered a message of compassion, telling Americans that he is fully committed to feeling their pain and, in the case of attractive young women, their breasts.

"As your president, I feel your pain," Clinton said from a podium overlooking a crowd of supporters and nubile campaign volunteers. "I would also very much like to feel your firm, plump breasts."

"The American people need to know that someone in Washington cares," he continued. "And the women of this country need to know that someone in Washington is willing to cup their breasts in both hands and give them a gentle squeeze."

Voters are praising Clinton's new vision for America.

"I met with President Clinton privately to discuss my economic situation, and he really seemed to understand how I feel," said Jennifer Langer, a 22-year-old nursing student from Little Rock. "That massage really helped."

Added Langer, "President Clinton was right: Going through tough financial times can really make you tense."

Said Georgetown University political-science professor Marcia Miller, "President Clinton is very concerned about the social and political issues facing our country today. In fact, he has asked me to counsel him privately to develop what he called a 'hands-on approach' to a number of key national issues."

As part of what he dubbed his "Feel America" campaign, Clinton has earmarked more than $380 million in federal funding for the hiring of attractive female White House aides, emergency blouse-removal programs, and the lowering of the federal neckline. He added that beginning Saturday, he will hold weekly "town hall" meetings at various bars in the Washington, D.C.-area to discuss the challenges facing America's hot young single mothers.

"Now is the time for our nation to pull together, very close together," Clinton said. "We must have the courage to stand by each other, and even brush up against one another and cop a feel."

Tipper Gore Jerks Arrhythmically At Inaugural Ball

LITTLE ROCK, AR—Tipper Gore, celebrated crusader for decency and wife of newly elected Vice President Al Gore, jerked arrhythmically to a variety of musical numbers at the gala Inaugural Ball Wednesday.

Dedicated to restricting minors' access to objectionable music through her Parents' Music Resource Center, Gore appeared unable to master even the most basic concepts of rhythm as she awkwardly lurched to and fro, celebrating her husband's victory without any semblance of grace or style.

"I'm not much for this modern music, which is filled with images of rape and sodomy, yet is sold to our kids. But just because I don't have the slightest ability to relax and follow simple dance steps doesn't mean I'm incapable of enjoying myself," Gore said, clumsily rotating her pelvis and bobbing her arms as if in great discomfort.

Gore and her husband amused onlookers while attempting to slow-dance to "The Blue Danube." The experiment was aborted after approximately two minutes, when a red-faced Tipper Gore called the composition "immoral and grossly sexual."

Seattle Parking Lot Named Hippest Parking Lot Of 1993

Parking-Industry Execs Locked In Bidding War To Sign, Lease Spaces

SEATTLE—Trend-conscious motorists are enduring waits of up to six weeks to park their vehicles in what *Spin* magazine is calling "America's Hippest Parking Lot of 1993": Seattle's Second-and-Bell municipal lot.

Located adjacent to three coffee houses, a piercing lounge and a recording studio, the lot boasts 52 parking spaces in one of Seattle's most fashionable neighborhoods.

"Forget the William Street parking facility," the *Spin* article said. "In 1993, the place to park is Second-and-Bell."

Explaining the lot's success, Seattle Public Works Administrator Charles Kim cited "the right mix of location, attitude and places where you can park your car. Second-and-Bell isn't about publicity. It's not about following the crowd. It's about defying authority and doing your own thing."

"We drove all the way from Portland to park in Second-and-Bell!" said motorist Jenny Loomis, 21, excitedly clutching her validation stamp. "We once parked in the lot on the corner of Grove and Walker in 1991, but it was nothing like this."

Not everyone is excited about Second-and-Bell's increasing popularity, however.

"This used to be the coolest lot around," said Seattle cashier Dan Baines, 23, who had been using the lot for years before it found success. "I used to feel like Second-and-Bell was mine. But now all the poseurs are coming out of the woodwork."

"It'll never be the same, man. The scene's all ruined," 24-year-old Chad Knowles said. "They've even raised the hourly rates. Second-and-Bell totally sold out."

the ONION

Saturday, May 29, 1993 — AMERICA'S FINEST NEWS SOURCE — ★★★ 50 CENTS

INSIDE

New MTV Show About Idiots Who Watch MTV Big Hit Among Idiots Who Watch MTV

Entertainment, page 1C

Snoop Doggy Dogg: 'Fuck'

Page 16C

Boris Yeltsin Reported In Good Health Following Burial

Page 11A

LOTTO

6 12 13 27 4

The Lotto. It's like a stock market for the poor.™

WEATHER

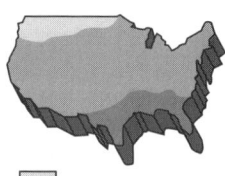

- Extreme rainfall; North
- Extreme flooding; South
- Extreme Summer; participating Taco Bell locations

DOW

Traders were relieved after the World Trade Center bombing upon learning that no money had been damaged. +4

Uneducated Forklift Driver To Address Nation On Rush Limbaugh Radio Show

Call-In Address Scheduled For 1:11 To 1:14 p.m. EST

Nation Eagerly Awaits Ohio Man's Profound Insight Into Current Events

LIMA, OH—Roy Shybinski, an uneducated 33-year-old forklift operator from Lima, is making final preparations for his national radio address tomorrow on *The Rush Limbaugh Show*.

Shybinski, who has been "waiting a long time to speak my mind about this draft-dodging, pot-smoking Clinton bozo," will speak to an expected audience of 32 million when he calls Limbaugh's radio program shortly after 1 p.m. EST.

"I wouldn't trust this sneaky draft-dodger any farther than I could throw him," Shybinski said from his living room, where he will deliver his much-anticipated message via telephone. "And believe me, with all the Big Macs he eats, I couldn't throw him very far."

Added Shybinski: "Hail to the Chief? More like *Inhale* to the Chief."

Political observers are eagerly anticipating the three-minute radio address.

"I am very much looking forward to hearing Mr. Shybinski's sophisticated insights and trenchant social and political commentary," Sam Donaldson of ABC News said. "This is a man who has much to contribute to our national dialogue. If ever there were a man who deserved a national forum in which to express his views, it is Roy Shybinski of Lima, Ohio."

Shybinski scheduled his address so as not to interfere with his 3 p.m. viewing of *Wheel Of Fortune* and his subsequent use of the bathroom.

Left: Roy Shybinski
Above: Rush Limbaugh

Comedians Struggling To Find Angle In Bobbitt Case

Across the nation, stand-up comedians are struggling to come up with a humorous angle on Lorena Bobbitt's penis-severing knife attack on husband John Wayne Bobbitt.

"I use a lot of current-events material in my act," said comedian Andy Walker, a regular at L.A.'s The Laff Barn, "and this is a pretty popular story. The only problem is, what joke can I make?"

"This is a real tough one," Royal Oak, MI, stand-up comic Tony Campanelli said. "I'd love to spoof the incident, but how?"

Said Campanelli, "If there was some element about it that was interesting to people, or if there were some kind of underlying social context to it all, I could do something with it. But I don't see anything."

Even radio shock-jock Howard Stern, who has built an audience of millions with his sometimes edgy humor, is having trouble making light of the news event.

"There is no way to talk about the Bobbitt case in a light or satirical way," Stern said. "Where is the humor?"

Despite their difficulties, comedians remain vigilant. "The details of the case may yield some humorous aspect," Campanelli said. "Maybe it's the brand of knife used in the assault; maybe the street they live on has a funny name. I maintain hope that the wacky part—the one funny detail of this event—will make itself apparent in due time."

Homeless Catch On To 'Grunge' Trend

SEATTLE—How big is this year's "grunge" trend? It's so big that even our nation's homeless are getting in on the act.

Here in Seattle, the unofficial grunge capital of the world, thousands of homeless people are catching the grunge spirit, dressing in old flannel shirts and wearing their hair in the unkempt style favored by such artists as Eddie Vedder and Chris Cornell.

"Spare change?" asks George Osager, 46, a homeless Vietnam veteran and, judging by his trendy ripped jeans and unwashed hair, a big Kurt Cobain fan. "I'm looking to get something to eat."

Like many grunge rockers, Osager shuns the corporate world: He's never worked in an office building and doesn't plan to any time soon. "Right now, I'm on disability," he says, echoing the anti-mainstream, "no-sellout" ethos of bands like Pearl Jam and Nirvana.

The homeless aren't just dressing like their grunge heroes, either: Like Cobain and many other grunge rockers, an estimated 70 percent of U.S. homeless people have a drug or alcohol problem.

"I've been an addict for nearly 20 years," says Paul Innes, a homeless San Franciscan whose drug of choice is heroin, the same one favored by members of such bands as Nirvana, Stone Temple Pilots and Alice In Chains. "Sometimes I just want to crawl into a hole and die."

With that kind of angst-ridden, self-loathing attitude, Mr. Innes, you could be the next Kurt Cobain!

A homeless man sports the latest styles.

Gay Servicemen March For Right To Love Men, Kill Men

ARLINGTON, VA—More than 500 members of Servicemen United for the Right to Gay Equality rallied outside the Pentagon Friday, calling for the right to love men and kill men.

"It is unconstitutional to keep us out of the U.S. military solely because of our sexuality," said SURGE president Lee Rothamer. "Gays, like everyone else, should have the right to love whomever they wish, and kill whomever their commanding officer deems in need of killing."

The group is demanding that gays be given the freedom to use advanced military weaponry to shoot, bomb, run over, impale, burn or vaporize their fellow man.

Gerald Atzen, a former Navy lieutenant given a dishonorable discharge in 1992 because of an "improper homosexual relationship," addressed his fellow rallygoers: "My whole life, all I've ever wanted to do is kill men," he said. "But just because of my attraction to men, the government has denied me my right to satisfy this bloodlust. This is hypocrisy at its worst."

Members of SURGE, an offshoot of the National Gay and Lesbian Task Force, vow to continue to fight discrimination against gays and raise public awareness that it is natural and acceptable for a man—regardless of sexual orientation—to want to take the lives of others.

"How many lives have been ruined by these unjust military policies?" Atzen asked. "How many gay officers hide the truth in shame? How many dreams of slaying another human being in the name of one's country have been senselessly denied out of prejudice and ignorance?"

155

the ONION

WEDNESDAY, NOVEMBER 2, 1994 — AMERICA'S FINEST NEWS SOURCE — ★★★ **50 CENTS**

INSIDE

Spielberg Reveals The Two Secrets Of His Success: Monsters, Jews

Movies, page 12C

Striking Baseball Players Demand 10-Hour Work Week, $2.4 Million Minimum Wage

Sports, page 19D

Mail-Related Killings This Week

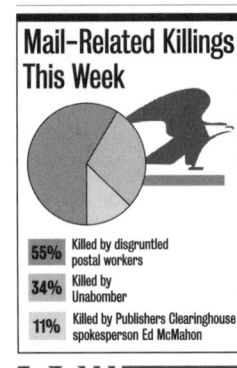

- 55% Killed by disgruntled postal workers
- 34% Killed by Unabomber
- 11% Killed by Publishers Clearinghouse spokesperson Ed McMahon

DOW

The Dow fell sharply yesterday when it was mistakenly firebombed by bungling ATF agents and burned to the ground. **−294**

Michael Jordan Shot For His Sneakers

CHICAGO—Chicago Bulls star Michael Jordan is in critical condition following a Tuesday street-corner mugging in which he was shot for his Air Jordans.

The assault occurred outside Chicago Stadium at approximately 11:15 p.m., shortly after the end of a Bulls-Pistons game. According to one witness, Jordan was approached by a group of teens who demanded he remove his Nikes. When he refused, one of the teens shot Jordan in the chest and ran off with the $110 shoes.

"Once again, the value our society places on these sneakers as status symbols has led to violence," Chicago Police Chief Richard Holdt said. "How many more people have to suffer because of these expensive shoes?"

Jordan is expected to be hospitalized for at least three weeks, and will likely miss 20 games as a result of the shooting.

The Jordan incident is the fifth Nike-related assault in Chicago this month. No suspects have been named in the case.

Michael Jordan

Republican Revolution Of '94: Everything's Different Now

WASHINGTON, DC—Capturing both houses of Congress in a stunning electoral sweep Tuesday, the Republican Party is proclaiming a bold new era in American politics.

"The Republican Revolution of 1994 has arrived," U.S. Rep. Newt Gingrich (R-GA) said. "From now on, everything will be different."

Gingrich predicted that within 30 days of the new Congress' installation, the national unemployment rate will plummet below one percent, crime will virtually cease to exist, and every citizen will be able to live the American Dream and own his or her own home.

"The days of Washington gridlock, corruption and politics as usual are over," Gingrich said. "Now that the Republicans have seized power on Capitol Hill, we are going to reinvent the way government operates. From now on, the government will work for the people, not the other way around."

Gingrich predicted that the Republicans' "Contract With America" will become a document as revered as the U.S. Constitution, and that schoolchildren for decades to come will commit to memory its hallowed words.

Across America, a palpable sense of change is in the air. Life is expected to improve for millions, thanks to decisions the Republican-controlled Congress will make in the coming months.

"This really is a revolution," said Nathan Doby, 37, a New Orleans dock-worker. "The election was just yesterday, but I can already tell that America's social and political landscape will be forever altered as a result of the Republicans' victory."

Princeton University political-science professor Scott Torcaso agreed. "I compare the historical impact of yesterday's Republican victory to that of the American Revolution of the 18th century. Before the Republican Revolution of 1994, our system of government was bloated, corrupt and inefficient. After the Republican Revolution of 1994, it will be streamlined, corruption-free and a model for the free world."

U.S. Rep. Newt Gingrich (R-GA)

Mountain Dew-Related Sky-Surfing Deaths On The Rise

WASHINGTON, DC—Sky-surfing fatalities among "Generation X" have risen nearly 800 percent since 1992, according to a report issued Monday by the National Safety Council.

By the end of 1995, the report warned, an estimated two million twentysomethings will die in popular "Gen-X" activities such as sky-surfing, snow-jumping, para-gliding, bungee-jumping, Dew-slamming and mountain-bike skydiving.

The report also indicated that males between the ages of 18 and 24 are at a high risk of being killed by cans of Mountain Dew speeding at supersonic speed toward their heads.

Concerned parents are blaming Mountain Dew parent company Pepsico. "Gen-Xers jump off cliffs after school, dive out of airplanes on weekends and flip through the air on snowboards all day long," said Joanne Henke, a spokesperson for Concerned Parents of America, "and it's all because Mountain Dew is glorifying these radical acts in its commercials."

Said Pepsico spokesperson Allen Simons, "Mountain Dew is merely holding up a mirror to society."

In response to the report, the Consumer Protection Agency announced it will launch a TV ad campaign encouraging Gen-Xers to refrain from extreme stunts and urging them instead to sit around, watch TV and do nothing with their lives.

Computer-Industry Leaders Call For Creation Of Masturbation Superhighway

PALO ALTO, CA—Computer-industry leaders concluded Tuesday's historic Global Info-Technology Summit with a call for the development of a "Masturbation Superhighway," a revolutionary computer network they claim will give millions of computer users instant and discreet access to the pornography of their choice from anywhere in the world.

"Within five years, you will be able to sit down at your computer and, at the click of a mouse, download everything from cum-drunk, tight-pussied teen virgins to triple-penetration fuckfests," said Marc Andreesen, CEO of a recently formed breast-server called Netscape. "This extraordinary new technology will forever change the way we jack off."

"No longer will a man have to travel to his local porn shop to get the latest photos of dildo-loving big black mamas," Andreesen added. "When the electronic global village is a reality, he will be able to do so right in his own home. This is the promise of the Masturbation Age."

156

the ONION

MONDAY, APRIL 24, 1995 — AMERICA'S FINEST NEWS SOURCE — ★★★ 50 CENTS

INSIDE

Ted Kaczynski, David Koresh, Timothy McVeigh Meet For Conspiracy-Theory Anti-Government Militia Cult Right-Wing Kook Summit

Page 7A

Rubber-Faced Fartsmith Is America's Sweetheart

Page 1C

TV TODAY

- 7:00 crap
- 8:00 re-run crap
- 8:30 sit-crap
- 9:00 docu-crap

WEATHER

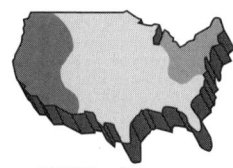

- Warm front over central plains
- Storm front approaching from Northeast
- West Coast niggaz be frontin'

Al Gore Caught In Love Tryst With Endangered Tree Owl

WASHINGTON, DC—Scandal engulfed the Clinton Administration once again Sunday, when allegations were made public that Vice President Al Gore engaged in an illicit sexual relationship with an endangered tree owl, then urged the winged nocturnal predator to lie about the affair under oath.

According to an anonymous source within the administration, the vice president first met the owl during a meeting with anti-logging activists in Washington State's Olympic National Park, admiring the bird in its tree perch and praising it for its "majestic plumage." Suspicion was aroused when the bird began making repeated visits to Gore's White House office, which is more than 3,000 miles from the owl's Pacific Northwest habitat.

Gore, long known for his strong pro-wildlife stance, denied the charges of an inter-species sexual liaison, insisting that his relationship with the woodland creature was "purely environmentalist in nature."

Experts on bird mating, however, say the owl's extensive molting and twig-gathering behavior, as well as its alleged lining of a nest with clumps of grass and feathers, suggest that the bird was sexually active during the weeks it spent with the vice president.

In addition, an unnamed Secret Service agent claimed that Gore ordered him to dispose of several fecal pellets found in the White House. He said the pellets contained the bones of small rodents.

A federal grand jury will convene Friday to determine whether the owl will be charged with perjury for an April 17 deposition in which ornithologists recorded the bird emitting a complex series of hoots denying the affair. Gore, if found guilty of encouraging the endangered owl to lie under oath, could face congressional censure on charges of perjury, obstruction of justice and owl-fucking.

Left: Vice President Al Gore. Right: the tree owl with which he has allegedly been sexually involved.

Grieving Families Of Oklahoma City Bombing Victims Turn To Angels

OKLAHOMA CITY—The survivors of last week's tragic Oklahoma City bombing now face their most daunting task yet: painstakingly putting the pieces of their shattered lives back together. It will not be easy, but these courageous souls have help, thanks to their deep faith in angels.

"My personal angel is looking down on me," said area florist Beatrice Winfield, who lost her husband in the explosion. "God sends angels to watch over those who need them the most."

Winfield carries a porcelain figurine of an angel at all times to remind her of her special spiritual guardian.

"Just as God is looking after my baby now, His Divine emissary is helping me get through this," said Madeline Pruitt, whose daughter Courtney was in the ill-fated day-care center that bore the worst damage from the explosion. "If it weren't for my guardian angel and my faith, I don't think I'd be able to get through this horror."

But faith is not needed by all the brave souls of Oklahoma City: Some already have proof of angels. "I was visited in a dream by an angel, so I know firsthand how real they are," said Arnold Crary, who lost his wife Linda in the blast. "That angel came down and spoke to me, and I knew then and there that he was watching over me."

Whatever becomes of the disaster's survivors, they are sure of one thing: Their ongoing efforts to rebuild and heal will be watched over with grace and caring by the many angels who have come to inhabit Oklahoma City.

"Whatever becomes of the blast site, whether it's a new federal building, a park or a memorial," said local resident Jean Freemont, "it is sure to be a blessed and successful endeavor, what with all the angels looking over it and all."

No angels could be reached for comment.

The Alfred P. Murrah Federal Building in Oklahoma City. Those who lost loved ones in the blast are taking comfort in divine angels.

Nation's Whites Eagerly Await Windows 95 Launch

REDMOND, WA—With just five days to go before the historic release of Microsoft's Windows 95 operating system, whites across the U.S. can barely contain their excitement.

"I can't tell you how long I've waited for this," said San Francisco white Richard Schoelke. "It's all anybody at the office has been talking about for weeks. From the big conference room to the mailroom, everywhere you go, you can see the anticipation in people's eyes. We're talking about the greatest software upgrade of our time."

To celebrate the launch, whites across the country are planning release parties and Windows 95-themed barbecues. Still other whites said they plan to wait in line overnight in front of superstores like Office Depot and Best Buy in order to be among the first whites to purchase the product when stores open their doors at 8 a.m.

"It's hard for me to express just how much Windows 95 means to me," said Frederick Worthington, a white accountant from Grand Rapids, MI. "All I know is, when I get that software home and install it on my PC, I am going to be the happiest white on my block, if not the entire subdivision."

The product all caucasians want.

157

the ONION

THURSDAY, AUGUST 10, 1995 — AMERICA'S FINEST NEWS SOURCE — ★★★ 50 CENTS

INSIDE

Head Deadhead Dead

Page 4C

Dallas Cowboys Receiver Suspended For Failure To Possess Cocaine

Sports, page 12D

Macintosh-PC Rivalry Comes to Head in Violent Chat Session

Page 1D

TV TODAY

7:00 Soothing flashing lights on picture box

DOW

The Dow was slow in early trading, but gained momentum following the addition of a slammin' techno soundtrack. +11

LOTTO

19 30 11 8 4

Whoomp! There the winning number is!

O.J. Finds Killer

LOS ANGELES—After months of tireless searching, a triumphant O.J. Simpson announced Wednesday that he has found the killer of Nicole Brown Simpson and Ron Goldman.

Simpson, who had been on a personal crusade to uncover the truth about the double homicide ever since it occurred on June 13 of last year, personally delivered 27-year-old Hermosa Beach auto mechanic Stuart Rogers to LAPD headquarters, telling law-enforcement officials that he had "found your man."

"At last, justice is served," Simpson told reporters. "This should prove to everyone that they rushed to judgment when they saw me panic-stricken and fleeing police in my Bronco, and when they heard that my blood-soaked glove and traces of my DNA had been found at the scene of the crime, and when they found out that I had a long history of abusing my wife and suspected she was having an affair with Mr. Goldman. The fact that I have found this man, Stuart Rogers, clears up the confusion once and for all."

Law-enforcement officials praised Simpson's dedication to finding the killer.

"Mr. Simpson is a model citizen who has singlehandedly tracked down the lowlife who perpetrated this great tragedy upon his family," said L.A. Police Chief Willie Williams. "He is to be commended for solving this case."

Simpson, who forsook golfing, book-writing and all other activities to devote himself fully to clearing his name, spent the past 14 months obsessively studying police reports, forensic evidence and crime-scene photos in his quest for the truth. He also interviewed an estimated 200 people with connections to his ex-wife or Goldman in search of leads.

"Once, I saw him in the crime lab at 2 a.m. and I suggested he go home or take the weekend off and enjoy a game of golf to relax," LAPD Officer Byron Peterson said. "O.J. got mad and snapped back, 'Don't you get it? I am trying to find the scumbag who killed my wife and her good friend Ron. I will not rest until I find this man.'"

With the killer found, numerous key players in the Simpson trial have come forward to offer him their apologies.

"I am deeply sorry for doubting you and working so hard to convict you," said lead prosecutor Marcia Clark. "I now realize that I jumped to conclusions based on false assumptions."

"Thank goodness we lost the case," prosecutor Christopher Darden said. "An innocent man could have gone to jail."

In a statement released early Thursday morning, Fred Goldman, father of Ron Goldman, called Simpson "a true hero for finding the man who killed my son. Thank you, O.J."

Numerous prominent media figures have come forward to apologize to Simpson, as well. Said *The Tonight Show*'s Jay Leno: "From the bottom of my heart, I apologize for all the jokes I have told at O.J.'s expense. I was wrong to imply his guilt and laugh at him."

David Letterman also expressed his regret, saying, "I should not have made fun of you, O.J. I'm sorry. I am glad you have found this dangerous killer. Way to go."

O.J. Simpson triumphantly enters the L.A. County Sheriff's office with the real killer of his wife Nicole and her friend Ron Goldman.

Alec Baldwin Signs Two-Year Deal To Care About Environment

Movie star Alec Baldwin has signed an unprecedented two-year, $12 million deal to care about the environment, according to a report in Wednesday's edition of *Daily Variety*.

Beating out the Tibetan Freedom Foundation in a fierce bidding war, the Environmental Defense Fund won exclusive rights to Baldwin's concern through August 1997.

As part of the deal, the *Hunt For Red October* star will care about the depletion of the world's rainforests, the greenhouse effect and off-shore oil drilling for the next two years. He will also appear at no fewer than 12 gala celebrity benefits.

Baldwin will worry about the plight of the environment beginning Sept. 1, immediately following the completion of his three-year contractual obligation to care about animals.

Baldwin's agent, Leo Cohn of ICM, said the deal was "a great move" for Baldwin.

"The environment is a good issue for Alec at this point in his career," Cohn said. "And he will care about it deeply until August 31, 1997."

Cohn said Baldwin is coming off a string of medical and human-rights-oriented issues, and was very concerned about getting typecast.

The exclusive agreement will prohibit the actor from caring about AIDS or children's leukemia.

Alec Baldwin

Ricki Lake Guest Think She All That

NEW YORK—In a scathing public indictment Wednesday, a *Ricki Lake* audience member rose from her seat and declared that show guest Tamika Williams, 19, "think she all that, but she ain't."

The accusation, issued at Lake's New York studio, was made by Laquanda Alberts, 28, of Brooklyn.

Many witnesses on the scene concurred with Alberts' statement, expressing their approval by clapping, squealing and shouting statements of encouragement.

"You go, girl. Word," yelled a supportive Lakeisha Rogers, 24, who pumped her fist wildly in the air.

The incident marks the first time Williams had been accused of thinking she all that before a live studio audience. She responded by claiming that it was, in fact, her friend, fellow *Ricki Lake* guest Yolanda Lee, who think she all that.

Lee accused Williams of being a "stupid bitch-ass troublemaker."

"She always be butting in when Devon and I trying to be alone," Lee said. "How 'bout that time when Devon and I gonna take [Lee's son] Tyreece to the mall, and there Tamika be standing there all like, 'Where we going?'"

Williams responded to Lee's allegations, saying, "Tyreece ain't Devon's kid anyways, on account of because Yolanda be running around all night long, so the ho don't even know who Tyreece be from."

"She got her goood," said unemployed, pregnant audience member Brianna Elkins, 22.

Elkins also noted that Williams is not doing anything Lee has not done herself: After the first commercial break, Lee admitted that she became pregnant with the child of Devon's brother Antwaine when Antwaine was still dating Kameelah.

Williams then addressed Lee directly. "If you be all worried Devon gonna run off, that ain't my problem," she said, bobbing her head furiously from side to side. "You got to do better at keeping your man happy, 'cause if you don't, somebody else will."

"Ain't like that Yolanda gonna end up with Devon anyway, 'cause you can see right now they ain't committed," added Elkins in defense of Williams.

Devon could not be reached at press time.

the ONION

SUNDAY, MAY 26, 1996 — AMERICA'S FINEST NEWS SOURCE — ★★★ $2

INSIDE

John Tesh Splits Time Between Awful Careers
Page 11C

Chris Farley: The Next John Belushi?
Page 1D

John Grisham Embarks On 40-City Airport-Gift-Shop Book Tour
Page 6D

Bob Dole: 'Bob Dole'
Page 3A

TV

'Must-See TV' Now Enforced By Law
Page 19C

LOTTO
21 7 2 4 14
The Lotto now accepts food stamps.

DOW
Campaigning to gain support among brokers, presidential candidate Ross Perot dropped by the NYSE floor yesterday and offered $1 million per vote. **+28**

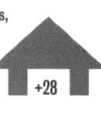

Oprah Secedes From U.S., Forms Independent Nation Of Cheesecake-Eating Housewives

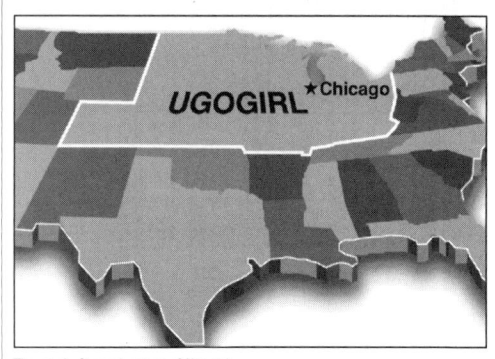

The newly formed nation of Ugogirl

Twenty million American housewives, led by daytime talk-show host Oprah Winfrey, seceded from the U.S. Saturday, forming the independent nation of Ugogirl.

Ugogirl, a nurturing, supportive republic, will be subject to a set of laws and provisions which prioritize access to healthy, low-fat recipes, creative home-decorating tips and inspirational stories of personal triumph over adversity. The new nation will have its own congress, constitution and national anthem, Whitney Houston's rendition of "I'm Every Woman."

"We women just weren't being heard," said Ugogirlian Nancy Gordon, a former housewife from Charleston, SC, who helped unanimously elect Winfrey the fledgling nation's President For Life. "It was time to do something about it."

Though situated within the U.S., Ugogirl will be recognized by the U.N. as a "sovereign nation with attitude and sass."

"The secession is not surprising," said Rick Blair, the new U.S. Ambassador to Ugogirl. "If Oprah could get all those women to go out and actually purchase a book, she could get them to do anything."

The idea for the independent nation grew out of a recent "Oprah Made It Happen!" segment of *The Oprah Winfrey Show*, a recurring feature on the program in which viewers share their dreams. Usually, the dreams involve reuniting with a long-lost sister or meeting Fabio, but, on a segment last month, Sherri Hanson of Mobile, AL, asked for the autonomous country.

"I just love Oprah and I could totally see her as presi-

Oprah Winfrey

> Ugogirl is a nurturing, supportive republic with attitude and sass.

dent," Hanson said. "She is such a strong person and she understands people so well."

Many housewives joined Winfrey in the creation of the caring new nation after the host invited guests to relate personal tales about the shortcomings of the present U.S. government. Several stories involving failings of its health-care system brought the studio audience to tears.

In the future, elected representatives plan to discuss office-skirt lengths, living with diabetes, post-divorce dating (how soon is too soon), and women's dramatic stories of their lifelong battles with weight gain.

Christian Coalition Holds Million-Man Potluck

A million right-wing Christian men converge on Washington to enjoy potato salad and buttered rolls.

WASHINGTON, DC—Carrying noodle casseroles, potato salad and honey-glazed hams, Christian Coalition members from across the U.S. gathered on the National Mall Saturday for a historic Million-Man Potluck.

"We've come here to show the world our Christian unity and strength," said David Bannister, 34, of San Jose, CA. "We also want to show the world what wonderful cooks our wives are. My Laurie made her famous chicken pot pie for the event. Try it—it's out of this world."

All day, speakers addressed the crowd, stressing the importance of preserving "our treasured role in America as first-class, white, male citizens."

They also offered recipes for homemade desserts and helpful hints on how to keep vegetables fresher longer.

"We must stay together as a people, bound by the principles of Christian charity and God's eternal love," said Christian Coalition member Ronald Hulett, standing in front of the Lincoln Memorial as he addressed a crowd estimated at 850,000. "We must also remember that cole slaw spoils easily, so it's important to make sure the container is sealed nice and tight."

Nation's 14-Year-Old Boys Demand More Precise TV Ratings System

WASHINGTON, DC—A group of 14-year-old boys lobbied Congress Friday, calling for more specific TV-content ratings.

"If a teenage boy is to make an informed decision about whether or not a particular show is worth watching, he needs to know exactly what it contains," said Portland, OR, 14-year-old Russell Bennett, president of Teenage Boys for TV Ratings. "For example, is there sexually suggestive content? Violence? Profanity? Partial nudity? Without such knowledge, we risk wasting our time on clean shows that are suitable for family viewing."

Among the ratings called for: TV-N, for programs that feature nudity of any kind; TV-S, for programs that feature sexually suggestive situations and themes; and TV-V, for programs that contain awesome violence.

"Television producers must be accountable for the content they put out," Bennett said. "We need some way to sift through the vast wasteland of responsible programming to find the really good stuff."

159

the ONION

TUESDAY, MARCH 4, 1997 — AMERICA'S FINEST NEWS SOURCE — ★★★ 75 CENTS

INSIDE

Pants Inflation Worst Since 1974

Page 1D

JonBenét Ramsey Investigators Uncover Poor Posture, Lack Of Congeniality

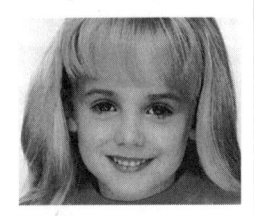

Page 11B

Larry King Continues Steady Descent Into Madness

Page 8C

TV TODAY

8:00 People's Choice Awards (CBS): Christopher Reeve receives a standing ovation for his severed spinal cord.

DOW

The DOW shed 45 unwanted points yesterday, thanks to the remarkable new fat substitute Olestra. −45

Federal Seat Of Power Moves To Mall Of America

The new U.S. capitol in Bloomington, MN

New U.S. Capitol Open 24 Hours, Boasts 400 Stores

BLOOMINGTON, MN—The U.S. federal government officially relocated to the Mall Of America Monday.

"Our D.C.-based government was growing increasingly isolated and out of touch with America's 250 million consumers," President Clinton said during a food-court press conference. "By moving to this deluxe, 400-plus-store facility, we've entered a new era of American leadership and shopping."

Said House Speaker Newt Gingrich (R-GA), "Finally, Congress, the Supreme Court and Foot Locker are all under one roof."

The new U.S. Capitol, legislators said, boasts many advantages over its predecessor. "The Mall offers luxurious climate-controlled weather for comfortable year-round legislating," said Senate Majority Leader Trent Lott (R-MS). "From voting on an Omnibus Motor-Voter Registration Act revision to looking for that perfect graduation gift, America's congressmen can do it all right here at the Mall Of America."

Clinton will host an Arab-Israeli peace summit later this month at the mall's Camp Snoopy.

MAD COW UPDATE

British Beef Cleared For Irish Consumption

LONDON—Two weeks into the "Mad Cow" scare that has caused panic throughout the United Kingdom, England's Health Secretary has declared British beef safe for Irish consumption.

"This beef should be perfectly safe for the Irish to eat," Health Secretary Stephen Dorrell said Monday. "Our top scientists have investigated the matter thoroughly, and they are almost 60 percent certain that Irish people who consume British beef will not die of fatal brain diseases."

According to British Agriculture Minister Douglas Hogg, more than four million pounds of British beef will hit Irish grocery-store shelves later this week. More than one million pounds will be shipped to Dublin grocery stores and butcher shops alone, most of it at no charge.

Hogg encouraged Irish ethnics to eat "as much English meat as possible."

"Meat from British Hereford cattle is high in many essential nutrients, such as protein, iron and Bovine Spongiform Encephalopathy," he said. "Eat some every day, micks."

A "mad cow" on its way to Ireland.

Philip Morris Denies 'Marlboro Babies' Cartoon Targets Minors

LOUISVILLE, KY—Responding to anti-smoking lobbyists' charges Monday, Philip Morris vehemently denied that its new "Marlboro Babies" cartoon characters, featured prominently in recent print ads, target children.

"Once again, the tobacco industry is being forced to defend itself against ridiculous, paranoid accusations," Philip Morris CEO Steven Hatchins said. "The Marlboro Babies and their lovable sidekick, Puff the puppy, in no way encourage children to smoke."

Philip Morris introduced the cuddly smoking kids last month following the success of its "Filter King & The Nico-Teens" billboard campaign, a marketing move the tobacco giant also denies was aimed at minors.

"We intend adults, and adults alone, to enjoy the antics and adventures of this rag-tag group of mischievous, chain-smoking moppets," Hatchins said. "Remember, kids: Only in the make-believe land of Smokadonia can someone under 18 get Marlboro-brand cigarettes from an older friend or go to a vending machine in an empty hotel lobby and buy some for themselves."

According to a story in the April 30 edition of *Advertising Age*, Philip Morris has already spent $480 million on Marlboro Babies-related advertising since introducing the characters last month. Expenditures include print and billboard ads, rebate mailings and the distribution of free Marlboro Babies promotional products, including baseball caps, yo-yos and lunch boxes.

Corruption At Highest Level Of U.S. Government Bores American Public

The American people reacted with yawns to corruption at the highest levels of government Monday, as President Clinton, House Speaker Newt Gingrich or some other prominent official became embroiled in another scandal involving financial impropriety, sexual indiscretion or lying.

According to a just-released ABC News poll, 94 percent of Americans "couldn't possibly care less" if the high-ranking official, whomever it may be, was involved in any wrongdoing, while 91 percent "don't give a rat's ass" about anything involving illegal campaign contributions or publishers' advances or stays in the Lincoln Bedroom. Eighty-nine percent described themselves as "not at all outraged" by various allegations of marital infidelity.

"About seven or eight scandals ago—I think it was that Travelgate one—I was kind of upset, I guess," said Raymond Purcell of Orchard Park, NY. "But now I'm just bored."

"I read that 10 years ago, somebody—Clinton?—was involved in some kind of illegal loan or property thing," Albuquerque, NM, resident Lorraine Bannon said. "That doesn't interest me at all."

the ONION

SATURDAY, SEPTEMBER 6, 1997 — AMERICA'S FINEST NEWS SOURCE — ★★★ 75 CENTS

INSIDE

The Spice Girls: Can Scantily Clad Young Women Make It In The Entertainment Industry?

Page 9D

Millions Of Unused Mother Teresa Contributions Revert To Charles Keating

Page 7B

TV TODAY

NICK	Dukes Of Hazzard
TNT	Dukes Of Hazzard
TNN	Dukes Of Hazzard
TBS	Dukes Of Hazzard

DOW

The Dow soared yesterday, prompting many traders to quip, "Show me the money!" +17

WEATHER

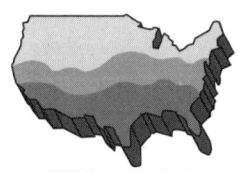

- Harvests devastated by drought
- Property devastated by tornado
- Life savings devastated by Psychic Friends Network

---

50 Percent Of U.S. Population Now Immobile

An immobile Lansing, MI, couple.

A study released Friday by the Department of Health and Human Services indicates that an unprecedented 50 percent of U.S. citizens are immobile.

"Half of all Americans are either motionless or limited to a small number of daily movements within their homes," HHS Secretary Donna Shalala said. "The immobile are America's fastest-growing demographic group."

Experts attribute the increase in immobility to the rising emphasis on convenience, as evidenced by the popularity of remote controls, in-home employment and catalog shopping.

"As far back as the '50s, the availability of home air-conditioning made staying at home a romantic status symbol," said University of Massachusetts sociologist Paul Jeffries. "In recent years, Nintendo, the Home Shopping Network and credit-card phone orders have carried the domestication of humans sev-

U.S. Immobility

- 9% Slumped in seats
- 41% Could get up, but don't want to
- 50% Completely immobile

eral steps further. Today, the typical citizen works out of the home, whether typing at his or her personal computer, stuffing envelopes or simply collecting public-assistance checks. Americans have little reason to leave their couches, let alone their homes."

With the number of stationary Americans only likely to rise, businesses are working to develop products that suit the needs of the motionless. Sears plans a 1999 release for its much-touted HomeStation universal furniture appliance, featuring a sofa, bed and toilet with a house-control panel mounted in the arm. Toshiba is expected to unveil first-generation robotic servants and pets within the next five years.

"In the future," Sony Chairman Hideo Watanabe said, "children will be born directly into a form-fitting environment console, which they will never learn to distinguish from their actual bodies."

'Teeny Baby' Trend Big With Inner-City Teens

Low-Birth-Weight Infants Fun To Collect, Say Youths

LOS ANGELES—Across the U.S., inner-city teens are going wild for "Teeny Babies," soft and cuddly low-birth-weight infants that are fun to collect.

"I've got two Teeny Babies, but I totally want more," said 16-year-old Sheila Reece, whose newest Teeny Baby, Bryce, was born Friday weighing just four pounds, six ounces. "Teeny Babies are so much fun to cuddle and hold."

Girls as young as 12 love to play "mother" to the adorable underweight children, which come in all different colors.

"My Michael Teeny Baby, he's got blond hair like Dean, but I've also got Renée, and she's got big brown eyes," said Tami Richards, one of countless L.A. teens who have dropped out of school to devote more time to their favorite hobby. "My friend Thuy got a little Vietnamese Teeny Baby that's the cutest thing I've ever seen in my life. I wish I had one of them."

"No one's sure who started the Teeny Baby craze, but one thing's for certain: It's taking America's urban areas by storm," said Gail

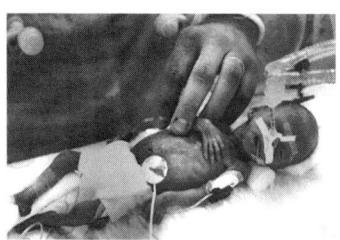

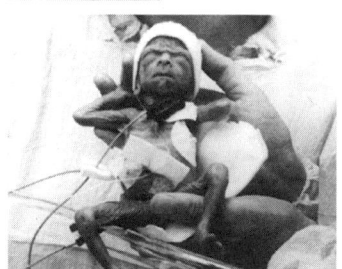

Two of the popular Teeny Babies

Freemont, director of the Los Angeles Department of Health and Human Services. "Some of the 18-year-olds have three or four Teeny Babies, and they still want to collect more. I don't see this craze slowing down any time soon."

Princess Dies As She Lived: In Incredible Plushness

PARIS—Princess Diana is being remembered as a "wealthy, wealthy woman" following her death in a Paris auto accident last week.

"She died precisely as she lived," said Diana's brother, the Earl Spencer, "in obscene comfort, surrounded by silk pillows, velour, silver-lined comforters and incredibly luxurious amenities."

The car carrying Diana was

'I'll Never Forget How Rich She Was,' Says One Di Fan

described by French police as a custom-built Mercedes SL600 featuring leather upholstery, a fully stocked wet bar and a television console fed by a roof-mounted satellite dish. Diana's companion, fabulously wealthy Harrod's heir Dodi Fayed, was also enjoying these indulgences at the moment of impact.

Also killed in the crash was driver Henri Paul, who was reportedly drunk on a $600 bottle of Cristal champagne.

Right: Princess Diana

Frog With Human Head Warns Against Dangers Of Genetic Engineering

SAN FRANCISCO—A six-legged frog with a human head held a swampside press conference Friday to warn of the dangers of tampering with the basic building blocks of human and animal life.

Addressing top executives from the nation's leading genetic-engineering firms, the mutant six-legged, amphibi-human hybrid called for an immediate moratorium on inter-species DNA experimentation.

According to the grotesque parody of nature, current standards of regulation within the $42 billion genetics industry are woefully inadequate and in need of immediate reform.

"Please... I beg of you, my human half-brothers... do not create... others like me..." said the hideous abomination. Moments later, the frog was brained with a shovel by a frightened scientist, as hundreds of horrified onlookers cried out for someone to "kill it, for God's sake, kill it."

161

the ONION

TUESDAY, DECEMBER 23, 1997 — AMERICA'S FINEST NEWS SOURCE — ★★★ 75 CENTS

INSIDE

Audiences Captivated By *Titanic*'s $29 Million Opening Weekend

Moviegoers Swept Away By Breathtaking $10,710 Per-Screen Average

Page 1C

Alphas Speak Out Against Epsilon Cloning

Page 1C

TV TODAY

8:00 Tonight on CNN: How the nation's media react to media perceptions of the media

WEATHER

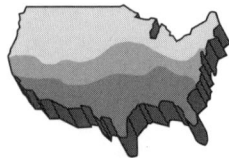

- Twisters, presented by Warner Bros.
- Volcanoes, presented by 20th Century Fox
- Armageddon, presented by Touchstone

DOW

Fed Chief Alan Greenspan's warning against "irrational exuberance" went unheeded by traders, who rolled around in giant piles of $1,000 bills while being fellated by hookers.

+247

Clinton, Paula Jones Square Off On 'Jerry Springer'

CHICAGO—President Clinton vehemently denied accusations of sexual misconduct against Paula Jones Monday, calling her "a lying ho-bag" during a taping of the *Jerry Springer* TV program.

Speaking before a raucous, hooting studio audience, Clinton said, "I have never committed a single act of sexual harassment against Paula Jones. Nor have I ever placed that [expletive] troublemaker in a hostile work environment. As I recently told Secretary of State Warren Christopher, she one crazy-ass bitch."

The president, pointing at Jones, added, "Now please quit talking [expletive] about me."

Clinton was joined by First Lady Hillary Clinton after the first commercial break. Jones addressed her directly by saying, "You know what your man is doing when he ain't at home?" Mrs. Clinton refused to respond and spent much of the show with her arms folded, scowling at the president.

The scene soon deteriorated when Jones leapt up and charged at the president with fists flying, prompting wild cheers from audience members. Jones then took off one of her high-heeled shoes and swung it at Clinton.

"Ms. Jones, you ain't [expletive], girl!" Clinton exclaimed, as bodyguards pulled the two apart. "I am president of the United States. I am forever, bitch!"

Clinton appeared on the popular daytime talk show at the urging of top advisors, who had hoped it would give him a chance to clear the air about the mounting sexual-misconduct allegations against him.

During the one-hour show, audience members had a chance to speak directly to the guests.

"Y'all need to talk this out for real," audience member Shawanda Riley said. "And you, in the suit [gesturing to Clinton], y'all can't just be talking all the time—you gotta learn to listen, too."

Springer then announced a pair of "surprise guests," suspected Clinton lovers Gennifer Flowers and Elizabeth Ward Gracen, the former Miss America contestant who claims to have had a 1983 liaison with Clinton.

Hillary Clinton, stunned by the unexpected appearance of Gracen, charged at her and started pulling her hair, but was quickly restrained by stagehands. "She got no business being here!" Mrs. Clinton said. "Ain't nobody told me she'd be here!"

When given a chance to speak, Gracen said, "I was telling the truth when I said that I had sex with Mr. Clinton." Pausing, Gracen then added, "But I didn't say I liked it." The snappy quip elicited an eruption of cheers from the studio audience.

During the final moments of the show, Flowers rose from her seat and asked, "You want to see what the president saw?" then unbuttoned her blouse to reveal her bare breasts.

"YOU'RE A NO-GOOD LYIN' DOG!"

President Clinton and Paula Jones on *Jerry Springer*.

Seven Percent Of World's Resources Still Unconsumed

A report released Monday by the U.S. Department of the Interior indicates that 7 percent of the natural resources that existed before the dawn of the Industrial Age still remain unconsumed.

"The global environmental crisis has been greatly exaggerated, as there are still plenty of resources to go around," Deputy Secretary of the Interior Russell Kohl said. "In addition to more than 30 tons of fossil fuel, the planet still has literally hundreds of acres of tropical rainforest."

Exxon celebrated the announcement by spilling the contents of a supertanker.

Blipping, Beeping Gizmo Wins Hearts Of Japanese

TOKYO—Blipping, beeping gizmo-mania is sweeping Japan.

From Tokyo businessmen to Osaka schoolchildren, all across Japan, people are going crazy for a new, pocket-sized device that blips, bleeps, flashes and whirs.

"I love the digital blepping machine!" said 33-year-old Hideki Kumagai of Nagano. "When I squeeze it, it makes noises and lights blink!"

"I like the way it has buttons you can press," said Shoko Osage, 9, of Tokyo. "I have all five colors."

Even more popular than 1995's "Plastic Blinking Shrieking Device," more than 45 million blipping, bleeping trinkets have been sold in Japan in the past four months. Retailing for about $16, the wildly popular gizmo has reportedly sold on the black market for upwards of $400.

A new version of the toy, which not only blips and bleeps but also trembles, is slated for release next week.

Golden Globe Awards Sweep Awards-Show Awards
Popular Awards Show Takes Home 46 'Awardies' At Gala Awards Show

HOLLYWOOD, CA—For the second straight year, the Golden Globe Awards swept the "Awardies," Monday's annual gala awards show honoring the best in awards-show achievement.

Though awards were given out in hundreds of categories to maximize the total number of awards awarded, the big winner of the evening was the Golden Globes, which took home 46 Awardies, including "Best Awards-Show Telecast," "Best Celebrity Award Presenter," "Best Supporting Celebrity Award Presenter" and the coveted "Best Awards."

Honors also went to the Academy Awards, Grammy Awards, People's Choice Awards, Clio Awards, Cable Ace Awards, VH1 Fashion Awards, MTV Movie Awards, GQ Man Of The Year Awards, Screen Actors' Guild Awards, *Sports Illustrated* Sportsman Of The Year Awards, Celebrity-Contestant Game-Show Awards, TV Bloopers & Practical Jokes Awards and USA Network Rerun Crap Awards.

A celebration of the glamorous Hollywood tradition of glamorous Hollywood awards shows, the nationally televised event was a star-studded awards-show spectacular, featuring appearances by everybody who is anybody in the awards-show industry.

Among the highlights of the evening's telecast were highlights of the best awards-show telecasts, guest appearances by celebrity presenters from past awards shows, and a show-stopping musical salute to the best musical salutes from the year's most spectacular awards-show show-stoppers.

In total, 864 Awardies were handed out to 362 awards shows. The night, however, clearly belonged to the Golden Globe Awards. The Golden Globes "won so many Awardies," quipped host Billy Crystal, "next year they're gonna have to call this the Golden Globe Awards Awards!"

the ONION

SATURDAY, JANUARY 10, 1998 — AMERICA'S NEWS SOURCE — ★★★ 75 CENTS

INSIDE

Clinton Denies Lewinsky Allegations: 'We Did Not Have Sex, We Made Love,' He Says
Page 4A

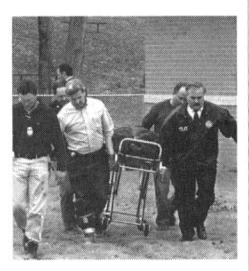

Educators Praised As U.S. Kids Lead World In Schoolyard Shooting Accuracy
Page 2A

Whitewater Probe Celebrates 10th Anniversary
Page 13A

WEATHER

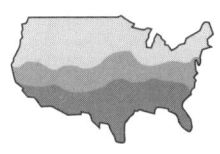

- Mid- to upper 70s
- Low to mid-80s
- The '90s are back

DOW

The Dow fell sharply yesterday when Jerry Seinfeld asked, 'What's the deal with the Dow?'
-106

Drugs Win Drug War

WASHINGTON, DC—After nearly 30 years of combat, the U.S. has lost the drug war.

Drug Czar Barry McCaffrey delivered the U.S.'s unconditional surrender in a brief statement Friday. "Drugs, after a long, hard battle, you have defeated us," he said. "Despite all our efforts, the United States has proven no match for the awesome power of the illegal high."

"In retrospect," McCaffrey added, "this was not a winnable war."

McCaffrey then handed over power to *High Times* magazine editor Steven Hager, who will head the new U.S. Office of Drug Policy, replacing the now-defunct DEA.

"We must all get behind drugs now," outgoing DEA Chief Thomas Constantine said. "I recommend we all get really, really baked."

With the defeat, drugs will begin a full-scale occupation of the vanquished U.S. Massive quantities of crack, heroin, PCP, LSD, marijuana and other drugs will flood the nation legally, saving America's estimated 75 million drug users billions of dollars on their yearly drug budgets.

U.S. Drug Czar Barry McCaffrey ceding power to nation's stoners.

Street gangs, working in conjunction with Colombian coke lords, will assume leadership of America's inner cities, and federally backed marijuana farms are expected to begin appearing throughout the rural Midwest and Northern California by the end of the year.

Drug kingpin Amado Fuentes said it was "inevitable" that the U.S. would surrender. "We knew we would eventually win this war," Fuentes told reporters from his impenetrable Mexico City palace. "America's relentless campaign of anti-drug slogans, TV public-service announcements and elite elementary-school D.A.R.E. forces were a formidable enemy in this war. But in the end, my well-armed and well-financed army was victorious."

Killer Robots Storm Home Of Bill Gates' Childhood Bully

SEATTLE, WA—Walter Conrad, a 46-year-old sporting-goods retail manager, was assaulted in his home by an army of killer Microsoft robots Friday.

Conrad, who had tormented and teased Microsoft CEO Bill Gates when the two were in junior high school together, suffered minor injuries in the attack. He sustained an estimated $120,000 in property damage.

Bill Gates

According to a Seattle Police Department report, at approximately 8:20 p.m., six robots wielding large iron fists and saw-blade hands entered Conrad's home and relentlessly pursued him. He only managed to escape death, police said, because of the robots' "lumbering pace." The robots were later traced to a secret, subterranean compound in nearby Redmond.

"He will not escape my armies next time," Gates said in a multimedia announcement, in which his image was broadcast on thousands of 40-foot-high closed-circuit screens across the U.S. "He will not escape."

Wealthiest One Percent Complete Construction Of Private Escape Pod

EAST HAMPTON, NY—America's upper crust breathed a sigh of relief Friday, when Global Tetrahedron Multinational, Inc., announced the completion of a $98 billion private escape pod for the nation's wealthiest one percent.

The impenetrable pod, which spokespersons for Global Tetrahedron called "a triumph of American high-tech ingenuity and exclusivity," boasts a complete environmental-control and life-support system, high-efficiency escape-velocity boosters and a luxuriously equipped interior. A ticket for the pod costs $1 billion.

Entertainment moguls Steven Spielberg, Michael Eisner and Ted Turner, as well as former President George Bush, have already purchased seats.

Said AT&T CEO C. Michael Armstrong, also a ticket-holder, "I feel a great sense of security knowing that, in the event that the world becomes uninhabitable due to social, economic or environmental decay, I will be rocketed to safety in extreme comfort, enjoying the finest in dining and entertainment."

Officials for Global Tetrahedron stressed that, in the event of domestic upheaval, seating on the pod is strictly "by reservation only."

Kenneth Starr Taunts Clinton With 'Sittin' In A Tree' Song

Kenneth Starr

WASHINGTON, DC—Special Prosecutor Kenneth Starr launched his latest salvo against President Clinton Friday, taunting him with the humiliating "Sittin' In A Tree" song.

Appearing before a special session of Congress to determine whether to move forward with impeachment proceedings against the president, Starr said, "Bill and Monica / Sittin' in a tree / K-I-S-S-I-N-G."

Repeatedly looking down at his notes, Starr continued, "First comes love / Then comes marriage / Then comes Clinton with the baby carriage."

Starr concluded by adding, "Sucking his thumb / Wetting his pants / Doing the hula-hula dance."

Starr said he has not ruled out the possibility of singing the song again at a later date, this time at a louder volume and directly to the president's face.

Upon conclusion of the song, U.S. Rep. Henry Hyde (R-IL) asked Starr to present evidence that Clinton and former White House intern Monica Lewinsky's lips actually touched. Starr responded that while he had only circumstantial evidence proving that kissing took place, witnesses reported seeing the two seated next to each other near the White House swingset.

Starr noted that, regardless of the nature of the contact, it was very likely that the president had exposed himself to girl germs.

163

2000 ★ A New Millennium Dawns ★ 2000

the ONION

SATURDAY, JANUARY 1, 2000 — AMERICA'S NEWS SOURCE — ★ ★ ★ $1

INSIDE

Jews, Arabs Forge New Era Of Peace
Page 12A

Planet Temporarily Closed Due To Computer Crash
Page 3A

Could A Rich White Male Be Our Next President?
Election Preview, page 6B

Meteors Headed For Earth Today

Size of	Time
Detroit *	8:27 a.m.
the moon *	11:20 a.m.
a mini-van	2:45 p.m.
Iceland *	5:02 p.m.
Taj Mahal *	10:30 p.m.

* indicates extinction-level mass

TV TODAY

VH1 — John Mellencamp's Slightly Rockin' New Year's Day Brunch

WEATHER

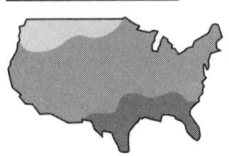

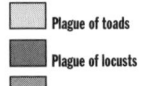

- Plague of toads
- Plague of locusts
- Plague of infomercials

DOW

-1348

The four horsemen of the apocalypse swept through the NYSE trading floor yesterday, smiting thousands of wicked moneylenders and Jews.

Christian Right Ascends To Heaven

Leaders of the Christian Right follow Jesus into His Heavenly Kingdom.

TULSA, OK—At the stroke of midnight, Jan. 1, 2000, the clouds opened above the Bible Belt and a golden staircase appeared for all born-again Christians who do not bear the Mark of the Beast to ascend into Heaven and enjoy Everlasting Salvation.

Night turned to day as Jesus Christ appeared at the top of the staircase in a blinding white sun-beam to select only 1,000 believers for ascension into Heaven, as outlined in the Book of Revelation.

"Follow Me," the bearded, unkempt Jew told His assembled flock as He unrolled a papyrus scroll bearing a list of names. The list was a veritable Who's Who of the Christian Right. "Pat Buchanan, Bob Dornan, Jerry Falwell, Fred Phelps, Ralph Reed, Trent Lott..." Jesus read on, as those named followed Him into the clouds.

Millionaire cable-TV executive and right-wing politician Pat Robertson smiled gleefully as he slowly climbed the stairs. "I've been waiting for this moment all my life," he said, his three-piece suit shimmering in the beatific glare.

"I am going to a place where everybody is like me, filled with Christian love and understanding," said conservative talk-show host and two-time presidential candidate Buchanan. "There will also be a shared hatred of gays."

Sources close to Jesus say He and Buchanan will meet privately later this week to discuss a gay-killing meteor, which could smite the Earth's wicked Sodomites by as early as 2002.

"Remember, Jesus loves you," said Christ, waving from atop the golden staircase, flanked by Robertson, Buchanan and Falwell, who also waved down to the damned.

"So long, suckers!" Falwell exclaimed.

Noted astronomer and atheist Carl Sagan, whose skull is now the drinking gourd of Satan, spoke from the fourth level of Hell, saying, "Save me, Jesus. I was wrong to value scientific reasoning over divine faith. Please, take me with you."

The chosen Christians are expected to enjoy an eternity of worshipping God and singing hymns in Heaven. "I expect it will be a great deal like being in Sunday service, except it will never end," Robertson said. "I am very excited about it."

All Corporations Merge Into OmniCorp

UNITED NATIONS—In a multimedia press conference held Friday at the U.N., top executives from the world's three remaining corporations announced a final merger, uniting the planet's financial resources under the newly created OmniCorp.

Under the terms of the record $9.2 quadrillion merger, the Global Tetrahedron Conglomerate gains controlling shares of its final two competitors, Time-WarTurABCDisSonylumbiaAT&T and GM-LockheedZweibSKGBank, creating what company spokespersons called "an unstoppable juggernaut wielding unparalleled wealth and power."

As a cost-saving measure, dealmakers also negotiated the absorption of all world governments into OmniCorp, making the corporate behemoth the sole ruler of humankind.

"We stand at the close of a century of progress and at the dawn of a new millennium," said OmniCorp spokesperson Ed Rohl. "One hundred years ago, the average working Joe was at the mercy of the big corporate trusts. Now, as a new century looms, we can celebrate just how far we have come."

Key members of OmniCorp's board of directors, including Walt Disney, were cyrogenically unfrozen and revived by a team of shadow-government technicians. They are expected to assume overlord duties as early as Thursday.

Muhammad Ali K.O.'s Ronald Reagan In Nursing-Home Scuffle

YORBA LINDA, CA—Former boxing great Muhammad Ali knocked out former president Ronald Reagan during a lunchroom scuffle at the Sunny Hill Rest Home in Yorba Linda Friday.

Ali and Reagan had been seated at the same table for their usual midday meal of cream of potato soup, fruit cup, strawberry gelatin and juice. According to witnesses, Ali hit Reagan after the 40th president attempted to take his fruit cup.

"At first, Muhammad was very patient with Ronald, merely holding out his trembling hand to keep him from taking his fruit cup," said Sunny Hill orderly Karen Colbert. "But when Ronald continued to pester him for it and wouldn't leave him alone, Muhammad got angry."

The three-time world heavyweight champion rose from his wheelchair for the first time in weeks, walked slowly around the table and delivered a blow to the former president, which connected with Reagan despite his feebly raising his arms to shield his face. The blow, though weak by professional-boxing standards, was powerful enough to shatter Reagan's jaw and knock him out of his wheelchair, breaking his hip.

"It was a return to Muhammad's old championship form," said Dr. Arthur Putnam, who oversees Ali's treatment for Parkinson's Disease. "He had his eyes wide open and level, his hands were up and cycling, and his wind was good."

Ali declined comment on the issue, instead returning to his meal. Reagan, though heavily sedated and not permitted to speak, told reporters, "Pill lady? Pill lady."

In a Complex and Changing World, You Need to Stay Misinformed.

the ONION's **FINEST NEWS REPORTING**

Get the <u>new</u> book from The Onion,® America's finest news source.

AT BOOKSTORES EVERYWHERE

THREE RIVERS PRESS
New York
www.randomhouse.com

To subscribe to The Onion, call 1-800-695-4376 or visit www.theonion.com/subscribe